The Making of Fornication

HELLENISTIC CULTURE AND SOCIETY

General Editors: Anthony W. Bulloch, Erich S. Gruen, A. A. Long,
and Andrew F. Stewart

The Making
of Fornication

*Eros, Ethics, and Political Reform
in Greek Philosophy
and Early Christianity*

Kathy L. Gaca

UNIVERSITY OF CALIFORNIA PRESS

Berkeley   Los Angeles   London

University of California Press
Berkeley and Los Angeles, California

University of California Press, Ltd.
London, England

© 2003 by the Regents of the University of California

Library of Congress Cataloging-in-Publication Data

Gaca, Kathy L.
   The making of fornication : eros, ethics, and political reform in
Greek philosophy and early Christianity / Kathy L. Gaca.
       p.   cm. — (Hellenistic culture and society ; 40)
   Includes bibliographical references and index.
   ISBN 0-520-23599-1 (cloth : alk. paper).
      1. Sex—Religious aspects—Christianity—History of doctrines.
2. Philosophy, Ancient—Influence.   3. Sexual ethics—History.
I. Title.   II. Series.
BT708 .G33   2003
241'.66'09015—dc21   2002012604

Manufactured in the United States of America
10   09   08   07   06   05   04   03
10   9   8   7   6   5   4   3   2   1

The paper used in this publication is both acid-free and totally chlo-
rine-free (TCF). It meets the minimum requirements of ANSI/NISO
Z39.48-1992 (R 1997) (*Permanence of Paper*). ♾

For you, my readers, Jonathan first of all

Great and hardly unknown among mortals
I am the goddess named Cypris, Aphrodite . . .
Those who worship my power I honor
And whoever disdains me I ruin.

EURIPIDES, *Hippolytus* 1–6

Demonic gods do not die easily.

TATIAN, *Oratio* 15.14

CONTENTS

ACKNOWLEDGMENTS

My research for this book was generously supported by doctoral fellowships from the University of Toronto Classics Department, a grant from the American Association of University Women, the Hannah Seeger Davis Postdoctoral Fellowship in Hellenic Studies at Princeton University, and a fall-term sabbatical leave from the College of Arts and Science and the Classical Studies Department at Vanderbilt University.

Books, like drama, involve a strong element of the collective endeavor. I am happy to recognize and to bring onstage, as it were, the many colleagues, friends, readers, family members, and librarians who have helped make this production possible.

Jonathan Bremer has provided wonderful intellectual camaraderie, support, and love while at the same time being one of my most intelligent and critical readers. He is peerless at giving warm hugs and sagacious advice.

John Rist, Howard Jacobson, and Tim Barnes have been scholarly models to emulate, John for his philosophical acumen and conviction that history is of significant concern in dealing with ethics, Tim for improving my skills at historiography, and Howard for showing why the fields of classics and Greek biblical studies belong together. Howard inspired my interest in classics from the first Latin declension, and has remained an important mentor since then. I am most grateful to the three of them.

Peter Brown, Tony Long, and John Dillon have taken a sustained interest in this project. Each of them offered perceptive comments that have made this study more coherent and lucid. Elizabeth Asmis and Brad Inwood likewise read the manuscript or portions thereof at various stages in its progress, Brad on several occasions. Their thoughtful comments have helped me improve various arguments considerably.

Dimitri Gondicas, Alexander Nehamas, and other members of the Program in Hellenic Studies at Princeton University provided a stimulating intellectual environment and gracious hospitality during my postdoctoral year of research with the Program. Faculty members of Princeton's Department of Classics, including Elaine Fantham, Ruth Webb, Richard Martin, and Froma Zeitlin, further enhanced my stay by encouraging me to participate in departmental colloquia and lectures.

My colleagues in the Classical Studies Department at Vanderbilt University have nurtured my development as a scholar. Robert Drews and Susan Ford Wiltshire in particular recognized the import of this project. They and my other colleagues, Chris Brunelle, Carter Philips, Tom McGinn, Dan Solomon, and Barbara Tsakirgis, were always a great audience when I presented various sections of this work during our informal colloquia. My gratitude also to Dennis Hall for Vanderbilt University's partial funding of the book cover.

Other scholars, editors, and readers provided very helpful comments on portions of this work. They include David Runia, Mimi Bonz, Roger Shiner, Elizabeth Adkins, Johan Thom, Graham Gould, Vernon K. Robbins, A.-J. Levine, and Hugh Mason. It has also been a great pleasure and privilege to work with the editorial staff of the University of California Press. In particular, I would like to thank the acquisitions editor, Kate Toll, for her expertise, guidance, and good cheer. Many thanks to Jennifer Eastman as well for her thoughtful contribution as copyeditor. She is a fine practitioner of the art. I am also very grateful to the masked chorus of anonymous readers who presented first-rate advice on the manuscript or sections thereof.

Various parts of this work were presented at the American Philological Association, the Society of Biblical Literature, the Classical Association of the Midwest and South, and the Vanderbilt Philosophy Department. Of the presentations given, I would especially like to thank Daniel Patte for selecting my 1999 *Harvard Theological Review* article for an SBL 2000 panel discussion, and John Phillips and Donald Klinefelter of the Philosophy and Religion Department at the University of Tennessee, Chattanooga, for generously inviting me to present a lecture on my study.

Michaela Milde and my sister Pat Gaca read an early draft of the whole manuscript and offered many helpful comments. I have benefited in particular from Michaela's expertise in Greek tragedy and from Pat's editorial advice. Hagith Sivan offered excellent advice on making the introduction appeal to a broad readership. Mark Anderson and my brother Fred Gaca read the chapter on Plato and offered insightful suggestions. John Kloppenborg provided useful bibliography on New Testament material.

While still working on my doctoral thesis, I joined the Classics faculty at Ball State University as a visiting assistant professor. Many thanks to my former colleagues there, especially Bill Magrath, Christine Shea, Walter Moskalew, and Leo Hodlofski, for encouraging me to continue my research while teaching, and for sharing some strategies on how to accomplish this goal while teaching four courses per term. Their talents and dedication to classics impressed me then, and even more in retrospect.

Librarians and libraries at the above institutions played a major role in supporting my research. My respect and gratitude to them all, and especially to the interlibrary loan departments of Vanderbilt University and Ball State University for their pivotal contributions to this project.

My parents, Fred and Anna, strongly nurtured the intellectual and educational advancement of my brothers, sisters, and me. My father has unflaggingly supported this book project and my career as a college professor. Though my mother passed away several years ago, she was an exemplary supporter of gender equity. My mother, father, and older siblings also were the first to encourage me to love books and libraries. Little did they know the profession they were getting me into! My family's love, intelligence, and witty sensibility sustain me in this endeavor.

Several sections of this book were published in earlier versions, as follows, while the work as a whole was in progress.

A section of chapter three was published as "Early Stoic Eros: The Sexual Ethics of Zeno and Chrysippus and Their Evaluation of the Popular Greek Erotic Tradition," reprinted from *Apeiron: A Journal for Ancient Philosophy and Science* 33 (September 2000), pp. 207–38, by permission of Academic Printing and Publishing.

A briefer version of chapter four appeared as "The Reproductive Technology of the Pythagoreans," reprinted from *Classical Philology* 95 (April 2000), pp. 113–32, © 2000 by the University of Chicago. All rights reserved.

Chapter eight was published as "Driving Aphrodite from the World: Tatian's Encratite Principles of Sexual Renunciation," *Journal of Theological Studies* n.s., 53 (April 2002), pp. 28–52.

Excerpts of chapters seven and nine were published as "Philo's Principles of Sexual Conduct and Their Influence on Christian Platonist Sexual Principles," *Studia Philonica Annual* 8 (1996), pp. 21–39; reprinted by permission.

ABBREVIATIONS

G-P   Greek Anthology. *The Greek Anthology: Hellenistic Epigrams*. Text (vol. 1) and commentary (vol. 2) edited by A. S. F. Gow and D. L. Page. Cambridge: Cambridge University Press, 1965.

G-P *Philip.* *The Greek Anthology: The Garland of Philip*. Text (vol. 1) and commentary (vol. 2) edited by A. S. F. Gow and D. L. Page. Cambridge: Cambridge University Press, 1968.

LS   *The Hellenistic Philosophers*. Vols. 1–2. Edited with translation and commentary by A. A. Long and D. N. Sedley. New York: Cambridge University Press, 1987.

PHP   Galen. *On the Doctrines of Hippocrates and Plato*[3]. Vols. 1–3. Edited with translation and notes by Phillip de Lacy. Berlin: Akademie Verlag, 1978–1984.

Primary source and other standard abbreviations not presented above follow (or, in the interest of clarity, are fuller than) the abbreviations listed in these reference sources:

A Greek-English Lexicon[9] (= LSJ). Edited by Henry G. Liddell, Robert Scott, Henry S. Jones, and Roderick McKenzie, with Revised Supplement edited by P. G. W. Glare and A. A. Thompson. Oxford: Clarendon Press, 1996.

The Oxford Classical Dictionary[3] (= OCD). Edited by Simon Hornblower and Antony Spawforth. New York: Oxford University Press, 1996.

A Patristic Greek Lexicon. Edited by G. W. H. Lampe. Oxford: Clarendon Press, 1968.

The SBL Handbook of Style: For Ancient Near Eastern, Biblical, and Early Christian Studies. Edited by Patrick H. Alexander et al. Peabody, Mass.: Hendrickson Publishers, 1999.

Chapter 1

Introduction

Ancient Greek Sexual Blueprints for Social Order

In this study I aim to resolve an important philosophical and historical problem about the making of sexual morality in Western culture: Do the patristic sexual rules of second-century Christianity differ notably from the Greek philosophical sexual principles that the patristic writers used to help formulate their own? Alternatively, are these Christian rules in unison with the Greek philosophical basis that they claim to have? These questions are of great significance for understanding the didactic motives of those patristic writers who later came to be known as church fathers,[1] because their sexual teachings have set an enduring and far-reaching standard of ecclesiastical sexual morality.

By the beginning of the second century c.e., patristic writers actively began to adapt ideas about regulating human sexual conduct from Plato, the Stoics, and the Pythagoreans as they developed their own teachings about permissible and impermissible sexual activity.[2] Tatian, Clement of Alexandria, and Epiphanes exemplify divergent early trajectories of this adaptation. Tatian was an ardent Christian advocate of complete sexual renunciation, also known as the "encratite" position, and Epiphanes was a Christian Platonist and a Gnostic supporter of more libertine sexual principles. Both

---

1. Translations from Greek in this work are my own. In my study "church fathers" are a subset of "patristic writers." They are patristic writers who have been deemed edifying by one or more branches of Christianity, such as Roman Catholicism. "Patristic writers" are not necessarily church fathers and some were declared heretical, such as Tatian and Epiphanes.

2. By "sexual activity" I refer to acts that involve genitals and generally orgasm as well, that is, ἀφροδίσια, not to sexually arousing behavior in general. "Sexual intercourse" denotes vaginal-penile copulation. I use the adjective "heterosexual" on occasion strictly to refer to such copulation, not to denote a sexual identity.

Tatian and Epiphanes drew on the Stoics for some of their teachings, and Epiphanes borrowed from Plato as well. Clement, also a Christian Platonist, censured both Tatian and Epiphanes for going to opposite extremes. He used Plato, the Stoics, and the Pythagoreans to develop putatively more moderate sexual guidelines. He is recognized today as a church father partly because he shaped a more workable set of Christian sexual regulations somewhere between the encratite and libertine positions. To what extent did these three patristic writers carry forward, transform, or abandon the sexual principles of their philosophical forebears?

Long before the emergence of Christianity, starting in the fourth century B.C.E., Plato, the Stoics, and the Pythagoreans produced sexually grounded political theories designed to create a more just and harmonious society. By their reasoning, human reproductive and other sexual mores are central to any endeavor to attain social order, justice, and well-being. Without the right procreative and other sexual principles, wide-scale disorder and inequity become the ingrained norm that falsely poses as the good society. For different reasons, Plato, the Stoics, and the Pythagoreans all found Greek society poorly constructed in its sexual foundations.[3] In response, they went to work like city-planning contractors and put in their utopian bids to construct sexual systems that would create new and improved societies. These blueprints for new civic order appear in various writings, such as Plato's *Republic* and *Laws*, Aristoxenus's *Pythagorean Declarations*, and Zeno's now lost *Republic*. The writings had little or no immediate social influence beyond their authors' philosophical circles. The male citizens of Athens howled with laughter at communal sexual reforms of the sort seen in Plato's *Republic*, and a number of readers were shocked at the communal sexual proposals in Zeno's *Republic*.[4] Though the Pythagoreans did establish their countercultural community in Croton and elsewhere in cities of southern Italy, other inhabitants violently disbanded their organization and drove the Pythagoreans out of town and out of the region as well.[5] Thus the philoso-

---

3. A few words are in order about my use of historical and philosophical patterns of verbal discourse. Past tense verbs are the norm in historical narrative when I refer to persons and actions in a historical manner, such as here, "the Stoics found . . ." I use present tense, however, when explicating ideas and themes, such as "the Stoic Chrysippus argues."

4. Plato, *Rep* 457b7–d5; R. G. Ussher, ed., *Aristophanes:* Ecclesiazusae (1973), xiv–xx; DL 7.34; M. Schofield, *The Stoic Idea of the City* (1991; reprint, 1999), 3–13; A. Erskine, *The Hellenistic Stoa: Political Thought and Action* (1990), 10–5; and P. Vander Waerdt, "Zeno's *Republic* and the Origins of Natural Law" (1994), 277 n. 19.

5. D. Musti, "Le rivolte antipitagoriche e la concezione pitagorica del tempo" (1990), 35–65; B. L. van der Waerden, *Die Pythagoreer: Religiöse Bruderschaft und Schule der Wissenschaft* (1979), 202–22; K. von Fritz, *Pythagorean Politics in Southern Italy: An Analysis of the Sources* (1940; reprint, 1977), 68–102; and E. Minar, "Pythagorean Communism" (1944), 34–47, along with his more detailed study *Early Pythagorean Politics in Practice and Theory* (1942; reprint, 1979).

phers had good reason to doubt, as Plato did near the end of his life, whether their ideal city plans would ever have any influence over human sexual behavior and society.[6]

Aspects of the Platonic, Stoic, and Pythagorean plans eventually did become more influential through the nascent Christian church as it developed its own sexually grounded bid for a new social order. This development started in earnest by the second century, when the patristic writers began adapting various regulatory elements from the Greek philosophers, as well as from the Greek Bible (or Septuagint), the apostle Paul, and Philo of Alexandria. The proto-ecclesiastical bid eventually won imperial approval. Near the end of the fourth century, the Roman emperor Theodosius I in effect awarded the contract to the church when he made orthodox Christianity the sole permissible religion in the Roman Empire.[7] At this time the sexual and broader political reforms promoted by the church proceeded on a much more ambitious scale than they had hitherto. This especially holds true for the religious sphere of Christian sexual reform. Polytheistic religion in antiquity was intimately connected with sexual and procreative conduct, for people worshipped gods embodying sexual power, such as Aphrodite, Dionysus, Hera, and Zeus. Through the arm of Christian empire, ecclesiastical sexual principles began to regulate the way to live, make love, and be religious in the lands of the later Roman Empire.

A millennium later, Christian sexual morality set forth on an even more ambitious venture into the world, hand in hand with European colonialism. Through this wide-ranging movement of Catholic and Protestant empire, the ecclesiastical sexual reforms that began to take shape by the second century C.E. have informed the sexual basis of Western culture. The inhabitants of Europe, the Americas, and various other regions live and make love in the domains of these religious sexual rules. This holds true even for the many persons, Christians and non-Christians alike, who resist Christian sexual morality and its predominantly marital orientation. The Christian pattern of family values remains powerful in the United States and elsewhere,

6. Plato in the *Laws* remains convinced that "no one will ever posit a more correct or better definition [of the ideal city] in its preeminence toward human virtue than one in which the private ownership of women, children, and all other goods is everywhere and by every means eliminated from human life," 739b8–e3. Nonetheless, by this time Plato has come to believe that such reform is not workable given entrenched human possessiveness—my house, my family, my slaves. Only "gods or children of gods dwell happily in the fully communal city," *Laws* 739d6–e1.

7. Theodosius's religious policy is well presented by A. H. M. Jones, *The Later Roman Empire, 284–602: A Social, Economic, and Administrative Survey* (1964), 167–9, 938–43; R. MacMullen, *Christianity and Paganism in the Fourth to Eighth Centuries* (1997), 1–73; and P. Chuvin, *A Chronicle of the Last Pagans* (1990), 69–72.

even though its grip has slackened somewhat in major cities and is increasingly more open to challenge. Still, we should entertain no fantasies that we live in a society of post-Christian and genuinely pluralistic sexual rules.[8] In the interest of leading the examined life, we should be eager to know how the encratite, proto-ecclesiastical, and libertine patristic plans for Christian sexual reform stand in relation to the corresponding sexual designs for social order offered by Plato, the Stoics, and the Pythagoreans. All three branches of the question are enlightening to investigate. Each in its own way enables us to grasp the import of the Christian sequel to the philosophers' designs that we find ourselves living with.

MOTIVES AND METHOD OF THIS STUDY

My inquiry is motivated by a concern similar to one of the several that led Foucault to turn to Greek and Roman antiquity in his studies of sexuality. As he asks at the outset of *The Use of Pleasure,* "Why is sexual conduct, why are the activities and pleasures that attach to it, an object of moral solicitude [in Western civilization from antiquity to the modern day]? Why this ethical concern?" Foucault recognizes that the relationship between the sexual principles of early Christianity and "Greco-Roman paganism" are central to the answer, and he expresses a sustained interest in this question.[9] Nonetheless, *The Use of Pleasure, The Care of the Self,* and his published interviews make little progress toward establishing the relationship.[10] On the one hand, Foucault downplays the idea that a sharp difference separates Christian sexual codes and related normative themes from those in Greek philosophy and Greco-Roman culture at large. "We are not talking about a moral rupture between tolerant antiquity and austere Christianity . . . ; the codes in themselves did not change a great deal . . . [and] the themes are the same."[11] On the other, he grants that sexual austerity intensifies in some way under Christianity, which makes it "a mistake to infer that the sexual morality of Christianity and that of paganism form a continuity."[12] Foucault

8. M. Wiesner-Hanks, *Christianity and Sexuality in the Early Modern World: Regulating Desire, Reforming Practice* (2000), 216–67.

9. *The Use of Pleasure* (1985), 14–5, 249–51; *The Care of the Self* (1986), 143–4, 235–40; and "On the Genealogy of Ethics: An Overview of Work in Progress" (1983), 229–52.

10. Least of the problems is that his incomplete and once anticipated fourth volume of *The History of Sexuality (The Confessions of the Flesh),* which concerned patristic sexual principles, will remain unpublished, following the directives in his will, *Use of Pleasure,* 12, and D. Macey, *The Lives of Michel Foucault* (1993), xix–xx, 466.

11. "Genealogy of Ethics," 244, 240. See too *Use of Pleasure,* 14–5, 249–51, and *Care of the Self,* 143–4, 235–40.

12. *Use of Pleasure,* 20–1. Similarly, "some of [the] interdictions change; some of the prohibitions are much stricter and much more rigorous in early Christianity than in the Greek pe-

nonetheless favors a thesis of continuity over one of discontinuity, and he is far from alone in this respect. Numerous other scholars also regard Hellenistic moral philosophy as the austere prescription-generating substratum of Christian sexual morality.[13] Hence, despite Foucault's occasional hesitations, the continuity theory has broad credibility, has increased in popularity since his work, and is settling in comfortably as the right way to think. By this understanding, the sexual ethics of Plato and the Hellenistic philosophers, the Stoics in particular, provided early Christians with a prototype to adopt, with the result that Christian sexual morality followed rather fluidly from its philosophical predecessors. This view, if correct, would mean that the church fathers launched the philosophers' sexual reforms on a scale that Plato, the Stoics, and the Pythagoreans never imagined—not a small town utopia here and there, but first the Roman Empire and later the New World as well. The differences separating the Hellenistic philosophers and church fathers would be relatively minor compared to their largely shared code of sexual morality. The former sing the Hymn to Zeus while the latter say the Lord's Prayer, but the philosophers are honorary pre-Christian church fathers in their sexual restrictions and ascetic discipline.

---

riod," "Genealogy of Ethics," 240. Foucault suspects that the main difference between Greco-Roman and patristic Christian morality rests not with the code of sexual dictates but with other factors in morality that pertain to regulating "the relationship to oneself," which Foucault divides into four aspects: ethical substance, the mode of subjection (viz., the means whereby persons are induced to comply with a code of rules), the formation of self, and the ethical end or telos, "Genealogy of Ethics," 240–3, cf. *Use of Pleasure*, 26–8; and A. Davidson, "Ethics as Ascetics: Foucault, the History of Ethics, and Ancient Thought" (1994), 115–40, and "Archaeology, Genealogy, Ethics" (1986), 228–30.

13. "Christianity did not bring into the world a new code of sexual behavior," J. Behr, "Shifting Sands: Foucault, Brown, and the Framework of Christian Asceticism" (1993), 18, and more recently, *Asceticism and Anthropology in Irenaeus and Clement* (2000), 4–5. So too A. Davidson ("Archaeology, Genealogy, Ethics," 231): "Foucault believed, and many other more traditional historians have defended the same view, that there was no great moral rupture between the Greek and Christian moral codes [viz., sexual regulations]. Many of the more significant prohibitions remain the same, and even where there are important changes, the themes remain similar." Likewise M. Poster ("Foucault and the Tyranny of Greece" [1986], 207): "To the surprise of the reader, [Foucault] shows that at the level of codes things have not changed all that much. The Greeks and Romans were often like the Christians and moderns in preferring monogamous, heterosexual, and procreative sex." E. Clark ("Foucault, the Fathers, and Sex" [1988], 622) further stresses "continuities of theme beyond those Foucault himself had recognized," though she admits (622 n. 6) that it is an odd omission for him to consider no Jewish writings whatsoever in his study. A fairly representative example of the increasing emphasis on continuity since Foucault appears in D. Martin (*The Corinthian Body* [1995], 200), "Christianity has sometimes been considered . . . as playing the role of the oppressive mother superior to the gay and sexually liberated pagan culture of Greece and Rome. Most recent works on sexuality in the ancient world, however, have shown this to be an oversimplification, if not totally inaccurate." Foucault's *Care of the Self* is first in Martin's supporting citation, 289 n. 3. In ensuing chapters I challenge more specific aspects of this scholarly position.

My argument, however, is that encratite sexual renunciation and the ecclesiastical sexual program, as exemplified by Tatian and Clement, respectively, differ radically from their counterparts in Greek philosophy and from marriage practices in Greek society at large, both in terms of their code of sexual rules and in the other factors of ethics that Foucault delineates.[14] Unlike Foucault, who concentrates on sexual ethics as it affects the formation of the self in individuals, and mainly in individual males, in antiquity,[15] I stress its effect on the community as well. This political dimension captures much about ancient sexual norms that Foucault de-emphasizes, such as the roles of women and children along with men as a populace. This dimension also reveals that marked transformations in sexual norms occurred in the encratite and ecclesiastical teachings, depending partly on how the encratites and early church fathers adapted select ideas from the sexual ground plans of the Greek philosophers. It is critical to identify the break between Greek principles of sexual morality and their redeployment in early Christianity.[16] Only then may we recognize the strongly religious rationale that separates the sexual reforms of the encratites and church fathers from those of Plato, the Stoics, and the Pythagoreans, and from popular Greek morality as well.

By contrast, the relationship between Plato, early Stoicism, and so-called libertine Christianity, as exemplified by Epiphanes, is one of substantive and thoughtful continuity regarding sexual mores. Epiphanes regards the Platonic and early Stoic sexual principles as the right models for a Christian way of life. Clement, however, condemns Epiphanes for heresy because the ecclesiastical sexual mores that Clement champions cannot be reconciled with the Platonic and early Stoic sexual reforms. The terms of this dispute between Epiphanes and Clement epitomize the discontinuities between ecclesiastical and Greek philosophical sexual morality that I will demonstrate in this study.

There are three main reasons why many scholars emphasize apparent connections between Greek moral philosophy and Christian sexual morality at the expense of the disparities. Foucault's *The Use of Pleasure* and *The*

14. I do not, however, use Foucault's terms "telos," "mode of subjection," and so on, for which see A. Davidson, "Ethics as Ascetics," 115–40, and "Archaeology, Genealogy, Ethics," 228–30.

15. A. Richlin, "Foucault's History of Sexuality: A Useful Theory for Women?" (1998), 138–60.

16. P. Brown (*The Body and Society: Men, Women, and Sexual Renunciation in Early Christianity* [1988], xvi) recognizes that it is misguided for "the sharp and dangerous flavor of many Christian notions of sexual renunciation . . . [to be] explained away as no more than inert borrowings from a supposed pagan or Jewish 'background.'" These notions, I plan to show, are the result of several revolutionary syntheses of such borrowings.

Care of the Self exemplify these problems, but he is in no way unique.[17] First, in order to understand the Greek ideas that precede and inform the patristic sexual principles, Foucault and others study Plato and the later Stoics,[18] but they either do not study the early Stoics Zeno and Chrysippus at all, or they give them scant mention. The early Stoics, however, formulate an original theory of communal eros that the later Stoics reformulate, discarding the communal aspect and replacing it with established Greek customs of marriage and the family. Stoic eros, in both its early communal form and its later marital guise, challenges the ingrained Greek conviction that eros is a divine force that capriciously subjugates mortals to its power. The Gnostic Christian Platonist Epiphanes adapts and promotes early Stoic eros in a communal Christian form. Foucault and other scholars, however, portray the marital sexual ethic of the later Stoa as though it were a universal Stoic position and as though the later Stoic ethos of marriage, the family, and the state were compatible with its Christian counterpart. This portrayal is misguided on both counts. The later Stoics do not represent Stoic sexual ethics as a whole, for they reject the broad communal grounding of early Stoic eros. Seneca and Musonius go even farther among later Stoics, for they repudiate the shared early and later Stoic view that sexual eros can and should be rehabilitated through ethics rather than remaining an incorrigibly harmful passion that is best avoided with a stony disposition. Finally, the patriotic family values of the later Stoics are opposed to Christian family values on deep-seated civic religious grounds. The common scholarly understanding of Stoic sexual ethics erases early Stoic eros altogether and erroneously uses Seneca's and Musonius's antipathy toward eros to make Stoicism as a whole seem like the sexually repressive foundation of the Christian family and state. Nothing could be further from the truth. This understanding of Stoic sexual principles is the fallout of the skewed terms that the church fathers used to lend a Stoic cachet to the non-Stoic, and

17. *History of Sexuality*, vols. 2 and 3 (*Use of Pleasure* and *Care of the Self*), have other inadequacies as well if one reads them as a social history of sexuality in antiquity, D. Cohen and R. Saller, "Foucault on Sexuality in Greco-Roman Antiquity" (1994), 35–59, and M. Lefkowitz, "Sex and Civilization" (1985), 460–6. Suffice it to say that Foucault would have been well-advised to omit the series title *History of Sexuality* when he published *The Use of Pleasure* and *The Care of the Self*, for the two books are not historiography and they do not concern broad sectors of an ancient populace. In these studies he instead concentrates on the modes through which some literate and learned Greek and Roman men constituted themselves as agents of sexual conduct, *Use of Pleasure*, 26–8. His method emulates P. Hadot's approach (in *Philosophy as a Way of Life: Spiritual Exercises from Socrates to Foucault* [1995]) of engaging in "philosophical exercises" on Epictetus and the like, A. Davidson, "Ethics as Ascetics," 115–40, and see also J. Behr, "The Framework of Christian Asceticism," 2–9.

18. For Plato, *Use of Pleasure*, 38–52, 61–2, 71–2, 123–4, 135–6, 167–70; for later Stoics, *Care of the Self*, 150–85.

indeed anti-Stoic, sexual norms that they promote as the biblical God's mandate.[19]

Second, the dictate that people should make love strictly for reproduction and only within marriage is not the generically Hellenistic or Stoic moral doctrine that many scholars, including Foucault, maintain that it is.[20] This sexual principle has a specifically Pythagorean provenance, and its central imperative is incompatible with Stoic sexual ethics, early and later alike. Given the prevalent but mistaken view that this sexual regulation was common currency in Hellenistic moral thought, its appearance in Philo and the church fathers seems a simple carryover of a widespread Greek philosophical view into the Christian sexual morality of the patristic period. This impression is false. Like the infinitesimal triangles that shape the elements of Pythagorean reality,[21] the sexual dictate to marry and make love strictly for reproduction is a distinctive, even peculiar, artifact of Pythagorean thought, which transmutes and naturalizes into a biblically grounded church doctrine through the scriptural exegesis of Philo and Clement.

Third, neither Foucault nor others make use of the Septuagint to account for early Christian sexual norms, even though it is the preeminent text from which Philo and Paul formulate their innovative ideas about God's sexual and social program for his people. Unless the Septuagint is taken into account, we gain little worthwhile information about how Christian sexual principles stand in relation to the philosophers' political plans for sexual reform. To investigate the formation of Christian sexual morality without considering the Greek biblical norms that inform it is like trying to understand *Moby Dick* while setting the whale aside. This study gives the Septuagint its due.

My work, which is a study in historically grounded ethics and political philosophy, directly complements the social history of early Christian sexual asceticism and related didactic ideology. As scholars such as Brown, Elm,

---

19. For example, U. Ranke-Heinemann (*Eunuchs for Heaven: The Catholic Church and Sexuality* [1990], 1–6) maintains that "sexual pessimism and hostility toward the pleasures of the flesh are a legacy from the ancient world which Christianity has preserved in special measure to this day. . . . Th[e] growing derogation and disparagement of sexual activity during the first two centuries A.D. was spearheaded by the Stoa, the great school of philosophy that existed c. 300 B.C.–A.D. 250." So too J. Broudéhoux, (*Mariage et famille chez Clément d'Alexandrie* [1970], 136), "Il est clair—et nous l'avons souligné maintes fois dans le detail—que l'ascétisme de Clément est largement tributaire de l'influence qu'a exercée sur lui la philosophie païenne, singulièrement la morale stoïcienne." G. Sfameni Gasparro, C. Magazzu, and C. Spada, eds. (*The Human Couple in the Fathers* [1998], 165) concur that Clement evinces "a clear pessimism of Stoic parentage in dealing with the passions [of] conjugal love." I demonstrate why this way of thinking is misguided in chapters three, four, seven, and nine.

20. *Use of Pleasure*, 167–8, *Care of the Self*, 151–4, 166, 178–9. Other problematic scholarship on this topic is cited below in chapter three, n. 5, and chapter four, nn. 9–10.

21. Plato, *Tim* 53c4–56c7.

and Rousselle have shown, by the second century, prominent sectors of the Christian populace started to put highly restrictive sexual principles into practice. Christian monks took to the desert to battle sexual fantasies and nocturnal emissions. Female virgins renounced marriage in order to adore Christ as their spiritual Bridegroom. Married couples opted for the sanctity of a marriage liberated from sexual relations altogether, or at least once their pious duty of reproduction was finished.[22] Brown's *The Body and Society* and Elm's *Virgins of God* concentrate mainly on such patristic and monastic sexual practices, their institutional background, and the notions of the body underlying them.[23] Rousselle similarly studies patristic and pre-Christian sexual practices and related ideas about the body.[24] Further, Clark has demonstrated that by the late fourth and early fifth centuries, the church fathers Jerome, Augustine, and Chrysostom systematized the Christian denial of the sexual body by infusing the ideal of sexual abstinence into their biblical hermeneutics.[25] These works of social history, however, have not ventured to investigate the motivating philosophical and religious principles behind Christian sexual asceticism, let alone examine the relationship between Christian sexual reforms and the antecedent reforms of Plato, the Stoics, and the Pythagoreans. One finishes reading such works with a lingering puzzlement about the rationale that informed the ardent Christian upsurge of widespread antisexual behavior. Surely the stimulus was not one of merely irrational frenzy due to some undetectable potion that early Christians drank. To find an explanation would be eminently worthwhile, seeing that ascetic practices are central to early Christian society.[26] Rousselle ac-

22. P. Brown, *Body and Society*, 213–4, 224–6, 259–84, and S. Elm, *Virgins of God: The Making of Asceticism in Late Antiquity* (1994), 253–330.

23. P. Brown (*Body and Society*, xiii) studies "the practice of permanent sexual renunciation . . . in Christian circles . . . [and] the notions of the human person and of society implied in such renunciations" from the latter part of the first century to 430 C.E. S. Elm's purpose (*Virgins of God*, viii) is to explore "how the monastic form did evolve and change," especially Benedictine monasticism, and also to examine the role of women in the development of monasticism.

24. A. Rousselle (*Porneia* [1988], 5) makes "an attempt at a historical study of [pagan and Christian sexual] behavior" and of the attitudes toward the sexual body implied by such behavior. K. Cooper (*The Virgin and the Bride: Idealized Womanhood in Late Antiquity* [1996], ix–x) sketches out the likely reception of Christian ascetic ideology by literate Romans who were morally earnest yet not renunciatory extremists.

25. E. Clark, *Reading Renunciation: Asceticism and Scripture in Early Christianity* (1999), 3–11, 104–76.

26. As V. Wimbush maintains ("The Ascetic Impulse in Early Chritianity: Some Methodological Challenges" [1993], 478), sexual and nonsexual asceticism is likely to "be a most important heuristic key to understanding ancient Christianity and much of what developed into dominant western cultural values and assumptions." For the more general social theory that informs Wimbush's position, see R. Valantasis, "A Theory of the Social Function of Asceticism" (1995), 544–52.

cordingly hopes that the work she has done "might prepare the way for a historical account of [the] ideas" that helped instigate Christian sexual asceticism and its great wall of commentary.[27] A historically grounded account of this sort would need to be philosophical in its approach in order to explicate the Greek philosophical and biblical theories about right social order that have shaped Christian conceptions of permissible and forbidden sexual conduct.[28] This is the account I plan to give. My aim is to establish a clear understanding of the underlying principles that made many early Christian sexual restrictions take the radically ascetic forms they did.[29]

My study is consequently oriented toward texts and their prescriptions—the sexual politics being formulated—not toward actual sexual practices or strategies of biblical interpretation that take shape in multiform response. This approach reflects the literate and even bookish nature of early Christian sexual morality, which proceeds from various texts taken as authorities to didactic precepts in written and oral forms.[30] One can still see this process at work in church services and televangelism: As it is written, so must you behave. What makes the patristic writers so innovative in their sexual reforms, however, is the number and kinds of books that they wave around as authorities. Unlike today's televangelist, the patristic writers have not yet pared down to one Holy Bible, with a virtually exclusive emphasis on the sexual teachings of Paul, the Pentateuch, and Prophets. They use extracts from Plato, the Stoics, the Pythagoreans, and Philo as well. Thus the philosophers are as important as scripture in comprehending the second-century production of patristic Christian sexual norms.

To the extent that my study deals with the Old and New Testaments, it can proceed only with a strong element of scriptural interpretation. This

27. A. Rousselle, *Porneia*, 5.

28. Whereas my work focuses on Greek philosophical, biblical, and patristic sources, Brown and Elm deal primarily with patristic sources, Rousselle mainly studies late Greco-Roman sources, such as medical writings and Roman laws, and patristic Christian sources, and Cooper concentrates on patristic writings and Christian apocrypha.

29. E. Clark (*Reading Renunciation*, 18, 22–7) regards the motivations of Christian sexual asceticism as an insoluble question because previous attempts to account for the sexually renunciatory behavior among early Christians have proven unconvincing. This judgment is premature. The attempts that she finds lacking are largely single-cause conjectures made by social historians, such as the theses that Christian sexual asceticism came about because members of congregations wanted to avoid priestly control or because women sought release from their traditional roles in marriage and the family. A different methodology, such as the philosophical one offered here, holds far more promise.

30. This is not to suggest, of course, that all patterns of morality presuppose texts and literacy even though early Christian sexual principles do, for numerous patterns of morality far antedate literacy. Kinship protocols, to name one example, play a major role in shaping the norms of preliterate societies, a fascinating example of which is explored by E. Deloria, *Speaking of Indians* (1944; reprint, 1998), 24–74.

hermeneutical project is not bible studies for its own sake, but serves the above interest in ethics and political philosophy. Through biblical exegesis I seek to elicit the normative grounding and transformations that take place in the rules of forbidden and permissible sexual conduct that Paul and Philo generate from the Septuagint.

ORGANIZATION AND SOURCE SELECTION

The first two parts of this work elucidate the relevant Greek philosophical and biblical sexual dictates and their motivating rationales. In the first part, I explore the arguments that Plato, the Stoics, and the Pythagoreans offer to support their respective conceptions of justifiable and unjustifiable sexual conduct. This task requires groundbreaking effort for the early Stoics and Pythagoreans in particular, given the fragmentary sources, and for Plato as well in significant respects. The sexual principles of Plato, the Stoics, and the Pythagoreans form an integral unit of my study for several reasons. First, they thought they held the key to reshaping and improving the sexual and social world of Hellenic society. Regardless of whether we concur with their grand aims—and most of us will not—their proposals stand as models of disciplined and engaged moral reasoning about the grounding of ethics, political theory, and social justice in human sexuality and reproduction.[31] The premises from which Plato, the Stoics, and the Pythagoreans argue are largely improbable or outmoded, but this does not diminish the lucidity, creativity, and earnest engagement of their ethical reasoning. Their sexual reforms would still be fascinating and worth knowing, even if they had remained a dead letter historically. Second, aspects of their sexual principles have had great historical impact through Christianity, albeit in transmuted guises. Third, Plato, the Stoics, and the Pythagoreans take a common stance toward popular Greek beliefs about the gods. The philosophers constructively reshape, but never categorically denounce, ancient Greek beliefs about the gods and the grounding of sexual activity in a polytheistic religious experience. The reformed presence of the Greek gods is crucial for appreciating sexual and civic reform in the Platonic and early Stoic model cities.[32]

31. I use the term "sexuality" strictly as a succinct way to refer to "the state of being sexual," not in more loaded senses that Foucault (*Use of Pleasure*, 3–6) has argued are not yet formulated in antiquity and should not be anachronistically projected onto it, such as men and women "having a sexual orientation" toward males, females, or both. "Sexuality" as employed here is directly relevant to my study of antiquity, for Greek biblical, philosophical, poetic, and patristic writings reflect the authors' acute awareness that humans are sexual beings.

32. My work here does not include an extended treatment of Aristotle or Epicurus, because they do not share the socially reformist ambitions that the Plato, the Pythagoreans, and the Stoics do. Aristotle was too conservatively inclined for him to put in a reformist bid. The

The second part of my study concentrates on the Septuagint sexual laws and on the normative sexual poetics of the Pentateuch and Prophets. Here I explicate the heavy and divergent didactic use to which the apostle Paul and the Jewish Middle Platonist Philo put these prescriptive texts. Philo and Paul, who are each in his own way pillars of ecclesiastical sexual morality,[33] make strikingly new adaptations of the Septuagint sexual rules and poetics regulating the relationship of God and his people. The biblically motivated sexual principles that they each formulate are the sine qua non for showing how and why the sexual reforms of the early church diverge markedly from those of Plato and the Stoics, and, to a lesser but still significant extent, from the Pythagoreans as well. Philo reconfigures several Platonic, Stoic, and Pythagorean sexual principles in light of the sexual laws and normative poetics of the Septuagint Pentateuch. Paul even more strikingly reinterprets these Pentateuchal norms in relation to the Prophets' religious didacticism, and he does so in a highly emotive and restrictive manner.[34] Encratite and ecclesiastical patristic writers in turn formulate their sexual regulations by the implicit motto "In God We Trust," but the god they trust for their ideas about forbidden sexual behavior proves to be a malleable entity whose dictates are defined by the innovative Septuagint hermeneutics of Paul, Philo, or both. Thus it is critical to concentrate as a unit on the Septuagint Pentateuch and Prophets along with Paul's and Philo's exegesis of them.

My concentration on Paul among early Christian writers reflects the his-

---

Greek status quo worked reasonably well enough, with adjustments, on his view. Epicurus and his followers in the garden sought more to retreat from conventional society than to change it. Epicureanism, further, was anathema as far as Philo and the church fathers were concerned. They so completely misunderstood Epicureanism as a doctrine of dissolute hedonism (e.g., Philo, *Opif* 163) that they gave it little or no serious consideration. At most they used the occasional Epicurean comment criticizing sexual pleasure as an added rhetorical flourish to their own distinctive reasons for fearing sexual pleasure, such as Clement, *Strom* 3.3.2. Among the church fathers, the name "Epicurean" served as a derogatory name among the church fathers, not unlike "Fascist" in the twentieth century according to R. Jungkurtz, "Fathers, Heretics, and Epicureans" (1966), 3–10. C. Glad (*Paul and Philodemus: Adaptability in Epicurean and Early Christian Psychagogy* [1995], 1–12) sees arguable thematic similarities between Epicurus's and Paul's protreptic method and several didactic teachings (none pertaining to sexuality), just as N. De Witt does (*St. Paul and Epicurus* [1954], but see W. D. Niven's review of De Witt [1955], 45). Neither Glad nor De Witt show anything more than these topical similarities; they do not demonstrate that early Christians such as Paul historically drew upon Epicureanism.

33. I am not suggesting that Philo aspired toward this role, for he was recruited postmortem as the church's Pentateuchal consultant on God's sexual mandate.

34. It is nothing short of extraordinary that Paul's use of the Septuagint has been heavily downplayed in Pauline studies, B. Rosner, *Paul, Scripture, and Ethics: A Study of 1 Corinthians 5–7* (1994), 1–25. As Rosner indicates, Paul's occasional polemicizing against biblical law has been mistakenly taken to mean that the Septuagint did not greatly influence his teachings.

torical prominence that his sexual precepts gained by the second century in Christian circles. Paul is by far the most dominant voice in encratite and ecclesiastical understandings of permissible and impermissible Christian sexual conduct.[35] As a missionary he urgently warned his religious communities to avoid the dangers of sexual fornication and other forms of sexual disobedience against God. The teachings attributed to Jesus, by contrast, address with this topic far less, though Matthew 5:27–8 is important.[36] Paul thus was well positioned to inaugurate Christian sexual principles in Hellenistic culture. He is the earliest known proselytizer for Christ in the Greek-speaking world, and from the first century to the present his letters have remained influential in shaping and reshaping Christian sexual norms.

I do not utilize two other fairly popular approaches to interpreting Paul's sexual principles, for the first proves inaccurate and the second goes too far afield. First, I refrain from portraying Paul as though he were a Hellenistic philosopher in his sexual principles, for that is not what he is. Though various aspects of Paul's thought indicate some acquaintance with Hellenistic moral philosophy,[37] there is no connection whatsoever between ancient

35. The use of 1 Corinthians 7 to formulate Christian sexual principles goes back to the apostolic fathers, Ignatius, *Pol* 5.2. For the outpouring of patristic sexual dictates based on Paul's letters, and on 1 Corinthians 7 in particular, note, for example, Tatian, fr. 5 (Whittaker); Clement, *Strom* 3.51.3, 68.1–4, 79.1–82.6, 88.1–4, 95.1–97.3, 107.5–108.1; Tertullian, *Exhort cast* 3.1–4.6, 9.1–10.5, *Monog* 3.1–10, 11.1–13, *Cult fem* 2.9.1–8, *Uxor* 1.3.1–6, 1.5.1–7.5, 2.1.1–2.9, 2.7.1–3, 2.5.1–7.5; Methodius, *Symp* 3–14; and Ambrose *De virginitate, De institutione virginis,* and *Exhortatio virginis,* as annotated in the scripture index of F. Gori, ed., 284; Athanasius *Virg* 2–3; and see too E. Clark, *Reading Renunciation,* 259–329. Jerome unforgettably describes the peerless stature that 1 Corinthians 7 gained in the formation of church sexual rules by the later fourth century. At the outset of his polemic against Jovinian's somewhat more lenient sexual ethic, he declares, "I will put the apostle Paul in the front line, and I will arm him as a very powerful general with his own weapons, that is, with his own dictates. For [Paul as] the teacher of the Gentiles and the schoolmaster of the church *(doctor gentium et magister ecclesiae)* replied at great length to the Corinthians when they made inquiries on this question [concerning sexual guidelines to follow]. Whatever he has established let us regard this as the law of Christ speaking in him," *Adv Jov* 1.245a–266c. M. F. Wiles *(The Divine Apostle: The Interpretation of St. Paul's Epistles in the Early Church* [1967], 4–5) shows that by the end of the second century, Paul's stature in his Christian missionary groups was on par with the Old Testament and Gospels. On Paul's early prominence, see further A. Lindemann, "Paul in the Writings of the Apostolic Fathers" (1990), 25–45, and P.-A. Fevrier, "Aux origines d'une exigence chrétienne" (1988), 179–80.

36. As W. Klassen states ("Foundations for Pauline Sexual Ethics as Seen in 1 Thess 4:1–8" [1978], 165), "[I]t is also striking to note how important the vice [of fornication] is to [Paul] in contrast to Jesus, who says little about it." See too L. Countryman, *Dirt, Greed, and Sex: Sexual Ethics in the New Testament and Their Implications for Today* (1988), 104–9, 190–214, and W. Schrage, *The Ethics of the New Testament* (1988), 226.

37. T. Engberg-Pedersen, *Paul and the Stoics* (2000), 1–31; A. Malherbe, "Hellenistic Moralists and the New Testament" (1992), 267–333, and *Paul and the Popular Philosophers* (1989); and C. Glad, *Paul and Philodemus,* 1–12.

Greek sexual morality in any form, popular or philosophical, and Paul's cardinal dictate that God's people must avoid sexual fornication in worship of other gods.[38] It is the Septuagint, not Greek philosophy or popular culture, that provides the precedent for this defining feature of Paul's sexual regulations. Second, I do not address how Paul's sexual rules relate to the rabbis'. My interest is in exploring the connections between the Septuagintal, Pauline, and patristic sexual principles, which means that it is tangential to my concerns to compare the positions of Paul and the rabbis on fornication and related matters. There is no transparent connection, further, between Paul and the rabbis, for the Pharisaic background that Paul claims in Philippians 3:5 differs in numerous major ways from the Pharisaism presupposed in the Hebrew-based rabbinic tradition, as scholars such as Sandmel, Sanders, and Neusner have established.[39] Thus it is not illuminating to

38. To see a good indication of this point, one need only compare the Pauline vice lists with the vice lists in Hellenistic philosophy. Though both sets of vice lists have common ground, as noted by A. Malherbe, "Hellenistic Moralists," 325–6 n. 278, the vice of πορνεία is entirely absent from the lists in Hellenistic philosophy but occurs frequently and near the beginning of the Pauline lists, Gal 5:19–21, Col 3:5, 2 Cor 12:20–21, Eph 5:3–5, and see A. Vögtle, *Die Tugend- und Lasterkaloge im neuen Testament: exegetisch, religions- und formgeschichtlich untersucht* (1936), 13–4, 223–5. Though the vice list at Rom 1:28–31 does not include the word πορνεία, Paul does not need to, as he dramatically highlights the danger of sexually fornicating idolatry just before the list, in Rom 1:18–27. For the Greek and Roman vice lists, none of which mention πορνεία, see the examples cited by A. Malherbe, "Hellenistic Moralists," 325–6 n. 278; H. Lietzmann, *Einführung in die Textgeschichte der Paulusbriefe an die Römer*[4] (1933), 34–6; and A. Vögtle, *Die Tugend- und Lasterkaloge*, 120–47, which include, among others, Dio Chrysostom, 1.26, 1.28; DL 7.110–4; Cicero, *Tusc disp* 4.5.9–10.24; ps.-Aristotle, *Virt et vit* 2.1249; Plutarch, *Mor* 556b; and the several lists that appear in von Arnim's chapter on Stoic passions (SVF 3.377–490), such as the selections from Andronicus's subheadings on the various manifestations of the four canonical Stoic passions, SVF 3.397, 401, 409, 414. In relation to Paul, L. Countryman (*Dirt, Greed, and Sex*, 3 n. 2) is right to maintain that Hellenistic philosophy contributes nothing of substance to New Testament sexual principles.

39. S. Sandmel (*The Genius of Paul* [1958], 15) demonstrates that "one cannot say that [Paul] was closely identified with Palestinian Judaism before his conversion." J. Neusner ("The Use of the Later Rabbinic Evidence for the Study of First-Century Pharisaism" [1983], 223) as well has shown that "the two sets of materials—the New Testament and the rabbinic literature—really cannot say much to one another in matters of detail," at least in terms of using the latter as assumed background of the former. E. P. Sanders (*Paul and Palestinian Judaism: A Comparison of Patterns of Religion* [1977], 1–12) likewise levels compelling criticisms against using rabbinic sources to construct superficial connections between rabbinic and Pauline thought. Finally, P. Alexander ("Rabbinic Judaism and the New Testament" [1983], 244) highlights important historical reasons to avoid reading the rabbinic tradition into Paul. "The way in which New Testament scholars without more ado read back into pre-70 Judaism post-70 Rabbinic traditions is totally unjustified" due to religious changes in Judaism after the destruction of the temple in 70 C.E. and the crushed rebellions of 135 C.E. The findings of Sandmel, Neusner, and Sanders are now standard, A. Segal, *Paul the Convert: The Apostolate and Apostasy of Saul the Pharisee* (1990), xiv–xvi, and D. Boyarin, *A Radical Jew: Paul and the Politics of Identity* (1994), 2, 6–10.

assume that rabbinic sources are the manifest background for Paul's sexual principles.[40]

In the third and last part of my study I show how the Greek philosophical and biblical sexual principles are reworked in three very different sectors of patristic Christian thought—the sexually encratite, the proto-orthodox, and the more libertine positions. Tatian, drawing mainly on Paul, the Septuagint, and the Stoics, advocates that Christians must renounce sexual activity altogether in order to be saved. His argument won him the reputation for being the leading voice of the encratites from the second century onward. Clement counters the encratite position by maintaining that reproduction within marriage is a worthy Christian practice, and to defend this teaching he draws on the full scope of Greek philosophical and biblical principles studied in the first two parts of my work. Despite the common scholarly view that he represents a healthy middle ground between the renunciatory and libertine extremists,[41] I demonstrate that his sexual principles are not moderate. Though Clement opposes Tatian by advocating the viability of procreative sexual relations, he does so in a manner that puts him but one dubious step away from the encratite position. Epiphanes is important for the philosophical and historical reasons that have made his conception of virtuous sexual conduct little known today—and misunderstood where known, with rare exception. He argues that the communal sexual principles of Plato and the early Stoics are the right model for Christians to follow, rather than the Septuagintal and Pauline sexual legacy, which he expressly criticizes for being misguided and unjust. Clement's polemic against Epiphanes indicates that it was a matter of some real debate which pattern of sexual conduct Christians should follow, Clement's or Epiphanes'. The historical outcome of this debate is important for recognizing the gulf that separates the Greek philosophers and the church. Epiphanes was silenced as a lasciv-

40. The reverse comparative procedure is more defensible on chronological grounds—to see how Paul's letters help clarify, by way of similarities and differences, themes that are recorded in the rabbinic tradition from the second century C.E. onward. Chronological concerns aside, though, it is still worthwhile to compare the views that Paul and the rabbis harbor about various topics such as sexual fornication, without assuming that the rabbinic tradition represents Paul's background. P. Tomson's study (*Paul and the Jewish Law: Halakha in the Letters of the Apostle to the Gentiles* [1990], 1–53) generally tries to avoid this assumption. Nonetheless it is questionable to use rabbinic evidence to control and fill in what Paul "must mean" on topics where he is terse or convoluted, as he frequently is, while the rabbis carefully explain their positions, as they tend to do.

41. For example, according to P. Karavites (*Evil, Freedom, and the Road to Perfection in Clement of Alexandria* [1999], 89), Clement adopts a "middle of the road approach" simply because he is neither a libertine nor a proponent of sexual renunciation. For the same reason, G. Sfameni Gasparro, C. Magazzu, and C. Spada, eds. (*The Human Couple*, 163) maintain that Clement "is the first Christian author in Greek to treat in a complete and balanced manner the subject of matrimony." See too J. Broudéhoux, *Mariage et Famille*, 43–5.

ious heretic while Clement made a major and formative contribution to ecclesiastical sexual morality.

THE SEPTUAGINT: ADDITIONAL CONSIDERATIONS

I use the Septuagint as a source in its own right to explore the Hellenistic ways of reading Greek scripture that helped generate the encratite and ecclesiastical sexual ethics of Tatian and Clement.[42] The most formative players in this hermeneutic arena antedate the Christian idealizing of Hebrew as the preferred vehicle of scriptural truth, for the *hebraica veritas* movement takes hold only later with Origen and becomes more prominent with Jerome. For Paul, scripture is exclusively or predominantly Greek.[43] The Septuagint Pentateuch likewise provides the basis for Philo's conception of the

42. On the importance of using the Septuagint as a primary source for Hellenistic Judaism and Christianity, J. Wevers is forceful in *Notes on the Greek Text of Exodus* (1990), xvi, and he reiterates his position in *Notes on the Greek Text of Deuteronomy* (1995), xiv: "It is time to stop this nonsense . . . [of] treat[ing] the LXX as a grabbag for emendations. . . . It is time to go back to the LXX and read it for what it is, a humanistic document which should be pondered both for its own sake and for understanding the Hebrew text." This position is also maintained by E. Schürer et al., *The History of the Jewish People in the Age of Jesus Christ* 3.1 (1986), 478; H. Orlinsky, "The Septuagint as Holy Writ and the Philosophy of the Translators" (1975), 108, 112; S. Jellicoe, *The Septuagint and Modern Study* (1968), 352–3; and G. Jouassard, "Requête d'un patrologue aux biblistes touchant les Septante" (1957), 307–27.

43. On the priority of the Septuagint for Paul, see R. Hays, *Echoes of Scripture in the Letters of Paul* (1989), x–xi; D.-A. Koch, Die Schrift als Zeuge des Evangeliums: Untersuchungen zur Verwendung und zum Verständnis der Schrift bei Paulus (1986), 48–101; E. Ellis, Paul's Use of the Old Testament (1957), 12–20; E. Ellis, The Old Testament in Early Christianity: Canon and Interpretation in the Light of Modern Research (1991), 53 n. 7 and 64 n. 62; and O. Michel, Paulus und seine Bibel (1929; reprint, 1972), 55–68, who quotes Vollmer's estimation that Paul "lebt ganz in und mit dem griechischen Text," 55. Vollmer exaggerates somewhat, for Paul's thought is a product of Hellenistic culture and not only of the Greek biblical tradition, but the observation holds true for Paul's notion of forbidden sexual conduct, as my study shows. The question concerning Paul's Old Testament is not whether he used a Septuagint text primarily, which is beyond doubt, but how best to explain the divergences between Paul's Old Testament citations and the modern critical edition of the Septuagint. The divergences may reflect fluidity in early Septuagint recensions, liberty in Paul's use or memory of Greek scripture, or a combination of both factors. Hays (Echoes of Scripture, 5–21, 154–92 and passim) has argued that Paul's exegetical thought is boldly creative and allusive, which would indicate that his style of using the Septuagint is one reason for the divergences. S. Keesmaat (*Paul and His Story: (Re-)Interpreting the Exodus Tradition* [1999], 15–53, esp. 26) fittingly describes this aspect of Paul's technique as "flexible reappropriation." The textual scholar E. Ellis (*Paul's Use of the Old Testament,* 12–28, 148–9) more cautiously considers the possibility that Paul through his own mind and recollection helped to transmute the Greek scriptural sources on which he drew. Ellis's textual evidence, though, needs further updating and reassessment, according to J. Barr, "Paul and the LXX: A Note on Some Recent Work" (1994), 593–601.

biblical God's sexual rules.[44] Tatian and Clement also presuppose the Septuagint, largely as interpreted by Paul for Tatian; and as interpreted by Philo and Paul for Clement.[45]

Despite the great impact that the Septuagint or Greek Bible has had on Christian sexual morality and Western culture, it remains a surprisingly underutilized work outside of Old Testament textual scholarship, where it generally is treated as a textual handmaiden for emending the Hebrew Bible or for reconstructing the lost Hebrew base texts from which most books of the Septuagint were translated. Granted, the Septuagint is like the foreign Hagar in relation to the Hebrew Sarah, but it is nonetheless the progenitor of the religious and sexual restrictions advocated by Philo, Paul, the encratites, and church fathers. The Greek Bible is a major source in its own right given its role as a catalyst of sexual and social change in the mores of the Hellenistic world.

Unlike the Hebrew Bible, the Septuagint has also played a morally problematic role in relation to Greek and Jewish culture alike. When Alexander the Great and his Macedonian successors brought Hellenizing imperialism to the ancient Mediterranean world, they promoted Greek as the dominant language of literature and education. In these social conditions, where Greek meant high culture, the Hebrew Pentateuch, Prophets, Psalms, and other books gradually made their international debut through a Greek translation, the historical details of which remain obscure.[46] Rules against sexual fornication (πορνεία) were introduced through translation as well. The debut went largely unnoticed in mainstream Greek education, but in synagogues and perhaps other alternative venues to Greek learning, the Greek biblical writings became central to the religious and cultural life of Hellenistic Judaism and from there to early Christianity. Within early Christianity, the Septuagint facilitated a counterexpansionist goal that took shape around the figure of Jesus and is exemplified by the apostle Paul in his mission and letters. According to Paul, the Septuagintal God, in con-

---

44. Philo's Pentateuch is Septuagintal, E. Schürer et al., *History of the Jewish People* 3.1, 479–80; S. Sandmel, "Philo Judaeus: An Introduction to the Man, His Writings, and His Significance" (1984), 31–2; and V. Nikiprowetzky, *Le commentaire de l'Écriture chez Philon d'Alexandrie: Son caractère et sa portée* (1977), 51–81, and the relatively few exceptions are arguably understandable as Greek variant readings, P. Katz, *Philo's Bible: The Aberrant Text of Bible Quotations in Some Philonic Writings and Its Place in the Textual History of the Greek Bible* (1950), 96–7, 125–38. Nikiprowetzky also judiciously reviews the primary textual evidence and competing scholarly views to reach the verdict that Philo was ignorant of Hebrew.

45. On the primacy of the Septuagint for Tatian and Clement, see chapter eight, n. 3 and chapter nine, n. 2 below.

46. A thoughtful and recent contribution to this question appears in M. Müller, *The First Bible of the Church: A Plea for the Septuagint* (1996), 38–67. E. Schürer et al. (*History of the Jewish People,* 3.1, 474–93) remains valuable as well.

junction with Christ, speaks a globally oriented Word to Greeks, other Gentiles, and Jews alike in the ancient Mediterranean world. God exhorts Paul and his followers to deliver his sexual and other religious norms to everyone, beginning with the Greeks, the conquistadors of high culture. Jews too, though, are urged to repent and be saved.[47] In this early Christian movement the Septuagint made its powerful presence felt in a transmuted way, through the allusions, citations, innovative exegesis, and new religious assumptions promulgated in early Christian writings, Paul's letters especially. Paul, despite his ambivalence to Pentateuchal Law, presupposed and depended on central Septuagint norms to impart God's authority "as it is written" for Christians to follow, such as his imperative to flee from fornication (1 Cor 6:18). In Paul's day, we must remember, the Septuagint provided the only Greek texts bearing the numinous force of the biblical God's authority. Paul had no Gospels, no Acts, no New Testament pastoral letters to consult. He had the Greek Bible, mainly the Prophets, Pentateuch, and Psalms, combined in a volatile way with his own heated mind in his prescriptive teachings. With the development of Christianity, the Septuagint gradually became dissociated from the Hellenistic Jewish constituency it originally served and started to become more the extended preamble for the book that gets good only at the end. The Hebrew Bible, by contrast, did not submit to paving the way for Christianity. The rabbinic trajectories of biblical interpretation and religious life deriving from the Hebrew scriptures have at best coexisted uneasily with the Greek Bible and its Christian legacy, for the Hebrew testament has not become "old" within Judaism. The Septuagint is thus the only Old Testament available for comprehending the formative Christian principles of sexual and social order.[48]

PROBLEMS WITH FORNICATION

Paul and other participants in his transitional religious milieu (viz. Jewish, God-fearing, Jewish Christian, and Christian) avidly warn God's people to flee from fornication (πορνεία).[49] They also share an alarmist tone on the

47. Paul arguably wavers, though, on whether he thinks Christianity completely supplants historical Israel, A. Segal, *Paul the Convert,* 276–84.

48. I thus support the position that the Greek and Hebrew Bibles and their respective traditions are, as R. Hays puts it (*Echoes of Scripture,* 11) "parallel phenomena, related but distinct dispositions of [Israel's scriptural] heritage. In light of the linguistic and cultural differences between these two streams of scripture and exegesis, "we are undertaking a valid and necessary . . . task when we inquire independently into the way in which any [Jewish or Christian writer] uses scriptural texts," such as Paul's use of the Septuagint.

49. Other participants include the anonymous authors of, for example, the *Testaments of the Twelve Patriarchs,* the *Didache,* and a few Gospel passages. For these and other warnings against fornication, note *T 12 Patr* 3.11–4.11; Matt 15:19–20; Mark 7:21–23; Acts 15:20, 15:29,

matter—the sky is falling, the sky is falling, unless God's people run as fast as they can from sexual fornication. Nonetheless, the writers who deliver this warning, such as Paul, take far more for granted about the practice than they ever explain, because fornication and its pressing dangers were an everyday part of their religious jargon and culture. To seek from their texts what fornication means and why it is wrong is like following Josef K in his quest for a straight answer from the courts, because this method of inquiry takes us into an inconclusive swirl of unstated assumptions about the significance and culpability of πορνεία. Modern New Testament dictionaries that explain the early Christian meaning of sexual fornication are largely based on this unavailing method and terminate in vague definitions that are ubiquitous in scholarship on early Christianity, such as "sexual immorality," "unchastity," "extramarital sex," and "sexual irregularity."[50] Definitions of this sort leave blanks about what constituted immoral sexual behavior from an early Christian perspective, what shaped its aura of irregularity, and why fornication had a lurid glow.

The Greek Pentateuch and Prophets, by contrast, allow entry into the inner sanctum of what Paul and other early Christians presupposed by sexual fornication and why they felt the need to shun it so compelling. The Septuagint is a rich source and it rewards careful study on biblical sexual principles and the place of fornication within them. With this understanding that the Greek Bible alone makes possible, we then can see the striking changes that take place in the substance of the imperative to flee fornication as voiced by Philo, Paul, Tatian, and Clement in their divergent syntheses of the sexual norms in the Pentateuch, Prophets, Plato, the Stoics, and the Pythagoreans. We are also better able to appreciate why Epiphanes

---

21:25; 2 Cor 12:20–21; 1 Tim 1:9–10; Rev 21:8, 22:15; and (with πορνεία first) Gal 5:19–21; Eph 5:3–5; Col 3:5; *Didache* 3.3; and *Barn* 19.4.

50. *BAGD* ad loc. and F. Hauck and S. Schulz, "πόρνη, πορνεία" *TDNT*, vol. 6, 579–95. New Testament scholars remain without a clear consensus about its meaning, despite numerous attempts to resolve the problem by studying the New Testament and roughly contemporary parallels, L. Countryman, *Dirt, Greed, and Sex*, 72–4; W. Klassen, "Pauline Sexual Ethics," 165; M. Dumais, "Couple et sexualité dans le Nouveau Testament" (1977), 48–56; B. Malina, "Does Porneia Mean 'Fornication'?" (1972), 10–17. Other scholars on early Christianity and Hellenistic Judaism tend to adopt one or another definition as it appears to fit the context. See G. Dautzenberg, "Φεύγετε τὴν πορνείαν (1 Kor 6,18). Eine Fallstudie zur paulinischen Sexualethik in ihrem Verhältnis zur Sexualethik des Frühjudentums" (1989), 285 nn. 61–2; H. Attridge, *The Epistle to the Hebrews* (1989), 387–8. Recent examples of this common hermeneutic include J. Glancy ("Obstacles to Slaves' Participation in the Corinthian Church" [1998], 491, 497), who maintains that "πορνεία in a narrow sense refers to prostitution," more broadly to "sexual irregularities," and on occasion to "sexual activity outside of marriage." P. Borgen too (*Early Christianity and Hellenistic Judaism* [1996], 240, 243–4) refers to πορνεία as "adultery" and as "unchastity."

declares that central ecclesiastical doctrines about fornication are inadvisable and even, as he put it, ludicrous on Platonic and early Stoic grounds.

Hence, as one main trajectory of my study, I explore the Greek biblical idea of sexual fornication (πορνεία) and its dangers. This regulatory idea is is alien to Greek culture, and it is pivotal for understanding the gulf that separates the sexual reforms of Paul and his patristic supporters from those presented by Plato, the Stoics, and the Pythagoreans. As such, πορνεία in the biblical Greek sense of "fornication" should not be confused with πορνεία in the non-biblical Greek sense. Biblical πορνεία refers to acts of sexual intercourse and reproduction that deviate from the norm of worshipping God alone. Πορνεία as "fornication" requires biblical monotheism to be intelligible as a sexual rule, insofar as sexual intercourse and procreation are fornicating, and forbidden, by virtue of not being dedicated to the Lord alone. In the non-biblical Greek sense, however, πορνεία means "prostitution" and has nothing to do with worshipping God alone. Πορνεία as "fornication" never loses its integral association with biblical monotheism, even though its significance transforms through the innovative sexual restrictions of Philo, Paul, Tatian, and Clement.

Just as the Greek biblical idea of fornication requires careful study in order to understand its transmutations in Paul, Philo, Tatian, and Clement, so too do the sexual reform plans of Plato, the Stoics, and Pythagoreans. We cannot comprehend the philosophers' sexual blueprints for improved civic order merely by giving them sketchy treatment, and then by pointing out in a similarly piecemeal way how the patristic writers assimilate select bits from the blueprints for their equally brave new world of Christian sexual morality. We must go down, as it were, yesterday, into the philosophers' envisioned cities of sexual and social reform, starting with Plato and then proceeding to the Stoics and Pythagoreans.

PART ONE

Greek Philosophical Sexual Reforms

Chapter 2

Desire's Hunger and Plato the Regulator

Plato's ideas about human sexual desire (ἐπιθυμία) and sexual activity (ἀφροδίσια) are a critical part of his social reforms in the *Republic* and *Laws*. Why is Plato (ca. 429–347 B.C.E.) interested in curbing what we loosely— and he not at all loosely—call our sex drive? Why does sexual desire seem far more problematic to him than do desires for less intense pleasures, such as the longing for a cool drink under a shady tree? What does he think unrestrained sexual activity puts at risk? Plato finds something significant at stake, for he maintains that individual sexual conduct and collective sexual mores should undergo restrictive reform in order to create a better social order. The sexual principles that he offers are central to his ethics and political philosophy.

Plato's sexual reforms also have great significance in the history of sexual morality in Western culture. In a transmuted form, his ideas influenced the sexual prescriptions of the Jewish Platonist Philo and Christian Platonist church fathers, such as Clement. Plato's dream to break and bridle Greek sexual mores finally gained authoritative power in this Alexandrian religious venue, which was itself undergoing a turbulent, and at times violent, transition between the times of Philo (ca. 30 B.C.E.–45 C.E.) and Clement (ca. 150–216 C.E.), for this was when Christianity in Alexandria was developing partly from, and partly in opposition to, Judaism in Alexandria. In this venue, however, Plato's ideas succeeded only in a limited way and on religious terms distant from his own. He would have needed an interpreter to understand how the problems that he associates with uncontrolled sexual desire were written into the Tenth Commandment that Philo and Clement produced. My concern in this chapter, however, is to elucidate Plato's principles of sexual and reproductive conduct along with their underlying mo-

23

tivations and ambitious social aims. The Jewish and Christian Platonist reworking of his principles is the subject of later chapters.

This chapter focuses on the features of human sexuality that Plato aims to
regulate more closely, not on his full range of ideas about human erotic experience. These features include the impulse for genital stimulation, which
Plato thinks has a strong proclivity to become corrupt, the related impulse
to reproduce, and the broader social practices a populace must follow to behave with appropriate sexual and procreative decorum. Plato aims to minimize and preferably to eliminate what he regards as ingrained customs of
sexual unrestraint that have myriad harmful effects on the individual and
society. In their place he seeks to install civic mores that are motivated by
and consistent with the virtue of sexual moderation that he formulates in
the *Republic, Laws,* and other dialogues.

To Plato's mind, of course, human erotic experience goes well beyond
the irrational sexual appetite and the desire to reproduce. He appreciates
that persons become aroused for reasons beyond the sexually appetitive, as
shown in his explorations of the Platonic love for the beauty of the body, for
the beauty of the soul, and for the form of Beauty itself (*Symp* 201d1–212a7,
Phdr 243e9–257b6). Though Plato is well disposed toward Platonic eros, he
does not try to mandate its attainment among his prospective guardians and
citizens.[1] In the *Republic* and *Laws,* he writes like a sex educator, legislator,
and philosophical city founder, not, as in the *Symposium* and *Phaedrus,* like
a transcendental prose poet on fire for Beauty. My study follows suit. I concentrate on Plato's sexual regulations, the conception of genital and reproductive urges that informs them, and the broader nexus of customs he
would establish to control those urges. Platonic eros is relevant here mainly
for the forceful distinctions he makes between it and the appetitive desire
for genital pleasure and procreation.

ATTRIBUTING IDEAS TO PLATO

Plato allows us access to his ideas in his middle and later writings, even
though he wrote dialogues with many voices rather than treatises in his own
voice.[2] Here I am concerned strictly with the middle and later works, such

1. This is not to suggest that Plato's reforms would deny the experience of Platonic love to
the inhabitants of his model cities. In his view, the reforms would facilitate it, whereas sexual
indulgence degrades it.

2. On the topic of attributing ideas to Plato from his dialogues, see, for example, T. Szlezák,
Reading Plato (1999); J. Klagge and N. Smith, eds., *Methods of Interpreting Plato and His Dialogues*
(1992), 1–12, 73–92, 201–19, 221–43; the divergent viewpoints in C. Griswold, ed., *Platonic
Writings, Platonic Readings*[2] (2001), 171–232; and G. Press, ed., *Who Speaks for Plato? Studies in
Platonic Anonymity* (2000), 15–26 and 201–10.

as the *Republic* and *Laws,* because these dialogues contain his ideas about sexual desire and sexual reform. In these writings, the primary dialectician offers a number of coherent ideas, including principles of sexual conduct, that Plato seriously maintained at the time he wrote them.[3] This is not to suggest, however, that Plato doctrinally adhered in perpetuity to those ideas, used them to construct a grand system, or tried to contain the full compass of his thought in his writings.[4] I mean only that Plato supported the favored dialectician's ideas for some time and is to be held responsible, as author, for being their promulgator. This main figure in the drama, who is often, but not always, Socrates, presents a set of ideas that diverges greatly from the more Socratic set in Plato's early dialogues, especially the aporetic writings. Vlastos and other scholars have inferred that the later set is Plato's and worth studying as such.[5] Aristotle corroborates that this traditional hermeneutic of the middle and later writings is correct, and he explicitly states that Socrates in the *Republic* and the Athenian stranger in the *Laws* reflect Plato's views. To doubt Aristotle's reliability about which ideas are Plato's would be skepticism taken to an extreme, for he was a member of the Academy for twenty years, during the middle period, and he was by and large an intelligent respondent to Plato's thought.[6] Since the favored dialectician in

---

3. T. Szlezák (*Reading Plato,* 118) thoughtfully presents this point: "[O]nly one figure is competent [in the middle and later dialogues], namely, the representative of the philosophy of Ideas. . . . [T]he dialectician, as a man with a philosophical advantage which cannot be caught up, stands in opposition to people in the philosophical conversation . . . who can be very ungifted or very gifted but who in every case are still undeveloped. In view of this inequality, the dialectician must make himself the leader in the conversation. . . . [W]hat finally appears . . . to be consolidated by agreement must be taken seriously by the author to be valid."

4. For several reasons Plato did not regard the written version of his ideas as definitive. He found greater intellectual clarity, completeness, and seriousness of purpose in active dialogue, *Phdr* 276a1–9, 277e5–78b4, and he thought one would not gain certain knowledge of metaphysical principles through writing and reading, T. Szlezák, *Reading Plato,* 118.

5. G. Vlastos, *Socrates, Ironist and Moral Philosopher* (1991), 45–106, esp. 45–6. See too the contributions of Kraut, Irwin, Woodruff, and Dorter in C. Griswold, ed., *Platonic Writings, Platonic Readings,* 171–232. The locus classicus for this way of reading Plato's middle and later dialogues is Paul Shorey, "The Unity of Plato's Thought" (1903; reprint 1980), section one of which is reprinted as "Plato's Ethics" in G. Vlastos, ed. (1971), 7–34.

6. It is important to distinguish between Aristotle's statements that the main interlocutor in the *Republic* and *Laws* reflects Plato's views and Aristotle's more questionable interpretations of what the interlocutor means by his arguments. I commit only to the former. "We are bound to believe Aristotle when he tells us that Plato *said* a particular thing but not when he tells us what Plato *meant,*" A. E. Taylor and J. Burnet, cited by H. Cherniss, *Aristotle's Criticism of Plato and the Academy* (1944), xi–xii. T. Irwin brings the significance of Aristotle's testimony (*Politics* 1266b5, 1271b1, 1274b9–10) to the fore in *Plato's Ethics* (1995), 5–11. Aristotle's statement that the main interlocutors of the *Republic* and *Laws* reflect Plato's views is especially valuable for my purposes, because these dialogues are central sources for Plato's sexual principles.

the middle and later dialogues presents sexual principles that belong reliably enough to their author, I call them Plato's here.[7]

THE HUMAN DESIRE FOR SEXUAL ACTIVITY AND ITS PLEASURES

Plato considers sexual desire to be a kind of physical appetite for sexual relations, just as hunger and thirst are physical appetites for food and drink. Sexual desire, hunger, and thirst are the three core appetites. "For human beings all things depend on a threefold need and appetite. . . . [T]hese are [appetites for] food and drink. . . . The third [is] sexual desire (ἔρως)" (*Laws* 782d10–83a4). Plato makes a similar statement in the *Republic:* "We call [the human soul's] appetitive part (ἐπιθυμητικόν) by this name because of the intensity of the appetites (ἐπιθυμίαι) for food, drink, and sexual activity (ἀφροδίσια)."[8] He reiterates this position more informally elsewhere by grouping sexual desire into this trio of appetites. The body has its "appetites and pleasures," which include "whatever one drinks, eats, and uses for sexual activity," and philosophers give them low priority among their main concerns in life (*Phd* 81b1–6, see also 64d2–6). Persons who suffer from "appetitive licentiousness" (ἀκολασία) reveal this condition by "getting drunk, stuffing themselves, and indulging in sexual activity."[9] Plato in the middle and late dialogues thus both explicitly and implicitly indicates that he considers sexual desire to be a core physical appetite along with hunger and thirst.

The Platonic physical appetites aim for the specific pleasures that come from sating a bodily want. The appetitive aspect of the soul, given its craving for sexual relations, food, and drink, is "comrade of satieties (πληρώσεων) and its pleasures" (*Rep* 439d6–8). As Plato sees it, persons stimulated by the appetites more precisely want the replenishment provided by,

7. J. Arieti succinctly presents the decentralized hermeneutic of Plato's dialogues that I do not adopt. "I would like to toss out the premise of virtually all work on Plato: that he is writing the kind of philosophical work in which the philosopher writes as clearly, as straightforwardly, and as soundly as he can," "How to Read a Platonic Dialogue" (1995), 121.

8. *Rep* 580e2–4. Plato uses various terms for the sexual appetite: "appetite" (ἐπιθυμία) *Phd* 81b3–4, 83b6–7, *Rep* 329c7, 437d2–9, 439d6–8, 580e2–81a1, *Tim* 91b3, 91b7; "innate compulsion" (ἀνάγκη ἡ ἔμφυτος) *Rep* 458d2–7; "sexual desire" (ἔρως) and "sexual desires" (ἔρωτες) *Tim* 42a6–7, 69d4–5, 91a2, *Rep* 573b6–7, 573d4–5, *Laws* 782e3, 783a1, 836a6–7, 839a7 (λύττη ἐρωτική). He clearly distinguishes eros meaning "sexual appetite" from Platonic eros. As explored further below, the sexual appetite is innate while Platonic eros is an acquired aspiration that one learns from Platonic philosophy and feels as a desire for the form of Beauty or the Good. See further T. Irwin, *Plato's Ethics,* 301–6 and C. Osborne, *Eros Unveiled: Plato and the God of Love* (1994), 86–111, 226.

9. *Rep* 425e5–26b2, *Prot* 353c1–8. This grouping of three main appetites also appears in works of disputed authorship whose provenance is certainly early Platonism, such as *Seventh Letter* 326d1–5, 335b2–6 and *Hipp Maior* 299a1–6.

say, having recently finished a beverage (*Phileb* 34d10–35b7) rather than wanting its other pleasant aspects, such as finding it enticing to look at and refreshing to drink in and swallow. Hence the physical appetites in human experience are inseparable from the pleasures that accompany replenishment. The pleasant feelings that occur from eating when one is hungry or drinking when one is thirsty are paradigmatic instances of such pleasures. Plato similarly considers sexual activity to be sufficiently like eating and drinking to class it with them. To our minds the sexual appetite might seem a somewhat unusual member of the trio. Human beings do not die from sexual abstinence as they do from being deprived of water and food, and it is questionable whether lovers feel full from engaging in mutually stimulating sexual relations, even though they may feel satisfied or spent and not want another immediate round of lovemaking. Plato, however, nowhere sees need to explain why his appetitive schema applies as readily to human sexual desire as it does to hunger and thirst.[10] He clearly thinks that just as persons want and feel pleasure from consuming food or drink when hungry or thirsty, so too sexual pleasure is a genuinely consuming passion. Human beings naturally want to sate this appetite on a regular basis when they become sexually depleted, and they enjoy doing so.

The desire for sexual replenishment and its pleasure is an inherent part of human nature in Plato's view. He describes it as "innate" ($\emph{ἔμφυτος}$),[11] though it manifests itself not at birth but later in life. Plato differentiates sexual desire in this respect from its counterpart appetites. "For human beings . . . [the appetites for] food and drink arise immediately once they are born. The third, . . . sexual desire, arises last" (*Laws* 782d10–83a4). The sexual appetite starts to become active quite early in life as Plato sees it, for he would sternly regulate "the sexual behavior of male and female children (παῖδες), as well as that of women for men and men for women" (*Laws* 836a4–b1). Once awakened, its periodic craving eventually diminishes, but not until persons are well advanced in years.[12]

10. Plato's linking of sexual desire with hunger and thirst is a good example of the incomplete yet intriguing aspects of his thought, which both E. R. Dodds ("Plato and the Irrational" [1945], 16) and G. Grote (*Plato and the Other Companions of Socrates*, vol. 4 [1888], 290) eloquently appreciate about Plato's writings.

11. *Rep* 458d2–3, *Phdr* 237d7–8.

12. Plato describes the cessation of the sexual appetite through a witty allusion to Homeric heroes grieving at a funeral. Most elderly men "lament" (ὀλοφύρονται) the loss, Cephalus notes, rather as though they were Achilles or Odysseus weeping for a dear but dead comrade, *Rep* 329a5–8. Writers in the Greek erotic tradition are not quite as resolute as Plato that the sexual appetite declines in old age. Mimnermus (fr. 1) and Euripides (fr. 23) echo Plato's view that old age is devoid of sexual desire, but for Longus (*Daphnis and Chloe*, 2.5.2) the elderly retain erotic spark. As the god Eros tells the graybeard Philetas, "After just one kiss, old age will not help at all to stop you from pursuing me."

Plato has theological and physiological reasons for considering the sexual appetite to be inherent in human anatomy. First, the gods instilled the sexual appetite into human nature when they created mortals in accordance with the demiurge's specifications.[13] Second, sexual desire is a function of specific bodily organs, such as the liver and genitals.[14] Third, in the *Republic* and in later dialogues the three physical appetites also belong to the irrationally appetitive part (ἐπιθυμητικόν) of the embodied soul.[15] The sexual appetite is accordingly an inherent part of the human body in Plato's view, and the force of this embedded design of the gods is felt throughout most of one's lifetime.

The sexual appetite has a wide-ranging palate according to Plato. It is "ready to try everything" of a sexually pleasurable sort (*Tim* 69d4–5), be the pleasures homoerotic, heterosexual, or some other pattern. Men, for instance, sate this appetite with males as well as females.[16] The sexual appetite, further, develops an elaborate taste for the illicit if it is not properly controlled. When it is particularly intense and left to its own devices, such as happens when people sleep, it stimulates them to dream with bold craving for sexual relations with any animate being, be it animal or human, mortal or immortal. All are on the fantasy menu, especially if the desired target is off limits, such as a god or goddess or a man's own mother (*Rep* 571b2–72d9). The main requirement of the sexual appetite, then, is an indiscriminate pleasurable friction from diverse sources, rather like a cat ready to rub up against any leg, be it a person's, a table's, or a chair's. Most alluring to the undisciplined sexual appetite, however, is the leg that is forbidden.

Plato nonetheless maintains that the sexual appetite of most people is driven in turn by an urge for the pleasures of reproductive intercourse. In the human physiology of the *Timaeus*, the sexual appetite of women is ruled by a procreative imperative. Their wombs are "an inner animal with a yearning for reproduction."[17] The sexual appetite of most men is also under the

---

13. The demiurge instructed that "the human soul must have sexual desire mingled with pleasure and pain," *Tim* 42a6–7, see also 91a1–d5.

14. Plato attributes physical appetition in general to the liver, *Tim* 70d7–71b3, and he attributes sexual appetite to the genitals as well, *Tim* 91b4–7.

15. *Rep* 439c5–d2, 580d3–81a1; *Phdr* 246a3–b4, 253c7–e5; *Phileb* 35d1–3; *Tim* 69c3–d6. In the *Timaeus* the appetitive part of the soul is mortal. The demiurge's assistant gods "constructed an additional kind of soul, a mortal one, in the body," which is subject to "fierce and compelling passions, pleasure first of all," 69c5–d1. In the *Phaedrus*, however, "all soul is immortal," including the appetitive part, 245c5–46b4.

16. *Symp* 208e1–3, 210a7–8; *Rep* 329b8–c4; *Phdr* 256c1–7.

17. *Tim* 91b7–c7. Here Plato adapts the idea of the wandering womb that goes back to the Hippocratic tradition, though M. Adair ("Plato's View of the Wandering Uterus" [1996], 153–63) is perhaps right that for Plato it is more the reproductive urge than the womb itself that courses about the female body.

sway of the procreative imperative. Semen, which Plato locates in the spinal marrow, wants to come to fruition in human form.[18] Semen prior to emission is willful in this manner because it is already partly alive and seeks to become a complete human animal. It "breathes" within the marrow and instigates a "life-giving" or "reproductive sexual appetite" ($\zeta\omega\tau\iota\kappa\grave{\eta}$ $\dot{\epsilon}\pi\iota\theta\upsilon$-$\mu\acute{\iota}\alpha$).[19] Thus, even though the sexual appetite seeks pleasurable rubbing quite apart from any reproductive goal, women's wombs and the semen in the male spinal cord direct this appetite toward procreation for the vast majority of human beings, male and female alike.[20] I refer to the combined force of the sexual appetite and the procreative urge as "sexual desire" hereafter in this chapter.[21]

The procreative imperative is nonetheless not an absolute master. Some men and women have a more pronounced homoerotic directive than a reproductive one. The recognition that Plato gives to homoeroticism, however, is limited to sexual love between males that eventually accords greater value to intellectual pursuits than to genital pleasures. The primary sexual directive that persons experience, as he puts it, depends on whether their inclination is motivated mainly by the immortal soul or the perishable body. Some men, whose stimulus is the soul, turn toward like-minded younger males. Though they are sexually involved at first, their intellectual engagement with each other gradually makes sexual pleasure less interesting and less frequent. Males in this relationship produce metaphorical progeny that

18. 91a1–b6. To locate semen in the spinal marrow was a respectable Hippocratic theory in Plato's time and later, J. Jouanna, *Hippocrates* (1999), 271–2.

19. 91b2–3. Plato here provides an anatomical explanation of the normative Greek view that one central purpose of heterosexual copulation should be to reproduce offspring, e.g., [Dem] 59.122, Cicero, *Fin* 3.62 = SVF 3.340.

20. In the creation myth in the *Timaeus,* however, Plato suggests that reproductive pleasures are lower on the scale of nature than restrained male homoerotic sexual pleasures. As this myth would have it, procreative intercourse became part of human nature only after some of the originally all-male race of human beings failed the demiurge's challenge to regulate their sexual and other appetites properly, 69c3–d6, 70d7–71a3. Due to this failure, the souls of the men who succumbed to sexual excess transmigrated into the bodies of women, who appear in the "second creation." Only at this point do the gods instill the reproductive urge into human nature, 41d4–42e3, 90e1–91a4. In terms of the Timaean creation myth, consequently, male homoerotic sexual relations are the primordial, and hence the first natural kind, of shared human sexual experience. Plato, however, maintains the opposite position in *Laws* 636c1–7, where he elevates the stature of reproductive sexual relations and marginalizes homoerotic practices, B. Brooten, *Love between Women: Early Christian Responses to Female Homoeroticism* (1996), 41.

21. Though Philo, Clement, and Epiphanes are indebted to Plato's conception of sexual desire, they do not maintain his distinction between the sexual appetite and reproductive urge. They classify the Platonic sexual appetite and reproductive urge under the one rubric of sexual $\dot{\epsilon}\pi\iota\theta\upsilon\mu\acute{\iota}\alpha$, that is, the sexual appetite or appetitive sexual desire, as I indicate later in chapters seven, nine, and ten.

Plato finds more worthy and enduring than children, such as poetry, philosophy, and law codes.[22] Other men, the vast majority, have a stimulus that is more the body, and they turn toward women to reproduce children. Plato does not consider the male homoerotic drive that remains vigorously sexual and does not fit his model of Platonic eros. He is also at best oblique in acknowledging that some women too have a homoerotic inclination, and he accords this relationship no intellectual honor whatsoever.[23] Plato's thoughts about homoeroticism are useful, despite their obvious limitations, as they show that he finds the reproductive imperative to be far from universally dominant.

Plato claims that the appetites for the pleasures of sexual activity, food, and drink are irrational. He defends this position through his much questioned argument about distinct sources of motivation in the human soul, namely, physical appetition, spirit, and reason.[24] Conflicting desires about whether to have a particular drink, for instance, indicate to him that there is a struggle between the appetitive and rational forces in the soul. Such conflict reveals "the presence in the soul of that which urges (τὸ κελεῦον) and that which restrains (τὸ κωλῦον) from drinking. That which restrains is something different from that which urges." The restraining force is "reason" (λογισμός) (*Rep* 439b3–e1). Physical appetition, by contrast, is "irrational" (ἀλόγιστον) (439d7–8), on the grounds that the conflict would not occur if the physical appetites were rational. Thus, for Plato the appetites are irrational given his conception of what happens in the human psyche when one both wants and does not want to have a drink, eat food, or engage in sexual activity.[25]

Plato further maintains that the irrational physical appetites function in

22. As portrayed in the *Symposium,* this relationship begins in a sexually active way and proceeds to more sublimated expressions of desire for beauty. The dominant lover initially "loves the body" of his more submissive partner in an intense way, 210a7, b5. ("Love of the body" is a circumlocution for sexual intimacy, cf. Xenophon, *Oec* 10.4–5 and Antipater in Stobaeus, 4.508.16–17.) Then the dominant partner moves toward a more disembodied love of beauty in which sexual activity plays a diminished role. At this point the lovers long to give metaphorical birth to great works, whereas women and their male lovers long to give birth to offspring, 208e1–10b3. See further A. W. Price, *Love and Friendship in Plato and Aristotle* (1989), 15–54 and E. E. Pender, "Spiritual Pregnancy in Plato's *Symposium*" (1992), 72–86.

23. In the *Symposium,* it is the character Aristophanes who discusses female homoeroticism, 191d3–92a1.

24. R. Robinson, "Plato's Separation of Reason from Desire" (1971), 38–48; J. Annas, *An Introduction to Plato's* Republic (1981), 109–52; T. Irwin, *Plato's Ethics,* 203–22; J. Annas, *Platonic Ethics, Old and New* (1999), 134–6; J. Cooper, "Plato's Theory of Human Motivation" (1984), 3–21; and C. Kahn, "Plato's Theory of Desire" (1987), 95–101.

25. Plato further supports his claim that the appetites are independent of reason by arguing that they give rise autonomously to lawless dreams and fantasies while reason sleeps, *Tim* 71a3–7, *Rep* 571c3–d4.

an antirational, and not merely arational, way. Since the appetites for food, drink, and sexual activity have no access to reason, they cannot know when enough is enough. They are aggressive in their ignorance, which leads them, contrary to reason, to strive always to exceed the limits of healthy appetition, to provoke human agents to consume or indulge far more than they should. Hunger, for instance, inevitably leads to gluttony unless reason hems it in and controls it. Were it not for the wise restraining power of reason's rule, human beings would end up in a ruinously excessive appetitive condition, rather like the legendary wine-drinking and pleasure-seeking Sardanapallus or the destructively voracious Erysichthon.[26] "The innate physical appetite for pleasures [of replenishment] . . . irrationally draws one toward [such] pleasures. If it prevails in us its name is licentious violence (ὕβρις). 'Licentious violence' is polyvalent. . . . [For example,] when the physical appetite prevails over better reason in relation to food and dominates among the appetites, it is gluttony [and the person is gluttonous] . . . and as for the names of the sibling appetites, the appetite that gains sway is clearly the suitable term to apply to the person," such as "drunkard" for persons with an excessive passion for wine.[27] Plato underscores the antirationality of the three sibling appetites with a number of natural and political metaphors. The appetites are a wild animal or an unruly, lawless mob that is incorrigibly persistent in its desire to rebel against reason's limits. When they gain the upper hand, the soul experiences a kind of civil war or tyrannical overthrow, an appetitive coup.[28] The appetites, then, inherently try to storm the citadel of reason because they really do want to eat cake, big slices of it.[29] Although Plato's metaphors are vivid, his position is not compelling. He does not justify why he shifts from arguing that the physical appetites are irrational to asserting that they are imperiously antirational, with the use of suggestive imagery displacing argument. Plato's conception of the physical appetites seems more grotesque than plausible, for it suggests that a sex-mad version of the Monty Python glutton evinces the human appetitive condition its purest unregulated form. This seems dubious. Plato is nonetheless earnest—be careful to control your appetites, or the explosive

26. J. Cooper gives a good explication of reason's desire to rule, "Plato's Theory of Human Motivation," 6–7 and n. 9.

27. *Phdr* 237d5–b5. J. C. B. Gosling and C. C. W. Taylor (*The Greeks on Pleasures* [1982], 115–28, 137–8) offer a valuable critique of Plato's position that the appetites for pleasure are insatiable.

28. Wild animal imagery appears in *Tim* 70e4, 91b6; *Rep* 439b4; and 572b4–5, while metaphors of mob rule occur in *Rep* 444b1–8, 571b5, 573b6–7, 573d4–5; and *Laws* 689b1–c3.

29. The image of the citadel or acropolis is Plato's. "The spirited part is placed nearer the head and between the neck and lungs in order that, being obedient to reason, it share forces with reason and hold back the clan of appetites when they refuse to compliantly obey the command from the citadel," *Tim* 70a6–7.

glutton will be you. Human reason must remain vigilant to prevent the appetites from wreaking havoc and driving persons into destructive excess.

Among the three appetites, in Plato's view, the sexual appetite has the strongest and most incorrigible propensity to excess. From later childhood through old age it stimulates the "greatest and sharpest need ($\chi\rho\epsilon\acute{\iota}\alpha$)" and "the fiercest and most intense" feelings of appetitive pleasure. The sexual appetite is also especially "tyrannical" in its impulse to overthrow reason (*Laws* 783a1–2, *Rep* 573b6–d5). As Sophocles maintains, with Plato's approval, sexual eros is "a raving and fierce master."[30] The sexual appetite is thus even hungrier than hunger for the greater part of one's life.[31] Its power "persuades and drags the majority" to seek out and venerate sexual activity and its pleasures, just as geometrical proofs persuade the mind to inquire into and admire the beautiful truths about Number that they demonstrate. In fact, "erotic compulsions are probably fiercer than geometrical proofs" among the populace at large given the crazed intensity of fricative pleasure.[32] The reproductive urge adds impetus to the sexual appetite (*Tim* 91a1–d5), for this urge too is "autocratic, like an animal disobedient to reason," and its "raging lusts" force most people to give in to the reproductive imperative (*Tim* 91b5–7). Sexual desire thus never learns to cooperate with reason, given its double-barreled force. At most it can be controlled by a fear of punishment for going beyond reason's limits. This is why the sexual appetite in the *Phaedrus* bears the brunt of a cruelty to which Plato never subjects hunger and thirst. "The charioteer, as though recoiling from the starting gate, yanks back more intensely the bit from the mouth of the wanton horse, thoroughly bloodies its jaws and evil-speaking tongue, and, making the horse sprawl to the ground on its limbs and hips, gives it a painful lashing." The beatings do not stop until the sexual animal finally cowers in a corner, forced somewhat into compliance because it is hobbled by terror.[33] Even in this condition, however, its swollen eyes retain a lascivious glimmer. The bad sexual horse still "has something to say to the charioteer and expects to enjoy some small treats for all its pains" (255e5–7). Human sexual desire thus poses the greatest challenge Plato sees to reason's mastery over the rampant ways of appetitive pleasure. So relentless is it that it must be blud-

---

30. *Rep* 329c3–4, cf. Soph. *Antig* 781, 790, 800–1. M. Nussbaum (*The Fragility of Goodness* [1986; reprint, 2001], 152) also notes Plato's conviction that the sexual appetite "is the most powerful among the appetites."

31. Plato even likens the sexual appetite to figurative gluttony. When the dominant lover wants to make love to an attractive youth, he wants to devour him like a ripe fruit, *Laws* 837b8–c3.

32. *Rep* 458d5–7, 403a4–6. Plato's point is that for every Euclid who is swayed by the intellectual pleasure of a well-executed theorem, countless others are swayed by the pleasure of sexual activity.

33. *Phdr* 254d5–e10. This image of subjection also appears at 256b2–3.

geoned into following reason's command, and even then its rebellious spirit remains unbroken.[34]

The continual struggle between the physical appetites and reason is central to Plato's conception of ethical human conduct. Human beings are virtuous when they regulate their appetites in a manner conducive to their own and the city's greater well-being. Conversely, they corrupt society and themselves when they give their appetites free rein. "Virtue (ἀρετή) is the outcome for those who conduct themselves well in relation to their three-fold need and appetite, and the opposite is true for those who conduct themselves badly in relation to them" (*Laws* 782d10–e3). Persons behave with appetitive virtue if they act only on what Plato calls "necessary and salutary appetites" (*Rep* 558e1, 559c3–4). He considers appetition necessary and healthy to the extent that persons benefit from it physically, and they so benefit when the appetites cannot be avoided without inducing harm to bodily well-being. "The appetites that we cannot deflect and that are healthy for us when acted on are rightly called necessary."[35] An ideal of nutritive simplicity also informs Plato's conception of appetitive virtue. He imagines that the dietary aspect of a good appetitive regimen would be met with the humble fare of the Greek countryside: wine in small amounts, bread, greens, and cheese for the main meal, chickpeas and figs afterwards, and roasted acorns for the occasional snack (*Rep* 372b1–c9). The sexual appetite is likewise beneficial when its pleasures are kept to a salutary minimum (*Laws* 784e5–85a1). People become wicked, however, when their ap-

---

34. Plato's position that the sexual appetite is incorrigible poses a difficulty for the common modern view that he thinks each soul part properly learns to carry out its own limited function of its own accord, with this cooperative distribution of soul labor leading to soul justice or temperance. T. Irwin (*Plato's Ethics*, 238) exemplifies this view: "temperance [according to Plato] involves . . . agreement by the non-rational parts that the rational part should rule; this agreement implies that each part does its own work, so that temperance requires justice." While a number of Plato's comments about the irrational part of the soul (τὸ ἐπιθυμητικόν) lend themselves to this interpretation, he does not allow that sexual desire ever learns to assent to reason's rule and to conduct itself like a tamed horse by the rule of moderation. At best the wild sexual horse "is ruined with fear" (*Phdr* 254e8) from reason's repression until it weakens and fades away of its own accord in old age. Hence for Plato justice in the soul is temperance with a billy club, which reason wields to keep the sexual appetite in reluctant submission. On this matter Plato differs from Posidonius, for instance, who maintains that human beings can and should train the irrational appetite in its entirety to obey reason, just as one trains a young colt to obey its master: by running it, tiring it, and by letting it have its fill of "the desires suitable to its nature" (οἰκεῖαι ἐπιθυμίαι) until the irrational appetite shows its obedience to reason by proceeding of its own accord "in a more measured fashion" F166, Edelstein and Kidd. J. Cooper ("Posidonius on Emotions" [1998], 90–3) offers a worthwhile analysis of this aspect of Posidonius's psychology and ethics.

35. *Rep* 558d11–59a1. Plato in the *Philebus* further considers necessary pleasures to be "true" and unnecessary, "false." This topic is carefully explicated by C. Hampton, "Pleasure, Truth, and Being in Plato's *Philebus:* A Reply to Professor Frede" (1987), 253–62.

petites are "unnecessary and lavish." In this condition they seek gratification in elaborate kinds as well as quantities. Broad culinary diversity, for example, is "bad for the body, bad for the soul, especially for its intelligence and capacity to be moderate." Persons who are wicked in their appetitive behavior are "stuffed on pleasures" (*Rep* 559b8–d10), be they gluttons, drunkards, sex maniacs, or some potent combination of the three. The appetites' voracity therefore drives an ongoing contest between virtue and vice in human affairs. The appetites seek vicious excess, and reason tries to restrain them within the limits of appetitive virtue. Showing proper restraint in dietary and sexual behavior is thus central to Plato's conception of what it means to be morally responsible.

Excessive pleasures are unhealthy partly because they upset the balance of pleasure inherent in appetitive human experience. Appetitive pleasures, as Plato sees them, are not simply pleasurable, but a mix of pleasure and pain.[36] When they are immoderate, the pain overwhelms the pleasure (*Laws* 733a6–34e2), such as groaning from the feast. Pain indicates a body in unhealthy distress, which is something "neither to choose nor desire" (*Laws* 733b1–2). Persons given to overindulging thus behave contrary to their bodily well-being. Sexual pleasure best exemplifies this health concern, for it is an especially intense mix of pleasure and pain.[37] By Plato's diagnosis, then, excessive sexual pleasure is like the self-inflicting of wounds, because the pain far outstrips the pleasure.[38] The disease is sexual madness (*Tim* 86b1–e2, *Laws* 783a2), and its symptoms are "a kind of panic" for sexual activity, burning with sexual desire, and becoming crazed during copulation and orgasm.[39] Persons cannot be blamed for suffering this condition if they have not learned how to control their sexual desire, but they are blameworthy to knowingly resist Plato's treatment, as shown further below.[40]

---

36. For worthwhile criticisms of Plato on mixed pleasure, see J. C. B. Gosling and C. C. W. Taylor, *The Greeks on Pleasure*, 115–28, 137–42 and M. Nussbaum, *The Fragility of Goodness*, 141–63. Like Gosling, Taylor, and Nussbaum, many people in Plato's day would have resisted his negative assessment of mixed appetitive pleasures. As Plato states, people by and large actively liked to "assuage either hunger, thirst, or similar things that the emergent nature [of the pleasure] fulfills. They take joy in its emergent nature by regarding it as a true pleasure. And they say that they would not accept living without experiencing thirst, hunger, and all other things attendant upon such kinds of distress," *Phileb* 54e4–8.

37. Plato uses the adjectives "very piercing" and "most fiery" (*Rep* 403a4, *Laws* 783a1–2) to describe the sharpness and burning that he associates with sexual desire and pleasure.

38. The preponderance of the pain that Plato ascribes to excessive pleasure is one likely reason why he calls it ὕβρις or "violence," *Phdr* 238a1–2, 250e5, 253e3; *Laws* 783a3, 837c5.

39. The sex-mad orgasm "makes one leap, causes all sorts of changes in skin color, bodily position, and breathing irregularities, . . . and it makes one shout in a crazed manner," *Phileb* 47a3–9. It is a "sexual panic" and a "total blow" to the body, *Laws* 783c10–d1, *Phileb* 47a8.

40. Persons given to sexual madness would be especially vociferous against Plato's constraining sexual reforms, *Laws* 839b3–6.

The contest posed by the sexual and other appetites goes far beyond the health concerns of the populace. In Plato's view, if one or another of them goes unchecked—and sexual eros especially—they stimulate and commandeer numerous other desires of an acquisitive, extravagant, or violent sort.[41] On this topic too, though, Plato is more eloquent than cogent. At best he sketches how and why unchecked appetition provokes this proliferation of desires by giving a quick guided tour of delinquent male character types who are afflicted and even criminal in their appetitively stimulated vices, such as the democratic man. The sexual appetite of Plato's tyrannical man, for instance, not only produces and rules over his desires for love affairs and for drinking parties, it also provokes him to steal from his own parents and neighbors and to loot temples in order to indulge these desires in a spendthrift way (*Rep* 573b6–75a7). Similarly, the man dominated by sexual passion is likely to commit any sort of murder as a crime of passion.[42] Uncontrolled sexual desire, hunger, and thirst stimulate other desires as a means to attain these core appetitive ends, such as the tyrannical man's desire to have money for drinking parties so that he can seduce the drunken participants who stir his ardor.[43] Plato's claim about proliferating desires, however, cannot adequately be explained as a means-end argument, for here he goes beyond such an argument without justifying why he does so. "Murder of any sort" is in many instances not explicable as a means to fulfill uncontrolled sexual desire, hunger, or thirst. Plato is contending that all vicious desires are propagated from the unregulated core appetites, and from sexual desire especially. The unrestrained appetites bring about "injustice, licentiousness, cowardice, ignorance, folly, and in general, every vice ($\sigma\upsilon\lambda$-$\lambda\dot{\eta}\beta\delta\eta\nu$ $\pi\hat{\alpha}\sigma\alpha\nu$ $\kappa\alpha\kappa\dot{\iota}\alpha\nu$)" (*Rep* 444a10–b8). A tree of vices to illustrate this idea would have a three-pronged taproot, with the longest root at the center being uncontrolled sexual desire.

Plato further contends that on a broader social scale the proliferation of desires goes beyond individual vices and leads to chronic wars of conquest and famine (*Rep* 373d7–74a2, 372b8–c1), with the greedy in power rapaciously consuming resources at the expense of the weaker in need.[44] As he would have it, then, sexual eros and the other two core appetites, unless

41. *Rep* 559c3, 559d9–10, 580e5.

42. *Rep* 571d1–2, 574e4. In another passage: "The majority are always looking down, bent toward the ground. They feast, stuffing themselves and copulating. Out of excessive desire for such things they kick and butt with horns and hoofs of iron, and kill one another due to their insatiability," *Rep* 586a6–b6.

43. J. Annas (*Plato's* Republic, 130) and J. Cooper ("Plato's Theory of Human Motivation," 10) note this means-end aspect of proliferating desires.

44. G. Vlastos ("The Theory of Social Justice in the *Polis* in Plato's *Republic*" [1977], 3–25) thoughtfully elucidates Plato's conviction that the populace in an ideal social order should make equally moderate use of material goods and physical necessities.

held in check by reason, are the origin of human-motivated social ills because they stimulate all vices from avarice to zealotry. If only we minded the necessary limits of sexual activity and ate and drank moderately, the society of peace and justice would be ours for the taking.

Plato sharply differentiates the sexual appetite from Platonic eros for bodily and transcendent beauty. The sexual appetite is inherently and dumbly drawn toward the fricative "pleasure of sexual activity," while Platonic eros is stimulated by a cognizant awareness of beauty in a beloved person and it recoils from the rub-a-dub-dub of sexual activity. Contrary to the straining of the sexual appetite toward pleasure, it strains with an opposing erotic intensity to perceive the nature of Beauty itself.[45] Unlike the innate sexual appetite, Platonic eros is acquired, a learned taste for Beauty or the Good, which one gains through becoming enlightened by Platonic metaphysics.[46] The sexual appetite cannot acquire or sublimate into developing this taste.[47] Its satisfaction requires heated friction of the genitals. By contrast, Platonic eros finds its ecstasy in the "sweetest" pleasure of seeing visible and transcendent beauty (*Phdr* 251e5–2a1). This pleasure is as sweet as sweet can be because it is free of the pain that accompanies genital pleasure. Sweet pleasure is experienced in its purest unmixed way through the study of geometry, when persons envision "the straight and the round, . . . [which] are always beautiful in themselves and have their own pleasures. These are not at all like the pleasures of scratching" (*Phileb* 51c3–d1). Sexual pleasure, by contrast, is a deep-seated scratching that involves "intensely

---

45. *Phdr* 254a2–7, b5–c3. Note, for example, the frequency of the verb "pull in an opposing direction" (ἀντιτείνειν) in the description of the soul as chariot, with the charioteer and the spirited part straining toward Beauty in opposition to the sexual appetite, which pulls against them toward sexual pleasure, 254a7, 254c3, 256a6.

46. *Phdr* 237d8–9. This contrast between the innate sexual appetite and the acquired Platonic yearning remains valid for both speeches, even though the contrast appears in Socrates' first speech about eros in the *Phaedrus,* not in the second or palinode speech. The palinode speech reaffirms that there is an innate drive for sexual pleasures, as opposed to an acquired Platonic taste for Beauty. In the palinode, Socrates recants only that the concept of eros applies strictly to the innate sexual appetite, which is the argument of the first speech, 238b7–c4. Instead, Socrates maintains in the palinode, eros has two very different senses—the innate sexual appetite as opposed to Platonic eros to behold Beauty.

47. The sexual appetite's inability to comprehend Beauty is also clear in *Phdr* 247c6–7: "The colorless, shapeless, and intangible being that truly is, is visible solely to mind, the pilot of the soul." The sexual appetite remains down in the bilge, blind to what the pilot or mind alone sees. Here I concur with C. Kahn ("Plato's Theory of Desire," 98–101) and support what A. W. Price (*Love and Friendship,* 83–4) regards as the "the less attractive" but more accurate interpretation of Plato's conception of the appetite for sexual pleasure: The "erotic appetite can be inhibited but not civilized." The charioteer's violent beating of the sexual horse supports this interpretation, for the aggression leaves the horse shaken but not subdued.

sharp, piercing, and burning" sensations (*Rep* 403a4, *Laws* 783a1–2).[48] Therefore, the sexual appetite is point for point the unregenerate opposite of Platonic eros.

Unlike the pleasure of studying geometry, however, the overall human experience of falling or being in love with another person combines the conflicting impulses of the sexual appetite and Platonic eros. This heady experience of being in love is a mixture of the two, not pure Platonic eros, and should never be confused with Platonic eros alone. Plato noticed such confusion brewing in his own day and attempted to clarify matters. As he explains in *Laws* 837b6–d2, Platonic eros remains unconditionally antisexual in its desire and end. It absolutely "forbids one from plucking the bloom" of sexual activity. Instead it thrills the soul with a desire to behold the form of Beauty itself, partly through the stimulus of seeing the bodily beauty of beloved persons. The experience of being in love is a "third sense" of eros, the "mix of [the two kinds of] eros." Platonic eros proper refers to the antisexual component, while the sexual appetite is the intensely sexual component.[49] Even though Plato deploys erotic imagery rivaling that in Sappho's poetry to describe the desire of Platonic eros to view Beauty,[50] eros in this sense has a pronounced aversion to sexual contact, contrary to sexually appetitive eros. The motive of Platonic eros is a longing to behold "the nature of beauty seated on a pure throne," not, as eros does for Sappho (fr. 1.1), to sexually worship Aphrodite seated on her "exquisite throne." To Plato, consequently, the sexual appetite as "wicked horse" is like an inflamed sa-

---

48. Plato seems not at his most perceptive to describe sexual pleasure in terms more suitable for a poison ivy rash, where the desire to scratch is ferociously intense and the pain predominates over pleasure once an afflicted person gives in and scratches.

49. G. Vlastos (*Platonic Studies* [1981] 39–40) is thus mistaken to characterize Platonic eros as "a peculiar mix of sensuality, sentiment, and intellect," and to emphasize that this definition "should count as the original and always primary sense of 'Platonic love.'" What he regards as the original and primary sense Plato regards as a tertiary and muddled sense that leads to "puzzlement and opacity" about what he means by Platonic eros, *Laws* 837b6–d2. Vlastos here overcorrects the misguided scholarly view in his day that persons stimulated by Platonic eros remain completely unruffled by any sexual ardor.

50. Plato especially draws on erotic tropes at *Phdr* 251c5–52a1, such as the outflow of eros from the eyes and the inability to sleep when the beloved is absent. The consummation of Platonic eros proper, however, occurs from "seeing the [beloved]," which is accompanied by a quasi-orgasm of dammed-up waters being released once eye contact is made. By contrast, the consummation of eros in Sappho and other erotic literature is sexual—eros requires, as Longus states, "kisses, embracing, and lying down together with naked bodies," *Daphnis and Chloe*, 2.5.7. Platonic eros reaches its climax by "looking rather than sexually interacting" (ὁρῶν μᾶλλον ἢ ἐρῶν), *Laws* 837c4–6. When Platonic eros temporarily prevails in the aroused soul of the lover, he regards the "sexual satiating of a body with a body" (τὴν περὶ τὸ σῶμα τοῦ σώματος πλησμονήν) as a "violent outrage" (ὕβριν).

tyr's groin in the soul's irrational faculty,[51] while Platonic eros is an ecstatic rapture that makes the soul's rational faculty flutter and throb with longing for the unadulterated pleasure of viewing Beauty in and of itself.

Human beings, insofar as they are embodied agents, do not experience Platonic eros on its own. Lovers are in a two-fold—and to Plato conflicting—state of agitation. Through reason they seethe with Platonic eros for Beauty, but through the sexual appetite they whinny for sexual pleasure.[52] Neither impulse comprehends or has any share in the other's longing, at least as Plato construes them.[53] Platonic eros, further, is no rarified substitute for sexual desire. On his view it is the more authentic eros, though it is not humanly possible to experience it in an unmixed form given the persistence of the sexual appetite.[54] Plato accords little or no beauty to sexual pleasure, even though he accords considerable beauty to the human body. Such pleasure, far from having aesthetic merit, is at worst a violent outrage and at best a grotesque comedy with its contorted bodies, panting, and shouting. Not least among its unattractive qualities is sexual desire's oblivi-

---

51. As A. W. Price aptly notes (*Love and Friendship,* 79), the bad horse in the palinode speech (*Phdr* 242d11–57b6) is "horrid." It is a "horse of wickedness" (ὁ τῆς κακῆς ἵππος) (*Phdr* 251d6–52a1), for it stands for the incorrigible sexual appetite in particular rather than for the physical appetites in general. The bad horse in the metaphor of the soul as chariot is sexual because it illustrates the first of the two kinds of eros in the palinode speech, namely, the irrational sexual appetite.

52. The verb Plato uses is χρεμετίζειν, which refers to the loud neighing or whinnying of horses, *Phdr* 254d4.

53. D. Halperin and M. Nussbaum diminish the opposition that Plato makes between the two. In fact, they meld the two together. Halperin's underlying premise in "Plato and Erotic Reciprocity" (1986), 80, is that "Plato refuses to separate—he actually identifies and fuses—the erotics of sexuality . . . and the erotics of philosophical inquiry." In "Platonic *Erōs* and What Men Call Love" (1985), 171, he similarly states that "My assumption throughout this paper . . . is that Platonic eros [is not reducible to sexual desire] but does indeed *also* make sense as an analysis of the intentionality of sexual desire and demands to be taken seriously as such." Nussbaum (*The Fragility of Goodness,* 220, 216) likewise maintains that in the *Phaedrus,* "sexuality broadly interpreted . . . permeates the whole of [the lovers'] madness." This is a sexuality in which sexual desire and intellectual aspirations "flow together so that the person feels no gap between thought and passion, but, instead, a melting unity of the entire personality." Interesting as their thoughts are about the fusion of erotic arousal and stimulated intelligence in human beings, they leave Plato far behind, for he allows no fusing or melting unity of the sexual appetite and Platonic eros. Their position that he not only allows but "refuses to separate" the two kinds of eroticism is an exaggeration that has likely been facilitated by Vlastos's erroneous position (see above, n. 49) that Platonic love in the "original and primary sense" is mixed (viz., both sexual appetite and Platonic eros straining in opposite directions), which Plato in the *Laws* expressly denies is his original and primary sense of eros.

54. *Phdr* 248a1–5 indicates that the sexual appetite precludes even the most disciplined person from being aroused only by Platonic eros. "The human soul that follows and best resembles the god lifts the head of the charioteer into the outer region . . . but is disturbed by the horses and is hardly able to look at the things that really are (τὰ ὄντα)."

ousness to beauty and its capacity to transmit this insensibility to the person as a whole.

Plato extends the harmful repercussions of excessive desire beyond the body and society and into the afterlife of the immortal soul. This afterlife concern is no ancillary matter, for his thought is permeated with the Pythagorean dualism of body and soul and with a cosmic dualism between the realms of being and becoming.[55] As his primary aim in ethics and politics, Plato strives to enlighten embodied souls through social and political change, and his sociopolitical reforms are a means to this end. "Not only once have we said . . . that tending the soul comes first, of the three things that properly matter to human beings [namely, soul, body, and material goods]," for "the soul is truly the most honorable concern for all."[56] The immortal soul, when embodied, is at great risk of being lured into myriad vicious and painful pleasures by the appetites. Appetite-driven concerns entice the soul and person as a whole into thinking that only the physical world of flux exists (*Phd* 81b1–5), and that pure being is a Platonic fiction. The soul, once beguiled, loses its ability to recollect its immortal nature and becomes burdened with bodily and earthly qualities (83a1–e3), buried alive with clods of proliferating vices (81e5–6). Souls that fail to recollect their nature cannot ascend to the Good or Beauty after they depart from the body at death (*Phd* 80d5–84b8). Instead they remain unenlightened, banished from their birthright in pure being, and from there descend into lower animal forms, encased in fur or fins, and never gazing upward again.[57] Excessive sexual and other appetitive behavior thus must be curbed for pressing reasons of concern to the soul that go beyond bodily health and the good society, important though these are. Plato in the *Republic* and *Laws* is eager to do whatever it takes to restrict appetitive behavior individually, socially, and politically in order to facilitate the philosophical quest of immortal souls for the intelligible world. The clampdown begins with sexual desire.

Even though sexual desire is the most recalcitrant troublemaker of the

55. C. de Vogel provides a sound explication of Plato's dualism in *Rethinking Plato and Platonism* (1986), 171–9, and see too G. Vlastos, "The Theory of Social Justice," 30–4 and J. C. B. Gosling and C. C. W. Taylor, *The Greeks on Pleasure*, 83–7.

56. *Laws* 743c5–e6, 731c5–6. Plato presents this position more fully at *Rep* 443c9–44a2.

57. Though Plato's soul-body dualism comes to the fore especially in the *Phaedo*, he reaffirms this view in the *Phaedrus* and *Timaeus*, albeit with a tripartite construct of the soul. In the *Phaedrus*, excessive sexual appetition distracts the soul from recollecting its immortal nature and the soul does not ascend toward Beauty, *Phdr* 248c2–e5, 250e1–51a1, 253d1–55a1, 256b7–d3, cf. *Phdr* 238a6–b3. In the *Timaeus*, Plato portrays the human condition as a contest in the soul between the appetites and reason; and reason must win the struggle. Souls in which reason loses are drawn into hedonism and sink lower on the scale of nature, 41d4–42e4, 91d5–92c3.

core appetites, Plato argues that it is both harmful and unfeasible to starve
or deny it altogether. The sexual horse should be given its requisite carrots
now and then, for a strict regimen of moderation exemplifies Plato's notion
of sexually appetitive virtue. Like hunger and thirst, sexual desire is unavoidable and beneficial to a degree (*Rep* 559c3–7). To this degree, persons ought to be sexually active for health reasons, because a "great compulsion" (ἀνάγκη) drives human nature to fulfill the necessary appetites
(*Phd* 64e4–6).[58] Plato's more precise plans for reproductive reform are explored in the following section. Suffice it here to say that he allows moderate
sexual hedonism for persons who have completed their procreative service
for the good of the city. He does not try to restrict necessary and beneficial
sexual activity throughout the human life span to the purpose of reproduction because he thinks sexual desire is far too compelling for so restrictive
a limit. Complete sexual abstinence, further, would be unfeasible and inad-
visably extreme even if some individuals were to prove able to emaciate
their sexual desire. Moderation exemplifies Plato's conception of virtuous
sexual conduct.[59]

Plato underscores his position that sexual renunciation would be unhealthy by associating diseases with the total deprivation of sexual pleasure.
If, for instance, women refuse to sate their urge for reproduction, their
wombs precipitate respiratory ailments and other signs of ill health.[60] Men
too undergo a suffering on par with Io's if they leave their sexual appetite
unfed (*Tim* 91b4–7). They become maddened from the stings and bites inflicted by their inner sexual horsefly. This physiological torture is especially
unbearable if a man has more than the usual abundance of seed teeming in
his spinal marrow (*Tim* 86c3–d2). In order to avoid such diseases, persons
should regard a law-abiding sexual moderation and "not complete sexual abstinence" as proper.[61] To live by this standard would admittedly be about as
exciting as a steady diet of chickpeas and acorns, brightened by the occasional fig. This is exactly how Plato thinks we should live, with the gift to be

58. Plato thus does not grant the position seen in Epicurus, that sexual desire is a natural
but unnecessary appetite, fr. 456 (Usener).

59. See further G. Klosko, *The Development of Plato's Political Theory* (1986), 103–13.

60. *Tim* 91b7–c7. For similar reasons Plato in *Laws* 930c2–6 states that it is inadvisable for
a young widow to remain without a second husband.

61. *Laws* 841b4–5, cf. 784e5–85a1 (and note Euripides, fr. 428, for a very similar view).
Thus even the model ascetic philosopher in the *Phaedo* would be sexually active within reason.
His soul should refrain from the physical appetites, 82c2–4, but only "as far as possible," 64e4–
6, 83b7, that is, in compliance with the moderate and necessary use of the appetites for sexual
activity, food, and drink, *Phd* 64d2–6, 81b1–6. Nussbaum is not persuasive that "the *Phaedo*'s
true philosopher can completely dissociate himself from it [the sexual appetite] with no danger," *The Fragility of Goodness,* 152. The model philosopher should engage in sexual activity
even by Plato's austere version of the golden mean.

simple in the sexual and sibling appetites and the ensuing gift to be free from vicious desires, social inequity, and widespread indifference to the Good.

PLATO'S PROCREATIVE ETHICS AND COMMUNAL SOCIAL IDEAL

Plato firmly believed that uncontrolled sexual desire had been allowed to run wild and plague the human condition. As far as he was concerned, its potential to run rampant was fully realized in Athens and elsewhere, with his fellow Greeks being afflicted with chronic sexual madness and yet denying that they were sick in the slightest. "Human sexual desires are the source of countless woes for people individually and for entire cities."[62] As far as Plato's contemporaries were concerned, though, nothing made them happier than sexual pleasures—and the more intense and frequent the experience, the better.[63] What they called happiness Plato regarded as a widespread addiction to the leader of the hedonistic pack, sexual desire, and to its spawn of other violent desires waging gleeful despotism over reason and moderation. To his mind sexual desire held the lead because of its composite make-up, the ferocious sexual appetite with the equally wild reproductive urge riding on it bareback. Given this magnitude of the woes and their ostensible origin, Plato put reproductive and other sexual reforms first on his agenda to ameliorate the embodied conditions of the soul in society.

The reproductive regulations in the *Republic* and *Laws* are pragmatic in intent and motivated by Plato's aim to rationally patrol sexual desire for the duration of its power, from early youth through old age. To accomplish this project, "an audacious lone man," he declares, must fearlessly intervene in the appetitive status quo, "guided only by reason and having no backers to support him" (*Laws* 835c2–8). Plato as maverick philosopher takes matters into his own hands through political philosophy, rather than directly on the political scene in Athens, for he fears that his ideas toward sexual and social reform would be unanimously voted down. Young adult males would protest the loudest, he thinks, for by his understanding young men are oversexed, "teeming with semen" in their spinal marrow (*Laws* 839b3–6). Rather than submit his proposals to a democratic vote, Plato started to teach young men philosophy, and as a recurrent theme in his ethics and political theory, he strove to reverse the conventional Greek measures of virility and happiness: Sexual restraint is the mark of a real man and genuine happiness,

---

62. *Laws* 836a8–b2. I interpret the word "countless" (μυρία) in 836b1 as an allusion to "countless woes" (μυρία ἄλγεα) at *Iliad* 1.2, for which note E. B. England's commentary on the *Laws* at 836b1.

63. Plato attributes this viewpoint to his contemporaries in a number of passages, such as *Laws* 840b6–7, *Phdr* 256c3–5, and *Phileb* 47b2–7, 65c1–e1.

while sexual pleasure is for sissies.[64] And in a more long-term investment beyond his immediate students, Plato wrote the *Republic* and *Laws*, not as bookish utopias, but as plans for real social change toward a future of appetitive restraint.[65]

Plato presumes the ancient Greek norm that the persons to target for procreative regulations are the central enfranchised group in a city, the guardians in the *Republic* and the citizens at large in the *Laws*. The regulations serve partly to perpetuate the group and the distribution of labor within it. As in Greek society, Plato does not offer other possibilities, such as requiring a slave class to perform reproductive labor on a surrogate basis, or employing other social outsiders as procreative laborers to do the job. He has eugenic reasons for requiring the citizens and good guardians to reproduce their own social kind. In the *Republic*, city officials regulate the guardians in a preferential system that gives the best and most restrained

64. There are several interesting illustrations of this new convention. In the *Laws* boys must abstain from all unnecessary sexual relations in order to become men. They are to regard this effort as a true male athleticism, following the ancient practice of athletes refraining from sex prior to a contest in order to ensure a more potent performance. The triumph of Plato's students, though, is better than winning in the Olympics, for they win immortal "victory over sexual pleasures," *Laws* 839e5–40c10. Plato also teaches that boys in a democratic society (a group that would have included all of Plato's Athenian students) are almost certain to lose this contest unless they mend their ways. The son of a democratic father "is led into all kinds of lawlessness" by the appetites and will be seduced to transform into the dread tyrannical man, *Rep* 572d5–e1. The *Timaeus* teaches that unless young men moderate their appetites, they will be reincarnated as girls, 41d4–42d2, 90e1–91a4. These teachings are hardly Plato at his most admirable or convincing. His inversion of male sexual prowess nonetheless had considerable success in later Greek philosophy, where it takes on an intensified machismo. In the late Cynic epistles, for instance, Plato's athletic theme becomes a "war" ($\pi\delta\lambda\epsilon\mu\sigma$) against sexual pleasures, Epistles 5, 12, 46 of ps.-Diogenes in A. Malherbe, *The Cynic Epistles* (1977). For Plato's disparagement of women as an inferior type of human being and the tension between this and his relatively enlightened proposals for female guardians in *Republic* 5, see J. Annas, "Plato's *Republic* and Feminism" (1979), 24–33; E. Spelman, "Woman as Body: Ancient and Contemporary Views" (1982), 109–31 and "Hairy Cobblers and Philosopher Queens" (1988), 19–36; M. Buchan, *Women in Plato's Political Theory* (1999), 91–4; and G. Vlastos, "Was Plato a Feminist?" (1989), 288–9.

65. Plato states that his reforms are no fantasy or "dream" pertaining only to a hypothetical populace, *Rep* 450d1, which J. Annas notes, *Plato's Republic*, 185–6, as does A. Gouldner, *Enter Plato: Classical Greece and the Origins of Social Theory* (1965), 171, 197–8. Nonetheless, Plato's reforms are frequently regarded today as "a pipe-dream [and] thought-experiment," J. Winkler, *The Constraints of Desire: The Anthropology of Sex and Gender in Ancient Greece* (1990), 18, and see too P. Vander Waerdt, "Politics and Philosophy in Stoicism" (1991), 196. M. F. Burnyeat ("Utopia and Fantasy: The Practicability of Plato's Ideally Just City" [1992], 175–87), however, refutes this view. As C. Kahn (in his 1993 foreword to G. Morrow, *Plato's Cretan City*, xxvii) aptly puts it, "Plato . . . had aspired to a public career of political reform. He ultimately chose the life of philosophy as a continuation of politics by other means," and by writing the *Republic* and *Laws* foremost. See also C. Bobonich, *Plato's Utopia Recast* (2002), 374–479.

guardians the greatest opportunity to procreate; the worst guardians, the least; and only the offspring of the best are to be raised once they pass inspection (*Rep* 459d4–6ob5). The guardians have no choice but to comply. In the *Laws,* however, all the citizens must reproduce their fair share and regard it as unholy to do otherwise (783d8–84e1, 721c2–8). They too, though, are to aspire toward moderation themselves and to reproduce restrained offspring. Male citizens face stiff penalties if they do not marry female citizens (721d1–6, 774a1–c2). Once married, the bridegrooms and brides must direct their attention toward procreation. Female overseers police the married couples to make sure that they obey (783e4–84c4). The obligation to procreate therefore applies to the guardians on a preferential scale in the *Republic,* and to the citizens without exceptions or preferential system in the *Laws.* In both plans, however, Plato's regulations aim to create a more purebred strain of human beings in control of their appetites.

Due to his assessment of the appetites, Plato regards society as a mixed blessing. On the one hand, human beings are not self-sufficient and require things to meet their basic needs or "necessary desires." People have rightly gathered into a city or polis to cooperate, share, and fulfill the needs of one another (*Rep* 369b5–d12). Reproduction, for example, is one such civic need, for without a symbiotic populace, there are no persons to work and sustain the division of labor. Plato deems society good to the extent that it satisfies the necessary desires that lead to individual and collective well-being. The physical appetites, however, relentlessly push human beings as political animals to transgress the limit of necessary desires, and sexual desire is the strongest culprit. Civic mores should impede this corruption by encouraging the enlightened rule of reason in the person of the philosopher king.

According to Plato, the customs of private property and the free market inevitably breed appetitive excess and violence. Society becomes inflamed with vices when men have too much wealth in persons, goods, and resources at their disposal on which their own appetites and those of their families may feed and proliferate. Even if a city begins with material simplicity and restraint, it is only a matter of time until it ends up frenetically unrestrained when its inhabitants "buy and sell, [using] the marketplace and coinage as a means of exchange" (*Rep* 371b4–8, 372e2–3). As Plato sees it, in a free market there are no checks on what people may want to acquire, own, and consume for themselves and their kin. Excess is encouraged as though it were economic prosperity, and this unleashes the mob of appetites and related desires rather than keeping them subdued. As a result, an initially restrained city "will not satisfy." Its inhabitants will demand more luxury goods, and thereby make their once healthy community feverish (373a1–8). In such a diseased city, "men think they will be happy by owning land, big fine houses, fine furnishings, . . . gold, silver, and all other such things . . . and they spend money as they wish, such as giving it to mistresses"

(419a4–9, 420a4–6). To rehabilitate the city from acquisitive license, Plato would prohibit private ownership, unrestricted consumption, and the free market. Given his diagnosis, a communal social order is the cure.

In the *Republic* Plato finds a Pythagorean-inspired communalism the most attractive option to implement for his envisioned city of Kallipolis. This social order works in the voluntary cooperative spirit that "friends should hold goods in common (κοινὰ τὰ φίλων),"⁶⁶ though the social pattern is also mandated administratively by enlightened philosophical rule. Plato works from a Pythagorean model partly because he and the Pythagoreans alike sought to institute "as many impediments as possible on the exercise of human sexual activity (ἀφροδίσια)" for the good of the city,⁶⁷ as explored further in chapter four. Plato thus approaches his plans for communal sexual reform in a Pythagorean spirit, for he too aims to help friends help one another keep their sexual and other desires in beneficial check, with guidance from the wise king. He is utterly serious in this endeavor, given all that he sees at stake.

The first kinds of property that Plato would free from the ownership of men are women and their capacities for reproduction and nurture. Women gain first priority because the principles by which members of a society reproduce offspring are his fundamental law of social order. Procreative customs, he states, play a pivotal role in determining whether social customs in general are restrained or dissolute. "The beginning of [human] generation is the first law that the lawgiver would establish by regulating marriage customs," because the patterns of "marriage, procreation, and raising children . . . have a great and complete bearing on whether the social order proceeds rightly or wrongly."⁶⁸ If this primary law mandates, as Athenian society did in his day, that men own wives and daughters—wives as household managers and mothers of their children, and daughters to be exchanged in marriage to other men—then the society is bound to be disorderly and feverish. Plato thus long ago had the basic insight for which Engels is better known.⁶⁹ He appreciates that the work of reproduction and childrearing sets the pattern of society itself, and with it the quality of life that the people have, female and male members alike. Plato too advocates a kind of socialism, albeit on a city, rather than nation, basis. What brings him to this in-

---

66. *Rep* 424a1–2, 423e6–24b1, 449c4–5.

67. Iamblichus, *vit Pyth* 209–10.

68. *Rep* 449d1–6. Plato supports this position through the main dialectician in *Laws* 720e10–21a8, even though Adeimantus rather than Socrates is the one who voices it in the *Republic*. Plato accordingly gives very careful attention to reproductive sexual mores in the *Republic* and *Laws*, *Rep* 423e6–24b1, 449c2–73e5; *Laws* 631d6–32a2, 720e10–21d6, 771c7–76b4, 782d10–85b9, 835d3–42a3, 925a2–c3, 929e9–30e2. G. Grote appreciates the import of Plato's emphasis on regulating procreation, *Plato*, vol. 4, 169–80, 342–7.

69. *The Origin of the Family, Private Property, and the State* (1972, originally published 1884).

sight, however, sets him apart from Engels and makes his socialism puritanical.[70] Because disorderly sexual desire and its progeny of vices are to blame for social and psychological corruption, he gives top priority to reining it in. In so doing Plato strives for a two-in-one efficiency. By regulating procreation as the first law of social order, he constrains the sexual appetite as well. The two-fold control mechanism that he devises works rather like a twisted leash that confines a dog by its neck and leg at the same time, though Plato's double leashing is deliberate. His communal rallying cry thus is not the Marxist-feminist "Workers of the world unite!" with a driving concern for female solidarity and freedom from male-mandated reproductive norms.[71] Rather, he is the first voice of the Platonist Temperance Union. "Citizens, rein in your sexual desire! The reproductive urge first and the rest will stay in tow!" A Pythagorean communalism of the women best facilitates this aim because it severs sexual desire from possessiveness and consumerism, helps restrict sexual activity to the beneficial degree, and in other ways encourages an appetitively subdued society.

First, the communal pooling of women and reproductive labor removes kinship-based factionalism and the related competition for wealth in the city. Plato thinks "there is no greater evil than the fragmented city" (*Rep* 462a9–b3). A city must strive to be politically unified and psychologically holistic, so that it responds quickly to suffering in its parts, just as the human body responds to a sharp blow to a finger (*Rep* 462b4–6, 462c10–d3). Traditional procreation within marriage, however, hinders civic unity because it motivates families and clans to rival one another to acquire more for their own households at each other's expense (*Rep* 462b8–c5, 464c5–e2). Families, preoccupied with their own material prosperity, tend to neglect and even contribute to suffering in the city outside of the kinship circle that claims their primary loyalty and identity (*Rep* 462a9–e3). Alcmaeonid pain is likely to give pleasure to the rival Pisistratid clan. Both groups are ready to dishonor their rivals and put them at a disadvantage, even though they are all fellow Athenian citizens.[72] Plato's communal reforms in reproduction

70. E. Barker (*Greek Political Theory: Plato and His Predecessors*[3] [1947], 211–7) explicates the salient differences and similarities between Platonic and modern socialism. His explanation gets right to the heart of the matter and antedates the heated and largely anachronistic controversy provoked by K. Popper in *The Open Society and Its Enemies*[5] (1971, first published 1945, under the duress of World War II). Barker senses and tries to defuse the reading of totalitarianism into Plato's *Republic* in his 1947 preface, x.

71. M. O'Brien, *The Politics of Reproduction* (1981), 123–5. This is not to deny that Plato had a desire to emancipate Athenian women. He states that he would like to free them from the "sunken and shadowy life" (*Laws* 781c6) to which they were relegated.

72. Reproduction of kin also leads to divided loyalty between family and city. If, for example, a city goes to war, male citizens face conflicting obligations—to fight, and risk death, or to do whatever possible to remain alive so as to support their aging kin. Plato recognizes the

and childrearing would dismantle the acquisitive bastions of kinship groups so as to produce a genuinely collective civic body committed to moderation.

Second, the communal pooling of women is of great benefit to women themselves. It frees them from the burden of running the domestic side of family-oriented acquisitiveness, such as purchasing goods for the household and maintaining it. Through this freedom they are much better positioned to help shape a holistic and unified city. When women are privately managed as wives, mothers, and daughters, the ensuing social order assumes that a married couple's desires to have their own children, house, and household goods are basic subsistence needs rather than acquisitive wants. A wife in this system belongs to a particular man and is the mother of his children. She is habituated to want her family's comforts foremost even if the cost, including her energy, would be better spent on a community project that matters to everyone. Her daily tasks inefficiently replicate the so-called women's work being done by neighboring wives and mothers in a house-by-house choreography that leaves them all with less time and initiative for more collective social pursuits.[73] Their energy would not be drained in a society that shared the raising of children and other domestic work. Women find their opportunities to work for the collective good curtailed in societies where men and their families sharply distinguish among themselves between "my property and not my property" (*Rep* 462c4–5, 464c5–e2). The problem becomes even more apparent the more consumer-oriented the society becomes, which Plato thinks is inevitable in a society that extols the family, property, and mercantilism. The women have bigger houses, more furnishings, and so on, whose upkeep is a their responsibility regardless of whether they own female slaves, or, in the modern day, machines. Plato explains this argument by analogy with female guard dogs. If the dogs, like Athenian women, were restricted to feminine roles such as tending the pups and cleaning the den, then the pack as a whole would suffer. The female dogs would not go hunting as they do along with the male dogs to help meet the entire pack's need for sustenance (*Rep* 451d4–52a1). This would be especially true if the den kept getting needlessly bigger and more elaborate due to covetous canine visions of the good life. Plato's communal reforms do away with the separate households that lead to unnecessary replication and proliferation of appetitive demands. Women are then freed along with the men to shape a holistic and unified city, rather than remaining pawns to the passions to have and to own.

Plato remains true to his conviction that the communal city ideally should

---

force of this γηροβοσκία obligation in *Laws* 930e3–32d8. His communal procreative reform would unify the city by eliminating such conflicting allegiance.

73. As J. Annas (*Plato's* Republic, 183) states, Plato is dissatisfied that "half the citizens [are] sitting at home wasting effort doing identical trivial jobs!"

supplant the society that privileges private ownership, favors the family, and encourages consumption.[74] In the *Republic* he is optimistic that his proposals are feasible and practical. This reform would work successfully, so long as philosophers become kings and their subjects are collectively raised and educated according to the principle that friends should hold goods in common.[75] Sexual communalism remains an elite practice in the *Republic*, however, restricted to the guardian class.[76] In the *Laws* Plato reaffirms and broadens his conviction that communal reproduction and childrearing are the best way to ground a society. If he could, he would extend these reforms to all citizens, not only to an elite guardian class. "No one will ever posit a more correct or better definition [of the ideal city] in its preeminence toward human virtue than one in which the private ownership of women, children, and all other goods is everywhere and by every means eliminated from human life" (739b8–e3). Nonetheless, Plato by this time is resigned to thinking that such reform is not possible on a pragmatic level. Only "gods or children of gods dwell happily in the fully communal city" (*Laws* 739d6–e1), but mere mortals seem incapable of such enlightenment. Plato surrenders to the apparent inevitability of familial norms in the *Laws* because of the flood of reactionary responses that his communal sexual proposals elicited, an onrush that has only recently abated.[77] The citizens of his envisioned city

74. E. Barker (*Greek Political Theory*, 219–20) eloquently conveys Plato's misgivings about the family as a social unit in his day: "'Every Englishman's house is his castle,' we say. 'Pull down the walls,' Plato would reply, 'they shelter at best a narrow family affection; they harbour at the worst selfish instincts and stunted capacities. Pull down the walls and let the fresh air of a common life blow over the place where they have been.' . . . [The home] is condemned again as a place of wasted talents, dwarfed powers, where the mind of the wife is wasted on the service of tables (460D), and 'little meannesses' abound."

75. Plato vitiates the idea of communalism in *Republic* 5 by describing the male guardians alone as "friends" (φίλοι) and grouping the female guardians and children as part of the communal resources the friends have in common, 449c4–5, 457c10–d3; M. Buchan, *Women in Plato's Political Theory* (1999), 121; M. Foucault, *Use of Pleasure*, 53 n. 2. A genuinely communal society would regard all morally mature agents as friends and treat children as friends in the making. The early Stoics formulate this idea, as shown in the next chapter.

76. *Rep* 450c1–5, 451b9–c7, 457b7–c1, 457c10–d3. As noted, however, by R. Mayhew (*Aristotle's Criticism of Plato's* Republic [1997], 130–7), even the *Republic* contains several intimations toward universalizing communalism to all the city dwellers.

77. The image of the flood is Plato's, *Rep* 457b7–d5. Aristotle's arguments against Plato's communal society appear in *Pol* 1261b16–64b24, the uneven quality of which R. Mayhew studies, *Aristotle's Criticism*, 59–122, and see too A. W. Price, *Love and Friendship*, 179–205. A prominent lampoon of communal sexual mores appears in Aristophanes, R. Ussher, ed., *Aristophanes:* Ecclesiazusae, xiv–xx. The precise relationship between *Republic* 5 and Aristophanes' *Ecclesiazusae* cannot be securely determined from available evidence, though Plato's communal theory might be reworking Aristophanes', M. F. Burnyeat, "Utopia and Fantasy," 180–5. More reactionary scholars, such as A. Bloom, have tended to dismiss or distort the reforms in *Republic* 5, as explored succinctly by C. Pierce, "Equality: *Republic* V" (1973), 1–11 and in greater detail by N. Bluestone, *Women and the Ideal Society: Plato's* Republic *and Modern Myths of Gender*

of Magnesia must make do with the given conditions of family and marriage, but still try to be moderate in all respects. For example, the rich and powerful should marry persons of modest means so that the ensuing generations of families are at most moderately affluent and roughly on par with one another (*Laws* 772e7–73e4). Here Plato is trying to deploy marriage to do what he knows a communal city would accomplish more effectively: to prevent social cliques of the wealthy from producing more of their own social kind, at the expense of shaping a more holistic and egalitarian city of moderation and justice for all.[78] In the *Laws,* however, he shrinks from enforcing even this method of severing the reproductive urge from family wealth and power, unlike the forceful separation of the two that he sets out for the guardians in the *Republic.* "To mandate these things by law would be considered laughable and would stir up anger among many" (*Laws* 773c3–8). Instead, the citizens must themselves learn to see the merit of marrying into appetitive temperance and voluntarily seek this middle class mean. In the *Laws,* Plato thus aims only to instill the norm of frugal economic parity within the more traditional Greek framework of marriage and the family. This alternative is second-rate in his view (*Laws* 739e4), because it leaves in place the appetitive breeding ground that should be supplanted for the moderate society to become a living reality—the individual male ownership of women, their wombs, and children in the family.

PLATO'S EUGENIC AIM IN HIS PROCREATIVE REFORMS

Plato in the *Republic* and *Laws* further restricts sexual desire through eugenic constraints on reproduction. Some of the measures derive from popular Greek culture, where they promoted generic well-being of the offspring and community at large. Plato, though, reshapes these measures to support his own conception of appetitive health. The guardians and citizens must obey population control measures, procreate only during their prime, abide by incest prohibitions, and conduct religious ceremonies in order to have the gods bless and ensure the production of healthy offspring. A few of Plato's other eugenic measures, though, go beyond retooling popular practices already in place. These measures aim even more pointedly to se-

---

(1987) 22–73, 154–62. Since the 1970s, *Republic* 5 has rightly been taken not as a comic interlude but as an earnest proposal. In addition to Pierce, see J. Annas, "Plato's *Republic* and Feminism," 24–33; S. Okin, "Philosopher Queens and Private Wives: Plato on Women and the Family" (1977), 345–69; N. Bluestone, *Women and the Ideal Society,* 77–154; G. Vlastos, "Was Plato a Feminist?" (1989); and M. Buchan, *Women in Plato's Political Theory,* 114–23, 135–48.

78. As P. A. Brunt observes ("The Model City of Plato's *Laws*" [1993], 263–8) a central moral aim of Magnesia is to restrain the love of money and reduce the gulf between "the Haves and the Have-nots," so much so that the citizens should not even trade with outside peoples.

lect for appetitive restraint so as to create a new order of lean human beings on the run like greyhounds toward virtue.

The guardians in the *Republic* and the citizens in the *Laws* must produce offspring in a limited number and of the best possible kind (*Rep* 456e3–8). In the *Republic* the ideal population should be large enough so that the city is self-sufficient and not so large as to preclude the city from being politically and psychologically holistic. "The guardians must guard in every way that the city will be neither big nor small but of adequate size and unified" (*Rep* 423c2–4, 460a5–6). The city officials monitor the frequency with which the guardians engage in procreative intercourse. The officials must, for example, take into account population losses due to natural deaths, wars, and diseases (*Rep* 460a2–6). In the *Laws* Plato is more specific about the preferred demographics of the polis. The adult male segment of the population and its concomitant number of households should amount to no more than the choiceworthy Pythagorean number 5,040.[79] The wives should bear at least two offspring, one of each sex. Though Plato does not quantify the upper limit that each couple should produce, he does have such a limit in mind (*Laws* 930c6–d1). Once married couples produce a "generous quantity of offspring," they must stop engaging in reproductive intercourse (*Laws* 784b1–3). The guardians and citizens thus must procreate strictly within the means of their community and respect its need for population control (*Rep* 372b8–c1). This rule hems in sexual desire, for it is a civic duty to avoid sexual relations that lead to births exceeding demographic interests. Population control further curtails the appetites more generally by sparing the city from having too many mouths to feed.[80]

The guardians and citizens also must reproduce only during their prime of life so as to give birth to the healthiest possible offspring. For Plato, the prime is an age span during which human beings are "at their peak" of mind and body, ripe for producing the best offspring (*Rep* 461a1–2). For females it starts between 16 and 20 and extends to 40 years of age. For males it starts between 25 or 35 years of age, or "whenever a man reaches his peak as a runner," up to the age of 55.[81] This rule is very strict. Since the guardians are committed to producing "the best possible men and women" (*Rep* 456c3–4), transgressors who procreate outside of the age limits must either abort

79. *Laws* 737e1–3. The number 5,040 is an admirable choice from a Pythagorean perspective because it is a multiple of all the numbers from one through ten. P. D. Bardis ("Overpopulation, the Ideal City, and Plato's Mathematics," [1971], 129–31) sees additional symbolism in Plato's choice of 5,040.

80. J. Mulhern ("Population and Plato's *Republic*" [1975], 273, 280) is right that for Plato the demographic issue "is at least as much the composition as the size of the population," but he is mistaken to say that Plato's concerns have "comparatively little to do with numbers."

81. *Rep* 460e4–7; *Laws* 772d5–e2, 785b2–5. M. Foucault (*Use of Pleasure*, 121–2) similarly notes that Plato prescribes these reproductive age limits in the interest of the offspring.

the fetus or expose the newborn infant. If they disobey, they commit a criminal act of impiety (*Rep* 461b9–c7). In the *Laws* too, overage citizens who transgress this rule are to be penalized and dishonored with public humiliations and the occasional beating (*Laws* 784e2–5). Plato thus curbs human sexual desire further by imposing a rule of quality control in addition to population control. The guardians and citizens must refrain from procreating until they are at the right age and the city needs newborn members to add its populace.

Incest prohibitions in the *Republic* and *Laws* serve partly to set another barrier to unregulated sexual desire. In the *Republic* he requires the guardians to obey a communal version of the traditional Greek rule to avoid parent-child incest.[82] In the *Laws* he reverts to the traditional Greek rules.[83] Sexual relationships between parents and children are "not in the least holy, but loathed by the gods and most shameful of shameful deeds" (*Laws* 838a4–c1). Though incest prohibitions prevent inbreeding, in Plato's cities they further tighten the reins of sexual desire, for the taboo in the *Republic* applies to guardians who are already retired from their reproductive duties and forbidden to produce more children, when the problem of inbreeding no longer applies. The guardians and citizens thus have to mind their place in the kinship structure as well as their age and demographic concerns before allowing themselves to engage in sexual activity.

In the *Republic* and *Laws* Plato insists that procreative relations elicit the benevolent involvement of the gods through the use of religious ceremonies. This requirement regulates sexual desire further by linking the reproductive urge with a piety that is both sexually explicit and solemn. The ceremonialism also reaffirms the presence and importance of the Greek gods, whom Plato has rehabilitated so that the gods are supremely good and impervious to corruption—models of divine virtue for the citizens to emulate.[84] The worship of Plato's noble Olympians is required to ensure that

82. In the *Republic*'s schema of prohibited incest, all children born within the seventh and tenth months after a communally celebrated procreative marriage event are off limits to those guardians who copulated during that event. The guardians in this group are the aggregate parents of all the offspring. The same incest prohibition applies to the guardians' grandchildren, that is, to the offspring produced by their collective children. These grandchildren too are the product of a festive event of copulation, *Rep* 461c1–7, d2–e2. Plato, however, allows sexual relations between the aggregate of siblings born as a result of each reproductive festival in Kallipolis, *Rep* 461d2–e3.

83. *Laws* 838a4–c1, cf. Sophocles *Oed Rex*, 1360–6. In Athens incest rules forbade sexual relations between parents and children, and also between full siblings and half-siblings with the same mother (ὁμομήτριοι), C. Cox, *Household Interests: Property, Marriage Strategies, and Family Dynamics in Ancient Athens* (1998), 116 n. 42.

84. Plato's rehabilitated religious traditionalism in the *Laws* is so strong as to be reactionary, given its "vehemence . . . and virtuous indignation against the impugners of orthodox belief" in the gods of his city, G. Grote, *Plato*, vol. 4, 384, 381–6. As M. Piérart (*Platon et la cité*

the gods will recognize their mortal counterparts in virtue and favor the people's production of appetitively sedate offspring. The rituals especially serve "the gods of reproduction (θεοὶ γενέθλιοι)" (*Laws* 729c5–8), such as Hera and Zeus, who were important deities presiding over the birth process in ancient Greece. The guardians and citizens must incorporate ample religious ritual into their mating through traditional feasts, hymns, and sacrifices.[85] The gods receiving such worship gain in honor and strength, as is their due, and once gladdened in their hearts, the gods are then propitious toward the city and its reproductive efforts. The guardians and citizens thus are obliged to sustain the gods in order to bear appetitively well-bred children, and to raise children worthy of sustaining the rehabilitated gods, just as the Greeks had long been doing by Plato's day, though without his refurbished Olympian theology and express eugenic aims. The generations to come, Plato insists, are required to hand on this living torch of worshipping the good gods.[86] He therefore supports the traditional polytheistic web connecting the Greek gods, city, adults, and children together in a symbiotic community, though his community and its Olympians are dedicated to appetitive virtue.

To Plato, as to the Greeks, the inaugural act of marital intercourse is itself a religious ceremony, such as the wedding night in the *Laws* or a communally reproductive event in the *Republic*. In the *Laws*, a personified deity of reproductive "Beginning" (ἀρχή) presides over this initiation. She ensures reproductive continuity across generations and its ceremonial exchange between the citizens and their gods. This goddess "maintains all things provided that she receives due honor from those who make use of her" (*Laws* 775e2–4). A male citizen thus would be outrageously impious if he refused to be a husband and father and abandoned this civic symbiosis with the gods. "It is never holy for a man to willingly and deliberately be deprived of a wife and children" (*Laws* 721c6–8). The goddess of reproductive Beginning helps prevent this impiety from occurring. As immortal over-

---

grecque: *Theorie et realité dans la constitution des Lois.* [1974], 353) likewise notes about the *Laws*, "L'aspect le plus marquant qui se dégage de l'examen de l'organisation du culte est le respect profond que Platon porte à la tradition grecque." See too P. A. Brunt, "The Model City," 252–3; G. Morrow, *Plato's Cretan City* (1960; reprint, 1993), 434–96; M. Morgan, "Plato and Greek Religion" (1992), 227–47; E. R. Dodds, *The Greeks and the Irrational* (1951), 219–24; and O. Reverdin, *La religion de la cité platonicienne* (1945), 218–41, 244–50. Hence if Plato lived in Porphyry's day, the question is not whether he would harbor sentiments *adversus Christianos* but how much more trenchant his criticisms would be. M. Morgan (*Platonic Piety: Philosophy and Ritual in Fourth-Century Athens* [1990], 100–57) ventures to interrelate Plato's religious piety and traditionalism with the *Republic's* epistemology and educational reforms.

85. *Rep* 459e5–60a2; *Laws* 716d4–e2, 774e9–75a6.

86. *Laws* 721b6–c6, 773e5–74a1, 776b2–4, and see also T. Van Eijk, "Marriage and Virginity, Death and Immortality" (1972), 209–11.

seer, she accompanies the newlyweds to the bedroom and sees to it that they carry out their procreative responsibility for the city and the gods.

Plato also proposes specialized methods of selecting for temperance that go beyond adapting popular Greek reproductive mores. In the *Republic* he proposes selective breeding, by analogy with purebred dogs, horses, and the like.[87] Through a rigged system of lots of which the guardians are unaware, "the best" female and male guardians, that is, the ones most virtuous in their appetitive discipline, should have the most frequent opportunity to mate. The guardians who prove somewhat inferior and less restrained should have the least frequent opportunity—and only with other inferior guardians (459d7-9). Their offspring are to be secretly taken away by officials and almost certainly left to die, along with the visibly defective offspring of the superior guardians.[88] Appetitive moderation is thus its own limited hedonistic reward in the *Republic*. Since the best guardians are most capable of managing their sexual desire, they win most of the available occasions for experiencing sexual pleasure while they are passing on their traits.[89] In the *Laws*, however, Plato abandons the breeding altogether and prefers to mate husbands and wives who complement each other psychologically as well as economically. The dispositions of the spouses should carefully counterbalance or offset whatever personality extremes the two partners may have. The intended result is to achieve the golden mean of temperance in the character formation of the offspring. For example, a rash man should marry and mate with a placid woman. This "will benefit the civic order" because their personalities will blend and form offspring who are more balanced

87. 456e6–7, 459d7–60c5, cf. 451d4–52a1.

88. 460c3–5. Plato is likely referring to infanticide here, though it has been argued that the inferior offspring are removed to the lower social classes of laborers and farmers. The latter interpretation seems dubious, though, for in 460c3–5, Plato states that "the officials will hide away (κατακρύψουσιν)" the offspring in an "unspeakable and secret place." By contrast, he designates that legitimate children (viz., those produced through the ceremonies) who are not visibly defective but prove not to be of golden caliber "will be thrust out (ὤσουσιν) to the craftspeople or farmers," *Rep* 415b6–c2. For discussion of the question see J. Mulhern, "Population and Plato's *Republic*," 274–7; W. K. C. Guthrie, *A History of Greek Philosophy*, vol. 4 (1975), 481–2; G. van N. Viljoen, "Plato and Aristotle on the Exposure of Infants at Athens" (1959), 63–6; and J. Adam, *The Republic of Plato*[2] vol. 1 (1963), 357–60.

89. Plato expressly refers to these more frequent opportunities as a prize (γέρας), *Rep* 460b1–5. Here he adapts the idea, prominent in the *Iliad*, that sexual activity is a prize for valor, *Il* 1.109–20. In the *Republic*, though, the prize is a sexual and procreative opportunity, whereas in the *Iliad* it is a civilian female captive who becomes the warrior's reward, his spear-prize concubine. In this respect as well, Plato privileges the male over the female guardians. Just as the males are the friends and the females belong to the aggregate that they share in common, so too the males win reproductively sexual enjoyment of the females in their ascetic harem, but not vice versa.

and restrained.[90] Plato thus ventures into innovative methods to implant the norm of appetitive virtue across generations. He is ready to be a political animal breeder or a marital chemist mixing character—whatever it takes to realize his reforms.

Plato offers a final eugenic plan in the *Laws,* and only in this dialogue, that is of great importance for the prominence it gains in Middle and Christian Platonism, albeit in a much transmuted form. The citizens of the hypothetical city of Magnesia must engage strictly in temperate and deliberately reproductive sexual relations when they first marry. This restriction pertains only to "the procreative union" (ἡ τῆς παιδογονίας συνουσία) (838e5–6), and it is in force either until the couples have produced their requisite number of children or throughout their prime of life, if they do not meet the quota. The rule ceases to apply once they produce sufficient offspring or pass their prime.[91] Plato imagines that the rule would be in effect for no more than ten years on average per couple (784b1–3). During this time their sexual interests and activity must be exclusively procreative. "The bridegroom must direct his mind to his bride and reproduction, and the bride must do the same," especially when no children are born yet (783e4–7). Newlywed husbands in particular are prohibited from ejaculating in a willfully nonreproductive way. They must refrain from homoerotic sexual activity, masturbation, and sexual acts that are either actively contraceptive or performed with fingers crossed to prevent conception. They also must avoid intercourse that is carelessly indifferent to whether pregnancy will ensue (838e4–39a6). Through this conditioning, the citizens during their procreative duty should ideally come to find nonreproductive sexual activity as unthinkable as incest and avoid it voluntarily (837e9–38e1). In case the citizens still prove sexually unruly, however, Plato has backup forces ready. The female overseers, police, and city council must, if need be, stop them from shirking or transgressing their reproductive obligation. Transgressors must be stigmatized in public; their names posted in public view. They are prohibited from attending marriage and birth ceremonies, and other citizens may beat the reprobates with impunity if they dare to attend such ceremonies.[92] The married couples thus must keep their sexual activity strictly procreative during their period of childbearing. The goddess Beginning is with them in the bedroom to reinforce compliance and a reproductive dragnet keeps them under surveillance.

90. *Laws* 773a7–b5. See further W. Fortenbaugh, "Plato: Temperament and Eugenic Policy" (1975), 291–6.

91. G. Grote (*Plato*, vol. 4, 345) recognizes the temporary nature of this strictly reproductive regimen.

92. *Laws* 783a1–e1, M. Piérart, *Platon et la cité grecque*, 161–3.

The procreant male citizens in the *Laws* receive a list of sexual prohibitions against masturbating and so on because Plato finds them his main regulatory problem, oversexed as he thinks men are in their ideas about virile happiness, especially in youth. Keeping the young women in line seems less difficult to him because Athenian social mores already recognized no sexual venue for female citizens beyond marital sex, unlike the many venues that men were openly accorded—to the city's detriment, as Plato saw it.[93] As he puts it, through his anatomical displacement of the social imperative, the womb naturally commands women to become mothers, while men must undergo full-scale reprogramming.

Plato facilitates his goal to inculcate appetitive restraint by construing the temperate and reproductive regimen as a work of art for the procreant citizens to make. Reproductive activity, as he describes it in the *Laws* alone, is a skillful craft, and like other crafts, it requires a purposeful and controlled technique to do well. "All persons who are partners in any enterprise produce fine and good products when they direct their mind to themselves and the activity, and do the opposite when they are inattentive" (*Laws* 783d8–e4). If the prospective parents are not deliberate and sedate in their acts of reproduction, then they fail in their duty to be master artisans of offspring. Like careless woodworkers whose furniture wobbles, they produce badly wrought offspring who are bound to become dissolute. To drink and then copulate is particularly reprehensible, rather as "drinking and driving" is today. Intoxication interferes with the sexual craftsmanship required to shape embryos that are "well-built, steady, and tranquil" (775c4–d4, 674b5–6). Plato further insists that the citizens can master this procreative skill only through life-long appetitive restraint in all respects. They cannot be undisciplined in other respects and then try to look restrained when they copulate to reproduce, such as by holding their breath or taking a sedative. Day after day they must avoid all the "diseased, violent, and unjust" activity that Plato associates with uncontrolled appetition (775d4–e2). Thanks to this overall habituation to temperance, parents imprint their sober craftsmanship on the embryonic character of their offspring. They also bring the newborns into a society where rampant desires have in theory become unthinkable due to the vigilant monitoring of the appetites that concentrates primarily on sexual desire as the deepest root of all vice. This eugenic proposal is the consummate touch to the program of sexual restraint that Plato works out in the *Republic* and *Laws,* his key way to eliminate the profusion of human wrongdoing that uncontrolled sexual desire unleashes.

93. As discussed in chapter four, Athenian husbands in Plato's day were allowed to engage in sexual relations with concubines, prostitutes, female slaves, and younger men. Wives, though, were allowed to copulate only with their husbands. Whatever sexual activity wives may have practiced without overt social recognition remains an obscure but important question.

The sexual program in the *Laws* is far more restrictive than the one in the *Republic* due to its twist on reproduction as purposive craft. In the *Republic* Plato argues only that city officials must monitor the frequency and coupling patterns of the guardians' procreative activity (460a2–6, 459d7–9). He does not demand that this activity be temperate and attentively purposeful. In the *Laws* Plato not only adds this major qualifier, he arms it with policing mechanisms for the procreant citizens (784a1–e1). The *Republic*, moreover, never specifies that guardians in their prime must engage only in reproductive sexual relations—it states only that their acts of procreation are to be strictly regulated. The *Republic* does not rule out autoeroticism, for instance, let alone stigmatize reproductive guardians for "killing the human race" if they occasionally masturbate to climax, whereas male citizens are so stigmatized in the *Laws* (838e7–8). Plato in the *Laws* creates a society that is more repressive due to this regimen of strict procreation that has no precedent in the *Republic*.

Plato's greater severity in the *Laws* is partly a compensatory measure for having to accommodate the family, clans, and the marketplace in Magnesia. Since these customs give sexual desire a ready way to breed myriad vices, he grants the reproductive urge and sexual appetite far less latitude. In the *Republic*, by contrast, the communal guardians are precluded from having sexual desire run wild through the conduits of the family and free market. Plato, if given a choice, would control sexual desire by eliminating these conduits rather than leaving them in place and having to clamp down on sexual desire. By the time he wrote the *Laws*, though, he found to his dismay that people refused to surrender familial clans and the market. Sexual desire thus pays the price and gets put under maximum security.

Despite the marital and procreative orientation of the *Laws*, in no dialogue does Plato require his citizens to engage in exclusively marital sexual relations. In the *Republic*, of course, he would prefer to do away with marriage altogether for the guardian class. In the *Laws*, where marriage is the norm, he takes it for granted that male citizens in their prime will occasionally impregnate female slaves as well as wives, though he requires this practice to remain discreet. "If a female slave mates with . . . a free man, her offspring must belong to her master."[94] Plato's position here is compatible with his eugenic rule that a procreant male citizen must not ejaculate into a woman unless he intends to make her pregnant (*Laws* 839a1–3). Because this rule is not as strong as requiring a male citizen to inseminate only his

---

94. 930d3–e2. Plato vacillates only on the question whether male citizens should be allowed to impregnate females slaves in their own, rather than only in other men's households, 841d5–e4, 930d3–e2. Within a man's own household, the female slave and child are to be exiled only if the case gains public notoriety.

own wife, the men remain free to exercise a reproductive prerogative with female slaves so as to replenish the slave labor force on a locally grown basis. And though Plato does not say as much, if the men are temperate and purposive while copulating with female slaves, they in theory improve the slave breed too—better workers who eat less. The *Laws* therefore does not mandate strictly marital sexual practices,[95] while the *Republic* eliminates marriage outright for the main enfranchised group.

Plato in the *Laws* and *Republic* leaves the sexual behavior of the citizens and guardians unmonitored after they complete their reproductive service to the city. He is quite confident that they will heed the limits of necessary and beneficial sexual pleasure, for by this time they are disciplined to be moderate and their reproductive urge has quieted down. Plato also thinks that those who are finished procreating inevitably will be sexually active because of the sexual appetite's driving force for much of the human life span. Assuming the *Laws'* ten-year average period of reproduction, most of the women would be only in their later twenties and most of the men would be around forty, hardly too old for eros. In the *Laws*, likewise, postreproductive sexual activity "should remain silently unregulated" so long as the citizens remain moderate, avoid incest, do not procreate, and refrain from copulating with citizens who are still serving reproductive duty (784e2–85a3). Even more permissively in the *Republic,* guardians past their prime need only obey incest rules and avoid reproducing. Otherwise the men are "free to have sexual activity with whomever they please, . . . and likewise the women" (461b9–c1), whereas Plato offers no such carte blanche in the *Laws*. In the *Laws*, further, he keeps plans to enforce sexual moderation on standby, for the sexual appetite needs an extinguisher in case the citizens break away from their controlled burn.[96] This outbreak is more likely to happen to them than to the communal guardians, for the family and private ownership fuel sexual desire.

Though Plato does not specify when postreproductive sexual behavior crosses the line from being necessary to unnecessary, what matters most is that necessary sexual activity takes place discreetly, not lewdly on display (784e5–85a3). Thus, even though he is stern in his restrictions, he is not so severe that he would require sexual abstinence from the guardians and citizens who have completed their reproductive service to the city. In fact, as he states in the *Laws,* citizens who have finished reproducing should regard moderation and "not complete sexual abstinence" as honorable, and they

95. In the *Laws* Plato initially entertains the idea of having his citizens be monogamously sexual after they finish their procreative duty to the city, but then states that this is unattainable, 840d9–41b5.

96. The city officials may, for instance, put the citizens through various physical workouts in order to redirect the nutriment that otherwise fuels their sexual appetite overmuch, 841a6–8.

should act accordingly (841b4–5, 784e5–85a1). In so doing they serve Aphrodite properly (841a9–b2), which she naturally compels them to do until they become elderly. Plato therefore never seeks to limit all sexual activity to a strictly procreative function, even though this position has been attributed to him, both in Jewish and Christian Platonism and in the modern day.[97] In the *Laws* the citizens adhere to a strictly temperate and deliberately reproductive function only for the time they must engage in their baby-making craft. In the *Republic* no such restriction applies. To Plato, then, temperate sexual hedonism is the mark of appetitive virtue, not sexual renunciation apart from the perfunctory performance of reproduction. This principle respects the force that Plato accords to the sexual appetite and is in keeping with the Apollonian tenor of his ethics, μηδὲν ἄγαν, "nothing in excess."

CONCLUSION

Sexual desire according to Plato is the most incorrigible of the inherently antirational physical appetites and gives rise to myriad ills individually and socially. It has plagued the human condition in its uncontrolled or poorly regulated form, and thus must be curtailed to the necessary degree. The sexual appetite, when successfully domineering, both deters the embodied soul from attaining enlightenment and places it at risk of reincarnating as a dumb animal, never to desire Beauty or even to think again. As a bodily health problem, further, excessive sexual desire and activity bring distress due to the gross imbalance of burning pain over pleasure. Finally, individual vices, crime in the streets, and warfare between cities and states are the seedy fruits of sexual desire, hunger, and thirst—and sexual desire especially. The inhibition of sexual desire and the other appetites would consequently bring great benefits for individual health, the social good, and the enlightenment of the embodied soul, and the last benefit for Plato is the most important of all.

In the *Republic* and *Laws* Plato does not present one fixed plan to rein in sexual desire, but he aims to control it by managing the reproductive urge in a variety of ways. Despite the absence of systematic fixity, he supports several constant plans across both dialogues. First, he advocates communalism, and reproductive communalism especially, in order to eliminate divisive clan groups and the marketplace through which the appetites run riot. Cru-

---

97. P. Hall (*Cities in Civilization* [1998], 27) is representative of this interpretation: Plato's "ideal city of Magnesia, described in the *Laws*, is an utterly joyless place in which . . . sex would be solely for procreation." W. K. C. Guthrie (*History of Greek Philosophy*, vol. 5, 354–5) is Hall's source. Note also J. Brundage (*Law, Sex, and Christian Society in Medieval Europe* [1987], 16 n. 30), who attributes strict procreationism to both the *Laws* and *Republic*. I address this marked overstatement of Plato's position further in chapter four.

cial though this reform is, in the *Laws* Plato despairs of its feasibility and constructs a second-best plan, while still preferring his communal ideal. The compromise system retains the family along with trade in the marketplace. As a compensatory measure, he constrains sexual desire even more firmly as the primary origin of vices. Second, Plato advocates procreative age limits and strict measures of population control in the interest of appetitive restraint and the greater good. Third, he requires the guardians and citizens to honor the gods through Greek religious ceremonies in order to enhance the greater symbiotic community of noble gods and well-behaved mortals through the reproduction of children destined for appetitive virtue.

In addition to the constants, Plato promotes several eugenic options to inculcate sexual and other appetitive restraint. In the *Republic* he encourages breeding only the better-restrained guardians; in the *Laws* he has persons mate with spouses of counterbalancing personality traits and economic backgrounds. As his most ambitious and historically significant plan, Plato in the *Laws* maintains that reproduction is a skill that requires life-long controls on the appetites, especially during the delicate craftwork of procreative sexual intercourse. To prevent the slipshod production of children, he requires the ever-temperate citizens to be strictly and deliberately reproductive in their sexual activity, but only while serving their time of providing newborn human resources for the city. After the citizens have performed their service, Plato directs them to continue paying their virtuously moderate sexual dues to Aphrodite, which the sexual appetite presses them to do until its yearning for fricative pleasure fades away much later in life.

Despite Plato's repertoire of eugenic plans, their common goal is to regulate procreation so that uncontrolled sexual and reproductive activity become passé customs that a new breed of human beings have transcended —the once sex-hungry men in particular. If Plato had his way, sexual practices and their progeny of vices would undergo major reduction and reform. So effective would the social reconditioning be that the citizens of the future would look back upon Plato's fellow Athenians as primitive sexual savages, much as we pride ourselves for our greater brain capacity over Australopithecus.

The early Stoics Zeno and Chrysippus, as I argue in the next chapter, strongly dissent from Plato's conviction that sexual desire is antirational and wildly prone to interfere with the good of the soul, individuals, and society. Though the early Stoics are critical of Greek sexual mores, their criticisms and proposed sexual reforms differ greatly from Plato's. Plato, as we have seen, is ready to do whatever it takes to prevent the sexually appetitive beast from spawning its wanton desires. The early Stoics deny that there is any such beast. To understand their arguments, we should now enter the early Stoic city of eros and then explore how later Stoics rework the sexual principles of Zeno and Chrysippus into a tamer and more traditional social form.

Chapter 3

Crafting Eros through
the Stoic Logos of Nature

Like Plato, the early Stoics Zeno (335–263 B.C.E.) and Chrysippus (280–207 B.C.E.) sought to improve moral life in ancient Greek society. They too stressed the need for communal sexual and reproductive reforms, though for reasons that go beyond Plato's aim to rein in acquisitive desires and that reveal much about the early Stoic conception of sexual eros as a method of training in reason and ethics. The early Stoic city of eros is evocative of, yet in substantive counterpoint to, Kallipolis in Plato's *Republic*.[1] The early Stoic principles of sexual and procreative conduct are thus of interest historically for what they reveal about the envisioned early Stoic city as an artifact of ancient political philosophy.

Zeno and Chrysippus are also of immediate contemporary interest, because they are among the most original thinkers about human sexuality and its socialization. They stimulate deeper reflection today on the relationship between social norms and human sexuality. To put some of the questions in terms more like the Stoics' own, what kind of sexual animals are we? Are we a definable species in this respect? How have conventional ideas about human sexual nature shaped us to become the political animals that we are through our upbringing, education, and other acculturating factors? How can unconventional ideas modify sexual practices and their cultural outcome, at least in theory? Regarding questions such as these, early Stoicism is of great value, not so much for the answers that Zeno and Chrysippus offered, but for the adventurous experiments in disciplined reasoning that they made in their inquiries.

The socially engaged sexual principles of the early Stoa deserve greater

---

1. The relationship is partly one of a "reply to Plato (cf. Plut. *Stoic. repugn.* 1034e–f)," as P. Vander Waerdt notes, "Politics and Philosophy in Stoicism," 186.

appreciation than they have hitherto received in the philosophy and history of ethics, sexual desire, and the body. Though Schofield, Rist, and Inwood have done some valuable work,[2] their contribution has often gone unnoticed in recent studies on desire, sexuality, and the body in antiquity. In most recent work the highly restrictive and marriage-oriented sexual principles of Seneca and Musonius, two unrepresentative Roman Stoics, are commonly taken to represent Stoic sexual ethics as a whole. Foucault, for example, has nothing to say about the early Stoics in his *History of Sexuality*. He presents the later Stoic marital ethic as though it were generically Stoic, and he includes Seneca and Musonius within this Stoic-based schema.[3]

Early Stoic sexual ethics differs in vital ways from its later counterpart and also from the popular ancient Greek view of eros as a destructive passion. All Stoics, be they early or later, agree that people should refrain from eros and sexual activity to the extent that eros is a passion, for passions in the technical Stoic sense are undesirable on several grounds. Passions, as "excessive and unnatural soul impulses," are contrary to right evaluative reasoning, lead to uncontrolled and unreflective actions, damage one's well-being, and conflict with human nature. They thereby preclude the attainment of right reasoning, which is the one virtue recognized in Stoicism, as it alone guarantees infallibly appropriate actions.[4] For Zeno and Chrysippus, though, eros is not inherently a passion, while two influential later Stoics, Seneca and Musonius, agree with the popular view and presuppose that eros inherently is a passion. The early Stoics, however, dissent and maintain that this ingrained view of eros misleads people and subjects them to habitual passions in their sexual relationships. In an effort to reform this deep-seated belief, Zeno and Chrysippus sought to transmute the human erotic experience in light of their cosmology, theology, ethics, and political theory. Their idea of early Stoic eros promotes practices of responsible and mutually friendly sexual conduct on a community-wide basis, not the extirpation of the erotic experience or the restriction of sexual activity to marital reproduction.

---

2. J. Rist, *Stoic Philosophy* (1969), 65–68, 79–80; M. Schofield, *Stoic City*, 26–56; and B. Inwood, "Why Do Fools Fall in Love?" (1997), 55–69.

3. "Conjugal fidelity [is] exalted by the Stoics," so that "one must keep one's practice of sexual pleasure within marriage in conformity with its [viz., the Stoics' pro-marital] objectives," *Care of the Self*, 40, 184, cf. 155, and see 168–9 and 178–9 for his inclusion of Seneca and Musonius within his later Stoicizing notion of "Hellenistic moral philosophy," 165.

4. In the strict early Stoic sense, "virtue" comes about when reasoning motivates infallibly appropriate actions ($\kappa\alpha\tau\circ\rho\theta\acute{\omega}\mu\alpha\tau\alpha$). To be virtuous and wise, persons need nothing but this flawless reasoning and ensuing choice of how to behave, which alone are "in our control," as Epictetus puts it, *Ench* 1; and see Stobaeus 5.906.17–907.5 = SVF 3.510; Plutarch, *Comm not* 1063a = SVF 3.539 = LS 61T; and B. Inwood, *Ethics and Human Action in the Early Stoa* (1985), 201–15. Stobaeus references are to the volume, pages, and lines of the standard edition by C. Wachsmuth and O. Hense.

By contrast, Seneca (ca. 4 B.C.E.–65 C.E.) and Musonius (ca. 30–102 C.E.), revert to the view that eros inherently *is* the passion it is portrayed as being in the popular Greek tradition. This position is contrary to both the early Stoic and later Stoic views, for the later Stoics Antipater, Hierocles, and Epictetus retain the early Stoic idea that sexual relations can and ought to demonstrate mutual respect between lovers, though they relegate this prescriptive function of eros to the marital relationship alone. According to Seneca and Musonius, however, eros is irremediably impassioned. People should strive to be detached from sexual relations and to eliminate eros except where unavoidable in marital acts of procreation. This core aspect of Seneca's and Musonius's thought is Pythagorean, as shown in the following chapter. It is important to appreciate that Seneca and Musonius are not Stoic in their sexual ethics, for in much scholarship they have been described as characteristically Stoic by virtue of being repressed and repressive in their sexual principles,[5] even though their conception of eros and its dangers is contrary to both early and later Stoic thought.

In this chapter, I first discuss valuable recent scholarship on early Stoic sexual ethics. The next section explores the salient features of the Greek erotic tradition that Zeno and Chrysippus found so problematic. Then I explicate the sexual principles that the early Stoics formulate in response to the Greek tradition. Zeno and Chrysippus are treated as a unit because their notions of human nature and eros are consistent with one another and distinct from those of the later Stoics. Together they articulate what is here termed "early Stoic eros." In the following sections I study the later Stoics Antipater, Hierocles, and Musonius as one group and then Seneca and Epictetus as another,[6] because their ideas about eros are in several noteworthy respects internally consistent within each group and distinct from the other group. Seneca and Musonius, however, take the additional step of

5. M. Nussbaum (*The Therapy of Desire* [1994], 389–401, 439–83) maintains that the Stoics as a whole strive to extirpate erotic love except where unavoidable (e.g., in reproduction). I show the problem with her argument in n. 55 below. On the tendency to interpret later Stoic sexual principles in this manner, see also M. Foucault as cited above; J. Brundage, *Law, Sex, and Christian Society*, 18–21; J. Noonan, *Contraception: A History of Its Treatment by the Catholic Theologians and Canonists*[2] (1986), 46–9; L. Countryman, *Dirt, Greed, and Sex*, 62; P. Brown, *Body and Society*, 21; D. Biale, *Eros and the Jews: From Biblical Israel to Contemporary America* (1992), 37–8; along with D. Allison, "Divorce, Celibacy, and Joseph (Matthew 1:18–25 and 19:1–12)" (1993), 7; U. Ranke-Heinemann *Eunuchs for Heaven*, 1–6; J. Broudéhoux, *Mariage et famille*, 136; and G. Sfameni Gasparro, C. Magazzu, and C. Spada, eds. *The Human Couple*, 165. J. Brundage's comment (*Law, Sex, and Christian Society*, 18–21) is especially memorable: "St. Paul and the Stoic teachers certainly agreed in their negative views about . . . sex as a potentially destructive temptation that virtuous persons should resist, save for procreative marital sex."

6. Epictetus lived ca. 55–135 C.E. Hierocles lived during the reign of Hadrian (117–138 C.E.), but otherwise the dates of his life are not known. I discuss Antipater's identity and the likely time period he lived in in n. 86 below.

arguing that sexual relations should be practiced strictly for procreation within marriage and for no other reason, in order to keep the destructive nature of eros in check. Because this represents a Pythagorean prescription, as demonstrated in the next chapter, I reserve study of this aspect of their sexual ethics until then.[7]

EARLY STOIC EROS AS CURRENTLY UNDERSTOOD

Schofield raises several points that help our understanding of early Stoic eros.[8] First, a good number of Stoics wrote about eros, including Zeno and Chrysippus, which suggests that they had something original to say about the topic. Second, eros in the early Stoic sense is distinct from popular Greek eros in some respect that Plutarch enigmatically mentions but leaves unspecified. Third, whatever the early Stoics thought about eros, they would not have recommended the experience of eros as passion or harmfully excessive impulse, because passions conflict with the Stoic ethical aim of right reasoning and its corollaries of wisdom and virtue. Fourth, the exercise of eros as advocated by Zeno and Chrysippus creates harmony in the early Stoic city and social order,[9] for the god Eros, who presides over Zeno's ideal city, suffuses friendship, concord, and freedom in the community.[10] More specifically, early Stoic eros is "an impulse for the making of friends that becomes manifest through the beauty" of a person and his or her attractive moral character.[11] Thus it requires some method of human interaction insofar as people must do something together in order to become friends.[12]

7. The other Stoics not mentioned in this chapter, such as Cleanthes, Panaetius, Posidonius, and Marcus Aurelius, are left out because their extant writings have little or nothing to add that is not already clear from the Stoic sources studied here. Persaeus and Cleanthes wrote treatises on love and marriage, but nothing about their works is known, DL 7.36, 7.175.

8. M. Schofield's points appear in *Stoic City*, 27–31, 34–48. See DL 7.33 and 7.124 for the early Stoic stance that only the virtuous (and wise) are friends.

9. The social order ($\pi o\lambda\iota\tau\epsilon\acute{\iota}a$) is an ideal governance system run by early Stoic guidelines, while the city ($\pi\acute{o}\lambda\iota s$) or cities ($\pi\acute{o}\lambda\epsilon\iota s$) are a practical means to begin working toward this ideal, DL 7.33 = LS 67B; Dio Chrysostom 36.20 = SVF 3.329 = LS 67J; M. Schofield, *Saving the City: Philosopher-Kings and Other Classical Paradigms* (1999), 51–68. As Schofield further explicates (*Stoic City*, 22–92), Zeno envisions both a universal social order ($\pi o\lambda\iota\tau\epsilon\acute{\iota}a$) and a particular city ($\pi\acute{o}\lambda\iota s$), not one or the other, which is a question H. C. Baldry (*The Unity of Mankind in Greek Thought* [1965], 156–66) and others used to debate.

10. Given the early Stoics' insistence that eros is conducive to wisdom and friendship and that the wise are free in Zeno's city (DL 7.33, 121), it seems dubious for M. Schofield (*Stoic City*, 54) to dispute that Zeno connected eros with freedom in a politically meaningful sense. Early Stoic freedom is ethical and political in its tenor, as S. Bobzien points out, *Determinism and Freedom in Stoic Philosophy* (1998), 338–40.

11. Stobaeus 2.115.1–4 = SVF 3.650, in Arius Didymus, *Epitome* (1999).

12. Though Eros might help instill this social harmony partly through his cosmogonic force, as G. Boys-Stones has argued ("Eros in Government: Zeno and the Virtuous City,"

Fifth, to become friends in the early Stoic sense is the height of moral attainment, for in early Stoic thought the virtuous wise alone are friends.[13] Given that the practice of early Stoic eros facilitates this attainment, it plays a pivotal role toward shaping the good life in the early Stoic city, so much so that Zeno selects Eros to be the city's presiding deity. Hence the topic of eros is central to early Stoic ethics and political theory.

Schofield, however, offers a problematic interpretation of the physically sexual nature of early Stoic eros. He maintains that eros in this sense transforms into "a sublimated Platonic form of love" that ceases to be sexual once the goal of making friends is met.[14] Early Stoic eros serves strictly as a sexual propaedeutic conducted by the wise to help adolescents in Stoic training, the προκόπτοντες, advance toward the nonsexual goal of friendship, wisdom, and virtue. Using male homoerotic relations as his example, Schofield states that "if the lover succeeds in helping his beloved mature into virtue, it is no longer love but friendship which is an appropriate relationship with him. Friendship consummates love—and replaces it."[15] Sages attain a higher and nonsexual level of friendship together, as opposed to the sexual rudiments toward friendship that they share with the προκόπτοντες. "[I]t seems to follow that love in a sense aims to transcend itself" once eros becomes friendship. Schofield later reiterates this tentative inference with less cautious phrasing. Early Stoic eros itself, "Zenonian love proper," is "of course a sublimated Platonic form of love."[16]

Schofield's theory of sublimation tries to account for the difference Plutarch notes between early Stoic eros and popular Greek eros. The transcendent end of desexualized friendship would be the salient differentiating factor. Eros in the popular sense refers to physically sexual love and its various symptoms, the impassioned longing to embrace the desired person, responsive genitals, and the sexual activity of lovers. This is not to suggest that popular eros is reducible to its sexual physicality, only that there is no eros without it. By contrast, Plato's notion of eros undeniably stands apart from this popular idea, for in the *Symposium* and *Phaedrus* he argues that eros can and should subdue the sexual body within the limits of the sexual appetite's unavoidable needs.[17] Schofield's theory is dubious, however, even in terms of the other points he raises about early Stoic eros. If Plato's ideal of sublimation were the right model for understanding early Stoic eros, it

[1998], 168–74), the god does so more immediately in civic daily life through his role in human interaction.

13. DL 7.124, Stobaeus 2.108.15–18 in Arius Didymus, *Epitome*.
14. M. Schofield, *Stoic City*, 46, cf. 34, 56.
15. *Stoic City*, 34.
16. *Stoic City*, 34, 45–6.
17. I have explored this point in the previous chapter.

would be puzzling why the early Stoics would write numerous treatises about eros. Few are the words needed to affirm that a predecessor's idea is the correct one to follow.

For three reasons Schofield is mistaken to maintain that early Stoic eros platonically sublimates with the attainment of friendship. First, if he is correct that sexual relations between προκόπτοντες and sages cease once the adolescents become sagacious friends, then sages do not make love with one another, for sages are by definition friends. Diogenes Laertius, however, shows that among the wise, men and women enjoy each other sexually and pair off to do so as they see fit, without the restrictions of marriage and the related prohibition against adultery (DL 7.131). Wise Stoic friends cannot enjoy this sexual latitude if early Stoic eros were strictly a sexual propaedeutic. Thus early Stoic eros includes two levels of sexual interaction, the educative sexual activity of sages with προκόπτοντες and the fully friendly sexual activity of the wise with one another. Hence Schofield is mistaken to restrict the sexual practice of early Stoic eros to the educative relationship and to deny that "Zenonian love proper" is sexual.[18]

Second, there are metaphysical reasons for differentiating Platonic eros from early Stoic eros. Though early Stoic and Platonic eros both involve an erotically motivated ethical training of younger partners by older ones, Platonic eros inclines toward devaluing sexual activity in favor of seeking visions of the Good or Beauty "seated on its pure throne" beyond the world of genesis.[19] This orientation of Platonic eros away from sexual physicality is motivated by Plato's stance that the immortal soul must struggle to loosen the shackles of the sexual body in order to glimpse pure Being. Platonic eros provides the impetus for this effort.[20] The Stoics, however, reject Plato's metaphysical dualism. They support a holistic conception of the human soul, body, and the cosmos at large. There is no world of pure Being beyond the Heraclitean world of flux. There is no immortal soul. Even the Stoic gods are strictly immanent spirits and pantheistic principles of order in the world. Early Stoic thought, therefore, has stronger motive to regard Platonic eros as a misguided desire based on faulty metaphysics, not to absorb it as an interloper into their very different scheme of the world.

Third, Zeno's conception of eros in his *Republic* appeared unspeakably crude to ancient readers who were mindful of conventional propriety, partly because of his explicitly antinomian sexual ideas, as Schofield notes.[21] Pla-

---

18. Thus G. Boys-Stones ("Eros in Government," 170) too is in error to state that "Zeno certainly never suggests that intercourse between sages will be of the sexual variety."

19. *Phdr* 254a2–7, b5–c3, cf. *Laws* 837b6–d2.

20. See, for example, *Phdr* 246d6–e3, 254a2–c3, 256a1–e2.

21. Chrysippus's elaboration of Zeno's ideas added to the seeming scandal, DL 7.32–4, 187–9 along with M. Schofield, *Stoic City*, 3–13. I address this topic at greater length below.

tonic eros, by contrast, never elicited censorious ire of this sort in antiquity. Ancient readers would not have been outraged if early Stoic eros became chaste with the attainment of friendship. Therefore, early Stoic eros is not desexualized in its ultimate aims. On this pivotal matter, Rist remains correct. In early Stoic thought "love is not directed to physical satisfaction, though this will certainly be enjoyed—but to friendship."[22] Further, as Inwood observes, Pausanias's model of sexual pedagogy in Plato's *Symposium* better captures the didactic aspect of early Stoic eros.[23] Hence, *pace* Schofield, a Platonic type of sublimation is not what differentiates early Stoic from popular Greek eros.

THE GREEK EROTIC TRADITION

To understand the originality of early Stoic eros, we must turn to the long-enduring popular erotic tradition.[24] Ancient Greek views about eros consist of several tenets that Zeno and Chrysippus find problematic. First, eros is a divine force emanating from the gods Aphrodite and Eros that stimulates people to yearn to make love. Aphrodite "has tamed" human beings, gods, and animals, in *Homeric Hymn 5*, by arousing them to sexually engage in "the works of Aphrodite."[25] Second, when the gods of eros tame persons or gods, such as Zeus, they particularly quell their ability to rationally deliberate about their sexual desire and conduct. "Limb-loosening Eros subdues the mind and thoughtful will in the breasts of all gods and persons," as Hesiod states.[26] Third, Aphrodite and Eros often, and even habitually, exert their mastery contrary to the will their victims would exercise were they in their right mind, rather than possessed by eros. For instance, Aphrodite ensures

22. *Stoic Philosophy*, 68, 65, cf. Doyne Dawson, *Cities of the Gods: Communist Utopias in Greek Thought* (1992), 191. D. Babut ("Les Stoïciens et l'amour" [1963], 55–63) mistakenly finds Stoic eros to be thoroughly sublimated, as noted by Dawson, 218 n. 50.

23. For this argument see B. Inwood, "Why Do Fools Fall in Love?" 56–60.

24. This tradition spans from earliest archaic times to the Hellenistic period of the early Stoa and well into the Byzantine period.

25. 5.3–6. There are numerous examples of this and the other popular Greek tenets about eros discussed in this section, spanning from the archaic into the Hellenistic period and beyond, such as Pindar, fr. 123; Ibycus, fr. 287; Aeschylus, fr. 44, vol. 3; Euripides, *Hipp* 447–50, 1268–81, fr. 898; Plutarch, *Amat* 752a–b, 759e; Athenaeus, 599f; and Meleager G-P 20.

26. *Theog* 120–2, cf. Euripides, fr. 136, 161, 430, 1054. Anacreon similarly states that one who is sexually aroused through eros is crazed, fr. 428. To Sappho (fr. 47), eros shakes down the mind like a mountain wind against treetops—the mind, normally like the still canopy, becomes a maenad of branches under the elements of eros. Archilochus suggests that the conquest of reason by eros verges on a near-death experience, while Callimachus states that the better part of the soul temporarily does die or escape during erotic arousal, fr. 191, 193, G-P 4. See also K. Gutzwiller (*Poetic Garlands: Hellenistic Epigrams in Context* [1998], 214–16) on Callimachus's conviction that rationality fails utterly when confronted with erotic passions.

that the woman Sappho loves will quickly be amorous in return, "even if the woman is unwilling" to do so prior to Aphrodite's intervention.[27]

Fourth, the gods of eros become tyrannical and destructive when persons try to resist the gods' power, even when this would lead to a better course of action. The stepmother in Euripides' *Hippolytus,* Phaedra, reasonably tries to withstand the supremacy of Aphrodite, who is compelling her to seduce her stepson, Hippolytus, only for Phaedra to be victimized further by the goddess as punishment for trying to refrain. Persons who try to abstain from ill-considered sexual activity succeed only in making the erotic gods more ruthless at shattering their will and psychological stability. Thus Phaedra's nurse remarks, as though it were beyond dispute, that surrendering without question to sexual desire is better than restraint.[28] Sexually aroused persons must do the gods' bidding with alacrity, for the gods are going to make them do it anyway—and with greater suffering if they initially practice forbearance.[29]

Fifth, despite the agony of eros, the ancient Greeks thought that mortals have not genuinely lived unless their reason and will power have been incapacitated by eros. "What is life . . . without golden Aphrodite?" (Mimnermus, fr. 1). Greek sensibility toward eros has a forceful and violent tenor, unlike Tennyson's placid moralizing that it is better to have loved and lost than never to have loved at all. For the Greeks, persons do not know life until they have been "skewered to the bone" by sexual desire (Archilochus, fr. 193). They are not truly human unless Eros has come after their psyche with an axe.[30] So strong is this conviction that persons who seem impervi-

27. Fr. 1.19–24, Page. The idea that the gods of eros break human will takes several poetic forms. The gods hunt down or shackle the mind so as to unleash wild eroticism within, Ibycus, fr. 286; or eros intoxicates the will and wine potently mixes with its liquor, Anacreon, fr. 376; Callimachus, G-P 8.

28. *Hipp* 443–6, Similarly, "Eros the bittersweet cannot be conquered in his limb-melting ways," Sappho, fr. 130, and see Theognis 2.1386–9. Likewise Sophocles: "Eros is invincible, . . . Aphrodite the god plays unbeatably" with people, and the game makes mortals crazed, *Antig* 781, 790, 800–1. Aphrodite as Spartan war goddess plays into this imagery, for several poets recast her as a kind of dominatrix in battle gear, *Anth Plan* 174 (anon.), 177 (Philippus), and see too G-P Commentary, 334. Sophocles himself maintained that Eros wields tyranny from youth to old age, as Plato's *Republic* indicates, 329c1–4. It is more doubtful whether Euripides believed this idea, though he presents it in his plays, for Hecuba in *Troades* voices a view the early Stoics would support: The popular idea of Aphrodite is but a name for human folly—Helen's own mind became Cypris when she saw Paris, 981–90.

29. See further C. Calame, *The Poetics of Eros in Ancient Greece* (1999), 14–19, as well as B. Thornton, *Eros: The Myth of Ancient Greek Sexuality* (1997), 26–31, which is a good hermeneutical section of a work that is otherwise uneven, as H. King observes in her review of Thornton, (1998), 755–6.

30. To speak more precisely, but too abstrusely for the image to be vivid in English, Anacreon's image (fr. 413) refers to the axe-like, or "peine," side of a blacksmith's hammer. My thanks to Peter Himmelheber for the technical term.

ous to eros are thought to have something wrong with them. The roving-eyed Aphrodite has not seen fit to glance their way, while others rightly melt like wax under her heat (Pindar, fr. 123). Persons unscathed by eros are so austere their cognition seems blighted. As the poet Nossis states, "The person whom Cypris has not loved does not know what sort of flowers roses are" (G-P 1). Such a person thinks roses are simply flowers, whereas lovers know roses also represent the works of Aphrodite.[31] Popular Greek culture repeatedly affirms that eros is a visitation from Aphrodite or Eros that routinely compels mortals to act contrary to their better judgment. And the gods will punish those who are arrogant enough to presume to regulate their sexual conduct. Nevertheless, persons never touched by the agony are worse off in their numbness than the walking wounded.

The preceding cluster of ideas about eros are not merely literary tropes. They reflect a widespread conviction about the way eros works. Persons in love routinely believed that they were struck by superhuman powers, as indicated by the popular practice of erotic magic in ancient Greek and Hellenistic culture. Once smitten, they in turn would summon the divine powers through incantations in Greek and the magical language of abracadabra, urging the gods and other supernatural forces to skewer their prospective love victims as sharply as the gods have already transfixed them.[32] Thus in the terms set by the popular Greek tradition, mortals have only a few methods to contend with erotic fever. Before being struck, they have recourse only to abject pleading with the gods of eros, not to principles of rational sexual conduct that they should learn.[33] Once struck, the victims must in turn negotiate a deal with supernatural powers to take out a contract on the beloved, for the gods deploy eros like hit men for hire. Aside from magic rituals and appeals, Greek popular thought offers no other method for contending with eros that strikes from the gods when and where it will, for good or ill. Or so the ancient Greeks were conditioned to believe through their vehicles of popular morality—their rituals, prayers, drama, songs, and stories.

31. See too Euripides, fr. 269, 663. The poets hope that persons as yet unscathed by the madness will experience a mind-breaking erotic visitation. As Hermesianax states via fictional anecdotes, even the austere philosophers Pythagoras and Socrates have been pony-boys of Aphrodite in her chariot—with such fire has she heated them, 7 *Lib.* 3.79–94.

32. These magic rituals are primarily attested from Egypt, but evidence of such binding spells also comes from Athens, other parts of Greece, and North Africa, J. Gager, *Curse Tablets and Binding Spells from the Ancient World* (1992), 78–115. The female figurine (in Gager, *Curse Tablets*, 97–100) epitomizes this belief, pierced as it is with bolts expressing a male would-be lover's desire that a particular woman be as riveted by him as he by her. Aphrodite is important in these spells, C. Faraone, *Ancient Greek Love Magic* (1999), 133–41, and see further 41–95, 146–60 and J. Winkler (*The Constraints of Desire,* 71–98) for the tradition of erotic spells in general.

33. *Medea,* 627–642; and cf. *Hippolytus,* 525–33; Euripides, fr. 26.

EARLY STOIC EROS, ITS GROUNDING
AND DIVERGENCE FROM POPULAR GREEK EROS

Zeno and Chrysippus dissent from the Greek erotic tradition, in which the gods of eros exercise ruthless tyranny over human will and reason. In order to see the reasons why, we must explore early Stoic cosmology, theology, ethical theory, and related ideas about human sexuality and human nature as a whole.

Zeno and Chrysippus maintain the holistic position that nature and its gods are rational, that the human soul is an integral part of rational nature, and that human sexuality is integral to the rational soul. Seminal reason extends throughout nature as an immanent and creative divine force and imparts a beautiful order. "The active principle is reason ($\lambda \acute{o} \gamma o s$) in the material ground, which is God ($\acute{o} \ \theta \epsilon \acute{o} s$). This is eternal and crafts ($\delta \eta \mu \iota o \upsilon \rho \gamma \epsilon \hat{\iota} \nu$) each and every thing throughout the entirety of nature's material ground" (DL 7.134–6). This divine force is identified as Zeus in early Stoic theology, who is "the director of the order in all things" (DL 7.88). Nature therefore has a rational design throughout, and its designer is on the interior, Zeus in the form of physical spirit that shapes all entities.[34]

Zeus's seminal reason pervades the human soul, including human sexuality, as aspects of nature, and it does so in the form of structured and human-specific $\pi \nu \epsilon \hat{\upsilon} \mu a$. $\Pi \nu \epsilon \hat{\upsilon} \mu a$ in general is the breath or air that animates living creatures and the world as a whole. The human breath or soul ($\psi \upsilon \chi \acute{\eta}$), that is, the $\pi \nu \epsilon \hat{\upsilon} \mu a$ specific to human beings, extends throughout and enlivens the body. Though the soul is distinct from the body, the two are integrally connected in living human beings. The soul animates and informs active sentience and thereby distinguishes the person from a dead body.[35] The soul is a composite of seven seminally rational parts in addition to the governing part, or $\acute{\eta} \gamma \epsilon \mu o \nu \iota \kappa \acute{o} \nu$, which Chrysippus enumerates as the soul parts corresponding to the trachea, eyes, ears, nose, tongue, flesh, and sex organs.[36] The soul as the early Stoics see it thus goes beyond the five canonical senses and includes two other soul functions, the vocal and genital.[37] The human vocal function is one of Zeus's preeminent arrangements

34. Alexander, *Mixt* 225.1–2 = SVF 2.310 = LS 45H; Aëtius 1.7.33 = SVF 2.1027 = LS 46A; M. Pohlenz, *Die Stoa: Geschichte eine geistiger Bewegung* (1959; reprint, 1984), 93–8, 108–10. For a good argument that Zeno's cosmology is grounded in Polemo's Timaean physics, see D. Sedley, "The Origins of Stoic God" (2002), 41–77.

35. See also A. A. Long, "Soul and Body in Stoicism"(1982), 34–49.

36. Galen, *PHP* 3.1.9–15 = SVF 2.885.

37. The word translated "genitals" or "sex organs" is $\acute{o} \rho \chi \epsilon \iota s$, which signifies "testicles," "ovaries," and by extension, human genitals and sexuality. Though Zeno and Chrysippus support the reproductive function of the sex organs, DL 7.110, they do not regard it as the genitals' only function, as I explain further below.

of πνεῦμα, for persons make their rational nature intelligible and audible through spoken utterances, or λεκτά.[38] The genital function is likewise an important configuration of seminal reason as soul πνεῦμα, for it is the vehicle through which persons formulate and have an active sexual nature. Human sexuality thus has a rationally physical basis.[39] The soul, πνεῦμα, can be imagined as octopus-like, with the soul parts as quasi-tentacles extending to the sex organs, voice, and senses.[40] Human sexual arousal and activity consequently are not and should not be regarded as anti-rational or even irrational, contrary to the popular tradition on eros. The sex organs are not bodily functions remote from mind (unlike, say, the growth of hair or nails), for the structure of the early Stoic soul disallows this divide. The early Stoics find sexuality highly meaningful for the human experience, just like seeing, speaking, thinking, and the other soul functions. Chrysippus emphasizes this idea by giving the sexual function the honor of a named place in the soul.

The cosmogony underlying the metaphysics of the early Stoa is similarly consonant with the idea that human sexuality is rational. In early Stoic thought the relationship between reason (λόγος) and matter (ὕλη) is a sexual intermingling of Zeus and Hera on a cosmic scale, which means that the material ground has a divine nature, just as immanent reason does. Zeus's reason, as Chrysippus explains it in reference to a painting of Hera fellating Zeus, is the semen that Hera receives "into her body for the purpose of arranging all things in a beautifully ordered way." Though Chrysippus here is allegorizing an erotic painting, his sexual imagery is not provoked merely by its explicit content.[41] The early Stoics regard the cosmos as being rational because of the cosmogonic sexual activity that created it. To see why and how, it is worth exploring testimony from Dio and Aristocles.

Dio states that the mind of Zeus is infinite, brilliant, and undifferentiated at the dawn of a new Stoic world cycle. At this time Zeus, as limitless mind, is stimulated by sexual desire (ἔρως) to generate the differentiated cosmos once again. "He becomes mindful of Aphrodite" and "makes love to Hera" in her role as divine but amorphous material ground.[42] Their lovemaking is the "most complete sexual union" possible thanks partly to Zeus's meta-

---

38. Sextus *M* 8.69–74 = SVF 2. 2.187 = LS 33C; A. A. Long, "Language and Thought in Stoicism" (1971), 75–113; and B. Inwood, *Ethics and Human Action*, 43–4, 57–66, 73–7.

39. Chrysippus refers to the physical basis of human sexuality as "another such kind of seminal reason" that the sexual part of the soul has, *PHP* 3.1.11 = SVF 2.885.

40. It is Aëtius who describes the early Stoic soul as octopus-like, SVF 2.836 = LS 53H.

41. Origen, *Cels* 4.48; Theophilus, *Autol* 3.8 = SVF 2.1073–4.

42. Dio Chrysostom, *Oratio* 36.54–60, esp. 36.55–7. On the Stoic ideas in this cosmogony, see D. Hahm, *The Origins of Stoic Cosmology* (1977), 61 and D. A. Russell's edition, *Dio Chrysostom* (1992), 242–7.

morphic potency. His sexual desire transforms his pure and infinite mind into a phallic lightning bolt, and in this fiery rational form he makes love to Hera. Through orgasm Zeus transforms from the bolt of creative fire into wet semen, every drop of it rational, just like the mind from which it came. Hera, upon receiving the semen, subsumes within her the entirety of Zeus's rational being. In recognition of this elemental sexual union, the early Stoics identify Zeus's reason as "a kind of semen, which holds the principles and causes of all that has been, all that is, and all that will come to be," as Aristocles notes.[43] In this fluid manifestation of his fiery mind Zeus shapes "the entire generation of the universe." Through consummating his sexual desire, then, Zeus gives his immanent and pantheistic all to the material world, which the receptive Hera embodies as the orderly and generative cosmos. The early Stoics thus require Zeus's metamorphic ejaculation of himself as semen into Hera in order to create the rational cosmos.[44] Without Zeus's sexual arousal, there is no transformation of reason from limitless mind to rational semen, and without the receptive body of Hera, no shaping of a cosmos can happen. This worldview provides a highly amenable habitat for the early Stoics' ideas about rational human sexual conduct.

In early Stoic ethical theory, Zeus's reason in nature has organized people to engage in actions that are suited to their ensouled body and beneficial to its maintenance. "The primary orientation or aptitude ($o\grave{\iota}\kappa\epsilon\hat{\iota}o\nu$) for every animal is its constitution and its awareness of this." Integral to this orientation is that the animal has a natural awareness to "reject harmful things and accept things suitable" to its nature.[45] People should act in accordance with

43. Aristocles cited by Eusebius, *Praep Evang* 15.14.2 = LS 46G = SVF 1.98.

44. D. Hahm (*Stoic Cosmology*, 60–82, esp. 64, 66, 68) is likely right that the early Stoic cosmogony is modeled on the gestation of an embryo, but he is too quick to equate the model with "birth" itself. The cosmos is Hera's inseminated body, not a third and separate entity born from her body—unlike, say, the birth of Cronus from Gê by Uranus in Hesiod's *Theogony*. Zeno nonetheless claims a precedent in Hesiod's *Theogony* for the early Stoic cosmogony. For other parallels in Ancient Near Eastern and Presocratic cosmogonies, see D. Hahm, *Stoic Cosmology*, 64–68. The Stoics, though latecomers to this tradition of sexual cosmogony, augment it philosophically by making Zeus's semen the pantheistic ground of a rational design and of rational norms in the world and human beings. In this connection, M. Levine's statement about Presocratic cosmology is worth noting (*Pantheism: A Non-theistic Concept of Deity* [1994], 41), for it also holds true of the Stoics: "The Presocratics relied on the concept of an ordering principle or force to explain the operations of nature, and its . . . divinity. The principle(s), and nature as a whole, are seen as having moral . . . properties associated with them. This is radically different from post-enlightenment ideas of nature, . . . where no values are taken as inherent, and where associating moral judgements with nature makes no sense." For the Stoics too, nature has moral properties, thanks to Zeus's immanence as rationally purposive semen.

45. DL 7.85–6. On the primary orientation, see B. Inwood, *Ethics and Human Action*, 184–94; G. Striker, "The Role of *Oikeiôsis* in Stoic Ethics,"(1983), 144–67, and "Following Nature: A Study in Stoic Ethics,"(1991), 2–13, 35–50; N. White, "The Basis of Stoic Ethics" (1979),

this principle by rejecting what is detrimental to human nature and accepting what is suitable to its well-being, for instance, eating when one is hungry, so as to stay alive. Circumstances may at times warrant another course of action, such as deciding to starve when one is kept in unjustifiable captivity.[46] Only on rare occasion, however, would starving be appropriate. This principle of appropriate behavior applies to human sexual conduct as well. Thus the early Stoic primary orientation leads to practices of beneficial sexual conduct. What counts as beneficial depends on how Zeno and Chrysippus further interpret human nature, as discussed below.

The early Stoics regard sexual pleasure in itself to be morally unproblematic, so long as it results from sexual activity in accordance with human nature.[47] Similarly, the pleasure one experiences when drinking water to quench thirst is appropriate because the need for water is an inherent part of our primary orientation. The early Stoics liken pleasure from appropriate actions to the health that animals and plants evince when they are in a nurturing environment. "Physical pleasure is generated after nature has itself by itself sought and received those things which are in harmony with an animal's constitution. In this manner animals are happily content and plants flourish in full bloom" (DL 7.86). Just as glossy fur and the symmetry in blossoms are natural and beautiful signs that mammals and flowering plants are in an environment suited to their needs, so too is human sexual pleasure a kind of bloom arising from sexual conduct practiced in accordance with human nature. Far from being problematic, such pleasure is rather a supervenient joy.[48]

143–78; and T. Engberg-Pedersen, *The Stoic Theory of Oikeiosis: Moral Development and Social Interaction in Early Stoic Philosophy* (1990), 7–64.

46. Since sages may find that an extenuating condition justifies an otherwise unnatural action (DL 7.121–3, Sextus *M* 11.64–7 = SVF 1.361 = LS 58F), they, and not rules about $\kappa\alpha\theta$-$\acute{\eta}\kappa o\nu\tau\alpha$, are the final arbiters of right action, B. Inwood, "Rules and Reasoning in Stoic Ethics" (1999), 107–27; P. Vander Waerdt, "Philosophical Influence on Roman Jurisprudence? The Case of Stoicism and Natural Law" (1994), 4854–6; but consult P. Mitsis as well, "Natural Law and Natural Right in Post-Aristotelian Philosophy: The Stoics and Their Critics" (1994), 4829–50. On appropriate action, see Cicero *Fin* 4.14 = SVF 3.13; Stobaeus 2.85.12–86.4 = SVF 3.494 = LS 59B; Cicero *Fin* 3.17, 58–9 = LS 59D, 59F; and J. Rist, *Stoic Philosophy*, 97–111.

47. J. Rist, *Stoic Philosophy*, 37–53 and B. Inwood, *Ethics and Human Action*, 145, 173–5.

48. Thus there is no evidence for the view that the early Stoics thought human beings should refrain from sexual activity per se. Zeno and Chrysippus grant only that persons should act with reservation as sexual agents, for any action in the world can be frustrated by chance factors. On the early Stoic view, persons and worldly concerns are "indifferent" ($\dot{\alpha}\delta\iota\dot{\alpha}\phi o\rho\alpha$) in the sense that they have no bearing on the Stoic virtue of flawless reasoning, not in the sense that they do not matter. This dictate of reservation does not imply that people should be aloof and unfeeling, as J. Rist has already shown, *Stoic Philosophy*, 52–3; and see too B. Inwood, *Ethics and Human Action*, 119–26, 210–15. The stereotype about the early Stoic sage's detachment and lack of emotion should finally be laid to rest.

Mature human action, including sexual behavior, is regulated by the ἡγεμονικόν, the governing or authoritative capacity of the unified yet manifold human soul. The ἡγεμονικόν, through its configuration of πνεῦμα, works like a combined mind and moral conscience. It begins to function maturely by the age of fourteen, though it takes a rigorous Stoic education and social environment to fully perfect.[49] Persons regulate human action by the evaluative decisions they make through this soul function. The ἡγεμονικόν formulates evaluative assessments in response to perceptions relevant to action, such as whether or not it is justifiable to engage in sexual relations with an appealing person in a particular situation. It then assents or dissents.[50] Each assent by the ἡγεμονικόν is also an emotive soul impulse (ὁρμή) to do something, such as the desire to make love. If the governing part of the soul reasons well, persons assent to propositions that are in accordance with and beneficial to human nature. If, however, the governing part of the soul functions poorly, the emotive decision is a passion, that is, "an unnatural movement or an excessive impulse" of the soul. The action ensuing from this impassioned impulse is detrimental to human nature. Passions make the soul and ensouled body diseased by virtue of being unnatural and excessive.[51] Wise persons with a perfectly functioning ἡγεμονικόν are extremely rare in conventional society, but in the disciplined early Stoic city sages would, in principle, exist as a noteworthy percentage of the populace.[52]

Genuinely irrational sexual activity by pubescent and more mature adults is precluded by the early Stoic notion of the rational soul. From the age of fourteen onward, an agent's sexual motives and activity are either rightly or wrongly rational, that is, well reasoned or falsely rationalized. Persons use their sexual organs well or badly depending on the evaluative propositions

49. For pubescent λόγος see SVF 1.149 = Iamblichus, *Anim* in Stobaeus 1.317.20–24; M. Schofield, *Stoic City*, 33 n. 21; and B. Inwood, *Ethics and Human Action*, 72–3.

50. The ἡγεμονικόν regulates voluntary actions and has a propositional content, Sextus *M* 8.69–74 = SVF 2.187 = LS 33C. See too A. A. Long, "Language and Thought in Stoicism," 75–113 and B. Inwood, *Ethics and Human Action*, 43–4, 57–66, 73–7.

51. The impulse is "turned away from right reason," Cicero, *Tusc disp* 4.5.11, 4.9.22. On passion as erroneous rational judgment and its harmful effect, see Galen *PHP* 4.5.13–14 = SVF 3.479; DL 7.110; B. Inwood, *Ethics and Human Action*, 127–73; and M. Nussbaum, *Therapy of Desire*, 366–86.

52. Persons who become wise are as rare as a phoenix due to conventional and non-Stoic mores of upbringing and education that hinder the human development of virtue. Virtue is eminently teachable according to the early Stoics, DL 7.91, and cf. Musonius 3.36.16–40.4 (Lutz), but not through a conventional education in Zeno's estimation, DL 7.32. Stoic educational and social reform is required to increase the population of sages. On this matter, I corroborate A. Erskine, *The Hellenistic Stoa*, 25 and Schofield's epilogue in *Stoic City* (1999), 147–52.

to which they assent.[53] If adolescent agents act on their sexual desire in ways unjustifiably contrary to human nature, this indicates that the governing part of their soul is poorly trained, not that there is anything intrinsically bad, demented, or harmfully god-possessed about sexual desire. Human beings are fully capable of acting with right reason sexually by the time their bodies sexually develop. Whether they act rightly or wrongly depends on whether they learn how to use their ἡγεμονικόν properly.

THE EARLY STOIC CRITIQUE OF THE GREEK EROTIC TRADITION

The early Stoics reject the popular Greek belief that the gods of eros possess and overwhelm the human rational faculty, leading mortals to harm themselves and others in their sexual relations. Chrysippus explicitly challenges tragedy for its portrayal of destructive eros.[54] Eros does not drive people to the acts of destruction and suicide that appear in the *Hippolytus* and other tragedies. People are possessed by the common conception of eros, not by eros per se. Habitual wrong thinking accounts for why people become passionately enamored both on stage and off. Chrysippus would say that the Greeks have assented to the widespread view that eros is an anti-rational affliction from the gods that mortals need to suffer in order to genuinely live. Through such thinking the Greeks start and fan the fire of eros as passion. What needs to be extirpated is eros as promulgated in popular thought, not eros as a whole.[55]

The early Stoics would reform several popular Greek ideas in order to transform the human experience of eros for the better. The first idea concerns the nature of the gods. In early Stoic thought, the gods are good, not domineering and malicious, for they heed the rational will of Zeus that pervades nature, including the human soul and its sexual part.[56] Eros and Aphrodite do not act like raging tyrants if persons refrain from sexual activity that is harmful and contrary to right reason. Hence the tragedians and pop-

---

53. Persons make use of "all bodily things (πάντα τὰ σωματικά) . . . well or poorly" depending on the quality of their reasons (Sextus *M* 11.61–63 = SVF 3.122).

54. Chrysippus's argument against eros in tragedy appears in verbatim fragments: Galen, *PHP* 4.6.23–39 = SVF 3.475.

55. Thus M. Nussbaum is mistaken to argue (*Therapy of Desire*, 389–401, 439–83) that the Stoics as a whole consider eros to be a passion that must be extirpated as fully as possible. She formulates her argument almost completely from Seneca and mainly from his *Medea*. Nussbaum is right about Seneca (as further shown in the next chapter), but not about Chrysippus.

56. "If there are gods," as there are in early Stoic thought, then "the gods are good," Chrysippus states in Alexander, *De fato* 37.210–14 = SVF 2.1005. On Zeus's goodness, see DL 7.147; Cleanthes, *Hymn to Zeus* 1–21 = SVF 1.537 = LS 54I; and B. Inwood, *Ethics and Human Action*, 19 n. 6. Early Stoic theology is thus reminiscent of Plato's, *Rep* 379a5–c8.

ulace at large have a misguided theology, for they misrepresent how the gods of eros interact with human sexuality, just as they wrongly caricature Zeus as Aphrodite's hapless victim.[57] To reform this misconception, the Greeks should adopt the early Stoic way of thinking about the gods.

Second, the Greeks should cease from abandoning themselves to their sexual impulses in fear of retribution from Aphrodite and Eros. The Greeks really believe, Chrysippus observes with dismay, that they must submit to their erotic impulses without question in order to avoid greater penalty for resisting. They stubbornly insist that they must "be allowed their erotic gratification, whether for better or for worse . . . even if they are wrong and it is not beneficial to them."[58] Chrysippus especially criticizes Euripides for contributing to this social conditioning in his now lost plays *Dictys* and *Stheneboea*, where his characters declare: "Aphrodite does not loosen the line even when she is rebuked. If you try to use force, she likes pulling the line even tighter."[59] Similarly, "Eros, when rebuked, pushes down even harder."[60] The early Stoics challenge this doctrine of unreflective surrender by repudiating the view that the gods are wicked and ought to be feared.

Third, popular Greek ideas about eros led to conceptions of a divided psyche that the early Stoics hoped to supplant with their monistic psychology. When persons suppose that they are swept away by their desire or heart, as Chrysippus's contemporaries did,[61] they blame their impulsive actions on an emotion or anatomical zone outside of their control, not on their own weakly trained powers of reasoning. This division of the psyche is problematic because it encourages people to think that they can never use knowledge or reflective deliberation to regulate their autonomous emotions.[62]

57. *Iliad* 14; Euripides, fr. 431; Asclepiades G-P 11, 14; Meleager G-P 19, and G-P Commentary ad loc. K. Gutzwiller (*Poetic Garlands*, 140–42) offers further insight into Asclepiades' portrayal of Zeus as victim of Eros.

58. Citations in this paragraph are to Galen, *PHP* 4.6.27–32 = SVF 3.475.

59. Galen, *PHP* 4.6.27, 32–3 = SVF 3.475.

60. Euripides fr. 340 and 665.

61. Galen, *PHP* 4.6.27, 32–3 = SVF 3.475.

62. This division takes various forms in ancient Greek thought, e.g., the emotive heart and the thinking agent who knows better (as in the viewpoint Chrysippus criticizes in SVF 3.745); or human "nature" ($\phi\acute{v}\sigma\iota\varsigma$) and the right thinking "mind" ($\gamma\nu\acute{\omega}\mu\eta$). The latter appears in another Euripidean fragment that the early Stoics take to task, Stobaeus 2.89.12. The conviction that reason is a force distinct from and weaker than emotions was widely shared in ancient Greek society. Plato attests its prevalence: "Among the majority, knowledge ($\dot{\epsilon}\pi\iota\sigma\tau\acute{\eta}\mu\eta$) seems to be the sort of thing that follows along, neither strong nor governing ($\dot{\eta}\gamma\epsilon\mu o\nu\iota\kappa\acute{o}\nu$) nor ruling. Not only do many regard knowledge as not ruling, they think that even though knowledge is often in a person, it is not knowledge but something else that rules, at times anger, at times pleasure, at times pain, occasionally eros, and often fear. Yes indeed, people in their thinking about knowledge regard it as a slave being dragged around by all the others," *Prot* 352b2–c2. Chrysippus, however, like Socrates, regards informed knowledge as being the strong governing principle of all impulses.

One key moral aim of the early Stoics' monistic psychology is to avoid this psychological divide and to promote responsible action through reason. If the ἡγεμονικόν adjudicates the actions of persons fourteen and older, as the early Stoics contend, then people should strive for right reasoning in all their behavior and stop blaming passionate decisions on an independent rush of feeling that carries them away.[63] Behavior motivated by sexual desire is no exception. People can and should learn to engage rightly and responsibly with the immanent divine powers of eros.[64] The early Stoics facilitate this learning by insisting that eros is governed by rational thought, not by its own frenzy. Get the thinking right, and ethically justified eros will follow.

EARLY STOIC EROS

The early Stoics define human beings as "a communal and mutually friendly animal"[65] and they construct their rehabilitated notion of eros from this definition. Insofar as human beings are "mutually friendly" (φιλ-άλληλον) by seminal design, appropriate erotic love for the early Stoics is neither harmful and contrary to friendship, as eros is in the popular Greek sense, nor is it austerely detached from friendly sexual arousal and activity, as reproductive marital sex becomes in ecclesiastical sexual ethics. Rather, eros motivated by right reason is "an impulse" (ἐπιβολή) on the part of sages "for the making of friends" (φιλοποιία) among persons who are νέοι, that is, adolescents or young adults. The impulse is stimulated by beauty.[66]

---

63. Chrysippus localizes the ἡγεμονικόν in the heart, or καρδία (SVF 2.838 = Aëtius, *Plac* 4.5.6). This reflects the early Stoic position that the heart, rather than the brain, is the vehicle of human reason, *PHP* 2.5.15–20 = SVF 2.894, and see further T. Tieleman, *Galen and Chrysippus on the Soul: Argument and Refutation in the* De placitis *Books II–III* (1996), 204. The rational command center is thus on the physical premises of the heart, where emotions conventionally come from in popular thought, screening them at source. The ἡγεμονικόν is not, so to speak, a weak absentee landlord elsewhere in the body, such as in the head, letting heartfelt emotions run unchecked.

64. For the early Stoics, Eros presides strictly over sexual relations that lead to friendship and virtue. Hence he "works to keep the city safe from harm," for "he is the god of friendship, freedom, and also is the provider of concord and nothing else," that is, no erotic madness or related afflictions, Athenaeus 561c = SVF 1.263 = LS 67D.

65. This characterization of the human animal is a reliably Stoic view, for Arius Didymus attests to it. Stobaeus 2.109.17–18 = SVF 3.686 = LS 67W, in Arius, *Epitome*. Other Stoic fragments reinforce the idea. See, for example, Cicero, *Fin* 3.65–9. On the importance of Arius Didymus as a source, see D. Hahm, "The Ethical Doxography of Arius Didymus" (1990), 2935–3055. For the worth of friendship and communalism in early Stoic thought, see Cicero, *Fin* 3.65–7 = LS 57F; DL 7.124; Athenaeus 561c = SVF 1.263 = LS 67D; and J.-C. Fraisse, *Philia: La notion d'amitié dans la philosophie antique* (1974), 333–419.

66. Stobaeus 2.115.1–4 = SVF 3.650, in Arius, *Epitome*. Other attestations are in DL 7.129, which refers to Chrysippus's περὶ ἔρωτος explicitly (= SVF 3.716, 718); Stobaeus 2.65.15–66.13 = SVF 3.717, SVF 3.721 (Scholia on Dionysius Thrax); SVF 3.722 (Alexander on Aris-

This friendship-building aspect of early Stoic eros is didactic;[67] it serves to train male and female adolescents alike in the arts of sexual conduct that show friendly reciprocity.[68] The ultimate goal of these didactic sexual relations is to help the younger partners progress toward the virtue of flawless reasoning and perfect friendship. For example, a Stoic wise man will "erotically love" ($\dot{\epsilon}\rho\alpha\sigma\theta\dot{\eta}\sigma\epsilon\sigma\theta\alpha\iota$) an adolescent male whose physical appeal and beauty of character stimulate the man to establish the sexual rudiments of friendship with the youth. This relationship is undeniably sexual; the intercrural position ($\delta\iota\alpha\mu\eta\rho\iota\sigma\mu\dot{o}s$) is one of the sexual practices cited.[69] Intercrural relations, further, are not the exclusively male homoerotic practice that Schofield thinks it is. As K. J. Dover notes, the practice is heterosexual as well and is first attested as such in Aristophanes' Birds.[70] This sexual position is not the only one practiced in the early Stoic city, for Zeno and Chrysippus encourage reproduction and female homoerotic activity, as demonstrated below. Educative sexual relations require time and commitment, not detached indifference, as Schofield well shows.[71] A genuinely mutual friendship between sages and $\pi\rho o\kappa\dot{o}\pi\tau o\nu\tau\epsilon s$ comes to fruition once the adolescents have attained consistently flawless reasoning and moral excellence. At this point friendly sexual relations continue as the sages see fit.

The friendship-building sexual relations facilitate the progress toward wisdom and virtue for members of the early Stoic city as a whole. If everything about these didactic sexual mores works according to plan, the city's populace has no unregenerate fools, unlike conventional society, which teems with them. Its inhabitants are at one of three general levels of ethical attainment: the virtuous wise men and women; the male and female $\pi\rho o$-$\kappa\dot{o}\pi\tau o\nu\tau\epsilon s$, who are advancing toward wisdom partly through didactic eros;

---

totle's *Topics* 2.109b13). Eros is defined as an $\dot{\epsilon}\pi\iota\beta o\lambda\dot{\eta}$, "an impulse before an impulse," Stobaeus 2.87.14–22 = SVF 3.173, in Arius, *Epitome,* and see too SVF 3.721, 3.722, 3.650. B. Inwood (*Ethics and Human Action,* 232–4) and M. Schofield (*Stoic City,* 29–30 n. 14) offer differing interpretations of $\dot{\epsilon}\pi\iota\beta o\lambda\dot{\eta}$.

67. On the similarities between the early Stoics' erotic didacticism and Pausanias's in Plato's *Symposium,* see B. Inwood, "Why Do Fools Fall in Love?" 56–60.

68. Stoic wise persons should actively seek out $\pi\rho o\kappa\dot{o}\pi\tau o\nu\tau\epsilon s$ as sexual partners with a view to fostering their propensity for virtue, DL 7.129; Plutarch *Comm not* 1073c = SVF 3.719; and Schofield, *Stoic City,* 32–4.

69. Sextus *PH* 3.245 = SVF 1.250. Scholars of early Stoic sexual principles rightly interpret this passage to mean "that [Zeno] enjoyed and enjoined physical relationships with young males, and with young females too (SVF 1.250)," G. Boys-Stones, "Eros in Government," 169; J. Rist, *Stoic Philosophy,* 68 n. 3; and M. Schofield, *Stoic City,* 44–5.

70. *Greek Homosexuality*[2] (1989), 98. For females, the position is doubly advantageous, for it is both stimulates the clitoris and prevents unwanted conception.

71. The commitment can last up to fourteen years or longer, from age fourteen to twenty-eight, M. Schofield, *Stoic City,* 33.

and the children, who are being raised in a more rudimentary and as yet nonsexual way toward virtue and wisdom.

Zeno applies the sexually didactic aspect of early Stoic eros to young women as well as young men. His inclusion of young women is no ancillary matter. Wise persons in the city "ought to engage in sexual relations (δια-μηρίζειν) with adolescent sexual favorites (παιδικά) no more or less than those of nonfavorites, females than males. Different rules do not apply to favorites as opposed to nonfavorites, females as opposed to males. Rather the same treatment for all is decorous and fitting." This principle of "the same treatment for all" touches upon a Socratic feature of early Stoic ethics, that males and females have the same capacity for moral excellence or virtue.[72] Virtue (viz., right reasoning) can and should be taught on the early Stoic view, and sexual training as they conceive of it is key toward this end. Since males and females are equally receptive to learning moral excellence, equal opportunity sexual didacticism is "decorous and fitting." Zeno recognizes that to give male homoeroticism privileged status would perpetuate favoring males over females, which conflicts with the socially cohesive aim of early Stoic eros. He further takes it for granted that numerous women would attain wisdom and virtue in the early Stoic city, for, as noted before, he states that among the wise, women and men would make love with one another as they see fit (DL 7.131). Hence, his directive to avoid gender bias in didactic sexual relations pertains to the sexual conduct of wise men and wise women alike. Therefore, bisexual practices would be the norm of didactic early Stoic eros.[73] Wise women would engage in friendship-building love with female as well as with male adolescents, just as wise men would.

The early Stoic requirement that sexual love should foster mutual friendliness would make Zeno's city a better place to live than conventional ancient Greek society in several major respects. The early Stoics stipulate that sexual relations are impermissible unless the participants give mutual consent, as Rist has observed. Rape is an extreme example of nonconsensual sexual activity and is especially unjustified.[74] When sexual activity is forced on unwilling partners, it abuses the mutually friendly tendencies that hu-

---

72. For Socrates, see Aristotle, *Pol* 1260a14–24 and Plato, *Meno* 72a6–73c5. Musonius expressly attests the Stoic support for this Socratic position 3.38.25–40.4 (Lutz), and Zeno assumes it at SVF 1.250 = Sextus, *PH* 3.245 and DL 7.131. See too M. Schofield, *Stoic City*, 43.

73. M. Schofield has no good reason to suggest that Zeno's early Stoic city would be sexually unbiased in theory but not in practice. His suggestion is based on his mistaken view that early Stoic ethical training via intercrural sexual activity is strictly male homoerotic, *Stoic City*, 43–6.

74. *Stoic Philosophy*, 65–6. This is why the early Stoics commend Menander's character Thrasonides for not sexually forcing his female partner against her will, DL 7.130. Zeno too favors refraining from forcing an adolescent who rejects sexual advances, Sextus *M* 11.190 = SVF 1.251.

man beings naturally have, to the early Stoics, for it traumatizes the victims and stimulates the aggressors to act in an inimical way toward them. For a similar reason the early Stoics would not permit sexual relations with persons under fourteen. Males and females who are not yet adolescents are as yet incapable of mature rational assent and thus are not ready to act sexually on their own cognizance. This early Stoic principle of mutual consent marks a major advance over common ancient Greek (and Roman) mores that regularly eroticize the sexual aggression of adult males and submissive fear from their targets, be they female or male.[75]

Further, even when mutual consent occurs, the early Stoics would rule out sexual relations that are solely or even mainly for the purpose of one's own gratification or some other motive of self-interest. These kinds of sexual activity fail to have friendship as their exclusive or primary motive. If, for example, male or female prostitutes consent to be hired, used, and paid, the customers have looked upon the prostitutes as being good merely for their own pleasure, which is a misuse of the mutually friendly purpose of human sexuality. Likewise the prostitutes should not be utilizing their sexual faculty to make money instead of to promote friendship. Similarly, a man should not adopt the ancient Greek custom of taking a wife primarily for legitimate offspring and domestic upkeep while considering her beneath his intellectual and emotional engagement.[76] Such marital customs are out of keeping with the Stoic aim of promoting shared ethical advancement toward friendship through wisdom and virtue.

Arius Didymus confirms the careful distinction that the early Stoics made between their sense of eros and the passion of eros in the popular sense. The "person who is worthy of love" ($\dot{a}\xi\iota\dot{\epsilon}\rho\alpha\sigma\tau\sigma$) in the early Stoic sense is also necessarily "worthy of friendship" ($\dot{a}\xi\iota\sigma\phi\dot{\iota}\lambda\eta\tau\sigma$), not merely "good for one's gratification" ($\dot{a}\xi\iota\alpha\pi\dot{\sigma}\lambda\alpha\upsilon\sigma\tau\sigma$). Hence early Stoic love is "the good love" ($\sigma\pi\sigma\upsilon\delta\alpha\hat{\iota}\sigma$ $\ddot{\epsilon}\rho\omega$), not an impulse contrary to nature.[77] Similarly, "the term 'one who loves' ($\dot{\epsilon}\rho\omega\tau\iota\kappa\dot{\sigma}$) also has two meanings." First, there are lovers in the early Stoic sense, who practice consensual and friendly eros to the best of their ability, either as sages or as $\pi\rho\sigma\kappa\dot{\sigma}\pi\tau\sigma\nu\tau\epsilon$. They must

75. For instance, "they say that one night undoes the hostility of a [captive] woman toward a man's bed," Euripides, *Tro* 665–6. Note also C. Sourvinou-Inwood, "A Series of Erotic Pursuits: Images and Meanings" (1987), 131–53 and the essays by Shapiro and Richlin in *Pornography and Representation in Greece and Rome*, ed. A. Richlin (1992), esp. 62 fig. 3.5, 64–70, 162, and 168. The early Stoics are the first known thinkers in Western culture to prohibit rape as a matter of principle. Apart from them, when more powerful male lovers in antiquity refrain from sexually coercing subordinates, they do so at their own discretion or by personal preference, e.g., Theognis, 2.1235–8 and Aristophanes, *Lys* 163–66.

76. ps.-Dem. 59.122 and Xenophon, *Oec* 7.18–19.

77. All quotations in this paragraph are to Stobaeus 2.65.15–66.25 = SVF 3.717, in Arius, *Epitome*.

responsibly retain their faculties when sexually involved with others and sustain a commitment to mutual amicability and virtue, regardless of the sex of the partners. Second, there is the impassioned type of lover, "the one who is blameworthy and vicious, such as the one who is maddened by love (ἐρωτομανής)." Erotically maddened persons are deluded in their love, because they think and act as though eros is domineering, irrational, and inimical to human well-being. Eros in this conventional Greek sense primarily requires sexual pleasure to quell the erotic fever—gratification first, and friendship rarely, if ever. People imbued with eros in this sense have learned a social lesson antithetical to early Stoic sexual ethics: Aphrodite and Eros are cruel overseers in a field of sexual exploitation where free adult males relentlessly have the upper hand.[78]

Erotic love according to the early Stoics should be communal as well as mutually friendly. The sexual impulse for establishing reciprocal friendship should likewise be communally oriented, not geared toward exclusive pairing, insofar as the human animal is also "communal" (κοινωνικόν) in its design.[79] Friendship itself is defined as being intrinsically communal, for φιλία is "a sharing in common of those matters that pertain to life" (DL 7.124). Human sexuality is a central "matter of life," for as Zeno and Chrysippus conceptualize it, eros plays a crucial role in achieving and sustaining a sagacious and friendly civic life worth living. Hence early Stoic eros is communal. The early Stoics are accordingly committed to the position that the human animal is sexually gregarious by nature,[80] which they indicate by the stances they take on marriage, sexual possessiveness of any extramarital sort, the raising of children, and incest prohibitions.

First of all, the early Stoics would abolish the conventional practice of marriage. Among the wise, men and women should make love to one another as they see fit.[81] They should not form married couples situated in nu-

---

78. The idea of early Stoic eros elicited some resistance from poets. Posidippus (G-P 1), who had some knowledge of early Stoicism, hopes to silence Zeno and champions the preeminence of "Eros the bittersweet" as portrayed by Sappho, fr. 130. K. Gutzwiller (*Poetic Garlands*, 157–8) appreciates the *recusatio* element of this epigram. My point is more specific: Posidippus is championing the popular Greek conception of eros (as epitomized by Sappho) against Zeno's notion of rational sexual eros. Euripides anticipates some features of early Stoics eros in a distinctive fragment about eros (fr. 897) that wins him the title "philosopher of the stage" from Athenaeus: Sexual eros can be a full education in wisdom and virtue, depending on whether one exercises it rightly.

79. Stobaeus 2.109.17 = SVF 3.686, in Arius, *Epitome.*

80. Greek philosophers debated whether human beings were designed for marriage in pairs or for communal sexual relations. For the former position, see Plato, *Laws* 840d2–e2; Aristotle, *NE* 1162a17; and Hierocles in Stobaeus, 4.502.15–19.

81. DL 7.131. Cynic ideas helped inspire antinomian early Stoic sexual principles, M. Schofield, *Stoic City*, 10–13, 23–4, 51–2; A. Erskine, *The Hellenistic Stoa*, 9–15; J. Rist, *Stoic Philosophy*, 54–80; and D. Dudley, *A History of Cynicism* (1937; reprint, 1980), 98–103, 187–99.

clear or even more extended biological families. Marriage stems from the mistaken premise that we are by nature paired rather than gregarious animals. As Zeno recognizes, further, husbands and wives are accustomed to be jealous and possessive of each other, which is incompatible with the goal of collective amicability and sharing. Hence marriage should become a thing of the past in the early Stoic social order, with the beneficial result that jealousy over adultery "will be made null and void."[82]

The early Stoics also would strive to eliminate extramarital forms of sexual possessiveness, since individuals need not be married to claim someone else as their own exclusive sexual partner. In the early Stoic city, this possessiveness is likely to appear in the sexual relations between sages and adolescents, for the latter are not yet wise. To counteract this problem (in addition to eliminating the problem of gender bias), Zeno directs sages to avoid claiming favorites even if they were partial toward some (SVF 1.250). Sages must set a nonpossessive role model for their young partners. Genuine sages are committed to imparting the rudiments of friendship and wisdom in an equitable way to a group of partners, not to the inequitable practice of having the sexual equivalent of a teacher's pet. As Zeno states, it is good for the wise to have many friends (DL 7.124, 131). Toward this goal, sages should foster a reasonable number of prospective friends through educative sexual relations, in addition to enjoying the accomplished friendship they share with their peers. Since nonmarital possessiveness obstructs sexual communalism, it too should be abolished along with marriage.

The early Stoic city should likewise be a collective in its reproductive and childrearing customs. Human sexuality naturally includes a procreative plan: "The very shape of the human sex and other reproductive organs declares the purpose of reproducing by nature." Given that the human animal is sexually communal and friendly, so too are its acts of reproduction. Thus, when the city denizens mate without exclusive pairing, they do so partly in order to procreate.[83] The upbringing of children should similarly be a community project, in which all the adults must show a parental kind of love for all the children alike in the city. "We will love ($\sigma\tau\acute{\epsilon}\rho\xi o\mu\epsilon\nu$) all the children equally in the way of parents" (DL 7.131). To the early Stoics, conventional reproduction is contrary to human nature, for these practices habituate parents to love their biological offspring more than their neighbors' children. This narrow-minded nurture prevents communal affection from taking root. For newborns and children to be deprived of a fully collective pa-

---

82. DL 7.31. M. Schofield, *Stoic City,* 26, J. Rist, *Stoic Philosophy,* 66.

83. Hence the only $\gamma\acute{\alpha}\mu o\varsigma$ countenanced in early (as opposed to later) Stoic thought is gregarious reproduction, for this practice alone accords with the communal and mutually friendly animal. On this question, see M. Schofield as well, *Stoic City,* 119–27. For the procreative purpose of genitals, see Cicero, *Fin* 3.62 = SVF 3.340 = LS 57F.

rental love stymies their moral development and makes the attainment of wisdom extremely rare and perhaps impossible to accomplish, for parents and children in families remain out of touch with their communal nature. Common nurturing alone gives the offspring the broad-based "natural affection" (φιλοστοργία φυσική) (DL 7.120) that they need to start developing ethically in their prepubescent years. Through this upbringing the children are ready to work further toward wisdom and friendship as sexually initiated adolescents. Thus the early Stoics would dissent from conventional family values on the grounds that they preclude the attainment of wisdom and virtue. As they see it, family-based nurture is too restrictive and possessive in expressing the love adults should devote to all children alike in the city.

If human beings are communal in their sexual nature, as the early Stoics maintain, then incest rules too should be abolished. Incest prohibitions help to maintain a society's kinship pattern by demarcating certain blood-related persons as being off-limits sexually. In this respect they complement marriage rules. In the fully communal early Stoic city, there is nothing contrary to nature about making love to biological relatives. As Chrysippus states, "Having sexual intercourse with mothers, sisters, and daughters . . . is irrationally slandered."[84] The slander is irrational because in the naturally grounded order of the early Stoic city, there is no marriage, no family, no clan groupings, no familial division of wealth. Incest taboos are at cross-purposes with this social order, for they presuppose the kinship divisions that the early Stoics seek to dissolve. The early Stoic social order is an aggregate of friends and prospective friends whose only division is one of age and accomplishment in moral progress. Its social structure quite simply cannot accommodate incest prohibitions and remain communal. Chrysippus even extends this unqualified communalism to acts of reproduction: "It is acceptable . . . that the mother procreate from the son, the father from the daughter, and the brother with the sister of the same mother." On this policy of reproduction, however, Chrysippus's position would lead to the risk of inbreeding, which would likely produce some individuals with genetic defects that impede their progress toward wisdom and its corollary of virtue. Thus, though the early Stoics are right to see that incest taboos are incompatible with a purely gregarious human society, to permit reproductive inbreeding runs counter to their aspiration of wisdom and virtue for all.[85]

---

84. This and other citations in this paragraph are to Plutarch, *St rep* 1044f = SVF 3.753 = LS 67F and Sextus *PH* 3.246 = SVF 3.745, cf. DL 7.188. Zeno likewise contends that incest prohibitions between a mother and son are misguided, Sextus *PH* 3.205, *M* 11.91 = SVF 1.256 = LS 57F.

85. The early Stoics' proposed abolition of incest rules is thus not a shameless Cynic posturing with no earnest aim or logic informing it. Further, it is not merely an illustration of their

ANTIPATER, HIEROCLES, AND MUSONIUS ON MARITAL HUMAN NATURE

A more conventional Stoic notion of human nature, appropriate sexual conduct, and social order was formulated sometime after Chrysippus (280–207 B.C.E.) and before Antipater. This philosopher was either Antipater of Tarsus (fl. ca. 133 B.C.E.) or Antipater of Tyre (fl. ca. 50 B.C.E.).[86] Though we do not know who first offered this modification, or when, Hierocles voices the new position most clearly. "Nature has made us not only gregarious (συναγελαστικούς) but also disposed to live in pairs (συνδυασκτικούς)."[87] In later Stoic sexual ethics, this definition becomes a new tenet displacing the earlier idea that human nature is communal, not paired, and that society must change accordingly. This about-face position is amenable to the basic structure of conventional society, supporting as it does heterosexual marriage and the family. Antipater, Musonius, and Hierocles are its three main

---

general principle that inappropriate behavior is acceptable under extenuating circumstances. Given the sexually communal nature of human beings, rejecting incest taboos is appropriate and observing them is inappropriate. Hence early Stoicism is not the source for Origen's statement that the Stoics find incest appropriate only in extenuating circumstances, *Cels* 4.45 = SVF 3.743. Chrysippus's own quoted words from his own work on the *Republic* (πολιτεία) disagree with Origen's testimony, for he states that "it seems right to me" (δοκεῖ μοι) not to recognize conventional incest prohibitions, such as were observed in Athens, SVF 3.745 = Sextus *M* 11.192, *PH* 3.246. My interpretation of the early Stoics' rejection of incest taboos considerably strengthens Doyne Dawson's (*Cities of the Gods*, 184–5) more tentative observations: "When Chrysippus laid out his massive defense of Zeno's ideals . . . he met the objection [about the occurrence of incest in a sexually communal society] and argued that in the circumstances of the ideal city there would be nothing wrong with occasional cases of unintentional incest." Later Stoicism is the more plausible source for Origen's statement, because the later Stoics redefine human nature as being designed for marriage in accordance with established social conventions, as explained in the next section of this chapter. Only by this Stoic conception of human nature does incest becomes permissible only in extenuating circumstances.

86. The Antipater studied here wrote two tracts, περὶ γάμου and περὶ γυναικὸς συμβιώσεως, and he is identified only as "Antipater" by Stobaeus. It is not clear whether the author in question is the more eminent second-century Stoic Antipater of Tarsus, whose *floruit* is around 133 B.C.E., or the lesser-known first-century Stoic Antipater of Tyre, who died around the mid-first century B.C.E. The latter wrote a book, περὶ κόσμου (DL 7.139), and is said to have introduced Stoic ideas to Cato Uticensis. Von Arnim ascribes the two tracts discussed here to Antipater of Tarsus in his 1903 edition of SVF (Antipater, 3.62–63), but he more prudently expresses doubts in his earlier *RE* article ([1894], 2515–16) on the two Stoics named Antipater.

87. Hierocles in Stobaeus, 4.502.15–19. This definition is consistent with and reminiscent of Aristotle's view that "the human being by nature is disposed to live in pairs (συνδυαστικόν) even more than he is a political [viz., community-oriented] animal" (*NE* 1162a17). W. Deming (*Paul on Marriage and Celibacy: The Hellenistic Background of 1 Corinthians 7* [1995], 69–89) discusses how the later Stoic arguments concerning marriage fit more broadly into the Cynic and Stoic marriage debate. See further O. Yarbrough (*Not Like the Gentiles: Marriage Rules in the Letters of Paul* [1985], 31–63), as well as the studies by Nussbaum, Brown, Biale, and Brundage cited at the outset of this chapter (see n. 5).

advocates, though Epictetus and Seneca support it as well.[88] Though the later Stoics continue to support some aspects of early Stoic ethics, such as the method of constructing a moral argument from a normative definition of human nature, they transform the import of early Stoic eros. The communally friendly purpose of sexual relations is confined to the marital bond and becomes a means toward mutual friendship only between husbands and wives.

Antipater endorses the position that human beings are naturally designed for marriage in pairs. Marriage "is among the most necessary and primary appropriate actions ($\kappa\alpha\theta\eta\kappa o\nu\tau\alpha$)" (4.508.2–3). Young men who are "the best by nature" show their talent for attaining virtue by taking a wife, and marriage is key to their moral progress (4.507.7, 16–20, 508.4). The marital relationship these couples share is superior to other kinds of friendly bonds. Marital friendship is perfect, like the inseparable blending of water and wine, whereas other friendly relations are a mere mix of separable beans (4.508.11–19). Husbands and wives bring about this perfect blending because they alone share much in common, their children, property, spiritual life, and each other's sexual bodies.[89] This is a good example of how the later Stoics reshape early Stoic sexual ethics into a marital pattern. In agreement with the early Stoics, Antipater thinks friendly sexual relations are crucial to establishing shared social cohesion and virtue, but he limits the sexual relations to marriage, which shrinks the early Stoic city of communal eros to domestic islands of two.

Musonius concurs with Antipater and argues that human beings are naturally created to be heterosexually paired in marriage. The demiurge himself mandated at the dawn of creation that young men who aspire to become wise must take a wife, live with her, and produce children.[90] "For what other reason [than marriage] did the demiurge cut apart ($\ddot{\epsilon}\tau\epsilon\mu\epsilon$ $\delta\iota\chi\alpha$) our race and make two sets of genitals, male and female, and instill a strong desire ($\dot{\epsilon}\pi\iota\theta\upsilon\mu\iota\alpha\nu$) and longing ($\pi\acute{o}\theta o\nu$) for association and common rela-

88. The arguments of Antipater, Musonius, and Hierocles are preserved by Stobaeus. Citations from Antipater and Hierocles are to Wachsmuth and Hense's edition of Stobaeus. References to Musonius are cited by the page and line numbers of C. Lutz's edition (1947) of his extant diatribes and fragments.

89. 4.508.16–17. Xenophon, *Oec* 10.4–5 presents a similar view of Greek marriage. Ischomachus and his young wife are joined "so as to be partners in each other's bodies" ($\tau\hat{\omega}\nu$ $\sigma\omega\mu\acute{\alpha}\tau\omega\nu$ $\kappa o\iota\nu\omega\nu\eta\sigma o\nu\tau\epsilon\varsigma$ $\dot{\alpha}\lambda\lambda\eta\lambda o\iota\varsigma$). "Body-sharing" was a euphemism for sexual intimacies in marriage, for the wife replies, "So people say, at any rate" ($\phi\alpha\sigma\grave{\iota}$ $\gamma o\hat{\upsilon}\nu$ ... $o\grave{\iota}$ $\ddot{\alpha}\nu\theta\rho\omega\pi o\iota$), in response to her husband's statement that she and he share in each other's bodies, and see further S. Pomeroy's commentary, *Xenophon*, Oeconomicus: *A Social and Historical Commentary* (1994), 306.

90. 90.24–92.9. Musonius claims that Pythagoras, Socrates, and Crates are the best philosopher role models for young men partly because they were married.

tionship with one another?"[91] Musonius's creation myth draws upon and alters that of Aristophanes in Plato's *Symposium*.[92] He omits the primordial pairs of male and female homoerotic lovers in Aristophanes' myth and retains only the heterosexual couple to reveal the creator's later Stoic intention that human beings form couples as husbands and wives. Hence marriage, as Musonius sees it, is such a pressing "appropriate action" for young men that extenuating circumstances have virtually no force to justify exemptions. Even Crates got married, and he was by choice a philosopher of extremely slender means.[93] Musonius's young male audience thus must follow this naturally ordained order by taking a wife and producing offspring within the domestic family.[94]

Hierocles likewise argues that, insofar as human beings are naturally "designed to live in pairs" of a heterosexual sort,[95] matrimony is an "appropriate and preferred" custom to follow.[96] Men should act accordingly by "sharing life with a wife" and producing children as "their truly divine fruit." The joys of this friendship are the greatest of all.[97] The happy rewards that Hierocles describes, however, are not mutual, for the husband has a clear advantage. When the married man comes home burdened with numerous troubles in his career and public life, his ever-untroubled wife should be like the pillow she provides to make her husband forget his cares, whereas the unmarried man has no comforter at home to assuage him (4.504.1–505.7). Hierocles thus adopts a somewhat different tack in his argument from the idealization of marital sharing offered by Antipater and Musonius. He tries to persuade his audience of young men that marriage is in the man's best interest because it provides wives to shelter beleaguered husbands from the stressful conditions men faced in the Greco-Roman civic order. Zeno and Chrysippus, by contrast, wished to eliminate the stressful conventions besetting men and women alike, not to use women as wives to alleviate the suffering of married men.

---

91. 92.8–17. Musonius's use of ἐπιθυμία to describe this urge does not signify the Stoic soul passion ἐπιθυμία. Rather, it is what Hierocles describes as a "natural sexual stimulus" (ἐξοτρύνουσα φύσις), 502.16–17.

92. Musonius's claim that the demiurge "cut apart our race" reflects *Symp* 189e6, 190d1–5, and his paired terms "desire" (ἐπιθυμία) and "longing" (πόθος) reflect participles at *Symp* 191a6–7, cf. Musonius 92.9–17. Like Musonius, Philo, *Opif* 151–52 has a creation narrative that is similar to Aristophanes' and also omits the homoerotic pairs.

93. 92.6–9, 94.30–2, 96.2–6, DL 6.87.

94. M. Foucault (*Care of the Self,* 151–2, 157) notes this aspect of Musonius' argument.

95. M. Foucault (*Care of the Self,* 153–4) further discusses this argument of Hierocles.

96. 4.502.11–20. Hierocles is more flexible than Musonius, however, for he qualifies his position: marriage is appropriate "unless there is a hindering circumstance," 502.14. His flexibility is more characteristic of Stoic ethics, which allows for justifiable deviations from nature's dicates.

97. 4.503.18–19, 503.24–505.7.

Antipater, Musonius, and Hierocles further argue that it is patriotic for men to marry and raise a family. Married citizens, families, households, and cities are to their minds the immutable components of what it means to be a political animal. According to Antipater, men must protect their fatherland (πατρίς) and help maintain its population through traditionally procreative marriage (4.508.2–6). Households must be staffed and run by husbands and wives, one each per house, with children already produced or in the making. If male citizens avoid this duty of marriage and the family, anarchy will prevail (4.509.12–15). Single-sex domestic pairs or groups living together are a sorry substitute for the heterosexual nuclear family. "The household and city alike are imperfect" if they are "of women only" or "of men only" (4.507.7–508.2). Hierocles similarly maintains that cities need traditional households in order to be proper cities. "The household of the married man is perfect and full," whereas "the household of an unmarried man is imperfect" and makes the city defective (4.502.5–7). By this argument, ancient cities cannot allow alternatives, particularly homoerotic alternatives, to the conventional household without becoming chaotic and corrupt. Sexually segregated arrangements are particularly anarchic, for these would allow for other patterns of sexual behavior in domiciles, such as homoerotic bonding or prostitution.

Musonius defends the same patriotic view with sonorous intensity. The true walls defending the city are not the rampart. Familial households provide the city's real defensive enclosures (περιβολαί), which each male citizen must keep and guard. For a man to fail in this duty would be worse than if Hector had abandoned Troy, because much more than the city is at stake. "The man who does away with the human institution of marriage does away with the home, does away with the city, and does away with the entire human race" (92.35–6). Citizens must pair off, climb into their household forts, and save humanity through the children they produce, not unlike paired-off bees protecting their domestic plot in the community hive (92.25–33). Particularly inimical to the city are the unmarried males. They are lone wolves loping along in the guise of citizens, for they have no share in the community, refuse to cooperate with it, and lack a sense of right and wrong (92.20–1). In addition to denying their marital nature, they are seditious toward the ancient civic order.[98] To ameliorate this problem, Musonius in effect urges "To arms, men, marry and become fathers!"

Marriage and reproduction are also obligatory acts of polytheistic civic

---

98. Zeno and Chrysippus, by contrast, reject the claim that one must show patriotic allegiance to the traditional social order, given its incompatibility with their conception of human nature. F. Devine ("Stoicism on the Best Regime" [1970], 328–9) has good observations on this point and provides additional reasons for disbelieving that the early Stoics advocated traditional patriotism.

piety for the later Stoics. According to Antipater, the naturally ordained method to reproduce citizens is integrally related to honoring the gods, as is right and just (4.508.2–6). "If [our] species should cease to exist, who will sacrifice to the gods? Some wolves or bull-killing lions."[99] Musonius similarly defends matrimony and reproduction on Stoic theological grounds. Hera, Eros, and Aphrodite are great and deserve reverence. Insofar as they are gods, they preside strictly over appropriate human actions, and in the front rank of such actions are marriage and procreation. "Where is Eros more justly present than at the legitimate union of a man and a woman? Where are Hera and Aphrodite more justly present as well?" (94.25–7). Here Musonius offers another glimpse of the way in which later Stoic sexual ethics transmutes early Stoic eros. In early Stoicism the god Eros is good and presides only over appropriately communal sexual activity, not over sexual relations unfit for human nature, such as those dominated by erotic mania or run by marriage and the private family. In Musonius's reworked version of this argument, Eros, the god of appropriate sexual behavior, now presides over heterosexual pairing. Young men must marry and raise a family as part of their due reverence to Eros and the other inherently good gods—and the more children they legitimately father, the better (94.20–32). A man commits a grave act of impiety if he does not sponsor a family. He "is unjust to his own kin, [since] he wrongs the gods of his fathers and Zeus protector of the family ($Z\epsilon\dot{v}s$ $\dot{o}\mu\dot{o}\gamma\nu\iota os$), who keeps watch on transgressions against the family. The one who wrongs the gods is impious" (96.22–98.1). Hierocles likewise argues that citizens must perform important rituals for the gods, which they can accomplish only by having a familial household in which to keep the fire of the gods going. As husbands and wives, they must show devotion to "the gods of marriage, birth, and the hearth" (4.505.12–14). Consequently, in later Stoic thought as explored thus far, citizens must dedicate their lives to marriage, children, and the household. Only in this manner do they fulfill their compelling obligations to defend the fatherland, honor the gods, and act in accordance with human nature.[100]

99. 4.508.7–8. Antipater is referring to the species of the human political animal, as he indicates in his opening sentence, which urges the young male citizen ($\nu\dot{\epsilon}os$ $\pi o\lambda\iota\tau\iota\kappa\dot{o}s$) to marry and reproduce, 507.7–8.

100. The sexual mores advocated in SVF 3.611 (Stobaeus 2.94.7–20) similarly reflect the later Stoic position that human beings are sexually paired by nature. M. Schofield's argument (*Stoic City*, 126–7) is correct that SVF 3.611 is incompatible with Zeno's notion of appropriate human sexual conduct, as my argument about early Stoic eros further corroborates. A. Erskine (*The Hellenistic Stoa*, 66, 121) is thus mistaken to use this testimony to explicate Zeno's conception of appropriate human sexual conduct.

SENECA AND EPICTETUS

Seneca and Epictetus are characteristic later Stoics in agreeing that human beings are designed for male-female sexual pairing and procreation.[101] As Epictetus states, matrimony is the bond "to which we are by nature oriented" (2.4.2–3). Seneca likewise thinks that marriage is the proper institution for sexual activity. He repeatedly censures breaches of marital fidelity, especially adultery by wives, and he idealizes Lucretia as the kind of faithful Roman woman a man should marry. "The woman who is chaste and noble must be praised."[102] The man who marries her chooses wisely and will be sure to have legitimate children and heirs.[103] Procreation and childrearing, when they take place, should occur within the marital union, and both practices are rightly to be expected of the vast majority of male citizens.[104] Seneca and Epictetus thus support the later Stoic position that human nature is heterosexually paired and reproductively oriented, and hence that it is by and large incumbent on persons to act accordingly for the benefit of society, just as Antipater, Musonius, and Hierocles argue.

Seneca and Epictetus do not accept, however, that marriage and reproduction are a sine qua non for virtue, which Musonius and Antipater maintain.[105] For Epictetus and Seneca, marriage and childrearing have many potential distractions and anxieties that can and often do detract from the equanimity needed to retain a sense of philosophical discipline and direction. These include worries over sick daughters and sons, jealousy and rage over a spouse's infidelity, as well as concerns for career advancement and wealth in order to support the family in a grand style.[106] Given these factors, the young man who is dedicated to wisdom should consider it advisable to disregard his natural sexual design and remain unmarried. As Seneca puts it, "Only rarely should the wise man undergo marriage," and the same holds

---

101. My thanks to A. A. Long for his helpful advice on this section.

102. To support the norm of the sexually monogamous wife, Seneca goes so far as to commend the Hindu institution of suttee. "Among the inhabitants of India there is a law, that the dearest wife is cremated with her dead husband. . . . The highest aspiration of the competing women, and the proof of their chastity, is to be considered the one worthy to die. . . . The wife who wins . . . has complete disregard of the flames ignited under her due to the praise heaped on her chastity," *De matrimonio,* 187 Frassinetti. C. E. Manning ("Seneca and the Stoics on the Equality of the Sexes" [1973], 170–77) further explores the reduced commitment that Seneca and other later Stoics evince toward giving women full opportunity to discover talents beyond wifely chastity and to fulfill their capacity for excellence.

103. *Ep* 94.26; *Ira* 2.28.7; *Ben* 1.9.3–5; *Helv* 16.3; *De matrimonio,* 186 Frassinetti.

104. Seneca *Ep* 9.17–18; Epictetus 2.7.19–22, 2.7.26, 2.23.37, 3.21.5, 4.5.7.

105. Musonius, 90.24–92.6, Antipater, 4.508.2–3

106. Epictetus 1.11.1–40, 3.22.70–73, 3.22.77; Seneca, *De matrimonio,* 186 Frassinetti.

for prospective wise men. The biggest problem that Seneca sees is the wife's proclivity for adultery. "It is indeed burdensome for the wise man to be in doubt about whether he is going to marry a good or a bad woman."[107] This is a classic instance of a Stoic argument from extenuating circumstances to justify an action other than the one that nature dictates.

Epictetus adopts a similar line of reasoning as Seneca. Young men who are ambitious and rigorous in their ethical discipline have ample justification not to marry and be responsible for a family, despite nature's dictate to do so. This decision, however, ought not be frivolous, for the youth has to be strong enough to endure the steep climb of the Cynic man's solo way of life as Epictetus portrays it. This Cynic wise man faces a demanding mission to set a virtuous example to the public through his devotion to the collective will of the gods.[108] He is the gods' "messenger, their advance guard, their emissary" (3.22.69–70). Considering this greater social purpose, young men who embark on this mission are best advised not to marry.[109] Epictetus rejects his former teacher Musonius's argument that "even Crates got married" on the grounds that Crates' marriage is close to impossible to replicate. Crates' wife, Hipparchia, was her husband's intellectual and philosophical peer, "another Crates," and the two of them mutually loved each other (3.22.76). Conventional marriages in antiquity, by contrast, were rarely if ever partnerships in the philosophical endeavor; they were more often like business deals between families. In such arrangements, the prospective spouses' compatibility as philosophers was not taken into consideration, unlike the main concerns of social status, connections, and wealth.[110] Hipparchia had to defy her parents in order to escape conventional wifely roles and become a bohemian philosopher-partner in Crates' enterprise (DL 3.67–72). Hence, while Musonius regards conventional marriage and reproduction as a young man's unavoidable duty for the greater social good, Epictetus thinks that the top moral leaders in the struggle against social corruption must not be burdened by a wife and family. In a better social world — one that valued philosophy as much as Crates and Hipparchia did — such men would marry and help raise children for the city, but until then, current circumstances warrant them remaining single, if they so choose, pro-

107. Seneca, *De matrimonio,* 186 Frassinetti.

108. For a full study about the greater social mission of the Cynic life according to Epictetus, see M. Billerbeck's commentary, *Vom Kynismus. Epiktet* (1979), 130–32.

109. 3.22.76, 3.22.70–77.

110. S. Treggiari, *Roman Marriage: Iusti coniuges from the Time of Cicero to the Time of Ulpian* [1991], 83–103, 107–19) discusses several of the traditional Roman concerns with marriage, such as rank and wealth. For similar Greek concerns, see C. Cox, *Household Interests,* 103–4, 135–41; C. Patterson, *The Family in Greek History* (1998), 75–87; and S. Pomeroy, *Families in Classical and Hellenistic Greece* (1997), 83–103.

vided that they model their lives and aims on Diogenes' noble way of life as portrayed by Epictetus.

Unlike Antipater, Musonius, and Hierocles, consequently, Seneca and Epictetus are sympathetic to the early Stoic position that conventional customs of marriage and the family stand in need of amelioration. Seneca would like a society free of adultery,[111] whereas Epictetus prefers one that accords higher priority to the discipline of philosophy. But because they uphold the later Stoic position that human beings are heterosexually paired by nature, for a man to remain single is the only alternative they see to marriage. Further, the person that Seneca and Epictetus imagine breaking the marital norm and remaining on his own is an individual male hero, the Cynic-Stoic Superman. Practically speaking, Seneca and Epictetus are probably right to portray this figure as male, and as a rare one at that. Women in antiquity would need collective social change to resist the pressures driving them to fulfill traditional familial roles, which neither Epictetus nor Seneca offer. Men were also by and large expected to become fathers, though they had some latitude to leave their home and city and seek other adventures in life.[112] The manly individualism of the rare sage in Seneca and Epictetus, however, provides little basis for social reform. As Zeno and Chrysippus understood, to bring about sustained reform, all social members must be included and cooperate, women, children, and men alike. The early Stoic notion of communal human nature puts such change at the center of the Stoic agenda, whereas the later Stoic notion of paired human nature leaves much of the social status quo in place.

We do not fully know why the later Stoics distanced themselves from the early Stoic position that human beings are communally sexual animals. Several contributing factors are clear enough, however, such as conventionally minded disapproval, concerns to develop a clientele of students, and the ready availability of counter-argument. A number of ancient writers, mostly non-Stoics, regarded the city of early Stoic eros as outright indecent. One otherwise little known Stoic similarly disapproved, Athenodorus, a librarian at Pergamum who attempted unsuccessfully to bowdlerize Zeno's *Republic*.[113] Stoics of like mind with Athenodorus would presumably have tried

---

111. To Zeno and Chrysippus, by contrast, adultery is but a symptom of unnatural married life. Adultery on their view would be a flawed attempt to heed the sexually gregarious call of nature, for adultery fails to lead to sexual communalism, and it frees no one from possessiveness, jealousy, worry, and anger.

112. They could, for instance, leave home and become mercenary soldiers, while young women had no fully reputable and readily available alternatives to marriage, excluding the occasional virginal priestess.

113. DL 7.34. The non-Stoic voices of disapproval include Cassius, Plutarch, Sextus Empiricus, and Origen. For the negative reaction of Athenodorus and of the non-Stoics, see

to revise early Stoic teachings on sexuality to make them more socially respectable. Concerns for building a Stoic educational system would also have facilitated this compromise with social propriety. In order for Stoic philosophy to become as influential as it did in ancient education, it would have had to accommodate marital conventions. Few are the parents who seek educators in sexual communalism and anti-family values for their children. Further, some later Stoics surely would have argued in a substantive manner against the early Stoic view that human nature is sexually communal, perhaps along the model of Aristotle against Plato's communalism (*Pol* 1261b16–64b24). Later Stoics would only have had to adopt some sort of neo-Aristotelian stance in order for the early Stoic communal utopia to fall to the family ideal for philosophical reasons as well as for propriety concerns.

The social mainstreaming of later Stoicism is an example of the process by which a revolutionary set of ideas gets tamed, loses touch with its origins, and thereby gains middle-of-the-road popularity.[114] Though the later Stoic advocacy of patriotic marriage is the most well known aspect of Stoic sexual ethics in the modern day, it is diametrically opposed to early Stoic ideas about the sexual and social conditions needed for people to attain wisdom and virtue in measurable numbers. If the shades of Zeno and Chrysippus could emerge and speak again, they would disavow the Stoic city that sets the patriotic bride and groom on its top tier.

CONCLUSION

The early Stoic design of human sexual nature has two related aspects. First, human beings as animals have the primary orientation to do what helps them stay healthy. Given this orientation, sexual arousal does not motivate erotic madness and its crimes of passion, such as murder and suicide. Neither do the gods motivate such passions, for in early Stoic theology the gods are good. In popular Greek thought, however, eros as a divine force quells human deliberation and has a harmful streak that intensifies in the face of reasonable attempts at sexual restraint; Aphrodite and Eros must be obeyed on command. Further, human life is deficient without this torture from the gods. By this way of thinking, in order for a relationship to be erotic, it must involve dominance and submission. There needs to be a male or quasi-

---

M. Schofield, *Stoic City*, 3–13; A. Erskine, *The Hellenistic Stoa*, 10–15; and P. Vander Waerdt, "Zeno's *Republic*," 277 n. 19. Some Stoic teachers did not disapprove of Zeno's *Republic*, but they prudently withheld it from their students until they were much farther advanced and proved themselves to be genuine philosophers, P. Vander Waerdt, "Zeno's *Republic*," 279 n. 25.

114. See further K. V. Wilkes, "Aspects of Stoicism: From Revisionary to Reactionary Ethics" (1983), 183–88. Early Christianity provides another example of socially radical ideas that are converted to support the familial status quo, as explored more fully in later chapters.

masculine person penetrating from the top and a female or quasi-feminine submissive or unwilling victim on the bottom. To be erotically aroused means that all lovers, masculine and feminine alike, are themselves slaves of the domineering gods. The early Stoics reject these ideas as the fraudulent product and perpetuating mechanism of impassioned thinking and sexual behavior. They instead argue, in light of their psychology and cosmology, that human beings from adolescence onward act on their own rational cognizance when sexually aroused, though they must learn to do so rightly and with mutual respect between lovers.

Second, human beings share species-specific features above and beyond the primary orientation. People are by nature communal and mutually friendly. To promote reciprocal friendship throughout the collective, Zeno and Chrysippus rule out narcissistic sexual hedonism, non-consensual sexual relations such as rape and sexual activity with underage persons, and other sexual practices that give priority to self-satisfaction over amicable relations. To ensure that the friendship is communal, they would also abolish marriage, sexual possessiveness and favoritism, and incest prohibitions. The early Stoics regard these practices as divisive and hence contrary to human nature. In place of such customs, many of which were an everyday part of ancient Greek life, Zeno and Chrysippus offer their principles of early Stoic eros. Pivotal to this communal "good eros" is sexual didacticism between sages and προκόπτοντες, female and male alike, which helps lead the young adults to wisdom and friendship. Children in the city under age fourteen receive parental love (στέργειν) from all the adults. After the young are raised with this broad-based affection, they are ready to be initiated as adolescent προκόπτοντες into the didactic sexual stage of their development and its continued principle of equitable sharing. These communal and friendship-building practices in childhood and young adulthood come to fruition in the attainment of wisdom and virtue, at which time the emergent sages reach their goal in this philosophical society and enjoy fully friendly relations with others of the same ethical attainment in the city. Women and men alike are among the wise, and the sagacious friendship they share with one another continues to include sexual relations.

Zeno and Chrysippus consequently never envision the sage as detached loner or advocate the extirpation of eros except where unavoidable in marriage. Sexuality is a valuable part of human nature, on par with thought, discourse, and perceptual engagement with the world. Human sexual interaction should help shape the rational and communally friendly microcosm of human society, just as in Stoic cosmogony, Zeus and Hera primordially unite seminal reason and material body to sexually shape the rational macrocosm of the world.

Early Stoic eros remains open to challenges that I have foregone discussing here. It is debatable whether human beings even have a definable nature and, if so, whether the early Stoic ideas are defensible and desirable. Inbreeding is clearly not advisable, for example, even though it accords with the logic of sexual communalism. Nonetheless, the ideas of Zeno and Chrysippus offer an ethical advance in major respects over ancient Greek sexual mores, such as their requirement that men and women alike learn how to deliberate, consent, and form bonds of affectionate commitment in their sexual relations from adolescence onward. There is value too in the early Stoic proposal that adults parentally care not only for their own offspring, but for every child in the community. Thus Zeno's and Chrysippus's innovative conception of eros is a challenging and mostly admirable exercise in moral reasoning, interweaving as it does early Stoic cosmology, theology, psychology, and ethical theory in an engaged critique of popular Greek eros and sexual mores. Early Stoic eros consequently merits greater recognition in the philosophy and history of ethics and political theory, especially in relation to sexuality, friendship, and family values.

The later Stoic view that human nature is heterosexually paired sets it at odds with the earlier conviction that it is sexually communal. According to Antipater, Musonius, and Hierocles, persons can attain virtue only if they patriotically embrace traditional marriage, the household, and childrearing in defense of their native cities and the gods. Seneca and Epictetus largely concur, though they would allow exceptions for extremely dedicated male philosophers who stand as lone moral beacons in conventional society. Despite the marked shift in the Stoic conception of human nature, the early Stoic conviction that sexual eros can and should be rehabilitated into "good eros" persists in a transmuted guise in later Stoic thought: Sexual relations can and should be used rationally to facilitate relationships of a mutually friendly and respectful sort, but only within marriage.

For the Roman Stoics Seneca and Musonius, by contrast, eros or sexual desire is nothing more than the passion that it was in popular Greek thought, as Nussbaum and others have already shown, and as I present further in the next chapter.[115] Seneca and Musonius concur that eros is as bad a domineering master as the tragedians and others claim, but rather than surrendering, as the poets advocate, they maintain that one must avoid eros with a stony disposition, aside from the unavoidable duty of procreation within marriage.[116] We would do well to cease from regarding this argument

---

115. In the next chapter I show the Pythagorean reasons why Seneca and Musonius regard eros in this negative light.

116. W. Stephens ("Epictetus on How the Stoic Sage Loves [1996], 194, 196, 206) initially attributes the same position to Epictetus: "In condemning all $\check{\epsilon}\rho\omega\varsigma$ as objectionable $\pi\acute{\alpha}\theta o\varsigma$ Epictetus stands with . . . Seneca and Musonius Rufus, and against the Greeks of the early Stoa," yet Stephens goes on to show that Epictetus has a sophisticated conception of Stoic love that is compatible in numerous respects with early Stoic eros, though Epictetus describes this conception more under the rubric of $\phi\iota\lambda\acute{\iota}\alpha$ and $\phi\iota\lambda\epsilon\hat{\iota}\nu$ than of $\check{\epsilon}\rho\omega\varsigma$ and $\dot{\epsilon}\rho\hat{\alpha}\nu$.

as a Stoic way of thinking at all, let alone as typically Stoic. The Stoic position that eros can and should be rehabilitated for the ethically beneficial purpose of mutual friendship—community-wide or within marriage—is incompatible with the position that eros is inherently a passion that one must avoid wherever possible.

Stoic sexual ethics overall maintains that sexual relations are justified and conducive to virtue, so long as they are directed toward mutual friendship. The friendship in question is communal or marital, depending on whether the Stoics are Zeno and Chrysippus or Antipater, Hierocles, and Epictetus. Seneca and Musonius, however, stand apart because they maintain that reproduction in marriage provides the sole acceptable justification for engaging in sexual activity. This sexual rule is at odds with the Stoic stance that the cultivation of mutual friendship provides a fully warranted and appropriate reason to copulate, quite apart from the procreative aims that such sexual activity naturally has on occasion. The strictly reproductive sexual principle is Pythagorean in its provenance and motives, as shown in the next chapter.

Chapter 4

The Reproductive Technology
of the Pythagoreans

Little is known about early Pythagorean sexual ethics, but several lineaments become clear from Plato and antedate him. These include determining, through geometry, the right time to reproduce, and advocating an appropriate method of copulation to ensure that the souls of offspring remain free of needless discordance. The overall purpose of these prescriptions is similar to Plato's in the *Laws:* to improve the human condition by developing a moderate breed of persons dedicated to practicing sexual and dietary austerity, with the dietary regimen serving to facilitate the spare use of sexual activity. To understand the Pythagorean sexual program, it is helpful to begin with their enigmatic geometry about the suitable time to reproduce.

THE NUPTIAL NUMBER

One of the more extraordinary ancient Greek ideas about regulating human conception is a Pythagorean theorem never taught in modern geometry. Though known as "the nuptial number," it pertains to procreation, not to marriage per se, and it dates at least from the time of Plato's *Republic.* The significance of the number here rests in the convictions that inform it, which help explain the Pythagorean ethic of harmonious and beneficial reproduction. Even though the nuptial number has had no discernible influence on ancient or modern sexual mores, it is a good overture to another aspect of Pythagorean sexual ethics that has had great influence in its transmuted Christian guise: "procreationism," the dictate that sexual relations should be practiced strictly in a temperate and deliberately reproductive way, and solely within marriage. This dictate dates at least from the time of Plato's last dialogue, the *Laws.* First, though, the nuptial number should set the tone.

The Pythagorean nuptial number in *Republic* 546b4–d3 is an abstruse eugenic principle that designates the most auspicious timing for producing human offspring. The timing and its geometric measure are notoriously complex,[1] but the formula has eminently clear moral and social goals. It aims to ensure that prospective parents produce offspring who have sound body and mind, experience good fortune, and help society become better through their improved moral character. Plato indicates this purpose in the *Republic,* where he applies the formula in earnest to the guardians, so that they make the best possible offspring to sustain their elite corps. "An entire geometric number is in charge of better and worse acts of reproduction. If the guardians are ignorant about this number and they bring the communal brides and grooms together at the wrong time, the children will not be well-formed (εὐφυεῖς) or fortunate (εὐτυχεῖς)" (*Rep* 546d1–3). The guardians are truly a golden race in the model city so long as they regulate their sexual intercourse by this formula, or so Plato maintains.

The Pythagorean nuptial number, though unknown outside of the *Republic* and the tradition of commentary on it,[2] contains several distinctive features that Pythagorean procreationism likewise evinces, as shown later below. First, the formulaic timing has a eugenic goal. Children who are the best in body, mind, and fortune are precisely the caliber of personnel Plato wants for ensuing generations of guardians.

Second, the nuptial number presumes the uniquely Pythagorean tenet that everything is structured by number in the form of geometrically related ratios.[3] These geometric structures have either a harmony, which leads to the

---

1. "For mortal begettings, there is a period comprehended by the first time in which augmentations dominating and dominated when they have attained to three distances and four limits of the assimilating and the dissimilating, the waxing and the waning, render all things conversable and commensurable with one another, whereof a basal four thirds wedded to the pempad yields two harmonies at the third augmentation, the one the product of equal factors taken one hundred times, the other of equal length one way but oblong—one dimension of a hundred numbers determined by the rational diameters of the pempad lacking in each case, or of the irrational lacking two; the other dimension of a hundred cubes of the triad. And this entire geometric number is determinative of this thing, of better and inferior births," tr. P. Shorey (1961). Shorey's translation better captures the numerological tenor of Plato's Greek than does Reeve's update of Grube's translation (1997). For modern attempts to figure out the mathematics of the nuptial number, see R. Waterfield, *Plato's* Republic (1993), 433–4, which is the interpretation Reeve favors. E. Ehrhardt has an alternative interpretation, "The Word of the Muses (Plato, *Rep.* 8.546)" (1986), 407–20.

2. M. Allen (*Nuptial Arithmetic: Marsilio Ficino's Commentary on the Fatal Number in Book VIII of Plato's* Republic [1994], 5–11) explores the ancient and renaissance tradition of commentators trying to solve the conundrum.

3. Γάμος is constituted by three dots for the male plus two dots for the female, with the male dots alternating with the female dots. All five dots in a row ingeniously symbolize a man and a woman copulating with a view to reproduction—two pairs of feet and another dot in between for the point of coitus, which for the woman is also the point of emergence for the

good life collectively and individually, or a discordance, which leads to corruption and misfortune.

Third, the harmonious ratios pertaining to the good life are not a given but must be sought through personal and collective human action. Discordance, conversely, should be diminished or abolished where possible. Human beings should lead their lives like a symphony, not like the dissonant squeaks and squawks in the warm-up before the performance. The attainment of harmony, further, requires intense constraints on human behavior, not liberties to do as one pleases. In the nuptial number, men and women who are trying to reproduce should copulate only at the most beneficial measure of time and not whenever they wish. This distinctive project of Pythagorean sexual ethics was already in its formative stage by the time Plato wrote the *Republic* and adapted the nuptial number for his purposes. The nuptial number is consequently instructive about the rudiments of the Pythagorean project, even though it never emerged from abstruse theory to become an influential norm regulating human reproduction.

PRELIMINARIES TO PROCREATIONISM

Now that the nuptial number has yielded some core features of Pythagorean sexual ethics during Plato's *floruit,* we are in a better position to appreciate the like-minded eugenic rule of procreationism. This sexual regulation is Pythagorean in its origins and guiding tenets. It dictates that men and women who engage in sexual intercourse should do so only in marriage and for the express purpose of reproduction, and that excitement during intercourse should be kept as sedate as possible. In a more extreme version, procreationism forbids all other sexual activity as reckless and morally reprehensible, be it homoerotic, autoerotic, or heterosexual deviance from strictly temperate reproduction within marriage. Pythagorean advocates of this sexual rule considered it key to improving the moral character of future generations.

Unlike the arcane nuptial number, procreationism is no ancient and abandoned oddity. Though it began as a distinctively Pythagorean doctrine, in its more extreme form it later came to be understood as God's law in ecclesiastical Christianity. In this adapted form the sexual principle went on to be one of the most potent dictates to monitor human sexual conduct in Western culture. This chapter concerns the Greek and Roman sources on procreationism that are not part of Hellenistic Judaism or Christianity, so that we may better understand its Pythagorean provenance and motives.

---

newborn. The symbolism is discussed by W. Burkert, *Lore and Science in Ancient Pythagoreanism* (1972), 33–4, 40, 476–7.

This dictate is first attested as a eugenic guideline in Plato's *Laws,* and in fragments from the *Pythagorean Declarations* of Aristoxenus,[4] which was written sometime in the latter half of the fourth century B.C.E. In addition to Plato and Aristoxenus, other proponents include the Neopythagoreans Ocellus Lucanus and Charondas, as well as Seneca and Musonius.[5]

PROCREATIONISM AS OPPOSED TO VALUING REPRODUCTION

At the outset, procreationism needs to be distinguished from other ancient norms that promote reproduction but do not limit morally permissible sexual activity to that function. The Stoics, for example, maintain that nature intends human beings to reproduce and that the shape of the genitals indicates this goal, but they also argue that friendship is the primary goal of sexual activity, quite apart from its reproductive function, as shown in the previous chapter.[6] Similarly, most ancient Greeks and Romans thought that the primary sexual roles of a free woman ought to be those of wife and mother, yet Greek and Roman sexual mores were never confined to a strictly reproductive purpose, even within marriage.[7] Though both Stoicism and ancient society make procreation central, neither of them limits permissible human sexual activity to reproduction, and hence they are not procreationist.[8]

4. Whether procreationism also belongs to pre-Platonic Pythagorean thought cannot be determined. Like the nuptial number, it first appears on record in Plato's writings, though it does not originate with Plato, as will be explained below. There is no compelling evidence for demonstrably pre-Platonic Pythagorean principles of human sexual conduct, though W. Burkert suggests one based on Plato's *Laws* 773e5–74a1: "One ought to beget children, for it is our duty to leave behind, for the gods, people to worship them," *Lore and Science,* 171 n. 42. Burkert's argument, however, is not persuasive. He maintains that *Laws* 773e5–74a1 reflects a pre-Platonic Pythagorean teaching because its content is similar to Iamblichus *vit Pyth* 86 and to the Babylonian *Gilgamesh,* which states that human beings were created to serve the gods. This idea, however, is ancient and widespread (e.g., the First Commandment). This religious value, further, is one that numerous and diverse priestly groups in the ancient Mediterranean world would have had a practical motive to promote. Hence *Laws* 773e5–74a1 and *vit Pyth* 86 are ancient expressions of a widespread piety that the Pythagoreans likely shared, but little marks them as definitively early Pythagorean doctrine.

5. Aristoxenus was born between 375 and 360 B.C.E.; the date of his death is unknown. The Neopythagorean Charondas has a *terminus ante quem* of the mid-first century B.C.E. and the treatise of Ocellus was probably written ca. 150 B.C.E. I discuss their dates below (nn. 29 and 31). Seneca lived ca. 4 B.C.E.–65 C.E.; Musonius, ca. 30–102 C.E.

6. Cicero, *Fin* 3.62 (SVF 3.340 = LS 57F), see also Hierocles, 502.15–20.

7. See, for example, ps.-Dem. *In Neaeram* 59.122; Menander, *Dyscolus* 842, *Samia* 727; R. Just, *Women in Athenian Law and Life* (1989), 135–51.

8. Athenian men, for instance, had great latitude to engage in sexual activity with younger men, concubines, prostitutes, and slaves of both sexes. Though married women chiefly served their husbands and families by producing legitimate children, in theory they too had other sexual venues, though we do not know to what extent female citizens (as opposed to noncitizens) exercised these options. Among women, there is evidence for homoeroticism and auto-

Modern scholars have largely failed to see the unusual nature of the pro-creationist dictate precisely because they have not distinguished it from wide-spread ancient norms that simply favor reproduction. They have accord-ingly found the pre-Christian origins of procreationism in Stoic thought as a whole, in Plato's *Republic,* and even in Hellenistic morality at large.[9] The idea that the Stoics are the originators and main proponents of this dictate is especially popular.[10] Thus the distinctively Pythagorean roots and motives for procreationism remain largely overlooked. This oversight has had a

---

eroticism with sex toys, Plato *Symp* 191e2–5; B. Brooten, *Love between Women,* 29–60; K. J. Do-ver, *Greek Homosexuality*[2] (1989), 102; and S. Blundell, *Women in Ancient Greece* (1995), 100–5 and figures 17–9. Moreover, D. Cohen (*Law, Sexuality, and Society: The Enforcement of Morals in Classical Athens* [1991], 133–70) suggests that Athenian wives had greater access to male lovers on the sly than was officially recognized. C. Patterson (*The Family in Greek History,* 114–32) ad-dresses this question further in response to Cohen.

9. D. Allison ("Divorce, Celibacy," 7) voices this position well. "Largely under the influence of Stoicism, many morally serious Greeks and Romans—and therefore many Christians after them—came to believe that the primary purpose of sex was procreation. It follows that, in gen-eral, men should refrain from 'sowing seed from which they are unwilling to have offspring' (Plutarch, *Mor* 144b [= *Coniugalia praecepta*]), and that, in particular, intercourse during preg-nancy was against nature, without good purpose, unseemly." J. Brundage (*Law, Sex, and Chris-tian Society,* 16) further contends that procreationism is a central teaching in Plato's political theory as a whole: "In the *Republic* and the *Laws* Plato argued that sexual relations ought to be restricted solely to procreative intercourse in marriage." W. Meeks maintains that the teaching is a widespread topos of Greek morality, "Pagan moralists habitually denounce 'passion' (*epi-thymia*) and 'pleasure' (*hēdonē*); the wise man indulges in sex for neither, but solely in order to beget children," *The First Urban Christians: The Social World of the Apostle Paul* (1983), 101. O. Yarbrough (*Not Like the Gentiles,* 11) and R. Harder (*Ocellus Lucanus* [1926; reprint, 1966], 122) hold the same view: Procreationism is "ein sehr weit verbreiteter Topos," as Harder puts it. A. Van Geytenbeek is rather anomalous in going to the other extreme, for he overly restricts the attested range of procreationism to Musonius, Philo, and Clement, *Musonius Rufus and Greek Diatribe* (1963), 72–3. S. Goldhill takes Van Geytenbeek at his word with one minor qual-ification, *Foucault's Virginity: Ancient Erotic Fiction and the History of Sexuality* (1995), 135 n. 51. Like D. Allison, H. Preisker incorrectly thinks Plutarch is a strict procreationist, *Christentum und Ehe in den ersten drei Jahrhunderten: Eine Studie zur Kulturgeschichte der alten Welt* (1927; reprint, 1979), 19 n. 36. While Plutarch mentions this sentiment, he believes that marital sexual activ-ity is justified if motivated by friendship (especially after a quarrel), and hence he is not a pro-creationist, *Coniugalia praecepta* 143d.

10. This scholarly position is prima facie plausible, for Seneca and Musonius, who support the dictate, are generally classified as Stoics. It does not follow, however, that procreationism is philosophically Stoic simply because two Roman Stoics happen to advocate it. In Stoic sexual ethics, as seen in the previous chapter, sexual activity is justified if practiced for the purpose of cultivating mutual friendship. Seneca and Musonius are anomalous as Stoics in supporting procreationism, as I demonstrate below. Scholars who contend that procreationism is a Stoic teaching include J. Noonan, *Contraception*[2], 46–9; L. Countryman, *Dirt, Greed, and Sex,* 62; P. Brown, *Body and Society,* 21; D. Biale, *Eros and the Jews* (1992), 37–8; along with D. Allison discussed above (n. 9), "Divorce, Celibacy," 7; U. Ranke-Heinemann, *Eunuchs for Heaven,* 1–6; and J. Broudéhoux, *Mariage et famille,* 136.

detrimental effect on our understanding of how the procreationist dictate in Hellenistic Judaism and patristic Christianity relates to its Greco-Roman precedents. Given the predominant scholarly view that procreationism is common currency in Hellenistic morality, its appearance in Philo and the church fathers seems simply to carry over a widespread Hellenistic sexual norm into Hellenistic Judaism and church doctrines. The carry-over comes, however, from Pythagorean thought rather than Hellenistic morality at large.[11] In order to see why, we must explore the procreationist dictate and its Pythagorean underpinnings.[12]

PROCREATIONISM AND ITS PYTHAGOREAN MOTIVATION

According to Aristoxenus, the Pythagoreans whom he was acquainted with favored restricting sexual activity to the maximum degree that they believed was both feasible and desirable for people to achieve.[13] "There should be as many impediments as possible on the exercise . . . of human sexual activity (ἀφροδίσια), which one must practice infrequently" (*vit Pyth* 209–10). As

11. The hypothesis that procreationism derives from the ancient Greek medical tradition is ruled out. The procreationist position is not attested in this tradition and is incompatible with prescribing contraceptive methods, which routinely appear there, such as in *De natura feminarum* 98 in E. Littré, ed., vol. 7, 414 (1839–1861; reprint, 1979); Galen, *De simplicium medicamentorum temperamentis ac facultatibus* 6.4.15–16 in C. G. Kuhn, ed. (1821–1833, reprint, 1964), vol. 11; and Soranus, *Gynecology* 1.61–3 in *Gynaeciorum libri IV* in J. Ilberg, ed. (1927). See also J. Riddle, *Contraception and Abortion from the Ancient World to the Renaissance* (1992), 16–30, 33–8, 74–6, 82–6, and H. King, *Hippocrates' Woman: Reading the Female Body in Ancient Greece* (1998), 132–56.

12. In arguing that procreationism is a distinctively Pythagorean doctrine, I am strengthening C. de Vogel's more limited observation that this sexual principle appears in some Pythagorean sources, *Pythagoras and Early Pythagoreanism: An Interpretation of Neglected Evidence on the Philosopher Pythagoras* (1966), 179–81. As de Vogel states, "moderation with respect to sexual activity (ἀφροδίσια) is mentioned several times"; she adds that Aristoxenus, Ocellus, and Musonius further support the idea that sexual intercourse should be directed only toward producing children in a restrained and lawful manner. She does not, however, attempt to demonstrate, as I aim to do here, that the teaching is originally Pythagorean, as opposed to a more widespread sexual norm that some Pythagoreans and Musonius happened to share.

13. The Pythagoreans whom Aristoxenus knew include: Xenophilus, with whom Aristoxenus studied prior to becoming a student of Aristotle, fr. 1 (Wehrli), Phanton, Echecrates, Polymnastus, and Diocles of Phlius. According to Diogenes Laertius, these were students of Philolaus and Eurytus, DL 8.46. Aristoxenus also knew about other Pythagoreans, such as Archytas. Aristoxenus's father, Spintharus, was a friend of Archytas and told stories about him, Iamblichus, *vit Pyth* 198, and see too W. Burkert, *Lore and Science,* 106–7 and 198. Aristoxenus somewhat tendentiously considered this group to be "the last of the Pythagoreans," for to him they were the last whose thought and ideas had merit since the time their community in Croton became fragmented, unlike the more uneducated followers of the Pythagorean way of life, who were lampooned in ancient comedy, Iamblichus, *vit Pyth* 251, and B. L. van der Waerden, *Die Pythagoreer,* 19, 164.

the main impediment these Pythagoreans set forth the teaching that all acts of heterosexual copulation ought to be directed toward purposeful and temperate reproduction. Their directive builds by binary concept division. They separate acts of reproduction that are temperate and according to nature from those that are violently performed and contrary to nature, and they presume that this division is exhaustive. Any act of procreation is either one or the other. The temperate acts are then further divided into deliberately and inadvertently reproductive acts. The Pythagoreans permit only the former, temperate and deliberately reproductive sexual activity. "One must do away with reproductive sex acts ($\gamma\epsilon\nu\nu\acute{\eta}\sigma\epsilon\iota\varsigma$) that are contrary to nature and done violently.[14] Among reproductive acts that are according to nature and done temperately, one must leave as admissible only those that are for the purpose of temperate and lawful reproduction of children."[15] Aristoxenus's Pythagoreans therefore believed that all acts of heterosexual copulation ought to be procreationist in purpose and method.

Aristoxenus's testimony does not allow us to definitely identify his Pythagorean sources as extreme procreationists, though they are strongly inclined in that direction. He states only that their reproductive intercourse must be temperate and deliberately procreative, but not also that this is the only kind of sexual activity allowed.[16] Thus the Pythagoreans could con-

14. The term $\gamma\epsilon\nu\nu\acute{\eta}\sigma\epsilon\iota\varsigma$ here refers to reproductive sexual activity for two related reasons. First, the context of Iamblichus, *vit Pyth* 209–10 pertains to methods of sexual intercourse. Second, the semantic field of $\gamma\acute{\epsilon}\nu\nu\eta\sigma\iota\varsigma$ and cognate terms primarily refers to the generative process from insemination through birth (e.g., $\gamma\epsilon\nu\nu\hat{\alpha}\nu$ "to reproduce"; $\gamma\acute{\epsilon}\nu\nu\eta\mu\alpha$ "that which is reproduced" or "offspring, child," for which see LSJ, ad loc). Note also Philolaus F13, "the genitals ($\alpha\grave{\iota}\delta o\hat{\iota}o\nu$) are the locale of insemination and reproduction ($\gamma\epsilon\nu\nu\acute{\eta}\sigma\iota o\varsigma$)." Since *vit Pyth* 209–10 pertains specifically to acts of sexual insemination and discusses their purposes and degrees of reproductive intensity, $\gamma\acute{\epsilon}\nu\nu\eta\sigma\iota\varsigma$ here signifies "reproductive sexual activity."

15. Iamblichus, *vit Pyth* 210. This passage belongs to an extended excerpt from Aristoxenus's *Pythagorean Declarations* ($\Pi\upsilon\theta\alpha\gamma o\rho\iota\kappa\alpha\grave{\iota}\ \grave{\alpha}\pi o\phi\acute{\alpha}\sigma\epsilon\iota\varsigma$) which appears in Iamblichus's treatise on the Pythagorean way of life, 209–13 (*vit Pyth*). The passage is also attested in an abbreviated form in the Hellenistic Pythagorean treatise of Ocellus, *On the Nature of the Universe*, 52–7. Section 55 in particular contains the procreationist dictate (sections 52–57 = 137.6–138.12 of H. Thesleff's edition). Stobaeus contains a truncated version of the excerpt from the *Pythagorean Declarations*, though he omits the procreationist passage (Stobaeus 4.878.15–879.14 = fr. 39 in F. Wehrli, *Aristoxenos* in *Die Schule des Aristoteles: Texte und Kommentar*[2] [1967]). On Aristoxenus's authorship of the passage and the more complete excerpt as it appears in Iamblichus's *vit Pyth*, see R. Harder, *Ocellus Lucanus*, 134–45; F. Wehrli, *Aristoxenos*, 58; L. Deubner and U. Klein, *Iamblichi: De vita pythagorica liber*[2] (1975), 113–15; and C. de Vogel, who collects the relevant ancient testimony in *Pythagoras and Early Pythagoreanism*, 269–70, sections 32b–c. See also W. Burkert, *Lore and Science*, 101 n. 17. All my references to Aristoxenus's *Pythagorean Declarations* are to the excerpts as contained in Iamblichus, *vit Pyth*.

16. Plato in the *Laws* similarly aims to restrict reproductive sexual intercourse ($\grave{\eta}\ \tau\hat{\eta}\varsigma\ \pi\alpha\iota\delta o\gamma o\nu\acute{\iota}\alpha\varsigma\ \sigma\upsilon\nu o\upsilon\sigma\acute{\iota}\alpha$) to deliberate and temperate acts, 838e5–6. Plato does not eliminate all nonreproductive sex acts except during the citizens' time of procreative duty.

ceivably have permitted other kinds (e.g., manual, oral, intercrural, anal), so long as vaginal-penile copulation remained strictly restrained and intent upon reproduction. If any other sexual activity had been permitted, however, it would have needed rigorous justification given their desire to put "as many impediments as possible on sexual activity." Further, whatever sexual latitude might make its way around such impediments would have to be exercised within marriage, as other Pythagorean rules restrict sexual practices to the marriage bond. Followers of Pythagoras ideally should refrain from sexual activity in their early youth, marry, and maintain marital fidelity thereafter, and in general they ought to make sparing use of sexual activity throughout their lives.[17] Hence even though Aristoxenus's testimony does not commit his Pythagoreans to the position that heterosexual copulation alone is permissible, they are unambiguously procreationist regarding such acts of copulation. Pythagorean sexual activity, further, is confined to marital agency, the bond of husband and wife, which in popular ancient Greek thought mainly serves the purpose of reproduction. The minds of the husbands and wives influenced by the procreationist regulation would likewise be accustomed to this marital norm and habituated to associate the marital sexual experience with copulation. Within the culturally specialized group of Pythagoreans, further, the married couples would have learned that temperate and deliberate reproduction alone is fit to be praised, prescribed, and performed within their social group. Hence this is the only type of sexual intercourse that is unambiguously without impediment in their system of social values. Pythagorean couples, as we have seen, must place "as many impediments as possible" on sexual activity. What trickles through these locks and dams on their sexual desire is either strict procreationism or a sexual norm verging closely on it.

The Pythagoreans advocate strictly temperate and purposeful reproduction for distinctively Pythagorean motives, some of which we have seen with the nuptial number. Random copulation is undesirable and discordant to the harmonic intervals of the soul being embodied. As Aristoxenus indicates, the Pythagoreans interpret conception and birth to be an act of guiding a soul into embodiment, or, more generally, an act of "leading someone into birth and existence" (*vit Pyth* 212). The guiding needs to be orderly and harmonious. If the prospective parents fail to be temperate and intent on reproduction while copulating, they are bad and even rather bestial leaders of the souls they guide into birth and existence. They reproduce "randomly and brutishly" and have children with bad moral character. Such unplanned parenting is unfit sexual behavior, due to the soul discordance

17. *vit Pyth* 47–8, 57, 210. The Pythagorean desire to restrict the exercise of the sexual appetite is a central part of their characteristic interest in controlling all physically appetitive behavior, J. Thom, *The Pythagorean* Golden Verses (1995), 127–30.

that the Pythagoreans associate with letting conception happen as it may. "Wretched offspring (μοχθηρὰ σπέρματα)" come from the "bad (φαύλης), discordant (ἀσυμφώνου), and disturbing blending (ταραχώδους κράσεως) in reproduction" that fails to be temperate and purposeful (*vit Pyth* 211). This concern about procreatively induced dissonance or "discordant blending" in offspring is distinctively Pythagorean, for persons and their souls must be structured as a harmony of ratios to have any capacity to become out of tune. Only Pythagoreans or Pythagorean-influenced writers conceptualize the soul, human body, and other entities in terms of ratios yielding either harmony or degrees of disharmony.[18] This idea was formulated at least a generation before Plato, moreover, for the Pythagorean Philolaus maintains that the soul has such a structure[19] and is harmonious

18. In Pythagorean thought, souls and all other physical entities are structured by number, which means in part that they are structured by numeric ratios, W. Burkert, *Lore and Science,* 40, and 28–52 passim, with the evidence from Aristotle evaluated therein. L. Zhmud attempts to reinstate and elaborate the theses of Frank and Cherniss (that Pythagorean number theory is an invention of Aristotle and Plato's successors in the Academy), but he does not effectively challenge Burkert's refutation of this argument in *Lore and Science,* 38 n. 50, 46 n. 97, and 86 n. 16; cf. L. Zhmud, *Wissenschaft, Philosophie, und Religion im frühen Pythagoreismus* (1997), 261–79, with Frank and Cherniss cited at 269–70 nn. 31, 34. C. Huffman (*Philolaus of Croton: Pythagorean and Presocratic* [1993], 64–74) has an interesting argument that Philolaus uses numeric ratios for epistemological purposes and thereby attempts to meet Parmenides' requirement for being and genuine knowledge. This argument, however, in no way precludes Philolaus from thinking that all things, such as soul, actually have numbers as their structuring principle, and he is quite emphatic that they do, F4. Huffman (55–6) overly downplays Philolaus's point about things having number in an effort to free him from seeming a number mystic, as P. Kingsley notes (1994), 94–6. W. K. C. Guthrie's discussion of Pythagorean number theory and cosmology remains worthwhile, *History of Greek Philosophy,* vol. 1 (1962), 233–306.

19. Philolaus is committed to the position that the soul has harmony as its ordering principle, by which he means that the soul is ordered by harmonic intervals in numeric ratios. In fragments from the opening of his lost book on nature, he claims that "nature in the cosmos has been harmoniously structured (ἁρμόχθη) from [two unlike principles, οὐχ ὁμοῖαι, F6] unlimiteds and limiters—both the entire cosmos and all things in the cosmos," F1. Compare F6, where he reaffirms and expands upon this point, and note also the stress on συναρμόχθη and ἁρμοσθέν in F2 and F7. Soul is one such entity, for Philolaus thinks that what animates human beings is soul (ψυχή) comprised of some substance or mixture of substances located in the heart, F13. The precise nature of soul substance is unclear. Thus by ἁρμόχθη in F1, Philolaus means that soul, like all else in the world, "is necessarily encased (συγκέκλεισθαι) by harmony" F6, and hence that it has harmony. Unfortunately, no extant fragments explicate precisely how he conceptualized the embodied soul as an attunement in relation to the body. Still, we get a general idea from the genuine fragments. As Philolaus states, "harmony" (ἁρμονία) has ordered the cosmos, and all things in it, through a variety of arrangements on his two principles (ἀρχαί) the "limiters and unlimiteds," F6. Soul in an ordered state (of incessantly vibrant motes or of air, perhaps, cf. Aristotle, *Anim* 404a16) would be one such arrangement. By ἁρμονία, further, Philolaus is referring to numeric ratios, which he maintains "knowable things have" and must have in order to be knowable, F6. These numeric ratios, finally, are concordant intervals, which Philolaus explicates in light of music theory, F6a. Therefore, accord-

in its well-ordered state.[20] Finally, the reproductive technology in question presumes at its core the earliest known Pythagorean tenet—that human nature is a dualistic composite of an immortal soul in a mortal body.[21] Only by presupposing this dualism can one intelligibly claim that reproduction somehow mixes the immortal soul and the body together in a way disturbing to the soul. Therefore, procreationism is the birth child of Pythagorean

ing to Philolaus the soul is structured by numeric ratios as harmonic intervals, at least in its ideal state. Consequently Macrobius is right to attribute the view that the soul is harmony to Philolaus (A23), despite Huffman's doubts (326–8), even though Macrobius would be more precise to say that the soul *has* a harmony according to Philolaus, rather than that it *is* harmony. The latter claim can and has led to two mistaken views of Philolaus's thought: First, the soul is reducible to the numeric ratios that lend it structure. Second, the soul is nothing other than an epiphenomenal attunement of the body itself—the mortal song of the body that necessarily dies out when a person dies. For the fragments of Philolaus and testimony cited above, see C. Huffman, *Philolaus of Croton*, 37–77, 93, 101, 123, 145–6, 226–7, 307, 323–6, 328–32.

20. Philolaus's notion of the soul as a harmonic structure of quantifiable ratios is distinct from the position that the soul is nothing other than an epiphenomenon of the mortal harmony or balance of substances that make up the human body. The latter position is the view Simmias offers in *Phaedo* 86d4 (viz., that the soul is a necessarily mortal "mix of bodily substances"). For Philolaus the soul's harmony is not merely a bodily epiphenomenon, for this would deny the soul any substantiality and harmonic structure of its own, which is contrary to Philolaus's soul theory, F13. Hence his conception of the soul as harmony is not reflected in Simmias's argument in the *Phaedo*. The provenance of Simmias's argument (*Phaedo* 85e3–86d4) is uncertain. It may come from an ancient Greek medical milieu, W. Burkert, *Lore and Science*, 272, or it may be Plato's own idea to test the Pythagoreans' position that the soul has harmony and is immortal. For the plausible view that Simmias's argument is Plato's invention, see H. B. Gottschalk, "Soul as Harmonia" (1971), 179–98. Thus Guthrie's discussion about Philolaus's attribution of harmonic intervals to the soul itself is on the right track, *History of Greek Philosophy*, vol. 1, 212–29 and 306–19.

21. DL 8.36 = Xenophanes DK 21B7. The transmigration of immortal souls (which presupposes soul-body dualism) is "the one most certain fact in the history of early Pythagoreanism," W. Burkert, *Lore and Science*, 120–3, esp. 120 n. 1. C. Huffman (*Philolaus of Croton*, 330–2) expresses reasonable doubt whether the Pythagoreans' belief in soul transmigration led them to have a defensible philosophical account of soul before Plato's day. Still, he takes doubt to an extreme to question whether the Pythagoreans, Philolaus included, believed in the soul's immortality. First, the Pythagorean belief in the soul's continual cycle of transmigration presupposes the soul's immortality. Second, according to Aristotle, Alcmaeon of Croton supported the soul's immortality on the grounds that soul is "always in motion" ($\dot{\alpha}\epsilon\dot{\iota}\ \kappa\iota\nu o\upsilon\mu\acute{\epsilon}\nu\eta$) and that it is divine or god-like 405a30–b1, see too W. Burkert, *Lore and Science*, 296 n. 95–97. The Pythagoreans according to Aristotle similarly believed that soul, which is comprised at least partly of motes or the air that moves them, is "manifestly in constant motion" ($\sigma\upsilon\nu\epsilon\chi\tilde{\omega}\varsigma\ \phi\alpha\acute{\iota}\nu\epsilon\tau\alpha\iota\ \kappa\iota\nu o\upsilon\mu\acute{\epsilon}\nu\eta$). This characteristic of incessant motion likely indicates that they too, like Alcmaeon, explicitly maintained that the soul is immortal by virtue of being in constant motion. Further, it is a prominent part of the Pythagorean tradition from Plato onward that the soul is divine or godlike, which is the other characteristic Alcmaeon of Croton ascribes to the immortal soul. On this tradition, see, e. g., Porphyry, *Pyth* 19 and B. L. van der Waerden, *Die Pythagoreer*, 116–22. Alcmaeon was acquainted with Pythagoreans in Croton and may have

thought insofar as the motives for promoting this reproductive practice are Pythagorean. Aristoxenus's testimony that this sexual regulation has a Pythagorean provenance consequently proves reliable for reasons internal to Pythagorean thought, and not for reasons depending more precariously on the reliability of Aristoxenus alone as a witness. Hence the regulation did not originate with Plato in the *Laws,* even though he is the first on written record to use it. Its proponents were either Pythagoreans themselves, such as the persons Aristoxenus knew, or, like Plato in the *Laws,* deeply influenced by the ideas of this sect.[22]

A passage in Plato's *Timaeus* helps further elucidate why the Pythagoreans think that willfully discordant procreation or "discordant blending" is harmful to human well-being and character. Acts of reproduction, Plato observes, bind an immortal soul into a mortal body in a manner inherently disturbing to the soul.[23] The soul is a structure of harmonic intervals, or "cycles" (περίοδοι), as Plato describes them, and the binding throws the embodied soul's intervals into some disharmony (*Tim* 43c7–d2). This discordance is partly unavoidable; it is what causes infants and toddlers to be helpless, irrational, and inarticulate (*Tim* 44a7–c4). However, if the disharmony is brought about through reproductive activity that is carelessly unrestrained, inadvertent, or both, then the harmful effects of embodiment on the soul linger even after the children mature. In such persons, the soul remains out of tune and thereby harms their ability to reason and act responsibly. Prospective parents consequently should rise above their deleterious ignorance and stop making wild love as though nothing were at stake for the soul and its delicate balance of harmonic intervals. Instead they must strive to be very restrained and deliberate so as to guide the soul into embodiment with the least possible turbulence. In this way they treat each soul they embody as the genuine Stradivarius that it is.

---

been one himself. By L. Zhmud's criterion Alcmaeon was Pythagorean because he is named as one in Iamblichus's doxographical list at *vit Pyth* 267 (*Pythagoreismus,* 67–8, cf. *vit Pyth* 267), by C. Huffman's criterion of evaluating what is known about Alcmaeon's ideas, he was not a Pythagorean (*Philolaus of Croton,* 11), and see further W. Burkert, *Lore and Science,* 289 n. 57.

22. Aristoxenus's testimony about procreationism does not depend on Plato's *Laws* for at least three reasons. First, there are no verbal echoes between the phraseology of Aristoxenus and Plato on procreationism. Second, Aristoxenus knew numerous Pythagoreans and had their oral traditions on which to draw for his understanding of Pythagorean sexual principles, DL 8.46. Third, there is one major difference between Aristoxenus's explanation of the procreationist rule and Plato's adaptation of procreationism in his hypothetical city of Magnesia, which I demonstrate below. The second point about oral Pythagorean traditions has considerable weight given the substantive differences between the *Pythagorean Declarations* and the *Laws* on procreationism and the absence of common phraseology.

23. *Tim* 42e5–44d2. This passage gives an account of birth and of early childhood even though Plato presents the account as a creation tale that happened once upon a time in the past, F. Cornford, *Plato's Cosmology* (1937; reprint, 1957), 147.

The Pythagorean supporters of temperate and deliberate reproduction give this sexual norm first priority on an agenda of social and familial reform. "The single greatest cause of wickedness and corruption," they maintain, arises from the common practice of adults producing future generations in flagrant disregard for the need to be restrained and purposeful about their reproductive task (*vit Pyth* 213). This is an urgent problem, for the vast majority of parents-to-be make love in a carefree and careless way (*vit Pyth* 210, 213), and in so doing allow the souls of their offspring to crash-land into embodiment. The parents have only themselves to blame for the results: children who are roughly thrown together and grow to be depraved adults. If only the parents acted as good leaders of souls into embodiment, as the Pythagoreans urge them to do, then children would be conceived properly. The parents would see the immediate reward for their efforts, sons and daughters at the head of the human class. Future society would also benefit greatly. The rapid recovery of psychic harmony in the offspring means that the community as a whole would improve by becoming sound in mind, body, and character. This desirable social change remains impossible, however, unless prospective parents cease reproducing with reckless abandon and become restrained technicians in the marital bed. Thus the Pythagoreans have a compelling reason to promote the procreationist dictate as the standard sexual norm for husbands and wives to religiously follow.

The Pythagoreans were already engaged in related measures to reform sexual mores toward procreationism, at least within their own groups. They offered two ways to encourage people to comply with their procreationist reform. First, a strict diet. Uncontrolled consumption of food and drink overstimulates the sexual appetite and leads it to transgress the limit of temperate and deliberate reproduction. Thus dietary restrictions are in order (*vit Pyth* 211). Second, people should take pride in being above animals on the Pythagorean scale of nature. They must refrain from blurring the difference by copulating as animals do, brutishly and randomly, oblivious to the unique human art of reproduction (*vit Pyth* 213). Therefore, people need to restrict their diet and to mind their assigned place in nature in order to attain the good society for future generations. They must be ever temperate, ever restrained, and never like wild animals—nowhere more so than when they guide souls into embodiment and thereby give future generations a greater eugenic edge.

Plato in the *Laws,* as shown in chapter two, likewise requires the citizens of Magnesia to behave in a strictly procreationist way during their years of reproductive duty. The motivation for his eugenic regimen is similarly Pythagorean. First, Plato blames intemperate sexual activity for bringing about the greatest harm to people individually and to entire cities (*Laws* 835c2–8, 836a6–b2). Unmanaged sexual activity gains such an alarming status in the *Laws* not simply because of the rampant consuming passions that Plato associates with the unrestrained sexual appetite in his dialogues as a whole. Rather, in his last dialogue, and there only, he is concerned about the presumed deleterious effects of uncontrolled sexual relations on the children thereby conceived and produced. Transgressing the temperate and deliberately reproductive purpose of sex is a kind of gross violence that harms the formation of the offspring, leading them to be "uneven, untrustworthy, and crooked in moral character" as well as in body (*Laws* 775d1– e2). The Pythagoreans held the same position, as seen above. In order to do away with "the single greatest cause of wickedness and corruption" in society, they too would like to put an end to the conventional laissez-faire style of reproduction and to replace it with purposive temperance (*vit Pyth* 213). Similarly, in the *Laws,* the citizens must marry and engage only in temperate and deliberately reproductive sexual relations when they enter their prime of life (*Laws* 783d8–e4). Plato, however, is distinctive in imposing a strict time limit on the procreationist restriction. In his hypothetical city the rule is in force generally no more than ten years on average per couple, for it applies only as long as the couples have not yet produced the requisite number of children (*Laws* 783e4–7, 784b1–3). Only during this period is Plato draconian about enforcing the procreationist norm.[24] After the citizens' time of reproductive duty, Plato grants and expects them to exercise greater latitude in their sexual behavior. In the *Laws,* the citizens will still be driven to serve Aphrodite through their sexual appetite on a regular basis until advanced old age, but they should do so temperately.[25] Plato permits these sexual relations and regards them as honorable, so long as the citizens do not reproduce or become outrageously licentious, such as by making a public show of it. Thus Plato in the *Laws* is very selective about the time frame in which he thinks Pythagorean procreationism is an advisable rule to follow.[26] He is extremely stern, though, during the time procreationism applies, because so much is at stake for the harmonious soul, society, and human race.

Several related Pythagorean measures to bolster procreationism also appear in Plato's *Laws.* Plato makes the same correlation as the Pythagoreans between excessive eating and uninhibited sexual behavior. The former fuels the latter. Plato accordingly advocates dietary restrictions as well as an exercise regimen in order to "divert the nourishment" elsewhere that otherwise makes the sexual appetite hyperactive (*Laws* 841a6–8). He likewise

24. *Laws* 837e9–38e1, 783a1–e1, 631d6–32a2.
25. *Laws* 841a9–b2, 841b4–5, 784e5–85a1.
26. In Aristoxenus's testimony about this sexual rule at *vit Pyth* 209–10, we see nothing of this major modification of the procreationist principle that Plato makes. This is the substantive difference between the procreationism of Plato and Aristoxenus that I adumbrated in an above note (n. 22).

concurs with the Pythagorean idea that human beings are above animals on the Pythagorean scale of nature and ought to stay there, as he makes very clear at the end of the *Timaeus*.[27] In the *Laws,* further, people "should be better than animals" in their sexual conduct, and they are better provided that they marry and follow the procreationist regimen. Otherwise they reproduce without purposefulness and restraint, in the style "of a four-footed animal," as Plato describes it in the *Phaedrus*.[28] Plato in the *Laws* consequently shares the Pythagorean conviction that society must undergo rigorous reform in support of procreationist eugenics: Eat food in limited amounts so as to avoid barnyard styles of copulation. Honor your standing as rational biped by reproducing strictly in the avant-garde style formulated in Pythagorean thought. Plato takes the additional step, however, of expecting his citizens to be sexually active without reproducing after they finish their procreationist duty. Nonetheless, the *Laws* makes the first known attempt to institute the Pythagorean craft of procreationism, albeit in an as yet hypothetical society and not as a lifelong measure.

CHARONDAS

The *Preambles to the Laws,* a Hellenistic Pythagorean treatise under the pseudonym "Charondas," advocates procreationism in an unambiguously strict sense. This work is independent of Aristoxenus and Plato for its source material and was in circulation prior to the mid-first century B.C.E. Precisely when the treatise was written, however, remains unclear.[29]

Charondas assumes that each man has or should have a wife and that the married couple should reproduce. To this extent his thought is consistent with mainstream Hellenistic sexual morality, but then he parts ways. He stipulates in no uncertain terms that the man must climax with his penis located nowhere else besides in his wife's vagina and for the purpose of re-

27. The scale of nature begins with men at the top, who are followed in descending order by women, birds, four-footed animals, belly-slithering animals, and underwater animals. The further down the type of animal, the less able the animal is to exercise appetitive restraint and the more remote are their embodied souls from being able to reason philosophically so as to recollect the soul's immortal nature, *Tim* 90e6–92c3.

28. 250e4–5. Nonprocreationist human reproduction is animal behavior from a Pythagorean perspective in part because it corrupts the embodied soul, and this corruption in turn causes the damaged soul to transmigrate later into one or another of the animal bodies, as mentioned in the preceding note, *Tim* 90e6–92c3.

29. For the pseudonymous text of Charondas, I cite the page and line numbers of H. Thesleff's edition, *The Pythagorean Texts of the Hellenistic Period* (1965). This work is earlier than the mid-first century B.C.E. because Cicero (106–43 B.C.E.) mentions it, *Leg* 2.5.14, and Diodorus Siculus (fl. 60–21 B.C.E.) also knew and used a portion of the same or a similar pseudonymous treatise, 12.11.3–19.2.

production alone. Any other purpose is wild, licentious, and forbidden. "Each man must love his legitimate wife and procreate from her. Into nothing else should he ejaculate (προιέσθω) the seed of his children (τέκνων τῶν αὐτοῦ σποράν). He must not waste or abuse that which is honorable in nature and custom. Nature made seed (σποράν) for the sake producing children (τεκνοποιίας), not licentiousness (ἀκολασίας)" (62.30–33). Here Charondas thinks in a Pythagorean manner by the exclusive disjunction he makes between ejaculating for procreation (τεκνοποιία) or for licentiousness (ἀκολασία). Unless a man ejaculates into his wife to reproduce, then he does so for licentious reasons, and such license is absolutely forbidden. Other justifications for sexual activity are left out of consideration, such as the Stoic goal of mutual friendship. Charondas thus goes by the strict letter of his procreationist law, and he would enforce this rule on a lifelong basis.

Charondas's unconditional procreationism is far more inflexible than Plato's use of the regulation in the *Laws*. Plato finds lifelong adherence to this rule both impractical and harmful. Aphrodite's power is too strong, so the citizens in reproductive retirement should honor her in a moderate and guardedly nonreproductive manner. Charondas disallows such permissiveness. He brings the Pythagorean goal of impeding human sexual activity toward its furthest possible limit while still allowing for the reproduction of the species. Only deliberately procreative sex acts in marriage remain permissible.

As Charondas and Plato clearly show, a reverence for semen goes together with the procreationist dictate. Charondas writes the procreationist ideal into the very words he uses to refer to the substance. Semen is "the seed of a man's children" and as such must be used strictly to produce them (62.31). Plato in the *Laws* likewise refers to semen as "procreative fluid" (γόνιμον) and contends that careless ejaculation is wrong for reasons that are apparent in the very name of the substance. Semen is strictly reproductive fluid during the time a man must father his required number of children (*Laws* 838e4–39a6). This solemnity about semen comes to the fore particularly when Plato and Charondas deplore its misdirected use. A man who misdirects his semen "kills" and "wastes" both "his children" and even the entire "human race" (62.30–33, *Laws* 837e7–8). Semen is one of the vehicles through which immortal souls come into embodiment, so to destroy this liquid is, in effect, to destroy a human soul. Charondas adheres to this viewpoint unconditionally. A man is duty bound to sow this sacred right-to-life substance only into his wife.[30] Plato's *Laws* likewise maintains that a

---

30. For these Pythagorean-based reasons, Clement of Alexandria similarly maintains that a man who ejaculates inadvertently engages in involuntary manslaughter, while the man who willfully does so is in effect a murderer, *Strom* 2.61.1–2. The idea that semen is a liquid constituent of soul appears in Aristotle, *Gen anim* 2.1.735a4–9, 2.3.737a16–18, and see D. Hahm,

man should not destroy semen, but only during his time of reproductive duty. Thereafter he should waste it in accordance with his undeniable sexual needs. As Plato sees it, let the vital substance die once it has reached its expiration date, rather than use it for producing deficient offspring.

OCELLUS

On the Nature of the Universe, which is attributed to "Ocellus," likewise supports the strictly procreationist position. This Hellenistic Pythagorean treatise, which dates to around 150 B.C.E.,[31] partly cites Aristoxenus's *Pythagorean Declarations* for its advocacy of this sexual regulation. Ocellus quotes Aristoxenus at length in sections 52–57. He also supports procreationism in his own words in sections 44–46.[32] I discuss Ocellus's own argument unless otherwise indicated.

Ocellus presumes the key Pythagorean tenet that sexual relations are motivated either for the production of children or for pleasure. The exclusive disjunction he posits is similar to the one that Charondas makes between reproduction or licentiousness. Ocellus likewise firmly maintains that only procreation within marriage is an acceptable purpose for human sexual activity. All the rest is hedonistic and unacceptable. "We do not engage in sexual relations (πρόσιμεν) for pleasure (ἡδονῆς) but for the procreation (γενέσεως) of children" (135.11–13). This regulation reflects the ordained purpose of the Pythagorean demiurge. This creator god shaped human beings and their sexuality deliberately and only so that they would participate in immortality through reproduction. Hence procreationist relations alone gain this god's approval (135.16–19). Ocellus also quotes and very much favors the argument from Aristoxenus, which states that of all possible acts of reproduction, only temperate and deliberately procreative ones within marriage are allowed (137.21–25). What Ocellus draws from this argument, however, is the hard-line position advocated by Charondas.

Stoic Cosmology, 70–1. The same sort of idea implicitly informs Pythagorean procreationism, given the strong concern to prevent men from killing their semen, as it were, by ejaculating in an expressly antireproductive manner.

31. The Ocellus in whose name the pseudonymous treatise is written was a Pythagorean, for which see Iamblichus, *vit Pyth* 267 and DK 1.440–1. The time by which *On the Nature of the Universe* definitely was written is the mid-first century B.C.E., but the date 150 B.C.E. is the likely approximate date of the treatise, F. Sandbach, *Aristotle and the Stoics* (1985), 63–4. See further W. Burkert, "Zur geistesgeschichtlichen Einordnung einiger Pseudopythagorica" (1972), 46; H. Thesleff, "On the Problem of the Doric Pseudo-Pythagorica: An Alternative Theory of Date and Purpose" (1972), 73; and R. Beutler, "Okellos" (1937), 2361–80. References to Ocellus are, as with Charondas, to Thesleff's edition.

32. Sections 44–46 are at Thesleff 135.11–136.9 and sections 52–57 from Aristoxenus are at 137.6–138.12.

Unless sexual activity is procreationist within marriage, then it is hedonistic —licentious, Charondas would say—and as such forbidden. Therefore, Ocellus enlists Aristoxenus's *Pythagorean Declarations* in support of absolute procreationism. We cannot be so sure that the same held true for the Pythagoreans with whom Aristoxenus was acquainted in the fourth century B.C.E., though they were very close to this position.

Ocellus, like Aristoxenus and Plato, reinforces the procreationist dictate by appealing to the Pythagorean scale of nature and ideas about excess nutrition. People who engage in unrestrained and nondeliberate procreative acts behave like irrational animals (136.4–6). To remedy such brutish conduct he prescribes just what his Pythagorean predecessors do, a dietary regimen that leaves no scraps on which the inner sexual animal may feed (137.26–138.3). Ocellus thus reaffirms the earlier Pythagorean view that excessive nutriment feeds the sexual appetite and brings us to make love below our zoological station—as though we were brutes in rut rather than master artisans of the right reproductive decorum.

Ocellus similarly endorses the older Pythagorean argument that procreationism chiefly serves the interest of the children. Offspring who are produced in anything other than a strictly purposeful way are "abject, ill-omened, and abominable (μοχθηροί, κακοδαίμονες, βδελυροί) in the eyes of the gods, demi-gods (δαιμόνων), people, households, and cities" (136.1–4). Procreationist sex acts avert this undesirable outcome and help set mortals right by the gods, in due accordance with Pythagorean piety.[33] Aristoxenus and Plato likewise maintain that strictly temperate and purposeful reproduction alone prevents offspring from having excessively discordant souls at birth. Ocellus, however, gives this position an astral twist. The souls of children who are produced inadvertently, intemperately, or both are born under a bad sign. They have been down since they began to crawl, afflicted with the life-long curse of having been embodied in a sexually abominable way.

As shown by the treatises of Ocellus and Charondas, the older Pythagorean doctrine of procreationism gains a favorable reception during the Neopythagorean revival of the later Hellenistic and early Roman period. The new version is not nearly as nuanced as those of Aristoxenus and Plato. First, it stresses the need for reproductive purpose yet loses sight of the point that the copulation also needs to be temperate. Temperance is needed to give the soul the smoothest possible landing during embodiment. Second, Charondas and Ocellus allow nothing other than strictly purposeful repro-

33. For the centrality of Apollo in the polytheistic piety of the Pythagoreans, see L. Bruit-Zaidman, "La piété pythagoricienne et l'Apollon de Délos" (1993), 261–9; for theurgy, P. Kingsley, *Ancient Philosophy, Mystery, and Magic: Empedocles and Pythagorean Tradition* (1995), 292–316; and for the gods worshipped by Pythagoreans, W. Burkert, *Lore and Science*, 112–14, 141.

duction within marriage, even for persons beyond their prime. Hence it is unlikely that they had anywhere near the clear grasp Plato reveals about the dualistic eugenics that originally motivated the Pythagoreans to formulate this regulation. One who grasps this reproductive principle would recognize, as Plato does, that it is problematic to advocate (as Charondas and Ocellus do) that for their entire lives married couples should make love only to reproduce. One must further specify how the couples should behave sexually once they are too old to produce offspring of first-rate quality. Despite its inflexibility, procreationism in its Neopythagorean form became popular enough to extend beyond its Pythagorean origins to thinkers known more as Stoics, as I will now show.

SENECA

Seneca advocates procreationism in its Neopythagorean version. Like Ocellus and Charondas, and unlike any Stoic other than Musonius, he presumes an exclusive disjunction between human sexual activity "for the purpose of pleasure" *(voluptatis causa)* or "for the purpose of reproduction" *(propagandi generis causa)*. Only purposeful reproduction is justifiable, and marriage is the only institution in which it may occur. Seneca's strict marital standard is unequivocal. He finds it intolerable for a man to have any sexual partner other than a wife, especially female partners, and he inveighs against adultery in particular.[34] If Seneca had his preference, he would like to see the Neopythagorean standard of sexual austerity become the predominant norm.

Seneca advocates unconditional procreationism out of concern more for the sexual agents themselves than for the offspring. He considers sexual desire for pleasure, *libido,* to be like a fire ready to rage out of control. He defines *libido* as a "destructive force *(exitium)* insidiously fixed in the innards." This force fulfills its violent tendency to harm sexual agents unless it remains within the confines of the procreationist limit. Like Plato, Seneca thinks that unregulated sexual desire spreads like wildfire to other kinds of all-consuming lust, or *cupiditas.*[35] Unlike Plato, however, he is convinced

---

34. *Ep* 94.26, *Ira* 2.28.7. Seneca consequently criticizes Roman practices of adultery and unchaste Roman women, *Ben* 1.9.3–5, *Helv* 16.3.

35. *Helv* 13.3. This passage from Seneca is as follows: *Si cogitas libidinem non voluptatis causa homini datam, sed propagandi generis, quem non violaverit hoc secretum et infixum visceribus ipsis exitium, omnis alia cupiditas intactum praeteribit.* Seneca's meaning is best interpreted as follows. "If one thinks that sexual lust is given to a man not for the purpose of pleasure but for propagating the human race, then all other lust will pass him by unscathed, since the destructive force insidiously fixed in the innards does not violently harm him." Such a man goes unscathed because he restricts his *libido* to its procreationist task and thereby prevents this *exitium* from giving rise to other rampant kinds of *cupiditas.* Plato likewise connects unrestrained sexual desire

that the only way to stop this calamity is to act on one's sexual desire only for reproduction within marriage. Therefore Seneca's sexual ethic is consonant with that of Charondas and Ocellus and more restrictive than Plato's use of procreationism in the *Laws*.

Seneca's procreationist doctrine is contrary to Stoic ethics even though he appropriates Stoic phrasing to describe it. The "wise person" *(sapiens)* who for Seneca is a traditionally married man, ought to make love to his wife "with reason" *(iudicio)* and not "with passion" *(affectu)*.³⁶ *Sapiens* is the Latin equivalent of the Stoic term σοφός and the contrast Seneca makes between acting with right reason or with passion is a Stoic one. Seneca's wise man, however, makes love to his wife "with reason" only if he engages in strictly reproductive sexual activity with her. Otherwise he would be making love for pleasure and hence "with passion." The later Stoics, by contrast, argue that sexual activity is justified if it is done to promote reciprocal affection within marriage. Seneca also rejects the core Stoic principle that love of beauty is an ethical stimulus of mutually friendly sexual relations, be it in marriage or communally. He regards such attraction to beauty as an egregious passion. "Love of beauty *(amor formae)* is the obliteration of reason, one step from insanity."³⁷ Seneca thus allows his strictly procreationist wise man only to have reproductive impulses with his wife, not to be sexually aroused by her beauty or to make love with her for friendship. Consequently, even though Seneca tends to be classed as a Stoic in many respects, he is anti-Stoic in his sexual ethics. It is utterly foreign to Stoicism to contend, as Seneca does, that one must do away with the experience of erotic love except for the reproductive urge within marriage.³⁸

Seneca is indebted to Neopythagoreanism for his procreationist dictate. He probably became aware of the rule through his involvement with the Neopythagorean revival in Rome.³⁹ The treatises of Ocellus and Charondas were in circulation in Rome by Seneca's day, for Cicero and Varro men-

---

with a proliferation of other kinds of cupidity, as shown in chapter two. For Seneca's procreationism see also M. Foucault, *Care of the Self,* 178–9.

36. *De matrimonio,* 188 Frassinetti, excerpted by Jerome, *Adv Jov* 319a.

37. *De matrimonio* 188 Frassinetti, from Jerome, *Adv Jov* 318c.

38. For other ways in which Seneca's thought is incompatible with Stoicism, see J. Rist, "Seneca and Stoic Orthodoxy" (1989), 1993–2012.

39. The renewal of greater interest in Pythagoreanism in Rome ca. 98–45 B.C.E. is discussed by J. Dillon, *The Middle Platonists* (1996), 117–9 and W. Burkert, "Pseudopythagorica," 40–3. M. Humm explores the broader question about the influence of Pythagoreanism in southern Italy and in early Roman society, "Les origines du pythagorisme romain: Problèmes historiques et philosophiques, I–II" (1996), 339–53, (1997), 25–42. See too L. Ferrero, *Storia del pitagorismo nel mondo romano (dalle origini alla fine della reppublica)* (1955). P. Kingsley (*Ancient Philosophy, Mystery, and Magic,* 317–34) challenges Burkert's thesis that Pythagoreanism died down before its Neopythagorean and largely Roman revival.

tion them by name.[40] Seneca might have had an opportunity to read one or both of them himself or to learn about their contents at a remove. Neopythagorean ideas were of great interest in the Roman intellectual milieu to which he belonged.[41] Be that as it may, he certainly employs the same formulaic disjunction between sexual activity for pleasure or for reproduction that Charondas and Ocellus employ. Further, Seneca promotes other aspects of the Pythagorean way of life and philosophy as well. He maintains the Pythagorean tenets that the body imprisons the immortal soul and that the soul must separate itself as much as possible from the weighty dregs of bodily existence.[42] He also states that the example of Pythagoras inspired him to become vegetarian for a time.[43] Seneca's endorsement of procreationism is consequently not as surprising as it might seem for those who think of Seneca as a Stoic. Rather, he admires the ascetic strain in Pythagorean thought as he learned it in Rome, so much so that he becomes an honorary Neopythagorean in his sexual ethics.

MUSONIUS

Musonius, though primarily Stoic, like Seneca, similarly promotes Neopythagorean procreationism. In *Diatribe* 12 he urges young men "to think that

40. Cicero, *Leg* 2.5.14, and Varro refers to Ocellus in a passage preserved by Censorinus (4.3, ed. O. Jahn, 125.10), and note as well W. Burkert, "Pseudopythagorica," 46, and H. Thesleff, "Doric Pseudo-Pythagorica," 73.

41. Seneca admired and studied with Quintus Sextius Roscius, a Roman who established a philosophical group known as the Sextii. This group was in the main Stoic but also had Pythagorean leanings. On this aspect of Seneca's life, see M. Griffin, *Seneca: A Philosopher in Politics* (1992), 36–42, and L. Ferrero, *Storia del pitagorismo*, 360–78. Seneca presumably also knew the Pythagorean astrologer Thrasyllus, who was prominent in the court of Tiberius and redacted Plato's writings. For the strong Pythagorean elements of Thrasyllus's thought and his association with Tiberius, see H. Tarrant, *Thrasyllan Platonism* (1993), 8–11 and fragments T19a–b as well as T13–16b, 222–230. My thanks to T. D. Barnes for noting the likely influence of Thrasyllus on Seneca's Pythagorean leanings.

42. The body is "this trivial body, the prison and chains of the soul" (*corpusculum hoc, custodia et vinculum animi*), while the soul is "sacred and eternal" (*sacer et aeternus*) unlike the body, *Helv* 11.5–7. Released from the body, the soul that quickly departs has an easy road to the gods because "it has dragged along the least amount of sediment and weight" (*minimum faecis, ponderis traxerunt*) from the body. Great souls find no joy lingering in the body, rather they chafe at its confines. "Thus it is that Plato declares that the entire soul of the wise man reaches out to death, ponders this, and always with this desire strives to be borne outward and away" (*sapientis animum totum in mortem prominere, hoc meditari, hac semper cupidine ferri in exteriora tendentem*), *Marc* 23.1–2.

43. *Ep* 108.17. For the Pythagorean provenance of vegetarianism in antiquity see W. K. C. Guthrie's collection and analysis of the ancient evidence, *History of Greek Philosophy*, vol. 1, 187–91, to which should be added Porphyry's *De abstinentia*. Note further R. Sorabji, *Animal Minds and Human Morals: The Origins of the Western Debate* (1993), 172–4.

the only just sex acts (δίκαια ἀφροδίσια) are those performed in marriage for the procreation of children" (86.4–6). Only this way of thinking constitutes right reasoning. All other sexual practices are "lawless" (παράνομα) to varying degrees. Adultery and male homoerotic sexual activity are "most unlawful" (86.8–10). Men's sexual relations with prostitutes, free unmarried women, and female slaves are unlawful, shameful, and blameworthy (86.10–12), though not quite so outrageously as adultery and male homoerotic relations. Musonius thus accepts the Neopythagorean stance that there are two and only two possible goals for human sexual relations: reproduction within marriage or pleasure. Unless sexual activity is marital and for the purpose of procreation, it is wrongly "on the hunt" for pleasure and thus unjust and lawless. This holds true "even in marriage" (86.7–8). Musonius therefore joins a small but growing chorus of men who promote procreationism in its inflexible mode.[44] He even brings new life to the Pythagorean image of brutish sexual activity. Men who are sexually deviant besmirch themselves "just like pigs" and they are happy rolling in the mud (86.27–29). With a touch of Circe's power, then, Musonius turns such men into swine. His magic trick would transform virtually the entire male populace of the Roman Empire, for in his day the dictate still had a long way to go before gaining greater prevalence by late antiquity.

As with Seneca, Neopythagoreanism is the most likely provenance of Musonius's sexual principle. Though very little is known about his life, Musonius was conversant with the intellectual milieu of Rome, which by then had a penchant for Neopythagorean ideas. His writings show that he admired the Pythagorean way of life. *Diatribe* 14, for example, indicates that Musonius knew enough about the life of Pythagoras to recommend it as a model worth emulating. In order for young men to become wise, they must adopt the married style of the philosophical life, which is best exemplified by Pythagoras and two other married philosophers (90.24–92.1). The Neopythagorean revival in Rome thus probably influenced Musonius just as it did Seneca.

Musonius and Seneca are the only known Stoics who advocate the procreationist dictate. They are completely anomalous as Stoics in so doing,[45]

---

44. On this aspect of Musonius's procreationist argument, see also M. Foucault, *Care of the Self,* 168–9.

45. Neither Marcus Aurelius nor Epictetus argue in favor of the procreationist restriction on human sexual behavior. Marcus Aurelius does not raise the topic, while Epictetus rejects the claim that marital sexual activity alone is permissible, and he tolerates some practices of non-marital sexual activity. Epictetus states that a male who engages in sex acts before marriage should partake only of acceptable customary ones and that males who remain sexually abstinent until marriage should tolerate males who do not, *Ench* 33.8. These extramarital kinds of sexual activity are customarily not motivated by a desire to reproduce. Musonius, by contrast, explicitly argues against the view that sex acts other than procreative marital intercourse are

for this Pythagorean rule conflicts fundamentally with the basic principles of Stoic eros. Therefore, it is completely misguided to infer anything about the tenor of Stoic sexual ethics from either Seneca or Musonius, as many scholars have done who have regarded procreationism as a Stoic sexual principle. Both Seneca and Musonius are ascetic Pythagoreans in Stoic clothing, at least with regard to their sexual ethics.

CONCLUSION

Advocates of procreationism support the principle that a temperate and deliberately reproductive goal within marriage is the sole justifiable and permissible goal either of sexual intercourse, or—more extremely—of sexual activity of any sort, especially if it involves ejaculation. This sexual regulation is Pythagorean and develops from uniquely Pythagorean concerns. The first concern is to limit the degree of discordance that immortal souls suffer during embodiment. The second and related concern is to remedy the individual and social corruption that the Pythagoreans attribute to heedless acts of discordant reproduction. Such practices are violent, licentious, and destructive to the harmonic intervals of the souls undergoing embodiment. The practices also harm the parental agents, as Seneca in particular indicates. The procreationist dictate is reinforced by several persuasive strategies. First, persons must diet and exercise to prevent the sexual appetite from being overfed. Second, they should regard unrestrained and nonpurposeful reproductive sexual activity as behavior fit only for brute animals. Third and most striking, they should revere semen and regard its willful misdirection as the destruction of a life. The Pythagoreans were in earnest about supporting this reproductive technology. In the Neopythagorean expression of this principle, however, greater stress is placed on the need for deliberate reproduction, as opposed to deliberate and moderate reproduction. Charondas, Ocellus, Seneca, and Musonius appear to have been somewhat distanced from the older Pythagorean eugenics that originally motivated procreationism.

The procreationist regulation at the outset showed a tendency to apply for the duration of the human life span, given the Pythagorean desire to "put as many impediments as possible on human sexual activity." Plato's *Laws* is the only demonstrable exception to this tendency, for Plato finds lifelong procreationism an unwanted and unfeasible proposition. He avidly supports a limited application of the principle, only for citizens in their prime who still need to reproduce. Thereafter the citizens are left to their own

---

acceptable practices, and he especially censures the sort of men who would have the audacity to engage in extramarital sexual activity of any kind, 86.8–24.

sexual devices so long as they do not get out of hand. Aristoxenus's Pythagoreans are undeniably strict procreationists with regard to sexual intercourse that may lead to conception. Though it remains somewhat an open question whether they prohibited all sexual activity other than copulation, they were nonetheless strongly inclined in that direction. Charondas, Ocellus, Seneca, and Musonius, however, show neither Plato's reflective modification of the procreationist principle nor the vestigial ambiguity of Aristoxenus. If the sexual activity is marital and reproductive in intent, then practice it, if not, stay away.

Procreationism in its aphoristic Neopythagorean form gains wider currency by the time of the early Roman empire. The stillborn nuptial number, by contrast, was at this time nothing but a puzzle for antiquarians, as Cicero attests.[46] Still, procreationism proves to have been as distinctive and strange a Pythagorean idea in its own way as the nuptial number is, even though it later underwent reprocessing and simplification. In this form, which was easy to teach and easy to grasp, the dictate gained enough popularity to elicit support from thinkers whose main affiliation was not Pythagorean, such as Seneca and Musonius; and it was well positioned to spread further into the Jewish Platonism of Philo and into ecclesiastical Christianity via Christian Platonism. By the second century of the common era, therefore, procreationism was well placed to gain a far greater regulatory hold on people's sexual lives than it ever had before.

46. *Att* 7.13.5, and see too M. Allen, *Nuptial Arithmetic,* 5–11.

PART TWO

Greek Biblical Sexual Rules and Their Reworking by Paul and Philo

Chapter 5

Rival Plans
for God's Sexual Program
in the Pentateuch and Paul

The Septuagint Pentateuch and Paul[1] define forbidden sexual conduct by measures designed to orient the society of God's people strictly toward his devotion and honor.[2] Impermissible sexual activity deviates from the First Commandment that one must worship God alone and permissible sexual conduct shows strict devotion to him.[3] Forbidden sexual activity includes

---

1. The Septuagint Pentateuch or a precursor to it was available by the early third century B.C.E., and the Greek Prophets and historical books were in circulation by 116 B.C.E., E. Schürer et al., *History of the Jewish People* 3.1, 476–7, and G. Caird, "Ben Sira and the Dating of the Septuagint" (1982), 95–100. Though chronologies of Paul's life have speculative features, his conversion dates to ca. 32–35 C.E. and he died ca. 60 by H. Koester's scheme, *Introduction to the New Testament*[2], vol. 2: *History and Literature of Early Christianity* (2000), 105–13.

2. Except where greater specificity is warranted, I refer to the peoples claimed for God in the Septuagint more generically as "God's people" or "the Lord's people." This generic designation is helpful for several reasons. First, the Septuagint sexual principles apply to all peoples who take the Greek version of Israel's scriptural heritage as their guide for how to live, whereas more historically specific names (such as Israelites, Jews, Samaritans, or God-fearers) do not have this inclusive reach. Second, the more generic name serves as a useful reminder that the Septuagint is at a Hellenized remove from its ancient cultural origins. Third, the general designation allows my study to avoid using terms entangled in the religious identity polemics of early Christianity, such as Paul's conception of Israel. In relation to the New Testament, I refer to the people who believe in Jesus Christ as "Christians," which is a shorthand way to say "the Christian branch of God's people."

3. There has been much valuable scholarly discussion in recent years about precisely what constitutes the religious ideal of biblical monotheism in various periods in antiquity and the limited extent to which the ideal applies to the diverse religious practices of pre-exilic Israel and Judah. A few preliminary points of clarification are thus in order. In my study I assume the minimal notion of monotheism implied by the First Commandment, which is that the people claimed for God or Yahweh must not worship gods other than or in addition to him. Further, in the scriptural texts I study it is also more frequently the case that alien gods are considered

certain kinds of fornication (πορνεία) as well as other kinds of sexual activity marked as rebellion against God, whereas religiously compliant sexual activity shows no such insubordination. This distinction between permissible and forbidden sexual conduct is simple in its structure, opposing as it does obedience and disobedience to a deity. This leading concern of biblical sexual morality, however, differs from those that inform the sexual principles of Plato, the Stoics, and the Pythagoreans. The Greek philosophers do not organize their primary sexual dictates by whether or not sexual and reproductive conduct shows obeisance to a god who requires exclusive worship. The ancient Greek populace did not do so either. The polytheistic organization of Greek culture precludes this requirement, even among philosophers who exalt the monarch of their rehabilitated Olympian pantheon as "God" (θεός).

Despite the outward simplicity of the biblical dichotomy between the sexually permissible and forbidden, neither the Septuagint nor Paul presents a straightforward explication of the specific contents of these categories. Paul's ominous warnings against sexual fornication make this particular activity seem the worst of deviance, but what does the practice involve, and how should it be prevented? If, for example, a Christian man copulates with a woman, a man, and an animal, is he a fornicator in any, some, or all cases? Questions such as these have been of pressing concern within Christianity at least since the second century, when Tatian, Clement, and other supporters of Paul started fleshing out what sexual activity was permissible for Christians, if any, and denying flesh to the forbidden.[4] A long prescrip-

---

to be real enough to be pose a demonic threat to worshipping God alone, not to be nonexistent fictions of a harmless sort. Hence the gist of the First Commandment as interpreted in Hellenistic times is that God's people must worship God alone and not any of the other baleful gods in the regions claimed for God alone. I do not address other interesting questions that are ancillary to my study, such as when the biblical God takes on the ontological status of being the One, when he loses the human-like extremes of emotion that he bears in the Prophets, what the relationship is between biblical monotheism and the lampooning of the material icons used in polytheistic worship (insofar as one can lampoon icon worship without necessarily being committed to biblical monotheism), when and where the idea finally becomes socially prevalent that there is no god but the biblical God, and the process by which Christianity works its three gods (the father, son, and holy spirit) into a trinitarian kind of one. R. Gnuse (*No Other Gods: Emergent Monotheism in Israel* [1997], 62–297) provides a valuable entry into this broader discussion with a copious bibliography, to which should be added the brief but valuable monograph by J. Levenson, *The Universal Horizon of Biblical Particularism* (1985). See also C. Newman, J. Davila, and G. Lewis, eds., *The Jewish Roots of Christological Monotheism: Papers from the St. Andrews Conference on the Historical Origins of the Worship of Jesus,* (1999), which explores "how Christian devotion in the first two centuries of the common era represents a manifestation of Jewish monotheism," x.

4. This tradition actually begins with Ignatius of Antioch, who tersely upholds Paul's idea that Christian marriages should be "in the Lord," *ad Pol* 5.2, as discussed further below.

tive tradition has developed since their efforts. To name but one much later instance, a seventeenth-century *Treatise of Fornication* begins with the query "*What the Sin is,* which the Apostle [Paul] here exhorts to fly, and that is Fornication." First on the author's agenda is to "define the *Thing* to be avoided," so that Christians might flee from its perils.[5] This endeavor goes back again and again to Paul's letters for the answers, and his starting point was the Septuagint.

In this chapter I too explore fornication and other sexual rebellion against God in the Septuagint and Paul, as well as the sexual behavior that they designate as safe and permissible. Unlike preachers of old and today, though, my interests are at a remove from the pulpit. I explore why Paul and his supporters have for centuries been urging Christians to run from the Thing like deer from all-consuming flames. What motivates and sustains this imperative? To answer this and related questions, I examine the Septuagint in order to understand what Paul, Philo, Tatian, and Clement adopt and modify from it.[6] The Greek Pentateuch, Prophets, and Paul are here treated as sexually grounded blueprints for a reformed social order, just like the Platonic, early Stoic, and Pythagorean reforms, for they similarly work toward social change and begin with reforms in sexual and reproductive mores. Despite the differences between the philosophical and biblical sexual principles of social reform, they all start off as ambitious programs at odds with current conventions, and they make genitals, wombs, and minds the center of regulatory change. This is not to suggest that the Septuagint is only political theory, for the Pentateuch, Prophets, and other books were part of a diverse living religion among Jews and God-fearers in Hellenistic culture, and Paul's Septuagint-based ideas were eagerly taken up by Christians of Greek and other Gentile backgrounds. As read by Philo, Paul, and their supporters, however, the Septuagint allows new sexual and reproductive mandates of social order to emerge, and these are my primary interest. I attempt no exploration of the religious history of ancient Israel and Judah, let alone make broad claims about what the Bible really means in any universal sense. My plan is to account for the religious sexual principles that Paul, Tatian, and Clement advocate from Septuagint and leave as their legacy for Christianized society to contend with.

As stated in the introduction, my findings from the Septuagint and Paul do not apply to Hebrew-based rabbinic Judaism.[7] There are myriad the-

5. W. Barlow, *Treatise of Fornication Upon 1 Cor VI.XVIII* (1690), 2.

6. Philo too plays a major role in this hermeneutical reshaping of God's sexual mandate relative to Clement and ecclesiastical Christianity, as I show in chapter seven. In this and the next chapter my focus is on the Septuagint and Paul.

7. What is meaningfully in the Hebrew Bible depends largely on the historical traditions of rabbinic exegesis and related literature. On the strictly literal—and historically less interest-

matic connections between the Greek and Hebrew aspects of Israel's heritage, and no rigid barrier separated Hellenistic and Palestinian Judaism from each other. Nonetheless, the adaptations that Paul makes to God's sexual program have a distinctive edge to them that contributes to ecclesiastical reasons for segregating Jews from Christians on religious and sexual grounds by the late fourth century.[8] To understand these developments and the social divisiveness to which they led, we must not regard the Greek and Hebrew exegetical traditions as though they were unanimous in the sexual norms they promote.

THE SEPTUAGINT PRINCIPLE OF SEXUAL REBELLION OR APOSTASY

The Septuagint Pentateuch forbids God's people from engaging in acts of religiously alienating rebellion, or apostasy, as one of its main underlying rules. Certain kinds of sexual activity are marked as apostasy, and these fit into two groups. First, sexual activity constitutes rebellion against God if it occurs while worshipping gods other than or in addition to the Lord. When members of God's people engage in such sexual relations, they transgress the premier commandment to worship God alone and no other gods.[9] One cannot be devoted to the Lord alone and at the same time make love in a polytheistic or other-theistic way, regardless of whether the sexual activity is sedately marital with a religiously alien spouse or the most unruly cultic practice imaginable.[10]

---

ing—level, though, the Septuagint Pentateuch's religious and sexual principles bear roughly the same general contents as the Hebrew Torah insofar as the Septuagint Pentateuch gives a reasonably careful translation of its Hebrew Vorlage, as J. Wevers has argued, *Greek Text of Deuteronomy*, xi–xiv. Nonetheless, the Septuagint translations have an exegetical tendency, A. van der Kooij, *The Oracle of Tyre: The Septuagint of Isaiah XXIII as Version and Vision* (1998), 1–19; H. Jacobson, *The* Exagoge *of Ezekiel* (1983), 21–2; and J. Beck, *Translators as Storytellers: A Study in Septuagint Translation Technique* (2000), 1–22. For more circumspect treatments than Wevers's of the Septuagint's accuracy, consider E. Tov, "Did the Septuagint Translators Always Understand Their Hebrew Text?" (1984), 53–70; J. Barr, "'Guessing' in the Septuagint," (1990), 19–34; P. Katz, "Septuagintal Studies in Mid-Century: Their Links with the Past and Their Present Tendencies" (1956), 197–208; and E. Bickerman, "The Septuagint as a Translation" (1976), 167–200.

8. This is not to assume that such was Paul's intention.

9. The warning to stay away from the apostasy of worshipping gods other than or in addition to the Lord is a continual refrain of the Pentateuch and other more historical books, for instance, Exod 20:4–6, 34:10–16; Lev 26:1–39; Deut 5:13–15, 8:19–20, 17:2–7; and 2 Chr 28:1–5. All Septuagint references in this study are to the Göttingen editions. I refer to 1–4 Βασιλέων as 1–4 Kgdms, but I refer to 1–2 Παραλειπομένων by the more familiar 1–2 Chr.

10. Prohibitions against religiously diversifying marriage appear at Exod 34:15–16, Deut 7:1–6, and against sexual rituals of a nonmarital sort at, for example, Num 25:1–9 and Mic 1:5–7.

Second, sexual activity is rebellious if it is a specific kind of defiling act, a sexual "abomination" ($\beta\delta\epsilon\lambda\upsilon\gamma\mu\alpha$) in the eyes of God. This classification is ambiguous, however, for the Pentateuch is not forthcoming about the criteria by which the sex acts in this group are considered abominations. Perhaps they were considered inherently repellant to God, or possibly their association with the worship of other gods sufficed to taint them. If the former, it is likely that priests or prophets who projected this opinion onto the biblical God regarded such sex acts as polluting, deviant, contrary to the natural order (such as a human being copulating with an animal),[11] a breach of a man's and family's property rights (such as adultery), or some combination of these and other possible factors. Some of the sexual abominations, however, are portrayed as ugly emblems of polytheistic rituals—the sort of thing those Canaanites routinely do in thrall to false gods.[12] Even though the blight associated with alien worship does not necessarily explain why certain sexual practices are marked as abominations, their association with other gods is still a significant part of what makes them seem repellant.[13] One function of labeling the sex acts as abominations, then, is to persuade God's people to turn from the worship of other gods and to devote their sexuality and reproduction strictly to the Lord. By the letter of Pentateuchal law, then, sexual activity is off-limits to the extent that it involves worshipping alien gods or is classified as an abomination. There is significant overlap between the two categories, because some sexual abominations are named as such partly because they involve the worship of other gods.

The Greek Pentateuch attributes fearsome risks to sexual and nonsexual rebellion, especially when the disobedience involves other-theistic worship. First, apostates forfeit their standing in the religious community, for they have abandoned the core principle of biblical monotheism inscribed in the First Commandment. Second, the rebels in theory also give up their lives. The religiously obedient should put them to death even if they are kin by blood or marriage. "If your brother on your father's or mother's side, your son or daughter, the wife in your embrace, or a friend as dear to you as your own life secretly appeals to you, saying let us go and worship other gods, . . . you will not consent or listen. . . . You will make a public proclamation about [the offender], with your hands set to kill him [or her] first, and the people's to do so last. They will stone [the offender], who will die because he [or she] sought to bring you into apostasy from the Lord."[14] Stories in

---

11. Lev 18:20–23, 20:15–16, 20:18, 20:23.

12. Lev 18:30, for instance, links the prohibited acts of incest with the customary abominations of Egypt and Canaan. Carved icons of alien gods are themselves an "abomination," and so too is any act of worshipping them, Deut 7:25–6, 13:15.

13. A. Tsitrone, "Sex et mariage dans la tradition juive" (1988), 105–7.

14. Deut 13:6–11, Exod 32:26–9.

Septuagint history amply reinforce this violent mandate.[15] Thus the rule against religiously alienating behavior is not minor etiquette. It is critical to monotheistic social order—so critical that persons in principle must surrender themselves or close kin to retributive death for engaging in sexual or nonsexual rebellion.[16]

In the Septuagint sexual fornication consists of sexual intercourse between men and women that transgresses the criteria of religiously acceptable copulation. Its heterosexual specificity is made clear from examples. Male Israelites, for instance, fornicate with Moabite women at the festival for Baal-peor (Num 25:1). Similarly, Jacob's daughter Dinah is subjected to fornication when Shechem rapes her at a festival.[17] The sexual activity would be an abomination but not fornication if Shechem's victim were a son of Jacob or if any son or daughter of Israel were to engage in autoeroticism or sexual activity with an animal (Lev 18:22–3, 20:13–6). It is important to appreciate this heterosexual specificity of the rule against fornication; it is not vaguely against sexual irregularities of any sort, but against men and women engaging in sexual intercourse outside of God's ordinance system.

Fornication in many instances involves sexual apostasy against God. Members of the Lord's people are implicated in religious rebellion if they

---

15. Phineas earns a hereditary priesthood by killing an Israelite sexual apostate and his female lover, for his action finally turns away the Lord's wrath over Israelites fornicating with Moabite women, Num 25:1–13. Similarly, in relation to nonsexual and/or sexual apostasy, the usurper Jehu, anointed king of Israel by the prophet Elisha, kills Jezebel's son Jehoram on the battlefield because of the apostasy instigated by his mother's "fornications and magical potions," that is, the Baal worship she brought from Sidon to Israel, 4 Kgdms 9:20–26. Jezebel herself is killed for instigating rebellion against God in a manner that fulfills Elisha's grim prophecy, 9:10, 9:30–37. Further, Hosea condemns Ephraim (viz., Israel) and its leaders and vows to kill their offspring on the grounds that they are religiously and sexually in rebellion against God, 9:16. Similarly, Amos warns the house of Jacob that its religiously defiant men and women will fall by the sword in Israel, 7:17; and Isaiah denounces the women of Zion and prophesies that their acts of apostasy will cause their sons and husbands to be killed by invading armies, 3:16–25, esp. 3:16, 24–25, cf. 1:21. Ezekiel envisions that God commands him to stir up an avenging horde of "just men" in the form of invaders to take horrific punishment against apostate Samaria and Jerusalem, "Lead a horde against them, hand them over to uproar and plunder. Stone them with the stones of mobs and hollow them out with their swords. They shall kill their sons and daughters and burn down their houses," 23:46–47.

16. M. Hengel (*Judaism and Hellenism: Studies in Their Encounter in Palestine during the Early Hellenistic Period* [1981], 287 n. 204) notes how critical and distinctive a rule this was among strong adherents of the Lord: "The Jewish religion was the only religion in the East and in the Hellenistic world in which the worship of foreign gods was fundamentally regarded as apostasy and could be punished with death."

17. Gen 34:2, 31. The following examples also help show that sexual fornication is heterosexually specific. If Tamar had made love to a man other than Judah, she would have fornicated with him, Gen 38:1–30, esp. 21, 24, 26. A bride found not virginal on her wedding night fornicated with a man before marriage, Deut 22:21.

engage in adultery,[18] incest,[19] or acts of sexual intercourse partly or fully in devotion to gods other than the Lord. For example, Israelite wives commit adulterous fornication and must be stoned to death if they have male lovers, regardless of whether the adultery occurs in a ritualistic setting (Hos 2:4) or not (Deut 22:22). Male Israelites, further, must abstain from sexual intercourse with women in other-theistic rituals or else they too must be put to death (Num 25:1–18). Finally, the men and women alike must not marry religiously alien persons, for this leads the couples and their children to worship other gods (Exod 34:10–16, Deut 7:1–6). These kinds of fornication are marked as apostate defiance of God and his covenant, and perpetrators of these activities must in principle be destroyed as rebels.[20]

The Septuagint, however, does not present the position that fornication is unconditionally rebellious behavior that warrants death. The Pentateuch adopts a more lenient stance under several circumstances toward fornication within the community of God's people. If, for example, an unbetrothed woman is raped or seduced, neither she nor the man involved is to be put to death.[21] Also, if a betrothed woman is raped, not she, but her rapist, is to die (Deut 22:25–27). Further, occasional sexual relations between female prostitutes and males among God's people are in several instances portrayed as an acceptable custom on the part of the men, not as flagrantly disobedient fornication.[22] Hence in Septuagint terms persons do not become apostates marked for death simply by virtue of fornicating. They do, however, rebel against God and should be eliminated if their sexual fornication implicates them in devotion to alien gods, in adultery or incest, or if they are males who rape betrothed females in the community.

The Septuagint does not limit its notion of sexual apostasy to forbidden kinds of intercourse between men and women, even though these are its

18. Lev 20:10; Deut 5:17, 5:21, 22:20–3; Exod 20:13, 20:17; Ezek 16:38–41; and L. Epstein, *Sex Laws and Customs in Judaism* (1948), 194–215. See too Num 5:11–31, along with A. Destro, *The Law of Jealousy: The Anthropology of Sotah* (1989), 1–157, and L. Epstein, *Sex Laws*, 216–34.

19. Sexual intercourse within the prohibited degrees of incest is apostasy and Leviticus prescribes that its agents be put to death, Lev 18:6–30, esp. 18:29.

20. The theme of retributive death for adultery, incest, and religiously diversifying marriage appears in, respectively, Deut 22:21–4, Ezek 16:38–40, Lev 18:29, Exod 34:14–6, Deut 7:2–4, and note also Hos 9:11–2, 16 for the idea that God targets offspring of religiously mixed unions for destruction.

21. If raped, the unbetrothed woman is to be married to the man who raped her, he must pay a fine to her father, and no divorce is to be permitted, Deut 22:28–9. If the unbetrothed woman is seduced, her seducer must recompense her father for the material value of the virginity her father has lost, Exod 22:15–6.

22. When Judah makes love to Tamar disguised as a sacred prostitute, *his* action is not portrayed as wrong, Gen 38:15–26, and Samson has uncensured sexual relations with a prostitute, Judg 16:1; see also S. Légasse, "Jésus et les prostituées" (1976), 140–1.

predominant concern. Also included are male homoerotic sexual relations, at least in certain positions,[23] and sexual activity between humans and animals (Lev 20:15–16). These prohibitions, however, are mentioned sparingly. Leviticus refers to these acts as abominations and prescribes a capital punishment against transgressors. "Let them be put to death."[24] The main concern of the Septuagint is to outlaw practices of adulterous, incestuous, or other-theistic sexual intercourse between women and men. This is a significant point. The Septuagint primarily strives to enforce the rule that God's people practice sexual intercourse and reproduction strictly in its image of religious sanctity. Only secondarily does it try to root out male homoeroticism and sexual activity of humans with animals. This insistence stems to a considerable degree from the desire of priests and prophets to draw God's people, their offspring, and their children's children toward the Lord and away from other gods, like iron filings toward one numinous magnet and away from others, despite their attraction.

THE QUID PRO QUO ATTRIBUTED TO THE BIBLICAL GOD

In order to understand the sexual prohibitions attributed to the Lord, it is pivotal to recognize that the Septuagint imparts a layer of religious significance to ancient concerns about sexual defilement or pollution. In the Pentateuch sexual defilement and dishonor are incorporated into a new order of wrongdoing—disobeying a deity who requires unconditional obedience and devotion. For example, even before the Septuagint's "Yahweh-aloneist" religiosity was a glimmer in the eye of Moses and his followers,[25] the dishonor

23. S. Olyan ("'And with a Male You Shall Not Lie the Lying Down of a Woman': On the Meaning and Significance of Leviticus 18:22 and 20:13" [1994], 179–206) argues that Leviticus 18:22 and 20:13 prohibit only male homoerotic anal intercourse, not male homoerotic relations of any and all sorts. Though he may be right, his argument is not compelling. As Olyan notes, in biblical passages, if a man lies with a women, he engages in vaginal sexual intercourse with her. From this textual given, Olyan infers that a male bodily orifice needs to be penetrated in order for a male to commit the prohibited act of lying "as a woman" with another man, and Olyan regards the anus being the only viable contender. This argument is not persuasive, for face-to-face intercrural sexual relations can also be construed as an act of penetrating the quasi-orifice where inner thighs and testicles meet in a man-woman-like style. As D. Boyarin shows ("Are There Jews in the 'History of Sexuality'?" [1995], 346), it was a matter of rabbinic discussion how to categorize heterosexual intercrural intercourse. The same question would also hold for male homoerotic relations. In short, the phrasing of Lev 18:22 and 20:13 seems too allusive to maintain with confidence that the Levitical prohibition strictly concerns anal penetration.

24. Lev 18:22–3, 20:13, 15–16. S. Olyan ("And with a Male," 181–3) has a good discussion of how anomalous Leviticus 18:22 and 20:13 are.

25. The apt term goes back to Morton Smith. See R. Gnuse, *No Other Gods*, 75–6 and n. 28 for complete bibliography.

of females being raped by male foreigners was already offensive. When Dinah is raped by Shechem, her brothers retaliate against him and his people because this outsider with a foreskin defiled their sister and ruined her reputation (Gen 34:1–31), not because Dinah stands ruined and repellant for betraying the First Commandment (albeit inadvertently) by having sexual contact with a male who worships alien gods. However, once the Pentateuch identifies various kinds of sexual activity as forbidden by the Lord, the sexual activity is also a betrayal of God and the strictly monotheistic society being commissioned in his name. The order of wrongdoing expands to include the factor of covenant-breaking defiance, especially, but not only, on the part of willful agents.[26] We cannot readily appreciate the Pentateuch's implacable requirement of capital punishment for certain kinds of sexual activity without appreciating the religious treason being associated with them. For example, adultery in the Pentateuch is never wrong simply because it transgresses a man's or family's property rights, even though this criterion of disapproval remains at work.[27] In Septuagint terms adultery is wrong primarily because it constitutes defiance toward one of God's commandments, and keeping the commandments is a required part of worshipping the Lord alone. The same holds true of other sexual transgressions. Within this religious system, further, a genuinely new sexual transgression appears on the scene, one that presupposes, and hence does not antedate, biblical monotheism as a norm: the danger of men or women making love and reproducing with partners who worship gods other than the Lord. Prior to the formulation of Yahwism, such non-Yahwist practices of marriage and procreation were the status quo in the ancient world.

The Septuagint offers a potent and disturbing rationale for eliminating agents of religious rebellion: If apostates remain alive in the community, God will disinherit and destroy the community or a substantial portion thereof. This danger is portrayed as a live threat, given its precedent in the fate that the Lord is said to have dealt to the sexually abominating Canaanites and others. "If you forget the Lord your God and proceed after other gods to worship and bow to them, I bear witness to you today by the sky and earth that I will destroy you, just as I destroyed the other peoples . . . because of their irreverence" (Deut 8:19–20, 9:4). It is as though the Canaanites were culpably remiss in failing to anticipate and conform in advance to the way of the Lord, and God responds by uprooting their religious culture, the sexual mores that were part of that culture, and a number of the people

26. The unintentional defiance of women among God's people who are raped, taken captive, and impregnated by religious male outsiders is a significant concern, as I demonstrate in the next chapter.

27. B. Rosner (*Paul, Scripture, and Ethics,* 158–61) sums up these other reasons for the biblical prohibition of adultery.

themselves.[28] He then grants and guarantees their land to Israel, but with a formidable stipulation: His people are to remain keepers of the new dominion only if they unconditionally obey his laws. The prohibition against worshipping other gods sexually and reproductively is crucial, for the degree to which biblical monotheism becomes a reality correlates with the theistic orientation shown in the people's acts of sexual intercourse, procreation, and religious patterns of childrearing. The people must not continue to devote their sexual and reproductive energy to other gods, as their ancestors used to do, for the biblical God now claims them exclusively as his own. In case the people lapse, they must atone for their failings and renew their commitment to worship God alone (Deut 4:29–31). Otherwise, God will see to it that they and their patrimony face a similar demise through genocide, exile, and slavery, with its sexual and other abuses.[29]

The covenantal proviso in the Septuagint functions rather like a Faustian bargain. God grants his people inviolable access to prosperity, protection, and hegemony, but only so long as they surrender the other-theistic rituals and sexual practices that they used to enjoy. A veritable heaven on earth is theirs, but the cost is the very soul of religious and sexual pluralism. The people must relinquish in perpetuity the ability to act on their own cognizance religiously and sexually, for in order to have no other gods but God, they must make love, reproduce, and raise children for the Lord alone. And while Faust could have turned the devil down, God's terms are imposed in the Pentateuch as an already binding contract that the Israelites cannot reject without being annihilated.[30] The Israelites thus become a collective of tragic heroes who must comply with their assigned fate if they wish to live, to receive God's blessing instead of his curse (Deut 30:15–20, 11:26–8). The Lord has warned them of the calamity to come if they disobey—the same disinheritance and destruction that God has already dealt to the Canaanites at their hands. Deuteronomy reaffirms the quid pro quo by ex-

28. Leviticus similarly states in the assumed voice of God, "You [my people] shall not defile yourselves in any of these ways; for in these ways the heathen, whom I am driving out before you, made themselves unclean. This is how the land became unclean, and I punished it for its iniquity so that it spewed out its inhabitants," 18:24–25. "I will give the inhabitants of the country into your power, and you will drive them out before you. . . . I will drive out [the forbidden tribes]," Exod 23:31, 34:11, with the people's sacred places being utterly destroyed.

29. This either/or ultimatum also appears in, for instance, Exod 23:23–33, 34:11–16; Lev 20:11–27; Num 25:1–13; Deut 4:25–31, 7:1–9:29, esp. 9:4–14, 29:10–28; and Ezek 20:27–39.

30. J. Levenson also observes (*The Universal Horizon of Biblical Particularism,* 19–20), "In the Bible one sees this curious simultaneous affirmation of choice and fate in Joshua's covenant ceremony at Shechem. In one breath he offers Israel the choice of which god(s) to serve, and then in the next breath avers that if they choose any other than YHWH, YHWH will annihilate them (Josh. 23:15, 20)."

pressly reminding the Israelites that they must never think they are above God's laws simply by having been chosen as his people. The Lord esteems obedience more than he esteems any particular people, for he takes equal joy in helping the obedient to flourish and in destroying the rebellious (Deut 9:4–7, 28:63). It would thus be utter folly for the Israelites to defy the strictly monotheistic sexual mores to which they have been appointed.

Given the Pentateuchal terms of God's protection, agents of religiously alienating sexual and reproductive practices are public enemies. In the interest of community security, the dissidents in principle must be purged through stoning or some other method to contain the religious treason and avert God's retaliation. Members of God's people who abide by this biblical teaching have ample scriptural grounds to kill sexual transgressors of God's laws. Even if they do not resort to violence, they have grounds to harbor intense loathing and intolerance toward the transgressors. Tolerance is reprehensible, for to turn a blind eye elicits retribution from a deity who already has a formidable record for brutalizing peoples because of their sexual devotion to alien gods. The force of this doctrine comes through in the chilling openness with which rebels are targeted for destruction, as though they were carriers of a plague rather than family members, friends, or neighboring tribal groups.

In conjunction with annihilating deviants, the people claimed for the Lord must also eliminate polytheistic mores and sacred sites from God's domain. "You will neither bow down to their gods, nor worship them, nor carry out their rites. You will destroy and lay them low and tear down their monuments ($\tau\grave{\alpha}\varsigma$ $\sigma\tau\acute{\eta}\lambda\alpha\varsigma$)" (Exod 23:24). Once the obedient do away with these rituals and the condemned sites, the other-theistic competition declines and makes way for the people to be safe and sovereign in the Lord.

The moral of Numbers' composite story about Moabite and Midianite women highlights the danger of sexually fornicating rebellion. When Israelite men engage in sexual ceremonies with Moabite women devoted to Baal, the men must be killed. As Moses tells the judges, "Each one of you put to death your kinsmen who have been initiated into the worship of Baal-peor" (Num 25:5). Though the narrative has a break where we would learn whether the Israelites carried out these orders, it would appear that initially they did not. In response God unleashes a scourge that kills twenty-four thousand Israelites, until God's ardent supporter Phineas rises up to prevent total extirpation. Phineas observes that an Israelite man, Zimri, has taken a Midianite woman, Cozbi, as a lover and, perhaps, as a wife. He encapsulates God's anger in his own indignation and impales the two of them together, making sure that his spear runs "through the woman's womb" in the Septuagint version (Num 25:8). This death-bearing thrust prompts God to relent. At least one man, Phineas, has unquestioningly obeyed his orders, and God thus spares the remaining Israelite people. Thanks to Phineas, he declares, "I did not utterly wipe out the Israelites in my jealous anger" (Num 25:11), and in reward God grants Phineas a priesthood to be passed down in his male lineage. The Lord's killing field through which Phineas picks his way toward priesthood is made up of public enemies who ostensibly deserved to die.

The Septuagint version of the Numbers incident specifies the anatomical locale of Cozbi's slaughter for a didactic reason. Even though Zimri is the transgressor, not Cozbi, Phineas skewers her through the womb in order to show that his people must cease dissipating the Lord's claim to power by producing and rearing children for gods other than or in addition to the Lord. The spear through her religiously alien womb declares that once and for all there is to be no more fornicating sexual rebellion in the Lord's community networks of kinship and marriage, no more syncretistic religious diversity borne through the children across generations. So pressing is this rule that the people must even surrender their disobedient kin in order to prove their loyalty to God alone.[31]

Jeremiah succinctly indicates the difference between the defilement of rebellious sexual fornication and pollutions that do not involve apostasy. Defilements of the customary sort have a simple and relatively unproblematic purification, such as ritual washing or periods of isolation.[32] These acts of purification cleanse the defilement and restore persons to the social order of the Lord. By contrast, Jeremiah asserts, no amount of soap washes away the defilement of fornicating rebellion and the defiance associated with it. As he declares in the assumed voice of God, "[Israel,] your rebellion (ἀπο-στασία) will teach you; and your wickedness will betray you. . . . You declared 'I will not be your religious slave. Instead I will go upon every high hill and under every shady tree and there I will be dissipated through my sexual fornication. . . .' 'You are defiled by your wrongful actions,' the Lord

---

31. The emphasis here on God before family, even if that means killing family members, gives one indication that monotheism as formulated in the Pentateuch likely did not reflect at the outset a broad-based outlook shared by the men, women, and children. Peoples in antiquity traditionally valued their loyalties to family and kin and resisted forms of social organization that attempted to supplant preeminent kinship priorities, as we have seen with the Platonic and the early Stoic efforts to communalize society. In this respect the "God before family" Pentateuchal principle seems a radically unconventional idea in its formulation. By the time of Philo of Alexandria and probably earlier, however, the principle had gained its ardent proponents. Philo, for instance, believes that God's people must prefer no kinship or friendship over obedience to God, so much so that they should put their "closest friends and most beloved relatives" to death—and be the first to seek them out—in the event that the friends and relatives participate in rebellion against God, *Spec* 3.126.

32. For example, menstruating women and women in childbirth rejoin daily life after a set time of isolation that purifies their defilement, and ejaculation renders a man unclean until he washes and evening falls, and the same is true of the woman with whom the man copulates, Lev 15:16–18, and see J. Neusner, *Purity in Ancient Judaism* (1973), 16–23.

states, 'even if you wash with cleansing soda'" (2:19–22).[33] When the defilement derives from religiously alienating sexual fornication, not even an ancient equivalent of lye or detergent gets out the stain. Bloodshed is the only effective method of purging sexual apostates, and it must be used to keep the community clean and secure. To all appearances, this violent religious principle meets with valiant resistance time and again. In terms of the Septuagint quid pro quo that Jeremiah supports, however, the principle is right and the resistance is wrong.

THE SEPTUAGINT PRINCIPLE OF RELIGIOUS ENDOGAMY

The biblical notion of sexual fornication conjures up images that outrage Jewish and Christian conventions of decency—men and women pulsating in acts of cultic intercourse while glassy-eyed idols play the voyeur. While the Septuagint does denounce orgiastic sexual rites, the more critical problem comes from reproductive intercourse in syncretistic intermarriages. Though more mundane, this marital fornication is more problematic precisely because it is woven into the everyday life of the community and affects the religious character of the offspring. "You must not intermarry with [the nations whom I am driving out before you]. You will not give your daughters to their sons nor take their daughters for your sons; if you do, they will draw your sons away from me [the Lord] and make them worship other gods. Then the Lord will be angry with you and will destroy you straightaway."[34] The occasional orgiastic festival is of more sporadic concern and easier to keep at bay.

---

33. G. Corrington Streete (*The Strange Woman: Power and Sex in the Bible* [1997], 85–89) has a fine discussion of Jeremiah's position here. Jeremiah's claim that sexually fornicating rebellion against God is an indelible pollution illustrates M. Douglas's important point about the updating and redeployment of ancient ideas about pollution and purity. As Douglas has shown, ubiquitous ancient ideas about pollution and purity tend to be renewed and reworked to support new regulatory norms, which in Jeremiah's case is the ideal social order of worshiping God alone. The schema of pollution and purity on which Jeremiah draws far antedates this monotheistic ideal, but he renews and transforms it by connecting purity with monotheism and pollution with other-theistic practices. Jeremiah is not alone in this respect, for other passages in the Pentateuch and Prophets do so as well, such as Lev 18:24–5, Num 25:1–3, and Hos 4:13. One might say that this redirecting of pollution and purity rules to support biblical monotheism is a distinguishing feature of the Pentateuch. For Douglas's general point, see *Purity and Danger* (1966), 94–113, 129–39, and J. Neusner, *The Idea of Purity in Ancient Judaism* (1973), 7–31, 108–36, along with Douglas's response, 138–142. B. Morris (*Anthropological Studies of Religion* [1987], 226–33) offers a worthwhile review of Douglas's argument. For pollution and purity schemas in ancient Greek society, see R. Parker, *Miasma: Pollution and Purification in Early Greek Religion* (1983), 18–307.

34. Deut 7:3–4, and see too Exod 34:15–16; 3 Kgdms 11:1–13, 16:31. See further G. Corrington Streete, *The Strange Woman* (1997), 50–1.

Members of God's people who marry persons of an other-theistic orientation and share in their spouses' religious mores engage in no trivial breach of the First Commandment. They enter into alien worship through their wedding, marriage customs, and childrearing, and so do their relatives who participate in the wedding, condone the marriage, and celebrate the children's religiously mixed coming-of-age ceremonies. The transgression of the spouses, moreover, has an unavoidably sexual aspect, for in the ancient world marital sexual activity was partly devotional, just as the wedding was. In antiquity, sexual arousal, activity, and reproduction were in part immanent divine powers, not simply human forms of energy.[35] Sexually aroused persons who make love and women who give birth share in and honor gods of sexuality and procreation, such as women in childbirth who cry out "Hera help me! Save me, I beg you!"[36] The gods who motivate, control, and have their presence in sexuality and reproduction vary by culture, such as Aphrodite, Eros, Zeus, and Hera for the Greeks,[37] or Yahweh for the Jews.[38] Since the practice of religiously diversified intermarriage is not for the Lord alone, it incompatible with obeying the First Commandment. When persons within God's community intermarry, they defy a core feature of the covenant, because their action impinges on the religiosity of future generations. Religiously mixed marital sexual activity therefore ranks high among the kinds of rebellious fornication to drive out of the community and to keep out in perpetuity.[39]

35. A. Tsitrone, "Sex et mariage dans la tradition juive," 105, and D. Pralon, "Les puissances du désir dans la religion grecque antique" (1988), 73–84.

36. Terence, *Adelph* 486–7. Tertullian condemns this and other polytheistic rituals related to bearing and raising children, *Anim* 39.1–4, and see further J. Waszink's commentary on the rituals he pillories, 440–47.

37. As C. Faraone (*Ancient Greek Love Magic*, 134) notes, "Just as Dionysus is experienced in part as the wild intoxication of wine or dancing, the divinity of Aphrodite seems to have manifested itself in intense sexual desire or in the orgasm itself." For this and other ways in which the Greeks participated in divine powers through their sexual behavior, see too V. Pirenne-Delforge, *L'Aphrodite grecque: Contribution a l'étude de ses cultes et de sa personalité dans le pantheon archaïque et classique* (1994), 418–28; I. Clark, "The Gamos of Hera: Myth and Ritual" (1998), 13–26; J. Redfield, "Notes on the Greek Wedding" (1982), 181–201; W. Erdmann, *Die Ehe im alten Griechenland*, 135–9; and V. Magnien, "Le mariage chez les Grecs anciens: Conditions premières" (1936), 305–20.

38. Gen 9:1, Deut 28:9–14, and *Anchor Bible Dictionary* (1992), s.v. "God as creator and giver of life," 2.1051–52. See H. Jacobson, *A Commentary on Pseudo-Philo's Liber antiquitatum biblicarum* (1996), 720 for additional biblical parallels.

39. *Jubilees*, in strong support of this prohibition, broadens it by insisting that if "any man among Israel gives his daughter or sister to any foreigner, he is to die" by stoning and the woman is to be burned, 30.7. The "giving" here is a giving in marriage, 30.13–15. Just as Dinah's brothers refused to give Dinah to Shechem as his wife, 30.3, so too must the people of Israel refuse to have any sexual involvement with peoples of the foreskin, 30.12. *Jubilees* is so severe because it upholds the Pentateuchal teaching that retribution from the Lord inevitably

Let us consider an example so as to better appreciate why religiously mixed marriages take precedence over orgiastic rituals and prostitution among the kinds of sexual fornication to eliminate. If a male member of God's people takes a religiously alien woman as a wife, she, depending on her background, would worship the queen of heaven, Ishtar, Aphrodite, or other deities of sex and marriage, such as Hera and Zeus. She would also practice domestic religious ceremonies of a sort alien to her husband's religion, such as rituals of birth and puberty for her children. She would teach her daughters and sons to follow her example (which by then is likely to be somewhat syncretistic with her husband's) when they marry and have children. She might also encourage her husband to follow her lead. And if her husband tried to be the autocratic Hosea in her household, she might resist or persuade him that their family is better off and better protected by continuing to worship the gods of her heritage, such as the queen of heaven, than by worshipping Yahweh alone. In defiance of Jeremiah, diaspora women in Egypt openly declare such a preference for Ishtar with the full support of their husbands, leaving the prophet to retort ominously, "We will see whose word will prevail" (Jer 51:15–28). By contrast, a male Israelite who visits a prostitute or secretly takes part in an orgy in an outlying town does not enter into the same degree of religious danger that the syncretistic husbands and children do, so long as he goes back home to his family and religion of biblical monotheism and teaches his children to do likewise.

The Septuagint prescribes two measures to remove the danger of syncretistic marriage from the midst of the Lord's people. First, marriages between members of God's people, such as the Israelites, and persons who belong to seven specific religiously alien groups in the promised land, such as the Amorites and Canaanites, are in principle absolutely prohibited.[40] The punishment for this apostasy, according to Deuteronomy, is a swift punitive death (Deut 7:4). The status of these seven ethnic groups is distinctive, however, because they are in active dispute with the Israelites over the patrimony of land.[41] Unlike them, members of religiously alien groups that

---

follows upon disobeying these marriage rules: "Every punishment, blow, and curse will come. If one does this or shuts his eyes to those who do impure things and who defile the Lord's sanctuary and to those who profane his holy name, then the entire nation will be condemned together because of all this impurity and this contamination."

40. On the specific peoples with whom marriages are absolutely prohibited as apostasy, see Exod 34:11, Deut 7:1–4, Judg 3:5–6. Some of Solomon's royal intermarriages transgress this command, 3 Kgdms 11:1–13. Ahab's marriage with Jezebel also transgresses this rule, for she is a Canaanite queen from Sidon, 3 Kgdms 16:31.

41. Gen 15:18–21; Exod 3:8, 3:17, 23:23; and in Joshua the disputed land is acquired by military conquest. Deut 12:8–9 precisely specifies that the unconditional rules of segregation from Gentiles apply to God's people in their dealings with other peoples in the historical promised land, not outside of its geographical limits. 1 Esdras and 2 Esdras further support the

have no connection to the land claim of the Israelites are not untouchable as prospective spouses, but are to be accommodated by the second measure. These Gentile outsiders may marry into God's people, provided that they willingly convert to the Lord alone and agree to impart the ways of biblical monotheism to their children.[42] The Moabite Ruth illustrates this point well. Since the Moabites are not one of the seven prohibited tribes in Deuteronomy, a Moabite woman may convert and, like Ruth, vow, "Your people are my people and your God is my God" (Ruth 1:16). With this declaration, the woman is no longer alien in the sense that matters for biblical monotheism. Once converted, she is rehabilitated from a biblical perspective and can be accepted as a wife and mother among the Lord's people.[43] If, however, Ruth has a sister who continues to worship the gods of her ancestral heritage, the sister remains dangerously alien. Were she to marry an Israelite, she and her husband would know no peace if the likes of Phineas and Jeremiah were in their neighborhood, for her husband has rebelled against God by joining with her in marriage, and he relegates his children and parents to the same alienated standing (Exod 34:15–16). Hence, intermarriages are acceptable only when they are no longer "interfaith" in the ancient sense of worshipping gods other than or in addition to the Lord. The principle of biblical endogamy is thus elastic, for it is open to many Gentiles, so long as they convert and sincerely vow to abide by the First Command-

idea that mixed marriages with religiously alien women in the land gravely endanger God's people as a whole. When Ezra's group comes back from exile, they find such a condition of sexual rebellion upon their return, for men of the community who did not go into exile have married women from the forbidden tribes. Ezra requires the divorce of the men en masse from the women, 2 Esdr 10:10–11, cf. 1 Esdr 9:7–10. Though the ruling in this narrative is drastic, it is relatively speaking nonviolent and could have been more hard-lined and Phinean. For Ezra, purging through bloodshed is not needed; the severing of families suffices.

42. Philo's marital sexual ethic exemplifies this rule, as I show in chapter seven. As indicated by the book of Tobit, however, a more cautious guideline coexisted with this rule in Hellenistic Judaism: Jews are best advised to stay on the safe side and marry within the lineage of their ancestors, Tob 4:12, A.-J. Levine, "Tobit: Teaching Jews How to Live in the Diaspora" (1992), 44, 48, and L. Feldman, *Jew and Gentile in the Ancient World: Attitudes and Interaction from Alexander to Justinian* (1993), 77–9, though the question of which practice was more prevalent in Hellenistic Judaism remains more open than Feldman suggests.

43. Joshua similarly reflects that the main criterion of membership in the Lord's people is religion, not birthright. When Jericho is destroyed Rahab and her family alone are spared, for she proves her devotion to the Lord by helping to betray Jericho, Josh 6:16–25. Ambiguity nonetheless arises in the Septuagint about which religious aliens are allowed to convert into eligible spouses, because the peoples designated as ineligible changes. For example, Moabites are not on the Pentateuchal lists of peoples with whom marriage is absolutely prohibited, though marriages with Moabites are not recognized as valid in Deut 23:4. Moabites are, however, on a postexilic list of peoples with whom marriage is absolutely prohibited, 2 Esdr 9:1, cf. 1 Esdr 8:66.

ment.[44] I hereafter refer to this principle and practice as "biblical" or "religious endogamy," for its criterion of the eligible marriage pool is whether the prospective spouses already follow or agree to follow the way of the Lord alone. Other kinds of endogamy practiced in the ancient world were more fixed and culturally closed. They tended to restrict eligible spouses by characteristics that persons have by birth and cannot change, such as ethnic status or Athenian citizenship, not by religious conduct that one can change through conversion.[45] The community of the Lord alone uses its marriage rules to balance the requirement to be impervious to the polytheistic sexual mores that surround them without becoming entirely closed as a group.

The production and rearing of religiously mixed children poses a special danger to the norm of biblical monotheism. To the extent that the children become polytheistic, God's share of compliant worshippers declines in future generations, and with the reduced populace, God's social recognition diminishes. The Pentateuch and Prophets are dedicated to counteracting this trend. By their teaching, if monotheistic devotion wanes through syncretism or secularization, cultural suffering will occur as divine retribution for such dissolute tendencies. This retribution can and should rekindle atonement and monotheistic ardor among the surviving people. The Prophets rebuke the syncretistic offspring, in an effort to gain them as devotees of the Lord alone. Hosea labels them "children of fornication" and "religiously alien children," and urges them to renounce the religiously mixed ways of their parents. He inveighs against the influence of religiously alien mothers in particular, and some of the offspring apparently include his own children by Gomer, Hosea's wife, who preferred to worship Baal and continued to do so.[46] Hosea's vituperative exhortations are meant to stigmatize and sting the

44. This marriage rule works by the principle of expansive religious particularism, which J. Levenson succinctly analyzes in its Jewish form, *The Universal Horizon of Biblical Particularism.* The practice of Gentiles converting to Judaism and then marrying into the group is an important aspect of the open membership policy in Hellenistic Judaism. D. Sim (*The Gospel of Matthew and Christian Judaism: The History and Social Setting of the Matthean Community* [1998], 16–17) succinctly discusses this policy, though not in connection with marriage.

45. Practices of endogamy of any sort have played a major role in keeping peoples differentiated into separate cultures. R. Benedict boldly observed years ago (*Patterns of Culture* [1934; reprint, 1989], 7–8), "Primitive man [viz., peoples at a pre-state level of culture]" rarely if ever "looked out over the world and saw 'mankind' as a group and felt common cause with the species. From the beginning he was a provincial who raised the barriers high. Whether it was a question of choosing a wife or of taking a head, the first and important distinction was between his own human group and those beyond the pale."

46. Hos 1:2, 2:6, 5:7. B. Seifert (*Metaphorisches Reden von Gott im Hoseabuch* [1996], 119–22) offers worthwhile cautionary remarks about reading too much autobiography into Hosea's marital poetics, but a core element of the prophet's own experience presumably holds true—Hosea did have a wife who continued to worship Baal and other gods, and their children, among many others, were following along this path of religious sexual diversity.

offspring into turning wholly toward the Lord. In addition, the Prophets pointedly remind the people about the Lord's conditional terms of protection—God will destroy them if they turn a blind eye to the religious diversity growing up in their midst. The Lord will either render mixed unions barren or kill any children born to Israel from them (Hos 9:16–17). Ezekiel draws attention to the same problem. The former denizens of the sacked city of Jerusalem had wrongly turned a blind eye to the presence of Amorite and Canaanite spouses and parents in their communities, who were unconditionally off-limits as marriage partners. As Ezekiel sees it, God rightly brought about Jerusalem's destruction because of this forbidden mixing of peoples and religious customs.[47] The offspring are an impure alloy of several metals, which the Lord will have to melt down to regain the pure silver (Ezek 22:17–22). Thus the procreation of children who worship gods other than or in addition to the Lord are at the heart of sexually fornicating danger, for this practice corrupts the Yahwists' brightest hope, the purely monotheistic generations of the future.

DIVERGENT RESPONSES TO THE BIBLICAL
MANDATE AGAINST SEXUAL REBELLION

The biblical dictate that God's people must eliminate sexual fornicators who are implicated in apostasy appears primitive and brutal, stemming from days when the Lord's adherents were too busy lashing out at competing gods to develop the Lord as a deity of forgiveness and mercy. A benevolent god, though, is more appealing and sophisticated than a deity who outdoes the stomping ogre of folklore in his dealings with his own and other peoples. Numerous devout teachers, such as Jesus and other rabbis, have accordingly tried to get beyond the violent terms of the covenant. They highlight alternative biblical passages, such as the tenet that God is "compassionate and gracious . . . forgiving iniquity, rebellion, and sin, and not sweeping the guilty clean away" (Exod 34:6–7).[48] Though they strive to leave behind the

47. Ezek 16:1–45, and on the forbidden parentage, 16:1–4, 45 and G. Corrington Streete, *The Strange Woman*, 91.

48. Other biblical passages similarly foreground the principle that God is compassionate and that he sets a high standard of clemency that his people should obey, Deut 4:29–31, 13:17, Luke 6:36. The didactic tale about Jesus taking a stand against stoning the adulterous woman at John 7:53–8:11 likewise challenges the appropriateness of stoning sexual apostates and encourages forgiveness. This tale is probably not part of John as first composed (but see J. Heil, "The Story of Jesus and the Adulteress [John 7,53–8,11] Reconsidered" [1991], 182–91), yet it is an early Christian teaching associated with Jesus (known to Papias), C. K. Barrett in *Peake's Commentary* 759d. The unconditional imperative to love your enemies is also likely relevant in this connection, Matt 5:43–8, Luke 6:27–8, 32–6. Further, in the rabbinic tradition there is a strong tendency to forgive rather than to exact a violent death penalty. The rabbis require that agents of adultery and other sexual apostasy meet extensive conditions that are virtually im-

use of terror to inculcate the worship of God, other proponents of the Lord, such as Paul and Philo, continue to promulgate the violent terms and have a divided conception of God.[49] On the one hand God is providence or agape, but the other hand is the Lord's fist clenched in wrath against agents of sexual rebellion and the community that fails to root them out. Persons who internalize the Pentateuch's ineluctable quid pro quo have a compelling motive to restrict permissible sexual activity and reproduction to marriages that comply with biblical endogamy and to demand the same protectionist standard of sexual conduct from all community members. This is not to claim, however, that they are necessarily so Phinean as to kill religious sexual deviants, be it in vigilante style or by verdict of biblical law.[50] Nonetheless, ardent followers of the Lord have solid Pentateuchal grounds for urging some form of violent and in principle deadly action against sexual apostates, so strong is the biblical abhorrence of allowing religious syncretism to seep into the Lord's domain through fornicating intercourse and procreation.

PAUL'S RELIGIOUS SEXUAL ETHIC AND ITS ADAPTATION OF THE SEPTUAGINT PENTATEUCH

The apostle Paul is a highly innovative advocate for the protectionism of an Israel that knows no cultural boundaries. He treats some basic tenets of the Septuagint Pentateuch and Prophets as variables open to change: The peoples to be claimed for the Lord become humanity at large, the biblical God is conjoined with Christ, and the promised land of pure dominion partly becomes a kingdom at the end of time.[51] Paul's core rules for Christians

---

possible to meet before a death penalty would be warranted, P. Tomson, *Paul and the Jewish Law,* 102; L. Epstein, *Sex Laws,* 211.

49. Philo's divided God of enlightenment and God of wrath is discussed in chapter seven.

50. It remains in debate whether some Hellenistic Jews and early Christians such as Paul actively sought to put persons to death within the religious community for defying God's core regulations; and if so, whether they took matters into their own hands like a lynch mob, submitted the matter to a due judicial process in which cooler heads might prevail, or felt satisfied with calling down death curses on the rebels. See T. Seland's worthwhile study on the question, *Establishment Violence in Philo and Luke: A Study of Non-Conformity to the Torah and Jewish Vigilante Reactions* (1995), along with the reviews by G. Sterling (1997, 368–70), D. Winston (1998, 372–4), and L. Feldman (1997, 154–5). It is not subject to question, however, whether ardent followers of God's laws supported the ideology that sexual and other nonconformists in the community should in theory be put to death through human and/or supernatural agency, for this they undeniably urge, as I discuss below (nn. 57 and 58). The debate turns only on how they lived by this violent word. I do not try to resolve this issue here. For my purposes, the animosity expressed toward sexually rebellious persons within the community suffices to show the strength with which Philo—and Paul too, as I later show—passionately upheld the terms of the Pentateuchal quid pro quo through their exhortations.

51. A. Segal (*Paul the Convert,* 158–69) has a good succinct discussion of Paul's apocalypticism.

to gain and retain hegemony in this domain, however, remain focused on eliminating practices of rebellious sexual fornication in the Gentile lands of the ancient Mediterranean. As argued here, Paul in his Christian mission strengthens the Pentateuchal prohibition against rebellious sexual fornication in three ways. He streamlines the prohibition into an unconditional format for all humanity to follow; he elevates its importance while setting aside other major aspects of biblical law; and he considers sexual intercourse in honor of other gods to be worse than nonsexual aspects of other-theistic worship or idolatry.

For two reasons, Paul's fervid sexual morality should not be regarded as a typical product of his being from a Hellenistic Jewish background. First, his zeal for the Lord was already extreme prior to his conversion to Christianity. On fire to uphold the Pentateuch in full, he persecuted Christians for deviating from it (Gal 1:13–14, Phil 3:5). Second, as a Christian he sustains and broadens his devotional zeal by reclassifying Gentiles as Israel and bearing an antipathy toward their polytheistic sexual mores that is modeled on the antipathy that the Prophets show toward the historical Israel's behavior of sexually fornicating in honor of other gods. These two features are key to understanding why Paul is severe and innovative in his insistence that sexual fornication must be driven from Gentile lands.

Paul believes that the violent terms of the Septuagint pact are true and apply universally to Gentiles as well as to God's historical people of Israel, Judah, and their descendants. God's realm is the known world, for all human beings are Israel, Gentiles and Jews alike (Rom 11:25–27). God is destined to bring his wrath against other-theistic sexual mores in the entirety of this domain. The Canaanites were but the first altercation in a much bigger battle about how human beings are to conduct themselves as religious agents sexually, reproductively, and in non-sexual respects. Paul accordingly teaches formerly Gentile Christians that they must abandon their hitherto traditional sexual worship of other gods. He tells the Corinthian Christians that God killed twenty-three thousand Israelites because of their sexually fornicating worship of alien gods and other acts of disobedience. The Corinthians must take heed of this example and abandon the gods to whom they used to direct their energy sexually, reproductively, and in other respects (1 Cor 10:8, 11–12). They also must remain vigilant to prevent others in their community from participating in such practices. If the Corinthian Christians are negligent, they too are destined for a horrible demise, just like the Israelites. Paul issues the same message to the Thessalonian Christian community. They must abstain from sexual intercourse in worship of other gods in order to avoid "the avenging Lord" (ἔκδικος κύριος) (1 Thess 4:6). The community in Rome receives notice as well. Paul states that God's wrath is emerging against some or all Gentiles for the sexual worship that they devote to their gods (Rom 1:18–27). The Roman community must refuse to have further dealings with such sexual practices or they too will be destroyed.

Paul does not recognize the Pentateuch's distinction between rebellious and nonrebellious sexual fornication. Christians on his view must unconditionally "flee from sexual fornication" (1 Cor 6:18), especially in the context of worshipping other gods.[52] He emphasizes this imperative by according fornication a prominent place in lists of vices that Christians must always avoid.[53] In order for sexually active Christians to comply with this imperative, they must make love strictly within the marriages that Paul deems to be sufficiently in the Lord, the parameters of which are demonstrated in the next section. Otherwise, they succumb to Satan (1 Cor 7:2–6). Paul is especially outraged by sexual fornication, as he indicates by his condemnation of the Christian man who makes love with the wife of the man's father (1 Cor 5:1–5).[54] Even without involving incest or adultery, sexual fornication constitutes surrender to Satan (1 Cor 7:5), and as such is unconditionally forbidden and rebellious. As Paul unequivocally declares, a man who sexually fornicates severs himself from the body of Christ (1 Cor 6:18). Paul does not distinguish between degrees of disobedient sexual fornication, as the Pentateuch does, because he is struggling to teach Christians that they must protect themselves and their children at all costs from the sexual and reproductive conduits of other-theistic worship that pervade their social world. To remain free of such Satanic influence, Christians must flee sexual fornication altogether and make love solely within the bounds of religiously acceptable marriage.[55]

Paul goes so far as to support the biblical principle of eliminating rebellious sexual fornicators in order to protect God's Christian people from divine retribution. His position about how to administer a death penalty is

---

52. Other Hellenistic Jewish and Christian writings similarly prohibit sexual fornication without mentioning any exceptions, *T 12 Patr* 3.11–4.11; Matt 15:19–20; Mark 7:21–23; Acts 15:20, 15:29, 21:25; 1 Tim 1:9–10; Rev 21:8, 22:15; and (with πορνεία first) Eph 5:3–5; *Didache* 3.3. *Barn* 19.4 too supports this position. See further B. Rosner, *Paul, Scripture, and Ethics*, 123–46, and G. Dautzenberg, "Φεύγετε τὴν πορνείαν (1 Kor 6, 18)," 271–98. It does not follow from these parallels, however, that Paul is in no respect unusual in how he conceptualizes and highlights the dangers of fornication. The position he adopts is highly distinctive in several major respects, as I argue in the next chapter.

53. For the unconditional command, see 1 Cor 6:18, 10:8; 1 Thess 4:3; and cf. 1 Cor 5:1–5. The vice lists appear in letters written by Paul and in his name at Gal 5:19–21, Col 3:5, 2 Cor 12:20–1, Eph 5:3–5, 1 Tim 1:9–10.

54. The biblical prohibition against adultery carries over into the New Testament, Matt 15:19 and Mark 7:22. Further, the adulterous woman in John 7:53–8:11 is told to "sin no more." Though Jesus pardons her in this tale, adultery remains a sin.

55. To Paul, in other words, marriage in the Lord "is an effective barrier against the demonic power of unchastity and the triumph of evil," W. Schrage, *The Ethics of the New Testament*, 204.

ambiguous, but undeniably harsh. In First Corinthians Paul judges that the man who fornicated with his father's wife must be sentenced to die (5:1–13, esp. 4–5, 13). As Paul makes clear, the sentencing applies to the man as an agent of sexual fornication (πορνεία), not as an adulterer or agent of incest, even though the man is both. Thus Paul's death sentence here cannot be regarded as a rare measure that applies only in the extreme case of incest and adultery. His judgment would be as stern were he to catch Christians sexually worshipping Aphrodite.[56] The terminology Paul uses in his death sentence, however, is ambiguous. The Corinthians must hand the man over to Satan "for the destruction of his flesh" (1 Cor 5:5). Paul perhaps means that the Corinthians must surrender the man to be put to death through supernatural and Satanic forces.[57] By this interpretation, the Corinthians must summon superhuman powers to bring about this end, but they themselves do not lay a violent hand on him.

It cannot be ruled out, however, that Paul aims to stir up zealots in the community to kill the man outright, problematic though such a procedure might be if Roman authorities were to find out. Deuteronomic precedent requires the death penalty, which Paul cites in delivering his condemnation. "Eliminate (ἐξάρατε) the wicked man from your midst" (1 Cor 5:13). Ἐξαίρω is the Septuagint euphemism for killing sexual apostates by human agency, such as stoning (Deut 17:2–7).[58] In other sectors of Hellenistic Ju-

---

56. As Paul states, unrepentant or "truth-suppressing" apostates are doomed to the wrath of God because of their sexually deviant worship practices, and they "deserve to die" as a result, Rom 1:18, 32. Revelation harbors similar violent sentiments, 2:18–29, esp. 22–23, and *Jubilees* does likewise, as mentioned above, 20.6, cf. 16.5–6.

57. Majority scholarly opinion favors that Paul calls for actual death to befall the man in some form, likely through supernatural agency, when he urges the Corinthian community "to hand such a man over to Satan for the destruction of his flesh" (παραδοῦναι τὸν τοιοῦτον τῷ Σατανᾷ εἰς ὄλεθρον τῆς σαρκός). "Die meisten erklären, es gehe um den Tod des so Verfluchten," W. Schrage, *Der Erste Brief an die Korinther* (1991), vol. 1, 376 n. 51. In addition to the numerous sources Schrage notes, see P. Tomson, *Paul and the Jewish Law*, 101–3; C. Senft, *La première épitre de saint Paul aux Corinthiens*[2] (1990), 73–4; W. Meeks, *The First Urban Christians*, 130; W. Orr and J. Walther, *1 Corinthians: A New Translation and Commentary* (1976), 188–9; C. K. Barrett, *A Commentary on the First Epistle to the Corinthians* (1968), 126; and T. Seland (who abstains from a verdict himself), *Establishment Violence*, 267–8.

58. Paul's command, ἐξάρατε τὸν πονηρὸν ἐξ ὑμῶν, is based on similar Deuteronomic commands, which follow the formula "you will eliminate the wicked man from your midst" (ἐξαρεῖς τὸν πονηρὸν ἐξ ὑμῶν αὐτῶν), Deut 17:7, 19:19, 22:21, 22:24, 24:7. This sentencing is synonymous with capital punishment, such as θανατῶσαι and λιθοβολήσουσιν αὐτήν . . . καὶ ἀποθανεῖται, Deut 17.7, 22.21, cf. 22:24 and ἀποθανεῖται, Deut 24:7. It is also worth recalling that the rabbinic tradition requires extensive precautionary measures before allowing any trial of a purported sexual fornicator, let alone the exacting of a death penalty. Paul, by contrast, delivers his condemnation (κέκρικα) based on hearsay alone, ὅλως ἀκούεται ἐν ὑμῖν πορνεία, 1 Cor 5:1–3. The rabbis likely came to insist on much greater procedural restraint before trying an alleged fornicator in part because they knew the deleterious

daism, further, the elimination of sexual apostates is required, just as the Pentateuch stipulates, and in several instances the prospective executioners are human rather than supernatural.[59] Finally, in Paul's phrase "the destruction of the [man's] flesh," the term used for "destruction" is ὄλεθρος, which has the same word root as the name Paul gives his angel of destruction in 1 Cor 10:10, ὁ ὀλοθρευτής, who sees to the massacre of the rebellious Israelites. Regardless of whether Paul has in mind a supernatural or conventional death penalty, and whether the Corinthians would have carried through his sentencing in any form, he unambiguously believes the Pentateuch's teaching that the man ought to be killed to avert the divine retribution to which the man has subjected the Christian collective through his sexual fornication. Paul is therefore deeply imbued with the Pentateuch's teaching that God's obedient people must take preemptive action to eliminate rebellious sexual fornicators in order to keep the community safe. Motivated by this antipathy toward agents of sexual defiance against God's

---

social effects of such precipitate judgments. Hence the competing and milder interpretation of what Paul means by his condemnation is in greatest likelihood erroneous. By this view, Paul hopes only to excommunicate or banish the sexual fornicator and perhaps to forgive him later. Scholars who opt for this interpretation (e.g., G. Fee, *The First Epistle to the Corinthians* [1987], 208–13, and R. F. Collins, *First Corinthians* [1999], 207) are engaged in a gallant but misguided effort to make Paul seem like a reasonable apostle of enlightenment in every respect. Rather than insisting, with G. Fee (212), that "Paul is on the ['restorative love'] side of things," such that he must have forgiven the man, interpreters of this passage should seriously question why Paul unconditionally opposes forgiveness when faced with sexual fornication, why he thinks the man must be extirpated through supernatural or possibly even human agency. The terms of God's Pentateuchal quid pro quo, as adapted by Paul for Christians, amply accounts for why he is so quick and resolute about condemning the man.

59. *Jubilees*, which dates to ca. 170–150 B.C.E., likewise insists that a man who makes love to his father's wife must be put to death through stoning by the community. "To eternity there is no expiation to atone for the man who has done this; but he is to be put to death, to be killed, and to be stoned and uprooted from among the people of our God," 33:13. *Jubilees* would have the woman put to death as well, 33.10. This is precisely the situation Paul addresses in 1 Cor 5.1–5. For a man to make love to his father's wife is forbidden under penalty of the death-bearing curse in Deut 27:20 and under penalty of death in Lev 18:8, 29. Philo similarly urges that persons he deems to be sexual apostates should be put to death. Prostitutes among the Lord's people, whom he considers to be apostates, should be "stoned to death," *Spec* 3.51, and stoning implies human agency. Philo also forthrightly states that men who engage in homoerotic sexual relations "are worth killing by those who obey the Law" (φονᾶν ἄξιον νόμῳ πειθαρχοῦντας), *Spec* 3.38. More ambiguously regarding whether human agents are to do the killing, Philo further insists that men and women who have sexual intercourse with animals also "must die" (θνηκέτωσαν) along with the animals, *Spec* 3.49–50. Adulterers similarly "must be punished with death" (κολαστέον θανάτῳ), *Spec* 3.11, 58. Philo advocates these harsh measures similarly because of the quid pro quo in the Pentateuch, as shown in chapter seven. As he sees it, the Pentateuch unconditionally requires the penalty of death for these practices (Lev 18:22–23, 29, 20:13, 15–16; Exod 20:13; Deut 5:17) to keep the community safe and sound.

will, he introduces this preemptive measure to Christianity as an unavoidable necessity for the collective good.

Paul, moreover, makes the Corinthian man's death sentence sound like a merciful and prudent measure for everyone concerned, the fornicator's included. In this respect he offers a radically different version of Deuteronomy's offer to choose monotheistic life over retributive death (Deut 30:15–20). So long as the Corinthians hand the man over to Satan for his destruction in the flesh, they do so to ensure that the man's "spirit be saved on the day of the Lord" at the resurrection (1 Cor 5:5). Their action provides the same assurance for themselves. To Paul, Christians would be negligent fools to throw away eternal life by tolerating fornicating sexual deviants among them. The life that matters most starts with the resurrection, unlike this transient life of the flesh, in which death is mere sleep until the grand awakening.[60] The Pentateuch, by contrast, does not suggest that the sexual apostates themselves benefit by their death, for it does not share Paul's conception of the resurrection. In the Pentateuch the advantage falls strictly to the community through the people's restoration to God. The corpses of the sexual apostates lie there for the benefit of the repentant survivors, not of themselves.[61] Paul therefore renews and strengthens the mandate that God's people must bring about the demise of sexual apostates. Among Christians in Gentile lands, the only good fornicators are dead ones, and it is good for them to be dead. Paul thus makes it possible, in theory, for Christians to wish with a clear conscience that fornicators in their midst meet their redemptive demise, and possibly even to take action to make that wish come true. Regardless of whether the death-bearing agent is demonic, human, or both, by Paul's teaching the hooded executioner is an angel of mercy.[62]

Even though Paul deplores the sexual abominations condemned in the

---

60. 1 Cor 15:1–28, with the dead described as sleeping at 1 Cor 15:18.

61. In Leviticus the people prevent the land from becoming enraged at them and from having God punish them as he punished the Canaanites, Lev 18:8, 24–30. In Deuteronomy God is portrayed as being determined to wipe out the members of God's people who pursue other gods, just as he claims to have done against the forbidden tribes, Deut 7:1–10, 8:18–19. The death penalty requires two or three witnesses of the alien worship committed, Deut 17:2–7. The didactic aim of these extremely severe penalties is to enforce religious obedience in the interest of greater prosperity, Deut 30:15–20, 31:16–23.

62. This Pauline position is at odds with the Gospel teaching of unconditional forgiveness and mercy in the face of wrongdoers, Matt 5:38–48. John 7:53–8:11 extends this principle even to adultery, as previously discussed. This unqualified principle of forgiveness is almost certainly an authentic teaching of Jesus, R. Funk, R. Hoover, et al., *The Five Gospels: The Search for the Authentic Words of Jesus* (1993), 143–47. If it is authentic, this would indicate that Jesus, like Aeschylus in the *Oresteia*, appreciates the problem of retributive violence and terror, and strives to counteract it as part of his life's work. Paul, by contrast, has not shaken free of the retributive vendetta against sexual fornicators and carries the doctrine over into Christianity through his letters.

Pentateuch, such as homoeroticism on grounds that he elaborates from Leviticus,[63] the danger of sexual fornication has much higher priority in his mission. He inveighs against homoeroticism but once in his letters,[64] while he repeatedly denounces fornication. This is because Paul's pinnacle of religious sexual danger remains, as in the Pentateuch, a heterosexual deviance—a male among God's people making love to a biblical harlot,[65] as Paul describes her (1 Cor 6:16–18), not a man making love to another man or a woman to a woman, though these also offend his conception of God's sexual mandate.

Paul elevates his prohibition against sexual fornication by his screening of other Pentateuchal rules. By the time he comes to avow that Jesus is the Christ, or savior, and takes this distinctive message of the Lord to the Gentiles,[66] he regards fundamental features of the Pentateuch as not binding on formerly Gentile Christians, such as the dietary laws and male circumcision. Extensive sections of the Pentateuch, in fact, do not carry over into the regulations that he presents to Christians in his letters.[67] Paul does not relent

63. The Pentateuch itself leaves female homoeroticism unmentioned and unregulated. On Paul's antipathy toward male and female homoerotic sexual behavior and its limited connection with Leviticus, see B. Brooten, *Love between Women*, 247–58, and P. Stuhlmacher, *Paul's Letter to the Romans: A Commentary* (1994), 37.

64. This is not to downplay that Paul's antihomoerotic comments in Romans 1:26–27 have had a long and pernicious influence in Western culture, as B. Brooten shows, *Love between Women*, 189–357.

65. For the meaning of "biblical harlot," see chap. 6, 165–72. Even though Paul elsewhere carefully insists that Christian widows marry "in the Lord" (1 Cor 7:39), it is interesting that here he makes a fearsome emblem of the danger posed by a Christian man entering into an intimate relationship with a biblical harlot, not the reverse—a Christian woman with a religiously alien man. The Pentateuch, by contrast, highlights both aspects in its warnings, such as Deut 7:3–4: "You must not intermarry with [the nations whom I am driving out before you]. You will not give your daughters to their sons nor take their daughters for your sons; if you do, . . . the Lord will be angry with you and will destroy you straightaway" because of the alien worship involved in the marital relationships, cf. Exod 34:16. Like Paul, however, 2 Esdr 10:10–11 and 1 Esdr 9:7–10 stress the problem of male members of God's people taking religiously alien women as wives—in this case women from among the tribes in the land, with whom marriage was forbidden.

66. Regarding Jesus Christ, I do not venture into the historical Jesus question, and for the most part deal strictly with the Christ figure as promoted by Paul and others, aside from several comparative points made in the notes about the teaching of Paul about sexual fornication and likely teachings of Jesus on the subject. The relationship between the historical Jesus and the Christ figure generates a steady flow of worthwhile studies, a few of which are P. Fredriksen, *From Jesus to Christ*[2] (2000), 18–64, 133–215; G. Dawes, ed., *The Historical Jesus Quest: Landmarks in the Search for the Jesus of History* (2000); and R. Funk, R. Hoover, et al., *The Five Gospels*, 24–34.

67. Paul's principle of selecting which biblical rules to keep and which to set aside probably depends on a proto-Mishnaic teaching that Gentiles should uphold the Noahide commandments, not biblical law in its entirety, as argued by M. Bockmuehl, "The Noachide Command-

at all, however, regarding monotheistic sexual obedience. Thus the liberty Paul thinks Christians have gained from following biblical law he does not extend to sexual and reproductive behavior (Rom 7:4–6). Instead he intensifies this prohibition by repeatedly presenting it in unconditional terms. Paul's letters consequently portray God more as though he were the monotheistic chief of an antifornication vice squad. The Pentateuchal God, by contrast, is not quite so fixated on his people's sexual behavior, because he has numerous matters of holiness to oversee: diet, war, circumcision, the Sabbath and other holy days, the arts of proper sacrifice, tabernacle-building, and so forth. The God whom Paul reshapes for Christians to follow has fewer regulatory functions. Central among God's remaining tasks is to keep watchful surveillance on Christian patterns of sexual and reproductive conduct.

Paul uses strong imagery to stress the threat that sexual fornicators pose for the security and integrity of the Christian community. Christian bodies, he states, are the temple of the holy spirit and fornication is a sin "against the body" (1 Cor 6:18–19), not unlike the desecration of a temple.[68] Nonsexual transgressions do not bear this pivotal danger.[69] Even though nonsexual sins are wrong, they are less intimately threatening because they are "outside the body," such as the transgression of Christians litigating in a pagan court (1 Cor 6:18, cf. 1 Cor 6:1–11). Further, if Christians are lax

---

ments and New Testament Ethics with Special Reference to Acts 15 and Pauline Halakhah" (1995), 72–101. Nonetheless, as demonstrated in the following chapter, the Noahide prohibition list itself does not explain why Paul gives the prohibition against sexual fornication top priority. Bockmuehl ("The Noachide Commandments," 98) states that prohibiting sexual idolatry is most fundamental for Paul simply because it is the most pressing issue confronting any missionary for the biblical God in Gentile culture. This explanation is on the right track but not sufficient. As E. P. Sanders notes (*Paul, the Law, and the Jewish People* [1983], 95), Paul's sexual prohibition at 1 Cor 6:15–20 "goes beyond Jewish law and is based on his interpretation of union with Christ." See too B. Rosner, *Paul, Scripture, and Ethics*, 130–7; W. Schrage, *The Ethics of the New Testament*, 172–4; and A. Schweitzer, *The Mysticism of Paul the Apostle* (1931), 125–30. In the next chapter I develop the great significance of this point in connection with Paul's striking adaptation of the Prophets' sexual poetics of monotheism.

68. B. Byrne ("Sinning against One's Own Body: Paul's Understanding of the Sexual Relationship in 1 Corinthians 6:18" [1983], 613) notes the strong sexual overtones in Paul's conception of "sinning against the body" and R. Kirchhoff (*Die Sünde gegen den eigenen Leib: Studien zu πόρνη und πορνεία in 1 Kor 6,12–20 und dem sozio-kulturellen Kontext der paulinischen Adressaten* [1994], 104–98) provides a careful study of this question as well. B. H. Throckmorton ("The ναός in Paul" [1982], 500–1) further explains Paul's claim that fornication is a sexual sin against the body as temple.

69. B. Fisk (*"Porneuein* as Bodily Violation: The Unique Nature of Sexual Sin in 1 Cor 6:18" [1996], 541, 544, 550) similarly recognizes that Paul situates the act of sexual fornication in a class of transgression and danger by itself. In conjunction with this point, Fisk also rightly sees that by πᾶν ἁμάρτημα, Paul means that "every other sin" besides fornication is "outside the body" because other sins do not involve the degree and kind of violation that Paul assigns to fornication alone.

about allowing fornicators in the community, then a pollutant permeates the whole community, which Paul visualizes as a yeast that pervades the entire loaf of bread (1 Cor 5:6–8). If, however, Christians show no tolerance toward sexual fornicators in their midst, they will be a pure, unleavened bread that no yeast as foreign ingredient can pervade.[70] Like the Prophets, Paul makes free use of metaphors to teach the norm of biblical monotheism. Flee from sexual fornication or else you desecrate your body as temple, and the community becomes an impure bread of death rather than the pure bread of life.

Paul's hostility toward other-theistic sexual fornication and its putative dangers is all the more noteworthy insofar as the biblical prohibition against idolatry does not adequately explain it. He regards sexual intercourse and procreation for other gods to be far worse than other nonsexual aspects of other-theistic or idolatrous worship. Though he continues to forbid Christians from worshipping other gods (1 Cor 10:14), just as the Pentateuch and Prophets do for God's historical people, he adopts a divergent stance on two equally idolatrous practices: dining on food and drink in worship of alien gods, as opposed to making love in worship of them. Regarding sacrificial food and drink, Paul maintains in principle that Christians must not dine "at the table of demons" (1 Cor 10:21), yet he tempers this stance considerably. Christians may partake of food offered to idols, but only so long as they are not expressly informed about its identity as a religiously alien offering. If they are so aware, they should abstain, but the matter is not a critical concern.[71] As he responds to the Corinthian Christians, "Food will not dedicate you to God. We are neither left behind if we do not eat nor do we prevail if we do eat" food offered to alien gods (1 Cor 8:8). When it comes to sexual intercourse in worship of other gods, however, Paul's stance dif-

---

70. Paul here assimilates the Pentateuchal command to eat unleavened bread for Passover with his notion that sexual fornication taints God's people with the pollutant of yeast, 1 Cor 5:6–8, cf. Exod 13:3–7, and note further W. Schrage, *Der Erste Brief an die Korinther*, vol. 1 (1991), 378–85.

71. Paul "only says that one may eat anything without inquiring into the possibility of its being previously sacrificed to idols. Though food itself is neutral and there is no need to inquire about its origins, one is expected to abstain if the food is somehow identified as idol food," A. Cheung, *Idol Food in Corinth: Jewish Background and Pauline Legacy* (1999), 297, 82–162. Cheung's interpretation here is more restrictive than the predominant scholarly interpretation. By the predominant view, Paul is very lenient about Christians dining on food and drink offered to other gods, but thinks Christians should abstain from doing so only if they are with weaker fellow Christians who have not yet become accustomed to Paul's position that to ingest such sacrificial food and drink poses no danger to their faith (1 Cor 8:7–13, cf. Rom 14:20). My point is even stronger if the prevalent interpretation were to be vindicated against Cheung's, for then there is a vast discrepancy between Paul's unconditional stance against sexual intercourse in honor of other gods and his completely laissez faire stance toward dining in the gods' honor.

fers radically. Christians under no circumstances are to politely ignore whether their sexual relations are in honor of gods other than the Lord, for to do so would be a reckless eliciting of divine retribution. Though "food is there for the belly and the belly is there for food," he contrasts this dictate by adding that "The human body, though, belongs not to sexual fornication but to the Lord, and the Lord belongs to the human body" (1 Cor 6:13).[72] To Paul, then, it is a comparatively minor matter whether Christians occasionally dine on sacrificial food devoted to other gods, but it is a pressing concern that their acts of sexual intercourse never be devoted to gods other than or in addition to the Lord. Hence, regarding the worship of other gods, heterosexual copulation perturbs and provokes him far more than the dining does, even though both are of the body and other-theistic. Since both practices are equally idolatrous, the danger of idolatry per se does not sufficiently explain Paul's alarmist stance against fornication. Why he singles out and elevates the danger of other-theistic sexual intercourse as he does is an important topic that remains to be explored in the following chapter.

PAUL'S PRINCIPLE OF RELIGIOUS ENDOGAMY

Paul upholds the Septuagint principle of religious endogamy and its strict protectionism, though he imparts an inchoate Christian direction to it. He also pragmatically adapts this principle in First Corinthians to accommodate a common situation in his early Christian mission—the religiously hybrid union that develops when one Gentile spouse converts to Christianity before the other spouse does.

Paul distinguishes between two kinds of married couples in his missionary communities. There are couples who are fully married by virtue of both being in the Lord,[73] and there are those who are not yet in this preferred

72. Even if this sentiment in 1 Cor 6:13 reflects a Corinthian Christian adage, it is one with which Paul agrees in 1 Cor 8:8. Though G. Fee (*First Epistle to the Corinthians* [1987], 383) thinks that 1 Cor 8:8 reflects a Corinthian adage, he grants that the sentiment "fully accord[s] with Paul's own point of view."

73. Paul's conception of eligible prospective spouses definitely excludes as yet unregenerate Gentiles. It is not clear, however, whether Paul after his conversion would have deemed Jews and non-Christian God-fearers to be religious aliens whom Christians should avoid marrying. It seems questionable whether he would have regarded Jews as alien, for his own cultural and religious heritage is Jewish, as he proudly states, Phil 3:4–6. In the early days of Paul's mission, further, the number of persons in Christ would have been small relative to the number of unmarried persons in the bigger and more established populace of Jews and God-fearers. Thus, if Paul were pragmatic, he would have allowed unmarried Jews and God-fearers to marry persons in Christ, and it is not clear how sharp of a difference he would have made between the three groups. Paul, however, offers no comment—neither antipathy nor a favorable disposition toward the forming of marriages between Christians and Jews or God-fearers. This question therefore must be kept open. To keep it open, I refer to Paul's marital norm as mar-

devotional class of marriage. In the second group only one spouse per couple has thus far converted to Christianity from a preexisting condition of being polytheistic worshippers of Greek and other gods.[74] Only the first group receives Paul's more honorific label "the married" (οἱ γεγαμηκό-τες); the others are "the rest" (οἱ λοιποί) (1 Cor 7:10–15). In the case of "the rest," because the couples were Gentiles at the time they wed, ancestral gods recognized their marriage and any childbearing done so far. These domestic partnerships remain at risk, for one spouse in each couple remains polytheistic and may teach his or her children to carry on this tradition. To Paul's mind, the families in question nonetheless show considerable promise of becoming fully rehabilitated, for the Christian spouse is obliged to make an effort to save the unconverted spouse and children.[75] Paul accordingly considers "the rest" to be in transition toward full Christian marriage. In the interim, however, he makes a hierarchical division between the two groups of couples. Only "the married" are fully married in the Lord, so only they must heed Jesus' absolute prohibition against divorce. The marriages of "the rest," however, are not unconditionally binding (1 Cor 7:10–11, 15), for their marriages are not yet fully genuine to Paul's mind, infiltrated as their sexual and domestic life still is by other gods of sex, birth, the household, and the public sphere. If the Gentile spouses do not consent to remain married to their Christian partners, then Christians have Paul's permission

---

riage "in the Lord" or with a similar paraphrase. By this I mean that Paul requires Christians who choose to be sexually active to marry a person recognized within their religious community as one of their own. The prospective spouses would be Christian or possibly Jewish or God-fearing, but exclude as yet unconverted Gentiles.

74. Patristic writers clearly grasp this point. As Ambrosiaster states (*comm in Rom* 81.75–6), Paul is dealing with "the case of two Gentiles, one of whom has become a believer." Similarly, Severian of Gabala maintains that "Paul does not mean that one should marry an unbeliever, only that one should stay with [an unbeliever] if already married," K. Staab, ed., *Pauluskommentare aus der griechischen Kirche: Aus Katenenschriften gesammelt und herausgegeben.* (1933), 250, both citations first taken from G. Bray, *1–2 Corinthians* (1999), 64. The same understanding holds true of early-twentieth-century commentaries that date back to the time when Christian scholars still felt no qualms about referring to Gentiles as "heathen." "There were some who had married before their conversion and now had a heathen wife or a heathen husband," A. Robertson and A. Plummer, *A Critical and Exegetical Commentary on the First Epistle of St. Paul to the Corinthians*[2] (1914), 141. A number of more recent commentaries fail to reflect this precision. To name but one instance, H. Conzelmann (*First Corinthians* [1975], 121) simply states that "the rest" are "Christians living in a Christian/pagan mixed marriage" without further specifying that these marriages were in origin purely religious alien unions that have become mixed through the conversion of one spouse to Christianity before the other, not marriages formed by a dedicated polytheistic bride marrying a Christian bridegroom or vice versa.

75. Early Christians were taught that converted spouses must strive to win their entire family for the Lord alone, including their now religiously alien spouses, cf. Hermas *Vis* 1.3.1–2, Tertullian *Uxor* 2.7. Hence such marriages are worth keeping intact from Paul's perspective, except in instances where the unconverted spouse refuses to cooperate and leaves.

to let that union dissolve. Finally, Paul sees need to reassure the Christian spouses among "the rest" that the religious danger emanating from their partners is defused by special dispensation. In these already existing marriages the Christian spouse sanctifies the Gentile spouse and thus neutralizes the danger that the intimate yet alien partner would otherwise pose to the Christian spouse and community at large (1 Cor 7:14). The bona fide "married" couples, by contrast, require no such reassurance, for these marriages fully meet Paul's standard of genuine marriage. There are no alien deities stirring the sheets of their marriage bed.

Though Paul extends a special dispensation to already formed Gentile marriages that become halfway Christian and promise to do so fully, he does not allow Christians to marry unregenerate Gentiles. Paul commands that many Christians "marry" ($\gamma\alpha\mu\epsilon\acute{\iota}\tau\omega\sigma\alpha\nu$) (1 Cor 7:9, 36, cf. 7:2).[76] By this imperative he means, as his own phrasing suggests, that they should join the preferred ranks of "the married" ($o\acute{\iota}\ \gamma\epsilon\gamma\alpha\mu\eta\kappa\acute{o}\tau\epsilon\varsigma$) by avoiding polytheistic partners and marrying a co-religionist in the Lord. First, Paul presumes that single Christians who marry must find the right balance between engaging in devotional prayer to the Lord and in marital sexual relations. The sexual activity serves the cooperative purpose of keeping Satan at bay (1 Cor 7:5). If Christians marry Gentiles, however, the Gentile spouses cannot carry out either of these two tasks. The couple can neither pray together in Christian monotheism nor ward off Satan through practices of sexual intercourse dedicated to God through Christ. Gentiles would not have heard of Satan, let alone vest the enormity of importance in keeping him at a distance that Paul and his fellow believers do. Only Christians who marry fellow constituents of God's people can pray and make love in the manner Paul requires of newly made marriages. Second, Paul expressly states that Christian widows may remarry "only in the Lord," that is, only with a man whom her religious community recognizes as belonging to their group (1 Cor 7:39).[77] Paul therefore makes it clear that the marriages he allows Christians to make must abide by his transformative conception of biblical endogamy: The marriages must be indissoluble unions of Christians married to Christians (or possibly to other members of God's people) or else to Gentiles who convert to being in the Lord. Single and widowed Christians who wish to be sexually active must marry only within this Pauline branch

---

76. Paul prefers sexual abstinence among especially committed Christians such as himself, but he does not require the practice, for he thinks that most Christians are not strong enough to remain sexually abstinent in their devotion to Christ. This topic, which has been much discussed in relation to Paul's evaluation of marriage, is not important for my argument here. D. Horrell concisely discusses the issue, *The Social Ethos of the Corinthian Correspondence: Interests and Ideology from 1 Corinthians to 1 Clement* (1996), 158–9, and E. Castelli provides an extensive bibliographical note on the relevant scholarship, "Asceticism and History in Paul" (1999), 183 n. 5.

77. W. Meeks, *The First Urban Christians*, 162–3.

of biblically monotheistic faith, make love only with their spouses, and rear children devoted to God alone.[78] The sanctions against transgressive mixing are great. If Christians willfully pair off with unregenerate polytheists, they commit sexual fornication by reverting to polytheistic religious mores, and they and their children are damned. Religiously defiant marriages of this sort are unacceptable in the Christian community because they provoke the wrath of "the avenging Lord," if not immediately, then at the more pivotal end of time.[79]

A passage in Second Corinthians shows the fervid anger early Christians could summon against Christians marrying Gentiles. Paul likely wrote this passage, but its authorship remains disputed. Regardless of whether he wrote it, borrowed it, or someone else inserted it,[80] its marital principle is substantively the same as the one Paul promotes in First Corinthians: Be Christian and marry a fellow member of God's people if you plan to marry.[81] Second Corinthians 6:14–7:1 forbids "believers" (πιστοί), who are members of God's people, from "entering into alien unions with unbelievers" (μὴ γίνεσθε ἑτεροζυγοῦντες ἀπίστοις).[82] The unions of primary concern

---

78. Over time, however, the Christian marriage rule hardens to become more exclusively for Christians only. By the late fourth century, Christians who marry must marry Christians or Gentiles who convert to Christianity; Theodosian law prohibits Jews and Christians from marrying each other. *Ne quis Christianam mulierem in matrimonio Iudaeus accipiat neque Iudaeae Christianus coniugium sortiatur. Nam si quis huiusmodi admiserit, adulterii vicem commissi huius crimen optinebit, libertate in accusandum publicis quoque vocibus relaxata, C.Th.* 9.7.5, and see further C. Haas, *Alexandria in Late Antiquity: Topography and Social Conflict* (1997), 122.

79. Ignatius of Antioch holds the same position on the basis of First Corinthians. He distinguishes sharply between marriages in Christ the Lord (γάμος κατὰ κύριον) and religiously alien marriages, which he refers to as γάμος κατ' ἐπιθυμίαν, "marriage in accordance with the forbidden desire" to religiously mix with Gentiles and perhaps any non-Christians in marriage *(ad Pol* 5.2). (I explicate this meaning of ἐπιθυμία later in this chapter). According to Ignatius, only marriages "in the Lord" are permissible and have the bishop's blessing, H. Rathke, *Ignatius von Antiochien und die Paulusbriefe* (1967), 28–39, and W. Schoedel, *Ignatius of Antioch: A Commentary* (1985), 272–3. For the consistent severity from late antiquity onward of the Christian prohibition of religious intermarriage, see, for example, L. Epstein, *Marriage Laws in the Bible and the Talmud* (1942), 183 n. 118, who sums up the salient evidence, and M. Wiesner-Hanks, *Christianity and Sexuality,* 256.

80. On the contested authorship of 2 Cor 6:14–7:1, see W. Walker, "The Burden of Proof in Identifying Interpolations in the Pauline Letters" (1987), 610 n. 2. V. Furnish (*II Corinthians* [1984], 375–83) judiciously sorts through the debated authorship issues involved, and leaves the question undecided. Scholarly opinion is more recently swaying in favor of Pauline authenticity, J. Lambrecht, *Second Corinthians* (1999), 122–8.

81. 2 Cor 6:14–7:1 differs from 1 Corinthians 7 (and from 1 Cor 7:13–14 in particular) only insofar as the former deals strictly with the making of marriages and does not address the status of marriages that become mixed through the conversion of one spouse before the other.

82. W. Webb, "Unequally Yoked Together with Unbelievers. I. Who are the Unbelievers (ἄπιστοι) in 2 Corinthians 6.14?" (1992), 27–44.

are religiously pluralistic marriages that lead to the syncretistic worship of alien gods.[83] "The believers" and "the unbelievers" are portrayed as though they were different religious species that must never be paired off together to copulate and reproduce hybrids. The participle ἑτεροζυγοῦντες refers primarily to the making of marriages, as opposed to other kinds of unions, for it applies a rule against mixed animal breeding in Leviticus 19:19 to

---

83. W. Webb ("Unequally Yoked Together with Unbelievers. II. What is the Unequal Yoke [ἑτεροζυγοῦντες]?" [1992], 179) concludes that ἑτεροζυγοῦντες refers to "any activity that forms a covenant-like bond with pagans and their idols," and this interpretation is supported by C. K. Barrett, among others, as discussed by V. Furnish (*II Corinthians,* 327). Entering into a mixed Christian-Gentile marriage, however, is the primary instance of the bond forbidden by the imperative μὴ γίνεσθε ἑτεροζυγοῦντες ἀπίστοις. The second element of ἑτεροζυγοῦντες is cognate with ζεύγνυμι, which refers to the "yoke" binding husband and wife together in marriage, LSJ II.2. In the ancient world, weddings and the practice of marital sexual intercourse are the paradigmatic instance of entering into a partnership, as indicated by the Greeks with the verb stem ζυγ-, to "yoke," which the Latin etymology of "con-*jug*-al" (viz., "being yoked together") similarly indicates. The author of 2 Cor 6:14–7:1 may also be prohibiting other kinds of partnerships, such as a shared business, but these are secondary to the primary concern with the enterprise of marriage and reproduction. Webb's objections ("What is the Unequal Yoke?" 167–73) to interpreting ἑτεροζυγοῦντες to refer primarily to mixed marriages are not cogent. In his first two objections he fails to recognize that Paul prohibits the *making* of religiously mixed marriages (as opposed to allowing mixed marriages to continue after one spouse converts to Christianity); his third objection is mistaken because it assumes that there is a "delayed nature" (171) to other-theistic practices in mixed marriages, which would allow newlywed Christians time to avoid falling into the worship of the gods revered by their new spouses. This is false in relation to ancient Greek practices, for the wedding itself and its preliminaries, such as the προτέλεια γάμων and the ἀνακαλυπτήρια, involve worshipping other gods, J. Oakley and R. Sinos, *The Wedding in Ancient Athens* (1993), 9–42; J. Oakley, "The Anakalypteria" (1982), 113–18; and V. Magnien, "Le mariage chez les Grecs," 305–20. As J. Toutain states in relation to the bride ("Le rite nuptial de l'anakalypterion" [1940], 349), "dans l'Antiquité grecque et romaine le mariage était, pour la fiancée, un acte religieux d'une importance considérable: le jeune fille . . . était admise, dès son arrivée dans la maison de son époux, au culte domestique de son nouveau foyer, ce qui constituait pour elle une veritable initiation." Fourth, Webb is not right to maintain that a prohibition against forming mixed marriages is too narrow a directive for Paul to address to the Corinthian Christian audience as a whole. From Paul's perspective, the rule is a pressing matter for the entire community to hear, especially parents with children who are likely to marry, as well as persons who are themselves in a position to marry. Webb's last objection very weak. He maintains that since 1 Corinthians 7 on marriage does not expressly raise the problem of idolatry in marriage, neither does 2 Cor 6.14. This objection fails because 1 Cor 8–10 deals at length with Paul's exhortation to avoid idolatry, and this exhortation would apply as a matter of course to the making of new marriages as well. Hence there is ample reason to regard the rule against being ἑτεροζυγοῦντες ἀπίστοις predominantly as a rule against forming religiously mixed marriages, and no reason whatsoever to doubt it. C. K. Barrett (*Second Corinthians* [1973], 196) is correct that the injunction means that "those addressed should avoid idolatry and moral defilement." My point is that for a Christian to inaugurate a new marriage with a Gentile is first on the list of forbidden types of idolatry and defilement.

spouse selection.[84] Leviticus 19:19 prohibits the mating of unlike animals. 2 Cor 6:14–7:1 recasts and extends this rule to mean that Christians should no more pair off with unconverted Gentiles than, say, sheep should mate with horses. Other striking imagery in 2 Cor 6:14–7:1 reaffirms this resolute marriage restriction by separating Christians from the lower species of idolatrous beast: Christians are vessels of righteousness, light, Christ, and the temple of God, while unbelievers are carriers of lawlessness, darkness, Beliar, and idols (2 Cor 6:14–16). Second Corinthians thus brings the fervor of Ezekiel or Hosea to the nascent social norm of Christian endogamy. Paul in 1 Corinthians 7 endorses the same substantive marriage rule,[85] though 1 Corinthians 7 uses less excitable rhetoric and is written more in the tone of marriage counseling.[86]

It is consequently a mark of deep historical confusion to portray the formative Christian idea of sexual fornication as though it refers simply to acts of sexual intercourse outside of marriage and classifies such relations as immoral because they are extramarital, such as premarital sexual activity among adolescents in the modern day. Paul's conception of sexual fornication refers to sexual intercourse that is for the most part marital but outside of the institution of marriage in the Lord, aside from the pragmatic dispensation he allows for transitional marriages that become mixed through the Christian conversion of one Gentile spouse before the other. He finds such relations immoral because they are religiously diversifying, not because they are extramarital.[87] Paul's stance on marriage is consequently one

84. On this precedent see also C. K. Barrett, *A Commentary on the Second Epistle to the Corinthians* (1973), 195.

85. Paul's advice about marriage in 1 Thess 4:3–8 is consistent with 1 Corinthians 7 and 2 Corinthians 6:14–7:1. O. Yarbrough (*Not Like the Gentiles*, 65–87) carefully explores the marital tenor of 1 Thess 4:3–8 and its concerns to keep sexual fornication out of the community.

86. C. K. Barrett (*Second Epistle to the Corinthians*, 192–7) and B. H. Throckmorton ("The ναός in Paul," 498–9) therefore remain correct that 2 Cor 6:14–7:1 may not be written by Paul but "does not express an unpauline view," as Barrett puts it, 197. H. D. Betz's argument that 2 Cor 6:14–7:1 is anti-Pauline is unpersuasive ("2 Cor 6:14–7:1: An Anti-Pauline Fragment?" [1973] 89, 88–108), because he omits mentioning the precedent for ἑτεροζυγοῦντες in Lev 19:19, even though 2 Cor 6:14–7:1 is interpreting this verse from Leviticus, and he instead maintains that "the 'yoke' of the πιστοί must be identical with the Torah," though neither Leviticus 19:19 nor Second Corinthians 6:14 is demonstrably relevant to τὸ ζυγόν meaning "Torah." Betz's argument, however, needs this relevance in order to be persuasive.

87. Scholars dealing with the Christian notion of sexual fornication consequently should cease defining it as "extramarital sexual relations" in relation to early Christianity. This definition, which occurs repeatedly in New Testament scholarship and elsewhere, is testimony to the conquest of Christian over polytheistic marriage norms in Western culture. Paul assumes that unless the marriage is acceptably within the range of being in the Lord, it is not a bona fide marriage and its marital sex is fornicating. Nonetheless he would never define sexual fornication as extramarital, for he is imbued with the biblically grounded view that sexual fornication is an intrinsic part of Gentile marriages and of newly made mixed marriages between Chris-

of fierce religious protectionism on par with the Prophets' own, albeit on different theological terms and in open new Gentile terrain.

Paul's norm of biblical endogamy proves revolutionary in relation to the traditional domestic and political culture of the Greeks and other Gentiles. In ancient Greek society, each city and its households provided the foundation, maintenance, and cultural existence of the gods and heroes. Central to these cities and their gods were the established local religious patterns of procreative relations among the citizens.[88] As Plato states, "one ought to beget children, for it is our duty to leave behind, for the gods, people to worship them" (*Laws* 773e5–74a1). Women and their reproductive bodies played a pivotal role in the household center of this Greek political system. Paul in his antifornication program aims to convert their bodies, domiciles, and cities into a new religious sphere with a far more centralized and exclusive focus on worshipping the biblical God alone through Christ.[89]

PAUL ON FORBIDDEN DESIRES AGAINST GOD'S WILL

Paul lends a psychological dimension of forbidden desire to the prohibitions he adapts from the Septuagint, such as his rule against sexual fornication. Transgressions against God do not simply include disobedient actions, but also the desire to commit such actions—the impulse itself, quite apart from whether one actually partakes of the forbidden activity. On this topic Paul is part of a broader Hellenistic Jewish and early Christian trend that stresses the danger of rebellious impulses very stringently.[90] In Matthew's

---

tians and Gentiles. As Wisdom 14:12 likewise states, "the invention of idols [viz., gods other than or in addition to the Lord] is the beginning of sexual fornication," and polytheistic marriage and reproduction are central to the problem (Wisd 13:17). Since Paul's time, however, Christianity has gained a monopoly over the very idea and practice of marriage in Western culture, on the grounds that unless the union is Christian, it cannot be marriage and instead is fornication. One result of this religious revolution in the marital sphere is that the semantic range of sexual fornication has shrunk, so that the term now seems a generic way to refer only to extramarital sexual intercourse. To name but a few of the ubiquitous instances in modern scholarship where sexual fornication is mistakenly defined or conceptualized as "extramarital" sexual intercourse in antiquity, see G. Dautzenberg, *Φεύγετε τὴν πορνείαν* (1 Kor 6, 18), 285 n. 62 (who cites, among others, H. Conzelmann and H. Balz); H. Crouzel, "Les sources bibliques de l'enkrateia chrétienne" (1985), 520; and J. Brundage, *Law, Sex, and Christian Society*, 58.

88. S. Pomeroy, *Families in Classical and Hellenistic Greece* (1997), 68–72, and J. Redfield and Fustel de Coulanges as cited by Redfield, "Notes on the Greek Wedding," 185.

89. The more organized and publicly political as opposed to domestic this sphere becomes through the church in its negotiations with the Roman imperial administration, the more its central power structure falls to men as the dominant religious functionaries.

90. H. D. Betz, *The Sermon on the Mount: A Commentary* (1995), 234–6; F. Büchsel, "*θυμός*, *ἐπιθυμία*," 169; B. Jackson, "Liability for Mere Intention in Early Jewish Law" (1975), 202–

Sermon on the Mount, for instance, adultery is no longer only an act of disobedient sexual behavior. When a man looks with desire at a woman who is forbidden to him as a sexual partner, he commits adultery "in his heart" (Matt 5:27–8), even if he does not make love to her. Paul as a missionary to the Gentiles, however, narrows the range of forbidden desire in the Hellenistic Jewish sense, which signifies that it is wrong to want to transgress any of the rules in biblical law, sexual and nonsexual alike. He thinks, as noted previously, that Christians must uphold but a few key Noahide rules from the Pentateuch (such as the prohibition against fornication), and not the Law in its entirely. The way Paul psychologizes sin is important to understand, for its anguished coloring plays a significant role in shaping the hairshirt ethos of ecclesiastical sexual morality, as we will later see.

Paul's understanding of wrongful "desire" (ἐπιθυμία) or wrongfully "desiring" (ἐπιθμεῖν) is thoroughly informed by a Hellenistic Jewish variant on the Septuagint Tenth Commandment. The variant is a two-word imperative οὐκ ἐπιθυμήσεις, which he cites and stresses in Romans 7:7 and 13:9. The Tenth Commandment in the Septuagint has the familiar lengthy form, which begins with the two-word imperative, οὐκ ἐπιθυμήσεις, followed by its complete set of direct objects, the neighbor's wife, house, field, servants, ox, and plow. This commandment in full prohibits men from coveting the people and goods belonging to other men in the community. It primarily protects the ownership privileges of male heads of the household (Exod 20:17, Deut 5:21). The persons and goods, wife included, are marked as inviolably a man's own insofar as other men must refrain even from wanting to take, let alone actually taking, any of them. In Hellenistic Jewish and early Christian exegesis, however, the phrase οὐκ ἐπιθυμήσεις occasionally stands on its own, as attested, for example, by Paul and Philo.[91] In this two-word form, the Tenth Commandment takes on a significance that subsumes and goes beyond coveting in the sense of "strongly desiring to possess." The newer prohibition teaches that it is wrong or sinful even to desire to act contrary to God's will. Adherents of the Lord must refrain from wanting to disobey God's laws in any respect, be it a coveting of another man's wife or plow, a longing to worship other gods, a yearning to toil on the Sabbath, or

---

15; and G. Moore, *Judaism in the First Centuries of the Christian Era: The Age of the Tannaim* (1927), vol. 2, 268–72.

91. The phrase οὐκ ἐπιθυμήσεις in Philo and Paul appears, respectively, at *Spec* 4.78 and Rom 7:7, 13.9. Note also 4 Macc 2:6, "the law says that we must not have desires (μὴ ἐπιθυμεῖν)" contrary to God, and *Didache* 3.3, "My child, do not become one who lusts (μὴ γίνεσθε ἐπιθυμητής)" against God's will, especially because such lust leads to religiously unacceptable sexual intercourse. For this sense of ἐπιθυμία and cognates, also see Num 11:34, Ps 105:14–15, Matt 5:27–8, John 8:44, Hermas *Vis* 1.1.8, 1.2.4, Ignatius, *Ad Pol* 5.2.

any inclination to transgress Pentateuchal regulations, whether or not the rebellious inclination involves coveting.

Paul's Christian didacticism is imbued with the Hellenistic Jewish sense of ἐπιθυμία as a wrongful inclination or impulse to transgress God's will. In 1 Thessalonians 4:3–5, he sternly reminds Christians that it is "the will of God" (τὸ θέλημα τοῦ θεοῦ) for them to refrain from sexual fornication. If they disobey, then they succumb to being "in the passion of desire" (ἐν πά-θει ἐπιθυμίας). The Thessalonian Christians suffer this sinful "passion of desire" not merely because they are heated with arousal, but because their sexual inclination is contrary to what God requires of them. They still want to engage in customs of sexual intercourse that the Lord forbids Gentile Israel to take part in, such as other-theistic copulation in the way of their ancestors.

In First Corinthians Paul likewise discloses that wrongful desire in his sense signifies an impulse to act contrary to his conception of God's will. He warns the Christians in Corinth not to be "those who desire wicked actions (ἐπιθυμηταὶ κακῶν)," by which he means the select Pentateuchal rules Christians must avoid: sexual fornication, idolatry, and resisting God's prophets or messengers (1 Cor 10:5–13). In this passage he teaches Christians these rules by drawing upon incidents in the Pentateuch that elicit divine punishment against disobedient Israel: the Israelites worshipping Aaron's golden calf (Exod 32:1–35), the Israelite men engaging in sexual fornication with the Moabite and Midianite women (Num 25:1–9), and the Israelite soldiers opposing Moses' orders (Num 14:1–39). Christians, as Paul's Israel, must learn to fear God from the negative example set by biblical Israel and its retributive suffering.[92] They must worship no gods but God, abandon practices of sexual fornication, and obey Paul's commands. In the Septuagint, however, the Israelites rebel against God only if they engage in the actions forbidden by the Pentateuch, while the Corinthians rebel against God simply by wanting to transgress Paul's more sexually specific compendium of Pentateuchal interdictions. The men sin against God if they even desire a forbidden woman, just as Flaubert's St. Antony later sins with desire despite himself when the Queen of Sheba captivates his gaze.[93]

---

92. M. Bockmuehl, "Noachide Commandments," 72–101, and W. Meeks, "'And Rose Up to Play': Mishnah and Paraenesis in 1 Corinthians 10:1–22" (1982), 64–78.

93. Paul's conviction that the desire to transgress is itself sinful later helps provoke Christian men to become monks in the desert and to fear divine retribution simply because they want to sexually fornicate. The Pentateuch differs considerably from Paul in this respect and does not promote such fear. Unlike the monks, the Israelites in the desert fear the repercussions of many transgressive actions, nonsexual and sexual alike. Though their proverbial stubbornness and contrary hearts are culpable (Exod 33:3, Deut 9:13), their desire to disobey the Lord is not itself the transgression that elicits retribution, whereas it is for the monks thanks in part to Paul's religious psychology of the wrongful desire to disobey God's orders.

The same principle holds true for Christian women in their desires for the forbidden. According to Paul, then, Christians who even want to make love in the religiously alienating wilderness outside of marriage in the Lord relegate themselves to the outer darkness of apostasy and destruction.

Paul also blames ἐπιθυμία in the sense "desire to disobey God" for sin that takes the form of rebellious action. In Septuagint Psalm 105, Paul notes, the apostate Israelites "felt wrongful desire (ἐπεθύμησαν ἐπιθυμίαν) in the wilderness" and thereupon "tested God in the desert" by their acts of transgression. Their foolish testing of God's resolve then led to their destruction by his hand.[94] To Paul this incident reveals two fundamental points: God means what he says in his vow to destroy the disobedient and save the obedient alone, and in order to avoid disobedience, God's people must avoid the stimulus of wrongful desire altogether. In short, they must obey Paul's aphoristic commandment οὐκ ἐπιθυμήσεις.[95] Paul enforces this commandment by making wrongful desire itself a sin.

In Romans 7:7–25, however, Paul expresses disbelief that mortals can obey οὐκ ἐπιθυμήσεις through their own will-power. As he sees it, the desire to transgress God's will is an overwhelming kind of contrary law in the bodily limbs of human beings, which struggles against the obedient "law of the mind" that worships God. The greater force of the bodily law enslaves human beings to the sin of wanting to defy God (Rom 7:23).[96] Paul accord-

---

94. Paul alludes directly to Septuagint Psalm 105:14 by his phrase "just as they [the Israelites] lusted (κἀκεῖνοι ἐπεθύμησαν ἐπιθυμίαν)" and "let us not tempt the Lord" (1 Cor 10:6, 9). Paul's fairly unusual noun form ἐπιθυμητάς at 1 Cor 10:6 similarly refers to and recalls another incident of God's retribution against disobediently desirous Israelites in Numbers 11. The apostates in Numbers 11 are destroyed as a "lustful people" (λαὸν ἐπιθυμητήν) (11:34) because of their persistent longing to rebel and return to Egypt, contrary to Moses' conception of God's will.

95. Hence Paul's notion of ἐπιθυμία is very much the antinomian inclination that H. Räisänen argues that it is ("Zum Gebrauch von ἐπιθυμία und ἐπιθυμεῖν bei Paulus" [1979], 85–99), so long as we understand by "antinomian" not deviance from biblical law as a whole, as opposed to deviance from the prescriptions that Paul takes from the Pentateuch and considers to be still binding on Christians. In my explication of Paul's commandment οὐκ ἐπιθυμήσεις, I support and extend J. Ziesler's important study ("The Role of the Tenth Commandment in Romans 7" [1988], 41–56), which itself builds from Räiäsenen and others. Ziesler (47–9, 52) somewhat overemphasizes the vestigial persistence of "coveting" in Paul's conception of desiring to act contrary to God's putative will, but he takes the important step of refuting the idea that Rom 7:7–25 deals with biblical law in general as opposed to the abbreviated Tenth Commandment in particular. J. Fitzmyer (*Romans* [1993], 466) similarly grasps this gist of Paul's imperative οὐκ ἐπιθυμήσεις, "Through such a commandment, the . . . conscience becomes aware of the possibility of the violation of the will of God so made known." Like Ziesler, however, Fitzmyer still thinks of the violation in an overly narrow way as a coveting of created things, even though coveting is but one aspect of desiring to disobey God's will.

96. As S. Stowers has persuasively argued ("Romans 7.7–25 as a Speech-in-Character (προσωποποιία)" [1995], 180–94), Romans 7:7–25 is a "speech in character" that pre-

ingly expresses considerable angst about the human condition, for he is convinced that these persistent wrongful desires subject God's people to a punitive state of being alienated from God, which he vividly describes as "the body of death" (Rom 7:24). Human beings are severed from God and hence dead because obeying οὐκ ἐπιθυμήσεις is simply out of their reach, even if their actions may achieve an outward show of piety. Paul sees only one route to freedom from this plight. Through Christ the Lord alone, people can be rescued from their servitude to the desires that Gods forbids. Thanks to Christ, Christian Israel is uniquely gifted to live by this commandment without any opposing impulses. Genuinely devoted Christians do not even want to question Paul's teachings. They submissively obey them in full.

Paul's conviction that human beings are utterly unable to obey οὐκ ἐπιθυμήσεις by their own will and discipline sets him apart from his Hellenistic Jewish background. No other known Jew or early Christian concurs with Paul on this matter.[97] The cardinal tenet of Judaism is that God is an eminently reasonable legislator whose laws both can and should be upheld in their entirety. As Deuteronomy states, "This set of commandments that I give to you today is not over burdensome or far from your reach" (Deut 30:11).[98] According to Paul, by contrast, people are uniformly abject slaves to the desires God forbids them to have,[99] so much so that Christ has had to intervene in order to make obedience and salvation possible. As signs of such enslavement, Paul's Christian communities have not yet submitted totally to his teachings. They still yearn to worship their native gods, to make

---

cludes a strictly autobiographical reading. He is also probably right that a number of formerly Gentile Christians likely would have understood Romans 7:7–25 to refer to a losing struggle of the mind over passion similar to that which Medea expresses on stage, Euripides, *Med*, 1056–80. Paul, however, is not referring to "acrasia" or "passion" in the same sense as Medea is. He is concerned with "passions" in the sense of "impulses that breach the didactic requirement to obey God's will to the full," whereas no Greek parallel on acrasia shares this biblically grounded goal, let alone Paul's conviction that retributive death follows upon the failure to control God-defying passions.

97. Philo, further, demonstrably disagrees that human will is slavishly unable to obey God's laws of its own accord, as I show in chapter seven.

98. Deut 30:11–14 in full is especially poetic and eloquent on this point, as are Septuagint Psalms 18 and 118: "This set of commandments that I give to you today, is not over burdensome or far from your reach. It is not up in the sky so that you say 'Who will go up to the sky and get it for us, so that we can hear it and act on it?' It is not across the sea so that you say, 'Who will cross the sea and get it for us, so that we can hear and act on it?' The words are very close for you to do, on your lips, in your hearts, and at your hands." See too Deut 4:2–10, 4:39–40, 6:4–9, 27:26.

99. J. Ziesler ("The Tenth Commandment," 41–2) further explores the distinctiveness of Paul's claim that the abbreviated Tenth Commandment brings about a kind of "moral paralysis."

love outside of marriage in the Lord, and to question Paul's authority. Still, as Christians, they have a decisive advantage over other branches of God's people, for they at least have received the interventionist grace that Paul considers necessary to obey οὐκ ἐπιθυμήσεις to the full. Only as obedient Christians will God's people finally drive desires for religious pluralism and sexual freedom far, far away from their formerly Gentile lands.

Paul's conception of wrongful desire (ἐπιθυμία), as I have argued, is grounded in his Greek biblical background and the Hellenistic Jewish goal to refrain even from wanting to transgress God's laws. It is consequently misguided to continue the Greek patristic habit of explicating Paul's notion of ἐπιθυμία as though it were directly informed by Plato's idea of the irrational appetite (ἐπιθυμία), the Stoic passion of excessive desire (ἐπιθυμία), or some combination of the two. Paul gives no indication of using or even knowing ἐπιθυμία in the Platonic or Stoic philosophical senses.[100] His conception of ἐπιθυμία as culpable desire is fully intelligible in terms of the Greek biblical background that informs his urgent concern to curtail the inclination to act contrary to God's will.[101] In this respect Paul differs markedly from Philo and Clement, even though his conception of forbidden desire helps shape and inform Clement's antipathy toward sexual desire, as is explained in chapter nine.[102]

100. New Testament lexica and related scholarship are prone to two habits that tend to obfuscate this fundamental point. First, they assimilate Paul's sense of ἐπιθυμία to ἐπιθυμία in the Stoic and/or Platonic philosophical senses, and, second, they present their assimilations as Paul's own. For example, F. Büchsel (*TDNT*, "θυμός, ἐπιθυμία," 169–71) asserts that "in Jewish Greek ἐπιθυμία and ἐπθυμεῖν can denote a sin. This usage is plainly dependent in part on the Stoic usage," and cf. BAGD, s.v. ἐπιθυμία. *Pace* Büchsel and the BAGD entry, the sin of ἐπιθυμία as Paul understands it can and should be explained strictly in Greek biblical terms, with no groundless assumptions that Paul must have drawn his sense of ἐπιθυμία from Stoic thought, even in part. As I have argued is the case for Romans 7 (and also for Psalm 105:14), the sin of ἐπιθυμία in Hellenistic Judaism and early Christianity is readily explicable as a religious psychology of sinfulness that is formulated by connecting the abbreviated Tenth Commandment with the problem of the entrenched rebelliousness of God's people, as Paul's interpretation illustrates in Romans 7. Neither the Stoics nor Plato have anything to do with this Pauline conception of ἐπιθυμία. This is not, of course, to deny that patristic writers later assimilate the Stoic and Platonic senses of ἐπιθυμία to Paul's, for they most definitely do, only that *we* should cease being uncritical recipients of the patristic tendency to bestow their Stoic and Platonic assimilations on Paul.

101. The Septuagint translations (excluding 4 Maccabees, which is not a translation) are themselves uninfluenced by Stoic, Platonic, and other Greek philosophy in their usage of ἐπιθυμία and cognates, as J. Freudenthal has shown long ago, "Are There Traces of Greek Philosophy in the Septuagint?" (1890), 205–22, and as J. Ziesler has more recently confirmed, "The Tenth Commandment," 46 nn. 15–18.

102. In chapters seven and nine, I demonstrate that Philo and Clement create highly innovative sexual principles in God's name partly by the way they conjoin the Platonic and Stoic senses of ἐπιθυμία with ἐπιθυμία in Paul's adapted Hellenistic Jewish sense.

CONCLUSION

In the Septuagint Pentateuch rebellious sexual fornication refers to heterosexual acts of copulation that deviate from biblical endogamy and from the closely related norm of worshipping God alone. Forbidden acts of sexual intercourse include marital intercourse with spouses who remain polytheistic, other sexual worship of alien gods, as well as adultery and incest. Not all fornication is apostasy, though, for the Pentateuch allows several exceptions. The Pentateuch's main regulatory concern in the sexual sphere is religiously diversifying intercourse and its ostensible dangers, even though male homoeroticism (in at least some copulating positions) and sexual activity with animals are also marked as rebellious in Leviticus.

Orgiastic sexual intercourse for alien gods forms the more salacious kind of religiously alienating fornication in the Pentateuch and Prophets, but religiously mixed marriages pose the more pressing and endemic problem. Religiously alien spouses and the mixed rearing of children are a conduit for the flow of alien worship into the community of people who are required to devote themselves strictly to God. In-laws and relatives among God's people are also implicated in the problem when they attend religiously mixed weddings and rituals of their children and grandchildren. Marriages of this sort provoke red-hot ire from Hosea, Ezekiel, and other persons of like mind, such as the author of 2 Cor 6:14–7:1, who may be Paul himself and who at least abides by the same doctrine of biblical endogamy that Paul presumes in 1 Corinthians 7. The prospect and perceived danger of marriage with polytheistic persons would have been relatively high in the social world of the Hellenistic cities, where numerous gods still retained cultural authority and the vast majority of the inhabitants were polytheistic. The Septuagint as Greek text was on the frontier in defending God's diaspora people from taking part in this religious melting-pot practice. It taught Jews and other persons who claimed identity as God's people that they must marry fellow believers, if they chose to marry, so that the weddings, marital relations, and other domestic and community rituals would show the single-minded devotion to God that the First Commandment requires.

The Septuagint Pentateuch offers a potent but morally problematic rationale for eliciting compliance with the First Commandment and its corollary of biblical endogamy across generations. God is said to promise his people security, prosperity, and dominion in the land he gives them as their patrimony in exchange for their exclusive devotion. The land of milk and honey is theirs in perpetuity so long as they cease to partake of polytheistic mores, especially in their sexual and reproductive behavior. If they fail to comply, however, especially by the marital sexual worship of other deities, God vows that he will disinherit and destroy many of them, just as he did to the Canaanites. Though many today would find this teaching misguided and dangerous if taken seriously, Paul found it true and too dangerous to ignore.

Paul regards the Greek biblical quid pro quo to be as indubitable and universal as the law of gravity. If members of God's Gentile Israel persist in the sexual worship of other deities, they will fall as surely as the apple that landed on Newton's head. The suffering instigated by "the avenging Lord" occurs either in this life, as the Prophets maintain, or in the even more permanent and precious afterlife, as Paul teaches. It would be hard to imagine a more potent formula for inculcating monotheistic sexual obedience, for it is fear-inducing; works at the formative social level of marriage, reproduction, and childrearing; and connects these sexual customs with dire consequences for deviating and with unsurpassed glory for compliance.

Paul reworks the Pentateuch's religious sexual program into his own highly restrictive code. Christians, he contends, must unconditionally "flee from sexual fornication," and this is the first and foremost of all the sexual and nonsexual transgressions they must avoid. Paul's antifornication marital principle, further, is easy to learn and the reward he promises is great: Christians who choose to be sexually active must take as a spouse a fellow member of God's people and then engage in marital sexual relations only. As their reward they and their children will be saved at the end of time. Paul allows only one grandfather clause to his nascent Christian rule of religious endogamy—the transitionally Christian marriage of "the rest." Christians who defy Paul's sexual rules, however, must in principle be extirpated by some ambiguous means for the putative good of all. If the community is so foolish as to turn a blind eye to sexual scofflaws, then they too are complicit in the defiance and are marked for judgment day.

According to Paul, it does not suffice for Christians to abstain from sexual intercourse in the worship of other gods and yet long for such ancestral mores. They must fully comply with his understanding of the commandment against forbidden desires (οὐκ ἐπιθυμήσεις). Christians alone, further, have received the ability to bend their will entirely in compliance with the Lord. Thanks to Christ's saving grace, obedient Christians do not look with desire even once, let alone twice or a third time, at the temples and rituals of the people they used to be, for there lies the dreaded way of fornication.

At this point we have come far in understanding the innovative gestalt of Paul's sexual morality, which is driven by his insistence that Christians must run away from sexual fornication foremost of all other-theistic dangers. The Pentateuch's sexual regulations on their own, however, fail to adequately motivate the emotive intensity of the restrictive sexual principles advocated by Paul and his patristic followers. To understand this extremely important dimension of early Christian sexual morality, we must turn to the sexual poetics of the Pentateuch, Prophets, and Paul.

Chapter 6

From the Prophets to Paul

*Converting Whore Culture
into the Lord's Veiled Bride*

Two didactic metaphors in the Pentateuch and Prophets exercise great emotive hold on Paul in his formulation of sexual rules for Christians to follow. The metaphors reinforce the requirement that God's people must obey his will sexually and in other respects, and that they must organize their society toward this end. I refer to the first metaphor as "spiritual fornication" and to the second as "spiritual adultery." Though it is common to see only one generic metaphor of fornication in the Old Testament, there are two and they have divergent implications for what it means to serve the Lord in sexual and nonsexual ways. The first metaphor appears in the Pentateuch and Prophets, while the second is exclusive to the Prophets and leaves an indelible signature on Paul's sexual ethic. Spiritual fornication uses sexual fornication as a symbol of religious disobedience, and it stigmatizes religiously alien women and dissident female members of God's people as harlots or whores. Spiritual adultery uses sexual adultery as a symbol of religious disobedience. It stigmatizes God's people, males and females alike, as though they were the Lord's promiscuous and fallen wife. The metaphor of spiritual adultery is more domineering in its tone, partly because it brands the people under God's covenant as the Lord's flagrant and slatternly adulteress. The two metaphors—and spiritual adultery foremost—stimulate Paul's conviction that sexual fornication is the most intimately threatening danger that Christians face and must eliminate from the lands of the Greeks and other Gentiles, starting first with their own sexual behavior.

Spiritual fornication and spiritual adultery are a central poetic means by which the Septuagint further elicits compliance with the reproductive basis of its laws for the monotheistic life. Whereas Plato thinks poets should be driven from the city to prevent unexamined metaphors from dominating a community's way of life,[1] the Septuagint elevates its poet-prophets to the height of being the prescriptive voice of God himself. While Plato and the Stoics strive to give philosophical reasoning the authority to articulate justice and morality, the Septuagint Prophets especially give suggestive poetics the upper hand to stimulate obedience to the Lord. Metaphors, however, are especially open to creative interpretation, and when they are didactic, the norms to which they may lead are not within the power of the original poets or even poet-prophets to foretell. Spiritual fornication and adultery are an excellent case in point, for their suggestiveness induces Paul to create strikingly new and restrictive norms of religious sexual obedience to Christ.

The Pentateuch, Prophets, and Paul employ the two metaphors in an effort to make sexual and nonsexual transgressions against God unthinkable rather than tempting. Given the imagery, however, sexual fornication is never far from the mind, for the metaphors sexualize transgression and associate it with a prostitute in God's temple—one seductive as Phryne posing as the nude Aphrodite. This is true especially for spiritual adultery, where the Prophets make explicit use of female sexual imagery. The heavy breathing that accompanies their didactic poetics, however, arises from a desire to expel the whore who causes sin from the domain of the Lord. Though both metaphors impart overtones of heightened flagrancy to sexual fornication, only the Prophets' metaphor of spiritual adultery inspires a sexual morality of its own through Paul's remarkable transformation of it in his emergent Christian sexual principles.

THE PENTATEUCH AND PAUL ON SPIRITUAL FORNICATION

In the Septuagint Pentateuch, various members of God's people occasionally fornicate against God or God's will by transgressing his commandments.[2] This metaphor associates the defilement and danger of sexual fornication with acts of defiance against God and his prophets. The insubordination may, but need not, involve sexual fornication, and it need not be sexual at all.[3] The book of Numbers best illustrates the workings of this meta-

---

1. A philosopher of great poetic skills himself, Plato is adept at deploying select metaphors for his own causes.

2. On some occasions I refer to the transgressions as being "against God's will" and on others I refer to them as being "against God." Precisely speaking, the spiritual fornication is against God's will, because it involves transgressing rules that God is said to want his people to obey. The sexual imagery involved in the metaphors, though, also makes it seem that the transgressions are an affront to God personally as well. My two phrases "against God" and "against God's will" serve as a reminder about this two-fold nature of the betrayal described by the metaphors.

3. In the previous chapter I discussed the defilement associated with sexual fornication in connection with, for example, Dinah being raped by Shechem or Israelites making love in the worship of gods other than the Lord, Gen 34:5, 27, Num 25:1–18.

phor. Numbers 15 states that God's adherents must not turn toward their own thoughts and inclinations at the expense of following God's laws, for to do so is fornication, that is, an act of fornicating against the Lord's will (Num 15:39). Though adulterers are among the transgressors who fit this profile, so too do agents of nonsexual disobedience, such as persons who dishonor their mother and father, take God's name in vain, and worship other gods in nonsexual modes. This point is made clear when Israelite soldiers protest Moses' command to attack the Canaanites. These Israelites commit fornication against God's will because they challenge the orders of God's prophet Moses (Num 14:2–3, 26–27, 33). In Leviticus, similarly, the Lord's people fornicate against God when they partake of religiously alien oracles and incantations (Lev 20:6), because such practices implicate them in worshipping other gods. Thus to be a fornicator against God persons need not be engaging in any practice involving their genitals, let alone sexually fornicating.

The Prophets also use the metaphor of spiritual fornication on occasion. God, they contend, has surrendered Samaria and Jerusalem to military conquest because his people worshipped other gods and thereby fornicated against his will, both nonsexually in various ways and sexually in their marriages and other ritual practices.[4] The conquests are the violent purgative that God in his quid pro quo has warned would follow upon unchecked practices of spiritually fornicating rebellion. In the incidents denounced by the Prophets, the people's disobedience includes rebellious sexual fornication, such as fertility rites and religiously syncretistic marriage.[5] The metaphor of spiritual fornication is not reducible to its sexual aspect, however, because it conceptualizes and denounces religious disobedience, sexual and nonsexual alike, in terms of sexual fornication.[6]

---

4. Deuteronomy states that the people will be devoured whole for fornicating after other gods, 31:16–18, cf. Judg 2:11–15; Jeremiah, that Israel will become an object of plunder, 2:14–25; Isaiah, that Zionite women will smell the rising dust of an approaching army, see their sons and husbands vanquished and killed, and find their beautiful dress replaced by a sackcloth, a rope around their waist, and their heads shaved, 3:16–26; Micah, that Samaria will be exposed down to the foundations and all its material wealth burned, 1:6–7; Amos, that some Israelites will fall by the sword, others die in an unclean land, and that their land will be apportioned to others, Amos 7:17. Natural catastrophes such as drought are also accounted for in these terms, Deut 11:17, Hos 4:1–3.

5. Spiritual fornication involves sexual fornication at Num 25:1–5 and Jer 5:7–8, for example. Sexual fornication also occurs in the fertility aspect of the rituals denounced, for instance, at Hos 4:13 and Jer 2:19–20, 3:6 according to the interpretation of S. Ackerman (*Under Every Green Tree: Popular Religion in Sixth-Century Judah* [1992], 185–94) and others.

6. Acts of spiritual fornication that are not sexual are diverse and wide ranging. Within the religious community, agents of such nonsexual fornication against God would include parents who permit their children to marry members of the forbidden tribes, Exod 34:15–16; persons who offer their sons to Molech rather than to the Lord, Lev 20:1–5; participants in sacrificial

Paul utilizes the Septuagint idea of spiritual fornication to teach the Corinthian Christians to obey his compendium of Pentateuchal rules. He stresses the need to avoid sexual fornication, resistance to his teachings, and idolatry in general (1 Cor 10:6–12). Were the Corinthians to question and resist Paul authority as God's apostolic messenger, they too would fornicate against God and be destroyed en masse, just as the Israelites were for their spiritually fornicating resistance to Moses.[7] "Do not protest (μηδὲ γογγύ-ζετε) as they [the Israelite soldiers] protested (ἐγόγγυσαν) and were destroyed by the terminator (ὑπὸ του ὀλοθρευτοῦ)" (1 Cor 10:10). Paul thus redeploys the Septuagint idea of spiritual fornication to instruct Christians in the way of the Lord.[8]

The metaphor of spiritual fornication uses sexual fornication as an opprobrious vehicle to reinforce directives to worship the Lord alone, be the directives Pentateuchal, Pauline, or other. In this metaphor, sexual fornication stands for any instance of dissent from the will ascribed to God, and especially to radical dissent, such as defying a prophet or apostle or making love in devotion to gods other than the Lord. In a modern example of such

---

feasts in honor of alien gods, Hos 9:4; and persons who follow religiously alien oracles, icons, and other sacred objects associated with gods other than the Lord, Lev 20:6, Judg 8:27.

7. Paul is explicitly referring to the incident in which the Israelites fornicate against God by rebelliously "protesting" (γόγγυσις) against Moses' commands, Num 14:2, 27, 36, 17:6, Septuagint Ps 105:25.

8. Paul's letters are not alone in this respect among writings that later became part of the New Testament. Revelation and John use spiritual fornication in a very similar way. In Revelation a female "slave," or prophet, is accused of being a "Jezebel woman," that is, of being as prominent an instigator of fornication against Christ as was Jezebel against Elijah's Lord, Rev 2:20, cf. 4 Kgdms 9:22. The fornication of the Christian "Jezebel" includes eating meat sacrificed to idols, Rev 2:18–29, which is not a sexual act, but is an act of rebellion in Revelation, and hence of fornicating against God's will. For the meaning of "slave" as "prophet" in Rev 11:18 and 22:9, see F. Mazzaferri, *The Genre of Revelation from a Source-Critical Perspective* (1989), 259. Likewise, in John, some Jews who "believe in Jesus" (8:31) but reject the claim that he is the son of God are for this reason said to worship the devil as their father god rather than worshipping God of Abraham, 8:18–19, 26–27, 31, 39–44. These Jews rightly infer that this accusation would, if true, mean that they are religiously alienated fornicators against God's will, or "of fornication born," 8:41, and they dispute its veracity, 8:33, 39, 41, 48, 52, 59. They especially dispute the implication that the devil is their father, 8:41–44. The fornication under dispute in John is a matter of religious doctrine, not of sexual practice. It advocates John's belief about Jesus (I believe in Jesus and that he is the son of God, cf. John 1:34) set in opposition to another, which it portrays as defiled and demonic (I believe in Jesus, but not that he is the son of God). John 8 therefore vilifies these Jews as fornicators against God because they believe in Jesus but do not accept the sonship claim. Hence the biblical metaphor of spiritual fornication is an active part of the texts that go on to become the New Testament. The problematic divisiveness of John 8 is discussed by S. Freyne, "Vilifying the Other and Defining the Self: Matthew's and John's Anti-Jewish Polemic in Focus" (1985), 136; T. Dozemann ("Sperma Abraham in John 8 and Related Literature: Cosmology and Judgement" [1980], 354–58) offers a useful historical perspective on the topic.

an opprobrious metaphor, we can imagine the leaders of a club rebuking disobedient members for "screwing with" the club's charter and rules.[9] In both "screw with" and "fornicate," the negative sexual imagery aggressively underscores the speakers' conviction that the transgressions are serious, shameful, and deserving of penalty. The metaphors have this didactic force because they associate insubordinate behavior of any sort with sexual activity construed in a dirty and crude way. The biblical metaphor, however, was considerably more visceral and forceful for its proponents than "screw with" is today, for from their perspective, sexual fornication was defiling and likely to be a dangerous act of other-theistic defiance against God with dreadful repercussions. Its sexual associations were meant to instill a deep psychological deterrent to disobeying the Lord by motivating God's people to obey all his rules with the seriousness they should already feel about the need to avoid rebellious sexual fornication through marriage in the Lord.

When the metaphor of spiritual fornication has its intended effect and takes hold,[10] its poetic method of inculcating compliance with God's will makes sexual fornication appear to be wrong in a manner that differs from and runs much deeper than the wrong of biblical lawbreaking itself. The metaphor makes sexual fornication a kind of paradigmatic scapegoat that stands for rebellion against God in its many diverse modes. As such the metaphor suggests that sexual fornication is the sin of sins, the viper of all religious wrongdoing.

The biblical dangers already associated with other-theistic sexual fornication partly explain why sexual fornication is the Septuagintal emblem of choice for all sin. Nonetheless, the choice was not inevitable. If some non-sexual poetic vehicle had been selected to teach the imperative to obey God, the Septuagint's normative poetics would instead suggest that the par-

---

9. I have opted to use the relatively mild "screw with" here, insofar as this is a work of scholarly discourse. The other more common and visceral English counterpart to "screw with," however, has greater force and would get the point across even more effectively.

10. It is unpredictable, though, how well its didactic aim would actually work in practice on individual recipients. Depending on historical circumstances, a number of persons within the community might not yet have accepted and internalized the perceived need for sexual relations to be strictly in the Lord, which the proponents are assuming is the case for their metaphor to get its didactic point across. Many persons apparently did not yet accept this norm in the pre-exilic period, at least as the Pentateuch and Prophets would have it, for these texts repeatedly denounce God's people for routinely practicing other-theistic sexual and nonsexual worship. And even persons who are devout practitioners of marriage in the Lord might question the soundness of religious leaders who stoop to use sexually crude language in their claim to speak for God. Ezekiel 16 and 23, for instance, are so outrageous that the chapters are subject to eliciting the latter sort of reader response. J. Muilenburg (in *Peake's Commentary* 495a, 507e) voices this not uncommon way of reacting to Ezekiel: There is something unsettlingly "abnormal" about the prophet for a number of reasons, not the least being the violently sexual mode in which Ezekiel expresses "almost unbridled rage and disgust" in Ezek 23.

adigm of sin is whatever the nonsexual metaphor happens to be. If, for example, the poetic emblem were the sacrifice of animals to alien gods, then disobedience would be a symbolic act of "slaughter" rather than "fornication" against God. The poetic aura of wrongdoing would cling to animal sacrifice as a paradigmatic sign of the forbidden, not to acts of sexual intercourse, and early Christians might have turned out to be ardent vegetarians with a happy sex life. As things stand in biblical poetics, however, sexual fornication is the chosen one of all wickedness; the sin of sins is sexual.

THE BIBLICAL HARLOT AND HER DANGERS
ACCORDING TO THE SEPTUAGINT

The metaphor of spiritual fornication informs what it means to identify women as "harlots" or "whores" (πόρναι) in the Septuagint. This topic is critical, for it is often misunderstood and this misunderstanding in turn obfuscates the sexual principles of Paul and his patristic supporters. The terms for "whore" and "fornicate," which in Greek are etymological cognates (πόρνη, πορνεύειν), are associated with each other through the metaphor. The determining factor of a woman's harlotry or whoredom in the biblical sense is not that she is sexually promiscuous, let alone that she is employed at a brothel, but that she is religiously promiscuous in her sexual, reproductive, and other ritual behavior, for she worships gods other than or in addition to the Lord. As scholars on the Prophets readily acknowledge, unless women are vessels of devotion to the Lord alone, they are harlots as far as the Prophets are concerned, quite apart from whether the women's sexual behavior is in fact promiscuous or involves formal prostitution.[11] The label πόρνη serves to vilify women for worshipping in a manner alien to the way of the Lord. Its central function is to deter male members of God's people from being attracted to such women and their other-theistic ways, for to do so is to spiritually fornicate (πορνεύειν) against the Lord with them. This is especially true when the men marry such women without first converting them. Mixed marriages create or perpetuate polytheistic

---

11. As G. Corrington Streete insightfully recognizes, "True 'whoredom' . . . is deviance from sanctioned religious authority, as it is from sexual authority," *The Strange Woman*, 51, 43; and the same is true of women labeled πόρναι, P. Bird, "To Play the Harlot" (1989), 76–80; S. Légasse, "Jésus et les prostituées," 138–9. F. Andersen and D. Freedman (*Hosea: A New Translation with Introduction and Commentary* [1980], 161, 157–63) likewise note that "*zōnā* [Septuagint πόρνη] alone, as we have shown, refers to any woman [who partakes of] sexual misconduct of any kind," and is regarded as guilty in so doing, without the woman having to be wantonly promiscuous or a professional prostitute. Women identified as πόρναι are mentioned in Gen 34:31, 38:15 (but Tamar is a πόρνη only from Judah's perspective at this point in the narrative, 38:24, 26); Lev 21:7, 21:14; Deut 23:18; Judg 11:1–3; 3 Kgdms 20:19, 22:38; Prov 5:3, 6:26, 7:10, 29:3; Jer 5:7; Ep Jer 4–11.

practices in the home, reproduction, and childrearing. Though the terms of biblical monotheism change from the Septuagint to Paul, the idea of the biblical whore functions consistently to dehumanize religiously alien and rebellious women as though they were all harlots, and as such unfit to be wives and mothers among God's people, unless they follow Ruth's example and rehabilitate themselves.

Biblical harlots fit into two types. Whores of the first type, religiously alien women, are πόρναι insofar as male members of the people spiritually "fornicate" (πορνεύειν) against God with them through religiously mixed marriage or other rituals.[12] Solomon's religiously alien wives and the Baal-worshipping Moabite women in Numbers 25 exemplify this group. In these cases the men are the fornicating transgressors both spiritually and sexually, for they are the ones who transgress the covenant, but the women are vilified as whores for imperiling the men's observance of the First Commandment. Biblical harlots of the second type are women among God's people who act as rebellious insiders. They are harlots (πόρναι) because they fornicate (πορνεύειν) against God through their sexual or nonsexual religious rites. The Prophets repeatedly denounce such practices among the women of the Lord's people as so much subversive whoredom.[13] Though other-theistic sexual intercourse is a prominent element in their whoredom, the women's spiritual fornication is not reducible to sexual fornication. The defamatory poetics of harlotry imputes that both types of women are sexually promiscuous or prostitutes, but the women need only be religiously alien to, or alienated from, the Lord by virtue of revering other gods in their sexual and other practices.

The biblical figure of the whore is an integral and potent feature of the Septuagint metaphor of spiritual fornication. When male members of God's people "screw with" his laws, and religiously alien women are involved as wives or in other capacities, the women are the whores with whom the men screw the laws. When the insubordination implicates female members of

---

12. Exod 34:15–16, 3 Kgdms 11:1–2, Ezek 16:27–29, Tob 4:12, 2 Esdr 10:10–17, cf. 1 Esdr 8:65–67. Various biblical passages warn male members of the Lord's people that the mores of religiously alien women lead them to apostasy, Num 25:1–5; Prov 5:1–23, 7:1–27. Other biblical passages blame religiously foreign women for making male members of the Lord's people deviate from their path, 3 Kgdms 11:4; 4 Kgdms 9:22; Prov 5:1–23, 7:1–27. Such women are biblical harlots or agents of πορνεία, 4 Kgdms 9:22, Hos 1:2, Prov 5:3. Prov 7:5 further describes this class of women as "alien and wicked." The pre-exilic Hosea protests against the ingrained habit of blaming only the female participants in rebellious rituals insofar as the name "whores" sullies their reputation alone, 4:14. He nonetheless contributes to the prejudice against which he protests, for he transforms his adulterous wife Gomer, not the many apostate male Israelites whom he castigates, into the very emblem of God's harlot people, Hos 1:2–2:25.

13. Hos 4.13, Isa 3:16–26, Jer 51:24–30, Ezek 23:48–9, Ecclus 23:22–27.

God's people in rebellion, then they are the whores screwing the laws, and they do so sexually with religiously alien or alienated men when acts of sexual intercourse are involved.[14] The biblical whore thus crosses ethnic lines and links female outsiders with insiders, Gentile women with dissident women claimed for the Lord, in an unusual collective of putatively lewd and wicked ladies of the night.

The nonbiblical and biblical Greek senses of πόρνη differ in important ways. In ancient Greek texts uninfluenced by the Septuagint, a πόρνη is a lower-class prostitute, as opposed to a higher-class ἑταίρα, or courtesan. Πόρνη in this sense is inherently sexual, for it refers to a sector of women in the profession of sexual activity for hire. The term stems from πέρνημι, which refers to the sale and exportation of female slaves for the sex trade in the ancient Mediterranean.[15] In the Septuagint and writings influenced by the Septuagint, however, πόρνη largely translates the Hebrew term *zonah*,[16] which refers to any woman who deviates from biblical monotheism in her religious conduct, especially, but not only, in the sphere of sexual intercourse, procreation, and childrearing. As with the Septuagintal πόρνη, its defining criterion is that the woman is other-theistic rather than sexually promiscuous. Prostitutes are but a minor subset of this, the genuinely oldest female profession in the world, women conducting the worship of gods other than or in addition to the Lord, partly through their sexual behavior.

Advocates of monotheistic protectionism nonetheless insinuate, through their description of the women's bodily gestures, that biblical harlots are indeed sexually promiscuous or prostitutes at heart. The whores wink, make enticing movements with their feet, and boldly look men in the eye instead of keeping their eyes downcast.[17] This stereotype is misleading in at least two ways, even when it refers to actual sexual behavior of the women. First, it associates willfully seductive sexual conduct with all women who are classified as whores. A number of the women in question, however, are victims of rape and forced impregnation as captive wives, concubines, and slaves. Even if they are coerced into converting, they remain religious aliens at core, for unlike Ruth, their conversion is not voluntary. Such women have no incen-

---

14. The claim in Matthew and Luke that Jesus associated with harlots (πόρναι, Matt 21:31, Luke 15:30) raises an interesting possibility to consider. It is conceivable that Matthew and Luke mean that Jesus associated with religiously alien and alienated woman and taught them to follow him, not merely that he aimed to leave brothels with fewer employees by converting some prostitutes. If so, then Jesus would have been carrying out a mission that included Gentile women as well as religiously alienated Jewish women in his vicinity.

15. LSJ, s.v. πόρνη.

16. E. Hatch and H. Redpath, *A Concordance to the Septuagint and Other Greek Versions of the Old Testament* (1897; reprint, 1998), s.v. πόρνη.

17. On the seductive bodily gestures of harlots, see Prov 6:25, 7:5–27; Isa 3:16; Ezek 16:25; Ecclus 26:9.

tive to worship the Lord alone and have good reason to resist the practice and to teach their children to do likewise. Further, when Israelite warriors take captive wives or concubines from tribes with whom intermarriage is forbidden,[18] the Israelite captors fornicate against God themselves. They take as long-term sexual partners and childbearers women who by biblical principle cannot sexually mix with the Lord's people and should, when captured, instead be put to death or sold to Gentiles outside the promised land. Similarly, when daughters of Israel or Judah are abducted, they too as captive women are victims of rape and subjugation by Gentile males.[19] Both groups of women are thus forced into sexual and likely procreative unions of a religiously prohibited sort. These women are not dragged off as captives because they seductively winked from the city walls or played footsies with attacking soldiers. The figure of the biblical harlot, however, grossly stigmatizes female sexual victims of ancient warfare as whores who were asking for it.

Second, even when biblical harlots are sexually involved in a voluntary way with male Israelites, the sexual activity is likely to occur within a religiously diversified marriage deemed respectable by the spouses and approving kin. To the extent that the women winked and wiggled, they would have done so partly to keep the home fires burning in their relationships with their husbands. The Phoenician Jezebel, for example, is, as far as we know,

---

18. Deut 21:10–14 presumes the custom of taking female prisoners of war as captive wives. Despite this permission, a female prisoner taken as a captive wife does not say of her own volition, like Ruth, "your people will be my people and your God will be my God." Rather she is informed through physical degradation that she is her captor's and his God is hers. Women in this position consequently remain religiously alien at heart and the marriage is technically an act of fornication against the Lord's will on the part of the Israelite husband. Further, female prisoners taken as captive wives would mainly have come from the peoples with whom marriage is absolutely forbidden. The biblical injunction is for the Israelites to conquer and annihilate these peoples, and certainly never to marry them, Exod 34:11, 15–16. Israelite soldiers nonetheless are said to have taken alive and kept at least some of the women, on occasion against express orders, as in the retaliatory attack over the Moabite and Midianite incident in Num 31:9–18. The ancient militaristic custom of taking female prisoners of war into sexual servitude therefore conflicts with the biblical rule against marrying religious aliens on two grounds: many of the women are unconditionally off limits as wives by biblical regulations, and even if some of them are not in this class, they nonetheless remain religious aliens at heart. Physical degradation of the sort described in Deut 21:10–14 is a sign of enslavement through capture, O. Patterson, *Slavery and Social Death: A Comparative Study* (1982), 7–9. On Deut 20:11–14, see H. Washington, "'Lest He Die in the Battle and Another Man Take Her': Violence and the Construction of Gender in the Laws of Deuteronomy 20–22" (1998), 205–7 and S. Thistlethwaite, "'You May Enjoy the Spoil of Your Enemies': Rape as a Biblical Metaphor for War" (1993), 65. Female captives are degraded sexually and forced into indentured reproduction as well through concubinage and marriage by spear point, G. Lerner, *The Creation of Patriarchy* (1986), 76–100.

19. Deut 28:32, Judg 2:14, 2 Chr 28:8, Joel 4:1–6, Bar 4:30–5.

sexually faithful to her Israelite husband, King Ahab. But Jezebel is a harlot or doer of whoredom no matter what she might do sexually (4 Kgdms 9:22), because she is married to Ahab and yet passionately promotes the worship of Baal and Baal's prophets against Yahweh and his prophets. The religious deviance of wives among God's people on occasion does involve sexual adultery, as in the case of Hosea's wife, Gomer, who makes love with a man or men in rituals for Baal.[20] Still, what determines Gomer's fornicating promiscuity is that she too worships another god. From a biblical perspective, however, the women in such marriages have turned their domiciles into houses of quasi-prostitution, because they seduce their husbands and children away from the Lord in honor of the gods and religious practices of their own people and ancestors.

Women who find themselves in communities regulated by images of the biblical whore would quickly learn that to win any respect in their community, they must keep their eyes downcast, their hips and feet still, and their sex organs and wombs devoted strictly to God in the names of their husbands. If they fail, they too would be portrayed as though they were card-carrying members of a hostile religious union, the United Sisterhood of Whores against the Monopoly of the Lord.[21] In this social order, women's rituals for other gods are delegitimated as the behavior of loose women luring families away from God. Girls and women who are habituated to this norm would have added religious reason to feel traumatized and guilty if they are subjected to wartime acts of rape and forced impregnation for new masters. First, the bodily violations alienate them from God in addition to being an assault on their persons, for the sexual activity signifies that they have become biblical whores, especially when they give birth to offspring subject to alien religious mores. Second, the stereotype of the biblical harlot as a seductive woman would lead them to suspect that they must have done something flirtatiously wrong in their devotion to God and ought to repent, for otherwise the almighty Lord would never have allowed the soldiers to conquer their cities and sexually brutalize them.[22] Warped as the

---

20. 4 Kgdms 9:22, Hos 1:2–3.

21. Scholars who uncritically refer to the biblical harlot as a prostitute inadvertently perpetuate the stereotype, such as Y. Sherwood's labeling of Homer's wife Gomer as a "prostitute" in the title and text of *The Prostitute and the Prophet: Hosea's Marriage in Literary-Theoretical Perspective* (1996). This excessive literalism should be put to rest, except for instances where a biblical harlot is demonstrably a prostitute, rather than one of the many women who are "promiscuously" alien to, or alienated from, the biblical God.

22. F. Andersen and D. Freedman (*Hosea*, 157–63) are thus misleading to maintain that sexual wrongdoing or guilt on the part of the women is involved in the biblical allegations about female religious promiscuity: "*zōnā* alone refers to any woman guilty of sexual misconduct of any kind."

image is of the biblical whore, it potently regulates women's sexual and other religious conduct when and where it wields psychological force.

PAUL'S USE OF THE BIBLICAL HARLOT STEREOTYPE

Paul makes the biblical whore the emblem of polytheistic sexual culture among the Gentiles; and he regards this whore culture as a feminine stand-in for Satan. In so doing he intensifies the Greek biblical position that religiously alien harlots wickedly entice God's people into religious rebellion.

Paul presents an exclusive disjunction between two opposing religious groups, two corporate entities of religious culture, the religiously alienating body of the whore and the rightly devotional body of Christ.[23] He refers to these two entities as "the limbs of the harlot" ($\mu \acute{\epsilon} \lambda \eta \; \pi \acute{o} \rho \nu \eta s$) and "the limbs of Christ" ($\mu \acute{\epsilon} \lambda \eta \; X \rho \iota \sigma \tau o \hat{v}$) (1 Cor 6:15). Obedient Christians belong to the latter, while Gentiles and fallen Christians belong to the former. Christians who disobey Paul's version of biblical endogamy are severed from their union with Christ's body and absorbed into the dreaded "limbs of the harlot." By contrast, Christians who shun religiously alien sexual intercourse remain in "Christ's limbs" and retain Christ's spirit (1 Cor 6:15–17). When a Christian man makes love to a woman outside of a marriage that Paul deems acceptably in the Lord, such as the man with his father's wife (1 Cor 6:15–17) or with, say, a fiancée devoted to Isis or Aphrodite, he becomes "one body" with the harlot. This harlot with whom the man sexually joins is not to be identified solely with the actual woman with whom he copulates, though she too is a biblical whore from Paul's perspective and her sexual body is involved in the man's transgression. The man also joins the bodily "limbs of the harlot," which symbolize the unregenerate culture of Gentile females and males, excluding Gentiles who are already married to recently converted Christians. Aside from this exception, Gentiles are off-limits as sexual partners unless they convert to the Lord alone. Otherwise, they are the baneful sexual doorway to the body of religious culture in opposition to Christ, the "limbs of the harlot." The body of the harlot in 1 Corinthians 6 thus has very long limbs, for she represents all polytheistic societies of the ancient Mediterranean world as one corporate entity in exclusive opposition to Paul's monotheistic collective, the growing body and limbs of Christ in pure devotion to God. The constituent members of the whore's corporate limbs are the vast majority of Gentile women and men, whom Christians must avoid marrying or having as sexual partners in any capacity, unless they are already married to them.

23. In a manner similar to Paul, Revelation conceptualizes polytheistic culture on the outside of his Christian Israel as the harlot Babylon, 17:5.

Paul's opposition between the limbs of the harlot and the limbs of Christ epitomizes his sexual mandate. Christians have but three legitimate sexual options in life. They can remain virginal or celibate, marry fellow members in the Lord, or convert the Gentile spouses they already have to Christianity. People born Christian in turn have only the first two options. Failure to comply keeps the seductive Gentile whore alive by adding fallen Christians to her members through mixed marriages and other sexual practices. But through the practices of marriage and childrearing in Paul's religious framework, the limbs of the whore should die off. In this way the formerly pluralistic harlot may transform, born anew as Christ's limbs and chaste bride-to-be.

Paul succinctly offers the same teaching about the dangerous limbs of the harlot in 1 Corinthians 7, where he replaces the whore with Satan. Christians who sexually fornicate, he asserts, succumb to Satan and fall away from Christ (1 Cor 7:5). As Satan is to Christ, so "the limbs of the biblical harlot" are to "the limbs of Christ" in 1 Cor 6:15. The corporate whore in 1 Cor 6:15 is thus the semantic equivalent of Satan in 1 Cor 7:5, for sexually disobedient Christians are succumbing to the same wicked entity in both cases. Paul thus strengthens the Septuagint stereotype that harlots and their religious cultures are inherently wicked, dangerous, and must be shunned at all costs. To his mind the polytheistic peoples, gods, and societies in the ancient Mediterranean are the limbs of Satan in transvestite guise, the devil with a blue dress on. No Christian should ever marry into her body, let alone procreate there.

Paul starkly emphasizes that to make a religiously mixed marriage is the most dangerous transgression Christians can commit. As noted in the previous chapter, he teaches that transgressions that do not involve sexual intercourse are sins that Christians commit "outside the body," but the Christian who sexually fornicates sins "against his [or her] own body," such as a Christian man "cleaving (κολλώμενος) to a whore," rather than marrying a woman who already is or voluntarily becomes a member of the Lord's people. By the participle "cleaving" (κολλώμενος), Paul unambiguously signifies the danger of taking a biblical harlot *in marriage*, for he alludes to the marital cleaving (κολλώμενος) of Adam and Eve in Genesis 2:24.[24] Though the meaning "prostitute" is virtually ubiquitous in interpretations of ὁ κολλώμενος πόρνῃ at 1 Cor 6:16, it is misguided and based on the an-

---

24. 1 Cor 6:16–18. As G. Dautzenberg has shown ("Φεύγετε τὴν πορνείαν (1 Kor 6,18)," 277–82), Hellenistic Jewish and early Christian references to Gen 2:24 unanimously "beeziehen Gen 2,24 auf die Ehe. Bei Zitation des ganzen Verses ist kaum ein andere Auslegungshorizont möglich." Paul fits into this tradition by my interpretation of 1 Cor 6:16 and its use of Gen 2:24. W. Schrage (*Der Erste Brief an die Korinther*, vol. 2, 24–33) thoroughly discusses the participle κολλώμενος and its marital connotations as well.

cient Greek meaning of the term rather than the biblical Greek sense of what πόρνη means in Paul's letters. The so-called whore in this case is any woman who is religiously alien to, or alienated from, Paul's missionary communities. She is not only a prostitute plying her trade in Corinth, let alone a more specialized cult prostitute of Aphrodite.[25] The harlot could just as easily be a daughter under the watchful eye of her conservative Greek parents, a real girl-next-door type whose mother is a priestess of a goddess or god,[26] for Paul is referring to the danger of a Christian man joining in a marital or other committed sexual partnership with any woman dedicated to gods other than or in addition to the Lord.[27] According to Paul, then, every individual Christian must make sure that spouses and families in the community gain or keep their orientation toward God alone to avoid succumbing—and in many cases reverting back—to being constituent members of the polytheistic harlot. Christians already married to Gentiles must work to convert their spouses, and unmarried Christians must never take Gentile doers of religious harlotry as prospective spouses, such as a Christian man cleaving to a Gentile woman as his newlywed wife.

25. H.-D. Saffrey ("Aphrodite à Corinthe: Réflexions sur une idée reçue" [1985] 359–74) warns against exaggerating Corinth's reputation for Aphrodite's prostitute-priestesses and presuming that Paul in 1 Corinthians 6 must be referring to men visiting them. J. Héring (*The First Epistle of Saint Paul to the Corinthians* [1962], 45) exemplifies this tenuous interpretation: "Perhaps we should remember that *'pornai'* were in general sacred prostitutes, slaves attached to the service of a pagan temple (notably to a temple of Venus-Aphrodite), who were supposed to put those who worshipped there in communion with the deity they served—a further reason for looking upon union with such as having a strongly negative religious value."

26. R. Kirchhoff (*Die Sünde*, 196, cf. 35) is one of the few interpreters who carefully points out that πόρνη in Paul's letters does not simply mean "prostitute": "Πόρνη nennt Paulus nicht speziell eine Prostituierte, sondern jede Frau, mit der ein christlicher Mann nach Paulus' Meinung nach nicht sexuell verkehren darf." To translate 1 Cor 6:16 as "prostitute" perpetuates the Christian side of the biblical ideology that women who are not devoted to the Lord alone are a bunch of whores whom male members of God's people must shun. This overly narrow interpretation of πόρνη is a good example of the hermeneutic trouble that comes from not giving the Septuagint its due for understanding Paul.

27. One unfortunate implication of understanding of πόρνη to mean strictly "prostitute" in 1 Cor 6 is that it makes Paul's religiously protectionist marriage rules seem motivated primarily by a judicious desire to do away with the ancient double standard, in which husbands were free to visit prostitutes while wives were expected to be sexually faithful to their husbands. A. Wire (*The Corinthian Women Prophets: A Reconstruction through Paul's Rhetoric* [1990], 76–9) offers an interpretation of this sort: "By challenging the practice of going to prostitutes, Paul indicates the existence of a double standard that commonly applied in Corinthian marriages.... The immorality he exposes is male. The solution he calls for is marriage ... in Paul's plan to put an end to immorality." Paul's pattern of Christian marriage happens to avoid this double standard, but not primarily out of an interest in fairness for wives. Rather, he prefers exclusive Christian monogamy as the key way to keep religiously alien influences out of the family and community in the Lord.

THE PROPHETS ON SPIRITUAL ADULTERY

The biblical harlot takes on another, more forceful configuration in the Prophets, where the metaphor of spiritual adultery serves to identify her with God's people themselves as the Lord's wife turned adulterous whore. This metaphor and its figure of the adulterous wife especially helped stimulate the antifornication sexual ethos that Paul brought to the formation of Christianity in Greek and other Gentile lands.

All of the major and some of the minor Prophets occasionally describe the covenant between God and his people as a marital covenant,[28] with the Lord as the husband and his cities or communities of people as his collective wife or wives.[29] This metaphor enables the Prophets to portray acts of religious disobedience, both sexual and nonsexual, as adultery against the Lord, not simply as fornicating against him. In the book of Hosea, for example, Gomer is both the prophet Hosea's wife and the religious community as God's wife. Hosea similarly adopts a complementary dual role. He is both the husband of Gomer and God the husband of his people. Hosea has this double vision because he is outraged to learn that Gomer and other community members have engaged in sexual practices in worship of Baal. He berates and threatens Gomer on two grounds simultaneously. First, on a personal basis she has committed adultery against him. Second, the rebellious people represented by Gomer have committed spiritual adultery against their husband, the Lord. The people are thus God's figuratively adulterous

28. Though there is a latent marital poetics of sorts in various passages of the Pentateuch, there is still a world of difference between the Pentateuch and Prophets in this respect. There are traces of the idea that the covenant is a marriage in the Pentateuch (D. Carr, "Gender and the Shaping of Desire in the Song of Songs and Its Interpretation [2000], 238–9), but the imagery is not deeply ingrained because marriage is traditionally a heterosexual pairing, while God and Israel alike in the Pentateuch are chiefly portrayed as masculine entities, and they bond in primarily masculine ways, such as the Lord being the Israelites' invincible commander in war, J. Schmitt, "The Gender of Ancient Israel" (1983), 115–25. Starting with Hosea and in later Prophets, by contrast, there is the full-blown development of an explicit marital poetics along with the engendering of Israel as a feminine entity, G. Corrington Streete, *The Strange Woman*, 76–80. Since God's people are not strongly symbolized as the Lord's wife in the Pentateuch, it is not surprising that there is, as J. Galambush (*Jerusalem in the Book of Ezekiel: The City as Yahweh's Wife* [1992], 37) has noted, no Pentateuchal evidence for portraying God's rebellious people as his adulterous wife.

29. The cities and peoples that represent the Lord's wife are mentioned in Hos 5:3, 9:1; Jer 3:6–14; Ezek 16:1, 46, 23:4; Isa 1:21. On the marital symbolism, see G. Corrington Streete, *The Strange Woman*, 76–100 and J. Galambush, *Jerusalem in the Book of Ezekiel*, 20–23, 35–59. The following studies are helpful as well: A. Fitzgerald, "The Mythological Background for the Presentation of Jerusalem as a Queen and False Worship as Adultery in the Old Testament" (1972), 403–16; J. Schmitt, "The Virgin of Israel: Referent and Use of the Phrase in Amos and Jeremiah" (1991), 365–87; P. Bird, "To Play the Harlot," 75–94; P. A. Kruger, "Israel, the Harlot (Hos. 2:4–9)" (1983), 107–16; D. Clark, "Sex-Related Imagery in the Prophets" (1982), 409–13; C. Cohen, "The Widowed City" (1973), 75–81.

wife, just as Gomer is Hosea's literally adulterous wife.[30] Likewise, in Jeremiah God denounces the people of Judah as his wife for committing spiritual adultery through sexual and other acts of polytheistic worship, and he angrily issues Israel a bill of divorce for similar reasons (Jer 3:6–9).[31] Ezekiel also describes, scurrilously and at length, how Samaria and Jerusalem have become the Lord's slatternly wives due to their acts of sexual and non-sexual rebellion (16:1–63, 23:1–45).[32] The Prophets thus poetically link literal adultery with spiritual adultery against God. Like the rhetorical image of spiritual fornication, spiritual adultery aims to reinforce monotheism as the norm to which God's people must conform with inviolate fidelity.

The metaphor of spiritual adultery in the Prophets, though similar to spiritual fornication in didactic intent, offers a more emotively forceful approach to inculcating the norm of biblical monotheism. In biblical terms, sexual adultery is a major act of infidelity to spouses and God's laws alike, given its prohibition in the Decalogue, whereas sexual fornication is not necessarily an act of rebellion against God's laws, even though it is shameful and defiling. For example, an Israelite man who rapes the unbetrothed daughter of another Israelite man in the community has committed sexual fornication, but he has not committed apostasy. If, however, the man commits adultery with another man's wife in the community, the man and woman

30. Gomer is a religiously alien woman, or "harlot," who was purchased as a wife by the prophet Hosea; she is also a symbol for the Lord's adulterously unfaithful people. Hosea too is a dual persona (he is both the prophet and the Lord) who anticipates that Gomer (and "Gomer," the people of God) will adulterously disobey him (and "Him"), 2:7, 3:1–3. Hosea warns that He/he will strip and punish "her"/her for dual adultery, 2:5, 8, 12–13. In order to make the dual Gomer recognize that he is her only Lord, Hosea urges her children to condemn her, 2:9, 2:4. Y. Sherwood (*The Prostitute and the Prophet*, 134–8) explores these metaphorical amalgams of identity (God/prophet and people/wife) more thoroughly, as does B. Seifert, *Metaphorisches Reden von Gott im Hoseabuch*, 87–263. These earlier studies remain useful: J. Schmitt, "The Wife of God in Hosea 2" (1989), 5–18; M. Friedman, "Israel's Response in Hosea 2:17b: 'You Are My Husband'" (1980), 199–204; and H. H. Rowley, "The Marriage of Hosea" (1956–1957), 200–33.

31. For Israel to be issued a bill of divorce indicates "her" symbolic status as (former) biblical wife. In Jeremiah symbolic adultery occurs because Israel has become idolatrous and has "gone up to every high hill" and fornicated beneath every tree, 2:19–20. Jerusalem is alienated from the Lord through symbolic adultery for similar reasons, 13:27.

32. Ezekiel names Samaria and Jerusalem in a sexually specific way as Oholah and Oholibah in chapter 23, 23:1–4, but does not use such nicknaming in chapter 16:1–63. Once the youthful and innocent Jerusalem has sexually matured, the Lord consummates his marriage with her and makes her his honored wife, 16:8–14. The same holds for Samaria. The two cities later fall to the status of adulterous harlots, that is, "wives" who have become religious aliens through violating their religious fidelity toward the Lord alone. Ezekiel is particularly violent and lewd in his spiritual adultery poetics, G. Corrington Streete, *The Strange Woman*, 94, 90–8; J. Galambush, *Jerusalem in the Book of Ezekiel*, 91–157; and R. Weems *Battered Love: Marriage, Sex, and Violence in the Hebrew Prophets* (1995), 72–8.

have both transgressed a commandment, and in principle both must die by stoning. The Prophets' metaphor of spiritual adultery pointedly connects the people disobeying God with the unconditional Decalogue wrong of a married woman sexually defying her husband and master. The metaphor of spiritual fornication does not have this precision because sexual fornication is not necessarily rebellious. Hence spiritual adultery delivers a different and much more forceful censure than spiritual fornication does. The Prophets sew a scarlet letter onto God's people for their infidelity, which the metaphor of spiritual fornication does not do.

The Prophets' marital poetics also has more domineering and violent overtones. By its disturbing association between biblical marriage and the Lord's relationship with his people, God's people ought to suffer violent retribution for their sexual and other disobedience, just as a wife ought to be put to death for failing to show sexual fidelity to her husband alone. Spiritual adultery thus casts the relationship between God and his people in terms of the most backwoods form of patriarchal marriage, where the husband has the power to protect or destroy, and the wife is allowed no shield to defend herself or her children. The Lord wields the upper hand against the feminine body of his people, and when they suffer from military or other catastrophes, God is punishing her in order to demonstrate that they are allowed peace and prosperity only if they uphold the covenant. As Ezekiel crudely puts it, the wife has to quit spreading her legs for other gods and remember that the Lord alone is her lover (16.15, 25, 26). Try as she might, she cannot get away from him, and she should not even try.

The metaphor of spiritual adultery has an intense religious doctrine built into it, because it rules out chance factors to account for the suffering of God's people. Absolute protection by God is an attainable norm to be gained through strict obedience. When disasters occur among the people, the devastation never simply happens but is the work of the angry Lord in all the force he has forewarned would be the cost of defying his covenant. When Samaria and Jerusalem are sacked, the Prophets are convinced that these catastrophes could have occurred only because the inhabitants went astray and elicited God's punishment. The people sorely provoked their almighty husband to acts of outrage through military forces. Behold the smoking ruins, the adulteress delivered to her stoning. If only the people would learn to worship God alone, they would remain safe from the alien armies who overthrow their cities, rape the women, kill the men, and sell surviving captives into religiously alienating slavery and sexual servitude.[33] When the surviving remnants of God's devastated people are able to gather again and

33. Ezekiel, for example, states that Assyrians and Babylonians are among the righteous men who punish Oholah (Samaria) and Oholibah (Jerusalem) "as adulterous wives," 23:9–10, 22–26, 45.

piece their lives back together, they must atone for their renegade past and become the model wife in their devotion to him. Then and only then will their domain fulfill its promise to be a peaceful land of milk and honey.

The Prophets shift the identity of the biblical harlot and the culpability associated with her to the people themselves through the metaphor of spiritual adultery. As the Prophets see it, the problem of disobedience to God lies with the unfaithful people as adulterous wife, not with religiously alien or Gentile women for luring God's men to defect from the Lord. In the metaphor of spiritual fornication, by contrast, female outsiders are blamed for being the enticing whores.[34] Proponents of the spiritual adultery metaphor recognize that the people themselves are the real harlot problem insofar as they and not alien women are obliged to follow the First Commandment and God's related sexual laws.[35] When an Israelite man takes an unconverted Moabite as a wife with his family's approval, they, not the wife, are the agents of whoredom. One troubling imputation of both metaphors, however, remains the same: Wicked religious behavior is still embodied as a woman, be she the seductress from the outside or the adulteress on the inside whom the Lord catches in the act with other gods. The Prophets' metaphor of spiritual adultery thus diminishes the xenophobia about outside women, but keeps the misogyny.[36] As Zechariah puts it, religious waywardness is woman—keep her in the barrel.[37]

PAUL'S TRANSFORMATIONS OF SPIRITUAL ADULTERY

The Prophets' marital poetics has rich potential to give rise to a more fully developed marital theology about the relationship between God and his people. Several developments of this sort appear in the later sections of Isa-

---

34. Jezebel offers the paradigmatic instance of this problem. Ahab marries Jezebel, a fervent Baal devotee, and then finds himself caught between equal and opposite fundamentalists, his wife and Elijah. Though Ahab is the wrongdoer by marrying a religiously alien woman, Jezebel goes down as the blazing whore for bringing Israel to fornicate against God in favor of Baal.

35. R. Weems (*Battered Love*, 64) likewise appreciates that "explicit sexual language and disgusting scenes of a sexually ravaged woman were intended to convince the prophets' audiences that they had no one to blame but themselves."

36. G. Corrington Streete (*The Strange Woman*, 89, 96–8) discusses several important ways in which the misogyny persists.

37. An angel proclaims that religious lawlessness is woman to Zechariah by bringing forth a covered barrel with a woman trapped on the inside. The angel removes the leaden cover, identifies the woman, "This is Lawlessness," and declares that she represents "the women's guilt throughout the entire land." To contain her, the angel forcefully thrusts Lawlessness back down into the barrel and casts the leaden stone back on top, Zech 5:5–8. The message could hardly be more blunt: Women, worship the biblical God alone, or else that is you in the barrel. For the significance of the barrel (rendered as $\tau\grave{o}$ $\mu\acute{\epsilon}\tau\rho\upsilon$ in the Septuagint), see C. Meyers and E. Meyers, *Haggai, Zechariah 1–8* (1987), 295–7.

iah and in Paul's letters and other New Testament writings. These include the desire to restore God's people to their glory as his wife, the belief that this marital union is destined to happen soon, and the conviction that people who refuse to become the renewed bride will suffer in perpetuity as the harlot whom God marks for destruction. This complex of ideas is much in evidence in early Christianity, nowhere more strikingly than in Paul's sexual dictates.

The later installments of Isaiah (viz., Second and Third Isaiah) further elaborate the Prophets' marital poetics. They promise that there will be a joyous wedding to restore the Lord's fallen wife to her former stature of being pristine and cherished.[38] Once the people are rehabilitated, they will reunite with the Lord in his bridal chamber of pure monotheism.[39]

Picking up on the theme of monotheism as marriage, Revelation, Paul, and other early Christian sources stress that the upcoming wedding includes Gentiles and has an imminent date. Their mission is to present a wedding invitation to the peoples they claim for God. In place of the polite r.s.v.p., however, stands an ultimatum to be in attendance, for they are not to be merely guests, but constituent members of the Lord's bride. The people must repent and join the monotheistic bridal collective or face certain destruction for persisting in their ancestral harlot mores of alien worship. This expression of impending celebration or violent retribution is a recurrent eschatological theme in the New Testament.[40] In Revelation, for instance, Gentiles who convert are saved because they have the religious and sexual characteristics of Christ's heavenly bride, Jerusalem, while the unconverted are destined for destruction as the polytheistic whore "Babylon."[41] In the Prophets, by contrast, the religious culture that God punishes

38. The Greek Pentateuch and Prophets alike share a recurrent theme about the Lord's people becoming joyfully rehabilitated and restored to God. The theme takes on strong marital overtones in the Prophets alone, Deut 4:29–31; Ps 105:43–8; Hos 14:1–9; Joel 2:12–17; Isa 12:1–3, 41:10; Jer 2:19, 3:12–18, 25:5–6; Bar 4:30–5:9; Ezek 16:60–63, 23.48–49.

39. The Lord proclaims that he has returned to his formerly abandoned people as "wife" now that she acknowledges her creator: "You will no longer be called abandoned and your land will no longer be called deserted . . . Just as a bridegroom rejoices in his bride, so shall the Lord rejoice in you," Isa 62:4–5, cf. 54:4–8.

40. In the Prophets, by contrast, God's acts of retributive destruction are more historically tangible. When God's collective wife turns into an adulterous whore, she is devastated within historical time by Assyrians and other armies. In the New Testament, God gains an apocalyptic edge. He no longer needs armies to function as the brute intermediaries of his retaliation, and his punitive methods are not limited to occurring within historical time.

41. Rev 17:1–18:24, esp. 17:1–6. Obedient Christians belong to the bride (19:6–9), whereas apostates belong to the defiled harlot Babylon. On the exclusive opposition between Christ's bride and the harlot Babylon, see also F. Mazzaferri, *The Genre of Revelation*, 10, and P. Hirschberg, *Das eschatologische Israel: Untersuchungen zum Gottesvolkverständnis der Johannesoffenbarung* (1999), 231–3.

for her spiritual adultery remains limited to God's historical people and the historical promised land. In Revelation, though, and Paul as well, these cultural restrictions are removed and the wedding plans universalize.[42] As Paul succinctly puts it, formerly Gentile Christians are "a sacred virgin" whom he has come to join "to Christ as to one husband" (2 Cor 11:2).[43]

Paul most clearly presents his marital poetics of monotheism at 1 Cor 6:13–18, where he describes the relationship between Christ and his people with phrasing that structurally matches his description of Christian spouses in the Lord at 1 Cor 7:4. The Christian body—both the individual and the corporate group—belongs to the Lord, not to sexual fornication, and the Lord belongs to the body (1 Cor 6:13–18). In a closely analogous manner, the wife and husband in 1 Corinthians 7 each belong to the body of the other, not to sexual fornication, and they are to exclusively devote themselves to each other sexually in order to keep Satan at bay. "The wife does not exercise sexual autonomy over her own body, but her husband does; and similarly the husband does not exercise sexual autonomy over his own body, but his wife does" (1 Cor 7:4). This shared ownership of the Christian spouses' sexual bodies within marriage functions as the religiously endogamous barricade "to prevent Satan from tempting" them through the sexual mores of their polytheistic surroundings (1 Cor 7:5). The same marital pattern defines the relationship between Christ and his people in 1 Cor 6:13–18, but this marriage also signifies Christian monotheism. Christians and Christ each belong to the other's body and limbs. As the betrothed collective, Christians must remain in the body of the Bridegroom Christ by fornicating no more after other gods, especially when this involves marital sexual intercourse and procreation. Thus when Paul declares that the bodies of Christians are the limbs of Christ, he means that they as a corporate entity are the female bride that Christ claims as his own on the model of Gen-

42. In Revelation the identity of the harlot includes all Gentiles, and it perhaps extends more broadly to include all non-Christians, Jew and Gentile alike, P. Hirschberg, *Das eschatologische Israel,* 283–301. I am not suggesting that universalizing tendencies are absent from the Prophets, for on occasion they do express the aspiration to enlighten Gentiles about the one true God, such as Isa 49:6, Jer 1:5. This goal differs notably, however, from Revelation's view that unconverted Gentiles are doomed unless they repent and are saved.

43. This marital image of the relationship between Christ and his adherents is also prevalent in the Synoptic Gospels, John, Revelation, and the Apostolic Fathers, Matt 9:14–15, 25:1–13; Mark 2:18–20; Luke 5:33–35; John 3:28–29; Eph 5:22–33; Rev 19:6–9, 21:2; *Did* 16.1; *Barn* 3.6; Ignatius *Eph* 5.1; *Smyrn* 12.2. See also C. Chavasse, *The Bride of Christ* (1940), 49–109; U. Bechmann, "Brautsymbolik" (1994); and, for adultery imagery in Rev 5:1 and 10:8–11, J. Ford, "The Divorce Bill of the Lamb and the Scroll of the Suspected Adulteress: A Note on Apoc 5, 1 and 10, 8–11" (1971), 136–43. Christians therefore have ample reason to think of themselves as a collective feminine entity in devotion to Christ as Bridegroom. As argued below, however, Paul's marital theology has some distinctive features that should not be assumed true of early Christianity at large.

esis 2:24. As "the two [Eve and Adam] will be one flesh" (1 Cor 6:15–17), so too are Christians with the body of Christ.[44] Paul could hardly be more forthright in his doctrine of marital monotheism, seeing how he declares that he has joined Christians to Christ as a virgin to one husband.[45]

Despite the spiritual nature of Christ's flesh, Paul imparts an innovative sexual tenor to the union of Christians and Christ. He is convinced, as demonstrated in the previous chapter, that only transgressions involving sexual intercourse violate the collective bride of the Lord, and that no other kinds of wrongdoing have this degree or kind of violation. Religiously diversifying sexual fornication is a far more dangerous transgression than nonsexual acts of alien devotion, such as eating food sacrificed in honor of alien gods. Paul thus takes up the Prophets' themes of the wedding and impending joy, and he does so with great universalizing fervor. Nonetheless, regarding the metaphor of God's wife, an interesting shift toward sexual specificity has taken place in Paul's poetics relative to the Prophets'.

Paul's intensifying of the danger associated with sexual fornication is puzzling when considered in light of the Prophets' marital poetics. Unlike Paul, the Prophets nowhere maintain that sexual fornication is the single most dangerous transgression that God's people as wife can commit. In their poetics, if the Lord's people commit an act of religious rebellion— sexual or nonsexual—then they make an adulterous wife of themselves, so to speak. This message casts the deviant feel of adultery around any act of transgressing God's will and thereby sexualizes disobedience in its entirety. Despite this adulterous aura around disobedience, the Prophets refrain from maintaining the position that Paul infers from their marital poetics, namely, that sexual fornication is the most profound possible betrayal of God. Granted, they find sexual fornication very dangerous to the extent that it is other-theistic and leads to mixing with forbidden tribes or other unconverted Gentiles, but so too is polytheistic worship that does not involve sexual intercourse, such as consulting oracles. In the Septuagint, further, sexual fornication is not necessarily an act of apostasy, for Israelite

44. B. Rosner (*Paul, Scripture, and Ethics,* 130–7) further explores the Greek biblical basis of Paul's marital conception of the relationship between Christians and Christ.

45. Paul indicates his marital theology further at Romans 7:4: "Thus, my brothers, you too have died to the Law through the body of Christ, so that you belong to another man, the one risen from the dead, in order to bear fruit for God." As J. Fitzmyer notes in scholarly language (*Romans,* 459), Christ as *Kyrios* becomes a sort of "second husband" and is the master of the Christian henceforth. D. Lloyd-Jones (*Romans: An Exposition of Chapters 7.1–8.4. The Law: Its Functions and Limits* [1973], 55) more effectively captures (and shares) the marital sensibility of the "Law of the Husband" passage in Romans 7:1–6: "Every Christian is married to Christ. You cannot be a Christian without being in that position. We are never detached. We are either married to the Law or else we are married to Him. The privileges belong to all who are Christian."

males may copulate with prostitutes, unbetrothed women, and perhaps female slaves without being branded apostates and triggering fears of God's wrath. Paul, however, sees something of major significance about the bodily violation involved in the act, such that sexual fornication becomes the most threatening transgression of all.

Paul sets sexual fornication in a class of danger by itself because of the body with which he associates the violation. On his view, the body is the collective of Christians as corporate bride and together they symbolically share an intimate female sexual anatomy, a virtual vulva.[46] Though this anatomy is in origin but a didactic image about religious fidelity in the Prophets' metaphor of God's wife, to Paul the anatomy is real enough that each and every Christian must participate in preserving it by avoiding sexual fornication first and foremost themselves, as though they were each a bride. In terms of biblical norms, which Paul presumes here, ordinary prospective brides must flee sexual fornication foremost of all transgressions, for it is only through impermissible sexual intercourse that a bride outrages her fiancé, the community, and God, so much so that she should be put to death (Deut 22:13–21). All her other transgressions pale by comparison because they are not, as Paul puts it, "against the body." Christians in their promised wedding with Christ are no exception, for they are the bride extraordinaire. Christians need to uphold the bride's chastity through their own sexual bodies; they must internalize the requirement through keeping their own genitals untouched by sexual fornication. To Paul, Christians obey this imperative so long as they practice either sexual abstinence or sexual activity that is sufficiently marital in the Lord.[47] Only by staying within these limits will their virginity of Christian monotheism remain intact and acceptable when Christ comes to take them at the end of time.[48]

46. In this respect Paul's marital theology seems distinctive in the New Testament, for other New Testament passages containing theological bridal imagery do not commit to Paul's position that the Christian community has a female sexual nature to protect, such that the rule against sexual fornication becomes the most pressing regulation for Christ's bride to follow. Paul's insistence that Christians shun sexual fornication thus does not stem only from the grounds of Noahide laws, as Bockmuehl would have it, "Noachide Commandments," 98. For Paul, Christians who sexually fornicate do not merely break a Pentateuchal law. They ruin the sexually charged promise of uniting with Christ's body as his eschatological bride, and this peerless opportunity is ruined for the entire Christian community as well.

47. Synecdoche, the trope that involves substituting a part for the whole, is helpful here for understanding Paul's position. To Paul, it would appear, every Christian is part of the corporate entity of Christ's bride and must behave sexually as though he or she were the whole bride. If they fail due to acts of sexual intercourse outside of marriage in the Lord, then their individual acts of sexual fornication transfer over and defile the collective bride.

48. In Paul's marital theology, it is as though the Sumerian goddess Inanna "of the wondrous vulva" and her impassioned sexual union with Dumuzi have gained a transmuted religious niche in the union Paul envisions between Christ's religiously compliant bride and her

Even though the Prophets do not vest the same degree and type of religious threat that Paul does to sexual fornication, their imagery of spiritual adultery is nonetheless conducive to Paul's position that God's people share a female sexual anatomy that needs much greater protection than it has hitherto received. On noteworthy occasions the Prophets call attention to the genitals and breasts of God's people as collective wife, especially to depict her religious disobedience and the retaliatory abuse she suffers from God. Hosea, for example, in his dual voice as the betrayed husband and Lord vows to punish his wife and people in a sexually degrading manner. "I shall strip her as naked as she was on the day of her birth. . . . I shall expose her sexual defilement to her male lovers" (2:4, 2:12). At the collective level Hosea projects onto the people the same sexual physiology that his degraded wife has. The people too will be stripped naked and have their defiled female genitals put on display. Similarly, in Ezekiel God's people have breasts and female genitals. God finds Jerusalem eminently attractive as a woman while she is youthful, promising, and religiously compliant. He admires her firm young breasts and sexually consummates his marriage with her (Ezek 16:7–8).[49] For this to happen, the people have, as it were, a vagina. When, however, the inhabitants of Jerusalem mature and become alienated from God, the once beautiful bride turns into a lewd nymphomaniac, so promiscuous in her religious adultery she has lost count of the number of gods she has fornicated after. "You offered yourself freely to every passer-by. . . . You spread your legs for any man who came along. . . . You committed fornication with well-hung Egyptians who copulated with you. In many ways you fornicated so as to provoke me" (16:15, 25, 26).[50] God's wrath takes the form of the religiously alien lovers turning against Jerusalem and raping her by sacking the city.

The Prophets' sexually explicit images for rebellion and its punishment

---

bridegroom. For the sacred marriage of Inanna and Dumuzi and its thematic parallels with the Christ story, see D. Wolkstein and S. Kramer, *Inanna: Queen of Heaven and Earth: Her Stories and Hymns from Sumer* (1983), 11–49, esp. 12, 37, and S. Kramer, *The Sacred Marriage Rite: Aspects of Faith, Myth, and Ritual in Ancient Sumer* (1969), 49–133. By Paul's teaching, though, the collectively Christian bride is very chastened and subdued in her sexual demeanor by comparison with Inanna. Unlike Inanna, Christ's bride does not go to the sheepfold, to the shepherd, and then lean back against the apple tree exulting in her sexuality, D. Wolkstein and S. Kramer, *Inanna*, 12. Rather, the individual human members of Christ's bride must keep their sexuality concealed and controlled "in the Lord," male and female alike. In this note I am strictly pointing out thematic similarities between Paul's martial poetics and the Inanna-Dumuzi myth, not maintaining that Paul historically drew upon this myth to formulate his marital poetics.

49. On the sexual imagery made possible by the adultery metaphor, see Ezek 16:1–63, 23:1–49; Hos 2:4–15; G. Corrington Streete, *The Strange Woman*, 76–100.

50. For Ezekiel's exaggerated perception of Egyptian penises, see G. Corrington Streete, *The Strange Woman*, 93, 95.

have a shock value that can overwhelm the metaphor. God's people are not really a woman, but the community has breasts and a vagina. Their spiritual adultery is not to be equated with sexual fornication, yet the rebellious wife has her legs spread to copulate with any male foreigner who comes along, especially if he is a well-endowed Egyptian lover. The retribution the people suffer is not actually the brutal exposure of a wife's sexual body by her outraged husband, but there she is, stripped naked and exposed to her former lovers, who turn against her and destroy her. In the Prophets this woman laid waste is a potent image of a conquered city that now lies abandoned by its presiding deity. Still, the city looks so much like the woman in the field of Käthe Kollwitz's "Raped" that it is hard not to see God's people as Paul saw her: the assaulted woman left to die unless someone comes to heal her with a balm of strict biblical monotheism, the active ingredient of which numbs her former desire for religiously diverse sexual practices.[51] The Prophets' metaphor of spiritual adultery thus has an electric charge that comes close to jolting one into making a literal interpretation. To keep their poetics in order, one must keep recalling to mind that God's brutalized wife is a metaphor, not a woman.

Paul does not participate in the mnemonic chant of "metaphor, not woman." In his marital theology the sexual force of the Prophets' metaphor takes on a more literal significance.[52] God's Christian people must avoid sexual fornication above all, men and women alike, for nothing outrages the Bridegroom more than a sexually defiled bride. If he finds her deflowered, he will destroy her. The same dangers do not hold for sins "outside the body." Even if Christians eat food sacrificed to alien gods, which occurs inside the body, the mouth is not the orifice that matters. If, however, Christians make love outside of marriage that is fully or transitionally in the Lord, they are lost; their destiny is worse than Eurydice's. Christ as Orpheus turns around not out of overwhelming love but because he is duty-bound to reject his bride turned adulterous whore, so that she plummets into the underworld, divorced forever from the Bridegroom, her deepest heart's desire. Paul finds this danger real and urgent, and his Christian mission to the Gentiles is dedicated to averting this outcome.

Paul's bridal image of God's Christian people also suggests that perpetual virginity is an ideal for Christians to adopt. Sexually active Christians, even religiously endogamous ones, do not fit the collective bridal profile as well as sexually abstinent Christians. Devoted female virgins fit the imagery

51. Plate 2 from "Peasant's War," 1907, in K. Kollwitz, *Meisterwerke aus dem Käthe-Kollwitz-Museum Berlin* (1995).
52. Paul imparts a strongly spiritual component as well to the relationship between the corporate bride and Christ, 1 Cor 6:17.

perfectly, for they are each like Christ's bride in miniature, porcelain dolls in their purity. Paul admittedly tries to prevent his marital symbolism from being taken to quite this literal extreme. Even though he prefers the standard of sexual renunciation himself (1 Cor 7:7–8), he makes it clear that sexually active Christians preserve the bride's purity adequately, so long as they are married in, or transitionally in, the Lord.[53] Married Christians, further, augment the body of Christ by bearing children in the Lord. Paul thus rejects the requirement of perpetual virginity for individual Christians. Nonetheless, his marital poetics fits like a chastity belt around this ideal: Insofar as the collective bride is vaginal, it is best to remain virginal.[54]

PAUL'S TRUTH-SUPPRESSING ISRAEL IN REBELLION

The marital ultimatum that Paul brings to the Greeks and other Gentiles is highly distinctive in another significant respect by comparison with the Septuagint. In Romans 1:18–23 he charges the Greeks or the Gentiles at large with being Israel in rebellion against God. According to Paul, some or all polytheistic people in the ancient Mediterranean manifestly know God and once recognized him. They appear not to know him now only because they have done precisely what the Prophets maintain about historical Israel in re-

---

53. Sexually active Christians refrain from deflowering the bride only so long as obey Paul's rules of monotheistic endogamy. As explained in the previous chapter, Paul requires that "each man have his own wife and each woman her own husband" among sexually active Christians, 1 Cor 7:2–3. He also requires that sexually active Christians belong to either his preferred group of "the married" or "the rest." The latter are formerly Gentile couples that are now halfway converted to Christianity and stand a good chance of becoming fully Christian, insofar as the Christian spouses should be working to save their Gentile spouse. Paul tersely explains the prima facie paradox that Christians can be sexually active without deflowering the bride by referring to the marital "joining" of Adam and Eve "into one flesh," 1 Cor 6:16, cf. Gen 2:24. Christians copulate in a permissible way only if they engage in sexual relations that Paul recognizes as sufficiently marital, like Adam and Eve, and thus they do not endanger the bride's acceptability to Christ. In other words, these couples alone can sexually "join" within marriage and still remain "joined" in their bridal bond with the body of Christ.

54. By late antiquity, Paul's conception of the upcoming marital union with Christ served to help promote the Christian ideal of virginity and celibacy as the best way for members of Christ's bride to live. Paul's marriage doctrine thus did not successfully prevent his rather literal marital poetics from taking on a normative life of its own in later writings that extol perpetual Christian virginity among females and males alike. His own preference for remaining single in his devotion to Christ (1 Cor 7:7–9) added greater impetus to the formation of this ideal. Scholars on the patristic period acknowledge Paul's influence on shaping the normative ideal of virginity in late antiquity, such as E. Clark, *Reading Renunciation*, 259–329; P.-A. Fevrier, "Aux origines d'une exigence chrétienne," 179–80; P. Brown, *Body and Society*, 45–57, 307–9, 376–7; and S. Elm, *Virgins of God*, 139–40, 166–7, but they do not yet appreciate that Paul's highly creative adaptation of the Prophets' marital poetics informs and helps inspire the ideal of sexual renunciation among his followers.

bellion: they "exchanged" their worship of God for worshipping many gods, and have been in idolatrous denial ever since. To Paul's mind the Gentiles in question are thus "suppressors of the truth" about God and "have no defense" for worshipping their ancestral gods.[55] Here he boldly classifies these polytheists as Israel in apostasy, God's renegade wife. If, as Paul contends, Israel encompasses all humanity, Jew, Gentile, and Christian alike (Rom 11:25–27), then the people he denounces for their rebellion in Romans 1:18–23 are his new apostate Israel. His mission is to bring them back to the Lord.[56] This rebellious branch of Israel is Paul's fantasy, but to his mind Gentile religious culture is an apostate enterprise that cannot be tolerated.

Paul is also convinced God has already long been punishing the truth-suppressing Gentiles with a sexual affliction that differs notably from the methods of retribution that God deploys in the Septuagint. Once the renegades started worshipping other gods, Paul asserts, God "surrendered" ($\pi\alpha\rho\acute{\epsilon}\delta\omega\kappa\epsilon\nu$) them to sexually "dishonoring passions" ($\pi\acute{\alpha}\theta\eta$ $\dot{\alpha}\tau\iota\mu\acute{\iota}\alpha\varsigma$) as punishment for their abandonment of him (Rom 1:21–7). He stimulated their forbidden desires to make heterosexual and homoerotic love in devotion to gods of their own devising.[57] In the Septuagint, by contrast, God "surrendered" ($\pi\alpha\rho\acute{\epsilon}\delta\omega\kappa\epsilon\nu$) his rebellious people to enemy armies and enslavement.[58] He administers this punishment in an effort to purge other-theistic sexual (and nonsexual) practices, he does not use other-theistic sexual practices as punitive torture. God in Romans, however, foments these sexual desires and practices so as to make his polytheistic rebels a society of deviants who are destined for destruction unless they cure their sexual affliction through the Lord alone.

In the Septuagint, moreover, other-theistic sexual desires and practices are recognized as alluring, though forbidden. The practices pose a temptation, so much so that God's punishment is necessary to deter his people

---

55. I have shown the importance of this point in "Paul's Uncommon Declaration to the Greeks: Romans 1:18–32 and Its Problematic Legacy for Pagan and Christian Relations" (1999), 171–7.

56. D. Boyarin (*A Radical Jew*, 232–6) has thoughtful comments about the difference between Paul and rabbinic Judaism on this matter: "The genius of [Pauline] Christianity is its concern for all peoples of the world; the genius of rabbinic Judaism is its ability to leave other people alone."

57. Sexual passions, however, are only the beginning of their punishment from God according to Paul. Rebellious peoples are also doomed and deserve eschatological death unless they repent and are saved by Christ, Rom 1:32.

58. Deut 28:32, Judg 2:14, 2 Chr 28:8, Joel 4:1–6, Bar 4:30–5. To make this claim Paul follows the Septuagint usage of the verb $\pi\alpha\rho\acute{\epsilon}\delta\omega\kappa\epsilon\nu$ for "hand over" or "surrender," Judg 2:14–15, 2 Chr 28:5, Ezek 23:9, Ps 105:41–2. The future tense is used in Deut 7:2 and Ezek 16:39 for God's vow to do the same to his rebellious people.

from indulging in them.[59] Paul in Romans 1:18–27 flatly denies that these sexual mores have any appeal; they are, in fact, sickening punitive instruments, the equivalent of the enemy soldiers who in the Prophets' schema act as God's outstretched hand against his people. To make matters worse, the afflicted people suffer their sexual punishment with willful abandon (Rom 1:26–27), burning with desire to comply with their devotion to alien gods such as Aphrodite, Dionysus, Hera, and Zeus.[60] Regardless of what the Gentiles themselves think about the merits of their religious heritage, as far as Paul is concerned they are crazed, for they have come to like the sexual abuse to which God surrendered them. Their only salvation is for Paul to buy them back out of their sexual slavery to other gods so as to restore them to their one Lord and husband (2 Cor 11:2). Just as Hosea strove to buy back his rebellious people as wife for the Lord, Paul strives to redeem his truth-suppressing Gentiles from their standing as the Lord's renegade wife (1 Cor 6:19–20).[61]

Paul's polemic against some or all Gentiles in Romans 1:18–32 is an innovative ideology drawn with considerable liberties from the Septuagint. There is nothing like it in either the Septuagint or the tradition of Hellenistic Jewish polemic against polytheism.[62] Hellenistic Jewish polemic criticizes Greeks and other Gentiles for being religious outsiders who are ignorant of God. Gentiles are theologically misguided and sexually defiled, and they would greatly benefit from monotheistic enlightenment, but they do not belong to Israel and thus can be left to follow their own religious and sexual mores. They are welcome to convert to the Septuagint way of the Lord but are under no compulsion to do so. Christians who follow Paul's polemic, however, cannot afford to tolerate the polytheistic sexual mores of the "truth-suppressing" Gentiles, for to leave these customs in place is to elicit God's punishment for allowing religious sexual deviancy in his new domain. Gentiles, as Christian Israel, are thus under strict orders to convert to Paul's revolutionary way of the Lord.

Though Paul does not specify whether his truth-suppressors are Greeks alone or Gentiles at large, by the second century encratite and ecclesiasti-

---

59. Similarly, God's people must avoid adultery and other forbidden sex acts, even though this behavior actively appeals to the people (Ecclus 23:18–19, Jer 5:8), because divine retaliation later causes widespread pain and grief, such as enslavement to foreign masters, Joel 4:3.

60. Non-Greek Gentile gods are included as well if Paul's notion of the truth-suppressors' cultural identity refers to Gentiles as a whole, including the Greeks. His description in Rom 1:18–32 is too nebulous to determine whether he himself thinks his truth-suppressors are Greeks alone or Gentiles as a whole, K. Gaca, "Paul's Uncommon Declaration," 173–7.

61. G. Klein, "Hos 3:1–3—Background to 1 Cor 6:19b–20?" (1989), 373–5. Klein's case that Hosea 3:1–3 informs 1 Cor 6:19–20 is convincing.

62. Here I summarize my argument in "Paul's Uncommon Declaration," 165–71.

cal patristic writers come to identify the apostates as Greeks either exclusively or primarily, as I discuss later in connection with Tatian and Clement.[63] They accordingly urge the Greeks in particular to renounce their religious sexual heritage as so much inherently punitive fornication, from orgiastic sexual activity honoring Dionysus in the mountains to procreative marital relations honoring Zeus and Hera γενέθλιοι at home. The patristic writers carry on Paul's mission by working to cure the renegade Greeks of the venereal condition to which God has subjected them because of their apostasy. This patristic agenda precipitates a radical discontinuity between Greek and Christian Greek sexual principles, as argued in later chapters.

CONCLUSION

The metaphor of spiritual fornication in the Septuagint connects disobedience toward God's regulations with the shameful and defiling act of sexual fornication, while spiritual adultery links disobedience with sexual adultery. Of the two metaphors, spiritual adultery is the far more potent and volatile tool for promoting the worship of God as sole lord and master. It casts transgressions against God's will in terms of a wife's intimate betrayal of her husband, and it retains the associations with defilement and shame that spiritual fornication has. Spiritual fornication is more restrained as a didactic metaphor, for it does not go beyond one corrective vulgarity—quit screwing with God's laws. The Prophets, however, transform the vulgarity of spiritual fornication into an outrageous pornography about the people's adulterous rebellion, in which Israel (or Jerusalem or Samaria) plays the nymphomaniac wife only to be forced to submit to her Lord once massive suffering teaches her that her foreign lovers have nothing compared to God's absolute power. With this religious pornography, however, the Prophets are trying to excite God's historical people to expel religiously alien sexual mores from the land, and to refuse to have sexual dealings with unregenerate Gentiles, especially in procreative marriage. Once the people attain and sustain strict monotheism, the violence ends and romance begins. God will rescue the damsel he has put into distress for her religious promiscuity, and together the couple will return in perpetual glory to the promised land.

The sexually possessive message of the Prophets' metaphor had a pro-

---

63. Paul's argument in Romans 1:18–32 starts to come into its own in Tatian's *Oratio ad Graecos*. Starting with Tatian, the new polemic that targets the Greeks in particular wins the endorsement of church fathers who read Romans in Greek and wrote in Greek themselves, such as Clement of Alexandria, Origen, Athanasius, Gregory Nazianzen, and John Chrysostom. The Romans polemic is also endorsed by Latin church fathers, such as Lactantius, Augustine, and Ambrosiaster. Augustine and Ambrosiaster, however, more broadly interpret the truth suppressors to be Gentiles at large, K. Gaca, "Paul's Uncommon Declaration," 177–98.

found impact on Paul, who transformed the breadth and sexual specificity of the teaching in his development of Christian sexual morality. In Romans 1:18–23 Paul delineates much or all of the Gentile world as Israel in rebellion, whose retribution is at hand for her polytheistic sexual blight; and in 1 Corinthians 5–7 he provides the antifornication template designed to transform her polytheistic "limbs of the whore" into the "limbs of Christ," or a "virgin to one husband," just as Eve was to Adam. In this vision Paul is a Christian Zechariah. An ecumenical harlot Israel of polytheistic Gentiles stands on one side of Paul; and on the other stands the whore society's alterego, Christ's chaste collective bride. The limbs of the whore need monotheism in Christ to be restored from her venereal rebellion against God, for otherwise she faces imminent devastation at his hand. The bridal limbs of Paul's Christian Israel, by contrast, are restored to pristine form, virginal, sleek, and sexy for Christ alone, just like the nubile Jerusalem, when her firm breasts caught God's eye and he consummated his exclusive claims upon her. Christian Israel must run like with wind from the fornicating ways of religiously diversified sexual practices, for this is the sole "sin against the body" that ruins her unadulterated monotheism in Christ. Unlike the Greek virgin Atalanta, who loses the race for her virginity because she picks up the apples of eros thrown to entice her, Christian Israel must intensify her flight when the apples of fornicating eros are tossed her way,[64] because she has real enough genitals to protect from the sexually transmitted disease of other gods. The fornicating mores that she must abandon, however, are the lynchpins of the Greek and broader Gentile cultural heritage, such as Greek courting festivals, weddings, marital and extramarital sexual rites, along with the rituals of birth and puberty for children born to be wild in their devotion to the gods.

The Prophets do not impart the same degree of virtual reality to the sexuality of the Lord's adulterous wife that Paul does to Gentile Israel, but they set up the explicit imagery that makes it possible for him to view salvation primarily as the rescuing of a whore culture's sexuality from the othertheistic sexual mores that God has punitively inflicted on her body. Still, Paul is not merely literalizing the Prophets' imagery of God's sexual punishment of Israel, though that is partly what he is doing. He recognizes that for his Christian ideal of biblical monotheism to become the dominant norm in the Gentile lands that he claims as Christ's domain, he cannot allow the focus on God through Christ to dissipate in religiously diversified mores of copulation and reproduction. To prevent this outcome, Paul concurs with the Prophets that the relationship of a model biblical wife to her

64. On the Greek erotic symbolism of apples in connection with Atalanta, see C. Faraone, *Ancient Greek Love Magic*, 69–78.

husband is the paradigm to use for instilling the worship of the Lord alone, though Paul is convinced that only Christ makes the vision attainable for an Israel that knows no bounds. Just as dutiful brides and wives exemplify docility and sexual obedience to the men who are their masters, so too must Gentile Israel learn to bend her volition and sexual mores to God alone. Paul's mission will succeed so long as this collective adopts their new identity as Christ's submissive bride.

Christ's body alone has what it takes to instill monotheism in the new Gentile domain, because the combination of his body and her sexuality provides an erotic incentive for Gentiles to convert and obey. This is a significant added feature in Paul's marital poetics that the Prophets do not have to the same degree. Thanks to the bride's virtual genitals and Christ's intimate claim upon them, devoted Christians thrill at the prospect of the time-stopping wedding night to come, and as a result they no longer even want to fornicate after the sordid polytheism that attracted them in the past. Like Eustochium, they are impassioned for Christ alone in their bedchamber of religiosity. There is nothing like this fervent sexual doctrine in pre-Christian Greek traditions, and even the Prophets pale by comparison. Paul's story about Christ bringing his once rebellious Gentile bride into a state of eager compliance, however, provides the solid basis of the devotional sexual mores that Christians must follow, just as the oak bed of Penelope and Odysseus rooted their union. In this doctrine, Paul is a master of knowing his primary Greek audience, for it is hard to imagine a more effective way to win the Greeks for the Lord than to stir their sexual ardor.

To preserve the erotic promise and reward, Paul administers an austere venereal cure. Gentiles who convert to Christianity share in salvation and marriage with Christ so long as they never transgress his sexual limits of marriage in the Lord. In readiness for their Bridegroom they have but three sexual choices in life. Christians may remain virginal or celibate, marry a co-religionist, or work to convert the polytheistic spouse they already had when they converted. If Christians practice either of the latter two options, their sexual activity must remain strictly marital. If, however, the people fail in their required sexual devotion, they succumb to the Satanic whore culture of other-theistic mores and will take obedient Christians down into destruction along with them. This their community must never tolerate under any circumstances.

Though Paul adopts his marital poetics from the Septuagint Prophets, he radically reworks its significance. The Prophets shape Paul's view that God's people are a collective feminine entity whose greatest glory is to be joined in holy matrimony with God as supreme male deity. The Prophets also goad Paul's hostile disposition toward other-theistic sexual and reproductive behavior. They too conjoin this hostility with the passionate conviction that to worship the biblical God alone is the only authentic way to live, make love, and procreate. Despite his debt to the Prophets, however, Paul's revolutionary mission is his own hermeneutic invention. The Prophets aim to enforce the norm of biblical monotheism and its supporting laws among God's historical people, Israel and Judah and their descendants. Paul's goal is to drive polytheistic sexual practices from the borders of the known world and to replace them with his emergent Christian brand of religious endogamy and biblical monotheism in Christ the Lord.

The regulations of the Septuagint Pentateuch and its considerably less florid poetics of spiritual fornication are also important for understanding the sexual foundation of the city of God as envisioned by Philo of Alexandria. As I argue in the next chapter, Philo's religious sexual ethic is an innovative synthesis that combines the Pentateuchal laws and sexual poetics of spiritual fornication with the sexual reform plans of the Pythagoreans and Plato.

Chapter 7

Philo's Reproductive City of God

Middle Platonists, by the current scholarly view, favored Plato's metaphysics but departed from his conviction that civic society as a whole—men, women, and children—needs appetitive reform in order to create better living conditions for the good of the soul, from the modest use of simple food to temperate sexual relations.[1] As Plato maintains in the *Republic* and *Laws,* the social collective must refrain from the inherently consuming passion for sexual pleasure and from the numerous other desires that accompany it, such as the hunger for more territory and other wealth. Only in this way do human beings stand a chance of attaining a likeness to God, with even brighter prospects for their future progeny. Middle Platonists set this social engagement aside and opted for solo asceticism instead—the philosopher as holy man using Plato as his personal trainer. Accurate as this assessment is for much of Middle Platonism, it does not hold true for the Jewish Middle Platonist Philo (ca. 30 B.C.E.–45 C.E.) or the Christian Middle

---

1. For example, P. Merlan ("Greek Philosophy from Plato to Plotinus" [1967], 83) maintains that in Middle Platonist thought, "the political . . . aspects of [Plato's] dialogues have largely been relegated to the background" in favor of his metaphysics; and J. Rist ("Plotinus and Christian Philosophy" [1996], 389) agrees: "Many features of the Platonic dialogues have been omitted or downplayed in Plotinus's presentation of Platonism: above all the social and political themes and the concern with public life which permeate the whole of Plato's work. . . . Such reflections . . . could be affixed to virtually all (if not all) pre-Plotinian writers in the Platonic tradition, perhaps even back to the first generation after the master's death."

Platonist Clement, who rework select aspects of Plato's *Laws* and *Republic* to develop Alexandrian versions of the city of God, a biblical Magnesia.[2]

PHILO AND HIS DOUBLE SET OF *LAWS*

Only the *Timaeus* is fully appreciated thus far for the formative role Plato's writings play in Philo's Middle Platonist thought.[3] The cosmological *Timaeus*, however, readily assimilates only to the first couple of chapters in Genesis. After Genesis 3 cosmology yields quickly to the rules and normative tales concerning what members of Israel should and should not do as a society open to proselytes, such as worshipping God alone and not coveting another man's property, as well as dietary regulations concerning clean and unclean food, and many other matters impinging on the daily life of men, women, and children alike. The *Laws* (οἱ νόμοι) of Plato provides a suggestive companion piece to Moses' *Law* (ὁ νόμος) or, more descriptively, *Laws* (οἱ νόμοι).[4] Beyond the virtually identical title of the two works in Greek, Plato's *Laws* covers the same regulatory terrain, albeit with different rules: what the members of Magnesia should and should not do as a closed city 5,040 families strong, such as worshipping Plato's rehabilitated Greek gods and refraining from unnecessary desires for private property, as well as dietary regulations meant to eliminate appetitive indulgence on a community-wide basis, nowhere more so than in the sexual sphere.

Despite the differences in the specific laws of Plato and Moses, Philo and the Christian Platonists such as Clement (who built upon Philo), found it irresistible to regard Moses' *Law* and Plato's *Laws* as part one and part two of the same dispensation. They assimilated the two works, where feasible, and included some features of the *Republic* in the mix. They interpreted roughly similar themes in the Septuagint Pentateuch and Plato as evidence

2. My description of Philo as a Jewish Middle Platonist is consonant with the sense in which G. Sterling ("Platonizing Moses: Philo and Middle Platonism" [1993], 110–11) and D. Runia ("Was Philo a Middle Platonist? A Difficult Question Revisited" [1993], 130) have argued that it is appropriate to regard Philo as such. As Sterling phrases it, "Philo's Moses was not a Hebrew Moses; he was a Middle Platonist. It is from this perspective that I think *we* can speak of Philo as a representative of Middle Platonism . . . for Philo, Plato and Moses are intellectually one."

3. As D. Runia and others have demonstrated, Jewish and Christian Platonists read the *Timaeus* as a key to the metaphysics allegorically hidden in the Genesis cosmology, *Philo of Alexandria and the* Timaeus *of Plato* (1986), 20–2, 71–362, and see too J. Dillon, *The Middle Platonists*, 139–83. In so doing they were significantly reworking the Middle Platonist tendency (for which see D. Runia, *Philo and the* Timaeus, 57 n. 126, 46–57) to regard the *Timaeus* alone as the "Platonists' Bible," as Jaeger puts it.

4. Though the proper and most common title of the Pentateuch in Greek is the singular (ὁ νόμος), its more descriptive name takes the plural form νόμοι or οἱ νόμοι), Josephus *Ap* 1.8.38–41, and see E. Schürer et al., *History of the Jewish People*, vol. 2, 316–21.

that Plato had learned from Moses,[5] and used allegory to smooth the rough edges of the synthesis.[6]

Plato's and Moses' laws seem to agree on three general points. First, sound legislation originates from a single god within a culture, God or ὁ θεός, who sounded like the same deity, or close enough, to synthesis-inclined readers in Alexandria. Plato makes this argument about the legislative role of God in the opening of the *Laws,* while in Genesis 1:1 God speaks as lawgiver for nature; and then for mortals later in the Pentateuch, through Moses as intermediary.[7] Second, Plato's conception of the theocratic state in the *Laws* arguably captures the gist of Moses' envisioned social order in the Pentateuch, as Josephus maintains.[8] Third, Plato delivers his regulations in the *Laws* with a firm and assured hand, as the Pentateuch does, though the Pentateuch does it in a more stern and fixed manner. To Philo and the Christian Platonists, consequently, it was clear that Plato's *Laws* in its own way bore God's social mandate, and this conviction facilitated their amalgamating of Plato's and Moses' dictates for social order.[9]

---

5. D. Wyrwa, *Die christliche Platonaneigung in den Stromateis des Clemens von Alexandrien* (1983), 122, 122–33; N. Roth, "The 'Theft of Philosophy' by the Greeks from the Jews" (1978), 64–7. Plato (429–347 B.C.E.) was dead at least fifty to seventy-five years before the Pentateuch was produced in Greek. The Septuagint Pentateuch was extant in some form by the early third century B.C.E., and on linguistic grounds was probably produced then, E. Schürer et al., *History of the Jewish People,* vol. 3.1, 476.

6. David Dawson, *Allegorical Readers and Cultural Revision in Ancient Alexandria* (1992), 73–126.

7. The Athenian: "My guest friends, is it a god [or God] or some person who is responsible for the arrangement of the laws on your behalf?" (θεὸς ἤ τις ἀνθρώπων ὑμῖν, ὦ ξένοι, εἴληφε τὴν αἰτίαν τῆς τῶν νόμων διαθέσεως;) Clinias: "A god [or God], my friend, a god [or God], to speak most fairly" (θεός, ὦ ξένε, θεός, ὥς γε τὸ δικαιότατον εἰπεῖν), *Laws* 624a1–6. Though Clinias immediately goes on to qualify that the θεός in question is Zeus as lawmaker among the Cretans, and Apollo among the Spartans, phrases such as θεός, ὦ ξένε, θεός helped facilitate the melding of the Platonic and Pentateuchal *Laws,* for in the latter too the divine being responsible for the arrangement of the world and laws alike is often referred to as θεός. Genesis 1:1 begins with an evocatively similar sounding deity, "In the beginning God made heaven and earth" (ἐν ἀρχῇ ἐποίησεν ὁ θεὸς τὸν οὐρανὸν καὶ τὴν γῆν) primarily through the giving of regulatory commands, though elsewhere ὁ θεός is ὁ κύριος and κύριος ὁ θεός, such as Num 1:1 and Deut 1:6.

8. *Ap* 2.164–67 and Y. Amir, "*Theokratia* as a Concept of Political Philosophy: Josephus' Presentation of Moses' *Politeia*" (1985–1988), 83–105.

9. The syntheses appear in Philo's *Special Laws* and his other writings, Clement's *Paedagogus* and *Stromateis,* and especially books 12 and 13 of Eusebius's *Praeparatio Evangelica,* which systematically intertwine regulations from Plato's *Laws* with the Pentateuch. One indication of the Jewish and Christian Platonists' interest in Plato's political philosophy appears in the relative frequency of their citations of the *Laws,* as given in the apparatus of citations for Philo and Clement, respectively, by L. Cohn and P. Wendland and O. Stählin et al. This contrasts with the relatively scant use of the *Laws* in other branches of Middle Platonism, as indicated in brief by J. Dillon's index of citations from Plato in *The Middle Platonists,* 486.

A biblical piety nonetheless prevails in Philo's (and Clement's) melded laws of God, for the Pentateuch comes first and Plato respectfully second to Hellenistic Jewish thinkers, at least as a matter of religious principle. The Pentateuch thus regulates the hermeneutic relationship to a considerable extent. Passages in Plato must show some prima facie congruence with the Pentateuch to be eligible as a borrowing, while aspects of Plato's thought that do not fit with the Pentateuch are left aside, such as Plato's conviction that communal sexual reforms and rehabilitated Greek polytheism are both necessary and desirable in order for human beings to live like the gods.[10] In practice, however, Plato is as much Moses' teacher as his student, especially in Philo's reworked program to restrain sexual desire.

Philo's sexual principles are part of an innovative agenda for social order that borrows from Plato and the Pentateuch, makes sense only in relation to both, and yet represents neither without noteworthy transformation. This is especially true for Philo's reinterpretation of the problems Plato sees with sexual desire, which Philo presents in his take on the aphoristic version of the Tenth Commandment: "You will not desire" (οὐκ ἐπιθυμήσεις). In Philo's synthesis, forbidden desire (ἐπιθυμία) in the Hellenistic Jewish sense, which signifies any inclination to defy God's will, becomes primarily sexual in light of Plato's conviction that uncontrolled desire (ἐπιθυμία) for sexual pleasure is the single biggest source of individual and social corruption. Conversely, the biblical problem of spiritual fornication, or "screwing with" God's laws, is recast as an affliction that is caused primarily by sexual desire in the appetitive part (τὸ ἐπιθυμητικόν) of Plato's tripartite soul.

Though not a Christian, Philo is a major figure in the development of early church ideas about permissible sexual conduct. He in effect revisited Mt. Sinai and brought down a tenth commandment with a freshly minted meaning, one that Plato helped inscribe. Philo's innovative sexual agenda greatly helps explain why Christian Platonist church fathers later strive to quarantine sexual desire. The church fathers' sexual restrictions and related notion of forbidden desire develop from Philo's synthesis and are not understandable without it. Previous scholars on Philo's sexual ethics, however, have studied its Jewish and Middle Platonist components, not the utterly new sexual program that he produced from these components and bequeathed to the church through Christian Platonism.[11] Philo's major role

10. For similar reasons, Plato's aporetic dialogues generally contribute little or nothing to this project of synthesis, for they show little kindred spirit with the prescriptive Pentateuch. Unlike Socrates in the *Euthyphro,* Moses gives every appearance of knowing what holiness is, for he presents numerous rules to ensure its protection, whereas Socrates raises more probing inquiries than answers.

11. I. Heinemann, *Philons griechische und jüdische Bildung: Kulturvergleichende Untersuchungen zu Philons Darstellung der jüdische Gesetze* (1932; reprint, 1962), 261–92, S. Belkin, *Philo and the*

in the making of Christian Platonist sexual asceticism has not yet received the recognition it deserves.

As argued here, Philo has two main criteria by which he distinguishes morally impermissible from permissible sexual activity: First, is the sex act practiced "for pleasure" rather than "for procreation"? The Pythagoreans and Plato are Philo's sources for this procreationist criterion. Second, does the sexual activity entail rebellion or apostasy from God? The Septuagint Pentateuch is the source for Philo's conception of sexual apostasy. He assimilates these two criteria to a limited degree. The uncontrolled sexual appetite for pleasure, Philo contends, is the primary motivator of rebellion against God, both directly and through the many vices it propagates. He does not, however, grant the reverse, that all sexual activity for pleasure, rather than for reproduction, constitutes apostasy from God. He nonetheless comes close to maintaining the latter position in various ways, and in response to Philo, Christian Platonists such as Clement later take up this position and put it at the center of their highly restrictive sexual dictates. To understand this development, we must begin with Philo's understanding of the desires that God forbids.

PHILO'S REVOLUTIONARY CONCEPTION OF FORBIDDEN DESIRE

Philo's Jewish Middle Platonist notion of forbidden desire combines two Hellenistic ideas that are philosophically distinct and originate in different cultural milieus. The first is the Hellenistic Jewish concern about the desire ($\dot{\epsilon}\pi\iota\theta\upsilon\mu\acute{\iota}\alpha$) to disobey God's laws, which we have previously explored in connection with Paul. The second is the Middle Platonist problem of excessive physical appetites ($\dot{\epsilon}\pi\iota\theta\upsilon\mu\acute{\iota}\alpha\iota$) for the pleasures of food, drink, and especially sexual activity, contrary to reason's judicious sense of moderation. In Greek biblical terms, the desire to disobey God's regulations is wrong on theological and pragmatic grounds, theologically because the rules in principle derive from a divine being who is beyond fallibility, pragmatically due to the fearsome repercussions associated with transgressing, such as disinheritance and destruction. In Platonic terms, the uncontrolled sexual and other physical appetites are wrong because of the myriad psychological and social vices to which they ostensibly lead. Philo makes the Middle Platonist problem of the excessive sexual appetite a dominant concern of the Septuagint Decalogue, for he regards the sexual appetite as the most fiendish instigator of spiritual fornication. He does so by synthesizing the Hellenistic

---

Oral Law: The Philonic Interpretation of Biblical Law in Relation to the Palestinian Halakah (1940), 219–70.

Jewish and Middle Platonist problems in his explanation of the abbreviated Tenth Commandment, οὐκ ἐπιθυμήσεις.

In branches of Hellenistic Judaism and early Christianity uninfluenced by Plato, the abbreviated Tenth Commandment taught that God's people must refrain even from wanting to disobey the Pentateuchal laws. Paul, as we have seen, understands it in this non-Platonic way, though he reduces the number of biblical rules for Christians to follow, while intensifying the rules against sexual fornication and religiously diversifying procreation. Philo's approach to sexualizing Pentateuchal law differs markedly from Paul's because he brings Plato's sexual ethics and political theory into the picture.

Philo accepts Plato's theory of the irrational physical appetites as well as his position that the sexual appetite is the most domineering and recalcitrant of the lot. Philo concurs with "those philosophers who researched the nature of the soul and found that its nature is tripartite: reason, spirit, and the irrational appetite" (*Spec* 4.92–4). He further agrees that the appetites are an unavoidable part of our human and animal nature: "Nothing escapes from the irrational appetites completely" (*Decal* 173–4). These inborn urges, however, are miscreant drives. Contrary to reason, they are insatiable in their primary desires for too much sexual pleasure, food, and drink. As Philo puts it, the soul's irrationally appetitive part "dwells [near the navel and diaphragm,] farthest from the royal abode of reason, for it is the most insatiable and unrestrained of beasts and is fed in those regions where digestion and copulation are located" (*Spec* 4.94).[12] Human beings must keep their appetites under rational guard by curbing their wild sexual desire through restricting the intake of food and drink.

Uncontrolled sexual desire, or eros, is especially problematic for Philo and his predecessor Plato. Sexual eros on Plato's view comes into its own as a raging tyrant once surplus nutriment fuels its voracity. The combined sexual appetite and reproductive urge, when fattened and left to their own devices, are the main root of depraved minds and social mores because they stimulate a proliferation of other passions. Philo fully agrees with Plato on this matter. Sexual eros is "the passion at the origin of wrongdoing" (ἀρχέκακον πάθος) (*Spec* 4.85). To prevent it from spawning other corrupt passions, people must keep it under strict control.

Philo transfers and attributes Plato's plans for appetitive and social reform to Moses and God through his gnomic Tenth Commandment. As he

---

12. On the strongly Platonic element of Philo's concept of irrational appetition (ἐπιθυμία), see too D. Runia, *Philo and the* Timaeus, 301–11; P. Frick, *Divine Providence in Philo of Alexandria* (1999), 158–62; and J. Bouffartigue, "La structure de l'âme chez Philon" (1998), 59–60.

observes in *Special Laws* 4, οὐκ ἐπιθυμήσεις makes God speak with terse ambiguity and "deliver an oracle" in the mode of Apollo.[13] Like Apollo's dictate "nothing in excess" (μηδὲν ἄγαν), οὐκ ἐπιθυμήσεις has Apollo's open-ended brevity. Philo reinterprets this commandment in a Platonic spirit that is very much in keeping with "nothing in excess," as though οὐκ ἐπιθυμήσεις meant "you will restrain your physical appetites from becoming excessive," the sexual appetite especially. By οὐκ ἐπιθυμήσεις in this sense, God too teaches the Platonic doctrine that depravity is grounded primarily in the unrestrained sexual appetite and its progeny of vices. Moses brought this commandment down in order to free God's people from intemperate sexual relations, feasting, and wine-drinking, as well as their many progeny, such as acquisitive greed and political tyranny (*Spec* 4.87–91, 95–6). To underscore this point, Philo cites, directly from *Republic* 575b6–9, a list of the proliferating vices that he attributes to breaking his version of the Tenth Commandment (*Spec* 4.87). In God's social order these iniquities would become a thing of the past, so long as the people heed the commandment οὐκ ἐπιθυμήσεις by getting their appetitive urges under control, especially sexual desire.

Restricting diet is an important part of taming sexual desire for both Philo and Plato. Philo regards Moses' dietary laws as the one sure regimen that reduces sexual desire and thereby subdues its offspring of vices. Moses established the dietary prohibitions in Leviticus because he knew that the prohibited types of animal flesh, such as pork, are particularly laced with an aphrodisiac surplus (*Spec* 4.100–18). Insofar as "eros has often filled the known world with unspeakable disasters," Moses strove to cut off this appetitive proliferation at its nutritive source (*Spec* 4.85, 95–6). By prohibiting the listed meat, poultry, and fish from the people's diet (*Spec* 4.100–18), he "contrived the putting out of appetitive desire, as though he were withholding wood from a fire" (*Spec* 4.118). Moses thus "began to train and chastise the appetite centered on the belly" (*Spec* 4.96), because he knew God's people needed to put their "love-mad" sexual behavior on the right kind of diet (*Spec* 3.9–10). Thanks to Moses' foresight, virtuous social order is readily within reach, on their lips and at their hands. So long as they keep the forbidden food off their plates, sexual restraint will follow, and with this control in place the many other vices die off. Philo consequently sees no mystery behind the obscure reasons why Leviticus prohibits the eating of animals that, for instance, have cloven hooves but fail to chew the cud. Moses clearly had Plato's appetitive reforms in mind.[14]

13. *Spec* 4.78, cf. *Decal* 142, 173–4.

14. Philo's allegorical method of interpreting the dietary laws allows him to minimize the differences between the dietary regulations of Judaism and the programs of appetitive restraint

Philo's commandment οὐκ ἐπιθυμήσεις would mean "you will not have appetitive desire," if he were to interpret it at face value. He adopts no such literal reading, however, for he concurs with Plato that persons neither can nor should try to extinguish the appetites altogether. Though the appetites are incorrigibly wicked when given free rein, to escape them completely would be as undesirable and unfeasible as trying to remove the liver, the appetites' central locale,[15] for they are what motivate us to stay alive and to produce the next generation. Philo thus softens an otherwise impossible οὐκ ἐπιθυμήσεις into a feasible rule, as though the commandment were οὐκ ἐπιθυμήσεις ἄγαν—you will not have excessive appetition. To heed this rendering of the Tenth Commandment, God's people need the sage scriptural guidance of God, Moses, and Plato, combined with their own human effort to exercise moderation. They do not need anything like the extraordinary intervention that Paul thinks mortals must get from Christ in order to obey his distinctive and non-Platonic rendering of οὐκ ἐπιθυμήσεις. Paul's rule requires the extirpation of desires that conflict with his conception of God's mandate for Christians, such as the desire to practice polytheistic sexual intercourse and procreation. Philo's Platonic rendering of this commandment does not involve such extirpation, at least in relation to the physical appetites.

Philo, however, does not simply transfer Plato's appetitive program unchanged to the Pentateuch. He reinterprets Platonic appetition—and sexual desire foremost—in light of the Hellenistic Jewish prohibition against the desire (ἐπιθυμία) to disobey God's will. Though Philo likely is not the only proponent of Jewish Platonism to reevaluate the Platonic physical appetites in this way, he is the only one known to do so.[16] On his view, the sexual

---

in Pythagoreanism and Platonism, and see too R. Grant, "Dietary Laws among Pythagoreans, Jews, and Christians" (1980), 299–310.

15. As I show in chapter nine, Philo's understanding of οὐκ ἐπιθυμήσεις undergoes still greater change in the Christian Platonism of Clement, who takes Philo's Tenth Commandment at its literal word to mean that God commands Christians not to be appetitive at all, at least with regard to sexual desire. Philo, like Plato, would find this interpretation to be impracticable and detrimental.

16. It is not clear whether Philo's step is original or derives from a broader Jewish Platonist milieu, because so little is known about Jewish Middle Platonism apart from Philo. For an attempt to reconstruct a broader and more liberal Jewish Platonist background than Philo's from his works, see R. Goulet, *La philosophie de Moïse: Essai de reconstitution d'un commentaire philosophique préphilonien du Pentateuque* (1987), and D. Runia's review (1989), 590–602. Runia has no doubt that Philo had exegetical predecessors of a likely Jewish Platonist sort, 600–2, but he questions whether Philo is quite the derivative reactionary that Goulet portrays him as being. Runia would still allow Philo to be an original contributor to Jewish Middle Platonism even though he is also a defensive guardian of Pentateuchal laws. B. Mack ("Philo Judaeus and Exegetical Traditions in Alexandria" [1984], 227–71) explains the broader difficulty with ascertaining Philo's intellectual place in Hellenistic Judaism.

and other physical appetites are inherently bad because their inborn proclivity to be unrestrained is also a proclivity to transgress God's will as written in the Pentateuch. "The irrational appetite" (ἐπιθυμία), and the sexual appetite in particular, "is the beginning of wrongs and violation of the Law" (*Opif* 151–2). Physical appetition in general is "the origin of unjust acts" (*Decal* 173), "a great and excessive wickedness, truly the origin of all wrongdoing," and "most shameful and cause of the most shameful deeds" (*Spec* 4.84, 95). The sexual appetite, though, is the worst of the lot given its persistent itch for the illicit, which for Philo means that its most deep-seated urge is to sexually defy biblical social order and to spawn myriad other wrongs in rebellion against the Lord. Moses consequently "cast the irrational appetite off with loathing" to the fullest extent possible (*Spec* 4.95), and he taught his community to do likewise, most pithily through the oracular Tenth Commandment. The sexual appetite must be bridled, as Plato urges, but for Philo it must be bridled because it is at core an impulse to stimulate sexual behavior that shows religious defiance toward God.

Philo's Tenth Commandment is innovative as a Decalogue rule because it valorizes sexual desire as the main source of all wickedness. The Hellenistic Jewish Tenth Commandment in its two more traditional forms does no such thing. The commandment in its complete Septuagint form prohibits covetousness on the part of male property owners for the property and persons belonging to other men. Though forbidden coveting includes a man's desire to sexually arrogate for himself another man's wife or servant, this coveting is no worse than wanting to steal the ox and plow or to displace another man's family from his home. Further, the shortened form of this commandment is not sexually specific, for it prohibits God's people from wanting to transgress any of his laws, nonsexual and sexual alike. Philo's version of οὐκ ἐπιθυμήσεις, however, prohibits unrestrained sexual desire as the primary origin of all religious defiance and corruption in the city of God. As Plato states, "Human sexual desires are the source of countless woes for people individually and for entire cities" (*Laws* 836a8–b2). God's people accordingly must make every effort to impound their sexual desire. The other two versions of the Tenth Commandment require nothing of the sort.

Philo, however, differs dramatically from Plato by insisting that sexual and other appetition is a "great and excessive wickedness, truly the origin of all wrongdoing" (*Spec* 4.84). Influenced as he is by the sinfulness of desiring to disobey God in Hellenistic Judaism, such as we see in Romans 7 on ἐπιθυμία, Philo loses touch with Plato's central point that appetitive sexual desire is valuable within reason and beneficial when exercised to the necessary degree required for good health. For Philo it has no redeeming merit because there cannot possibly be any merit in wanting to act contrary to God's will.[17] Philo's poetic imagery highlights the unconditionally negative value that he associates with eros and its feeding grounds. Just as no fuel escapes being consumed by fire, nothing gets away from the appetites (*Decal* 173). They function like poison and poisonous animals, such as snakes. The appetites sack and burn down the soul if one lets them, for appetitive passions are a "city-destroyer of the soul" (*Spec* 4.86, 95). The appetites, though part of human nature, are inherently poisonous, shameful, evil, and snake-like, because they are a deep inner affliction to rebel against God, nowhere more so than the erogenous zone. Further, though Philo and Plato concur that unrestrained eros is the leading source of wrongful actions, Philo's conception of right and wrong is biblically based. For Plato, people who give free rein to sexual desire primarily transgress the greater wisdom of human reason, not a god who requires unconditional obedience to him. Philo reworks Plato's moral problem of the appetites in a Hellenistic Jewish mode that intensifies and alters the dangers that sexual desire poses. Sexual desire is inherently wicked and its primary yearning is to break away from the regulatory confines of the Pentateuch.

Philo markedly revises the traditional Greek biblical idea about the root of wickedness against God by vesting grave danger in sexual desire and its fricative pleasures. In Hellenistic Judaism and early Christianity, the primary danger of wickedness and rebellion against God is the desire to follow alien gods. The Wisdom of Solomon states this position most succinctly. The worship of alien gods or "idols" is "the beginning and end of all evils." (Wisd 14:27). Though religiously diversifying sexual behavior is central to this danger, the fundamental problem is still the alien or syncretistic worship, not the sexual activity itself. Acts of sexual fornication are the secondary fallout of such worship, for without alien gods and forbidden patterns of worship, there can be no sexual fornication. In other words, "the invention of idols is the beginning of sexual fornication" (Wisd 14.12).[18] In biblical

17. Philo's negative evaluation of human sexual desire is also noted by J. Cohen, *"Be Fertile and Increase, Fill the Earth and Master It": The Ancient and Medieval Career of a Biblical Text* (1989), 74, and D. Runia, *Philo and the* Timaeus, 346.

18. Paul in Romans 1:18–32 preserves this traditional biblical sequence of vices as well: Polytheistic peoples first wrongly contrived to worship false gods. Because of the idolatry, they then succumb to sexual fornication along with numerous other sexual and nonsexual vices. To cure the sexual vices, they need to stop the idolatry. "Like Paul, the work [Wisdom of Solomon] attributes the beginning of vice to idolatry and emphasizes sexual evil" as the first vice ensuing from idolatry, S. Stowers, *A Rereading of Romans: Justice, Jews, and Gentiles* (1994), 92; and see further O. Yarbrough, *Not Like the Gentiles*, 10–11, and H. Jacobson (*Commentary on Pseudo-Philo's* Liber antiquitatum biblicarum [1996], 301–2), who notes that there was an additional associative link made between idol worship, seductive music, and sexual vices. The traditional conviction that alien worship is the source of sexual vice is far from being a thing of the past in more avid branches of modern-day Christianity. For example, T. Weir and M. Carruth (*Holy

terms, consequently, God's people must concentrate not on curtailing sexual desire per se, but on eliminating the worship of other gods in their midst in order to ensure the security of biblically monotheistic marriage and reproduction in the Lord. As the Pentateuch states, God's people must tear down the sacred sites of other gods and ritual practices in the promised land (Deut 7:5), for there lies the purported origin of wrongdoing, especially in the sexual domain of human behavior. For Philo, however, the "origin of wrongdoing" and "of violation of the Law" (*Spec* 4.84, *Opif* 151–2) is innate sexual desire and its tendency to excessive pleasure, as Plato argues, not the worship of competing gods in the vicinity. Eros is what needs dismantling. Religiously alien sexual worship is simply one venue invented to accommodate the nefarious ways of eros.

Philo, however, does not leave behind the alarmist biblical stance toward the worship of other gods.[19] Eros becomes the baneful idolatry of the soul. Philo identifies sexual desire as a kind of spiritual fornication against God that implicates the soul in psychologically worshipping Aphrodite in her inborn guise as the harlot Pleasure. Philo loosely explains this biblically grounded notion of soul fornication by putting the Stoic terminology of soul passions to an entirely new use.

On Philo's view, the inborn appetite to defy the Lord is inherently culpable and as such fit to be described with the terminology and definitions that the Stoics use for excessive desire ($\dot{\epsilon}\pi\iota\theta\upsilon\mu\dot{\iota}\alpha$) in the sense of a culpable soul passion. Sexual and other appetition is intrinsically, as the Stoics define soul passions, "an unmeasured and excessive impulse" ($\ddot{\alpha}\mu\epsilon\tau\rho\sigma\varsigma$ $\kappa\alpha\dot{\iota}$ $\pi\lambda\epsilon\sigma$-$\nu\dot{\alpha}\zeta\sigma\upsilon\sigma\alpha$ $\dot{\sigma}\rho\mu\dot{\eta}$) and "an irrational ($\ddot{\alpha}\lambda\sigma\gamma\sigma\varsigma$) and unnatural movement ($\kappa\dot{\iota}$-$\nu\eta\sigma\iota\varsigma$ $\pi\alpha\rho\dot{\alpha}$ $\phi\dot{\upsilon}\sigma\iota\nu$)" of the soul. As such its very function is culpable, for "every passion ($\pi\dot{\alpha}\theta\sigma\varsigma$) is blameworthy ($\dot{\epsilon}\pi\dot{\iota}\lambda\eta\mu\pi\tau\sigma\nu$)."[20] The substance of Philo's notion of appetition, however, is not at all Stoic.[21] Appetition is inherently wicked on the grounds that it strives to disobey God, starting with

---

Sex: God's Purpose and Plan for Our Sexuality [1999], 135) declare that "The origin of the Kingdom of Sexual Perversion is found in false religion."

19. Philo still thinks that idolatry is egregiously wrong and dangerous, *Spec* 3.29, but he dislodges it from its status as the origin of evil. I am not arguing that Philo necessarily maintains this position in a rigorously consistent way throughout his writings, only that he offers it as an innovative idea; later this idea becomes influential among the church fathers, as demonstrated in chapter nine on Clement.

20. *Spec* 4.79, cf. *Decal* 142–3, 173–4.

21. The formal definitions that Philo uses for appetition ($\dot{\epsilon}\pi\iota\theta\upsilon\mu\dot{\iota}\alpha$) and passion ($\pi\dot{\alpha}\theta\sigma\varsigma$) are Stoic. Compare, for instance, Plutarch *Virt mor* 441c = SVF 1.202; DL 7.110; Stobaeus 2.88.8–90.6 = SVF 3.378 = LS 65A, in Arius, *Epitome;* Galen *PHP* 4.5.144 = SVF 3.479. Philo's writings are so imbued with Stoic phrasing about the passions that von Arnim uses passages from Philo as a corroborating witness for Stoic definitions and descriptions of the passions, such as SVF 3.388, 3.392, and 3.406.

the sexual urge against the Tenth Commandment and transmogrifying from there to a full-scale assault on biblical social order. It is in this Jewish Platonist sense that irrational appetition is a passion, for the impulse to go against God is "unmeasured, excessive, unnatural, and culpable."[22] In Stoic thought, by contrast, excessive desire ($\epsilon\pi\iota\theta\upsilon\mu\iota\alpha$) as passion has nothing to do with forbidden desire in the Hellenistic Jewish sense. The Stoic passion of excessive desire is "unmeasured, unnatural, and culpable" in the sense that it is a faulty evaluative decision and impulse that conflicts with right human reason and should be corrected through Stoic education, not in the sense that it is an innate, irrational, and inherently wicked affliction that strives to defy a supreme deity and can only be suppressed. In Philo's writings, further, the four canonical Stoic passions, desire, pleasure, fear, and remorse, become a canon of two: the irrational appetite and its pleasures. The Stoic definitions of the passions that Philo uses are thus like a label that at first glance looks Stoic, but the contents have changed. The innate sexual appetite is an excessive passion because it itches to defy a god who requires full compliance with his rules.

Philo appropriates the Stoic terminology of the passions to recast the biblical danger of spiritual fornication in psychological terms. For the Stoics, the passions cause a soul "disease" ($\nu\acute{o}\sigma\sigma s$), but for Philo, the soul becomes "fornicated" ($\pi\epsilon\pi\sigma\rho\nu\epsilon\upsilon\mu\acute{e}\nu\eta$) and thus "defiled" through its appetitive desire and pleasure.[23] The new malady that Philo ascribes to the appetite-dominated soul presupposes the Pentateuchal metaphor of spiritual fornication and its didactic message. This metaphor serves to deter God's people from insubordination by casting the opprobrium of sexual fornication on transgressions in general. Philo is doing the same thing here in a Platonizing psychological vein, for he is utilizing the Pentateuch's sexual slur—quit "screwing with" God's laws—to depict appetitive eros as the source of all such spiritually fornicating transgressions, which for Philo starts with religious sexual defiance of the Lord and generates countless other vices from there. Philo situates spiritual fornication and its defilement in the soul (the soul's third part in particular) because that is where he, following Plato, locates sexual desire, hunger, and thirst. This new religious affliction of soul fornication further underscores the non-Stoic nature of Philo's passions of

22. Philo cites Stoic sources frequently enough that one can claim on prima facie grounds that he thinks like a Stoic and regards the physical sensation of pleasure as morally neutral or "indifferent," which would include appetitive sexual pleasure. A. Le Boulluec entertains an interpretation of this sort, "La place des concepts philosophiques dans la réflexion de Philon sur le plaisir" (1998), 136. Philo, nonetheless, does not grant this neutrality to appetitive sexual pleasure. On his view, the experience of sexual pleasure shows that this rebellious inclination is wrongfully at work to some degree, and he strives to keep it contained.

23. *Spec* 1.281–82, *Fug* 153, *Cher* 51, *Spec* 4.79.

desire and pleasure. Even if the sexual and other appetites do not successfully provoke God's people into rebellion, that is what these snakelike and
fornicating passions of the soul hiss to do. Similarly, the irrational sexual
and other appetites are "shameful idols of the soul" (*Praem* 116–17), like
inner psychic icons of alien gods luring God's people to turn away from
the Lord and to worship the appetites instead. If the idolatrous enticement
succeeds, the soul succumbs to fornicating against God, first sexually and
then in many other ways spawned by eros. Once a soul succumbs, human
regimens of purification are worthless at restoring it. Even the strict Pythagorean regimen fails.[24] Only the Lord God can save the soul that is fornicated beyond human remedy (*Spec* 1.282). Though Philo draws upon the
Stoics and Plato to articulate this notion of soul fornication, neither the Stoics nor Plato would recognize Philo's religious sexual ethic as their own, for
Philo's presupposes the Pentateuch and its didactic metaphor of spiritual
fornication.

Through imagery of the biblical harlot, Philo elaborates his position that
the sexual appetite strives to fornicate against God's will. To understand this
imagery, one must realize that Philo, like Paul, presumes that the biblical
innuendoes about harlots are true: Such women embody the seductive and
largely sexual lure to abandon the Lord. Appetitive Pleasure, Philo asserts,
is a biblical whore (πόρνη) (*Sacr* 20–21). She gives alluring looks, walks
suggestively, and boldly holds her neck upright (*Spec* 3.8).[25] Likewise in the
Septuagint, women labeled as harlots use the same stereotype gestures of
enticement to lure male members of God's people to their religious ruin.[26]
Pleasure is Philo's preeminent biblical whore because appetitive sexual pleasure is what lures God's people to transgress the aphoristic Tenth Commandment and other biblical laws. Philo, through his claim that Pleasure is
a biblical whore, emphasizes the danger of disobeying God that he associates with excessive appetitive pleasure. He also perpetuates the stereotype
that the woman unconstrained by biblical monotheism embodies religious
anarchy, be she a flesh and blood Jezebel or Philo's Jezebel, Pleasure.

The biblical whore Pleasure as Philo conceptualizes her, however, is no
ordinary woman and the pleasure that he fears is not generically appetitive.
She is the goddess Aphrodite and her pleasure is sexual. The cosmic force

24. Pythagorean purifications are described by Plato, *Phd* 79e8–84b8, and studied further
by W. Burkert, *Lore and Science*, 166–92; W. K. C. Guthrie, *History of Greek Philosophy*, vol. 1,
182–95; R. Parker, *Miasma*, 290–9; and P. Kingsley, *Ancient Philosophy, Mystery, and Magic*,
252–5, 285–6.

25. The allegorical figure of Pleasure in Philo is similar to the figure of Vice in Prodicus's
story about Heracles and also to the seductive "foolish woman" in Proverbs 9, cf. Xenophon,
Mem 2.1.21–34; Prov 9:1–18, esp. 9:13; and see further A. Le Boulluec, "La réflexion de Philon
sur le plaisir," 129–30.

26. Prov 6:25, 7:5–27, Isa 3:16, Ezek 16:25, Ecclus 26:9.

of Pleasure, Philo states, instills sexual arousal and sexual pleasure in living creatures, including human beings. "Pleasure is a mighty spirit throughout the world." The creatures of "the air, water, and land" eagerly copulate when stimulated by her powers (*Spec* 3.8, *Sacr* 23). Here Philo is simultaneously describing and debasing the power of Aphrodite by way of literary allusion, for the mighty spirit of sexual arousal that he ascribes to the whore Pleasure is Aphrodite's main attribute as presented in the *Homeric Hymn to Aphrodite*. Aphrodite as awesome goddess in the *Hymn* likewise stimulates all creatures of "the air, water, and land" to become aroused and eagerly copulate (5.1–6). The sexual dominion she wields over animate beings is a central part of Greek religious and world order. For Philo, by contrast, Aphrodite as Pleasure is not a genuine goddess who merits reverence, as she was for the Greeks. She is the cosmic madam of religiously alienating sexual desire. God's people must avoid Aphrodite's strong attraction and sexual power for the same reason that Jeremiah commands the Jewish women and men in Egypt to drive Ishtar from their religious lives. Insofar as sexual pleasure is an alien yet alluring deity, her force is inimical to upholding the commandment to worship God alone.

Philo, though, regards Aphrodite as a goddess whose power and presence are much more pervasive than her statues in various temple precincts indicate. He locates her in sexual desire, genital contact, and orgasms, just as the Greeks themselves did.[27] For Philo, though, Aphrodite wields her sexual power in the soul's appetitive zone in an effort to lure God's people into her realm of hedonistic sexual rebellion, just as Septuagint harlots try to draw Israelite men into fornicating rebellion. Pleasure gives the provocative "glance and nod" of the biblical harlot, and she even "whinnies" like the male adulterers whom Jeremiah likens to stallions in heat (*Spec* 3.8, Jer 5:8). The peoples and animals in her thrall barely wait for her imperious glance and nod before copulating in recognition of her power (*Spec* 3.8). Persons devoted to God must protect themselves as much as possible from her indwelling hold on the soul. If they fail, they revere Pleasure rather than God. Their fornicated souls become the domicile of the "shameful soul idol" par excellence, Venus de Milo herself. By this revolutionary understanding of the origin of transgressing God's laws, the very nature of human eroticism becomes the pursuit of the inner whore goddess who incessantly nods and winks and whinnies—come on over, seek sexual pleasure, abandon God, and worship me.

Despite his Platonism, Philo differs greatly from Plato in the central danger that he sees in sexual arousal and pleasure. Though Plato is his source for the idea that uncontrolled eros is the taproot of all wrongdoing, Philo

---

27. C. Faraone, *Ancient Greek Love Magic,* 134, and D. Pralon, "Les puissances du désir," 73–84.

supports this position largely because he considers Aphrodite a religiously alienating threat to the Lord's people. Plato, by contrast, takes it for granted that Aphrodite is a real goddess, that her sexual power is unavoidably part of nature and human behavior, and that this power is good within moderation. Plato supports the Greek custom of worshipping her, so long as the practice proceeds in a beneficial and temperate manner. Philo sees nothing good about Aphrodite. His antipathy toward her has as its counterpart Jeremiah's toward Ishtar—the goddess of sexual power must be stopped from intermingling with the way of the Lord. Plato does not share this hostile disposition about goddesses being in charge of the sexual domain.

Philo, as argued thus far, develops a forceful new program against sexual desire through his synthesis of Hellenistic Jewish and Platonic ideas about wrongful desire. He maintains that appetitive sexual desire is intrinsically the main root of all wrongdoing against the way of the Lord. As Philo vividly puts it, sexual desire is the fornicating soul passion in pursuit of the indwelling harlot Pleasure or Aphrodite. When left to its own devices, the whore also multiplies into many other kinds of lawless behavior against God. Plato's position that uncontrolled sexual desire is the primary source of corruption thus rings true for Philo, but for very different reasons. The fricative genital pleasure to which the sexual appetite is drawn is in effect forbidden worship, a form of hedonistic idolatry that God's people must avoid in order to abide by his monotheistic terms of social order. Through this synthesis of Hellenistic Jewish and Platonic ideas about wrongful desire, Philo imparts a more coercive way to control the exercise of sexual desire than Plato ever invented: fear of the Lord's wrath against those who sexually fornicate after other gods, and also against their communities. Philo, as I now argue, aims to quell this inborn impulse to sexually serve Aphrodite or Pleasure by promoting the lifelong practice of procreationism for God alone. Procreationist sexual behavior, after all, is "for reproduction" and not "for pleasure." Philo regards this Pythagorean sexual restriction as the Pentateuch's key way to rout fornicating sexual pleasure in perpetuity and thus to ensure the security and prosperity of God's obedient people.

PHILO'S CRITERIA OF PERMISSIBLE AND IMPERMISSIBLE SEXUAL ACTIVITY

Philo, given the fearsome danger that he attributes to sexual desire, maintains the procreationist view that sexual activity among God's people should be motivated only for the purpose of reproduction, and strictly within the marriage bond. All other sexual relations are "for pleasure" and as such fornicate the soul.[28] In his biographies of Abraham, Joseph, and Moses, for

28. Philo is a strict adherent of the position that procreation within marriage is the sole justifiable purpose for engaging in sexual activity, as has already been observed by I. Heinemann,

instance, Philo portrays the biblical patriarchs as exemplars of the strictly reproductive sexual behavior that God's people must emulate in order to keep sexual desire under tight control. Abraham's sexual relations with Hagar are strictly for reproduction, not for pleasure.[29] Abraham further thinks that Isaac should make love to Rebecca only for the procreation of children, not for pleasure (*QG* 4.86). Joseph too fends off the advances of Potiphar's wife by declaring his procreationist virtue: "Before acts of legitimate marital intercourse, we do not know other women, but come as chaste males to chaste females, not with pleasure as the end, but for the production of legitimate children" (*Jos* 43). Moses as well remains oblivious of sexual pleasures except insofar as they are necessary for "the sowing of legitimate children" (*Mos* 1.28). According to Philo, therefore, the patriarchs lived by the procreationist rule and thereby set the example of properly restrained sexual devotion to the biblical God.

Philo's reputation as "the Pythagorean Philo" among the early church fathers is borne out by the austerity of his sexual ethic, which is Pythagorean in origin. He objects to married couples engaging in sexual intercourse for any purpose other than reproduction. Husbands who exceed the limit with their wives make love "licentiously, not with other women, but with their own wives" (*Spec* 3.9). Philo rules out the possibility that married couples may reasonably engage in sexual relations for other purposes, such as fostering mutual friendship, as the Stoics argue, or keeping Satan at bay, as Paul maintains. Philo belongs fully to the later Pythagorean tradition of Ocellus and Charondas, who likewise maintain that sexual relations can only be rightly for procreation or reprehensibly for pleasure. Philo also learned the procreationist dictate at least in part from Ocellus, for he read "the treatise of Ocellus Lucanus, titled 'On the Nature of the Universe'" (*Aet* 12) and found its teachings eminently valuable.[30] Philo's thought shows other Pythagorean tendencies as well, such as his conviction that overeating or eating the wrong foods makes one oversexed. His endorsement of procreationism is therefore but one aspect of his broader endorsement of Pythagorean ideas,[31] which is true of Seneca and Musonius as well. Philo's procreation-

---

Philons griechische und jüdische Bildung, 267–8; S. Belkin, *Philo and the Oral Law,* 219–20; A. Van Geytenbeek, *Musonius Rufus and Greek Diatribe,* 73; and J. Cohen, *Be Fertile and Increase,* 139.

29. *Abr* 249. Philo allows for the polygamy of the patriarchs, such as Abraham's sexual relations with his concubine Hagar, but otherwise he assumes the norm of the paired married couple.

30. I. Heinemann, *Philons griechische und jüdische Bildung,* 267–9; S. Belkin, *Philo and the Oral Law,* 219–20; and note R. Beutler's summation of Philo's allusions in "Okellos," 2365–74.

31. On Philo's Pythagorean reputation and other Pythagorean aspects of his thought, see D. Runia, "Why Does Clement of Alexandria call Philo 'The Pythagorean'?" (1995), 1–22; J. Dillon, *The Middle Platonists,* 139–83; and A. Petit, "Philon et le Pythagorisme: un usage problématique" (1998), 471–82. Runia, Dillon, and Petit are mainly interested in the Pythago-

ism, however, differs in a noteworthy way from its Neopythagorean and Roman Stoic counterparts. He regards the sexual dictate as the formal mandate of the biblical God.

Procreationism gains greater breadth and normative force once Philo incorporates it into the Pentateuch and makes it the only acceptable way to be sexually active in worship of God. Leviticus 18:19, for example, prohibits a man from having sexual relations with a menstruating woman in order to avoid uncleanness. Philo ascribes a new motive to this law. The husband is meant to be strictly a "good farmer" of his wife's womb, and as any farmer knows, flooded fields cannot be successfully planted.[32] The husband must not make love with his wife during her period because he knows she is at flood stage (*Spec* 3.32–3). The procreationist husband, moreover, fears his seed will perish in his wife's menstruating womb (*Spec* 3.33), for deliberately nonreproductive ejaculation destroys "the seed of one's children," as Charondas asserts, and it thereby helps destroy humanity, as Plato earnestly maintains in the *Laws*.[33] Once the wife's menstrual period ends, however, Philo exhorts the husband to take courage and sow as he sees fit to help produce a flourishing crop of children in the Lord. Philo thus provides a new rationale for the prohibition in Leviticus against a man copulating with a menstruating woman. The husband is not avoiding uncleanness, he is following God's procreationist rule. Pythagorean reproductive technology has now joined forces with the biblical God.

Philo similarly recasts Leviticus 18:22, which prohibits a man from lying with a man "as though with a woman," and refers to such activity as an abomination. To Philo, male homoerotic lovers are foolish and reprehensible farmers in the reproductive agribusiness God requires of them, for they labor over fields known to be sterile at the expense of fruitful ones (*Spec* 3.39–40). These men also deliberately make cities desolate by emasculating their inherently procreative seed (*Spec* 3.37–42).[34] Philo thus justifies Leviticus

---

rean and/or Middle Platonist basis of Philo's metaphysics, while I am concerned with Philo's indebtedness to, and innovative adaptation of, Pythagorean sexual ethics.

32. On the general ancient Greek idea that female sexuality is like a fertile field to be sown, see P. DuBois, *Sowing the Body: Psychoanalysis and Ancient Representations of Women* (1988), 39–85.

33. Charondas 62.30–33 and Plato, *Laws* 838e5–39a3.

34. Philo glorifies masculinity as a symbol of metaphysical transcendence and abhors behavior that on his view effeminates the male and mires him in the sensual immanence of the physical world, R. Baer, *Philo's Use of the Categories Male and Female* (1970), 45–9, 65–9. Males in the passive homoerotic position especially raise Philo's ire, as H. Szesnat has shown ("'Pretty Boys' in Philo's *De Vita Contemplativa*" [1998], 97–106), because Philo believes that the passive partners suffer "the female disease" of being in the woman's position: "The man-woman counterfeits his nature," *Spec* 3.38, contrary to the law that Philo infers from Lev 18:22. As D. Runia observes (*Philo and the* Timaeus, 346), "Philo's deprecatory views on the female sex can only be

18:22 on the same grounds that Plato gives in the *Laws* against male citizens copulating with one another during their time of reproductive service to the city. If the male citizens transgress this rule while they are on procreative duty, they are destroying the human race (*Laws* 838e4–39a6). Plato in the *Laws*, however, does not disallow male homoerotic relations once the men are retired from duty. Philo's anti-homoerotic procreationism is binding throughout a man's lifetime. The biblical God would not have it otherwise on his view, for to make love for any reason other than reproduction within marriage is to fall into fornicating pursuit of Aphrodite as Pleasure.

Philo reinterprets the Septuagint Pentateuch in a striking way by maintaining that it supports procreationism. The Pentateuch promotes the value of reproducing families devoted to the honor and glory of God, for this is central to biblical ideals, as the Pentateuch shows in numerous ways.[35] This biblical directive is not procreationist, however, because it does not limit religiously acceptable sexual behavior to marital reproduction alone; while this is the restriction that Philo instates under the rubric of God's law.[36] Philo's procreationist conception of God's sexual mandate sets his sexual ethic apart from the sexual rules one can reasonably claim are contained in the Law. Not surprisingly, then, his Pythagorean-based views are incompatible with those of Paul and the rabbis, whose principles of sexual conduct remain closer to their respective biblical backgrounds in Greek and Hebrew.[37]

---

understood if one recognizes that they are coupled to fundamental metaphysical, psychological and physiological assumptions. . . . Even so they do him little credit."

35. For example, the honor owed mothers and fathers by their children is second only to the honor owed to the Lord, Exod 20:12, Deut 5:16. Further, the primordial man and woman and Noah's family are commanded to "grow and multiply" by the voice of the Lord, Gen 1:28, 9:1. Finally, extensive genealogical lists show an interest in maintaining social continuity through the reproduction of offspring, Gen 4:25–5:32. On the importance of procreation in Judaism and the priority assigned to it in Jewish marital sexual regulations, see also J. Cohen, *Be Fertile and Increase,* 13, 27–35, 76–82, 125–40, 167–80; A. Mattioli, *La realtà sessuali nella Bibbia: Storia e dottrina* (1987), 77–171; and L. Epstein, *Sex Laws,* 141–7, and *Marriage Laws,* 293–4.

36. Procreationism as a Pythagorean-influenced Jewish belief also appears among married Essenes, according to Josephus, *Bell Jud* 2.160–61. These Essenes likewise make love strictly "for procreation" and not "for pleasure." Their sexual morality—or at least Josephus's portrayal of it—is influenced by Pythagoreanism. For the broader influence of Pythagoreanism on these Essenes (or on Josephus's testimony about them), see P. Gorman, "Pythagoras Palestinus" (1983), 30–42, who significantly modifies and updates I. Lévy, *La légende de Pythagore de Grèce en Palestine* (1927). It is important not to simply take Josephus at his word that the Essenes were Pythagorean procreationists, as opposed to being cast in this light by him, for Josephus supports procreationism and loosely describes it as a Jewish position, *Ap* 2.199 and W. Meeks, *The First Urban Christians,* 228 n. 136.

37. The rabbinic tradition is not procreationist because of its position that a husband is not freed from the conjugal duty of marital sexual relations simply because he and his wife have

Though Philo's reading of procreationism into the Pentateuch is innovative, it is not arbitrary. On his view, God's Law and philosophical conceptions of natural law "are in mutual accord."[38] Persons who adhere to the Pentateuchal rules live "according to nature's intent" (*Opif* 1–3). Philo's sense of natural law, further, is infused with the Pythagorean stance that human sexual conduct should be strictly procreationist. As he states, "Servants of God fulfill the law of nature" by practicing strictly reproductive sexual relations in marriage.[39] Given that God's law and Philo's procreationist idea of natural law are in mutual agreement, proper sexual obedience to God's law must meet the procreationist standard. Philo's Jewish Middle Platonist exegesis thus serves not to distort the Law as he sees it, but to uncover the hidden wisdom of its procreationist norm.[40] This is not to diminish the fact that his hermeneutic effort transforms biblical sexual principles in light of Pythagoreanism. Philo's procreationist conception of biblical law is one of the revolutionary results of interpreting the Pentateuch as a document of normative nature.

There is a major difference in religious tenor between Philo's procreationism and that of Greek and Roman advocates of the rule. The norm of strictly marital and reproductive sex is Philo's key way to harness sexual desire in strict devotion to the Lord and to prevent it from following its in-

---

produced all the children that they plan to have. A husband owes his wife conjugal rights to sexual relations on at least a weekly or bimonthly basis. The only time he must abstain from marital sexual relations with her occurs during his wife's menstrual period. Otherwise "the Rabbis, unlike Philo, ... considered even those sexual relations not seeking procreation a marital obligation," S. Belkin, *Philo and the Oral Law*, 219, and O. Yarbrough, *Not Like the Gentiles*, 27. D. Boyarin (*Carnal Israel: Reading Sex in Talmudic Culture* [1993], 109–13) further indicates why rabbinic sexual principles preclude strict procreationism. Paul, moreover, is not a procreationist because he maintains that the need to avoid sexual fornication provides sufficient justification for Christians to engage in marital sexual relations in the Lord, 1 Cor 7:1–3.

38. See D. Winston, "Philo's Ethical Theory" (1984), 381–8; D. Runia, *Philo and the Timaeus*, 535–8; R. Horsley, "The Law of Nature in Philo and Cicero" (1978), 35–59; and H. Najman, "The Law of Nature and the Authority of Mosaic Law" (1999), 55–73. On Stoic natural law (which Philo identifies with Pentateuchal Law), see P. Vander Waerdt, "Zeno's *Republic*," 272–7; G. Striker, "Following Nature," 2–13, 35–50; and M. Colish, *The Stoic Tradition from Antiquity to the Early Middle Ages* (1990), 31–32 n. 62.

39. *Decal* 119. Philo further promotes the procreationist dictate under this natural law rubric in *Praem* 108 and *Her* 163–4.

40. Y. Amir reasonably concludes ("Philo and the Bible" [1973], 8), "Philo's commitment to Scripture is real, however strange his allegorical interpretation may appear to us as a method of exegesis." As David Dawson (*Allegorical Readers*, 78–82, 109, 118, 238) more extensively shows, the ethical dictates that Philo attributes to the Pentateuch are consistently meant to impart greater depth to God's Law, not to transform the Pentateuch into another school of Greek ethics, and see too V. Nikiprowetzky, *Le commentaire de l'Écriture chez Philon*, 181–92. My study of Philo on procreationism confirms this point, for his intention in attributing procreationism to the Pentateuch is likewise to attain the deepest meaning of the biblical sex laws.

herently lawless tendency to pursue alien gods, be they Baal, Ishtar, or the soul-dwelling harlot Aphrodite or Pleasure.[41] Greeks and Romans who favor procreationism, by contrast, are not biblical monotheists and do not regard sexual activity and its pleasures as a hostile divine power. Plato, Musonius, and the other Greek and Roman advocates of procreationism regard reproductive sexual relations as an intrinsic and obligatory part of worshipping their gods. This polytheistic piety is one of their arguments in favor of procreationism. As Musonius and Plato argue, citizens egregiously shirk their religious and civic duties unless they produce restrained children in order to foster Aphrodite and other gods of the city and to sustain the symbiotic relationship between gods and mortals.[42] The First Commandment rider of Philo's sexual ethic, however, segregates procreationists married in the Lord from the polytheistic social world surrounding them. Once this procreationist norm is in place, the hitherto elusive attainment of untroubled monotheism and prosperity will belong to the Lord's people in perpetuity. Philo's Pythagorean and Roman Stoic counterparts share neither his theological separatism nor his belief that procreationism is the way to the promised land.

In addition to his procreationist dictate, Philo has a second criterion for distinguishing impermissible from permissible sexual activity. This criterion, which adheres to the letter of Pentateuchal law, is motivated by the Septuagint's unconditional requirement for religious and sexual obedience to God. In the Septuagint, sexual and nonsexual actions that break the covenant rules elicit a death penalty in some form so as to avert God's wrath against the community. Philo concurs. If, in his estimation, a sex act constitutes apostasy from the Lord, it is absolutely forbidden and its agents should be put to death.[43]

In ardent support of the Pentateuch, Philo urges that agents of sexual rebellion within the community be killed in the interest of public security. If an act of sexual fornication implicates the agents in adultery, it warrants the death penalty for both parties. "[Adulterers] are common enemies of the entire human race and must be punished with death."[44] For the same religious reasons Philo rigorously upholds what he regards as the blanket Levitical death penalty for agents of male homoerotic and human-animal sexual relations. Men who make love to other men are "worth killing by those who obey the Law" (*Spec* 3.38). Men and women who copulate with animals like-

41. *Spec* 1.331–32, *Migr* 69, *Spec* 3.29.
42. Plato, *Laws* 729c5–d8, 773e5–74a1, 841a9–b2; Musonius 194.20–32.
43. *Spec* 3.11, 31, 49–51.
44. *Spec* 3.11, 58; cf. Lev 20:10; Deut 22:20–3; Exod 20:13, 20:17. In cases of suspected adultery, Philo concurs with the Pentateuch that the wife under suspicion should undergo the sotah ritual, *Spec* 3.52–63. This ritual, he contends, is a trustworthy test of the woman's purity because it is conducted not before "the tribunal of men" but before "the tribunal of nature," which on his view is identical with the will of God, as we have previously seen.

wise "must die" along with their four-footed sexual partners.[45] In the Pentateuch, these three kinds of sexual activity—adultery, male homoerotic sexual relations (in some, many, or all positions), and sexual activity of humans with animals—are unambiguously marked as rebellion and the penalty of death is their purification.[46] Philo advocates this code with a Phinean spirit in word if not deed for his Hellenistic Jewish community.

Philo further believes that when a sex act is marked as an abomination in the Pentateuch, it counts as rebellion and its agents deserve to be put to death. He accordingly extends a death penalty to several kinds of sexual activity that the Pentateuch classifies as an abomination but does not assign a specific penalty. Philo thinks, for example, that it is an abomination for female members of God's people to become prostitutes. He bases this rule loosely on Deuteronomy 23:18–19, which prohibits the women from becoming a specific kind of cult functionary and states that women who transgress this rule commit an abomination. This functionary is interpreted in the Septuagint as being a "female bearer of fruit" ($\tau\epsilon\lambda\acute{\epsilon}\sigma\phi o\rho os$) or temple "harlot" ($\pi\acute{o}\rho\nu\eta$), for her cult and sexual standards deviate from the way of the Lord as defined by Deuteronomy.[47] Deuteronomy leaves the question open as to how the people should respond to women who take on this forbidden temple role. Philo would have them killed. He takes the opprobrious term "abomination" in Deut 23:19 as a signifier that women in the community who become prostitutes are in rebellion against God. Such women are a source of "communal defilement" ($\kappa o\iota\nu\grave{o}\nu\ \mu\acute{\iota}\alpha\sigma\mu\alpha$) as well as "a pest and a bane," and thus must be stoned to death (*Spec* 3.51, cf *Jos* 43). Neither the Pentateuch nor the rabbinic tradition supports a death penalty for prostitution.[48] For Philo, however, the women must be killed because the abomination of their presence imperils the security of the people.

45. *Spec* 3.49–50. Leviticus (18:22–23, 29, 20:13) classifies as abominations human-animal sexual activity and male homoeroticism, and prescribes death as the required purification. See further B. Brooten, *Love between Women*, 246–7, 257–8, 283, and H. Szesnat, "'Pretty Boys,'" 87–106. Philo formulates an additional reason for doing away with persons and animals involved in sex acts together. The persons and the animals must die because they will produce monsters rather than children, *Spec* 3.49. Creatures like Pasiphae's Minotaur thus are a real possibility for Philo.

46. For adultery see Exod 20:13; Lev 20:10; and Deut 5:17, 22:13–23; and for male homoerotic and human-animal sexual activity see Lev 18:22–23, 29, 20:13, 15–16; and Exod 22:18.

47. Deut 23:18–19 states only that the woman's earnings are an abomination that must not be brought as an offering at the house of the Lord. On the Septuagint translation in this passage, see M. Gruber, *The Motherhood of God and Other Studies* (1992), 22–24 n. 9.

48. Previous scholars on Judaism in antiquity have argued that Philo's strong hostility toward female prostitutes should not be taken as a representative Jewish view. L. Epstein (*Sex Laws*, 165, 152–7, 164–7), for example, shows that "rabbinic law agrees that there is no death penalty for prostitution, no matter what kind," and S. Belkin (*Philo and the Oral Law*, 256–61) corroborates this point.

Philo likewise shows his chilling severity toward agents of sexual abominations in his support of a Deuteronomic rule against reconciling after a marital separation. This rule states that a woman and her first husband commit an abomination when they reconcile if the woman has had a second husband during the separation (Deut 24:4, cf. Jer 3:1). Though Deuteronomy does not state what measures the religious community should take, if any, against this transgression, Philo declares that the couple must be put to death for the abomination (*Spec* 3.30–31). He believes that the woman transgresses "ancient and divine sanctions" by cohabiting with a man while her first husband is still alive. Further, if the first husband takes the woman back upon her return, he commits "two of the worst transgressions, adultery and pandering" (*Spec* 3.31). Philo's disposition against the perpetrators of sexual abominations is exceedingly harsh as a cautionary measure to keep his community on the safe side of religious obedience and God. He does not want to risk letting sexual abominations go unpunished given the grave threat that they pose for the community according to the Pentateuch.

Philo, following Leviticus, maintains that acts of incestuous fornication are also dangerous and must be avoided. He considers a sex act to be incest if it transgresses the heterosexual relations among kin prohibited in Leviticus 18 (*Spec* 3.26–8). Philo finds the first Levitical prohibition, incest between a mother and her son, to be particularly dangerous: "No unholy act is more impious than to bring a father's bed to shame" (*Spec* 3.14). He refrains, however, from advocating that agents of incest be put to death through human agency, but asserts that divine Justice ($\Delta i \kappa \eta$) takes action of her own accord against agents of incest, as shown by the examples of Oedipus and Persian royalty (*Spec* 3.15–19). $\Delta i \kappa \eta$ is the Greek force of cosmic justice best known for righting such imbalance.[49] Philo therefore thinks that incestuous transgressors are doomed, but he does not urge the people in the community to strike them down as a preventive measure.[50]

Philo makes his uncompromising position against sexual rebellion clear in his creative retelling of Numbers 25, where some Israelite men fornicate with Moabite and Midianite women during rituals in honor of Baal. The men commit apostasy on two counts, disobeying the First Commandment

49. H. Shapiro, "Dikē" (1986), 3.1.388–91, and H. Lloyd-Jones, *The Justice of Zeus*[2] (1983), 79–81, 131–2, 161–2.

50. Philo's position here is somewhat puzzling, for as he states, $\Delta i \kappa \eta$ brings community-wide devastation, such as the plague at Thebes, *Spec* 3:15–19. Since this retribution encompasses the innocent as well as the guilty, it would stand to reason that Philo would advocate, say, that Tiresias act like Phineas and kill Oedipus and Jocasta on their wedding night rather than letting them live in incest for years and produce four children, only to have numerous unwitting Thebans suffer and die later in the plague. Philo does not advocate this position, however—he leaves the punishment of incestuous agents and their community at large to the broad punitive strokes of $\Delta i \kappa \eta$.

and making love to religiously alien women. Philo reveals the security danger that he associates with rebellious sexual fornication by attributing a conspiracy to the women. The Moabite women, he asserts, deliberately passed themselves off as prostitutes in order to seduce and weaken their enemies, the Israelite soldiers (*Mos* 1.296, 300),[51] as though the women knew that the Israelites remained powerful only so long as the men stayed untouched by their religiously alien sexuality. The Moabite women accordingly had "sexual intercourse with whomever they wished" among the Israelite soldiers, like guerrilla versions of Delilah behind enemy lines. By copulating with the men, they unleashed a "communal defilement" (κοινὸν μίασμα) that tainted the community and threatened its security because of God's vow to retaliate against his defiant people (*Mos* 1.303–4).[52] To ward off the disaster, the Israelite Phineas takes on his vigilante role. Filled with "righteous wrath" (ὀργῆς δικαίας) (*Mos* 1.302), he kills an Israelite and a Midianite woman. Other Israelites zealously follow suit and carry out violent purification on a mass scale. "They cleanse (ἐκκαθαίρουσι) the defilement of the [Lord's] people" by massacring twenty-four thousand of their kinsmen who had sexual relations with the Moabite women (*Mos* 1.301–4). This purge, on Philo's view, is the plague mentioned in Numbers 26.1. The Israelites responsible for slaughtering their kinsmen remain "pure" (καθαροί) (*Mos* 303), and Phineas is a hero who rose to the defense of the Lord.[53] The surviving Israelites are bloody but pristine because the slaughter of rebellious kinsmen is necessary to preserve the way of the Lord.[54]

In agreement with the Pentateuch, however, Philo recognizes that there are kinds of sexual fornication that are not apostasy and do not warrant the death penalty. As stated in Exodus and Deuteronomy, if a man rapes an unbetrothed virgin, she is corrupted and her father should redress the problem in one of the two ways. The father must either marry his daughter to the rapist in the interest of social purity, or take a dowry from the man without

51. Philo's conviction about a sexual conspiracy among the women partly stems from and elaborates the "crafty trickery" (δολιότης) that Num 25:16–18 attributes to the Midianites.

52. Prostitutes within the community have the same dire effect on God's people as Philo sees it, for they too bring "communal defilement" (κοινὸν μίασμα) and hence must be killed (*Spec* 3.51).

53. Philo calls Phineas "fine and good" (καλὸς καὶ ἀγαθός) because of his deed and thinks that the hereditary priesthood that Phineas received as a result is a fitting "reward" (γέρας) for his bravery, *Mos* 1.301, 304, and see further T. Seland, *Establishment Violence* (1995), 103–8, 132–6.

54. The episode of Phineas and its exegesis is an important aspect of the debated question whether zealous Hellenistic Jews actively engaged in vigilantism against apostates, as opposed to advocating such behavior without following through in action, T. Seland, *Establishment Violence*, 42–74, 103–8.

marrying his daughter to him.[55] If, however, a man rapes a virgin betrothed to another man, the rapist should be stoned to death but the woman should be spared, provided that she demonstrates through outcries, when demonstrable, that the act is against her will (*Spec* 3.72–8).[56] Furthermore, Philo states that if a man rapes a woman separated from her husband or widowed, "there is to be no death penalty" (*Spec* 3.64). Since the woman is no longer owned as the wife of a specific man, this act of rape does not implicate her attacker in adultery. Philo considers this sexual crime to be only half as grave as adultery, and he would subject the rapist to a flogging or a fine.[57] He therefore still recognizes the Pentateuchal position that there are gradations of wrong when it comes to sexual fornication—not all sexual fornication is outright rebellion. On this topic Philo differs from Paul, who urges Christians to flee sexual fornication unconditionally or else suffer divine wrath en masse when Christ comes to claim them.

Philo likewise concurs with the Pentateuch that marriages between members of God's people and foreigners are acceptable, so long as the foreign spouses have converted to the way of the Lord. It is misguided, Philo thinks, for his religious community to restrict eligible spouses only to persons born as members: "Intermarriages with foreigners lead to new kinships that are not at all inferior to blood-relationships." Such marriages are to be commended, for their religious outreach makes the way of the Lord more widespread and welcoming (*Spec* 3.25). Philo sternly reminds his community, however, that conversion must not proceed in the other direction, away from the Lord into religious diversification. If foreign spouses bring othertheistic practices to the marriage and God's community, then their marriages and families fall away from God and the community is imperiled. Such religiously deviant marriages are "the beginning and end of the utmost suffering" for God's people in the future (*Spec* 3.29).[58] Philo therefore endorses the Pentateuchal idea that membership in the Lord's community is to be measured more by its monotheistic code of behavior than by

55. Exod 22:15–16, Deut 22:28–29. Philo permits unbetrothed women who are raped to select either of the two options if their fathers are dead.

56. Philo here is consistent with Deut 22:23–27.

57. Philo neither claims to have nor has Pentateuchal authority for his position that raping a widow is only half as grave as adultery, *Spec* 3.64, cf. *Philo*, ed. F. H. Colson and G. H. Whitaker (Loeb series), note c ad loc.

58. Philo can safely be considered an advocate of proselytizing to the extent that he promotes outreach customs of marrying spouses who convert to Judaism and welcoming this practice in the community. To what extent Hellenistic Jews engaged in missionary practices beyond supporting the practice of Gentiles converting as spouses remains an active question, P. Borgen, *Philo of Alexandria: An Exegete for His Time* (1997), 206–24, and T. Still, *Conflict at Thessalonica: A Pauline Church and Its Neighbours* (1999), 249 n. 71.

its bloodline. He praises the marriage that supports this code, for it brings more persons to the light of God, while he deplores the marriage that abandons the code and plunges the family into the abyss of religious alienation.

Philo's conception of sexual apostasy and the social peril he links with it are based on in his exegesis of the Septuagint Pentateuch, not on his Middle Platonist learning. Regarding which sex acts are apostasy, he adheres to the strict letter of the Law, and in several instances he is more extreme. For instance, both Philo and the Pentateuch maintain that sexual fornication is apostasy if it involves a man making love to another man's wife, but not if it involves a man raping an unbetrothed virgin. Similarly, male homoerotic and human-animal sexual relations put their agents beyond the pale in their disobedience toward God, but raping a widow does not. Philo, however, would stone prostitutes for their abomination, which the Pentateuch does not countenance. Despite Philo's greater stringency, the Pentateuch provides the basis from which he develops his ideas about sexual rebellion against God, its grave social dangers, and the types of sexual activity that he classifies as rebellion.

PHILO'S LIMITED SYNTHESIS OF HIS CRITERIA OF IMPERMISSIBLE SEXUAL ACTIVITY

Philo could easily have argued that married couples commit rebellious idolatry anytime they make love for pleasure rather than for procreation, given the procreationist cast he imparts to biblical law. As he clearly states, God's mandate is that sexual activity should be marital and only for procreation. To experience the pleasurable end of sexual desire is to succumb to the soul harlot and idol Aphrodite. With a sweeping gesture, then, Philo could have regarded all sexual deviance from procreationism as the defiant and fornicating pursuit of Aphrodite. He nonetheless stops short of this uncompromising position.

Philo does not grant that sexual activity constitutes rebellion against God simply by occurring for pleasure rather than for reproduction. He distinguishes between two degrees of sexual wickedness. On the one hand there are "the great evils" of sexual licentiousness.[59] Sexual behavior is licentious when it exceeds its strictly reproductive function within marriage as ordained by God and nature. This behavior reveals that eros is ready to spring into lawlessness. Beyond this wickedness, however, lies the "even greater evil" (*Mos* 1.295–6) of eros successfully defying God through formally rebellious sexual activity, such as adultery, male homoerotic relations, and

---

59. Philo's term for "licentiousness" (λαγνεία) in *Mos* 1.295 is similarly defined by ps.-Andronicus as an "unrestrained appetite for sexual acts" (ἐπιθυμία συνουσιῶν ἄμετρος), SVF 3.397.

reconciled marriages of the sort Philo abhors. His assimilation of Pythagorean procreationism to the Pentateuch therefore remains incomplete. Sexual activity for pleasure rather than for procreation is apostasy only in circumstances where the Pentateuch outlaws it on a literal level or stigmatizes it as an abomination.

Philo sees two degrees of sexual transgression at work in biblical history and in his own society. If husbands make love with their wives for non-reproductive pleasure, he recommends the regimen of Moses' dietary laws, not death, for this class of sexual offenders.[60] Philo likewise remains content to rebuke men who seek out as wives women already known to be barren. These men are "adversaries of God" because they wish to "destroy their procreative semen," contrary to God's will and natural law (*Spec* 3.36). Verbal opprobrium suffices for spouses who exceed the procreationist limit in their marital sexual relations.[61] Even though the men are at grave risk of becoming apostates, they do nothing to stir Philo's Phinean ire so long as their wantonly nonreproductive sexual practices do not yet succeed in breaking out of the marriage bond.

By contrast, the Sodomites were drawn into religious rebellion due to the lawless proclivity of appetitive sexual desire. When they succumbed to their unrestrained sexual appetite for pleasure, they "threw off the yoke of sexual restraint" and committed "lawless acts of copulation" ($\dot{o}\chi\epsilon\dot{\iota}\alpha\varsigma\ \dot{\epsilon}\kappa\theta\epsilon\sigma\mu\omicron\dot{\upsilon}\varsigma$), for they broke the unconditional law against male homoeroticism that Philo sees in Leviticus (*Abr* 135). The Israelites likewise rebelled against God out of unbridled sexual desire when they fornicated with the Moabite women (*Mos* 1.295, 297). The Sodomite and Israelite incidents show eros fulfilling its deepest lust to defy God, which in turn leads the transgressors to be destroyed, in accordance with God's quid pro quo. These admonitory examples show Philo that God's people must adopt the norm of procreationism to prevent sexual desire from ever getting its rebellious way again.

Philo thus assimilates his two criteria of impermissible sexual activity together only to a limited extent. He does not identify all nonprocreationist sexual activity as apostasy, even though he regards biblical law as procreationist and identifies sexual desire as idolatrous soul whoredom working its way against God. Philo nonetheless refrains from categorizing "love-mad"

---

60. *Spec* 4.96–7, 3.9. Philo recommends Moses' dietary regimen because, as we have seen, he holds the Pythagorean view that a well-regulated diet is conducive to procreationist restraint, and he is also convinced that Moses' dietary laws are of peerless efficacy toward this end.

61. Philo nonetheless firmly believes that husbands and wives are obliged to be strict procreationists, even though he does not envision any divine wrath in store for transgressors. As N. Cohen observes (*Philo Judaeus: His Universe of Discourse* [1995], 268), the lack of coercive sanction against this or that transgression in Philo's writings is not synonymous with leniency on his part. Spouses in the Lord should internalize the importance of procreationist biblical law and follow through with willing compliance.

husbands and wives as apostates earmarked for destruction by the Lord. So long as the spouses' erotic madness stays marital, the community is not endangered and the couples may remain alive.

CONCLUSION

In support of Plato's political theory, Philo formulates a distinctively Jewish Platonist position that sexual desire is the primary root of rebellion against God. As he phrases this idea, eros is the "origin of wrongdoing" and "of violation of the Law" (*Spec* 4.84, *Opif* 151–2). Philo reaches this position by identifying the Platonic notion of sexual desire (ἐπιθυμία) with the Hellenistic Jewish concern about the inherently wrongful impulse (ἐπιθυμία) to transgress God's laws. He makes this identification most notably through his Jewish Middle Platonist explanation of the commandment against forbidden desire (οὐκ ἐπιθυμήσεις). Appetitive sexual desire is the leading threat against the security and hegemony of God's people because its aim of unrestrained pleasure transgresses Philo's aphoristic Tenth Commandment and presses toward greater lawlessness—licentiousness within marriage today, sexual abominations tomorrow. To emphasize this point, Philo adapts the biblical metaphor of spiritual fornication. Sexual desire and pleasure are fornicating soul passions. The lure of pleasure, and genital sexual pleasure specifically, emanates from the cosmic harlot Aphrodite. To pursue her beyond the procreationist limit is a kind of psychological idolatry, and this experience is fiery, poisonous, and snake-like—fit for abhorrence, never enjoyment.

To counteract the dangerous powers of Aphrodite, God via Moses sternly limits sexual desire among his people to the strictly reproductive and marital outlet. The patriarchs solemnly lived by this rule and the people at large must heed it as well. This procreationist dictate is a sure way for God's people to finally transcend the religious sexual rebellion that has burdened them in biblical history. Husbands who fail to show strictly reproductive prudence with their wives are reprehensible because they allow sexual desire to slither closer to its goal of striking out against God, but they activate Philo's preemptive alarm only by transgressing the Pentateuch on a more literal level.

Philo lays the ground for a paradigm shift in biblical sexual norms, but he remains relatively conservative himself. He gives Christian Platonist writers ample reason to find any transgression of procreationism an act of hedonistic defiance of God, even within marriage. Philo himself, however, stops short of maintaining this position. Even though he asserts that God's law is procreationist and blames acts of sexual apostasy on the excessive sexual appetite, he does not think that persons commit apostasy simply by transgressing procreationism. Sexual relations within marriage for pleasure rather than for procreation are the major exception he allows. Philo's conception of sexual rules thus turns out to be more traditionally Pentateuchal than his adventurous exegesis would initially indicate. Despite his venturesome ideas that the Pentateuch is procreationist and that the aphoristic Tenth Commandment is inspired by the dangers Plato sees in appetitive sexual desire, Philo reserves the preemptive death penalty for transgressors who commit sexual abominations. Only agents of abominations pose the threat of God disinheriting and destroying his people.

Clement of Alexandria, as argued in chapter nine, completes Philo's paradigm shift, for in response to Philo he identifies any deviation from God's procreationist law as sexually hedonistic rebellion against God. Clement adopts this position, however, partly in an effort to defuse the even more extreme argument in favor of sexual renunciation offered by his formidable predecessor in patristic sexual morality, the encratite Christian Tatian, to whom we now turn.

PART THREE

Patristic Transformations
of the Philosophical, Pauline,
and Philonic Rules

Chapter 8

Driving Aphrodite from the World

Tatian and His Encratite Argument

The motives Tatian had for advocating sexual renunciation in the early Christian encratite movement remain largely unexplored and merit better understanding.[1] Though not the first Christian encratite on record, his stature as an advocate of Christian sexual renunciation eclipsed that of his predecessors and contemporaries in Greco-Roman society.[2] Tatian, who

1. Previous scholars have explained other aspects of his encratism, not his reasons for promoting and living a life of sexual renunciation. G. Sfameni Gasparro (*Enkrateia e antropologia: Le motivazioni protologiche della continenza e della verginità nel cristianesimo dei primi secoli e nello gnosticismo.* [1984], 32–56, 368–71) maintains that Tatian's overall ascetic outlook arises because of the gap he sees between a primordial (and more pristine) human nature, which he longs to restore, and the current condition of humanity, which he regards as fallen and corrupt. She does not attempt to explain why Tatian sees need to reject sexual activity in particular in order to bridge this gap. R. Grant ("The Heresy of Tatian" [1954], 64, "Tatian and the Bible" [1957], 300–1) simply corroborates that Tatian considered marital sexual intercourse to be fornication and L. W. Barnard ("The Heresy of Tatian—Once Again" [1968], 4–5) does likewise. A. Vööbus offers the dubious suggestion that Tatian was a natural ascetic because he was Syrian, *A History of Asceticism in the Syrian Orient I: The Origins of Asceticism* (1958), 11–12, but F. Millar ("Porphyry: Ethnicity, Language, and Alien Wisdom" [1997], 242–4, 261–2) shows why it is misguided to attribute an ethnically Syrian way of thinking to writers from Syria. Though Millar deals with Porphyry, his points apply equally well to Tatian. P. Brown (*Body and Society*, 92–6) discusses the spiritual significance of Tatian's sexual renunciation.

2. Numerous church fathers from the time of Irenaeus through the Middle Ages have regarded Tatian as the leading figure among the encratites in Greco-Roman or Hellenistic culture, as well as in Syrian Christian culture, W. Petersen, *Tatian's Diatessaron: Its Creation, Dissemination, Significance, and History in Scholarship* (1994), 61–4, 79 n. 138, and 78–83. I am concerned strictly with his role in promulgating sexual renunciation in Hellenistic Christian culture. On his stature in this cultural milieu, see Clement *Strom* 3.79.1–86.1; P. Brown, *Body and Society*, 83–102; and A. Vööbus, *A History of Asceticism*, 36–7. Tatian's *Oratio* was especially well known among his writings, Eusebius, *HE* 4.29.7.

converted from Greek learning to, as he phrases it, the "barbarian" learning of the Septuagint, the apostle Paul's letters, and the Gospels, went on to become one of the more provocative, influential, and sexually alienated Christians in the second century.[3] He ardently supported the encratite idea that Christians must renounce all sexual activity in order to gain salvation and immortality. This prohibition extended to all acts of sexual intercourse, including those within marriage. Tatian further believed that only Christians would be saved and that it was in the interest of humanity to become Christian. His encratite stance would make human beings extinct were it adopted universally, yet his way of thinking was hardly unique in second-century Christianity, and he helped give added momentum to making sexual renunciation the preferred Christian way of life. Encratism became popular enough by Tatian's time and later, partly under his influence, that it alarmed a number of Greek and Roman church fathers, such as Clement of Alexandria, who denounced Tatian as the leader of the encratites.[4] We should try to understand why he adopted his sexually ascetic regimen, for his rationale helps us better understand why encratism seemed appealing to Tatian and other like-minded Christians rather than being ignored by them or dismissed as ludicrous.

Tatian's encratite ideas were also a catalyst for more authoritative ecclesiastical sexual norms. By provoking church fathers such as Clement and Jerome to react against some of his ideas, he challenged them to formulate alternative sexual principles that were more in keeping with biblical sexual norms and more sustainable, as they allowed Christian marital intercourse and reproduction.[5] To better understand early church sexual ethics, then, it is worthwhile to know in what respects the church fathers thought Tatian went wrong and what they thought he got right.

On one major point, as we will see, the church fathers endorse the ideas of Tatian (and Philo). They abhor Aphrodite,[6] though they do not accord

---

3. *Orat* 43.9–12. For Tatian's reading of the Septuagint, see W. Petersen, *Tatian's Diatessaron*, 69, and A. Sperber, "The New Testament and Septuagint" (1940), 193–4. As for his use of New Testament writings, "the majority of [Tatian's] allusions are to Pauline passages," G. Hawthorne demonstrates, "Tatian and His Discourse to the Greeks" (1964), 181–87, and see too R. Grant, "Tatian and the Bible," 301–2. Tatian's Christian notion of barbarian wisdom is explored by A. Droge, *Homer or Moses? Early Christian Interpretations of the History of Culture* (1989), 82–96, and G. Hawthorne, "Tatian and His Discourse," 175–7.

4. Eusebius, *HE* 4.28.2; Jerome, *Adv Jov* 1.239, *comm. in Amos* 6.247, *comm. in Titum,* 7.686; and Petersen, *Tatian's* Diatessaron 61–4, 78–83.

5. Clement, *Strom* 3.49.1–6, 3.79.1–86.1 (with Tatian named at 3.81.1, 3.82.2), and Jerome, *Adv Jov* 1.239. Clement's argument against the encratite viewpoint more broadly includes Marcion and Julius Cassianus as well, *Strom* 3.12.1–24.3, 3.91.1–95.3.

6. See, for example, Clement, *Protrep* 33.9, 35.2, 36.1, 53.5–6, 60.2; *Paed* 2.123.1–3; *Strom* 2.107.2–3, 3.10.1, 3.27.1–3.

her quite the same extensive range of power that Tatian does in response to popular Greek religion. Their antipathy to Aphrodite as seductive demon reveals a hitherto unrecognized motive behind early Christian sexual asceticism. Tatian interprets the conflict between God and Aphrodite in terms of the Stoic idea that the gods are elemental components of human beings and the world. He sees Stoic cosmology as a wicked but partially true science, and he uses it to reveal why sexuality is an evil diabolical invention that Christians must reject in order to worship God alone. This theological factor in Christian sexual asceticism has gone unappreciated in recent studies on sexuality in antiquity. Foucault, to name one example, largely leaves the gods out of his studies on ancient sexuality, which the ancient Greeks and early Christians never did.[7] The encratite argument of Tatian and his followers, however, reawakens our awareness of Aphrodite's once formidable sexual presence.

With the above concerns in mind I explore Tatian's reasons for thinking that Christians must reject sexual activity altogether in order to be saved. Toward this end I use the extant fragment from his *On Perfection according to the Savior* (fr. 5) and his *Oratio ad Graecos*.[8] Tatian's speech and fragments provide the only sustained and direct testimony of encratite thought available today. We must give first priority to explicating his arguments and presuppositions in order to understand the encratite advocacy of sexual renunciation.[9] In his extant writings, however, Tatian nowhere provides an

---

7. M. Foucault is able to offer his theory that an austere continuity unites the sexual morality of Greek, Roman, and early Christian writers partly because he fails to appreciate the ideological war of the gods at work in the first rule of the early Christian sexual code: "Flee sexual fornication." The likes of this rule are nowhere to be seen in Greek and Roman codes of sexual behavior.

8. I use the edition of M. Whittaker, *Tatian: Oratio ad Graecos* (1982) and cite passages by the page and line numbers common to her edition and that of E. Schwartz (1888). The text of Marcovich's edition (1995) has too many conjectural emendations, but otherwise contains valuable information. On the possible date range of 165 to 172 for the *Oration*, see M. Marcovich, 2–3 but note also R. Grant, "The Date of Tatian's Oration" (1953), 99–101.

9. It is inconclusive to deal piecemeal with Tatian's argument and presuppositions by using this or that passage to label his thought as Gnostic, Hermetic, Syrian Christian, Judaeo-Christian Baptist, or some combination thereof. R. Grant ("The Heresy of Tatian," 62–8) associates Tatian's encratite stance with Gnosticism, as does W. Petersen, *Tatian's* Diatessaron, 78, and G. Quispel selects passages from Tatian as proto-Gnostic to help explain Gnosticism, *Makarius, Das Thomasevangelium und das Lied von der Perle* (1967), 65–113. Though it is beyond dispute that Tatian's thought has Gnostic overtones, this does not explain his reasons for advocating sexual renunciation. Vööbus problematically associates Tatian's encratism with a Syrian outlook, as discussed above (n. 1). P. Beatrice explores the origins of the early Christian encratite movement in Judaeo-Christian Baptism, "Apollos of Alexandria and the Origins of the Jewish-Christian Baptist Encratism" (1995), 1251–71. The possible connections between this early encratism and Tatian's remain uncertain. Beatrice does not raise this topic because Tatian postdates the early time span of his study.

explicit manifesto in favor of sexual renunciation. Instead he presumes this norm and leaves clues here and there indicating his reasons for supporting it. Some detective work is needed to elicit the religious and philosophical motives of his encratite stance.

Tatian demonstrates his support for sexual encratism through two exegetical stratagems—his striking interpretation of Paul's ideas about uncontrolled sexual activity and fornication in 1 Corinthians 7, and his explanation of why Adam was driven from paradise. The motives behind his encratite position, however, he reveals more indirectly. Tatian's underlying rationale depends on a heady mix of Greek and biblical ideas on the Greek gods and their powers; the gods' origins and Stoic grounding in nature; and the human condition under the control of these immanent gods. These ideas reveal his combined cultural background in Greek religion and education, Stoic natural philosophy, and Greek scriptural teachings.[10] We can comprehend Tatian's fervent desire to eliminate sexual activity only if we grasp his Stoic-based cosmology and its drama of gods and mortals. His argument also helps show the conflicting theological ideas that helped motivate early Christian sexual asceticism in Hellenistic culture.

TATIAN'S ENCRATITE POSITION AS INDICATED IN HIS EXEGESIS

Tatian is the first known Christian writer to have seen the practical need to explain the significance of Paul's ideas about uncontrolled sexual activity. Paul suggests in 1 Corinthians 7 that if married Christian couples were to try to renounce sexual relations within marriage, they would risk succumbing to Satan, because most people are too weak for life-long sexual abstinence. Due to their "state of being uncontrolled" ($\dot{\alpha}\kappa\rho\alpha\sigma\acute{\iota}\alpha$) with respect to sexual activity (1 Cor 7:5), they would give in to sexual temptations forbidden by biblical law. To Paul's mind the gravity of such forbidden sexual activity is very severe, as he indicates by his summary condemnation of a man who had sexual relations with the wife of the man's father. Paul declares that the man must be put to death in some way that he leaves ambiguous, as discussed in chapter five. The man must be surrendered to Satan for "the destruction of his flesh" (1 Cor 5:1–5), for by sexually fornicating, he has succumbed to Satan's temptations.[11] Given Paul's fearsome judgment against

---

10. Though born in Syria, Tatian identifies himself as Greek by culture and education prior to his conversion. His pre-Christian identity as a Hellene was therefore an acquired one, like that of his Syrian compatriot Lucian, *Oratio*, 2.9–10, 43.9–12, and see also A. Vööbus, *A History of Asceticism*, 32–3, 37, and M. Elze, *Tatian und seine Theologie* (1960), 19–27. Tatian's allusions to Greek literature are listed in M. Whittaker, *Oratio*, 87. His knowledge about Greek sculpture is shown in *Oratio* 34.8–36.24.

11. According to Paul, sexual fornicators by definition succumb to Satan's temptations, as he indicates in his discussion of the Christian marital obligation: Married Christians must make

the man, the many early Christians who sought to guide their lives by Paul's dictates, as Tatian did, had a compelling motive to learn what kinds of sexual activity Paul considered to be uncontrolled fornication. Through this knowledge they could monitor their sexual activity to avoid succumbing to Satan and to the punitive outrage of fervent devotees in their community. Paul, however, nowhere neatly itemizes these types of forbidden sexual activity. He thus left two questions open to speculative interpretation: What kinds of sexual activity must Christians avoid practicing in order to remain free of Satan and community punishment? Second, what kinds of sexual activity, if any, are safe and free of distress? Paul's early exegetes stood to quell community fears about this danger if they could provide fellow Christians with clear rules to follow. Tatian was the first known person to offer an answer for his and their own apparent good.

By Tatian's understanding of 1 Corinthians 7, no sexual activity is safe to practice. All sexual activity is uncontrolled and Satanic fornication, including sexual intercourse within Christian marriage.[12] As Tatian states, in a fragment from *On Perfection according to the Savior*, Paul's phrasing indicates that sexual relations unavoidably enslave one to the devil. Tatian thinks that Paul does not really mean it when he ostensibly says in 1 Cor 7:2–5 that he allows each man to have a wife and each woman a husband, so that the couples may engage in marital sexual intercourse. Paul only seems to permit sexual relations within Christian marriage, but he is so reluctant in his wording that he actually indicates that such practices are in bondage to Satan. "Paul permits them [viz. Christian marital sexual relations] in so disapproving a manner that he in effect prevents the practice. By agreeing that [the couples] after their prayers may come together in the union of sexual corruption because of Satan and their lack of self-control (ἀκρασία), Paul has revealed that the one who would follow this advice is enslaved . . . to a state of being uncontrolled (ἀκρασία), to sexual fornication, and to the devil."[13] Christians therefore have only one way to avoid being a sexually acratic pawn of Satan. To gain proper control over their sexuality, they need to renounce any and all sexual activity as the "union of sexual corruption."[14]

---

love strictly with their spouses in order to help each other avoid Satan and the temptations to sexually fornicate that he presents to them, 1 Cor 7:2–5.

12. Tatian's position that γάμος is πορνεία is a characteristic feature of encratite thought, U. Bianchi, *La tradizione dell'enkrateia: motivazioni ontologiche e protologiche* (1985), xxv and C. Spada, "Un' omelia greca anonima 'sulla verginità'" (1985), 604 n. 3.

13. *On Perfection*, fr. 5 = Clement *Strom* 3.81.1–2. Jerome further corroborates Tatian's unconditionally negative evaluation of sexual intercourse: Tatian found "all sexual intercourse to be filthy" (*omnem coitum spurcum*), *Adv Jov* 1.239, and "every sexual union of the male with a woman to be unclean" and "a corruption," *comm. in Gal.* 7.526.

14. G. Sfameni Gasparro, "Motivazioni protologiche dell'*enkrateia*" (1985), 157–8. M. Elze (*Tatian und seine Theologie*, 116–20) further explains the disruption in harmony that Tatian as-

Tatian's interpretation of 1 Corinthians 7 differs significantly from the more straightforward interpretation of Paul's meaning. Paul states that Christians who wish to be sexually active should marry Christians, and then engage only in marital sexual relations.[15] On his view marriage in the Lord serves as a preventive from falling into practices of sexual fornication, such as incest or adultery, not as a venue in which to sexually fornicate. "Due to acts of sexual fornication (διὰ δὲ τὰς πορνείας), let each man have his own wife and let each woman have her own husband. Let the husband render the sexual duty to his wife and let the wife behave likewise for her husband" (1 Cor 7:2–3). Paul pointedly contrasts marital sexual intercourse in the Lord with sexual fornication.[16] Christian marital sex is a conjugal "duty" (ὀφειλή), or obligation (1 Cor 7:3), and this duty functions as a kind of sexual barrier against Satan with his many polytheistic and other lures. Christian couples must make love periodically in order to help each other keep Satan's temptations at bay. Hence the Christian conjugal duty has an apotropaic force according to Paul. Not unlike the sprinkling of holy water, it keeps the devil at a distance in his prowling.

Tatian, however, interprets Paul's prepositional phrase "because of fornicating acts" (διὰ τὰς πορνείας) to mean that Christians who marry do so in order to sexually fornicate under the cover of marriage. By this understanding, if Christians cannot refrain from sexual intercourse completely, which is what they must do in order to be saved, then they need to marry so as to give their sexual fornication a façade of legitimacy. The seeming legitimacy is fraudulent, however, for the institution of Christian marriage does not rehabilitate the sinfully fornicating nature of marital sexual relations.[17] Rather, marriage wrongly makes this egregious transgression seem normal

---

sociates with being sexual active. As shown by Elze, Tatian creatively elucidates this idea about disrupted harmony partly from Paul's statement that married Christians should "harmoniously [or: agreeably] abstain for a time (ἐκ συμφώνου πρὸς καιρόν)" from sexual relations in order to pray, 1 Cor 7:5.

15. Paul, I have shown in chapter five, assumes the norm of religious endogamy in the Lord in 1 Cor 7:1–39, where he accords preferential status to married couples made up of two spouses who worship the Lord alone. Paul does not condone Christians marrying Gentile persons who do not first convert to Christianity.

16. Sexual fornication in Paul's sense consists of sexual intercourse that is beyond the boundaries of marriage religiously permissible for Christians. This includes, as shown in chapter five, extramarital sexual relations; sexual intercourse in devotion to gods other than or in addition to the Lord, such as in marriages formed between Christians and Gentiles; and sexual transgressions of Pentateuchal prohibitions, such as incest and adultery.

17. J. Héring (*The First Epistle of Saint Paul to the Corinthians*, 45) captures the gist of Tatian's reasoning here, though he describes the viewpoint as one belonging to "ascetic gnostics" in general, not to Tatian in particular: "If fleshly communion with a 'πόρνη' = 'harlot' breaks the union with Christ, why is the same not true of the fleshly communion in marriage?"

and permissible. Tatian is not fooled by this specious normalcy. Christian marital intercourse is "sexual fornication" in a marital guise, as he declares in *On Perfection*. And such fornication deserves nothing but antipathy. "I loathe sexual fornication" (πορνείαν μεμίσηκα), he expressly states in his *Oratio* (11.27–8). Tatian recoils at the prospect of Christians marrying and making love within marriage because he concurs with Paul that fornication is a Satanic threat that Christians must "run away from" altogether (1 Cor 6:18). Tatian, however, flees sexual intercourse under any circumstances, even to the point of declaring that sexually active married Christians are fornicating slaves of the devil, and he is convinced that Paul agrees with his assessment. As Paul has shown, he declares, Christians who would marry and make love to their spouses are "enslaved . . . to sexual fornication and to the devil" (fr. 5, *On Perfection*). By Tatian's understanding, therefore, Christian leaders would be reprehensibly permissive to teach that Paul not only allows but requires most Christians to engage in marital sexual activity. The gist of this negligent doctrine would be that Christians are not only free but obligated to sexually succumb to Satan, so long as they are married. Paul's true intention rules out this reckless teaching. Even though he pretends to allow Christian marital sex, the disapproving scowl Tatian imagines him making reveals that Paul disallows it.

Tatian reinforces his conviction that sexual intercourse is a kind of devil worship in his interpretation of Adam's sin and fall. Adam, he maintains, became alienated from God because he engaged in sexual intercourse with Eve. Insofar as Eve is Adam's wife and sexual mate joined as "two into one flesh" (Gen 2:24),[18] Tatian excludes the possibility that the primordial biblical couple could have made love without defecting from God. If he believed that sexual intercourse were religiously permissible among couples devoted to God, he would not have banished Adam from paradise for making love with his wife. Tatian does expel him, however, which suggests that marital sexual activity is the original sin. He consequently sets marital sexual relations in the same league of fornicating danger as the one posed, on Paul's view, by a Christian man making love with his father's wife. Had the man made love with his own wife rather than with his father's, for Tatian his sexual sin would have been as heinous. The next important question is what makes Tatian misconstrue 1 Corinthians 7 so remarkably, what drives him to expel Adam from paradise for making love with Eve.

---

18. Tatian presumably denies salvation to Eve along with Adam because of this marital sexual fornication, though Epiphanius's testimony does not say as much, *Haer* 2.215–18 and A. Vööbus, *A History of Asceticism*, 36. Vööbus skillfully suggests several additional ways in which Tatian's *Diatessaron* imparts the message of sexual renunciation, *A History of Asceticism*, 42–3, which W. Petersen (*Tatian's* Diatessaron, 81) lists and relates to Matt 1:19, 1:24, and Luke 20:27–40.

THE OLYMPIANS' HOSTILE TAKEOVER OF THE WORLD

In this section I explore the Greek ideas that motivated Tatian to declare that sexual activity is contrary to the way of God. It should not seem surprising that his writing reflects Greek ways of thought. Though Syrian by birth, he identifies himself as having been thoroughly Hellenized through his education prior to his conversion to Christianity. "Men of Greece (ἄν-δρες Ἕλληνες), . . . I once was very eminent in your ways of wisdom."[19] To disclose the Greek underpinnings of his encratite position, I begin with his conception of the Olympian gods and then explore the pantheistic world of Stoic physics in which he situates his battle of the gods.

Tatian believes that the Greek gods tangibly exist and that they have the powers traditionally associated with them in Greek religion, Homer, and astrology. At the center are the gods of the Olympian pantheon. For example, as Tatian lists them in his *Oratio,* Athena is a warrior goddess, Poseidon a power of the sea, Aphrodite of sexual relations, Apollo of healing and lyre music, and Zeus their leader negotiates with the forces of fate.[20] In addition to the Olympians, there are numerous other gods, such as Gaia and various Titans. All these gods are real on Tatian's view. They are comprised of matter and spirit, though they do not have human flesh, properly speaking.[21] Nonetheless, their corporeality is substantial and subject to pain, for God destines the Olympians to eternal punishment for their sinful manipulation of the Greek people and their culture (15.7–16.2). The Olympian gods embody and still control the zodiac domain, through which they have shaped the human condition to be mortal and subject to the constraints of fate.[22] Tatian thus does not regard the gods as the defused figments of storybook mythology into which they metamorphosed when their realm of Olympus became uninhabited, "a museum in the night."[23] The Greek gods are genuine superhuman beings whose awesome powers are still at work in the zones traditionally associated with them, be it the sea, sex, and so forth. Their

19. 1.2, 2.9–10. All further references to Tatian are to his *Oratio.*

20. 8.21, 9.4, 10.23, 11.1. In addition to Aphrodite, Tatian names the following Olympians as fellow conspirators of Zeus: Artemis, Apollo, Hephaestus, Athena, Poseidon, Dionysus, Demeter, and Persephone. He does not mention Hermes or Hera. Non-Olympians whom he mentions include Gaia, Cybele, Cronus, and Asclepius.

21. 13.15–17, 15.14–15.

22. 9.23–10.5, and see also 8.4–5, 11.25. The Olympians, partly as astral or zodiac powers, have ruthlessly and "very unjustly" subjected the Greeks to "birth under the regime of fate."

23. R. Calasso, *The Marriage of Cadmus and Harmony* (1993), 378. For further study of the real and physical existence that Tatian attributes to the gods, see H. Wey von Schwarzenbach, *Die funktionen der bösen Geister bei den griechischen Apologeten des zweiten Jahrhunderts nach Christus* (1957), 70–3.

forces are reflected in astrology, and the Greek people who worship them are ruthlessly under their control.

In Tatian's estimation, the Greek gods are not the bona fide deities that they are in Greek popular theology. The Olympians are rebellious angels who committed high treason against God, and in response God disowned and cast them out from his presence. Once upon a time, as Tatian tells the story, "An angel who was more cunning than the rest of the angels by virtue of being first born revolted against God's law and then was proclaimed as God by his mortal (ἄνθρωποι) and immortal followers. Then the power of God's word banished the arch-leader of the rebellion and his followers," divine and mortal alike (7.24–9). The mortals who rebelled with the Olympians became the renegade angels' subjects and followers. Tatian's myth about the fallen Olympians is a variation on the story of fallen angels in the book of Enoch, in which the unnamed sons or angels of God in Genesis 6 defect from God and come to dwell on earth.[24] In Tatian's version, however, the head of the rebellion is "the leader Zeus" (8.18–19).[25] Because the people who defected at the same time did so to worship Zeus and his fellow Olympians, they are culturally identifiable: the early ancestors of Tatian's Greek contemporaries. Thus, as Tatian would have it, the Greeks have been a wantonly rebellious tribe of Israel ever since the days of Agamemnon and earlier, when their ancestors first abandoned God in favor of Zeus the usurper. Tatian harbors the view that the Greeks are in rebellion because he believes that Paul's accusation about truth-suppressors in Romans 1:18–32 is historically true and targets the Greeks as the apostate society.[26] Since their abandonment of God, the Greeks have been outrageous dupes of the rebellious Olympians, such as Aphrodite, Athena, and, of course, Zeus the leader.[27] The Greek gods are thus are a dangerous collective of God's adversaries, the Satanic gang of twelve with Zeus as the ringleader, and the Greeks are guilty fools for defiantly worshipping them.

Tatian accordingly deplores his Greek contemporaries for continuing to worship the Olympians. All the Hellenic religious festivals are corrupt to the core.[28] The celebrations wrongly serve to honor "evil demons" (24.18–21),

24. H. Wey von Schwarzenbach, *Bösen Geister*, 15 n. 40, and for the myth see *The Book of Enoch* 6:1–11:2 and E. Schürer et al, *History of the Jewish People*, vol. 3.1, 252.

25. Tatian's former teacher Justin similarly identifies the Greek gods as demons, *1 Apol* 5.1–4, H. Wey von Schwarzenbach, *Bösen Geister*, 186–90.

26. K. Gaca, "Paul's Uncommon Declaration," 171–7, 181–3.

27. 7.29–8.3, 8.18–9.23.

28. The culture that he castigates is thoroughly Greek, not a Gentile culture of mixed ethnicity. Tatian indicates his Hellenic audience by his repeated address to "the men of Hellas" (Ἕλληνες and ἄνδρες Ἕλληνες) at key points throughout his speech, 1.2, 4.20, 14.10, 15.8, 23.5, 30.26, 31.9–11, 43.9.

not "the blessed gods" (μακάρεσσι θεοῖσιν), as Homer thinks (8.12). Hellenic practices of this sort are not a religious heritage worth defending on civic and spiritual grounds, but damning indications of how badly the Greeks went astray when their brazen ancestors turned their backs on the god of Abraham and to follow the gods of Agamemnon. For Tatian, then, nothing could be more wrong than to believe, as the Greeks and Stoic philosophers did, that Zeus is "the best and greatest of the gods" and that his fellow Olympians are second only to Zeus as deities worth worshipping for their various powers.[29]

Tatian deploys Stoic physical cosmology to produce a demonology of the Olympians as elemental principles in the world.[30] He shares the Stoic position that the world is comprised of two cosmological principles, matter (ὕλη) and psychic or immanent spirit (πνεῦμα). He further agrees with the Stoics that the human soul and body are a human-specific composite of these elemental components.[31] Tatian's definition of spirit in relation to matter reveals his debt to Stoic thought. Immanent spirit, he states, is "spirit extending throughout matter" (πνεῦμα διῆκον διὰ τῆς ὕλης) (5.2, 10). This is the standard Stoic conception and definition of spirit (πνεῦμα) as cosmological principle. In Stoic physics, an immanent divine "spirit extends throughout the cosmos (πνεῦμα διῆκον διὰ τοῦ κόσμου) . . . and moves through the changing facets of matter (ὕλης)."[32] This creative involvement of divine spirit with matter shapes all entities in the universe and lends them their distinctive characteristics, including the gods, human beings, and the souls that make mortals alive, sentient, rational and sexually active. Tatian's conception of the physical human body also adopts a Stoic framework. Human bodies are an "intricate succession of sinews and bones" (19.2–3), just as the Stoics call the human body an intricate system (ἕξις) of "sinews and bones."[33]

Tatian, however, superimposes the biblical idea of God on Stoic physics and theology. God is himself a transcendent spirit, and he produced the mutable immanent spirit and matter. God then used these two elements to

29. *Hymn hom* 23.1, Cleanthes, *Hymn to Zeus*, SVF 1.537 = LS 54I.

30. Tatian's adaptation of Stoic physical principles has hitherto received passing mention, H. Wey von Schwarzenbach, *Bösen Geister,* 73 and M. Elze, *Tatian und seine Theologie,* 68. G. Hawthorne ("Tatian and His Discourse" [1964], 167, 177–8) astutely senses that Tatian is partly engaged in "a frontal attack on the Stoics," and on Stoic pantheism in particular, but he leaves this point undeveloped.

31. 5.2–5, 5.10–12, 12.18–22.

32. SVF 2.1027; and note also SVF 2.416 = Galen, *Intr* 14.698; SVF 2.441 = LS 47L = Alexander of Aphrodisias, *Mixt* 223.25; and SVF 2.1037 = Sextus Empiricus, *PH* 3.218.

33. A. A. Long ("Soul and Body in Stoicism," 42–5) aptly refers to this Stoic conception of the physical body as "the flesh and bones body." The Stoics, though, described the body as a system of "sinews and bones" (DL 7.139), just as Tatian does.

create and structure the world and everything in it, including human beings (4.29, 5.5). In Stoic thought, there is no transcendent creator or deity separable from the world. The primary deity and principle of rational order is Zeus as immanent spirit in its pantheistic and elemental diversity.[34] Tatian, by situating God over the Stoic cosmos as its creator, is able to reevaluate the Stoic pantheistic principle of immanent spirit.

In Tatian's remake of Stoic physical cosmology, the world and the immanent spirit that informs and shapes it were good and orderly as created by God—or at least they used to be, prior to the Olympian rebellion. In its origins, "the construction of the cosmos is good."[35] When the Olympians defected from God and instituted the regime of Zeus, however, the primordial order of cosmic spirit and matter changed drastically for the worse. Once Zeus and the gods rebelled, they infiltrated immanent spirit like squatters, threw it into wicked disorder, and have yet to be removed. From their strongholds in immanent spirit, the gods "rage like bacchants in their wicked habits," "wallow in filth," and plunge the Greeks down to their level and away from God.[36] The Greek gods thus function like toxins polluting the world's immanent spirit, dripping evil where goodness and purity once suffused the cosmos and human nature.[37] The world has thus been reconfigured and contaminated due to the gods' corrupt and freeform perversions of immanent spirit.

Despite his debt to Stoic cosmology, Tatian's evaluation of the world and its immanent spirit is radically anti-Stoic. As he sees it, nothing about the world as imbued by Zeus and his fellow gods can possibly be rational, for the Olympians are evil and crazed fallen angels who hold much of it in their maniacal possession. This antirational condition holds true of people too, and especially of the lunatic philosophers, who teach depraved ideas such as the Stoic view that Zeus is the pantheistic bearer of rationality and good order. "The human being is not a rational animal, receptive to mind and knowledge, as those squawking [philosophers] teach."[38] These views are di-

---

34. M. Elze too (*Tatian und seine Theologie*, 68) notes this difference between the Stoics' immanent God and Tatian's transcendent God.

35. 21.11–12, cf. 13.8–11.

36. 17.19–24, 24.15–17. On Tatian's position that the Greek gods are corrupt demons with domineering power over mortal lives, see H. Wey von Schwarzenbach, *Bösen Geister*, 68–70, 191–202.

37. Tatian's belief that the material world is manipulated by evil demons differs from the Gnostic stance that matter is inherently and pervasively evil. He maintains that matter is good but infected with hot spots, so to speak, of Olympian spirit evil. The biblical God, he further believes, can and should cleanse the locales. Hence Tatian is not a fully dedicated Gnostic, for he does not denigrate matter as such even though he urges that one must "reject matter" for as long as it is still infected by Olympian spirits, 17.29–18.4.

38. 14.16–21, 16.10–11.

ametrically opposed to Stoic philosophy. In Stoic cosmology, the gods make the world rational, holistic, and beautiful by their presence. "All that exists coexists and is unified since it has a spirit extending throughout it, by means of which the entirety coheres, is continuous, and is entirely of concordant feeling with itself."[39] Zeus shapes the primary identity of immanent spirit, for he is the seminal logos of immanent spirit and his guiding will makes the spirit rational.[40] The other gods, in obedience to Zeus, help shape living creatures to be sexually active, mortal, and subject to the unavoidable constraints of fate. In Stoic psychology, further, adult human beings are the rational animal par excellence.[41] The structure of their souls is inherently rational, though they need disciplined Stoic training to behave in a correctly sagacious manner. If men and women attain their disciplined best, which they should strive to do, they are consummate agents of right reason, thanks to Zeus foremost as indwelling spirit of reason.[42] Thus, where the Stoics see the human beings and the world as rational and holistic due to the immanent Zeus, Tatian regards them as wildly insane and dislocated from God because Zeus the demon has invaded the world.

As go the demonically corrupted elements of the physical world and human nature, so goes human society on Tatian's view. He finds the Olympian gods responsible for tainting everything about Greek culture and the arts in the civic institution (πολίτευμα) of Greek society (21.11–12). Greek theatrical performances, painting, and sculpture vividly reveal the larger cosmic problem that keeps the Greeks in bondage to the Olympian conspirators. So too do the avid faces in the audience, captivated as they are with deranged desire for Greek theater (26.8–10)—yet another worthless play by Euripides and the like. The Olympians both produce and eagerly view the obscene show of Greek culture, and they laugh incessantly at the mayhem they bring to mortal lives.[43] This show, however, is not simply a cultural one. The lewdness and violence of Greek theater and the other visual arts reflect the chaotic and base world as run by the gods, beyond the city walls and beneath the city foundations.

Tatian is especially provoked by the popular allegories about the Olym-

---

39. SVF 2.473 = LS 48C = Alexander of Aphrodisias, *Mixt* 216.14.

40. DL 7.134.

41. Cicero eloquently presents this Stoic viewpoint: "This animal, which we call the human being, endowed with foresight and quick intelligence, complex, keen, remembering things, full of reason and counsel, has been created by the supreme god with a particular distinguished status," *Leg* 1.22.

42. For human beings as agents of right reason and the role of Zeus therein in early Stoic thought, see B. Inwood, *Ethics and Human Action* (1985), 19 n. 6, 201–15.

43. 8.10–12, 24.18–25.15.

pians that the Stoics and other philosophers offered. In these allegories, matter and immanent spirit become more openly polytheistic, Mount Olympus on a cosmic scale. Matter and spirit provide a home for all the Greek gods as elements and forces, not exclusively for Zeus as immanent spirit and Hera as matter. Zeus as king of the gods remains the primary spirit element and rational ordering principle, and the other Olympian gods are physically with him in the spirit, just as they are on Olympus. Their diverse elemental powers, in compliance with Zeus's rational guidance, keep the world and human beings well ordered.[44] In Tatian's day and earlier, allegory provided a method more sophisticated than myth for conceptualizing the presence of the immanent gods, for it transformed the anthropomorphic and largely amoral gods of Greek myth into constructively good elements and forces. The Epicurean Metrodorus of Lampsacus, for example, regarded the Olympians as the very "grounds of nature" and as "the ordering patterns of the elements ($\sigma\tau o\iota\chi\hat{\epsilon}\iota a$)."[45] Tatian denounces Metrodorus's allegorizing worldview as an arrogant fraud, because the Greek gods bring derangement, not order, to the spirit that shapes and informs the cosmos (13.15–23). God's order was originally good, but since then the Olympians have instilled manic chaos in immanent spirit and have enslaved mortals to their wicked madness.[46] Tatian attacks philosophical allegory because it scandalously whitewashes the indwelling gods.

Tatian suggests that Paul supports his anti-Stoic agenda against the Olympian spirits. Paul in Galatians ominously warns that there are evil "elemental principles of the cosmos" ($\sigma\tau o\iota\chi\hat{\epsilon}\iota a$ $\tau o\hat{v}$ $\kappa\acute{o}\sigma\mu ov$), with which Christians must not associate (Gal 4:3, cf. Col 2:8, 20). These principles are dangerous spirit powers in the world.[47] Though Paul does not specifically identify these

44. The gods are an integral part of the spirit that pervades the cosmos according to the Stoics, SVF 2.1027 = Aëtius, *Placita* 1.7.33; SVF 2.1055 = Plutarch, *De def or* 29.

45. 24.9–10. Metrodorus, though Epicurean, is one of the more well-known proponents of the predominantly Stoic idea that the gods are beneficial formative principles of the cosmos. On Metrodorus, see Metrodorus (2), with bibliography in OCD^3, and for his role as a proponent of allegorizing the gods, see J. Tate, "On the History of Allegorism" (1934), 105, 108. Stoic allegory is further studied by A. Le Boulluec, "L'allegorie chez les Stoïciens" (1975), 301–21.

46. 13.17–19, 19.4–8.

47. In Hellenistic philosophy, such as Stoicism, the elemental principles ($\sigma\tau o\iota\chi\hat{\epsilon}\iota a$) are the divinely inspirited physical elements that constitute the world, such as air and fire. In the broader religious thought of this period, the elements as divine forces were also thought to be powers holding sway over human lives, such as the astral powers of the zodiac. Paul harbors a strong aversion and hostility to them. As H. D. Betz says, Paul regards the $\sigma\tau o\iota\chi\hat{\epsilon}\iota a$ as "demonic forces which constitute and control 'this evil aeon'" and oppress human beings unless Christ intervenes to liberate and save them, *Galatians: A Commentary* (1979), 204–5, with bibliography at nn. 30–31. J. Martyn (*Galatians* [1997], 393–402) more fully explicates the Greek

elemental forces as Olympian or other gods, the Greek term that he uses to describe these dangerous forces, "elemental principles" (στοιχεῖα), signifies in Stoic physics the divine components of the physical world and their principles of pantheistic order and movement.[48] Tatian, given his acquaintance with Stoicism, interprets Paul's warning as a coded message to beware of the fallacious portrayal of the gods as good in Stoic cosmology and allegory. The gods, Tatian states, manipulate and function as the "elemental principle" (στοιχείωσις) of life and wickedness.[49] Contrary to what the philosophers falsely teach, Zeus and his Olympian followers are antirational and evil elemental forces, not orderly ones.

Tatian develops a plan to restore the immanent spirit of the world and human nature to its once pristine state, in accordance with God's original intentions. To accomplish this cleansing, the Olympians must be driven from their strongholds.[50] The powerful gods cannot be taken down all at once, however, and they are not equally pernicious in their effects on human lives, even though they are all malicious in commandeering the world's spirit. Consequently, Christians must choose their battles, for the gods' expulsion needs some order of priority. The first to go should be the gods chiefly responsible for imposing the human condition of a finite and sexually active life, constrained as it is by fate and laden with miseries. Mortality is not a natural condition, as the Stoics and Greeks as a whole foolishly think it is. Rather, it is a sorry substitute for immortality, a wicked and dirty trick played on humanity by the gods, all so that they can howl their Homeric "quenchless laughter" (ἄσβεστος γέλως) at our expense (8.11–12). Mortals are meant to be immortal, blissful, and one with God.[51]

---

philosophical background of στοιχεῖα and hones several features of Betz's explanation. See further E. Lohse, *Colossians and Philemon* (1971), 94–8; R. G. Tanner, "St. Paul and Stoic Physics" (1982), 481–90; and F. Pfister, "Die στοιχεῖα τοῦ κόσμου in den Briefen des Apostels Paulus" (1910), 411–27.

48. On the Stoic elemental principles, see SVF 3.413 = LS 47A = Stobaeus 1.129; DL 7.135–6 = LS 46B. The divine substratum of Stoic elements is discussed by Cicero and Augustine, LS 47C = Cicero, *ND* 2.23–5, 28–30; SVF 2.423 = Augustine, *Civ. dei* 8.5; and see too the discussion of A. A. Long and D. Sedley, *The Hellenistic Philosophers*, vol. 1 (1987), 266–72.

49. Tatian indicates this implicit assumption at 9.23–4 and 19.2–8.

50. Tatian further explains his position by analogy. The divine creation is like the letters that combined into a language, which God invented and intended to express certain meanings, 18.26–19.25. When the Olympian gods defected from him, they changed the intended meanings into obscenities. Tatian's use of this analogy is new, but the idea goes back at least to Plato that letters, syllables, and syntax offer a useful analogy for explaining the structural components of other entities, *Pol* 277e2–78d6.

51. G. Sfameni Gasparro (*Enkrateia e antropologia*, 32–56) fully explores the conception of human nature that informs Tatian's conviction that mortals are meant to be immortal. See also her "Asceticism and Anthropology: *Enkrateia* and 'Double Creation' in Early Christianity" (1995), 127–46.

TATIAN AND THE EARLY CHRISTIAN DILEMMA
BETWEEN CHOOSING GOD OR APHRODITE

Tatian finds human sexuality sharply in conflict with God's intended world order. Aphrodite in her diabolical cunning has turned the dirtiest Olympian trick of them all, the seductive lure of sexuality built to perpetuate the unnatural condition of human mortality. She stands as the Olympian Satan who inhabits and constitutes the mortal darkness of sexuality, while God is purity and immortal light. Tatian regards Aphrodite as one of the most dangerous Olympians for reasons deriving from a conflict between the Greek notion of human sexuality and the biblical teaching against sexual idolatry.

Tatian believes the popular Greek doctrine that Aphrodite prevails over human sexuality and represents the very nature of sexual desire, activity, and pleasure. He regards this belief as obvious: "Aphrodite takes pleasure in the embraces of sexual union" that she stimulates through her powers (8.24). Here Tatian, like Philo, reflects the Hellenic belief in her existence and erotic force. As in Tatian's comment, the goddess in the *Homeric Hymn to Aphrodite* provokes and vicariously enjoys the erotic pleasure she arouses. "Cyprian Aphrodite provokes sweet desire" in humans and animals alike, and they are all subject to her rule. "Each and every mortal being is attentive to the works of Aphrodite with the shapely crown" (5.1–6). In Greek ideas about the Olympian gods and their powers, which Tatian shares, Aphrodite embodies the particularly compelling and domineering force of eroticism with its feverish excitement in the animate soul. The Greeks reaffirm this belief through their terms for sexual activity, "the works of Aphrodite" ($\check{\epsilon}\rho\gamma\alpha\ \text{'}A\phi\rho o\delta\acute{\iota}\tau\eta\varsigma$), or, more simply, *aphrodisia* ($\dot{\alpha}\phi\rho o\delta\acute{\iota}\sigma\iota\alpha$). Aphrodite is so inseparably a part of human nature for the ancient Greeks that she is "inborn in their joints" ($\check{\epsilon}\mu\phi\upsilon\tau o\varsigma\ \check{\alpha}\rho\theta\rho o\iota\varsigma$), as Empedocles memorably states.[52] From a Greek perspective Aphrodite's sexual gifts to humanity are largely a blessing, but they are also problematic, given the deep torment and suffering Aphrodite often brings along with the excitement of passionate love and arousal.[53] The Greeks, as Tatian would have been well aware, also put these beliefs into practice in their rituals and in their religious art. In pre-Christian antiquity they worshipped Aphrodite as the preeminent deity of eros, built temples to her, sculpted statues to embody her presence, and composed hymns, poetry, and prose narratives about her powers.[54] From this long-

---

52. Fr. 25/17.20–22, B. Inwood, *The Poem of Empedocles*[2] (2001).

53. On popular Greek eros and Aphrodite, see chapter three, in connection with early Stoic eros. The sexual power of Aphrodite is also an elemental or cosmological principle of erotic attraction in Presocratic and other philosophically informed poetry, Parmenides (fr. 12, 13), Empedocles (fr. 25/17, ed. Inwood), Aeschylus fr. 44, Euripides, fr. 898, and Lucretius 1.1–20.

54. Even a highly intellectual Greek such as Plato shared these beliefs. As he states in the *Laws* 841a9–b2, citizens serve "their mistress" ($\delta\acute{\epsilon}\sigma\pi o\iota\nu\alpha$) Aphrodite through sexual activity,

standing Greek perspective, which Tatian takes for granted as true, humans are living sexual beings thanks to Aphrodite's universal erotic power. To be sexually active means showing her the requisite worship. For the Greeks, accordingly, mortals must give Aphrodite her due respect, not dismiss her from mind and body.

For Tatian, however, there is nothing sweet or shapely about the desire Aphrodite provokes and takes pleasure in, as there is for the Greeks. True life and immortality rest with God, while death lies with Aphrodite. Tatian has a potent biblical motive for associating the sexual worship of Aphrodite with death. By the strict letter of Pentateuchal law, peoples devoted to God must in principle suffer retributive death if they worship gods other than or in addition to him (Exod 20:3–5, Deut 5:7–9). This is especially true of the sexual worship, for God particularly abhors dissidents who scoff at the First Commandment in their sexual behavior and hand this attitude on to their children. The apostle Paul reaffirms this doctrine in 1 Corinthians, which Tatian read and respected as the inviolable truth. "Do not become idolatrous, and let us not sexually fornicate as they [the idolatrous Israelites] fornicated."[55] Paul tersely points out that the Israelites died en masse when, in defiance of God, they sexually worshipped Baal with Moabite women (1 Cor 10:8). This biblical and Pauline teaching could hardly be more blunt. Stay away from sexual idolatry. Christians who fail to do so are doomed to die by God's anger, severed in perpetuity from him.[56] Since Tatian thinks that sexual arousal and activity are inherently in devotion to Aphrodite, he sees but one route to escape her all-embracing sexual power. Christians must renounce sexual arousal and activity in order to gain salvation and immortality.

Christians who took to heart Paul's warnings against sexual idolatry, as Tatian did, would especially shun Greek gods with sexual powers. This task would have been relatively easy to carry out for some of the gods. To avoid the phallic wine god Dionysus, for example, Christians simply had to stay home and remain sober when the Bacchic revels came around. Aphrodite was far more problematic, however, because of the widespread and enduring power accorded to her. Christian baptismal waters did not wash away the

---

as she compels them to do until they reach old age. Plato accordingly requires his citizens to worship her, but to do so with the propriety of sexual moderation.

55. Paul is referring to the incident in Numbers 25, 1 Cor 10:7–8, cf. 1 Thess 4:3.

56. Chapters five and six discuss this Pentateuchal and Pauline theme of God vowing to disinherit and destroy his religious communities or a substantial portion thereof if his people permit fornicating sexual idolaters and other apostates to remain in their midst. Tatian ardently believes this doctrine in his own distinctive way—mortality itself is God's retribution, and Christians must escape this punitive condition by denying sexual activity altogether due to its inherently idolatrous ways.

enduring Greek idea that the very nature of sexuality manifests Aphrodite's formidable power. Christians with a Greek or Hellenized background would be imbued with the idea that there can be no sexual activity without Aphrodite, just as Tatian was. They also learned through Christian conversion and catechism, however, that God punished sexual idolaters with death-bearing retribution. Sexual renunciation seemed the only guaranteed way to follow God and escape the death shroud of Aphrodite. Thus, like Tatian, Christians with a Greek cultural background had strong biblical grounds for putting Aphrodite near the top of the list of Olympians to overthrow. Her power seemed to pose an especially alarming threat to Christian immortality, rather as a Venus fly trap is inimical to the insects it draws into its fold and consumes.

Tatian's loathing of Aphrodite comes through most clearly in the disgust he shows toward Sappho, the goddess's most compelling poet. Sappho, in songs of great sensuous force, draws her erotic and poetic inspiration from "immortal Aphrodite on her exquisite throne" (ποικιλόθρον' ἀθάνατ'Ἀφροδίτα) (fr. 1.1), as Greeks were aware. "Cypris and Eros together nurtured Sappho," the poet Antipater of Sidon aptly says. So attuned was Sappho to Aphrodite that she became the Greeks' tenth Muse, "the Muse mingled with Aphrodite."[57] Her books thus contained extremely dangerous poetry for Tatian, none of it worth hearing or taking to heart, because to find Sappho's poetry appealing would be to collude with Aphrodite in her rebellion against God. Eroticism is central to the "death-bearing mores" (θανάτου ἐπιτηδεύματα) that the defiant Olympian gods have brought about in their counterfeiting of nature.[58] Sappho wrongly celebrates this false, rebellious, and death-bearing sexuality. To keep this threat at bay, Tatian calls Sappho a demeaning string of obscenities, rather as though he would blot out her poetry by scribbling ugly graffiti on her persona. "Sappho, the sex-mad and cheap little whore (γύναιον πορνικὸν ἐρωτομανές) sings licentiousness (ἀσέλγεια) about herself" (34.20–21). The special loathing Tatian reserves for Sappho thus stands as a telling indicator of his hostility toward Aphrodite.

Tatian was not the only Christian of his day to consider erotic writings such as Sappho's to be a baneful entryway into the erotic trap of Aphrodite. Christians in his religious community, as he proudly observes, worked hard to keep "licentiousness" (ἀσέλγεια) of any kind "far from their circle of

---

57. G-P Antipater 11–12; *Anth. Plan.* 310 (Damocharis); *Anth. Pal.* 9.506 ('Plato'); G-P Dioscorides 18; *Anth. Pal.* 9.521 (anon.); Plutarch, *Amat* 762f. For the widespread admiration of Sappho in pre-Christian Hellenic culture, see Plato, *Phaedrus,* 235c3; G-P Nossis 11; G-P *Philip* Antipater of Thessalonica 19, 72; Laurea 1; Pinytus 1; *Anth. Pal.* 9.184 (anon.); and 9.189 (anon.); Athenaeus 596d; and note also the Greek-inspired Catullus, 51, 35.16–17.

58. 15.15, 14.10–16.

purity" (πόρρω κεχώρισται). The women were especially diligent in the cleansing.[59] Christians, like their Greek compatriots, realized that erotic poetry stimulated readers to explore the power of Aphrodite in its iridescent depths. Sappho in particular "speaks words truly mixed with fire," and her poetry serves to "bring up heat from the heart," as Plutarch openly acknowledges.[60] From Tatian's encratite Christian viewpoint, however, the heat has become damnation. Sexually active Christians might as well be jumping to their deaths for the short-lived thrill of the leap, because they cast themselves down from God by sharing in the works of Aphrodite. Hence Tatian and his community vilified Greek erotic literature as smut that promoted Aphrodite at the expense of God and human well-being.[61] If such literature were to remain available in an increasingly Christian Greek culture, captivated readers would fall back into bondage to Aphrodite, with eros shackling the left ankle and retributive death the right. Christians in Tatian's community thus strove to dispose of the works of Sappho and others in their effort to escape the works of Aphrodite and attain salvation with God.

Tatian's project to drive Aphrodite from the world discloses a new and urgent motive in Greek society for alienating people from erotic experience. Prior to the rise of Christianity, no Greeks thought it possible or desirable to eliminate the powers and effects of Aphrodite. Though pre-Christian Greeks had their own reasons for being sexually inhibited, such as the medical view that males weaken from excessive seminal emission,[62] the Greeks never aspired to eradicate sexual desire and activity altogether, let alone overthrow the gods responsible for eros. Once Greeks and Hellenized persons converted to Christianity, however, they were required to stop worshipping the gods of eros as well as other deities, and to remove the gods from their midst. Their premier religious imperative was to worship the Lord alone, and this rule encompassed their sexual and reproductive be-

59. 34.20–23, 33.10–11.

60. With rather incongruous imagery that would seem frighteningly accurate to Christians of like mind with Tatian, Plutarch goes to the extreme of likening the erotically heated voice of Sappho to liquid flames from the mouth of the fire-breathing monster Cacus, *Amat* 762f.

61. What disturbs Tatian is not the homoerotic element of Sappho's poetry but its erotic element more generally, regardless of the sex of the partners. As far as he is concerned, Sappho is at least professionally heterosexual, for he regards her as a high-class prostitute (ἑταίρα), and as a love-crazed one as well, 34.10, 34.20–21.

62. M. Foucault, *Use of Pleasure* (1985), 15–17. The ancient Greeks had their share of other sexual inhibitions and aversions as well. Ancient Greek men, for instance, faced the prospect of severe censure for showing unreserved enthusiasm for sexual activity, especially if they openly enjoyed being penetrated anally, K. J. Dover, *Greek Homosexuality*[2], 23; J. Winkler, *The Constraints of Desire*, 45–6, 54; and D. Cohen and R. Saller, "Foucault on Sexuality," 40–1. Conversely, Greek women were pressured not to seem sexually aggressive or "masculine," B. Brooten, *Love Between Women*, 146–71.

havior. Regardless of whether they were sexually active or abstinent, their sexuality had to be devoted to God alone and to abandon fornicating after other gods. But to do away with Aphrodite would have had a deeply unsettling effect on those who still wanted to marry and give in marriage, for to their minds, as the example of Tatian vividly indicates, Aphrodite was synonymous with sexual activity and reproduction. The social demands to raise a family, however, have an enduring normative force that far antedated Greek Christian concerns about whether it was possible to make love without breaking the First Commandment to worship no other gods but God. Hence many of them continued to marry and reproduce.

Encratite Christians like Tatian, however, sought to cast Aphrodite from her throne by treating sexuality as the first idol to destroy. Like the Titans against the Olympians, they were ardent in this effort, for they believed Christians would reign immortal so long as they expelled sexuality from human nature. Tatian's reasoning in support of this view was simple and potent: Mortality is the punitive death brought about through Aphrodite's devices, which means that the goddess and her power must cease to function in order for Christians to be eternally one with God. The "demonic gods do not die easily," though, as Tatian grudgingly admits (15.14), for eros and mortality are not readily overthrown. Since then, however, Greek religious beliefs about Aphrodite, have proven more vulnerable, for Aphrodite is now an armless Snow White in the nude, not a viable deity to worship. Along with her demoted status the erotic sensibility of the pre-Christian Greeks has gone underground, aside from the lingering heat in fragments of Sappho and the like. This iconoclasm of ancient Greek eros has no precedent in Hellenic culture prior to the development of Christianity. The attack on Greek religious eros appears most visibly in Tatian's encratite argument simply because he continued to accord sexual powers in full to Aphrodite and thus saw need to eliminate sexual activity completely. Other proponents of biblical monotheism in Hellenistic culture were similarly hostile toward Aphrodite as a divine sexual power, such as Paul, Philo, and also Clement, as shown in the next chapter. Paul and Clement differ from Tatian only in that they believe it possible to obliterate Aphrodite and other alien gods without eliminating marital sex and reproduction.

TATIAN'S REASON FOR REINTERPRETING 1 CORINTHIANS 7

Tatian consequently reinterprets 1 Corinthians 7 because of his unshaken Greek conviction that Aphrodite wields absolute power over sexuality. As he sees it, all sexual agents are fornicators in her thrall, much like Paris and Helen whom Aphrodite imperiously drove into the marriage bed under strict orders to make love. Being married is surely no escape from her, for the Greeks do not allow for a special matrimonial category of ἀφροδίσια without Aphrodite, and, in fact, they accord her a special role in matrimonial sexual relations.[63] This is why Tatian believes that, according to Paul, even Christians who marry and make love to their spouses are "enslaved to . . . fornication and to the devil" (*On Perfection,* fr. 5). Aphrodite is Tatian's devil. Married Christians make a fatal error to assume that their marital sexual relations are exempt from her power of fornicating servitude.

Paul's religious assumptions about the divine power of sexual activity differ markedly from Tatian's. Paul, raised and educated as he was primarily in the Pentateuch and Prophets, does not share Tatian's complete identification of sexuality with Aphrodite. Instead, he assumes the biblically grounded opposition between permissible sexual relations, which are marital and devoted to God alone, and sexual relations in forbidden devotion to alien gods. Only the religiously alien relations are fornicating servitude to Satan, such as making love in worship of Aphrodite. To Paul's mind, the divine power of human sexuality is a matter of fighting fire with fire. The pure blue flame of Christian marital sex in the Lord alone stops the smoke of sexual idolatry from making its way into Christian communities, bedrooms, and future generations. For Tatian, however, all erotic fire is the deadly smoke kindled by Aphrodite. Tatian and Paul harbor conflicting religious assumptions, the one Greek and the other biblical, about the link between human sexuality and divine power. Tatian houses the entirety of sexuality in Aphrodite's temple, while Paul places marital sexual activity devoted strictly to the Lord in a monotheistic sanctuary set apart from sexual fornication. They both have no doubt, however, that deities rule over sexuality, that Christianity precipitates a battle between these powers, and that the Lord must prevail over the gods of eros through the Christianizing of Greek culture.

THE CONFLICT BETWEEN TATIAN AND THE CHURCH FATHERS

Tatian, with his persistent belief in Aphrodite, is not at odds with Paul alone. He discredits the core biblical teaching that God commends and presides over the reproductive relations of his people. In biblical theology there is no genuine god but God, and his omnipotence extends to ensuring the fer-

---

63. Aphrodite is "marital" (Euripides, fr. 781.14–26), and "the ruler of the marital bedroom" ($\theta\alpha\lambda\acute{\alpha}\mu\omega\nu$ $\mathring{\alpha}\nu\alpha\sigma\sigma\alpha$), adesp. fr. 213a *TrGF,* vol. 2 (ed. R. Kannicht and B. Snell). So too Musonius: "That marriage is a great and worthy practice is clear from this, that the gods who preside over marriage are great, as people believe, first Hera, . . . then Eros, then Aphrodite. We understand all three perform this function, to bring a man and woman together sexually. . . . Where does Aphrodite [along with Hera and Eros] more fittingly belong than presiding over the lawful sexual intercourse of a man and woman?" Musonius 94.20–32 (Lutz); see too Plato, *Laws,* 840e2–41b2; Plutarch, *Coniugalia praecepta,* 138c–d; P. Friedrich, *The Meaning of Aphrodite* (1978), 84–5, 116; V. Pirenne-Delforge, *L'Aphrodite grecque,* 418–28, and 21–5, 153–4, 187–8, 197–8, 200–2; and J. Oakley and R. Sinos, *The Wedding in Ancient Athens,* 11–21, 30–47.

tile reproduction of his people. Genesis, the New Testament Pastoral Epistles, Hebrews, and Ephesians strongly encourage God's people to marry, for marriage allows them to sexually fulfill his command to grow and multiply in his honor alone.[64] Even the sexually ascetic passages of the New Testament leave this marital and reproductive dictate intact. Both the unmarried Paul and Jesus' celibate disciples in Matthew openly concede that marital sexual intercourse is permissible for Christians, even though they opt out of the practice themselves in favor of sexual renunciation as their higher calling (1 Cor 7:7–9, Matt 19:11). Pragmatically speaking, further, it makes good sense for God to issue a procreative mandate. If he were not accorded the power to regenerate his people and yet required their exclusive devotion, he would likely be short-lived and impotent in his religious influence, a lonely eunuch in the kingdom of heaven. God's normative influence, however, has been far-reaching thanks in part to the biblical imperative to grow and multiply for his glory.[65] As far as Tatian is concerned, though, God's power is indeed absolute (*Orat* 5.19–20), but sexuality is a false and malevolent force from which God is entirely removed. Aphrodite's diabolical invention is not beyond him; it is beneath him. Tatian thus undercuts the biblical tenet that sexuality and fertility belong in God's absolute power.

Tatian also overturns the biblical motive for distinguishing between monotheistic sexual relations and sexual fornication in worship of other gods. The biblical idea of sexual fornication functions much like a negative advertisement campaign. It promotes monotheistic sexual relations and reproduction by making the religious competition look bad—the wicked work of the devil, rather than the good work of God. Members of God's communities must adopt the marital sexual behavior that allows them to remain within the monotheistic circle or their denominational portion thereof.[66] This campaign backfires, however, in encratite Christian thought, where Aphrodite still holds such sway that God appears neither to have nor to want

---

64. God's command "Grow and multiply" presupposes that his people can and should make love and bear children in devotion to him. Adam and Eve are the prototype couple in this respect, created as they are to be sexually joined as two-into-one flesh, Gen 1:28, 9:1. Bishops according to 1 Tim 3:2–5 should be married and have children. Ephesians and Hebrews likewise favor the practice of Christian marriage, Eph 5:22–33, Heb 13:4. On marriage and family in the Lord as advocated by the Pastoral Epistles, note too the commentaries by G. Knight (1992), and M. Dibelius and H. Conzelmann (1977) at Titus 1:6, 2:4, 1 Tim 3:2–5, and 3:12.

65. In the previous chapters I have shown that the biblical position is one of strongly advocating marriage, reproduction, and the family, but only provided that the customs are in devotion to the Lord alone.

66. The respective circles are open to new members as potential spouses, of course, for as previously noted, persons who convert and join a denomination in the Lord are in principle welcome.

any share in the human procreative market and its fornicating method of reproduction. Clement of Alexandria criticizes Tatian precisely on these grounds, for failing to recognize that the permissible marital sexual relations of Christians are "as far from fornication as God is from the devil" (*Strom* 3.84.4).[67] For Tatian and his fellow encratites, however, Christian marital sex is as far from God as Aphrodite is from God. The biblical terms for denigrating the idolatrous competition come to absorb and define human sexual activity as a whole.

THE SPIRITUAL ADULTERY OF THE GREEKS AGAINST GOD

Tatian reinterprets the Prophets' and Paul's ideas about God's punishment of his spiritually adulterous people. By his understanding, God has afflicted the rebellious Greek souls with cognitive blindness and mortality because of their truth-suppressing apostasy. The souls of the Greeks, he maintains, originally cohabited with the spirit of God in a marital union ($\sigma\upsilon\zeta\upsilon\gamma\acute{\iota}\alpha$).[68] Their souls then became his wayward wife by defecting from God and his rules. The Lord in turn renounced his spiritual marriage with their souls, just as he more formally issued his rebellious people a writ of divorce in Jeremiah 3:6–9. As Tatian puts it, "The spirit of God abandoned [the soul] because she refused to follow him."[69] Helen of Sparta, Tatian adds, similarly "fornicated" ($\acute{\epsilon}\kappa\pi\rho\nu\epsilon\acute{\upsilon}\sigma\alpha\sigma\alpha\nu$) against Menelaus to live with Paris in adultery (11.19–22), just as the adulteress Israel fornicated against God to pursue other gods as lovers instead. The embodied soul suffers horribly because of her spiritual adultery, and Tatian's portrayal of her suffering presupposes a medley of ideas about Greek soul therapy colored with Gnostic and trace Middle Platonist themes.[70] Unless the soul reunites with the Lord's spirit and regains her true nature as his spouse, she wanders in darkness, blind to her immortal nature, incapable of rational thought, and unable to regain self-knowledge.[71] In this blighted and acratic condition she remains trapped in

67. Clement has Tatian in mind here, for he mentions him by name at *Strom* 3.81.1 and 3.82.2, and pointedly criticizes his encratite argument at *Strom* 3.82.2 and 3.84.4.

68. 14.22, 14.26–8, 15.5. By "soul," Tatian is referring both to the collective soul that is betrothed to God and to individual souls that belong to the collective, which includes the Greeks on his view. He begins by discussing the singular and collective term "soul" and then shifts to plural and individuated "souls" in his discussion at 14.10–15.7. The shift occurs at 15.2–7.

69. 14.26–8, 15.5–7.

70. I am not suggesting that Tatian was formally or directly acquainted with Middle Platonist ideas, though he does reflect vestigial traces thereof from intermediaries, such as Justin or the like.

71. Tatian reveals more a Gnostic than a Platonist idea here by asserting that the soul without divine intervention is in utter darkness and has an abject incapacity for reason, as G. Quispel has shown, *Makarius*, 57–9. Tatian's marital poetics of the soul is similar to a teaching about the soul and her celestial Bridegroom in the Nag Hammadi text *The Authentikos Logos*, G. Man-

following rebellious demons (14.16–31), the Olympians foremost.[72] The Greek soul in adultery against God can never accomplish her task of enlightenment, afflicted as she is with the crazed spirit of diabolical gods such as eros contrived by Aphrodite.

According to Tatian, cognitive blindness to the true self is only the beginning of the soul's plight. The souls of the Greeks will perish unless they transcend their denial about the one true Lord and regain immortality through their marital union with him. In other words, the Greeks go from adulteress darkness to doom unless they become Christian and renounce their former gods. Every Greek soul, therefore, must "seek anew to be united with the holy spirit and to busy herself with this marital union (συζυγία)" (16.4–6), as Tatian's encratite Christians have done. The Greeks, by making the spirit of God their only devotional soul mate, will extricate their souls from mortality and dwell forever with God.[73] Sexual renunciation, of course, is a mandatory part of this elixir of immortality that Tatian distills from his blend of Pauline marital theology and Greek soul therapy.[74]

The theme of soul therapy allows Tatian to recreate the metaphor of adultery in the Prophets and Paul. He identifies God's rebellious wife as a collective of embodied Greek souls, whereas the Prophets and Paul identify her with God's people. For Tatian, the Greeks' rebellious souls are barred from self-enlightenment and immortality as their punishment for worshipping other gods. For the Prophets, by contrast, mortality is a natural part of the human condition and the people are punished with the atrocities of war, conquest, rape, slaughter, and slavery. To this bleak list of retribution for spiritual adultery, Paul adds sexual desires and practices of an othertheistic sort (Rom 1:18–27), which he regards as God's punishment in the flesh against the Gentile truth-suppressors, as shown in chapter six. Tatian

---

tovani, "La tradizione dell'*enkrateia* nei testi di Nag Hammadi e nell'ambiente monastico egiziano del IV secolo" (1985), 575–8.

72. In Middle Platonist soul therapy, the embodied soul's obliviousness to its immortal nature comes from being overly entranced by the appetitive pleasures of the body, not, as with Tatian, from abandoning a deity who requires exclusive worship. The cure for the delusion in Middle Platonism is Plato's regimen to curb the appetites' forceful pull toward excess so that the soul may recollect its immortality, as studied in chapter two. The *Phaedo* and *Phaedrus* are important dialogues for delineating this soul blindness and its cure, *Phd* 80d5–84b8 and *Phdr* 243e9–57b6. Both of these dialogues were also very popular in Middle Platonism, J. Dillon, *The Middle Platonists*, 9, 458, and M. B. Trapp, "Plato's *Phaedrus* in Second-Century Greek Literature" (1990), 141–73. Tatian gives no indication of knowing their contents directly.

73. 16.5–6, 14.22, 33.2–5.

74. Tatian's imagery of the soul's marriage with God's spirit "blocked out the possibility of sexual joining in ordinary marriage," as P. Brown aptly notes, *Body and Society*, 91–2. Tatian rules out this possibility because sexual arousal is inspired by the diabolical Aphrodite and manifests her very nature. It is impossible for the soul to be sexually stimulated and still remain united with God's spirit.

Hellenizes this punitive series by taking the Middle Platonist theme about the amnesiac soul and transforming it into a spiritually adulterous soul—a condition that brings not only blindness but mortal doom as well.

Tatian's therapeutic reworking of Christian marital theology in his exhortation to the Greeks offers a rather ingenious appeal to Greek sensibilities. Polytheistic peoples would have found the biblical propositions implicit in the Prophets' and Paul's marital poetics culturally alien: There is one god alone; this deity is a Bridegroom jealous of his people making love in worship of other gods; the people claimed exclusively for him are his wife or fiancée; and she is destined for brutal punishment if she commits spiritual adultery. These tenets would be difficult for Greeks even to understand, let alone believe. Tatian tried to meet this challenge by recasting spiritual adultery in terms that appealed to the popular Greco-Roman interest in healing one's soul through philosophical therapy.[75] In order for the soul to attain enlightenment, according to Tatian, it must liberate itself and fly aloft, just as it does in Platonic and Pythagorean thought. Tatian, though, changes the means of liberation and feminizes the soul. In his Christian therapy the soul must free herself not from excessive appetites but from the worship of the Olympian gods, Aphrodite especially, or else die as punishment for playing the whore against God.

Tatian's reference to the adulterous Helen is another, more inchoate, effort on his part to reshape biblical marital poetics in understandable Greek terms (11.19–22). From Homer and tragedy, the Greeks knew very well the disaster that followed Helen's abandonment of Menelaus. If they persist as the Lord's fornicating wife, like Helen to Menelaus, then their souls burn and fall like Troy because of God's anger against his wayward wife. To become good Christians, they need to see themselves as the culpable Helen; God as their outraged husband, Menelaus; and their gods as the slippery Paris who stole Helen away. The Greeks must repent and return to the Lord as Bridegroom, with chastity restored through conversion and kept intact through sexual renunciation. Thanks to soul therapy and the story of Helen, the Greeks can finally grasp the need to live by Tatian's encratite Christian marital theology in order to save their souls.

CONCLUSION

Tatian's argument that Christians must renounce all sexual activity in order to abide eternally with God arises from the turbulent encounter between two deeply rooted religious convictions about sexual activity. The first is

---

75. I. Hadot, *Seneca und die griechisch-römische Tradition der Seelenleitung* (1969), 10–95, and M. Foucault, *Care of the Self,* 39–68.

the longstanding Greek belief that Aphrodite represents and embodies the power of sexuality, with human beings as her eager yet tormented slaves. The second is Paul's adaptation of the Pentateuchal teaching that Christians must avoid sexual idolatry or else fall away from God and suffer punitive death. For Tatian and his fellow encratite Christians, these two beliefs combine to produce the innovative stance that sexual activity as a whole is unconditionally forbidden as idolatry and brings punitive mortality in its wake. Tatian's argument unforgettably reveals this collision of beliefs at the historical moment of impact: Because Aphrodite's power is universal, all sexual activity is deadly and irretrievably within the idolatrous domain of the devil.

Tatian reinforces his advocacy of sexual renunciation through his innovative use of Greek mythology, Stoic cosmology, and the didactic metaphor of spiritual adultery in the Prophets and Paul. In his religious mythology about the Olympian gods, Tatian is not unlike a Titan who has escaped and is looking to even the score. The Olympians, he asserts, long ago rebelled against the biblical God in order to infiltrate and infect the world and humanity. The gods have hitherto succeeded in their project of corruption thanks to the avid compliance of the Greeks, whose ancestors championed the gods' rebellious cause and egregiously turned their backs on the one true God they used to recognize. Since that time, the Olympians have submerged the Greeks' embodied souls in the darkness of spiritual adultery against God. More broadly still, the gods have transformed all of humanity into mortal and sexual beings, in place of the immortal beings they used to be and ought to become once again—angels impervious to Aphrodite's whips of sexuality and death. To return human nature to its primordial state, the gods must be overthrown, Aphrodite notably among them.

Tatian deploys Stoic natural science to describe the material process by which Aphrodite and the other gods carried out their coup against God. Zeus and his fellow Olympians descended into and took over the immanent spirit that informs and shapes matter constituting the world and human beings. Through their spirit presence in strongholds of matter, they have inflicted bacchic disorder on God's originally good cosmos and they have divorced Greek souls from God. Aphrodite is the most cunning elemental maenad of them all, for she has brought countless human beings to the grave through eros and reproduction. Christians, however, must now fight back to free themselves from their unnatural mortal constraints. They must reject all sexual activity as the only way to avoid Aphrodite's lure. Tatian projects this encratite viewpoint onto Paul in his interpretation of 1 Corinthians 7, though Paul believes that Christian marital sexual relations in worship of God alone are the antithesis of Aphrodite worship.

Tatian's principle of sexual renunciation has not, of course, become the dominant mode of Christian sexual mores. Christianity has instead built

much of its populace and denominational systems from physical regeneration, through Christians marrying, making love, and reproducing, just as
Paul and other New Testament writers allow or encourage.[76] In the second
century, however, Aphrodite was still too vital a religious and cultural presence in the Hellenized world for there to be a painless transition from the
works of Aphrodite to the worship of God alone. Tatian and Christian encratites of like mind concurred with the Greeks that eros was hot, impassioned, and overpowering—the goddess's counterpart to Zeus's lightning
bolt, not a monotheistic procedure to ward off the devil and produce children for God. While the Greeks felt compelled to surrender to Aphrodite
with fervent trepidation, Tatian's encratite group felt equally driven to cast
her down. Longing for immortal restoration with God, they condemned
everything about Aphrodite's fatal gift of erotic fire to humanity, including
erotic poetry, lovemaking, and reproduction. Like a fanatic Diomedes, Tatian took the lead in this assault on Aphrodite.[77] Paul preceded Tatian in the
Christian struggle against alien divine powers of sexuality, and Clement followed after both of them. But along with Paul and Philo, Clement argues
that the demise of Aphrodite is meant to facilitate the reproductive way of
the Lord, as explored in the next chapter.

76. Devout Christian marital practices sustain this ancient link between sexuality and divine power and they derive their authority from the marital norm that Paul and other early
Christian writers endorse: Christian marriage and it alone is "undefiled and its marital sex im-
maculate" (Heb 13:4), unlike human sexual activity powered by other gods.

77. Antisthenes and Clement of Alexandria somewhat similarly fantasize having Diomedes' opportunity to wound Aphrodite. Clement states, "I approve of Antisthenes when he says
'I would strike Aphrodite dead, if I were to catch her, because she has corrupted many of our
fine and good women,'" *Strom* 2.107.2–3. Tatian and Clement, however, truly believe that Aphrodite needs to meet her demise. They have a fervent agenda, while Antisthenes simply mor-
alizes about Aphrodite encouraging women to be more like Helen than Penelope.

Chapter 9

Prophylactic Grace in Clement's Emergent Church Sexual Ethic

The contribution of Clement (ca. 150–216 C.E.) to ecclesiastical plans for sexual reform has great historical value. His writings, like Philo's, are at the confluence where the Greek philosophical and biblical principles meet and undergo major reworking into emergent church doctrine. He is not later downstream simply handing on a fixed set of received teachings about permissible and forbidden sexual conduct. Clement develops his innovative and influential piecework of Christian sexual rules from Greek philosophical and biblical sources,[1] including the Pythagoreans, Plato, several later Stoics, Philo, the Septuagint Pentateuch and Prophets,[2] Paul, and a few passages from Matthew and John. In this pastiche, Clement transforms his borrowings into a revolutionary and intensely restrictive kind of sexual fornication that Christians must flee.[3]

Clement strongly believes, in response to Philo, that appetitive sexual desire is inherently lawless and instigates sexually fornicating rebellion against God. To Clement's mind, innate sexual desire is so dangerous that it makes procreationism in the Lord the only way to prevent sexually active Christians from going the defiant way of rebellious Israel. Accordingly he intensifies Philo's procreationist conception of biblical law by insisting that God

---

1. Clement's assemblage of sexual principles is rather complicated but patterned, as he intimates by the descriptive title he gives his main work on the topic, the "patchwork" *Stromateis* or *Miscellanies*. A. Méhat (*Étude sur les 'Stromates' de Clément d'Alexandrie* [1966], 96–112) more fully explores the significance of Clement's title.

2. For Clement's central dependence on the Septuagint form of the Old Testament scriptures, see the monograph by O. Stählin, *Clemens Alexandrinus und die Septuaginta* (1901).

3. Clement fully endorses Paul's position that sexual fornication is absolutely forbidden to Christians, *Paed* 2.101.1–2, 3.29.1; *Strom* 3.43.5, 84.4, 88.4.

condemns all sexual practices other than procreationism within Christian marriage for their hedonistic worship of Aphrodite and Eros, even if the sex "for pleasure" occurs within marriage. To underscore this point, Clement transforms the biblical meaning of adultery to describe this new danger of appetitive sexual rebellion "for pleasure." His new sexual ethic would go on to become one of the more authoritative sexual regulations in Western culture, for its core lineaments became early church doctrine and continue in a mitigated form today as Roman Catholic doctrine.[4]

Though Clement derives his notion of appetitive sexual desire largely from Philo, his antipathy to it is far more negative than Philo's. Clement reinterprets Paul's and Matthew's teaching that it is sinful even to desire to disobey God to mean that the very function of the sexual appetite is a forbidden desire to defy God, even if it does not successfully lead Christians into transgressing God's procreationist law. Clement's antipathy to sexual desire is so strong that he is convinced it must be denied altogether, even in the subdued form it takes to perform sober and purposive reproduction in the Lord. For this a miracle is in order. Through Christ's saving grace, married Christian procreationists experience a prophylactic remission from the sexual appetite and its inherent servitude to Aphrodite. They alone practice sex that is safe from the demon-driven sexual appetite, but only so long as they remain resolutely set on reproducing whenever they copulate.

Clement is especially determined to liberate Christians from innate sexual desire because of his interpretation of Paul's marital theology. According to Paul, the top priority of Christians is to remain free of fornicating sexual impulses and actions in order to keep the collective body of Christians ready for her Bridegroom. By this Paul primarily means that they must avoid other-theistic sexual relations and any desire to engage in them. Clement takes this requirement to mean that Christians must never yield to sexual desire, or else they besmirch the betrothed chastity of church and soul alike, and thereby imperil salvation. Thus, even though Clement advocates Christian procreationism to challenge Tatian's even more extreme argument that all sexual activity is forbidden devotion to Aphrodite, his sexual principles do not reflect a balanced or healthy middle ground between total renunciation and libertine sexual mores. Clement is convinced that almost all sexual activity is prohibited devotion to the Greek gods of eros. Christian procreationism is the only exception he allows, but only on the dubious ar-

---

4. *Humanae vitae* 2.8–17 in J. Smith, Humanae Vitae *A Generation Later* (1991), 42–54, 276–87, 340–70; G. E. M. Anscombe, "You Can Have Sex without Children: Christianity and the New Offer" (1981), 82–96; R. Lawler, J. Boyle, and W. May, *Catholic Sexual Ethics: A Summary, Explanation, and Defense*² (1998), 31–65, 151–75; and J. Noonan, *Contraception*², 126–31, 143–79, who explores Augustine's major influence on this aspect of Catholic sexual morality.

gument that Christ has intervened to save married Christian procreationists from being motivated at all by the harlot impulse of sexual desire.

CLEMENT'S CHRISTIAN ENDOGAMY

Clement abhors the dangers of other-theistic sexual fornication that religiously alien people and mores pose to the Christian community. To eliminate this problem, he uses the Pauline letters to endorse a Christian-specific version of marriage "in the Lord" that Paul formulated from the Septuagint. Among Clement's increasing population of co-religionists, those who are unmarried and inclined to be sexually active must marry persons of the opposite sex who are or become Christians.[5] They must not enter into sexual relations with persons who worship gods other than or in addition to God in Christ, for they are to "refrain from contact with the unclean," as 2 Corinthians 6:16–18 mandates (*Strom* 3.73.3). Clement identifies "the unclean" as the polytheistic peoples and culture of the ancient Mediterranean. Greeks, Romans, and others wrongly "continue to live in fornication," he asserts, here alluding to 1 Thessalonians 4:3–5, where Paul declares that Gentiles live in fornication by virtue of not worshipping God alone in their sexual, reproductive, and other religious acts (*Strom* 3.73.4). Through Paul's teachings, the biblical rule that segregates the Israelites from the Canaanites and other peoples in the historical promised land now severs Christians from the polytheistic cultures in which they live. The antipathy carries over as well. Like Paul, Clement considers the Greeks, Romans, and others to be debased primitives in their religious sexual mores, on par with the defiled, lewd, and violent Canaanites. Sexual and procreative intimacy with other-theistic peoples alienates Christians from God and subjects them to eventual disinheritance and devastation. Clement, therefore, upholds a Christian norm of biblical endogamy for the perceived safety and salvation of all Christians. In so doing he gives unmarried Christians but two choices for their sexual lives. They may remain single and virginal in perpetuity,[6] or, if they are going to be sexually active, they must take Christian spouses and circle their family wagons so as to keep the Gentiles at bay.

Clement reserves a special loathing toward Greek religion and Greek sexual customs in particular. In the *Protrepticus* he, like Tatian, supports Paul's accusation that the Greeks are egregious renegades who originally worshipped God, only to turn against him in a polytheistic coup (Rom 1:18–

---

5. Jews and Judaizing Christians are culturally remote to Clement, not a part of the Christian religion as he understood and practiced it: "No true dialogue with Jews or Judaizing Christians took place" in Clement's adaptation of ideas from Philo, A. van den Hoek, "How Alexandrian was Clement of Alexandria?" (1990), 185, and C. Haas, *Alexandria in Late Antiquity*, 105–6.

6. *Strom* 3.79.3–5, 86.1, and J. Broudéhoux, *Mariage et famille*, 107–13.

27).[7] In the *Stromateis,* however, Clement more prudently distances himself from this historical fiction and regains a more selective, yet cautious, appreciation of Greek philosophy and literature,[8] though his hostility to Greek religious and sexual mores remains. Christians must "have nothing to do with the customs of the Greek city," and especially with its religiously alien practices of marriage and reproduction, because "the way of the pagans" (ὁδὸς ἐθνῶν) is "a society antagonistic" to the Christian way of life.[9]

Clement makes his commitment to Christian sexual separatism especially clear by rejecting the later Stoics' patriotic argument in favor of marriage and reproduction. He initially considers redeploying this argument for Christian purposes, only to reconsider and recant it as a religious cause inimical to his own. Clement outlines the later Stoic conviction that men and women should marry and have children in order to honor and uphold the civic structure and polytheistic social order of their ancestors: "One must marry on behalf of the fatherland, the succession of children, and to fulfill our obligation to the cosmos (κόσμος) so far as we are able" (*Strom* 2.140.1). Later in the same work Clement repudiates this argument for being too connected with the cosmos and its gods to be useful for Christian ends—too much in thrall to the fornicating family mores that define "the way of the pagans" and their cities. "Do not partake of the customs of the polis," for the social order of "families, households, and cities pleases the cosmos (κόσμος) rather than the Lord" (*Strom* 3.97.3). The later Stoics' patriotic argument is displeasing to the Lord because it presupposes and supports the religious foundations of Greek civic culture, and the Greeks are "stubborn horses" for not turning unanimously toward God.[10] Stoic family and civic values are central to the problem of other-theistic fornication that Christians must flee. Hence Christians as practitioners of marriage in the Lord must turn away from the Greek city, and they must teach their growing families to do likewise.[11]

---

7. *Protrep* 81.2, 114.1, and K. Gaca, "Paul's Uncommon Declaration," 183–5.

8. A. Droge, *Homer or Moses?* 138–49; G. Boys-Stones, *Post-Hellenistic Philosophy: A Study of Its Development from the Stoics to Origen* (2001), 188–94; H. P. Timothy, *The Early Christian Apologists and Greek Philosophy* (1973), 59–80; C. Stead, *Philosophy in Christian Antiquity* (1994), 92, 112–3; and E. de Faye, *Clément d'Alexandrie. Étude sur les rapports du christianisme et de la philosophie grecque au IIe siècle*[2] (1906), 192–200.

9. *Strom* 3.97.3, 107.1. Clement similarly states that the Christian cross is the boundary marker separating Christian converts from their former social and religious identities, *Paed* 3.85.3.

10. The Greek for "stubborn horses" is ἵπποι σχληραύχενες, *Protrep* 89.3. Stubbornness is the hallmark characteristic of God's rebellious people, as in Deut 9:6 (λαὸς σκληροτράχηλος εἶ), cf. Exod 33:3, Deut 9:13.

11. Clement's conjoining of procreationism with biblical endogamy has proven historically durable and influential through Roman Catholicism, albeit in a somewhat softened form that de-emphasizes the intent to reproduce and emphasizes instead that it is wrong to try to pre-

CLEMENT'S PROCREATIONISM

Clement supports the procreationist rule in its later Pythagorean form. "Marriage," as he defines it, is "the first union of a husband and wife for the sowing of legitimate children."[12] If a husband engages in sexual activity strictly for procreation with his wife, he does so with "an earnest and temperate will," and his marriage is temperate (*Strom* 3.58.2, 86.1). If, however, he makes love to her for any other reason, his appetitive sexual desire wrongly indulges in wanton pleasure. Such relations are acts of lawlessness (*Paed* 2.92.2, 95.2–3). Clement also affirms the Pythagorean view that persons who engage in nonprocreationist sexual activity fail to act as true human beings who are superior to animals. They are "pigs and goats."[13] By now this sexual ethic is familiar from Charondas, Ocellus, Seneca, Musonius, and Philo. Clement even cites Musonius in support of procreationism,[14] though he recognizes that the provenance of this teaching is Pythagorean rather than Stoic. The Pythagoreans, Clement states, make love "only for procreation, not for pleasure" with their wives (*Strom* 3.24.1–2). To this extent his core sexual principle is indistinguishable from theirs. In this respect Clement too is ὁ Πυθαγόρειος, the very name he gives to his predecessor Philo.[15]

Following Philo, whose writings he knew and respected,[16] Clement recruits the force of God's word from the Septuagint Pentateuch to endorse

---

vent conception with anything but the rhythm method, *Humanae vitae* 2.8–17, in J. Smith, *Humanae vitae: A Generation Later*, 277–87. Though Philo as procreationist likewise requires that marriage and reproduction occur for the biblical God alone, Clement diverges from him at what becomes the parting in the marital ways of the Lord by the late fourth century, *C.Th.* 9.7.5. Philo's procreationist endogamy is Jewish, whereas Clement's is Christian and proto-Catholic.

12. *Strom* 2.137.1. Clement defines γάμος as "first union" rather than simply as "union" because he advocates strict monogamy (e.g., *Strom* 3.108.1) due to his understanding of the sexual norms involved in Paul's marital theology, as I discuss later in this chapter.

13. *Strom* 3.47.3, cf. *Paed* 2.98.3, *Strom* 2.143.3.

14. *Paed* 2.92.2, and see further J. Broudéhoux, *Mariage et famille*, 132 n. 131, and P. Wendland, *Quaestiones Musonianae: De Musonio Stoico Clementis Alexandrini aliorumque auctore* (1886), 31–2. Broudéhoux (*Mariage et famille*, 74–83) includes additional textual evidence for Clement's procreationism in his study.

15. *Strom* 1.72.4, 2.100.3, and D. Runia, "Why Does Clement of Alexandria call Philo 'The Pythagorean'?" 1–22.

16. A. van den Hoek, *Clement of Alexandria and His Use of Philo in the* Stromateis: *An Early Christian Reshaping of a Jewish Model* (1988), 23–230; E. Osborn, "Philo and Clement" (1987), 34–49; J. Van Winden, "Quotations from Philo in Clement of Alexandria's *Protrepticus*" (1978), 208–13; and S. Lilla, *Clement of Alexandria: A Study in Christian Platonism and Gnosticism* (1971), 5 n. 1. Clement is the first Christian to utilize and elevate the stature of Philo's writings among the church fathers, D. Runia, *Philo in Early Christian Literature: A Survey* (1993) 132–56, and R. Radice, "Le Judaïsme alexandrin et la philosophie grecque" (1998), 486–7.

his procreationist dictate. He concurs with Philo that the Pentateuch forbids a man from copulating with a menstruating woman because it is an act of sterile and antireproductive husbandry.[17] Clement also draws an explicit procreationist moral from other biblical exegesis in Philo. For instance, Philo maintains that the ritual of circumcision symbolizes the need for God's people to "circumcise," that is, curtail their excessive appetite for sexual pleasure lest they succumb to its rebellious drive.[18] Clement utilizes this notion of the circumcised sexual appetite to impart a procreationist twist to Ezekiel's outcry, "Circumcise the fornication among you!" To his mind, Ezekiel means that sexually active Christians fornicate unless they circumcise sexual hedonism by remaining strictly reproductive and marital in their sexual relations (*Paed* 2.95.2). Clement likewise presents an argument from silence to support Philo's claim that the patriarchs were devout procreationists. "You could not show an instance of any of the elders in the scriptures approaching a pregnant woman in order to have sexual relations with her. Rather, you would find men knowing women only after their pregnancy and lactation," for the patriarchs are biblical role models who would never defy God's law by obliterating their seed (*Strom* 3.72.1, *Paed* 2.92.1–3). Clement thus accepts and extends Philo's arguments that deep down the Pentateuch is a procreationist tract.

Clement's reinterpretation of Deuteronomy 21:10–13 especially shows that Philo is his Pentateuchal authority for procreationism. Their combined interpretation of this passage also indicates how distant both of them were from Stoic sexual ethics. Deuteronomy 21:10–13 lists regulations about how an Israelite soldier may take an enslaved captive woman as his wife. The man must leave her sexually untouched for thirty days before consummating his marriage. During this period the woman's head must be shaved and her nails clipped. Philo connects this passage with God's plan to rein in sexual desire. Deuteronomy, he thinks, prescribes the thirty-day period to prevent the man from being so unrestrained that he rapes the captive right away. The man is then free to take her at his will sexually, provided that he marry her first (*Virt* 110–14). Though Philo would much prefer that the man copulate with the woman only for reproduction rather than pleasure, he would not enforce that rule, so long as the man waits the month and recognizes her as his wife beforehand. Philo thus refuses to meddle in a husband's sexual prerogative over his wife.

Clement carries Philo's moralizing further. The head-shaving, nail-clip-

17. Clement supports Philo's stance that a husband must be a strictly procreationist farmer with his wife, *Paed* 2.83.1–3, 102.1–2; *Strom* 2.143.2–3.

18. On this allegorical interpretation of circumcision in Philo, see P. Borgen, *Philo, John and Paul: New Perspectives on Judaism and Early Christianity* (1987), 62. The use of "circumcision" to signify being obedient to God in one's heart and inclinations appears already in Deut 10:16.

ping, and month-long delay, he thinks, are eminently noble procreationist measures. During this waiting period the husband comes to find his bald prisoner so unattractive that after the thirty days are over, he no longer sexually wants her for any reason other than reproduction (*Strom* 3.71.4). Philo does not prohibit the husband from taking his captive wife against her will for his sexual pleasure, while Clement allows him to do so only because he is obliged to make his unappealing wife pregnant. Clement and Philo thus remain in the dark ages of Deuteronomy and the *Iliad* when the sexual power of men over their wives and captive women was unquestioned. They channel the men's power more expressly into procreation, but the power remains the husband's prerogative. Hence Clement and Philo are out of touch with the early Stoic principle that sexual relations should occur only by mutual consent among persons committed primarily to generating mutual friendship and good will through their sexual behavior, which the later Stoics still advocate as a rule within marriage.

Clement revises the biblical distinction between sacred and defiled sexual activity to reflect his stance that Christian procreationism is God's inflexible law. In biblical terms sexual intercourse is sacred provided that it remains in compliance with the Pentateuchal laws. Sexual intercourse that deviates from the requirement to worship God alone is by definition defiled and forbidden. Clement fully upholds this principle, but he adds a Christian procreationist twist: "Given that the Law is sacred, marriage in accordance with the Law is sacred" (*Strom* 3.84.2). Since biblical law mandates Christian procreationism, marital sexual relations that transgress this standard are defiled and wrong as well. Clement consequently interprets Baruch's statement "You were defiled in an alien land" (*Bar* 3:10–11), which refers to Jews in exile, to mean that Christians who engage in nonprocreationist sexual activity in Christian marriage are defiled in the alien land of sexual pleasure (*Strom* 3.89.2). Married Christians must cleanse this "stained and defiled practice" in order to keep their marriages sacred (*Strom* 2.143.3). Clement thus adjusts the biblical dichotomy between sexual purity and defilement to fit his Pythagorean-derived dichotomy between sex "for procreation" or "for pleasure." The sacred becomes the strictly reproductive aim within Christian marriage and the defiled signifies all other sexual relations and motives.

For Clement, Plato is a teacher of procreationism second only to Moses and is much in his debt, as shown in Plato's *Laws*. "The philosopher who learned from Moses taught, 'Do not sow seeds on rocks and stones, on which they will never take root'" (*Paed* 2.90.4).[19] From Clement's perspec-

19. Clement is loosely quoting *Laws* 838e4–39a6, where males in their reproductive prime "must not sow on rocks and stones where their semen can never develop."

tive, Plato's legislative supplement to the Law of Moses mandates that non-procreationist sexual activity of any sort is "an outrage to nature" that must cease altogether (*Paed* 2.95.3). Plato, however, never advocates that human sexual conduct should be restricted solely to the function that we share with rabbits. After the citizens of Magnesia have fulfilled their strictly reproductive service in accordance with the city's needs, they should exercise a moderate and nonprocreative sexual hedonism, which Aphrodite compels them to do through their appetitive sexual desire. Clement, however, treats the *Laws* as though Plato, in unison with Philo's Moses, advocated a lifelong regimen of avoiding sexual activity apart from deliberately reproductive relations within marriage.

Clement portrays procreationism as though it were an apostolic regulation as well. He attributes the doctrine to Paul, his "holy apostle of the Lord" (*Protrep* 81.3), for he finds the procreationist mandate latent in Paul's notions of the sinful flesh and the belly.[20] To Clement, Paul's conception of the sinful flesh refers to the Pythagorean theory that overeating damages the body and fuels unrestrained desire for sexual pleasure and its many harmful repercussions.[21] In this overfed condition, desire becomes even more ferociously intent on transgressing God's procreationist law.[22] Clement similarly imposes a procreationist hermeneutic on Paul's eschatological prophecy about the cessation of bodily needs after the resurrection: "Food is for the belly and the belly is for food, and God will put an end to both" at the end of time (1 Cor 6:13). Clement interprets this prophecy as yet another of Paul's Pythagorean reminders that human beings must avoid the aphrodisiac risk of overfeeding the inner sexual beast. Mortals must not eat to copulate, for that is the sinful flesh God is now bringing to an end through procreationist law.[23] Clement thus puts Paul's stamp of apostolic authority on his Pythagorean conception of "temperate marriage" (*Strom* 3.86.1). In so doing he strengthens the normative force of procreationism as a Christian doctrine, for Paul is the premier sexual and marital advisor in early Christianity.

20. R. Ward ("Musonius and Paul on Marriage" [1990], 284–7) succinctly explains why Paul is not a procreationist.

21. On Paul's broader (and nonprocreationist) notion of sinful flesh, see E. P. Sanders, *Paul and Palestinian Judaism*, 508–9, 546–8, 553–4; R. Bultmann, *Theology of the New Testament* vol. 1 (1951), 227–46; and P. Brown, *Body and Society*, 47–52.

22. At *Strom* 3.41.3–6, for instance, Clement explains that Paul is referring to the unrestrained appetites when he urges the Galatian Christians not to use their new found freedom in Christ as an "opportunity for the flesh."

23. *Strom* 3.47.3. Clement similarly supports the dietary correlation at *Paed* 3.66.1, and he agrees with Valentinus that Jesus exemplifies perfect appetitive restraint. So good was Jesus at keeping his diet free of superfluous nutriment that he had no need even to defecate, let alone experience sexual desire from eating and drinking too much, *Strom* 3.59.3–4.

Nonetheless, Paul would have had strong reservations about the advisability of procreationism, had he known about it. In 1 Corinthians 7, as previously shown, he maintains that married Christians must carry out their sexual duty with sufficient frequency as a safeguard to keep Satan at bay, that is, to avoid the temptations of sexual fornication, such as adultery and a Christian man copulating with a woman who remains resolutely Gentile. Paul allows Christian couples to let down their guard only for brief and mutually agreeable periods of time, when the spouses are too busy praying together to cast a roving eye. He would have found it overly risky to compel married Christians to refrain from sexual activity for nine months and even years at a time, which Clement thinks they must do while wives are pregnant and nursing. To Paul, Satan is too wily an opponent to require the procreationist standard from ordinary Christians who must marry. Not only is celibacy out of their reach, Clement's schedule of infrequency is as well.

Clement's extension of procreationism to Paul is not entirely arbitrary, however. Paul ardently supports and intensifies the Pentateuchal sexual laws: Christians must unconditionally shun fornication as the most intimate threat to their bridal chastity, and they must also obey the other biblical sex laws.[24] Insofar as the Pentateuch is an unimpeachable authority for procreationism in Clement's opinion, to his mind Paul automatically becomes one as well.

In short, Clement thinks that sexual activity is biblically lawful only if it occurs within Christian marriage and for reproduction alone. All other sexual practices are a fornicating defiance of God. Clement adopts this position because he takes Philo at his word that the Pentateuch is a bona fide procreationist treatise. Philo however, reads the Pentateuch from two distinct viewpoints, one as a fairly literal-minded biblical traditionalist and the other as a Pythagorean procreationist. When it comes to determining which sex acts count as rebellion against God, Philo is traditional. Clement brings Philo's dual perspective into one procreationist focus; and he draws Paul into this way of seeing as well.

SEXUAL DESIRE AS DIABOLICAL WHORE PASSION

Clement inflexibly holds sexually active Christians to the standard of marital procreationism in the Lord for two related reasons: He presumes Philo's innovative conception of sexual desire, and he takes this normative idea to a greater extreme given his understanding of what Paul means by forbidden desires. To demonstrate the combined force of these ideas, we must begin with Clement's debt to Philo on sexual desire.

24. In support of the Pentateuch, Paul prohibits incest, adultery, sex acts outside of marriage in the Lord, as well as male and female homoerotic sex acts, as discussed in chapter five.

Along with Philo, Clement believes that sexual desire is an innate and irrational appetite that is located in the appetitive part of the Platonic tripartite soul, along with the appetites for the pleasures of food and drink (*Paed* 3.1.2). In further agreement with Philo, he describes the very function of the sexual appetite and its fricative end of pleasure as a culpably harmful passion. To communicate this position, he too appropriates the negative significance of the Stoic passions desire (ἐπιθυμία) and pleasure (ἡδονή). Contrary to the Stoics, who regard these passions as misguided evaluative decisions with harmful emotive repercussions, Clement finds sexual desire to be innately and always blameworthy for the same reason that Philo rejects Plato's idea that properly controlled sexual desire is beneficial (*Strom* 3.4.1, 3.59.1). The very nature of sexual desire is to compel God's people to defy the biblical law of procreationism, and to descend from there even deeper into the forbidden, such as incest and orgiastic devotion to other gods (*Paed* 3.1.2). Persons who act on their sexual appetite for pleasure rather than strictly for reproduction in the Lord are thus "still led around by passions" (*Strom* 3.43.1, 57.1), because they deviate from God's will. The Septuagint-based notion of the desire to disobey God plays a major role in Clement's conception of sexual desire and its dangers, which he draws from Philo. Like Philo, then, Clement diverges widely from the Platonic and Stoic ideas about sexual desire that he redeploys. To emphasize the danger of defying the Lord, Clement too dresses appetitive sexual desire in a slinky new religious skin—it is the snake of sexual temptation and Eve's desire to disobey wrapped into one.

Clement regards the sexual appetite as the definitive social problem of biblical history. Along with Philo, he blames the Septuagint incidents of Israel and Judah apostasizing on sexual desire and its intransigent tendency to defy the way of the Lord. As Clement sees it, the Jews fell away from God on repeated occasions because they acted on their "alien sexual appetite," and as a result they were disenfranchised and sold to foreign peoples (*Strom* 3.90.2–3). He calls the sexual appetite "alien" because its aim is the forbidden fruit of sexual pleasure. Similarly, when Jeremiah cries out to male adulterers, "You have become in my eyes female-mad stallions" (Jer 5:8), Clement takes the stallions as a reference to the apostate sexual horse "for pleasure" in the Platonic chariot of the soul. So confident is he in this interpretation that he even attributes Jeremiah 5:8 to Plato (*Paed* 2.89.2). To act on the sexual appetite therefore is tantamount to riding a Satanic steed away from God. Christians must stay off this horse or they too are doomed to perpetuate the female-mad rebellions that have afflicted God's people throughout history.

Clement exceeds Philo in advocating that the way of the Lord requires unconditional procreationism because he combats sexual desire even more than Philo does. The two-word Tenth Commandment, οὐκ ἐπιθυμήσεις, signifies to Clement that any instance of sexual activity for pleasure rather than for procreation implicates its agents in apostasy, even within Christian marriage.[25] Further, married Christians are egregiously defiant, adulterers in fact, if they even want to make love for any reason other than reproduction. "You will not have appetitive sexual desire ($οὐκ\ ἐπιθυμήσεις$), for by the sexual appetite alone you commit adultery" (*Protrep* 108.5). God, Clement adds, keeps an especially close eye on this new class of adulterers and will punish them for the nonreproductive sexual desire they show within their marriages, just as God punishes traditional adulterers (*Paed* 2.99.3–100.3). He supports his claim by citing Ecclesiasticus 23:18–19, where God is said to watch for and punish men who make love to other men's wives (*Paed* 2.99.3). Though Clement recognizes the difference between these two kinds of adultery, he nonetheless contends that both sins are equally adulterous, and that Ecclesiasticus denounces both. Even though the inclination to transgress procreationism within Christian marriage is not adultery "against neighbors," it is adultery that the married couples commit "against themselves" (*Paed* 2.100.1). To Clement, then, the sexual stirring of desire between a man and a woman for any nonprocreationist reason is so dangerous that it becomes his main criterion of adultery,[26] regardless of whether the sexual desire stirs against neighbors or between spouses.[27] Given the deleterious nature of the sexual appetite, Clement marshals two commandments against it, $οὐκ\ ἐπιθυμήσεις$ and $οὐ\ μοιχεύσεις$. Philo refrains from this step, though he helps bring Clement to it.[28]

Clement condemns the sexual appetite for pleasure more harshly than Philo because he equates it with the desire to disobey God that Paul condemns as the death-bearing state of psychological sin. Paul, in his anguished reflections on $οὐκ\ ἐπιθυμήσεις$ in Romans 7, states that mortals are in sinful defiance of God's will if they even want to transgress the laws that remain binding on them, and especially the imperative to abandon sexual in-

25. Clement cites this commandment in its abbreviated form at *Protrep* 108.5, *Strom* 3.71.3, and 3.76.1, and he describes it at *Strom* 3.57.1–2.

26. *Strom* 2.145.3, 146.2. Clement also regards it as adultery for Christians to remarry while their first spouses are still alive. He would condemn these sexual relations regardless of whether the divorced and remarried persons make love strictly in a procreationist manner.

27. Clement implicitly recognizes another distinction between the two senses of adultery in that he, like Philo, supports the biblical principle that adulterers in the traditional sense must be put to death (*Strom* 2.147.1) and approves of Phineas's preemptive strike against sexual apostasy (*Strom* 3.32.1), but nowhere advocates capital punishment against Christians who commit nonprocreationist "adultery" within marriage. Clement leaves it to his ever vigilant God to exact retribution against married Christians who commit adultery "against themselves."

28. As shown previously, though Philo finds nonprocreationist sexual activity highly culpable, he classifies only those acts that transgress bona fide Pentateuchal sex laws as being formally in apostasy against God's will.

tercourse and reproduction in honor of other gods.[29] Clement, in light of Philo, takes Paul to mean that the very function of appetitive sexual desire for fricative pleasure is the fornicating sin of sins (*Strom* 3.76.1, 78.1). Paul's idea of forbidden desire (ἐπιθυμία) is unrelated to Plato's and to Philo's Platonizing view that sexual desire and its pleasures are the root of all wrongdoing,[30] but Clement does not see it that way. To his mind the Hellenistic Jewish and Platonic senses of culpable desire are intertwined, thanks to the way Philo braids them together and reconfigures the Platonic sexual appetite into the "original wicked passion" (ἀρχέκακον πάθος) against God (*Spec* 4.85). Thus, when Paul condemns even the desire to defy God's will, due to the deadly power of the lawless inclination, Clement and later church fathers understand him to be condemning the very function of the appetitive sexual desire as the snaky fornicating impulse to defy God.[31] This fusion of Paul's and Philo's positions on ἐπιθυμία is a radically new normative idea: the very experience of appetitive sexual desire is itself death-bearing and rebellious. Given the fusion, which Clement is the first on record to make, Christians wantonly defy God merely by desiring fricative sexual pleasure, which means that they surely cannot afford Philo's relative leniency toward husbands and wives indulging in nonprocreationist sexual activity together. Such indulgence is the fornication that Christians must flee. Clement's innovative conception of eros and its dangers is one of his key contributions to ecclesiastical sexual morality, and it is pivotal to understanding the heightened alarmism about eros that imbues the procreationism of later church fathers.

Matthew 5:27–8 provides Clement's main precedent for labeling sexual desire as adultery rather than simply as fornication.[32] Clement's position on ἐπιθυμία relative to Matthew's is nonetheless innovative and more restrictive, just as it is to Paul's. In Matthew, a man commits adultery in his heart when he looks at a woman who is biblically off-limits to him "with a view to desiring her" (πρὸς τὸ ἐπιθυμῆσαι αὐτήν).[33] Here Matthew contends, as

29. I have explicated Paul's biblically grounded idea of forbidden desire in chapter five.

30. Paul was not himself acquainted with Platonism, and he did not know Plato's conception of the sexual appetite and its nefarious vices.

31. Clement's interpretation of οὐκ ἐπιθυμήσεις becomes more prevalent in ecclesiastical thought after Clement, and partly in support of his views. In explanation of Rom 7:7, for example, Theodore of Mopsuestia interprets the commandment primarily as God's prohibition against "food, drink, and sex" along with the proliferation of other desires to which they lead, including the desire for "fame and fortune as well," K. Staab, ed., *Pauluskommentare aus der griechischen Kirche*, 126.

32. This identification appears, for instance, in *Protrep* 108.5.

33. See too *Strom* 3.71.3, 94.3, *Paed* 3.82.5–83.4. For the context and connotations of the Matthean dictate prior to its reinterpretation in Christian Platonism, see G. F. Moore, *Judaism*, vol. 2, 268–72 and W. D. Davies, *The Setting of the Sermon on the Mount* (1964), 101–3, 300–1.

Paul does in Romans 7, that it is wrong to want to act in defiance of God's will, though Matthew 5:27–8 deals specifically with a man's desire for sexual defiance with a woman.[34] Like Paul, Matthew retains traditional biblical notions about forbidden male-female sexual relations, such as adultery and fornication,[35] and these are linked to his prohibition of adulterous desire: It is adulterous for men even to want to commit adultery, make love to religiously alien women, and so on. For Clement, however, it is adulterous for a man and woman to want to make love at all unless their inclination to copulate is dedicated strictly to generating more children for God in a Christian social order.

Clement's new norm against sexual fornication marks the change in Christian sexual morality from the early views we see in Paul and Matthew to the ecclesiastical views of the developing church. Neither Matthew nor Paul gives any indication of knowing about, let alone advocating, a position like Clement's. The new norm is a paradigm shift about original sin that Clement adapts from Philo and takes to a further extreme through his interpretation of Romans 7 on forbidden desire. "Sexual fornication" in his sense, meaning "the inherent pleasurable end of the (demonized) Platonic sexual appetite," presupposes that the Platonic sexual appetite is at the heart of the Hellenistic Jewish problem of the desire to defy God's will.[36] This formative patristic sense of fornication is not to be found in the Septuagint and Paul.

Clement, however, is not alone in reshaping the significance of sexual fornication and its dangers. The Christian redaction of the Pythagorean *Sentences of Sextus* contends, in light of Matthew 5:27–8, that "Every man who is sexually unrestrained in his interaction with his wife commits adultery with her" (μοιχὸς τῆς ἑαυτοῦ γυναικὸς πᾶς ὁ ἀκόλαστος).[37] Clement is the first known Christian, however, to expressly identify this adultery of sex-

34. Paul's discourse on the οὐκ ἐπιθυμήσεις problem in Romans 7 deals with desires to commit transgressions against God in any sphere of behavior, sexual or not. For Paul, to be sure, sexual transgressions are the most dangerous, given his marital theology about Christ's collective bride. Nevertheless, Romans 7 treats οὐκ ἐπιθυμήσεις more broadly, whereas Matthew 5:27–8 focuses on a man's sexual desire for a woman who is prohibited to him on biblical grounds.

35. Matt 5:27, 5:32, 19:9.

36. P. Brown aptly describes this patristic view: Fornication is a "demon . . . perceived as a lurking, mute presence in the heart," "Bodies and Minds: Sexuality and Renunciation in Early Christianity" (1990), 481–2. Other modern patristic scholars have similarly observed that demonic "sexual fornication" (πορνεία) in patristic thought comes to refer to the end toward which the human sexual appetite or sexual desire inherently aims, such as A. Guillaumont, "Le célibat monastique et l'idéal chrétien de la virginité ont-ils des 'motivations ontologiques et protologiques'?" (1985), 84, and A. Rousselle, *Porneia*, 1. Clement is one of the first church fathers to promote this new meaning of sexual fornication.

37. *Sentences* 231.

ual unrestraint in Christian marriage with deviation from the strict procreationist narrow. The Christian redaction of the Pythagorean *Sentences* does
not have this specificity, for it does not designate what constitutes sexual unrestraint within marriage.[38] From Clement onward among the church fathers, the specification becomes clear—make love only for reproduction,
not for the adultery of sexual pleasure.

Clement uses Philo's trope of soul fornication to identify sexual desire
with the whorish worship of the Greek gods of eros. In so doing he reinforces
the view that sexual desire is intrinsically adulterous. If Christians make love
for any reason other than marital reproduction, they suffer a "prostitute
passion" (ἑταιρικὸν πάθος) that defiles the soul (*Paed* 2.98.3), and makes
it, as Philo would say, fornicated. Sexual pleasure is a prostitute passion because it represents the whore incarnate and her son, Aphrodite and Eros.[39]
Aphrodite is "a name for sexual activity" and Eros is synonymous with the
sexual appetite (*Protrep* 102.3, *Strom* 3.44.2). Eros as combined god and
sexual appetite is the diabolical "enemy" of Christians, and he "works death
from within" through "the desires and pleasures" that he stimulates. Christians must beat back every stirring of sexual ardor in order to be saved. If
they fail, this enemy god "arises from within" them as sexual desire, provokes their rebellion against God's procreationist law, and remains "always
present" in them even if they try to run away (*Quis dives,* 25.4–6). Woe to
Christians, then, who in their renegade hearts want to enjoy sexual pleasure

38. Some scholars, including M. Foucault (*Care of the Self,* 177) and U. Ranke-Heinemann
(*Eunuchs for Heaven,* 3) have mistakenly perpetuated the idea that Seneca means the same
thing as Jerome by the sentiment that "nothing is more defiling than to love your wife as an
adulteress" (*Adv Jov* 319a–b). Seneca means that it is tantamount to adultery for a man to copulate with his own wife while fantasizing that his partner is another man's wife: "If a man were
to make love with his own wife as though with another woman, he will be an adulterer, though
the woman would not be an adulteress" (*Si quis cum uxore sua tamquam cum aliena concumbat,
adulter erit, quamvis illa adultera non sit*), *Const* 7.4. Jerome, however, along with Clement and
the Christian redactor of the *Sentences* 231, means that it is adulterous for a man to make love
in an unrestrained way with his wife under any circumstances. For Seneca, by contrast, the critical factor is the arousing fantasy of adultery on the part of the man. Bickel (*Diatribe: Fragmenta
de matrimonio,* 361–2) is the first to conflate these two very different senses of "adultery within
marriage" in his edition of Seneca's *De matrimonio,* which is comprised of fragments taken from
Jerome's *Adversus Jovinianum.* There is no evidence for attributing the sentiment that we see in
Jerome, *Sentences* 231, Clement, or even Matthew 5:27–8 to Seneca or to any other Greek or
Roman source. The Greek claim that husbands who engage in unrestrained marital sexual relations treat their wives like prostitutes (e.g., Plutarch, *Coniugalia praecepta* 140c, 142c) is not
the same sentiment, *pace* H. Chadwick, *Sentences of Sextus,* 173, for it is not a claim about adultery in any sense.

39. As noted in the previous chapter, Clement abhors the Greek gods of eros, *Protrep* 33.9,
35.2, 36.1, 53.5–6, 60.2; *Paed* 2.123.1–3; *Strom* 2.107.2–3, 3.10.1, 3.27.1–3.

while making love, even within marriage. They cannot have it without falling into the deadly grasp of Aphrodite and Eros.[40]

To Clement, sexual pleasure poses the same degree of religious danger for Christians as biblical whores do in the Pentateuch and Prophets. Just as rebellious male Israelites meet their demise by chasing after "religiously alien women" (ἀλλότριαι γυναῖκες)[41] or whores in the biblical sense, so too do married Christians by wanting to pursue "religiously alien pleasures" (ἀλλότριαι ἡδοναί), or harlots in the sense of the "prostitute passion" (*Strom* 3.96.2, *Paed* 2.98.3). For Clement and Philo alike, this whore is Aphrodite. Clement, however, is much more severe than Philo about this harlot danger embedded in the flesh. Like Tatian, he is convinced that sexual pleasure is central among the "devil's passions" (διαβολικὰ πάθη) (*Strom* 3.81.4). Philo does not go this far. Even though he calumniates sexual pleasure as the biblical harlot Aphrodite on a cosmic scale, he remains enough of a Pentateuchal traditionalist to think that God's people commit apostasy only by seeking sexual pleasure in biblically forbidden relationships, such as religiously mixed marriages, not by seeking sexual pleasure per se. For Clement, however, Christians who defy the biblical law of procreationism are on par with male Israelites in hot pursuit of Moabite women, to the ruin of themselves and the Christian community at large.

For Clement, consequently, sexual pleasure within and outside of Christian marriage is the darkness of evil, death, and damnation, while Christian procreationism or virginity is the light of God, goodness, and salvation. He frequently reiterates this emergent church teaching. Pleasure, Clement declares, is diametrically opposed to God's goodness (*Strom* 3.43.2). He similarly reprocesses Matthew's adage about God and Mammon. Christians cannot serve both "God and pleasure" (*Strom* 3.26.2). And Christ did not come into the world to save humanity from sins of all sorts. He came to save us from "enjoying pleasures" (*Strom* 3.44.4, 94.3). Even angels fell from heaven because they failed to restrain their sexual appetite for pleasure.[42] Sexually ac-

---

40. Clement is of two minds on the erotic gods' status. In theory, he regards the gods as fictions or as projections of human emotions (as discussed by A. Droge, *Homer or Moses?* 125–32), but he continues to believe that most sexual activity involves servitude to the inner appetitive demons of sexual desire, Eros and Aphrodite. Therefore Aphrodite and Eros remain real and diabolical powers for Clement, regardless of his theoretical position about the nonexistence of the gods. As a general rule, a good way to test whether or not early Christians with a Greek background have gotten beyond believing that alien gods exist as demons is to discern whether they think sexual desire is free of indwelling alien gods. Clement fails the test.

41. Ἀλλότριαι γυναῖκες often means "religiously alien women" in the Septuagint, such as 3 Kgdms 11:1, 4.

42. *Strom* 3.59.2, *Paed* 3.14.2. Clement's claim that angels fell from heaven is an instance of mythologically reinterpreting Gen 6:1–4 in the manner of *The Book of Enoch* 6:1–11:2. Ta-

tive Christians are sure to plummet as well, unless they take heed and abide by procreationism. Likewise, when Paul in Romans 7 deplores ἐπιθυμία as impulse to disobey God's will, Clement understands him to be "berating hedonists" for acting on the sexual appetite (*Strom* 3.78.1). Even though Philo stops short of this extreme, he leads Clement to the ecclesiastical edge.

CLEMENT'S BRAVE NEW PROCREATIONIST IMPULSE

Clement so aggressively fears the diabolical nature of the sexual appetite that he finds the procreationism of his predecessors to be seriously deficient, Philo's included. In Platonic and Pythagorean thought prior to Clement, a married couple's desire to reproduce is stimulated by the sexual appetite for pleasure even when the sexual activity is marital, temperate, and deliberately procreative. Through the procreationist regimen the spouses artfully impose constraints on the otherwise wild sexual appetite and reproductive urge, which is for the good of their offspring and themselves. As even Philo acknowledges, sexual pleasure guides God's people to reproduce,[43] odd as it is for his winking and whinnying whore Pleasure to be any sort of guide. Clement fully understands this basic tenet of his predecessors. In the ascetic regimen of Plato and other Greek philosophers, he states, human beings should at most strive to be "irrationally appetitive with restraint" given the innate needs of the human appetites (*Strom* 3.57.1). Clement, however, finds this ascetic regimen inadequate, dangerous, and outmoded as far as sexual desire is concerned. Persons living by this discipline do not transcend their innate proclivity toward Aphrodite and Eros. Christians, however, are absolutely forbidden to have any such orientation, even in the vestigial manner that Philo allows as a means to the reproductive end. Christians thus need a radically new asceticism that would allow them to avoid the fornicating ways of sexual pleasure altogether. In their procreationist sexual conduct they must aspire "not to hold out while being irrationally appetitive (ἐπιθυμεῖν)," as the philosophers teach, "but to refrain even from the irrational appetite (ἐπιθυμεῖν)" and to gain complete mastery over it.[44]

---

tian creatively redeploys the same motif in his myth of the Olympians as God's fallen angels, as shown in the preceding chapter.

43. "The first sexual joinings of the male toward the female have pleasure as their guide, and through this pleasure acts of sowing and reproduction come about," *Opif* 161.

44. *Strom* 3.57.1–58.2, 3.69.4. Clement regards this difference as a major one. Merely to restrain the sexual appetite is still a gross enslavement to sexual pleasure that Christians must eliminate from their lives. To underscore this point, he caricatures Greek philosophical proponents of sexual restraint (Plato, Democritus, the Stoics, Epicureans, and Peripatetics) as libidinous slaves of sexual pleasure, *Strom* 2.138.2–6, because they failed to completely conquer the sexual appetite and instead tried to work with it as a natural given.

Clement's need for a new ascetic sexual discipline leaves him with a thorny problem, for in Pythagorean, Platonic, and Philonic terms, human beings cannot possibly "refrain even from the irrational appetite" unless they are dead. The appetites to make love, eat, and drink are necessary for regeneration, sustenance, and overall well-being. To Clement, however, the sexual appetite "works death from within." How, then, can Christians be sexually active at all, even as strict procreationists within marriage, without succumbing to the fornicating sexual appetite?[45] Clement has to develop something like a reborn sexual impulse in order for Christian procreationism to seem permissible. Otherwise, Tatian and his encratite followers would appear to be right after all. Making love under any circumstances enmeshes Christians in the worship of Aphrodite.

To Clement's mind, God has rescued Christians from the need to renounce sexual activity altogether. With Christ as intercessor, the Lord miraculously bestows the nonappetitive and passionless sexual capabilities of the Stoic sage exclusively on married Christian procreationists. Christians remain liberated from innate sexual desire, but only so long as they never transgress the limit of temperate and deliberately reproductive sexual relations within marriage. In place of appetitive sexual desire, God grants them a higher level of "natural impulses" ($\alpha i \ \tau \hat{\eta} s \ \phi \acute{u}\sigma\epsilon\omega s \ \acute{o}\rho\acute{\epsilon}\xi\epsilon\iota s$) for reproduction alone, without any admixture from the innate sexual appetite (*Strom* 3.82.1). In obedience only to this acquired impulse, the Christian couples desire only that which is sexually "appropriate," namely, legitimate Christian children, and they reject that which is sexually "harmful," that is, any and all other sexual purposes (*Strom* 3.69.2). Because their strictly reproductive aim is a "well-reasoned impulse" ($\acute{o}\rho\epsilon\xi\iota s \ \epsilon\ddot{u}\lambda o\gamma o s$) (*Strom* 3.71.4), they make love with a "chaste and controlled will" ($\sigma\epsilon\mu\nu\hat{\omega} \ \kappa\alpha\grave{\iota} \ \sigma\acute{\omega}\phi\rho o\nu\iota \ \theta\epsilon-\lambda\acute{\eta}\mu\alpha\tau\iota$) (*Strom* 3.58.2). The agreeable feeling they gain from this sexual experience is not pleasure but "enjoyment" ($\acute{a}\pi\acute{o}\lambda\alpha\upsilon\sigma\iota s$) of an "encratic" ($\acute{\epsilon}\gamma\kappa\rho\alpha\tau\acute{\eta}s$) sort.[46] Hence Christians alone of all people are free of sexual sin despite being reproductively active, because they are uniquely gifted with the ability to be "entirely impervious to thoughts motivated by irrational appetition" in their sexual conduct (*Strom* 3.69.4). Clement requires

---

45. J. Broudéhoux (*Mariage et famille*, 130) understates the problem that Clement faces: "il est dificile de soustraire totalement [des relations conjugales] à l'$\acute{\epsilon}\pi\iota\theta\upsilon\mu\acute{\iota}\alpha$ et à l'$\acute{\eta}\delta o\nu\acute{\eta}$."

46. *Strom* 3.85.2. D. Hunter ("The Language of Desire: Clement of Alexandria's Transformation of Ascetic Discourse" [1992], 99–105) and A. Louth ("Apathetic Love in Clement of Alexandria" [1989], 414–17) offer insights into the difference Clement articulates between the sexual appetite ($\acute{\epsilon}\pi\iota\theta\upsilon\mu\acute{\iota}\alpha$) and the sexual "well-reasoned impulse" ($\acute{o}\rho\epsilon\xi\iota s \ \epsilon\ddot{u}\lambda o\gamma o s$). They do not note, however, that Clement regards the latter as a special dispensation strictly for procreationist Christians that comes only through Christ.

this appetite-free standard of sexual behavior from all Christians, the "more simple" *(simpliciores)* and Gnostic Christians alike.[47] He insists that this Christian liberation comes about only through divine intervention in Christ,[48] though this gift is not inalienable. If married Christians deviate in the slightest from this procreationist rule, they are stripped of the sanctity of this higher impulse and fall back to what he calls the "old" and deadly condition of innate sexual desire and its "religiously alien pleasures" (*Strom* 3.95.1–96.2). Thus Clement really means it when he says that Christ came into the world in order to save us from pleasures (*Strom* 3.44.4, 94.3). Christ has brought the revocable gift of prophylactic grace that makes the nonappetitive reproduction of Christians possible. Its blessed recipients neither want nor feel sexual pleasure when they have genital contact with procreationist resolve.

Clement reinterprets a polemical distinction in the Gospel of John as proof that married Christian procreationists do not experience even vestigial sexual desire when they copulate. Christians are "children of God's will," not "children of the irrational sexual appetite ($\dot{\epsilon}\pi\iota\theta\nu\mu\dot{\iota}a$)."[49] To retain this freedom, Christians must never sexually transgress the procreationist limit, for otherwise they lose their identity as children of God's will and become delinquent agents of the sexual appetite (*Strom* 3.58.1–2). Nothing could be further from the topic of John's narrative than this unprecedented doctrine of sexual temperance that Clement formulates.[50] Hence

47. As Clement sees it, Christians at all levels must obey the commandments, as noted by O. Prunet, *La morale de Clément d'Alexandrie et le Nouveau Testament* (1966), 85, and he considers $o\dot{\nu}\kappa\ \dot{\epsilon}\pi\iota\theta\nu\mu\dot{\eta}\sigma\epsilon\iota\varsigma$ as a pivotal commandment for all Christians to keep, even if they do not advance beyond a state of moderate passions ($\mu\epsilon\tau\rho\iota o\pi\dot{a}\theta\epsilon\iota a$) to attain the perfectly passionless state ($\dot{a}\pi\dot{a}\theta\epsilon\iota a$) of the complete Gnostic. Further, strictly procreationist Christian marital behavior (or sustained virginity) must be stably in place in order for the broader Gnostic perfection to become attainable. Gnostic Christians must then go one major step further. They must rise even above the mid-range "good passions" ($\epsilon\dot{\nu}\pi\dot{a}\theta\epsilon\iota a\iota$) in addition to already transcending the culpable passion of the sexual appetite for pleasure, W. Völker, *Der wahre Gnostiker nach Clemens Alexandrinus* (1952), 220–54, 524–43. Obedient Christian procreationists in the *simplicior* class are not at this higher Gnostic level. In their state of $\mu\epsilon\tau\rho\iota o\pi\dot{a}\theta\epsilon\iota a$, they still feel an "encratic enjoyment," *Strom* 3.85.2, but not appetitive sexual pleasure, from their strictly reproductive sexual activity within marriage. For the distinction between two levels of *simplicior* and "Gnostic" Christian ethics in Clement's thought, see O. Prunet, *La morale de Clément,* 68–117, and S. Lilla, *Clement of Alexandria,* 103–17.

48. *Strom* 3.44.1, 57.1, 58.2, 95.1.

49. The distinction Clement is adapting appears at John 1:12–13 and is further developed in the polemical context of John 8:42–44.

50. As mentioned in chapter five, John is promoting one theological position and denigrating another: Jesus is the son of God; Jesus is not the son of God. On his view children of God's will believe the first tenet, while "children of forbidden desire" and "the devil" believe the second. Clement's exegetical wand transforms John's theological polemic into a biblical

when Clement states that procreationist sex acts within Christian marriage are "moderate,"[51] he means something radically different from all of his procreationist predecessors. Moderate Christian procreationism is completely untempered by the sexual appetite, not the work of tempered appetition.[52] Obedient Christians as sexually active children of God's will "refrain even from the irrational appetite ($\dot{\epsilon}\pi\iota\theta\nu\mu\epsilon\hat{\iota}\nu$)," because otherwise they are heinous fornicators.[53]

Clement's Christian procreationist ethic is incompatible with Stoicism even though, like Seneca, he uses Stoic phrases to describe it. To attain Clement's pseudo-Stoic disposition of passionless sexual conduct, persons need to be married Christians in order to receive the gift of prophylactic grace that protects them from the innate sexual appetite and its diabolical ways. Married Christians retain this passionless gift only by remaining on the procreationist path as "children of God's will." If they stray from the path in the slightest, they succumb to sexual desire and thereby become alienated from God and life in the only form worth having. By contrast, to attain the Stoic ideal of passionless sexual activity, persons must work long and hard in the philosophical discipline of Stoic physics, logic, and ethics. As a central part of this discipline in the Stoic way of life worth living, persons ought to engage in sexual relations toward mutual friendship and enlightenment, either communally or maritally, depending on the Stoic advocate. Though this training precludes sexual activity for a selfish type of pleasure, it welcomes the sexual desire and pleasure that accompany justifiable sexual relations. Clement's conviction that sexual desire and pleasure are inherently rebellious is opposed to Stoic thought, and the same is true of procreationism. Even the marital ideals of Antipater and Hierocles are wicked and dangerous from Clement's perspective, for they too attempt to conceal the sexual worship of Aphrodite and Eros under the sinfully cozy blanket of mutual friendship within marriage. Clement nonetheless does use convenient Stoic phrases to persuade married Christians that they may reproduce without fear of being enslaved to sexual desire. In his vision of ideal sexual mores, people must be Christian and marry Christians if they choose to be sexually

---

proof text that Christian procreationists, and they alone, are "children of God's will" rather than "of the irrational sexual appetite for pleasure."

51. *Strom* 3.58.2, 81.3, 86.1.

52. Clement further expresses his antipathy to the sexual appetite for pleasure in his interpretation of the phrase "putting an end to the works of the female" in the gospel of the Egyptians. He equates "the works of the female" with the sexual appetite that married Christians escape provided that they remain strictly procreationist, *Strom* 3.93.1–2. The encratite significance of the phrase, by contrast, serves to issue a call for the cessation of sexual activity and reproduction, T. Van Eijk, "Marriage and Virginity," 214–7.

53. *Strom* 3.57.1–58.2, 69.4.

active. Then they must cast off the sexual desire that afflicts them with hedonistic rebellion against God. In this mission, they must don procreationist armor embossed with Stoic phrases so as to crush their sexual appetite
underfoot: Believe in Christ and you are an imperturbable sage. Believe and
you transcend sexual pleasure. If you deviate from procreationism, the sexual appetite rears its hooded foreskin and strikes again. Despite the borrowed phrases, nothing about this vision is Stoic.[54]

Another example shows how anti-Stoic Clement's thought is in relation
to human sexuality, He severely criticizes the Stoic argument that "nature
made us well designed for procreative marital intercourse,"[55] on the grounds
that it is not nature but Christ's special dispensation that makes Christian
procreationism possible. People who argue that human beings should follow nature's design and reproduce, he maintains, should be ashamed of
themselves, for they believe that "the human body created by God is more
acratic than even irrational animals" (*Strom* 2.139.3–4).

Due to his fear of the erotic gods, Clement is much closer to Tatian than
his procreationist argument against encratism would initially suggest. To
Clement, Tatian is in error only because he does not see that Christian procreationism is the sole sacred exception to Aphrodite's sexual tyranny over
humanity. Yes, Christians must renounce the erotic gods' fornicating mastery over mortals, yet this does not mean that they should not have children,
for prospective Christian parents retain the one safe and fecund zone that
Clement demarcates. While Tatian finds sexuality one vast sea of Aphrodite,
Clement sees only one dry island in the seductive sea foam, where the Lord
alone rules. Here, where Odysseus would never have lingered, married
Christians live and make strictly temperate and reproductive love within
Christian marriage, while the rest of humanity drowns. Clement, far from
being a sexual moderate, is but one dubious step away from Tatian's encratite position.[56] He pointedly corrects Tatian's claim that all sexual intercourse is in thrall to "fornication and the devil" (*Strom* 3.82.1), but only by
making Christian procreationist marriage a miraculous exception to such
enslavement.

54. W. Richardson ("The Basis of Ethics: Chrysippus and Clement of Alexandria" [1966],
87–97) shows the many catechetical substitutions involved in Clement's reworking of Stoic
ethics, e.g., the logos is Christ, the προκόπτοντες are disciples of Christ, the patriarchs are
sages; one's "orientation" (οἰκείωσις) is toward God and the Pentateuchal commandments, as
opposed to "toward oneself" (πρὸς ἑαυτόν) in the Stoic sense of "orientation," which refers
to having an increasingly informed awareness of one's actions and motives. This is not minor
tinkering; it is the transformation of Stoic philosophy into Sunday school.

55. Cf. SVF 3.340 = Cicero, *Fin* 3.62.

56. I have now shown why it is misguided to maintain the common view that Clement's disposition toward sexual activity is "middle of the road," as P. Karavites puts it, *Evil, Freedom, and
the Road to Perfection,* 89.

THE SPIRITUAL ADULTERY OF THE CHRISTIAN CHURCH AND SOUL

Clement's ardent procreationist cause gains impetus from Paul's marital theology. He agrees with Paul that the Christian church is joined "to Christ as a sacred virgin to one husband (ἑνὶ ἀνδρί)" (*Strom* 3.74.1–2). If Christians in the affianced church succumb to thoughts and practices contrary to the Bridegroom's will, then the church as a whole "fornicates against her one husband (τοῦ ἑνὸς ἀνδρός), God the almighty" (*Strom* 3.80.2). The same is true of each Christian soul, which Clement regards as feminine and betrothed to God as promised husband.[57] For Clement, of course, Christians fornicate against God by transgressing or even wanting to transgress their sole procreationist outlet.[58] Here Clement performs another innovative synthesis, for he situates Paul's problem of spiritual adultery in a procreationist framework and links procreationism with Paul's marital poetics. Married Christians must heed primarily the procreationist limit to ensure that their community and souls remain pure virgins in their monotheistic devotion, for as Paul teaches, sexual fornication is the worst of all sins the collective bride can commit. Clement is thus like a vigilant father keeping his daughter sexually pure for the man who will claim her. He allows Christians to remove their chastity belts only for reproduction within Christian marriage, while Tatian would keep Christians entirely under lock and key until the arrival of the Bridegroom.[59]

---

57. *Strom* 3.84.3. Christian husbands, Clement adds, especially need to become habituated to the collective feminine gender that they acquire as members of Christ's prospective bride. He sees nothing incongruous about this idea, for he ascribes femininity to the souls of Christian men and women alike. To protect the chastity of the soul as inner bride, he writes rather like an advice columnist about regulating male Christian conduct. Christian men, he advises, make "good husbands of their Christian wives," so long as the men "remember their Bridegroom," *Protrep* 107.3. Christian procreationism is central to the lessons he thinks husbands must learn in order to mind their Bridegroom.

58. Though Clement is primarily concerned to rout acts of sexual fornication against God from the community, he fully agrees with the Pentateuch that spiritual fornication (viz., fornicating against God) need not be sexual in nature. He recognizes two other nonsexual meanings of "fornication" in addition to the sexual appetite's "love of pleasure." These are "idolatry" and "love of money," *Strom* 7.75.3.

59. Clement's feminization of the embodied and bridal soul strikingly differentiates his notion of the soul and of soul fornication from Philo's. According to Philo, the soul in its ideal state is masculine, purified of the femininity that unmans it, *Cher* 50, 52. It seeks union with God partly as a feminine principle of wisdom or Sophia, *QG* 3.21, 4.97, 4.145–6, not as an almighty bridegroom. Philo does not share the conception of spiritual adultery that plays such a formative role in the sexual regulations of Paul, Tatian, and Clement. This is the case partly because Philo makes very little use of the Prophets, which is where the biblical metaphor is developed of God as almighty husband and of the people as God's submissive wife. Philo's ideal of the manly soul would make for a very awkward adulteress, especially against God engendered as Sophia.

To Clement it is so critical for Christians to avoid spiritual adultery that he demotes his procreationism to his Christian marital theology in one important way. Christian spouses, he maintains, ought to imitate the monogamous relationship between Christ and the church by having only one spouse in Christ the Lord (*Strom* 3.80.3). Wives in particular must remain unconditionally devoted to their husbands, just as the church is to Christ. Clement reluctantly allows only one exception. A Christian may marry a second time, but only if his or her first spouse has died. Even this exception, however, deviates from pure monogamy and thus precludes a perfectly sacred marriage.[60] All further deviations from Christian monogamy, such as divorcing and remarrying, are an outright "fall" into sexual fornication against the body,[61] and hence into the worst sort of spiritual adultery against Christ. Women who fail to comply with this requirement are to be stigmatized as biblical harlots (*Strom* 2.147.2). Clement's ideal of Christian monogamy potentially conflicts with, and takes precedence over, his procreationist aim of reproducing children devoted to God alone. If, for example, a young, childless Christian widow wants to remarry in order to have children, Clement prefers that she remain a childless widow and he would label her next marriage second-rate.[62] If a wife were to leave her husband and have children with another man, Clement would allow the whore no dignity or tolerance.[63] Christian monogamy is thus such a compelling cameo of the relationship between the church and her Bridegroom that for Clement the inviolability of first marriage takes precedence over reproduction. Married women who fail to conform to this ideal are, at best, less than perfect widows who marry again once. Otherwise they are whores.[64]

60. *Strom* 3.82.4–5. Clement condones no more than one remarriage under any circumstances. J. Broudéhoux (*Mariage et famille*, 91–4) discusses his marital ethic in connection with its background in 1 Corinthians 7 and the pastoral epistles. Clement, in supporting this ideal of strict monogamy in the Lord, greatly elaborates and intensifies the New Testament teaching that married Christians must not divorce, Mark 10:11–12, Luke 16:18, 1 Cor 7:10, Eph 5:22–33, cf. Matt 5:32, 19:9.

61. *Strom* 3.89.1–90.1, 2.145.3, 2.146.2–3.

62. Plato in the *Laws*, by contrast, finds it inadvisable for a young widow to remain without a second husband (930c2–6), due to the sexual deprivation she would suffer. This is a good illustration of how Clement's theologically motivated belief in sacred monogamy is at a marked remove from Plato's ideas about why human sexual desire should be monitored.

63. Such a woman, Clement further asserts, is living in sin and dead to the commandments. If she repents and returns to her first husband, she is "reborn," that is, no longer dead to the commandments. Her rebirth means that her former identity as harlot "dies," or ceases, *Strom* 2.146.1–147.2.

64. Clement's goal to have each individual Christian marriage emulate that of Christ and the church markedly differentiates Christian monogamy from the Roman ideal of the *univira*. The Roman ideal is not at all motivated by a desire to model marriage on the community's intimate relationship with a possessive male deity. This point should be added to the other dif-

The city of God in Clement's *Paedagogus* outdoes Margaret Atwood's worst-case scenario of biblical social order in *The Handmaid's Tale*.[65] Married Christian couples must not kiss, sing, or dance in a stimulating manner,[66] for such behavior would tempt them to exceed the procreationist limit. Women must keep their bodies fully draped, with no adornments whatsoever, regardless of whether the decoration is showy footwear, jewelry, or make-up. They must neither sway in the slightest when they walk nor give flirtatious glances with their eyes, which are the only female body part aside from the hands that Clement would not cover with fabric.[67] Wives in particular must remain above the suspicion that they make themselves attractive or venture from home on their own religious enterprises, for these are the habits of a harlot, while women are now the handmaids of God and their husbands. Christian husbands too must mind their Bridegroom. Toward this end they must ejaculate in no part of their wives' bodies other than the vagina, and then only for procreation. Wives, for their part, must never take the initiative in this preprogrammed event of antierotic reproductive intercourse. On the bottom she belongs, like the field to the plow, rather than "playing the man,"[68] for the wife is subordinate to her husband (*Paed* 3.94.5), just as the church and the soul are subservient to God as almighty "husband" ($\dot\alpha\nu\acute\eta\rho$).[69] Since this community cares most about sustaining procreationist purity so as to be prepared for the Bridegroom, it is top public priority that the private marriage bed remain strictly a platform for reproduction.[70] Clement's patchwork of sexual principles thus forms a leaden coverlet for the Christian marriage bed. Married Christians, and especially women, must monitor any conceivable behavior, especially of a sexual sort, that might raise doubts about their procreationist dedication to the Lord (*Paed* 3.83.2). Though the Prophets and Paul provide the groundwork for Clement's severe marital theology, he imposes a far more restrictive sexual decorum than they do for God's woman to stand by her man.

---

ferences between Roman and Christian marriage ideals that M. Lightman and W. Zeisel have elucidated, "Univira: An Example of Continuity and Change in Roman Society" (1977), 19–32.

65. Clement's code of public decorum is extensive. *Paed* 3.46.1–83.4 contains one noteworthy cluster of such regulations, and see also P. Brown, *Body and Society*, 126–7.

66. *Paed* 3.80.1–82.4.

67. *Paed* 2.114.1–4, 2.116.1–27.3, 3.68.1–3, 3.69.3–70.4.

68. *Paed* 2.83.1–3, 3.21.3, and B. Brooten, *Love between Women*, 325–6.

69. *Strom* 3.74.1–2, 80.2–3, 84.3.

70. Clement elaborates the symbolism of Christian reproduction in order to help formulate a collective Christian identity, D. Buell, *Making Christians: Clement of Alexandria and the Rhetoric of Legitimacy* (1999), 131–79. His goal in promoting this symbolic identity is partly to ensure that sexually active Christians remain committed to practicing strict procreationism within Christian marriage.

CONCLUSION

As I have argued, Clement develops an innovative and highly restrictive pastiche of sexual principles from the Greek biblical and philosophical traditions, largely as mediated through Philo and Paul. Though Clement's procreationist position derives ultimately from Pythagoreanism, his attribution of this dictate to the Pentateuch is strongly indebted to Philo. He likewise depends on Philo for his conviction that the innate sexual appetite inherently desires to disobey God through religiously alienating sexual practices. Given these two ideas from Philo, Clement is passionately committed to the view that any deviation from procreationism reveals the sexual appetite fornicating against God in its hedonistic pursuit of Eros and Aphrodite. His position that appetitive sexual desire is itself adultery against the Lord, however, is not Philonic. Clement develops this idea from a Philo-informed notion of sexual desire combined with Paul's and Matthew's position that it is egregiously sinful even to desire to disobey the laws of God still binding on Christians, such as the imperative to shun sexual fornication. Clement, thanks to Philo, understands this rigorist position to mean that it is flagrant adultery to experience even a flutter of the sexual appetite with which human beings are born.

Clement's argument for doing away entirely with sexual desire forms an unforgettable aspect of his sexual ethic, combining as it does the strictures of Plato and biblical scripture. If one could capture his argument with an allegorical animal, the creature would have two fused heads attacking its sex organs as emblem of forbidden desire, one head Platonic and the other scriptural in origin, but both melded and transmogrified into one. Clement, however, regards the self-assault as the perfect gift from God, the saving release from the sexual appetite's fornicating pursuit of eros. He accordingly replaces sexual desire with a brave new procreationist impulse available only to married Christians who abide by his Pythagorean-based sexual ethic. Like Pelops' ivory shoulder, this new impulse glistens in its purity and has nothing to do with the flesh.

Because of his hostility toward sexual desire, Clement thwarts his own goal of advocating the defensibility and merits of Christian reproduction. Though he seeks to challenge Tatian's encratite argument that sexual renunciation is required for salvation and immortality, he nonetheless agrees with the encratites that innate sexual desire is fornicating servitude to Aphrodite and Eros. To get around the encratite position, Clement conjures an absolution from the sexual appetite that Christ grants to married Christian procreationists alone. They retain this grace only so long as they comply with Clement's conception of "marriage in accordance with the Law." Christians who marry must marry Christians, and they should marry only once, and certainly no more than a disreputable twice—and then only if their first spouses have died. Within this marriage, as replica of Christ and the church, married Christians must either abide by procreationism or abstain from sexual activity throughout their lives. Though Clement's antisexual gift of grace and repressive social mores would seem like a curse to many, to his mind these controls are absolutely necessary, because innate human sexuality is beyond redemption, damned by its Greek association with Aphrodite, Eros, and their powers. "Eros works death from within," as he unforgettably states. The miracle of prophylactic grace liberates Christians from deadly inborn eros without forcing them to sacrifice marital reproduction or salvation.

Clement's reborn procreationism stands a religious world apart from Greek philosophical sexual ethics, despite his borrowings from the Stoics, Pythagoreans, and Plato. Though Clement makes Christian procreationist monogamy sound somewhat Stoic by calling it "well-reasoned," "appropriate," and so forth, his sexual principles are contrary to Stoic sexual ethics on two basic counts. He is hostile to sexual desire and pleasure per se, and he insists that reproduction within Christian marriage is the only permissible function of sexual relations. Further, even though Pythagoreanism is the ultimate source of his emphasis on strict reproduction, only in Clement's Christian community is this procreationist dictate wedded to the preeminent religious purpose of minding Christ the Lord alone as Bridegroom. From this perspective Pythagoreans such as Charondas and his wife are still fornicators, even though they are strictly procreative fornicators, for they devote their acts of generation to the wicked enterprise of worshipping other gods. Finally, though Clement's repressive sexual and social mores are somewhat reminiscent of Magnesia in Plato's *Laws,* they are far more extreme. Plato would find Clement's envisioned city of God an ill-considered domain that greatly differs from his own. Contrary to Plato, Clement strives to eliminate sexual pleasure, offers but two life choices, procreationism or virginity, and he shows an absence of eugenic concerns about population control. Further, Clement denies the gods whom Plato rehabilitates in favor of an innovative marital theology that develops in a freeform manner from the Prophets to Paul to Clement. On all these counts Clement's ideal social order is markedly anti-Platonic.

Clement allows Christians to grow and multiply within marriage, but they must populate a land that is devoid of eros. Such is his legacy to the emergent social order of the church, which takes its formative laws of sexual and social order from Clement as well as from other church fathers who favor procreationism for the same or similar reasons as Clement.[71] The rubble of

71. "The doctrine that the Magisterium of the Church has often explained is this: there is an unbreakable connection between the unitive meaning and the procreative meaning [of the

Stoic, Platonic, and Pythagorean ideas that are used here and there to build this bleak basilica should no longer be confused with their original philosophical structures—the Stoa especially.

---

conjugal act], and both are inherent in the conjugal act. This connection was established by God, and Man is not permitted to break it through his own volition," *Humanae vitae* 2.12, translated in J. Smith, Humanae vitae: *A Generation Later,* 281.

Chapter 10

The Fornicating Justice
of Epiphanes

A Christian Platonist disputation from the second century memorably reflects the incompatibility between the principles of sexual order envisioned by Plato and the early Stoics and those of the Septuagint as reinterpreted by Clement of Alexandria in support of Paul and Philo. This debate concerns whether Christians should adopt the sexual mores advocated by Plato and the early Stoics or those championed by Clement. The main participants were Clement and a little-known philosopher named Epiphanes, both of whom had strong Christian Platonist leanings. Epiphanes' sexual principles were associated with those of the Gnostic Carpocratians,[1] while Clement's amailgam later helps define orthodox sexual morality in the church. Epiphanes' argument appears in his now fragmentary treatise *On Justice,* which Clement cites and denounces in the *Stromateis.* Their conflicting views draw upon a variety of Greek biblical and Middle Platonist tenets, which for Epiphanes includes Plato's proposals in *Republic* 5 and early Stoic political theory. The controversy shows that it was a live question in the second century

---

1. Epiphanes is little known except for having written *On Justice,* fragments of which are preserved by Clement, *Strom* 3.6–9. He was a younger contemporary of Clement and purportedly died prior to the age of twenty, Clement, *Strom* 3.5.1–3. Biographical testimony that is not above question on several matters associates Epiphanes with the Carpocratians, Irenaeus, *Adv haeres* 1.25; Clement, *Strom* 3.5.1–3, 9.2, 3.10.1; J. Oulton and H. Chadwick, eds., *Alexandrian Christianity: Selected Translations of Clement and Origen* (1954), 25–9; G. Bardy, "Carpocratiens" (1949); A. Torhoudt, "Épiphane" (1963); F. Bolgiani, "La polemica di Clemente Alessandrino contro gli gnostici libertini nel III libro degli Stromati" (1967), 95–9; and H. Liboron, *Die karpokratianische Gnosis: Untersuchungen zur Geschichte und Anschauungswelt eines spätgnostischen Systems* (1938), 15–8. The entry on Epiphanes in W. Smith and H. Wace, eds., (*The Dictionary of Christian Biography: Literature, Sects, and Doctrines* [1880–1900; reprint, 1984]) remains useful as well.

which of the two sexual patterns was worth following, the communal one promoted by Plato and the early Stoics, or Christian procreationist monogamy, which Clement regards as the biblical yoke to which sexually active Christians must submit. Both Epiphanes and Clement think their respective views of sexual morality and social order reflect the true spirit of Christianity.

THE HISTORICAL IMPORTANCE OF THE DISPUTATION
FOR SHAPING ECCLESIASTICAL SEXUAL PRINCIPLES

The second-century disputation between Epiphanes and Clement is historically significant because of the social decision it reveals. The forming of an ecclesiastical sexual policy involved a choice, to some degree conscious and deliberate, to set aside the more communal and egalitarian sexual principles advocated by the early Stoics and Plato in favor of marriage customs grounded in the Decalogue, Pythagorean-inspired procreationism, and Christian monogamy. The Christian Platonists who went on to become the fathers of the church firmly believed, along with Clement, that sexually active Christians must abide by the strictly reproductive version of marriage in the Lord that Paul advocated: "Let each man have his own wife and each woman her own husband," with divorce being forbidden among couples fully married in the Lord (1 Cor 7:2, 7:10–11). In so doing they repudiated and tried to silence other Christian Platonists, like Epiphanes, who offered alternatives.

Epiphanes' sexual principles are also important because he exhorted Christians to adopt Platonic and early Stoic sexual communalism at a time when Christianity was still a countercultural movement partly shaped by communal social ideals. His sexual principles had a remote chance of succeeding, for among second-century Christians the question was not whether communal principles were desirable, but what those principles should be and how far they should be taken. Some sectors esteemed communal sharing as the right way to live in imitation of Jesus and the apostles. The book of Acts, for example, commends the first disciples of Jesus for their selfless practice of communal property sharing.[2] "They held everything in com-

---

2. For the historical origins, extent, and tenor of these practices, see B. Capper, "Community of Goods in the Early Jerusalem Church" (1995), 1730–74; Doyne Dawson, *Cities of the Gods*, 258–63; M. Hengel, *Property and Riches in the Early Church: Aspects of a Social History of Early Christianity* (1974), 23–34; R. Gnuse, *You Shall Not Steal: Community and Property in the Biblical Tradition* (1985), 102–7; and E. Judge (*The Social Pattern of the Christian Groups in the First Century: Some Prolegomena to the Study of New Testament Ideas of Social Obligation* [1960], 30–52), who fully appreciates the demographic difficulties in trying to determine how extensive early Christian communalism was. G. Theissen's study is valuable in this connection (*Social Reality and the Early Christians: Theology, Ethics, and the World of the New Testament* [1992], 33–93), though he

mon," a passage that would have warmed the hearts of Plato, Zeno, and Chrysippus.[3] Jesus' disciples were also taught that they should give all they had so as to share it with the poor, rather than keeping their material goods communal only among their own coterie.[4] This apostolic ideal of equitable sharing did not disappear without a trace once Christianity became more fully absorbed into society, with its man-and-wife conventions of marriage, childrearing, and property ownership, for communal monastic orders developed in support of this ideal. Christian monasticism, further, is consonant with Plato's desire to curtail acquisitiveness so as to diminish the gulf separating the rich from the poor. Monks and nuns also aspire toward collective wisdom and virtue in their own way, just as the early Stoic city aspired to do, though the Stoics did not segregate the sexes and prohibit reproduction.

Epiphanes' communally sexual model of society was a pragmatic attempt to impart a more enduring basis to the inchoate communal customs of Jesus' first followers by grounding them in the sexual reforms of Zeno, Chrysippus, and Plato. To all appearances, the Carpocratians responded favorably to Epiphanes' proposals and honored him for his efforts (*Strom* 3.5.1–3). In the second century, then, Epiphanes' combined Platonic, early Stoic, and Christian social program was not yet unrealistic, for the force of ancient marriage traditions—Septuagintal, New Testament pastoral, Greek, and Roman alike—had not successfully pressured all Christians to conform to the familial status quo in which father knows best and the husband is the head of his wife and children.[5] In Epiphanes' day, the communal aspect of Christian ideals had not been relegated to same-sex monasteries and convents separated by walls from the Christian family as fundamental social unit. The question was still where to situate communalism in Christian society and whether the practice should involve sexual activity and reproduction. Epiphanes was in a reasonably auspicious time and place to put the much pilloried Platonic and the early Stoic aspirations into Christian practice. His egalitarian sexual principles thus have a genuinely Christian motivation,

---

concentrates on individual early Christians who gave up property and became itinerant in a manner reminiscent of solo Cynics who did the same.

3. Acts 2:42–45. One interesting passage in the earlier Jewish strata of the *Sibylline Oracles* sympathizes with such communal values: "The Heavenly one distributed the earth in common to all," 3.247. A later Christian passage in this work bears a similar sentiment, but transposes the communal ideal to life after the resurrection. In this paradise, "life and wealth will be common to all, and the earth will be equally shared by all, not divided by walls or fences," J. Geffcken, *Die oracula sibyllina* (1902), 8.205–7. No passage in the *Sibylline Oracles*, however, broadens this communal ideal to include sexual practices.

4. Matt 19:16–31, Mark 10:17–31, Luke 18:18–30.

5. Eph 5:22–9; Titus 1:6, 2:4; 1 Tim 3:2–5, 3:12; Xenophon, *Oeconomicus* 7.4–14, 7.29–34, 10.1; J. Grubbs, *Law and Family in Late Antiquity: The Emperor Constantine's Marriage Legislation* (1995), 67–8.

even though they have been wildly misrepresented since antiquity as the prurient fantasies of a libidinous heretic.[6]

THE SHARED PRESUPPOSITIONS OF EPIPHANES AND CLEMENT

Epiphanes and Clement, despite their differences in sexual morality, concur on some religious and social norms that inform their disputation. First, they both assume that there is a primary deity, God, and that God is a singular masculine entity. In this they follow Greek biblical, Platonic, and early Stoic traditions, which predominantly conceptualize the primary deity as God ($\theta\epsilon\acute{o}\varsigma$) with the singular number, masculine grammatical gender, and other masculine traits, such as identifying him as a father. They do not consider God as feminine, androgynous, or above gender. Nor do Clement and Epiphanes imagine God as a polytheistic many, though Epiphanes regards the sun as "the father of light" (*Strom* 3.6.2), whose rays pour forth in compliance with the providence of the primary God or $\theta\epsilon\acute{o}\varsigma$. Their leading divine authority is a figure symbolized as male.

Second, Clement and Epiphanes agree that God is the teleological creator of the world, not an aloof entity in the manner of Aristotle's unmoved mover. God designed and made the world and human beings to work according to a plan that mortals can and should learn to follow. He monitors how well his plan is being carried out. Human beings have little or no room to amend the plan. In relation to God they are like employees of a corporation in relation to the founding executive officer. They must follow the founder's general plan and abide by his specific rules, or else they are culpably out of line. Clement and Epiphanes do not ponder alternative views in this regard. They do not consider that the world might not have been created by or through any divine entity, or that even if it were so created, it need not have been done for any ends that mortals must follow. Rather, not unlike the Stoics, they both believe in a divine world order with an implanted code of conduct that God continues to oversee. The concern is to uncover the code and follow it properly.

Third, Clement and Epiphanes agree that God's plan includes a social program. Central to their respective programs is what Plato and the early Stoics consider a central law of social order, namely, the sexual and repro-

6. Following Clement, J. Oulton and H. Chadwick (*Alexandrian Christianity*, 25) denigrate Epiphanes' *On Justice:* "The work merely consists of the scribblings of an intelligent but nasty-minded adolescent of somewhat pornographic tendencies." J. Ferguson (*Clement of Alexandria: Stromateis Books One to Three* [1991], 259 n. 19) accepts and quotes Oulton and Chadwick's assessment in the most recent and authoritative English translation available of Epiphanes' fragment of *On Justice* in *Stromateis* 3. This opinion has made its way into more wide-reaching information sources. For instance, according to *The Columbia Encyclopedia*[5] (1993, s.v. "Carpocratians"), Epiphanes and Carpocrates were "notoriously licentious."

ductive mores by which people should live. Epiphanes and Clement share the philosophers' insight that sexual rules shape and perpetuate patterns of kinship, inheritance customs, and broader patterns of wealth distribution. Sexual mores are likewise integral to related core values, such as the family structure a society idealizes, which in turn influences myriad other ethical questions. If, for example, God's sexual plan is taken to be oriented toward the monogamous Christian family, then differing sexual mores of other religions are marginalized. The same is true of other sexual patterns in life that today are often not considered a religious issue, such as deciding to be an single mother, divorcing and remarrying, being lesbian or gay, or living life unmarried without joining a holy order. But if God's sexual blueprint is seen to be oriented strictly toward the Christian family or, alternatively, toward celibacy and virginity, as Clement argues, then persons with noncompliant sexual and religious lives—and this includes all of the above—would be seen as an intolerable deviance from the ordained blueprint. Sexual regulations therefore play a crucial role in shaping any social order and the degree of religious and other diversity it allows in its sexual practices. Epiphanes and Clement, like Plato and the Stoics, recognize this point and thus make sexual mores their preeminent law, the first item that they set on God's agenda for mortals.

Clement and Epiphanes, despite their shared assumptions about God, his creation, and his plan for human beings, differ markedly in the sexual norms that they each think are divinely mandated. They part ways over the question of whether their one true masculine god and creator is the biblical God recast in Philo's Pythagorean terms, as he is for Clement, or the God of Plato and the early Stoics, as he is for Epiphanes.

COMPETING GODS AND SEXUAL MORES

Epiphanes is an ardent communalist in his sexual and social principles. He endorses Plato's argument as formulated in the *Republic* and broadened into an ideal for all citizens in the *Laws*. God, Epiphanes maintains, has ordained that human beings must live by the principle of communal and equitable sharing (*Strom* 3.6.4). He appeals directly to Plato's *Republic* in support of this position. Laws and customs are unjust if they lead people to regard persons and goods as property to be owned individually as "that which is mine" ($\tau\grave{o}$ $\dot{\epsilon}\mu\acute{o}\nu$) and "that which is yours" ($\tau\grave{o}$ $\sigma\acute{o}\nu$) (*Strom* 3.7.2–3). This reflects Plato's claim in the *Republic* that the human distinction between "that which is mine and that which is not mine" ($\tau\acute{o}$ $\tau\epsilon$ $\dot{\epsilon}\mu\acute{o}\nu$ $\kappa\alpha\grave{i}$ $\tau\grave{o}$ $o\dot{v}\kappa$ $\dot{\epsilon}\mu\acute{o}\nu$) is the root of social vices and violence.[7] According to Plato, hu-

7. *Rep* 462c3–5, 464c5–e2.

man beings must liberate themselves from the private ownership of persons and goods in order to curtail the incorrigible appetites and the myriad vicious desires that spawn from the appetites.[8] People must also reduce their trade and consumption to a healthy minimum marked by simplicity. Toward this end Plato would implement a Pythagorean-inspired communalism that works through the same spirit of cooperation that Acts attributes to Jesus' disciples, in which "friends hold goods in common" (κοινὰ τὰ φίλων).[9]

As the first step of his plan, Epiphanes, along with Plato, emphasizes that men must renounce owning individual wives and instead practice communal sexual mores (*Strom* 3.8.1–2). He follows Plato's key argument that a communal sexual order is the only reliable cure for the problem of consuming passions. Women and their wombs have priority among the property Plato would free from male ownership. To sexually communalize the women dissociates sexual desire and the longing for children from possessiveness and consumerism, helps restrict sexual activity to the beneficial degree, and yields other advantages to the city, such as the abolition of kinship-based factionalism and competition over family wealth. Second, sexual communalism also frees women from being overly burdened by family-oriented childrearing and household maintenance, so that they are better positioned to help shape a holistic and unified city. It is the *Laws'* more universal dream of communal sexual reform that appeals to Epiphanes as a way to strengthen the Christian commitment to the communal society. Even though Plato in the *Laws* came to regard this dream as unattainable, Epiphanes does not share his resignation. Epiphanes tries to persuade Christians as a whole to see the merit of Plato's argument and to follow it as God's plan.

Epiphanes has well-articulated ideas about communal social justice and the divine providence supporting it. Justice, he states, is "sharing in common on a basis of equity" (κοινωνία τις μετ' ἰσότητος) (*Strom* 3.6.1, 8.2). Human beings must strive to live unfettered by divisive possessiveness and ownership in order to share and share alike. Such is the mandate of divine providence, as corroborated by natural phenomena, including the sun, the earth, and herd animals. "Common justice is given to all equally" (δικαιοσύνης τῆς κοινῆς ἐπ' ἴσης δοθείσης) by the providence of God, just as "the maker and father of all gives eyes for all to see, regulating by common justice equally (κοινῇ πᾶσιν ἐπ' ἴσης . . . δικαιοσύνη νομοθετήσας)" (*Strom* 3.6.2–3, 7.1). Similarly, by God's direction, the sun shines down and the earth brings forth sustenance for our benefit, without according more to the socially privileged than to the underprivileged, such as the rich and the

8. By Plato's diagnosis, as argued in chapter two, human appetitive nature is inherently given to excess. Families and society inevitably become corrupt when men and their families have too much wealth in persons and goods on which appetitive desires feed and proliferate.

9. *Rep* 424a1–2, 449c4–5.

poor, ruler and ruled, men and women, free and slave. Herd animals, which are likewise recipients of God's unstinting generosity, behave in accordance with Epiphanes' sense of justice and nature. They share the grazing land, do not subdivide into divisive family units, and are satisfied to want only what they need. From these natural signs of the sun and animal behavior, "communalism is shown to be justice" (δικαιοσύνη ἀναφαίνεται ἡ κοινότης) (*Strom* 3.6.4). Private property is therefore a fundamental wrong that social conventions unjustly perpetuate. Practices of arrogating "that which is mine as opposed to yours" came about "once communalism and matters of equity were transgressed" (ἡ δὲ κοινωνία παρανομηθεῖσα καὶ τὰ τῆς ἰσότητος) (*Strom* 3.7.3–4). There is no more basic transgression against Epiphanes' notion of God and natural law than the ingrained possessiveness of individuals and families. "Customs geared toward the private person have cut apart and eaten away at the communality of divine law written in nature" (*Strom* 3.7.2). The cornerstone of unjust private ownership, further, is men's claim to individual wives. Human beings, despite having an "innate communalism from justice (κοινωνίαν ὑπὸ δικαιοσύνης ἔμφυτον)," have denied their birthright and say, "'Let each man take one woman and have her,' even though all are able to share (δυναμένων κοινωνεῖν ἁπάντων), just as the rest of the animals show" that are gregarious sexually and in other respects (*Strom* 3.7.1, 3.8.2).[10] Insofar as marriage is the preeminent transgression of natural law, Epiphanes finds it the first wrong that must be righted. Sexual communalism is thus paramount to attain an equitable Christian society.

Epiphanes adapts early Stoic political theory as well as Plato's *Republic*.

10. The standard English translations of Epiphanes' fragments seriously misrepresent his argument that all persons, females and males alike, can and should strive to share alike in all respects, especially in their sexual and reproductive mores. J. Oulton, H. Chadwick, and J. Ferguson distort Epiphanes' words "all alike can share" (δυναμένων κοινωνεῖν ἁπάντων), *Strom* 3.8.2, by making it appear as though he were urging husbands in traditional marriages to pass their wives around to one another for sexual purposes, with the wives as pawns of the men's decisions about which wife to copulate with on any occasion. Oulton and Chadwick (*Alexandrian Christianity,* 44) translate thus: "Those who [wrongly deny their innate communalism] say, 'Let him who has taken one woman keep her,' whereas all alike can have *her*. . . ." Ferguson (*Stromateis* [1991], 261) similarly translates "Those who [wrongly deny their innate communal nature] say, 'A man should marry a single wife and stick to her.' Everyone can share *her*. . ." (my emphases). These translations take "everyone" (ἁπάντων) to refer only to the men as agents of sharing rather than to everyone, women and men alike. This exclusionary sense of "everyone" in turn requires the translators to infer the implicit presence of the feminine direct object pronoun "her" of δυναμένων κοινωνεῖν ἁπάντων, as above, "all alike can share her," whereas the point of Epiphanes' argument is that the community of men and women alike can and should share one another in their sexual and nonsexual dealings with one another. In other words, the pronoun to be inferred as object of κοινωνεῖν is not "her" (αὐτῆς) but "one another" (ἀλλήλων).

His conception of divinely mandated social justice is informed by early Stoicism, and his arguments about communal justice are early Stoic in substance and structure.[11] Epiphanes' position that justice is "a communal sharing on a basis of equity" (κοινωνία μετ' ἰσότητος) presupposes, as Erskine first noticed, the early Stoic position that justice involves the "knowledge of," and related practices to achieve and maintain, "communal sharing on a basis of equity" (ἐπιστήμη κοινωνίας ἐν ἰσότητι).[12] Not only is this formulation of justice attested as Stoic, it is the idea of justice that Zeno and Chrysippus logically would have formulated for two reasons. First, on their view, human nature is inherently "communal" and "mutually friendly" by the seminal design of Zeus, which rules out practices that undermine his natural dictate to be communal, such as conventional marriage and private ownership of persons and goods. Second, friendship is by Stoic definition a relationship of equity between persons of the highest ethical attainment, males and females alike. Persons who are not yet at that level are being trained to reach it. Thus it is eminently reasonable that communalism and equity would play a prominent role in early Stoic justice. Precisely what "communalism" means relative to early Stoic ideas about property ownership remains to be considered.

For the early Stoics, communal social justice primarily means, among other more ancillary matters, that conventional property ownership should be abolished. This is the case for several reasons. First, marriage and the family were the core institutions in antiquity through which property was divvied up, held, and passed on to future generations. The early Stoic city, however, rejects marriage and the family and is instead based on openly communal sexual mores. This means that conventional property customs could not have been part of this social order. Further, in the naturally grounded early Stoic city, the wise are, without hindrance, in charge of all goods and their distribution: "All things belong to the wise" (τῶν σοφῶν δὲ πάντα εἶναι). This collective and "perfect authority" (παντελῆ ἐξουσίαν) that the wise exercise (DL 7.125) precludes resources from being owned or managed by individuals or sub-groups who could subvert the authority of communal natural law, such as by arrogating silver mines and profits for themselves. Instead, goods and resources must be left strictly to the sagacious management of persons who have attained wisdom and virtue. They

11. A. Erskine (*The Hellenistic Stoa*, 112–6) is the first to have seen similarities between the communalism of Epiphanes and of early Stoic political theory. Erskine's argument has not yet convinced readers, but his case is stronger than his tentative arguments make it seem. S. White (1992), for example, states that "much of Erskine's case is speculative," 295 n. 2 and P. Vander Waerdt is unconvinced by his arguments that the early Stoics "'saw an equal or approximately equal distribution of property as desirable'(121)" (1991), 201.

12. SVF 3.264 = Stobaeus 2.60.9–62.14 in Arius, *Epitome;* A. Erskine, *The Hellenistic Stoa,* 115–7.

know how to distribute the goods by the principle of equity that complies with human nature being communal and mutually friendly. That principle is communal sharing, just as Epiphanes describes it.

Second, on the early Stoic view, conventional property ownership is violent and offensively contrary to nature. As Dio points out in a Stoic passage (40.40–41) very similar to Epiphanes', human beings are "worse than animals" in their practices of friendship and sharing with one another, for animals such as birds, bees, cattle, and horses "do not have disputes" over resources for food and shelter. Herd animals form tranquilly mixed groups that graze without disputatious turmoil over utilizing resources to meet their needs. Humanity, by contrast, has taken this natural bounty that ought to be shared equitably and peacefully as "a cause for enmity and loathing." Through their social conventions mortals have staked divisive claims on the use of nature, from women's wombs to the harvest to the lands and water rights. Other animals, both within and across species, have devised a workable system of mutual sharing that people alone have transgressed (40.40–41). Human society therefore should model itself upon communal animals to regain its place in the scheme of natural justice.

Third, the early Stoic city disallows the use of coinage (DL 7.33), the key medium in the exchange of movable goods in the Hellenistic period. In light of the previous considerations, it is safe to infer that the inhabitants of Zeno's city must go without coinage as a matter of Stoic principle: Filthy lucre must be eliminated because it facilitates the perverse practices of trade and private ownership.[13]

In order to attain early Stoic social justice, consequently, human beings must do away with private property and adopt practices of equitable sharing under the judicious supervision of the wise. The reforms begin with communal sexual mores and reproduction and include other fundamentals, such as the provision of food and shelter. To fail and abide by conventional norms is central to the folly that alienates human beings from their divinely ordained nature and makes the wise person rarer than a phoenix. Epiphanes concurs with this view of the early Stoics, and his argument follows their lines precisely. Human beings must live in accordance with their "innate communalism," as he puts it, in order for there to be social justice sexually, reproductively,[14] and in the other basic necessities of life. Therefore, Epiph-

13. *The Hellenistic Stoa,* 103–22. Zeno, Doyne Dawson notes (*Cities of the Gods,* 180–1), prohibits the use of coinage in his envisioned city (DL 7.33). Dawson (181) intuits the relevance of this rule to the question of property ownership in the early Stoic city: "[T]he absence of coinage and general economic austerity confirms what we would assume anyway, that there would be complete communism in property in the Stoic ideal world."

14. *Strom* 3.6.1, 8.2. As shown in chapter three, the early Stoics would also do away with other sexual norms that obstruct this endeavor, such as sexual dominance and victimization, sexual possessiveness, and incest taboos.

anes' conception of communal social justice is strongly informed by both early Stoicism and Plato's *Republic*. He is boldly antinomian in arguing against the sexual and other customs that impede God's plan for human beings to live without claims of exclusive ownership. In this respect too his argument has an early Stoic quality. Like the Cynic-influenced Zeno and unlike Plato, Epiphanes does not compromise or give up in the face of public disapproval. He is out to change the world, and Zeno's envisioned republic is central to his mission and model society.[15]

Epiphanes' arguments about the divine providence of the sun and unselfish animals especially reveal an early Stoic provenance. As Schofield has shown, the Stoic argument for social justice characteristically appeals both to a divine plan or teleology and to exemplary animals that abide by the plan. In the teleological argument, "the universe is designed" by and through Zeus to be "the common home of gods and men, who form a just community," but only so long as they abide by "the law" inherent in nature from Zeus.[16] To elucidate this plan the Stoics construct a kind of altruistic zoology, in which rather Disney-like animals live in collective harmony, without a hint of territorial or predatory behavior, and as such serve as models of natural behavior for human beings to emulate. The arguments of Epiphanes and Dio, as discussed above, both employ this Stoic method. The sun as "father of light" provides Epiphanes' primary natural model for how human beings should proceed in this communal endeavor, and this appeal to the sun too has a Stoic provenance.[17] "God has poured the sun out" so that it shines equally on all.[18] The earth likewise brings forth all that living crea-

15. This is not to assume that Epiphanes necessarily read Zeno's *Republic* directly, as opposed to an intermediate source, although nothing precludes him from having done so, for the text was apparently available on a select basis in Stoic circles, P. Vander Waerdt, "Zeno's *Republic*," 279 n. 25.

16. M. Schofield, "Two Stoic Approaches to Justice" in A. Laks and M. Schofield, eds. (1995), 206–7.

17. Dio 3.73 similarly utilizes the sun as an emblem of Stoic divine providence: "You see the sun, how greatly it surpasses human beings in blessedness, being a god, but it does not tire out in serving us and doing everything for our sustenance." As A. Erskine has further noted (*The Hellenistic Stoa*, 113 n. 19), it is an early Stoic trope to regard the sun as a brilliant divine herald of right reason and natural law. This trope is a Stoic-specific adaptation of the widespread ancient belief that the sun is a deity to be revered. On the broad religious resonance of the sun as deity in antiquity, see T. Africa, "Aristonicus, Blossius, and the City of the Sun" (1961), 120–2 and for its connections with Stoic thought, the brief monograph of J. Bidez (*La cité du monde et la cité du soleil chez les stoïciens* [1932]) remains useful.

18. Aristonicus's failed rebellion is an interesting historical incident that precedes, and is thematically similar to, Epiphanes' sexually communal social order and his use of the sun as a model dispenser of justice. Aristonicus tried to create a city of the sun that was, as T. Africa puts it ("Aristonicus, Blossius, and the City of the Sun," 119, 124, 110–24), "free of the scourges of monogamy and slavery." The Stoic Blossius joined Aristonicus in his effort and committed suicide when the revolution failed and the "Sun State died with [Aristonicus] in a Roman dun-

tures need, human and animal alike, without demarcating property lines (*Strom* 3.6.1–3). "No trespassing" signs do not grow as earth-borne weeds. Epiphanes completes this teleological argument by describing how animals live by the equitable plan. The selfless creatures that he cites are cattle (as in Dio) and pigs, though the Stoics also cite ants, bees, and birds in this connection, as Schofield points out and as Dio further corroborates.[19] Regardless of the specific animals cited, the gist of the early Stoic argument remains the same. Gregarious animals put people to shame because the animals live in and for the social collective, share the earth's cornucopia peacefully, and thus comply with God's natural law, whereas human beings have contravened providence by taking hold of persons and things for themselves (*Strom* 3.6.1–8.3). The human race, therefore, must look to the animals to bring their social order into communal shape.[20] Plato does not justify his communal society on any of these grounds. Thus, even though Epiphanes is indebted to Plato, the ideal social order he presents to his Christian audience is strongly early Stoic as well.

Epiphanes likewise draws on early Stoicism to expand the list of social oppositions that the apostle Paul requires Christians to transcend. In support of Paul, Epiphanes insists that Christian society move beyond the social divisions between "female and male, slaves and free persons" (*Strom* 3.6.2). He further urges, however, that Christians must transcend the division between "the fools and the wise" (ἄφρονάς τε καὶ τοὺς φρονοῦντας) and its counterpart, "the corrupt and the good" (φαύλοις καὶ ἀγαθοῖς) (*Strom* 3.6.2).[21] Unlike Paul's more obvious social oppositions, which conscientious persons might readily notice with or without the influence of Stoicism,[22] Epiphanes' assumption that conventional society splits cleanly into the fools

---

geon." Whether Aristonicus's Sun State was itself motivated by early Stoic political theory, however, remains an open question worthy of further investigation, for which see A. Erskine, *Hellenistic Stoa*, 161–5, 204. The thematic similarities between the social ideals of Aristonicus and Epiphanes would suggest that this might be the case.

19. Dio 40.40–41; M. Schofield, "Two Stoic Approaches to Justice," 198; cf. Cicero, *Fin* 3.62–3.

20. Chrysippus, as noted in chapter three, similarly recommends that people "look to the animals" in support of his idea that incest prohibitions are contrary to the nature of the communal human animal, Plutarch, *St rep* 1044f = SVF 3.753 = LS 67F.

21. Epiphanes cites the second pair in reverse, "the good and the corrupt" (ἀγαθοῖς καὶ φαύλοις) to create a chiastic structure (AB BA) with "the fools and the wise" (ἄφρονάς τε καὶ φρονοῦντας). In the interest of clarity I have here set this chiasm aside in favor of the more straightforward AB AB sequence, "the fools and the wise," "the corrupt and the good." This ordering of the two pairs better shows the Stoic provenance of the two oppositions: wise persons are good, while fools are corrupt.

22. This is not, of course, to suggest that the early Stoics failed to notice these more obvious oppositions, for they both recognized and objected to them.

who are corrupt and the wise who are good indicates Stoic training.[23] This way of analyzing the corrupt state of ordinary society is trademark early Stoicism.[24] Apart from sages, people in conventional society are irremediably corrupt fools, and they remain that way unless they receive, as they should, Stoic training in communally reformed social conditions.[25] Epiphanes is trying to make these conditions and training the Christian norm, as he divulges by urging Christians to create the communal conditions that allow them to rise above the opposition between the fools and the wise, the corrupt and the good.

In the extant fragment from *On Justice,* consequently, Epiphanes' argument for sexual and social communalism shows at least as much early Stoic as Platonic influence. Erskine is right to have ventured the outline of this thesis, though he demonstrates the early Stoic connections only tentatively and incompletely. Epiphanes would begin his Christian social reforms precisely where the early Stoics and Plato start, by abolishing marriage and the household. To realize God's plan for a society genuinely committed to sharing, Christians must first relinquish the sexual and reproductive ownership of women by men, and then do away with other forms of ownership. Epiphanes works to shape Christian society into a flock over which Zeno, Chrysippus, and Plato are shepherds as important as Jesus.

As Epiphanes plainly recognizes, the sexual regulations of the Pentateuch are diametrically opposed to the founding sexual principles of the early Stoic city and Platonic communal ideal, which to his mind are divinely ordained. The Tenth Commandment prohibits each man from coveting his neighbor's wife and other property, and it thereby implicitly authorizes each man in the community to have his own wife and other goods. This rule is intensified by strict Christian monogamy, in which a wife cannot leave her husband and marry another man without being maligned as a whore. Epiphanes accordingly challenges the Pentateuch for presenting its marital

---

23. Epiphanes here is arguing that the sun and earth, while offering their bounty, disregard the basic early Stoic distinction between fools as opposed to the wise. If this particular argument is early Stoic, which remains uncertain, it would indicate that the early Stoics regarded all citizens as equally deserving of life's necessities, regardless of how far they had to progress toward wisdom. In other words, the wise are not to be given any privileged treatment with regard to physical necessities. Their bowls do not get filled first with the most, and so forth.

24. See, for example, DL 7.124; Plutarch *Comm not* 1062e–f ; Cleanthes in Clement *Strom* 5.3.17 = SVF 1.559; Stobaeus 2.68.18–23 = LS 41I = SVF 3.663. H. C. Baldry (*Unity of Mankind,* 157) likewise remarks on "the sharpness of the antithesis between wisdom and folly which stood out so strongly in their [i.e., Zeno's and his immediate followers'] picture of human life."

25. In connection with this point, it is worth noting that Epiphanes thinks in an early Stoic spirit by finding conventional laws inadequate on the grounds that they fail to correct "ignorance" (ἀμαθία), *Strom* 3.7.2. Ignorance is precisely what needs to be corrected on the early Stoic view in order to make right reasoning and reflective communal living attainable.

regulation as though it were God's sacred and inviolable word. The Tenth Commandment phrase, "You shall not covet your neighbor's wife," cannot genuinely represent God's position, for the true and good God of the early Stoics and Plato objects to the male ownership of women and their reproductive capacities. Epiphanes consequently finds the commandment "quite ludicrous" (γελοιότερον) (*Strom* 3.9.3), given its flagrant opposition to divine providence and natural law. Epiphanes impugns this commandment because he knew Christians in his day were being pressured to obey it. If this biblical sexual rule of social order were to become the law of the land, it would induce Christians to turn their backs on the communal heritage of the apostles. Epiphanes urges them to strengthen this heritage by putting Platonic and early Stoic political theory into practice.

Epiphanes boldly links the Christian norm of paired marriage to original sin by alluding to the apostle Paul's comments in Romans about sin becoming manifest in the world. Sin "entered" (παρεισελθεῖν) the world, Epiphanes contends, when people first decided that it was a God-given right that a man "who has taken one woman into marriage should keep her as his own" (*Strom* 3.7.2–8.2). Societies built on the man-and-wife rule are sinful, corrupt, and illegitimate, not sacred, good, and genuinely lawful, as Paul and other supporters of the Pentateuch would have it. From this marital practice have flowed the other vices that Plato deplores and likewise blames on paired marriage, such as untrammeled greed, women's wasted domestic labor, and narrow clan loyalties at the expense of the collective good. Here Epiphanes deliberately subverts Paul's views about biblical law and marriage in order to bring his own condemnation of paired marriage to the fore. According to Paul, the biblical law of God is good, and it "entered" (παρεισ-ῆλθεν) the world in order to make people aware of their inclination to sin against God's regulations (Rom 5:20, 7:7–11). One especially dangerous sin, as Paul sees it, is to deviate from the biblical norm of paired marriage in the Lord. As he expressly states, among Christians who are sexually active, "Each man must have his own wife and each wife her own husband" in the Lord (1 Cor 7:2). Any other sexual pattern involves fornication, which Christians must unconditionally flee lest they provoke God's wrath and their community's outrage.[26] According to Epiphanes, by contrast, the "law" (νόμος) of men taking wives was what "entered" (παρεισελθεῖν) the world as original sin (*Strom* 3.7.2–3), and this practice has been the breeding ground of social vices ever since. Epiphanes' striking notion of the entry of original sin and its progeny thus uses Pauline phrasing to demote Paul's ideas about sin, biblical law, and marriage, and to promote in their place the communal ideals of Plato and the early Stoics.

26. 1 Cor 6:18, 10:8–9; cf. Rom 1:18, 1:26–7.

CLEMENT'S REACTION TO EPIPHANES' PLAN
FOR CHRISTIAN SOCIAL ORDER

Clement finds it extremely dangerous for Epiphanes to argue that Christians must be sexually communal in order to bring about a just society. Epiphanes, he asserts, deserves to be ostracized from Christianity, for his ideas are nothing but a "fornicating justice" (ἡ πορνικὴ δικαιοσύνη) that lures Christians back into the frenzied worship of Aphrodite (*Strom* 3.10.1). "How could this fellow (οὗτος) still be lined up on our side, and counted as one of us?" (*Strom* 3.8.4). Clement strikes Epiphanes from his list of true Christians because Epiphanes' ideal sexual rules transgress the rules of God as revealed in "the Law, the Prophets, and the Gospel" (*Strom* 3.8.5). God may have inspired much of Greek philosophy and literature,[27] but when it comes to the rules for sexual activity, reproduction, and right worship, there is no God but the biblical one and there are no permissible sexual rules but the rules of Christian procreationism that Clement infers from Philo, Paul, and the Septuagint.[28] Epiphanes, therefore, cannot be counted as a Christian. He "fights against God" (*Strom* 3.9.2) because his philosophical conception of God and the good society does not follow the set of latter-day Pythagorean authorities that Clement upholds.

Clement demonizes Epiphanes' early Stoic and Platonic conception of the ideal society for reasons having to do with the Pentateuchal quid pro quo. A fearsome danger of religious alienation and divine retribution lurks in any social pattern that deviates from Clement's conception of the biblical sexual mandate. If sexually active Christians exceed his rule of Christian procreationist monogamy, they become fornicators and elicit God's inerrant punishment. Epiphanes not only transgresses Clement's rule of sacred marriage, he would overthrow it altogether and stimulate the wicked rise of "religiously alien ideas that are opposed to the truth."[29] Orthodox church

27. D. Wyrwa expatiates upon this point, *Die christliche Platonaneigung in den Stromateis,* 298–322, and A. Droge does as well, *Homer or Moses?* 138–49.

28. Clement's adaptation of Pauline religious endogamy, which he sees endorsed in the Law, Prophets, and Gospel, is a central feature of what R. Williams ("Does It Make Sense to Speak of Pre-Nicene Orthodoxy?" [1989], 18) aptly describes as the "precarious evolution of a 'normative' Christianity" during the formative time when Christianity was "still an interwoven plurality of perspectives on what was transacted in Jerusalem."

29. *Strom* 3.80.2. Clement approves only of those aspects of Greek literature and philosophy that do not conflict with his religious tenets, including his procreationist conception of Christian sexual purity. When he sees a conflict, as he does with the Platonic and early Stoic bases of Epiphanes' argument for sexual communalism, then he is as hostile as Tatian or Tertullian toward "pagan" Greek ideas. Clement's sympathy for Greek philosophy is thus very selective. He admires and utilizes philosophy only to the extent that he thinks it can be safely adapted for Christian purposes. "Sa principale préoccupation a été de conserver, au profit de jeune christianisme, ce que la philosophie avait de meilleur," E. de Faye, *Clément d'Alexandrie,* 192–200, esp. 199, and more recently C. Stead, *Philosophy in Christian Antiquity,* 92, 112–3. A

fathers must conquer such ideas to ensure that Clement's restrictive sexual mandate prevails, lest Christians be ruined for their sexual defiance of the Law, the Prophets, and the Gospel according to Clement.

Clement's reaction to Epiphanes is accordingly marked throughout by tropes of the biblical antifornication polemic: the unreflective outrage, the label "fornicating justice," the smearing of the opponent as a lewd outcast, and the fantasy that Epiphanes' sexual principles are a mere pretext for orgiastic idolatry and rampant adultery. Such vilification tactics are the standard reaction whenever there is a challenge to the sacred sexual way of the Lord. For Paul and the Prophets, the challenge stems mainly from religiously diversifying marriage and childrearing, while for Clement, any deviation from Christian procreationism is the fornicating danger to fear and banish. Epiphanes especially provokes Clement's ire, for he not only gyrates to the wild drumbeat of communal sexual idolatry, he also has the audacity to proclaim that such fornicating justice is the only right way for Christians to live.[30]

Clement exculpates Plato while attacking Epiphanes, even though he recognizes that Plato's *Republic* 5 is one of the central sources for Epiphanes' sexually communal society. Clement boldly denies that Plato ever supported the sexual and social communalism that Epiphanes advocates. Plato in *Republic* 5, he declares, nowhere advocates the communalization of women for reproductive and other purposes. The unmarried female guardians are a "community" (κοινωνία) strictly in the sense that they are available as a collective of eligible brides until men marry them individually, just as seats in a theater are collectively available until each person in the audience claims one. Once each man takes his pick, the woman he selects as his wife belongs to him alone.[31] Clement denies the contents of *Republic* 5 in this manner because he requires Plato's ideas to be consistent with the Law,

---

striking example of his adaptation appears, as previously mentioned, in his catechetical reworking of Stoic philosophy, W. Richardson, "The Basis of Ethics," 87–97. Though not speaking about Clement specifically, A. H. Armstrong ("The Way and the Ways: Religious Tolerance and Intolerance in the Fourth Century" [1984], 8) captures the principle of selection at work in Clement's adaptation of Greek literature: "The classics could be, so to speak 'decaffeinated,' their pernicious pagan contents neutralized, and what was useful in them turned toward wholly Christian purposes."

30. It is only as of the late twentieth century that this distortion of Epiphanes' thought has begun to be superseded, thanks to the pioneering efforts of A. Erskine, *The Hellenistic Stoa*, 112–6, and Doyne Dawson, *Cities of the Gods*, 264–9. It is similarly in doubt now whether the Carpocratians as a whole can fairly be regarded as unbridled libertines, W. Löhr, "Karpokratianisches" (1995), 23–48.

31. *Strom* 3.10.2. Here Clement is redeploying the theater analogy to support private property, just as the later Stoics did to counter the early Stoics, who drew upon the theater and other public spaces as examples in their arguments for communal sharing, A. Erskine, *The Hellenistic Stoa*, 105–10.

Prophets, and Gospel, so much so that his Plato is an utterly compliant disciple of Moses (*Paed* 2.90.4). Plato in this persona would never have argued for reforms that nullify the sex laws of Moses and God. Epiphanes is a libidinous charlatan to think otherwise.

THE CHRISTIAN PLATONIST CONFLICT
OVER THE VALUE OF THE SEXUAL APPETITE

As Epiphanes was aware, some Christian Platonists in his day were interpreting the commandment οὐκ ἐπιθυμήσεις in Clement's manner, to mean that persons must not feel or act on appetitive sexual desire at all.[32] Epiphanes strongly disagrees with this interpretation. Since the sexual appetite, as Plato maintains, is innate and beneficial in moderation, it neither can nor should be rescinded: "Neither law nor custom, nor anything else is capable of making the sexual appetite (ἐπιθυμία) disappear" (*Strom* 3.8.3). God created such sexual desire, and in so creating he did well. "God" (θεός), Epiphanes states, in a manner reminiscent of the *Timaeus,* originally instilled "a vigorous and intense sexual appetite (ἐπιθυμία) in males for the maintenance of the human race" (*Strom* 3.8.3), which God in the *Timaeus* extends to females too, once they are created.[33] Mortals accordingly should act on their innate sexual desire to the beneficial degree. Since the Platonic God is by definition good and does not vacillate, he would never create the sexual appetite only to later disown and outlaw it as a demonic contrivance.[34] Epiphanes consequently finds Clement's injunction against the sexual appetite to be "ludicrous" (γέλοιον) (*Strom* 3.9.3). He is too careful a thinker to blur the distinction between the Platonic sexual appetite (ἐπιθυμία) and the Septuagint-informed notion of the wicked impulse to disobey God (ἐπιθυμία), which is what Clement does in light of Philo and Paul. For Epiphanes, sexual desire remains what it is in Plato's dialogues, a part of the demiurge's creation that is worth acting on to a moderate and not strictly reproductive degree.

Clement sternly disagrees that the sexual appetite has any redeeming

32. According to Clement, as we have seen, the Decalogue ends on a resounding note that must be obeyed unconditionally by all Christians, Gnostic and "more simple" alike: "You will not be sexually appetitive, for by the sexual appetite alone you commit adultery," *Protrep* 108.5.

33. Epiphanes in his extant fragment makes no statement about female sexual desire, but insofar as his god shares all gifts equally, Epiphanes would presumably attribute appetitive sexual desire to women as well as men from early adolescence onward, just as Plato does.

34. In the *Timaeus* God as demiurge produces the immortal soul to be embodied in human beings, though he delegates to his assistant gods the task of making both the mortal appetitive part of the soul (69c5–d1) and the bodies in which to implant the composite immortal-mortal soul, 41d4–43a6, 69b2–72d3. Epiphanes' creation schema omits the supporting role of the other gods and assigns the entire project to the demiurge.

merit. Though innate sexual desire is part of human nature, it is a wicked contrivance of Aphrodite and Eros, and it stimulates mortals to fornicate after these alien gods of sexual desire and pleasure. The apostle Paul unconditionally condemns the sexual appetite in Romans 7 and thus adds his voice to the refrain against sexual desire that Clement hears in the Law, Prophets, and Gospel (*Strom* 3.76.1). Christians must abstain from the sexual appetite altogether throughout their lives.[35] If Christians even want to make love with their spouses for any reason other than procreation, then their hearts have stirred with desire and the sinless sexual parole that Christ grants them is lost. Back the fornicators go to the chain gang of Aphrodite and Eros, who bring death from within through reawakening the sexual appetite. Epiphanes, by strenuously disputing this conviction, fights against God on this count too (*Strom* 3.9.2). He is enticing Christians to succumb to the diabolical sexual appetite that persists in human nature and tries to alienate them from God.

Epiphanes' and Clement's dispute about the worth of innate sexual desire illustrates the divergent influence that Plato had on patristic interpretations of Greek biblical sexual norms. Neither the Septuagint nor the New Testament writings maintain that God created an irrational sexual appetite, let alone that he has since condemned its workings. Rather, it is Plato who claims in the *Timaeus* that human beings are equipped with a sexual appetite by the demiurge's command. Epiphanes' argument about the divine origin of the sexual appetite and its beneficial capacity depends on this Platonic claim. Clement's hostility to the sexual appetite also presupposes ideas that derive from Plato, for to his mind οὐκ ἐπιθυμήσεις means "you will not be sexually appetitive," in light of Philo's Platonic revision, rather than the Septuagintal sense, "you will not covet," or the broader Hellenistic Jewish sense, "you will not desire to disobey God's laws." Epiphanes thus does not fight against the biblical God by challenging the view that the sexual appetite is lawless. He struggles against taking Philo's Platonic hermeneutic of οὐκ ἐπιθυμήσεις to Clement's extreme. Clement likewise does not wrestle with the devil, as he thinks he does, by attacking Epiphanes' more lenient and Platonic conception of the sexual appetite. Clement's devil arises from not examining whether his demonization of appetitive sexual desire has the biblical basis that he confidently asserts. Thus the conflict between Epiphanes and Clement over the value of innate sexual desire pits Epiphanes' God as Platonic demiurge of the sexual appetite against Clement's combined Philonic and Pauline biblical God as would-be annihilator of the sexual appetite. The Greek biblical contribution to this conflict is but the outer shell of the phrase οὐκ ἐπιθυμήσεις, which ceases to bear its strictly Penta-

35. *Strom* 3.57.1, 69.4, *Protrep* 108.5.

teuchal and extended Hellenistic Jewish meanings and comes to be a commandment against sexual desire foremost. The hermeneutics of this dispute over sexual ἐπιθυμία are Platonizing throughout, even though its textual field of play is the abbreviated Tenth Commandment.

CONCLUSION

The outcome of Epiphanes' and Clement's disputation is clear from contemporary Christian practices. Christian family values, which have been defined conservatively for a long time, have developed from the largely biblical sexual dictates that Clement supported. Epiphanes' Platonic and early Stoic sexual paradigm failed to influence the path of Christianity in any sustained way. The link between sexual communalism and Christian practice has at most resurfaced on occasion as short-lived countercultural experiments.[36] Still, the disputation is illuminating because of the critical stance that Plato, Zeno, Chrysippus, and Epiphanes share toward practicing traditional marriage, owning private property, and raising children within a strictly two-parent and heterosexual household, where mothers individually must do much of the domestic labor and childrearing. Epiphanes was responsive to these concerns in the second century C.E. thanks to the moral sensibility he gained from Plato, the early Stoics, and from Christianity as he understood it.

The conflict between Epiphanes and Clement is also worthwhile because it shows the heated discussion that was taking place among Christian Platonists about the value of appetitive sexual desire. Epiphanes represented Plato's voice of moderation on this topic, while Clement denounced the sexual appetite as the diabolical impulse that the gods of eros implanted in human beings to provoke hedonistic sexual defiance of the biblical God.

Epiphanes' book *On Justice* was "much talked about" in Alexandrian circles (*Strom* 3.9.2), and not merely for its notoriety. He was trying to extend and strengthen the communal and egalitarian tendencies that were present in early Christianity. Epiphanes strove to impart greater intellectual power and social durability to these tendencies by communalizing Christian sexual mores in accordance with the Platonic and early Stoic blueprints of communal social justice. His proposed reforms, further, were better positioned to be put into practice than the Platonic and early Stoic sexual re-

36. In the nineteenth century, for example, the Christian Oneida community in upstate New York practiced communal sexual relations and believed that such sexual mores provided the appropriate basis for their utopian religious community. Exclusive monogamy, by contrast, was deemed impure. This social experiment lasted approximately thirty years, until it succumbed to pressures to comply with Christian marital norms outside of the community, S. Klaw, *Without Sin: The Life and Death of the Oneida Community* (1993), 3–9.

forms had ever been, for in his day Christian society was in transition and showed communal tendencies. Plato and Zeno, by contrast, produced their communal political theories in Athens, where conventional families were deeply rooted, stable, and highly resistant to dissolution. Epiphanes' paradigm nonetheless failed and came to be grossly misrepresented as sheer lechery by Clement. Epiphanes challenged biblical sexual norms directly because he knew that advocates of biblically grounded marriage rules were pressuring sexually active Christians to marry, reproduce in the Lord, and thereby perpetuate the anticommunal status quo of family and property divisions. To Clement's mind, however, the burgeoning Christian church had to be protected from the promiscuity of Platonic and early Stoic political theory. To preserve the church's chastity as Christ's monogamous bride, he attacked Epiphanes' arguments as the fornicating den of iniquity. Epiphanes, Plato, and the early Stoics, however, give thoughtful reasons for regarding Clement's biblically based marriage system as the sacred den of inequity that remains with us today.

Chapter 11

Conclusion

The Demise of Greek Eros and Reproduction

Paul's ideas about sexual morality and social change were as revolutionary in their formulation as those of Plato, the Pythagoreans, and the early Stoics. In the first century C.E. there was no reason to think that his vision of driving fornication from Gentile lands would take hold with any greater success than Plato's socialist ideals of civic moderation and justice, the Pythagoreans' eugenic aims to improve moral character through procreationism, and the early Stoics' plans to train citizens to achieve right reason and action through mutually friendly and communal sexual eros.

Paul in his mission issues a universal and Christ-centered version of the Septuagintal imperative against the fornicating mores of the Canaanites and rebellious Israelites. Human sexual and reproductive mores must be devoted strictly to the biblical God through virginity or paired marriage in the body of Christ. This pattern of sexual devotion provides the only permissible basis of social order, for all of humanity, Gentile as well as Jew, is Israel and as such must serve God alone. Paul consequently insists that Christians of Gentile backgrounds, and Greeks first of all, must cease from dedicating any aspect of their minds or sexual bodies to their former gods. He vilifies the Gentiles' sexual heritage as wicked and deadly fornication against God, and portrays his new order of virginity or marriage in the Lord as the sole path to salvation and immortality.

In Romans 1:18–32 Paul stakes out a new position of major import for Christian sexual morality. A nebulous group of polytheistic peoples, Paul asserts, once recognized yet later abandoned God, on the model of rebellious Israel as portrayed by the Prophets. Though this apostate branch of Gentile Israel existed only in his fervid imagination, to him and his early patristic supporters this renegade culture was real, exclusively or primarily Greek, and needed to be redeemed from her affliction of God's venereal wrath.

Though Paul vilifies homoeroticism once under this rubric, the primary target of his antifornication reform is marriage and reproduction in symbiotic connection with gods other than the Lord. On his view, Christ offers the only escape and safe haven from the other-theistic family and civic mores that formed the groundwork of society among the Greeks and other Gentiles. It is important to recognize that Paul's antifornication reform was a genuinely new erewhon, despite its freeform basis in the Septuagint, and that it became the well-worn standard of Western culture only after undergoing two loosely philosophizing transformations. The first of these was the ecclesiastical view that sexual activity should cease apart from sedate reproduction within marriage, and the second was the more encratite-inclined view that truly dedicated Christians must join higher orders to keep Aphrodite and Eros at bay through complete sexual renunciation.

Foucault and others are therefore mistaken in maintaining that "the codes in themselves did not change a great deal" between Greek and Christian Greek sexual principles.[1] Paul's unconditional imperative to flee fornication was radically new to the Greeks and other Gentiles, and its aim was to supplant religious sexual existence as they lived it, or, in the case of the philosophers, as they conceived it should be lived. The antifornication social order that Paul aspired to form could never peacefully coexist with the religious sexual heritage of any Gentile gods, be they the reformed gods of the cities of Plato, the Stoics, and the Pythagoreans, or the gods of the many historical cities that have been politically transformed from the reproductive ground up through Christian endogamy, child-rearing, and education, such as Athens and Rome. Paul's innovative sexual rules precipitated a sharp and irreconcilable divide between ancient Greek sexual politics, philosophical and popular alike, and Christian sexual politics in devotion to God alone through Christ.

The sharp difference between Christian and Greek sexual morality makes itself especially apparent in Paul's sexually specific reworking of the heated poetics of the Prophets. He is like a biblical father dedicated to purifying his adopted Gentile daughter and keeping her pure for her future marriage in the Lord. Paul valorizes sexual fornication as the only sin that is "against the body" of individual Christians and of the Christian bridal collective, for such sexual behavior is the only human action that imperils the bride's virtual genitals and her prospective marital standing. An ordinary biblical bridegroom does not care with whom his bride eats, only with whom she copulates. On Paul's view, the same holds true for Christ relative to Christians, and for very similar reasons.

So marked is the opposition between Christian and Gentile sexual norms

---

1. Interview with Foucault, "Genealogy of Ethics," in H. Dreyfus and P. Rabinow, eds., 240.

that Paul's antifornication polemic reverses the classification of good women and bad women in Gentile lands. Prior to Christianity, Greek women who worshipped gods other than the Lord were everyman's grandmother, mother, sister, or daughter, and they were practicing respectable religious customs on behalf of their families and cities.[2] In Paul's terms, however, the women are whores (πόρναι), for they wantonly deviate from his conception and cultural parameters of biblical monotheism through their sexual, reproductive, and other ritual activities. The women's presence poses the danger that Christian men will fornicate (πορνεύειν) against God with them, primarily by marrying them without first requiring them to convert and to raise their children in Christ the Lord. In order for Greek women to be considered good in Christian terms, they must abandon their ancestral gods and obey the Lord, both Christ and their husbands, with downcast eyes, minds, genitals, and wombs. Alternatively, they can remain unmarried and devote their sexuality virginally to Christ alone. Greek women who do not accept this catechetical formula of goodness remain wicked harlots no matter how good they are by other criteria, such as the Stoic and Socratic criterion of pursuing excellence in reasoning and reflective action. Sappho is a premier case in point. Greatly admired by Socrates and other Greeks for being peerless in her reflections on Aphrodite, Sappho falls to being a lowly "sex-mad little whore" in terms of the Pauline antifornication standard by which Tatian measures her worth.[3]

To rout and keep whoredom at bay, the Greek biblical rule of endogamy in the Lord directly complements the antifornication principle. This marriage rule is likewise unprecedented in Greek and other Gentile culture, and Philo and Paul are among its vanguard bearers, each in his own distinctive way. Philo, who favors the open-door policy of the Septuagint, welcomes the conversion of Gentiles to Hellenistic Judaism and their marriage to members of God's people, so that more families come to live and raise their children by the Pentateuch. Conversely, he condemns marriages with unconverted Gentiles, which would lead his people and ensuing generations to whore after the alien gods of the Greeks and Egyptians in Alexandria. For Paul, the open door does not suffice. Gentiles must be recruited away from their native religions through his missionary program. Though Paul's apocalyptic worldview makes him doubt the need for marriage and reproduction at all, he nonetheless maintains a formative Christian version of biblical endogamy for Christians who remain or choose to become sexu-

---

2. See further M. Dillon, *Girls and Women in Classical Greek Religion* (2002), 37–138 and 209–300.

3. Ancient Greek women, of course, were no strangers to misogyny before Christianity; They were labeled debased animals, defective males, leaky vessels, and so on, but they were not called whores for following their religious heritage and passing it on to their children.

ally active. Aside from his one pragmatic allowance for marriages where only one spouse has so far converted to Christianity, Paul prohibits sexual activity between Christians and Gentiles under any circumstances, especially the rebellious fornication of Christians entering into marriage and procreation with unregenerate Gentiles. It would be hard to overstate the impact Paul's marriage rule has had in Western culture and beyond.[4] Every church wedding, baptism, and coming of age or confirmation ceremony reenacts his retrieval of Gentiles from their fornicating servitude to other gods and their restoration to their one and only master, the Lord through, in, and with Christ. Christian missionaries and European colonialism have helped make these practices a dominant norm, but it is through marriage and reproduction that they took hold, spread, and continue.[5]

The religious sexual blueprint that Paul adapts from the Septuagint marks a divide between Jews and Christians as well as between Greeks and Christians. Despite the similarities between the Septuagint and Paul on promoting and enforcing biblical monotheism, the Septuagint does not advocate Paul's mission to replace the religious basis of ancient Greek eros and other Gentile sexuality with a collective betrothal to Christ the Lord. Even though the Septuagint Hellenizes Yahweh's identity with names that sound generic, such as "God" ($\theta\epsilon\acute{o}s$) and "the Lord" ($\acute{o}$ $\kappa\acute{v}\rho\iota os$), neither God nor his people universalize in the Septuagint, as they do for Paul. In Greek biblical terms, God's people must stay away from, not do away with, the religious sexual mores of Gentiles outside the promised land.[6] The protectionism against religiously mixed marriages and other sexual disobedience remains focused on three groups, God's historical people, spouses who convert on the model of Ruth, and their progeny. Thus, even though Paul continues to identify and think of himself as Jewish, he imparts a nascent Christian and non-Jewish cast to his mission by making the body of Christ a necessary condition for marriage or virginity in the Lord and by making Israel a land without borders. He is therefore revolutionary relative to both Jews and Greeks in his religious sexual rules for social order. No amount of associating Paul's ideas with those of the rabbis and Greek philosophers diminishes this pivotal point.

4. Paul's marriage rule itself is unambiguous and firm, though some social pressures would have worked counter to its being always upheld early in the Christian movement. For example, a young Christian from a still halfway Gentile family might be induced by his or her relatives to marry a wealthier and better connected Gentile for social and economic reasons of concern to the family.

5. "Missionaries throughout the New World and Asia enforced religious endogamy by refusing to marry a Christian and non-Christian," M. Wiesner-Hanks, *Christianity and Sexuality in the Early Modern World,* 256, and see also L. Epstein, *Marriage Laws,* 183 n. 118.

6. Deut 4:15–20, for example, recognizes that heavenly bodies are worshipped by other peoples and is content to let such practices be, though Israel must not partake of them.

The encratite and proto-orthodox versions of Paul's antifornication sexual order diverge from the social orders of Plato, the Stoics, and the Pythagoreans in other philosophically important ways. These differences especially become clear from the new uses to which the philosophers' ideas are put in the patristic efforts to champion Paul's cause.

The difference between early Christian and Stoic sexual ethics comes to the fore in Tatian's support of Paul's position on weak will. Tatian is convinced that the harlot soul of the Greeks is utterly incapable of thinking or motivating right action on her own, mindlessly defiant wife of God that she is. Along with Paul, he finds this acratic condition to be obvious from widespread polytheistic worship in Greek society. Even though the truth-suppressing Greeks once knew and used to follow the supreme Lord, they succumbed to their worst inclinations by pursuing false gods and fornicating in their honor. This abject state can and must change through betrothal to the Lord. As Tatian puts it, only by remarrying the Lord's spirit and following the sacred texts of his nuptial agreement will the Greeks recover by enlightening their souls through obedience to God's word.

According to the Stoics, however, the problem of weak will should be addressed through a different method of enlightenment, by learning how to think and act rightly through logical reasoning grounded in natural philosophy. There is a reverential commitment involved in this threefold endeavor of studying ethics, logic, and physics. The Stoics think that the good and sagacious Olympian presence in the world and the human soul provides guidelines that human beings must work together to discern and live by in order to become disciplined rational agents, both sexually and in other respects. Gods such as Zeus, Hera, and Eros are worthy of devotion, but the devotion is philosophical.[7] The human soul and the world alike are shaped, informed, and empowered by Zeus's reason in cooperation with other gods, such as Hera and Eros. To live well persons must strive, through right reasoning, to understand natural forces and the human place in them, from the sun to animal behavior. Toward this end, they must not allow misguided social conventions to stand in the way, such as erroneous popular assertions about the gods. Zeno and Chrysippus accordingly challenge the widespread Greek belief that Eros and Aphrodite are domineering forces who ruthlessly subject human reason and will to their crazed powers of sexual mania.

As far as Tatian and Paul are concerned, however, the Stoics are dangerously misguided in the rational goodness and philosophical promise that they ascribe to the Olympians' divine nature. The only problem with

---

7. It is in this sense, I think, that it is most fitting to maintain, as A. H. Armstrong does ("The Way and the Ways," 3), that "one of the most deeply and passionately religious of philosophies [is] the Stoic."

popular beliefs about the gods is that Greeks have not gone far enough in recognizing the gleeful malice with which the immortals hold human will and destiny in their clutches, in seeing, for instance, Aphrodite's forked tail and flaming visage. God alone through Christ can rescue them from this blighted servitude to demons. Greeks who regard the gods as worthy of reverence madly perpetuate the bondage and suppression of the truth about God. The Stoics are especially dangerous, for their philosophy teaches that the nature of the gods guarantees that philosophy's threefold discipline of ethics, logic, and physics empowers people to live and make love rightly. Tatian demonizes and subverts Stoic cosmology because his antifornication ethic, like Paul's, is hostile to the theology of human reason that grounds the Stoics' Olympian project in ethics and politics.[8]

Philo and Clement adapt aspects of Plato's notion of appetitive sexual desire and the Pythagoreans' reproductive strategy to develop still another cure for rebellious fornication, the procreationist social order of the Lord. As with Tatian, here too the borrowings from Plato and the Pythagoreans meld with antifornication goals to produce sexual principles that Plato and the Pythagoreans would not recognize as their own.

Though Philo supports Plato's argument that uncontrolled sexual desire is the primary and most incorrigible source of all vices, he identifies the Hellenistic Jewish notion of desiring to disobey God ($\epsilon\pi\iota\theta\upsilon\mu\iota\alpha$) with the Platonic sexual appetite ($\epsilon\pi\iota\theta\upsilon\mu\iota\alpha$). Due to the sinfulness of desiring to disobey God, he strips appetitive sexual desire of any beneficial capacity and makes it inherently wicked. This is contrary to Plato's position that sexual desire is salutary in moderation, but consonant with the irremediably delinquent nature of the inclination to deviate from the Lord. Philo stresses the baneful quality of sexual desire with phrases that are Stoic in word but not meaning. Appetitive sexual desire is an inherently culpable "soul passion," because it is coiled to strike out against Pentateuchal social order through the fornicating pursuit of Aphrodite as Pleasure. The desire for genital sexual pleasure is blameworthy because it is obeisant to this whore goddess in the soul and, if uncontrolled, stimulates an all-out assault on God's laws and social order. Hence, members of Philo's religious community must adopt lifelong procreationism conjoined with biblical endogamy and childrearing to liberate themselves from the taproot of all transgression, Aphrodite's fornicating power of sexual pleasure. God subtly prescribes this regimen in the Pentateuch's combined law of nature and of Moses, because procreationism effectively controls the sexual root of apostasy and thus makes Israel able to

8. It is thus far off the mark to maintain, as Brundage puts it (*Law, Sex, and Christian Society*, 18–21), that "St. Paul and the Stoic teachers certainly agreed in their negative views about . . . sex as a potentially destructive temptation."

transcend its past record of rebellion, so that the people may regain their sovereignty and flourish under the Lord.

Plato, by contrast, finds nothing wrong with the sexual worship of Aphrodite. He presumes and supports the practice in moderation, with strictly procreationist intercourse being the norm in the *Laws* only during the relatively short span of reproductive service for the city. After this time, mortals should make love (and avoid reproduction) well into old age, for Aphrodite is too strong a power to deny, and her works are beneficial within limits. Further, Plato's earnest adaptation of Greek religiosity is such that he is rather like Porphyry in protecting his social order of rehabilitated gods and mores of appetitive virtue from foreign religious influence. Plato would thus be at best surprised, and almost certainly perturbed, to see how Philo and Clement use his reforms to support a social order dedicated to the Lord alone through lifelong procreationism or abstinence.

Even though Philo links sexual pleasure with fornicating after Aphrodite, he nevertheless gives this hedonistic whoredom some latitude in his religious community. First, he acknowledges Plato's position that the desire for sexual pleasure is an unavoidable aspect of human sexual activity, even when the dominant aim is procreationist. Appetitive sexual desire seeks fricative genital pleasure, nothing more, nothing less, just as Plato maintains. Philo is unruffled by this hedonism, so long as prospective parents in the Lord keep this soul fornication subdued through their procreationist resolve. Second, even though Philo distrusts sexual desire because of its wicked proclivity to subvert the way of the Lord, he refrains from identifying all sexual activity for pleasure as apostasy. Even if couples practice nonprocreationist sexual relations, they do not yet cross the line of being lawless, though their risky sex acts for pleasure empower the sexual appetite and stimulate its voracious hunger to transgress Pentateuchal laws with gleeful abandon. To Philo's mind, then, procreationism involves an unavoidable and acceptable degree of fornication, because Aphrodite's appetitive whoredom is the only way to be fruitful and multiply. And he still does not react like Phineas when acts of sexual pleasure in marriage cease to be subservient to this greater goal.

Clement, by contrast, considers the very nature of sexual desire and its pleasures to be the power of fornication that Christians must flee. Paul's aphoristic Tenth Commandment, "you will not desire" ($o\dot{v}\kappa\ \dot{\epsilon}\pi\iota\theta\nu\mu\dot{\eta}\sigma\epsilon\iota\varsigma$), signifies to Paul that to desire an action forbidden in his abridged Pentateuch subjects Christians to "the body of death," such as the most dangerous impulse to make love and reproduce outside of marriage in the Lord. To Clement, however, the Pauline imperative means that the primary forbidden desire to disobey God is the Philonic sexual appetite for genital pleasure, and that this desire is what entraps God's people in the death-bearing enslavement that Paul laments. Clement reinterprets Matthew in the same way as he does Paul. For Christians even to desire sexual pleasure constitutes defiant adultery against Christ in their heart. If Christians feel sexual desire at all, they ruin the collective Christian bride's virginity of pure monotheism, because the desire shows that the bride is whoring after Eros and Aphrodite rather than remaining faithful to her Lord. Christians, however, must do their utmost to prevent the church and soul from "fornicating against her one husband God the almighty" (*Strom* 3.80.2), even though that means doing away with sexual desire altogether. So committed is Clement to identifying sexual desire with forbidden fornicating against God that he performs a kind of search and replace function on scriptural passages to prove it. Christians cannot serve both God and sexual pleasure; Christ died for our sexual pleasures, and so forth. Unlike his predecessor Philo, consequently, Clement sees urgent need to free Christians from sexual desire, but without requiring them to renounce procreation as part of their mandatory project to demolish sexual desire, as the encratites did.

Clement candidly maintains that Christ has saved Christians from sexual pleasure by bestowing a revocable gift of sedated sexual behavior on married Christian procreationists alone. Like an ether mask on eros, this gift allows the married couples strictly to reproduce in Christ the Lord without any desire whatsoever for fricative genital pleasure. This sexual desire remains blessedly comatose, though, only so long as the couples are devoted strictly to reproducing Christian offspring whenever they copulate. Otherwise the deadly inner demon of eros reawakens, and Christ's gift of grace has been lost—immortality and salvation squandered due to lust for sexual pleasure. This is just as Tatian argues, albeit without Clement's reproductive escape clause. Married couples who obey Clement's antifornication regimen feel at most a slight encratic twinge when they copulate to grow and multiply for the Lord, but the twinge is not really sexual pleasure, and they would not want it even if it were. In this formative principle of ecclesiastical sexual morality, Clement promotes a prolific sexual austerity, for the production of Christian children is good for God's glory, but sexual desire is wicked. To keep the desire unconscious in perpetuity, women must be kept under wraps, for their sexual bodies and former religious practices are its main dangerous trigger.

Given his marital theology, Clement thinks that even the narrow path of Christian procreationism is too dissolute for Christians to follow under certain conditions, in which case they must renounce sexual activity. Childless Christian widows and widowers ought to remain single and without offspring so that their first marriage remains the perfect miniature of the church in her marital devotion to the Lord. They fail to sustain this perfection of betrothed readiness for Christ if they remarry. Though Clement does not prohibit them from remarrying once if their first spouses have died, he frowns on the practice because it indicates fornicating urges. If the second marriage too ends in the same way, however, he relegates the twice-bereaved spouse to a life of mandatory sexual renunciation. Any other sexual relationship is a precipitous fall into fornicating against "the one husband God the almighty," and this the community must not permit.

Though Philo and Clement agree with Plato that the uncontrolled sexual appetite is the single main source of all vices, they completely transform what they borrow from Plato's political philosophy about establishing sexual controls to shape the good society. The corrupt vices stimulated by unregulated eros for Plato are still regarded as criminal problems in the secular sphere of law and morality, from men robbing and stealing to acquisitive confrontations on a small and large scale. To eradicate this disorderly behavior, cooperative unity must replace divisiveness between the rich and the poor, peace needs to prevail where there once was war motivated by rampant greed, and human beings must live in egalitarian simplicity and minimal materialism in order to enlighten their souls. Toward this end, the sexually communal society is the best social order to adopt, for it makes divisive property ownership and cupidity a thing of the past. Philosophical dialogue should be the indispensable regulatory method to shape this society and aid reason in its struggle with the acquisitive vices. This method is, as a matter of principle, open to further reflection and amendment, just as we see in Plato's *Republic* and *Laws*.

For Clement and Philo, the criminal behavior that is Plato's main concern is subordinated to their main goal of promoting a social order of monotheistic holiness in the Lord. Even though Philo and Clement likewise believe that unregulated sexual desire produces unwanted litters of vice, the first beast to bring terror to their nation under God is the dreaded impulse to make love in honor of gods other than the Lord. This impulse is no crime at all in Plato's envisioned society, where rehabilitated Greek polytheism is the norm to defend and the citizens ought to sexually serve Aphrodite in moderation. Philo's city of the biblical God can coexist with Plato's city of virtuous Olympians, so long as the two cities have a border between them. For Clement, however, the Olympians are the first gods who must be driven out of his growing Christian society, Aphrodite and Eros foremost. With them goes an indispensable part of Plato's, and the early Stoics', city planning. Philosophical inquiry, finally, ceases to be the main regulatory method for Philo and Clement in their respective struggles to instill the sexual ordinances of marriage in the Lord. Biblical hermeneutics and poetic symbolism instead become the way to generate and sustain these norms. The project is to inculcate obedience to scriptural dictates that are in theory immutable, divine, and should never be amended[9]—despite the mercurial

9. Philo, *Mos* 2.14.

fluidity that God's laws have in the procreationist hermeneutic that Philo and Clement perform on the Pentateuch.

For similar biblically grounded reasons, Clement and Philo reinvent the Pythagorean principle of procreationism that they advocate as God's word. Like Plato in the *Laws,* the Pythagoreans advocate procreationism because the widespread custom of reproducing in a negligent, unintentional, and random way damages souls being reincarnated beyond moral repair, dooms future generations to rampant vices, both societal and individual, and subjects souls to later being embodied in lower animal forms. To protect souls from going the way of the squid, human beings must "put as many impediments as possible" on appetitive sexual desire. Central to this endeavor is the eugenic norm of procreationism. Once the practice becomes common, the well-bred generations to come will easily respect and live by Apollo's principle "nothing in excess." Philo's and Clement's respective takes on procreationism as God's law have a Pythagorean coloring only at the surface level of the exclusive disjunction between permissible sexual activity for reproduction within marriage or forbidden sexual activity for pleasure. In their monotheistic sexual regimens, Pythagorean concerns about reincarnation fall by the wayside, and procreationism is converted to serve the goal of protecting God's people from the temptress Aphrodite, who tries to captivate God's people through their sexuality and make pleasure worshippers of them. Strictly reproductive intercourse keeps them and future generations out of her seductive clutches, completely for Clement but incompletely for Philo.

The sexual rules advocated by Philo and Clement are Stoic in phrasing but anti-Stoic in substance. Clement and Philo consider sexuality to be a cross between Plato's antirational animal and the serpent in the garden, while the Stoics think that the only creature to be feared about sexuality is the perpetuation of harmful sexual beliefs and practices. Foremost among the beliefs is the popular Greek view of the domineering erotic gods, which for Philo, Clement, and Tatian escalates and transmogrifies into divine sexual evil in opposition to the Lord. The early Stoics strive to challenge the premises on which this escalation would later build. On their view, sexuality is an important aspect of rational human nature, on par with discourse, thought, and perceptual involvement with the world. In early Stoicism, consequently, men and women alike must learn how to deliberate, consent, and form bonds of affectionate commitment in their even mix of heterosexual and homoerotic sexual relations. Excluding Seneca and Musonius, the later Stoics continue to uphold the early Stoic conviction that sexual eros has a noble function, but they believe that marriage is the only bond of friendship with the natural grounding that warrants a sexual commitment and its guiding principle of mutual consent and respect. Philo and Clement, however, continue to condone the common ancient idea that sexual activity is a man's prerogative with his wife. Even though the prerogative becomes pro-creationist, when it is time for the man to sow, the wife must be his field. The Stoics repudiate the idea and the practice of the man's sexual prerogative over his partner or partners. It is therefore wildly off the mark to regard the sexual ethics of Philo and Clement as Stoic merely because they call it a "soul passion" to disobey God's procreationist law and a "well-reasoned im-pulse" to obey it.

The Christian Platonist Epiphanes, in his plans for sexual reform, seam-lessly joins the Platonic and early Stoic sexual blueprints for social justice with the egalitarian communal tendencies of early Christian society. He agrees with Plato, Zeno, and Chrysippus that conventional marriage must be abolished in favor of communal sexual mores, and his reasoning borrows from and supports their arguments. The social justice of cooperative shar-ing ought to become a reality, and can be attained only if kinship patterns through blood and marriage are superseded by an undivided and collective commitment to the common good. The first step is to free women from be-ing the sexual and reproductive property of husbands and families. Epiph-anes consequently argues against Greek biblical sexual mores in any form, for the Septuagint and Paul still promote paired marriage and the family, which maintains social iniquity through property divisions and the owner-ship of persons.

Epiphanes is also a strong enough Platonist to see why it is impossible and undesirable to eliminate sexual desire from human experience, which Christian Platonists such as Clement believe is mandatory for salvation. He tries to counter this belief by declaring it manifestly absurd to deny the sex-ual impulse with which all human beings are born. Epiphanes thus is "li-bidinous" only in the sense that he respects Plato's position that human be-ings have a libido and should act on it moderately and in the interest of social justice.

Clement's polemic against Epiphanes' fornicating justice is grounded in the conviction that "the Law, the Prophets, and the Gospel" alone au-thorize permissible sexual conduct. Since, on Clement's view, holy scripture demands either perpetual virginity or monogamous Christian procreation-ism conjoined with no sexual desire, Christians would flagrantly forni-cate against their husband the Lord if they followed Epiphanes' proposals and even wanted to enjoy moderate sexual pleasure, let alone if they actu-ally did so, especially on the magnitude of a communally sexual social or-der. Clement accordingly escorts Epiphanes from his church of bridal chas-tity as "not one of us." His closing of the door is a good symbol of the divide between the sexual morality of the church on the inside and of Plato, the early Stoics, and Epiphanes together on the outside. It is a rallying of the mind, sexual behavior, and society around the purported cause of one exalted deity and against alternatives that throw the deity and the cause into question.

Despite the Protean shapes of meaning that sexual fornication takes on from the Septuagint to Philo, Paul, Tatian, and Clement, one striking feature persists. Rebellious sexual fornication, however it is identified, triggers an alarmist condemnation to keep the way of the Lord untouched by the apparent threat. Philo sounds the alarm if Hellenistic Jews defy biblical endogamy by marrying unregenerate Gentiles or by performing other acts of sexual intercourse that he deems to be abominations in the eyes of God; Paul, if inhabitants of his limitless Gentile Israel do or want to do the same; Tatian, if they make love at all; and Clement, if they engage in sexual relations aside from procreationist intercourse within Christian marriage or if they even want to do so. Clement's jeremiad against Epiphanes' fornicating justice is a striking example of the alarm going off, but its classical expression is to be found in the Prophets, and especially in Hosea, Jeremiah, and Ezekiel. This fear and abhorrence of rebellious sexual fornication is motivated by the biblical doctrine that monotheistic sexual protectionism is the sine qua non of safety, prosperity, and hegemony for God's people. In the interest of the people's security, one regulatory arm of the Lord works from the administrative top down, through priests, prophets, kings, emperors, and bishops, to outlaw and banish sexual intercourse and reproduction for other gods. The other arm works through an excitable grassroots watchfulness, and perhaps even vigilantism on occasion, to reduce dissidence among the people at large. Here too prophets and other messengers of God, such as Paul, Tatian, and Clement, play a role with provocative denunciations. The two arms meet in a tight grip on the sphere of marriage, reproduction, and childrearing, where women have long been pivotal figures in shaping children's religiosity, from storytelling to the wedding rituals.

The Greek Bible cannot fairly be described as antisexual, for it does not impugn human sexual behavior as a whole, even though it incriminates forbidden alien worship and its patterns of sexual conduct. Among Greeks and other Gentiles, however, sexuality and the gods were closely intertwined, like a two-ply cord, so that the encratite and ecclesiastical abhorrence of sexuality devolves from the downward spiral of trying to separate the two strands. First comes the biblically motivated dictate to do away with sexual behavior to the extent that it honors alien gods such as Aphrodite, which both Philo and Paul advocate. Then with Tatian this becomes the imperative to eliminate sexual desire and activity because it is all Aphrodite. Clement gets around that snarl in the untwisting only because he invents the miracle of Christian procreationism, in which married Christians reproduce without any desire for the sexual life that to him means certain death. It is hard now to imagine that the religious danger vested in Greek sexual customs could have been so terrifying as to elicit these extreme restrictions, but that is largely because the gods and people who gave the customs their ritual, coherence, and meaning are gone.[10]

Several explanations for the historical phenomenon of early Christian sexual asceticism have emerged from this study. The Septuagint pact that God's people must worship the Lord alone or else suffer brutal punishment and death takes on expansive new meanings and cultural horizons in Philo's, Paul's, Tatian's, and Clement's reworkings of its antifornication mandate. Practices of intense sexual asceticism among converted Greeks and other Gentiles are precisely what one would expect to find in this populace for the reasons that Tatian and Clement reveal. Since alien gods such as Aphrodite remained so potent a presence in human sexuality, it seemed critical to put an end to exercising her sexual energy rather than to defy God and thereby inflict agony on one's own person, family, and community. Conjoined with this fear is a motive of self interest: the conviction that Christian devotees of the Lord will gain a blissful existence in eternity at the comparatively low cost of sacrificing the desire for all sexual pleasures, from erotic poetry to orgasm. Christians must either renounce sexual activity altogether in order to gain this rightful standing, as the encratites advocate, or else engage strictly in a procreationist procedure that altogether transcends the desire for genital friction, which, starting with Clement, becomes early church policy. Rather paradoxically, the erotic promise that Paul instills into his marital poetics passionately stimulates Christian sexual asceticism on another count as well. Christians must not merely flee sexual fornication for fear of being besmirched by other gods. They must also run toward Christ in breathless arousal to consummate their marriage with him, with perpetual virginity becoming the preferred mode by late antiquity.

The models of sexual reform offered by Plato, the Stoics, and the Pythagoreans form a hypothetical city of Greek sexual ethics divided into several districts. Encratites and church fathers came to this city with Father and Son hard hats and stone crushers. Some of what they found they reworked into genuinely byzantine antifornication mosaics—sexual renunciation and latter-day procreationism without eros. The rest they razed: Zeus as immanent Stoic logos; early Stoic Eros as god of sexual beauty, mutual consent, and communal harmony; and Apollo, whose principles of moderation and justice Plato and the Pythagoreans sought to attain through their respective plans of procreationist eugenics. Underneath them all lie the remains of Aphrodite, the disarmed torso of the formidable sexual power she once embodied in Greek philosophy and society alike. Other patristic writers, such

10. As A. H. Armstrong ("Some Advantages of Polytheism" [1981], 188) thoughtfully notes, "a return to Hellenic polytheism" would be "futile and unreal," an archaizing but empty nostalgia.

as Epiphanes, came to this city and tried to Christianize its Platonic and early Stoic districts with greater fidelity to the philosophers' plans for sexual reform. Epiphanes' ideas were likewise overthrown by the church fathers. The continuity he maintained with Plato and the early Stoics transgresses monogamous procreationism in Christ the Lord, which alone allows the nascent church to keep her monotheistic virginity, insofar as Christian reproductive relations are sexual only in name, not in motive or sensation. Not least of Epiphanes' heretical common bonds with the philosophers was the conviction that sexual morality should be attained through justice, dialogue, and reasoning, not through power, commandments, possessive metaphors, and submission.

BIBLIOGRAPHY

ANCIENT WORKS

Aeschylus. *Tragicorum graecorum fragmenta.* Vol. 3. Edited by Stefan Radt. Göttingen: Vandenhoeck & Ruprecht, 1985.

Ambrose. *Opere morali.* Vol. 2. *De virginitate, De institutione virginis, Exhortatio virginitatis.* Edited with introduction, translation, and notes by Franco Gori. Milan: Biblioteca Ambrosiana, 1989.

Anacreon and Ibycus. *Poetae melici Graeci.* Edited by Denys L. Page. Oxford: Clarendon Press, 1962. The poetic fragments of Ibycus are also in *Poetarum melicorum graecorum fragmenta.* Vol. 1. Edited by Malcolm Davies. Oxford: Clarendon Press, 1991.

Antipater. See Stobaeus.

Apostolic Fathers. *The Apostolic Fathers*[2]. Edited and translated by J. B. Lightfoot, J. R. Harmer, and Michael W. Holmes. Grand Rapids, Mich.: Baker Book House, 1989.

Aristoxenus. *Aristoxenos.* In *Die Schule des Aristoteles: Texte und Kommentar*[2]. Vol. 2. Edited with commentary by Fritz Wehrli. Basel: Schwabe, 1967. See also Iamblichus.

Arius Didymus. *Epitome of Stoic Ethics.* Edited with translation and commentary by Arthur J. Pomeroy. Atlanta: Society of Biblical Literature, 1999.

Athanasius. *De virginitate.* Edited by Eduard Freiherrn von der Goltz. Texte und Untersuchungen 29.2. Leipzig: J. C. Hinrichs, 1905.

Athenaeus. *The Deipnosophists.* Vols. 1–7. Translated by Charles B. Gulick. Loeb Classical Library. Cambridge, Mass.: Harvard University Press, 1927–1941.

Callimachus. *Callimachus.* Vols. 1–2. Edited by Rudolf Pfeiffer. Oxford: Clarendon Press, 1949–1953.

Catullus. *Carmina.* Edited by R. A. B. Mynors. Oxford: Clarendon Press, 1958.

Charondas. *The Pythagorean Texts of the Hellenistic Period.* Edited by Hölger Thesleff. Acta Academiae Aboensis 30. Turku, Finland: Åbo Akademi, 1965.

Chrysippus. *Stoicorum veterum fragmenta.* Vols. 1–4. Edited by Hans von Arnim. Leipzig: Teubner, 1903–1924. Reprint, Dubuque, Iowa: W. C. Brown Reprint Library, 1964.

————. *The Hellenistic Philosophers.* Vols. 1–2. Edited with translation and commentary by A. A. Long and D. N. Sedley. New York: Cambridge University Press, 1987.

Clement of Alexandria. *Protrepticus und Paedagogus*[3]. Edited by Otto Stählin and Ursula Treu. Die griechischen christlichen Schriftsteller. Berlin: Akademie Verlag, 1972.

————. *Clementis Alexandrini Protrepticus.* Edited by M. Marcovich. Leiden: Brill, 1995.

————. *Quis dives salvetur.* In *Stromata: Buch VII und VIII, Excerpta ex Theodoto, Eclogae propheticae, Quis dives salvetur, Fragmente*[2]. Edited by Otto Stählin and Ludwig Früchtel. Die griechischen christlichen Schriftsteller. Berlin: Akademie Verlag, 1970.

————. *Stromata*[4]. Edited by Otto Stählin, Ludwig Früchtel, and Ursula Treu. Die griechischen christlichen Schriftsteller. Berlin: Akademie Verlag, 1985.

Didache. See Apostolic Fathers.

Dio Chrysostom. *Dio Chrysostom, Orations VII, XII, XXXVI.* Edited with commentary by D. A. Russell. Cambridge: Cambridge University Press, 1992.

————. *Dionis Prusaensis quae exstant omnia.* Edited by Hans von Arnim. Berlin: Weidmann, 1896. Reprint, 1962.

————. *Dio Chrysostom: Works.* Vols. 1–5. Edited by J. W. Cohoon and H. L. Crosby. Cambridge, Mass.: Harvard University Press, 1932–1951.

Empedocles. *The Poem of Empedocles: A Text and Translation*[2]. Edited with translation and commentary by Brad Inwood. Toronto: University of Toronto Press, 2001.

Enoch, Book of. *Das Buch Henoch* (Greek fragments). Edited by J. Flemming and L. Radermacher. Die griechischen christlichen Schriftsteller. Leipzig: J. C. Hinrichs, 1901.

————. *The Ethiopic Book of Enoch: A New Edition in the Light of the Aramaic Dead Sea Scrolls.* Vols. 1–2. Edited by Michael A. Knibb in consultation with Edward Ullendorff. Oxford: Clarendon Press, 1978.

Epictetus. *Epicteti dissertationes ab Arriano digestae*[2]. Edited by H. Schenkl. Leipzig: Teubner, 1916. Reprint, 1965.

————. *Epictetus.* Vols. 1 and 2. Translated by William A. Oldfather. Cambridge, Mass.: Harvard University Press, 1925–1928. Reprint, 2000.

————. *Vom Kynismus: Epiktet.* Edited with translation and commentary by Margarethe Billerbeck. *Philosophia antiqua* 34. Leiden: Brill, 1979.

Epicurus. *Epicurea.* Edited by Hermann Usener. Leipzig: Teubner, 1887.

Euripides. *Euripidis fabulae.* Vols. 1–3. Edited by J. Diggle. Oxford: Clarendon Press, 1981–1994.

————. *Tragicorum graecorum fragmenta.* Edited August Nauck, with a supplement by Bruno Snell. Hildesheim: Georg Olms, 1964.

Eusebius. *Die Kirchengeschichte*[2]. Vols. 1–3. Edited by Eduard Schwartz and Theodor Mommsen. Die griechischen christlichen Schriftsteller. Berlin: J. C. Hinrichs, 1903–1909. Reprint, Berlin: Akademie Verlag, 1999.

Galen. *Claudii Galeni opera omnia.* Edited by Karl G. Kühn. Leipzig: Cnobloch, 1821–1833. Reprint, Hildesheim: Georg Olms, 1964–1965.

————. *On the Doctrines of Hippocrates and Plato*[3]. Vols. 1–3. Edited with translation and notes by Phillip de Lacy. Berlin: Akademie Verlag, 1978–1984.

Greek Anthology. *Anthologie grecque.* Vols. 1–13. Edited with translation and notes by Pierre Waltz, Guy Soury, Robert Aubreton, et al. Paris: Les Belles Lettres, 1928–1980.

———. *Anthologia graeca epigrammatum palatina cum Planudea,* edited by Hugo Stadtmueller. Leipzig: Teubner, 1894–1906.

———. *The Greek Anthology: Hellenistic Epigrams.* Text (vol. 1) and commentary (vol. 2). Edited by A. S. F. Gow and D. L. Page. Cambridge: Cambridge University Press, 1965.

———. *The Greek Anthology: The Garland of Philip.* Text (vol. 1) and commentary (vol. 2). Edited by A. S. F. Gow and D. L. Page. Cambridge: Cambridge University Press, 1968.

Hermas. *Le pasteur*². Edited with translation and notes by Robert Joly. Paris: Éditions du Cerf, 1968. Reprint, 1997.

Hermesianax. *Collectanea alexandrina.* Edited by J. U. Powell. Oxford: Clarendon Press, 1925. Reprint, 1970.

Hesiod. *Theogony.* Edited with prolegomena and commentary by M. L. West. Oxford: Clarendon Press, 1966.

Hierocles. See Stobaeus.

Hippocratic Corpus. *Oeuvres complètes d'Hippocrate.* Edited by Émile Littré. Paris: J. B. Bailliere, 1839–1861. Reprint, Amsterdam: Hakkert, 1979.

Homeric Hymns. *The Homeric Hymns.* Edited by T. W. Allen, W. R. Halliday, and E. E. Sikes. Oxford: Clarendon Press, 1936. Reprint, Amsterdam: Hakkert, 1980.

Iamblichus. *De vita pythagorica liber*². Edited by Ludwig Deubner and Ulrich Klein. Stuttgart: Teubner, 1975.

———. *Iamblichus: On the Pythagorean Way of Life: Text, Translation, and Notes.* Edited with translation and notes by John Dillon and Jackson Hershbell. Atlanta: Scholars Press, 1991.

Ibycus. See Anacreon.

Ignatius. *Lettres*⁴. Edited and translated by Thomas Camelot. Paris: Éditions du Cerf, 1969. See also Apostolic Fathers.

Irenaeus. *Contre les heresies.* Vols. 1–4. Edited with introduction and commentary by A. Rousseau and L. Doutreleau. Paris: Éditions du Cerf, 1965–1982.

Jerome. *Adversus Jovinianum, Commentaria in Amos, Commentaria in epistolam ad Galatos, Commentaria in epistolam ad Titum.* Edited by J. Martaine et al. Patrologia latina, edited by J. P. Migne, vols. 23, 25, 26. Paris: Vrayet, 1845.

Josephus. *Flavii Josephi opera.* Edited by Benedikt Niese. Berlin: Weidmann, 1888–1895. Reprint, 1955.

———. *Works.* Translated with commentary by Louis H. Feldman, Steve Mason, et al. Leiden: Brill, 2000–present.

Jubilees. *The Book of Jubilees.* Edited by James C. Vanderkam. Corpus scriptorum Christianorum Orientalium, Scriptores Aethiopici 88. Louvain: Peeters, 1989.

Lucretius. *De rerum natura.* Vols. 1–3. Edited with translation and commentary by Cyril Bailey. Oxford: Clarendon Press, 1950. Reprint, 1986.

Menander. *Comicorum atticorum fragmenta.* Edited by Theodor Kock. Leipzig: Teubner, 1880–1888. Reprint, Utrecht H & S Publishers, 1976.

Methodius. *Le banquet.* Edited by Herbert Musurillo, with translation and notes by Victor-Henry Debidour. Paris: Éditions du Cerf, 1963.

Musonius. *Musonius Rufus*. Edited and translated by Cora E. Lutz. *Yale Classical Studies* 10 (1947), 3–147.

———. *Musonius Rufus: Entretiens et fragments*. Translated with notes by Amand Jagu. Hildesheim: Georg Olms, 1979.

Ocellus. See Charondas.

Parmenides. *Parmenides of Elea: Fragments*. Translated by David Gallop. Toronto: University of Toronto Press, 1984.

Paul. *The Greek New Testament*[3]. Edited by Kurt Aland, Matthew Black, et al. New York: American Bible Society, 1983.

Philo. *Philonis Alexandrini opera quae supersunt*. Vols. 1–6. Edited by Leopold Cohn and Paul Wendland. Berlin: G. Reimer, 1896–1930. Reprint, Berlin: Walter de Gruyter, 1962–1963.

———. *Philo*. Vols. 1–10. Edited by F. H. Colson and G. H. Whitaker. Cambridge: Harvard University Press, 1956–1962.

Philolaus. *Philolaus of Croton: Pythagorean and Presocratic*. Edited with translation and commentary by Carl A. Huffman. Cambridge: Cambridge University Press, 1993.

Pindar. *Pindari carmina cum fragmentis*. Vol. 1, edited by Bruno Snell and Herwig Maehler. Vol. 2, edited by Herwig Maehler. Leipzig: Teubner, 1971 (vol. 1), 1989 (vol. 2).

Plato. *Platonis opera*. Vol. 1, edited by E. A. Duke et al. Vols. 2–5, edited by John Burnet. Oxford: Clarendon Press, 1995 (vol. 1), 1900–1907 (vols. 2–5). Reprint, 1972–1977.

———. *The Laws*. Edited by E. B. England. Manchester: The University Press, 1921.

Plutarch. *Moralia*. Vols. 1–7. Edited by W. R. Paton, I. Wegehaupt, et al. Leipzig: Teubner, 1959–1967.

Posidonius. *Posidonius*. Vols. 1–3. Edited by L. Edelstein and I. G. Kidd. *The Fragments*[2] (vol. 1), *The Commentary* (vol. 2, pts. 1–2), *The Translation of the Fragments* (vol. 3). Cambridge: Cambridge University Press, 1988–1999.

Sappho. *Poetarum Lesbiorum fragmenta*. Edited by Edgar Lobel and Denys Page. Oxford: Clarendon Press, 1955.

Seneca. *Des bienfaits*. Edited and translated by François Préchac. Paris: Les Belles Lettres, 1926–1927. Reprint, 1972.

———. *Dialogorum libri duodecim*. Edited by L. D. Reynolds. Oxford: Clarendon Press, 1988.

———. *Diatribe in Senecae philosophi fragmenta: Fragmenta de matrimonio*. Edited by Ernst Bickel. Leipzig: Teubner, 1915.

———. *Ad Lucilium epistulae morales*. Edited by L. D. Reynolds. Oxford: Clarendon Press, 1965.

———. "Gli scritti matrimoniali di Seneca e Tertulliano." Edited by Paolo Frassinetti. *Rendiconti dell' Istituto Lombardo* 88 (1955), 155–88.

Septuagint. *Das Göttingen Septuaginta*. Göttingen: Vandenhoeck & Ruprecht, 1931–present.

———. *La Bible d'Alexandrie*. Translations and commentaries directed by Marguerite Harl. Paris: Éditions du Cerf, 1986–present.

Pentateuch, vols. 1–5, edited by John W. Wevers, 1974–1991; Prophets (Duodecim Prophetae[3], Isaias[3], Ieremias[2], Ezechiel[2]), vols. 13–16, edited by Joseph Ziegler, 1967–1984; Psalmi[3], edited by Alfred Rahlfs, 1979; Sapientia Salomonis

and Sapientia Iesu filii Sirach[2] vol. 12, edited by Joseph Ziegler, 1962, 1980; Tobit vol. 9.1, edited by Robert Hanhart, 1983.

    La Genèse, translated and with introduction and notes by Monique Alexandre,
1986; *L'Exode,* Alain Le Boulluec and Pierre Sandevoir, 1989; *Le Lévitique,* Paul
Harlé and Didier Pralon, 1988; *Les Nombres,* Gilles Dorival, 1994; *Le Deutéronome,*
Cécile Dogniez and Marguerite Harl, 1992.

Sextus. *The Sentences of Sextus: A Contribution to the History of Early Christian Ethics.*
Edited by Henry Chadwick. Texts and Studies 5. Cambridge: Cambridge University Press, 1959.

Sibylline Oracles. Die oracula sibyllina. Edited by Johannes Geffcken. Leipzig: J. C. Hinrichs, 1902.

———. "The Sibylline Oracles." Translated by J. J. Collins. In *Old Testament Pseudepigrapha,* vol. 1, edited by J. H. Charlesworth, 317–472. Garden City, N.Y.:
Doubleday, 1983.

Sophocles. *Sophoclis fabulae.* Edited by H. Lloyd-Jones and N. G. Wilson. Oxford:
Clarendon Press, 1990.

Soranus. *Gynaeciorum libri IV.* Edited by Johannes Ilberg. Leipzig: Teubner, 1927.

Stobaeus. *Ioannis Stobaei anthologii.* Vols. 1–4. Edited by Curt Wachsmuth and Otto
Hense. Berlin: Weidmann, 1884–1909. Reprint, 1974.

Tatian. *Oratio ad Graecos and Fragments.* Edited and translated by Molly Whittaker.
Oxford: Clarendon Press, 1982.

———. *Tatiani Oratio ad Graecos.* Edited by Miroslav Marcovich. Berlin: Walter de
Gruyter, 1995.

———. *Tatiani Oratio ad Graecos.* Edited by Eduard Schwartz. Texte und Untersuchungen 4.1. Leipzig: J. C. Hinrichs, 1888.

Tertullian. *Tertulliani Opera.* Edited by E. Dekkers, et al. Corpus christianorum series
latina, vols. 1–2. Turnhout, Belgium: Brepols, 1954.

———. *De anima.* Edited with commentary by J. H. Waszink. Amsterdam: Meulen-
hoff, 1947.

*Testaments of the Twelve Patriarchs. The Testaments of the Twelve Patriarchs: A Critical Edi-
tion of the Greek Text.* Edited by M. de Jonge. Leiden: Brill, 1978.

———. *The Testaments of the Twelve Patriarchs: A Commentary.* By H. W. Hollander and
M. de Jonge. Leiden: Brill, 1985.

Theodosian Code. *Codex Theodosianus.* Vols. 1–2. Edited by T. Mommsen and P. M.
Meyer. Berlin: Weidmann, 1905. Reprint, 1990.

Theognis. *Iambi et elegi graeci[2].* Vol. 1. Edited by M. L. West. New York : Oxford University Press, 1989.

Xenophon. *Xenophon,* Oeconomicus: *A Social and Historical Commentary.* Edited with
translation and commentary by Sarah Pomeroy. Oxford: Clarendon Press, 1994.

Zeno. See Chrysippus.

MODERN WORKS

Ackerman, Susan. *Under Every Green Tree: Popular Religion in Sixth-Century Judah.* Atlanta: Scholars Press, 1992.

Adair, Mark. "Plato's View of the Wandering Uterus." *Classical Journal* 91 (1996),
153–63.

Adam, James. *The* Republic *of Plato*[2]. Vols. 1–2. Introduction by D. A. Rees. Cambridge: Cambridge University Press, 1963.

Africa, Thomas W. "Aristonicus, Blossius, and the City of the Sun." *International Review of Social History* 6 (1961), 110–24.

Alexander, Philip S. "Rabbinic Judaism and the New Testament." *Zeitschrift für die Neutestamentliche Wissenschaft* 74 (1983), 237–46.

Allen, Michael B. *Nuptial Arithmetic: Marsilio Ficino's Commentary on the Fatal Number in Book VIII of Plato's* Republic. Berkeley and Los Angeles: University of California Press, 1994.

Allison, Dale C. "Divorce, Celibacy, and Joseph (Matthew 1:18–25 and 19:1–12)." *Journal for the Study of the New Testament* 49 (1993), 3–10.

Amir, Yehoshua. "Philo and the Bible." *Studia Philonica* 2 (1973), 1–8.

———. "*Theokratia* as a Concept of Political Philosophy: Josephus' Presentation of Moses' *Politeia*." *Scripta Classica Israelica* 8–9 (1985–1988), 83–105.

Anchor Bible Dictionary, edited by David N. Freedman et al. New York: Doubleday, 1992.

Andersen, Francis A., and David N. Freedman. *Hosea: A New Translation with Introduction and Commentary*. The Anchor Bible. Garden City, N.Y.: Doubleday, 1980.

Annas, Julia. *An Introduction to Plato's* Republic. Oxford: Clarendon Press, 1981.

———. "Plato and Common Morality." *Classical Quarterly*, n.s., 28 (1978), 437–51. Also available in N. Smith, editor, *Plato*, vol. 3, 220–38.

———. *Platonic Ethics, Old and New*. Ithaca, N.Y. : Cornell University Press, 1999.

———. "Plato's *Republic* and Feminism." In *Woman in Western Thought*, edited by Martha Lee Osborne, 24–33. New York: Random House, 1979. Originally published in *Philosophy* 51 (1976), 307–21.

Anscombe, G. E. M. "You Can Have Sex without Children: Christianity and the New Offer." In her *Ethics, Religion, and Politics*, 82–96. Minneapolis: University of Minnesota Press, 1981.

Arieti, James A. "How to Read a Platonic Dialogue." In *The Third Way: New Directions in Platonic Studies*, edited by Francisco J. Gonzalez, 119–32. Lanham, Md: Rowman and Littlefield, 1995. Also available in N. Smith, editor, *Plato*, vol. 1, 273–86.

Armstrong, A. H. "Some Advantages of Polytheism." *Dionysius* 5 (1981), 181–8.

———. "The Way and the Ways: Religious Tolerance and Intolerance in the Fourth Century." *Vigiliae Christianae* 38 (1984), 1–17.

Attridge, Harold W. *The Epistle to the Hebrews*. Philadelphia: Fortress Press, 1989.

Babut, Daniel. "Les Stoïciens et l'amour." *Revue des études grecques* 76 (1963), 55–63.

Baer, Richard A. *Philo's Use of the Categories Male and Female*. Leiden: Brill, 1970.

Baldry, H. C. *The Unity of Mankind in Greek Thought*. Cambridge: Cambridge University Press, 1965.

Bardis, P. D. "Overpopulation, the Ideal City, and Plato's Mathematics." *Platon* 23 (1971), 129–31.

Bardy, G. "Carpocratiens." *Dictionnaire d'histoire et de géographie ecclésiastiques*. Vol. 11. Paris: Letouzey et Ané, 1949.

Barker, Ernest. *Greek Political Theory: Plato and his Predecessors*[3]. London: Methuen, 1947.

Barlow, William. *Treatise of Fornication Upon 1 Cor VI.XVIII*. London: Raven, 1690. Early English Books 1641–1700, Reel 304.16. Ann Arbor, Mich.: University Microfilms.

Barnard L. W. "The Heresy of Tatian—Once Again." *The Journal of Ecclesiastical History* 19 (1968), 1–10.

Barr, James. "'Guessing' in the Septuagint." In Detlef Fraenkel, Udo Quast, and John Wevers, editors, *Studien zur Septuaginta*, 19–34. Festschrift for Robert Hanhart. Göttingen: Vandenhoeck & Ruprecht, 1990.

———. "Paul and the LXX: A Note on Some Recent Work." *Journal of Theological Studies*, n.s., 45 (1994), 593–601.

Barrett, C. K. *A Commentary on the First Epistle to the Corinthians.* London: A & C Black, 1968. Reprint, Peabody, Mass.: Hendrickson Publishers, 1993.

———. *A Commentary on the Second Epistle to the Corinthians.* New York: Harper and Row, 1973.

Beatrice, Pier Franco. "Apollos of Alexandria and the Origins of the Jewish-Christian Baptist Encratism." *Aufstieg und Niedergang der römischen Welt* 2.26.2 (1995), 1232–75.

Bechmann, Ulrike. "Brautsymbolik." In *Lexicon für Theologie und Kirche,* edited by Walter Kasper, Konrad Baumgartner, et al., vol. 2, 664–5. Freiburg im Breisgau: Herder, 1994.

Beck, John A. *Translators as Storytellers: A Study in Septuagint Translation Technique.* New York: Peter Lang, 2000.

Behr, John. *Asceticism and Anthropology in Irenaeus and Clement.* Oxford: Oxford University Press, 2000.

———. "Shifting Sands: Foucault, Brown, and the Framework of Christian Asceticism." *Heythrop Journal* 34 (1993), 1–21.

Belkin, Samuel. *Philo and the Oral Law: The Philonic Interpretation of Biblical Law in Relation to the Palestinian Halakah.* Cambridge, Mass.: Harvard University Press, 1940.

Benedict, Ruth. *Patterns of Culture.* New York: Houghton Mifflin, 1934. Reprint, with a new foreword by Mary Catherine Bateson and a preface by Margaret Mead, Boston: Houghton Mifflin, 1989.

Bernos, Marcel, editor. *Sexualité et religions.* Paris: Cerf, 1988.

Betz, Hans Dieter. *Galatians, A Commentary.* Philadelphia: Fortress Press, 1979.

———. "2 Cor 6:14–7:1: An Anti-Pauline Fragment?" *Journal of Biblical Literature* (1973), 88–108.

———. *The Sermon on the Mount: A Commentary on the Sermon on the Mount, Including the Sermon on the Plain (Matthew 5:3–7:27 and Luke 6:20–49).* Minneapolis: Fortress Press, 1995.

Beutler, R. "Okellos," *RE* 17.2 (1937), 2361–80.

Biale, David. *Eros and the Jews: From Biblical Israel to Contemporary America.* New York: Basic Books, 1992.

Bianchi, Ugo, editor. *La tradizione dell'enkrateia: motivazioni ontologiche e protologiche.* Atti del Colloquio Internazionale Milano, 20–23 Aprile 1982. Rome: Edizioni dell'Ateneo, 1985.

Bickerman, Elias. "The Septuagint as a Translation." In *Studies in Jewish and Christian History.* Vol. 1. Leiden: Brill, 1976.

Bidez, Joseph. *La cité du monde et la cité du soleil chez les stoïciens.* Paris: Les Belles Lettres, 1932.

Bird, Phyllis. "To Play the Harlot." In *Gender and Difference in Ancient Israel,* edited by Peggy L. Day, 75–94. Minneapolis: Fortress Press, 1989.

Bluestone, Natalie Harris. *Women and the Ideal Society: Plato's* Republic *and Modern Myths of Gender.* Amherst: University of Massachusetts Press, 1987.

Blundell, Sue. *Women in Ancient Greece.* London: British Museum Press, 1995.

Bobonich, Christopher. *Plato's Utopia Recast: His Later Ethics and Politics.* New York: Oxford University Press, 2002.

Bobzien, Susanne. *Determinism and Freedom in Stoic Philosophy.* Oxford: Clarendon Press, 1998.

Bockmuehl, Markus. "The Noachide Commandments and New Testament Ethics with Special Reference to Acts 15 and Pauline Halakhah." *Revue biblique* 102 (1995), 72–101.

Bolgiani, Franco. "La polemica di Clemente Alessandrino contro gli gnostici libertini nel III libro degli Stromati." Festschrift for Alberto Pincherle, vols. 1–2. *Studi e materiali di storia della religione* 38 (1967), 86–136.

Borgen, Peder. *Early Christianity and Hellenistic Judaism.* Edinburgh: T & T Clark, 1996.

———. *Philo, John, and Paul: New Perspectives on Judaism and Early Christianity.* Atlanta: Scholars Press, 1987.

———. *Philo of Alexandria: An Exegete for His Time.* Leiden: Brill, 1997.

Bouffartigue, Jean. "La structure de l'âme chez Philon." In C. Lévy, editor, 59–75.

Boyarin, Daniel. "Are There Any Jews in the 'History of Sexuality'?" *Journal of the History of Sexuality* 5 (1995), 333–55.

———. *Carnal Israel: Reading Sex in Talmudic Culture.* Berkeley and Los Angeles: University of California Press, 1993.

———. *A Radical Jew: Paul and the Politics of Identity.* Berkeley and Los Angeles: University of California Press, 1994.

Boys-Stones, G. "Eros in Government: Zeno and the Virtuous City." *Classical Quarterly,* n.s., 48 (1998), 168–74.

———. *Post-Hellenistic Philosophy: A Study of Its Development from the Stoics to Origen.* New York: Oxford University Press, 2001.

Bray, Gerald, editor. *1–2 Corinthians.* Ancient Christian Commentary on Scripture. New Testament 7. Downers Grove, Ill.: InterVarsity Press, 1999.

Brooten, Bernadette J. *Love between Women: Early Christian Responses to Female Homoeroticism.* Chicago: University of Chicago Press, 1996.

Broudéhoux, Jean Paul. *Mariage et famille chez Clément d'Alexandrie.* Paris: Beuchesne, 1970.

Brown, Peter. "Bodies and Minds: Sexuality and Renunciation in Early Christianity." In *Before Sexuality: The Construction of Erotic Experience in the Ancient World,* edited by David Halperin, John J. Winkler, and Froma Zeitlin, 479–93. Princeton: Princeton University Press, 1990.

———. *The Body and Society: Men, Women, and Sexual Renunciation in Early Christianity.* New York: Columbia University Press, 1988.

Bruit-Zaidman, Louise. "La piété pythagoricienne et l'Apollon de Délos." *Métis* 8 (1993), 261–9.

Brundage, James A. *Law, Sex, and Christian Society in Medieval Europe.* Chicago: University of Chicago Press, 1987.

Brunt, P. A. "The Model City of Plato's *Laws*." In *Studies in Greek History and Thought*, 245–81. Oxford: Clarendon Press, 1993.

Buchan, Morag. *Women in Plato's Political Theory*. London: Macmillan, 1999.

Büchsel, Friedrich. "θυμός, ἐπιθυμία." *TDNT*. Vol. 3, 168–72, see G. Kittel et al., editors.

Buell, Denise Kimber. *Making Christians: Clement of Alexandria and the Rhetoric of Legitimacy*. Princeton: Princeton University Press, 1999.

Bultmann, Rudolf. *Theology of the New Testament*. Vols. 1–2. Translated by K. Grobel. New York: Scribners, 1951–1955. Originally published as *Theologie des Neuen Testaments*. Tübingen: J. C. B. Mohr, 1948–1953.

Burkert, Walter. *Lore and Science in Ancient Pythagoreanism*. Translated by Edwin L. Minar. Cambridge, Mass.: Harvard University Press, 1972. Originally published as *Weisheit und Wissenschaft: Studien zu Pythagoras, Philolaos und Platon*. Nuremberg: H. Carl, 1962.

———. "Zur geistesgeschichtlichen Einordnung einiger Pseudopythagorica." In K. von Fritz, editor, 25–55.

Burnyeat, M. F. "Utopia and Fantasy: The Practicability of Plato's Ideally Just City." In *Psychoanalysis, Mind, and Art: Perspectives on Richard Wollheim*, edited by Jim Hopkins and Anthony Savile, editors. Oxford: Blackwell, 1992.

Byrne, Brendan. "Sinning against One's Own Body: Paul's Understanding of the Sexual Relationship in 1 Corinthians 6:18." *The Catholic Biblical Quarterly* 45 (1983), 608–16.

Caird, George B. "Ben Sira and the Dating of the Septuagint." *Studia Evangelica* 7 (1982), 95–100. Texte und Untersuchungen 126.

Calame, Claude. *The Poetics of Eros in Ancient Greece*. Translated by Janet Lloyd. Princeton: Princeton University Press, 1999. Originally published as *I Greci et l'eros: Simboli, pratiche e luoghi*, Rome: Laterza, 1992.

Calasso, Roberto. *The Marriage of Cadmus and Harmony*. Translated by Tim Parks. New York: Knopf, 1993.

Capper, Brian J. "Community of Goods in the Early Jerusalem Church." *Aufstieg und Niedergang der römischen Welt* 2.26.2 (1995), 1730–74.

Carr, David. "Gender and the Shaping of Desire in the Song of Songs and Its Interpretation." *Journal of Biblical Literature* 119 (2000), 233–48.

Castelli, Elizabeth A. "Asceticism and History in Paul." In *Asceticism and the New Testament*, edited by Leif E. Vaage and Vincent L. Wimbush, 171–85. New York: Routledge, 1999.

Chavasse, Claude. *The Bride of Christ*. London: Faber and Faber, 1940.

Cherniss, Harold F. *Aristotle's Criticism of Plato and the Academy*. Baltimore: The Johns Hopkins University Press, 1944.

Cheung, Alex T. *Idol Food in Corinth: Jewish Background and Pauline Legacy*. Sheffield: Sheffield Academic Press, 1999.

Chuvin, Pierre. *A Chronicle of the Last Pagans*. Translated by B. A. Archer. Cambridge, Mass.: Harvard University Press, 1990. Originally published as *Chronique des derniers païens*. Rev. ed. Paris: Arthème Fayard, 1991.

Clark, David J. "Sex-Related Imagery in the Prophets." *The Bible Translator* 33 (1982), 409–13.

Clark, Elizabeth A. "Foucault, the Fathers, and Sex." *The Journal of the American Academy of Religions* 56 (1988), 619–41.

———. *Reading Renunciation: Asceticism and Scripture in Early Christianity.* Princeton: Princeton University Press, 1999.

Clark, Isabelle. "The Gamos of Hera: Myth and Ritual." In *The Sacred and the Feminine in Ancient Greece,* edited by Sue Blundell and Margaret Williamson, 13–26. New York: Routledge, 1998.

Cohen, Chayim. "The Widowed City." *Journal of the Ancient Near Eastern Society of Columbia University* 5 (1973), 75–81.

Cohen, David. *Law, Sexuality, and Society: The Enforcement of Morals in Classical Athens.* Cambridge: Cambridge University Press, 1991.

Cohen, David, and Richard Saller. "Foucault on Sexuality in Greco-Roman Antiquity." In *Foucault and the Writing of History,* edited by Jan Goldstein, 35–59. Cambridge, Massachusetts: Blackwell, 1994.

Cohen, Jeremy. *"Be Fertile and Increase, Fill the Earth and Master It": The Ancient and Medieval Career of a Biblical Text.* Ithaca, N.Y. : Cornell University Press, 1989.

Cohen, Naomi G. *Philo Judaeus: His Universe of Discourse.* New York: P. Lang, 1995.

Colish, Marcia L. *The Stoic Tradition from Antiquity to the Early Middle Ages.* Leiden: Brill, 1990.

Collins, Raymond F. *First Corinthians.* Sacra pagina. Collegeville, Minn.: Liturgical Press, 1999.

The Columbia Encyclopedia[5]. New York: Columbia University Press, 1993.

Conzelmann, Hans. *1 Corinthians: A Commentary on the First Epistle to the Corinthians.* Translated by James W. Leitch. Hermeneia. Philadelphia: Fortress Press, 1975. Originally published as *Der erste Briefe an die Korinther,* Göttingen: Vandenhoeck & Ruprecht, 1969.

Cooper, John M. "Plato's Theory of Human Motivation." *History of Philosophy Quarterly* 1 (1984), 3–21. Also available in N. Smith, editor, *Plato,* vol. 3, 27–47.

———. "Posidonius on Emotions." In *The Emotions in Hellenistic Philosophy,* edited by Juha Sihvola and Troels Engberg-Pedersen, 71–111. Dordrecht, Holland: Kluwer Academic Publishers, 1998.

Cooper, Kate. *The Virgin and the Bride: Idealized Womanhood in Late Antiquity.* Cambridge, Mass.: Harvard University Press, 1996.

Cornford, Francis M. "Mysticism and Science in the Pythagorean Tradition." *Classical Quarterly* 16 (1922), 137–50 and 17 (1923), 1–12.

———. *Plato's Cosmology.* London: Routledge and Kegan Paul, 1937. Reprint, Indianapolis: Hackett, 1957.

Corrington Streete, Gail. *The Strange Woman: Power and Sex in the Bible.* Louisville, Ky.: Westminster John Knox Press, 1997.

Countryman, L. William. *Dirt, Greed, and Sex: Sexual Ethics in the New Testament and Their Implications for Today.* Minneapolis: Fortress Press, 1988.

Cox, Cheryl A. *Household Interests: Property, Marriage Strategies, and Family Dynamics in Ancient Athens.* Princeton: Princeton University Press, 1998.

Crouzel, Henri. "Les source bibliques de l'enkrateia chrétienne." In U. Bianchi, editor, 505–26.

Dautzenberg, Gerhard. "Φεύγετε τὴν πορνείαν (1 Kor 6,18). Eine Fallstudie zur paulinischen Sexualethik in ihrem Verhältnis zur Sexualethik des Frühjudentums." In *Neues Testament und Ethik,* edited by Helmut Merklein, 271–98. Festschrift for Rudolf Schnackenburg. Freiburg im Breisgau: Herder, 1989.

Davidson, Arnold I. "Archaeology, Genealogy, Ethics." In D. Hoy, editor, 221–33.

———. "Ethics as Ascetics: Foucault, the History of Ethics, and Ancient Thought." In *The Cambridge Companion to Foucault,* edited by Gary Gutting, 115–40. New York: Cambridge University Press, 1994.

Davies, W. D. *The Setting of the Sermon on the Mount.* Cambridge: Cambridge University Press, 1964. Reprint, Atlanta: Scholars Press, 1989.

Davies, W. D., and Dale C. Allison. *A Critical and Exegetical Commentary on the Gospel according to Saint Matthew.* The International Critical Commentary. Edinburgh: T & T Clark, 1988–1997.

Dawes, Gregory W., editor. *The Historical Jesus Quest: Landmarks in the Search for the Jesus of History.* Louisville, Ky.: Westminster John Knox Press, 2000.

Dawson, David. *Allegorical Readers and Cultural Revision in Ancient Alexandria.* Berkeley and Los Angeles: University of California Press, 1992.

Dawson, Doyne. *Cities of the Gods: Communist Utopias in Greek Thought.* New York: Oxford University Press, 1992.

de Faye, Eugene. *Clément d'Alexandrie. Étude sur les rapports du christianisme et de la philosophie grecque au IIe siècle*[2]. Paris: E. Leroux, 1906. Reprint, Frankfurt am Main: Minerva, 1967.

de Vogel, Cornelia J. *Pythagoras and Early Pythagoreanism: An Interpretation of Neglected Evidence on the Philosopher Pythagoras.* Assen: Van Gorcum, 1966.

———. *Rethinking Plato and Platonism.* Leiden: Brill, 1986.

De Witt, Norman W. *St. Paul and Epicurus.* Minneapolis: University of Minnesota Press. 1954.

Deloria, Ella. *Speaking of Indians.* Lincoln, Nebr.: University of Nebraska Press, 1944. Reprint, 1998.

Deming, Will. *Paul on Marriage and Celibacy: The Hellenistic Background of 1 Corinthians 7.* New York: Cambridge University Press, 1995.

Destro, Adriana. *The Law of Jealousy: Anthropology of Sotah.* Atlanta: Scholars Press, 1989.

Devine, Francis E. "Stoicism on the Best Regime." *Journal of the History of Ideas* 31 (1970), 323–36.

Dibelius, Martin, and Hans Conzelmann. *The Pastoral Epistles: A Commentary.* Translated by Philip Buttolph and Adela Yarbro. Hermeneia. Philadelphia: Fortress Press, 1972. Originally published as *Die Pastoralbriefe*[4], Tübingen: J. C. B. Mohr, 1966.

Dillon, John M. *The Middle Platonists.* Rev. ed. Ithaca, N.Y.: Cornell University Press, 1996.

Dillon, Matthew. *Girls and Women in Classical Greek Religion.* New York: Routledge, 2002.

Dodds, E. R. *The Greeks and the Irrational.* Berkeley and Los Angeles: University of California Press, 1951.

———. "Plato and the Irrational." *The Journal of Hellenic Studies* 65 (1945), 16–25.

Douglas, Mary. *Purity and Danger.* London: Routledge and Kegan Paul, 1966.

Dover, Kenneth J. *Greek Homosexuality*[2]. Cambridge, Mass.: Harvard University Press, 1989.

Dozeman, Thomas B. "Sperma Abraham in John 8 and Related Literature: Cosmology and Judgement." *The Catholic Biblical Quarterly* 42 (1980), 342–58.

Droge, Arthur J. *Homer or Moses? Early Christian Interpretations of the History of Culture.* Tübingen: J. C. B. Mohr, 1989.

DuBois, Page. *Sowing the Body: Psychoanalysis and Ancient Representations of Women.* Chicago: University of Chicago Press, 1988.

Dudley, Donald R. *A History of Cynicism.* London: Methuen, 1937. Reprint, 1980.

Dumais, Marcel. "Couple et sexualité dans le Nouveau Testament." *Église et théologie* 8 (1977), 47–72.

Ehrhardt, E. "The Word of the Muses (Plato, *Rep.* 8.546)." *Classical Quarterly,* n.s., 36 (1986), 407–20.

Ellis, E. Earle. *The Old Testament in Early Christianity: Canon and Interpretation in the Light of Modern Research.* Tübingen: J. C. B. Mohr, 1991.

———. *Paul's Use of the Old Testament.* Grand Rapids, Mich.: Eerdmans, 1957.

Elm, Susanna. *Virgins of God: The Making of Asceticism in Late Antiquity.* Oxford: Oxford University Press, 1994.

Elze, Martin. *Tatian und seine Theologie.* Göttingen: Vandenhoeck & Ruprecht, 1960.

Engberg-Pedersen, Troels. *Paul and the Stoics.* Edinburgh: T & T Clark, 2000.

———. *The Stoic Theory of Oikeiosis: Moral Development and Social Interaction in Early Stoic Philosophy.* Aarhus, Denmark: Aarhus University Press, 1990.

Engels, Friedrich. *The Origin of the Family, Private Property, and the State.* Translated by Ernest Untermann, with introduction and notes by Eleanor Burke Leacock. New York: International Publishers, 1972. Originally published as *Der Ursprung der Familie, des Privateigentums und des Staats,* Hottingen-Zurich: Schweitzerische Genossenschaftsbuchdruckerei, 1884.

Epstein, Louis M. *Marriage Laws in the Bible and the Talmud.* Harvard Semitic Series 12. Cambridge, Mass.: Harvard University Press, 1942.

———. *Sex Laws and Customs in Judaism.* New York: Bloch Publishing Company, 1948.

Erdmann, Walter. *Die Ehe im alten Griechenland.* Munich: C. H. Beck, 1934. Reprint, New York: Arno Press, 1979.

Erskine, Andrew. *The Hellenistic Stoa: Political Thought and Action.* Ithaca, N.Y.: Cornell University Press, 1990.

Faraone, Christopher A. *Ancient Greek Love Magic.* Cambridge, Mass.: Harvard University Press, 1999.

Fee, Gordon D. *The First Epistle to the Corinthians.* The New International Commentary. Grand Rapids, Mich.: Eerdmans, 1987.

Feldman, Louis H. *Jew and Gentile in the Ancient World: Attitudes and Interaction from Alexander to Justinian.* Princeton: Princeton University Press, 1993.

———. Review of *Establishment Violence in Philo and Luke,* by T. Seland. *Journal of the American Oriental Society* 117 (1997), 154–5.

Ferguson, John, translator. *Clement of Alexandria:* Stromateis *Books One to Three.* Washington, D.C.: Catholic University Press of America, 1991.

Ferrero, Leonardo. *Storia del pitagorismo nel mondo romano (dalle origini alla fine della reppublica).* Turin: Università di Torino, Fondazione Parini-Chirio, 1955.

Fevrier, Paul-Albert. "Aux origines d'une exigence chrétienne." In M. Bernos, editor, 165–81.

Fisk, Bruce N. *"Porneuein* as Bodily Violation: The Unique Nature of Sexual Sin in 1 Cor. 6:18." *New Testament Studies* 42 (1996), 540–58.

Fitzgerald, Aloysius. "The Mythological Background for the Presentation of Jerusalem as a Queen and False Worship as Adultery in the Old Testament." *The Catholic Biblical Quarterly* 34 (1972), 403–16.

Fitzmyer, Joseph A. *Romans: A New Translation with Introduction and Commentary.* The Anchor Bible. New York: Doubleday, 1993.

Ford, J. Massingberd. "The Divorce Bill of the Lamb and the Scroll of the Suspected Adulteress. A Note on Apoc 5, 1 and 10, 8–11." *Journal for the Study of Judaism in the Persian, Hellenistic, and Roman Period* 2 (1971), 136–43.

Fortenbaugh, William W. "Plato: Temperament and Eugenic Policy." *Arethusa* 8 (1975) 283–305.

Foucault, Michel. *The Care of the Self.* Translated by Robert Hurley. New York: Viking, 1986. Originally published as *Le souci de soi,* Paris: Gallimard, 1984.

———. "On the Genealogy of Ethics: An Overview of Work in Progress." Interview with Michel Foucault by Hubert J. Dreyfus and Paul Rabinow. In *Michel Foucault: Beyond Structuralism and Hermeneutics*[2], edited by Dreyfus and Rabinow. Chicago: University of Chicago Press, 1983.

———. *The Use of Pleasure.* Translated by Robert Hurley. New York: Viking, 1985. Originally published as *L'usage des plaisirs,* Paris: Gallimard, 1984.

Fraisse, Jean-Claude. *Philia: La notion d'amitié dans la philosophie antique.* Paris: J. Vrin, 1974.

Fredriksen, Paula. *From Jesus to Christ*[2]. New Haven: Yale University Press, 2000.

Freudenthal, J. "Are There Traces of Greek Philosophy in the Septuagint?" *The Jewish Quarterly Review* 2 (1890), 205–22.

Freyne, Sean. "Vilifying the Other and Defining the Self: Matthew's and John's Anti-Jewish Polemic in Focus." In *"To See Ourselves as Others See Us": Christians, Jews, and "Others" in Late Antiquity,* edited by Jacob Neusner and Ernest S. Frerichs, 118–43. Chico, Calif.: Scholars Press, 1985.

Frick, Peter. *Divine Providence in Philo of Alexandria.* Tübingen: Mohr Siebeck, 1999.

Friedman, Mordechai A. "Israel's Response in Hosea 2:17b: 'You Are My Husband.'" *Journal of Biblical Literature* 99 (1980), 199–204.

Friedrich, Paul. *The Meaning of Aphrodite.* Chicago: University of Chicago Press, 1978.

Funk, Robert W., Roy W. Hoover, et al. *The Five Gospels: The Search for the Authentic Words of Jesus.* New York: Macmillan, 1993.

Furnish, Victor Paul. *II Corinthians.* The Anchor Bible. Garden City, N.Y.: Doubleday, 1984.

Gaca, Kathy L. "Paul's Uncommon Declaration to the Greeks: Romans 1:18–32 and Its Problematic Legacy for Pagan and Christian Relations." *The Harvard Theological Review* 92 (1999), 165–98.

Gager, John G. *Curse Tablets and Binding Spells from the Ancient World.* New York: Oxford University Press, 1992.

Galambush, Julie. *Jerusalem in the Book of Ezekiel: The City as Yahweh's Wife.* Atlanta: Scholars Press, 1992.

Glad, Clarence E. *Paul and Philodemus: Adaptability in Epicurean and Early Christian Psychagogy.* Leiden: Brill, 1995.

Glancy, Jennifer A. "Obstacles to Slaves' Participation in the Corinthian Church." *Journal of Biblical Literature* 117 (1998), 481–501.

Gnuse, Robert Karl. *No Other Gods: Emergent Monotheism in Israel.* Sheffield: Sheffield Academic Press, 1997.

———. *You Shall Not Steal. Community and Property in the Biblical Tradition.* Maryknoll, N.Y.: Orbis Books, 1985.

Goldhill, Simon. *Foucault's Virginity: Ancient Erotic Fiction and the History of Sexuality.* New York: Cambridge University Press, 1995.

Gorman, Peter. "Pythagoras Palestinus." *Philologus* 127 (1983), 30–42.

Gosling, J. C. B., and C. C. W. Taylor. *The Greeks on Pleasure.* Oxford: Clarendon Press, 1982.

Gottschalk, H. B. "Soul as Harmonia." *Phronesis* 16 (1971), 179–98.

Gouldner, Alvin W. *Enter Plato: Classical Greece and the Origins of Social Theory.* New York: Basic Books, 1965.

Goulet, Richard. *La philosophie de Moïse: Essai de reconstitution d'un commentaire philosophique préphilonien du Pentateuque.* Paris: J. Vrin, 1987.

Grant, Robert M. "The Date of Tatian's Oration." *The Harvard Theological Review* 46 (1953), 99–101.

———. "Dietary Laws among Pythagoreans, Jews, and Christians." *The Harvard Theological Review* 73 (1980), 299–310.

———. "The Heresy of Tatian." *Journal of Theological Studies,* n.s., 5 (1954), 62–8.

———. "Tatian and the Bible." *Studia Patristica* 1(1957), 297–306.

Griffin, Miriam T. *Seneca: A Philosopher in Politics.* New York: Oxford University Press, 1976. Reprint, with postscript, 1992.

Griswold, Charles, editor. *Platonic Writings, Platonic Readings*². New York: Routledge, 2001.

Grote, George. *Plato, and the Other Companions of Socrates.* Vols. 1–4. New ed. London: John Murray, 1888.

Grubbs, Judith Evans. *Law and Family in Late Antiquity: The Emperor Constantine's Marriage Legislation.* Oxford: Clarendon Press, 1995.

Gruber, Mayer I. *The Motherhood of God and Other Studies.* Atlanta: Scholars Press, 1992.

Guillaumont, Antoine. "Le célibat monastique et l'idéal chrétien de la virginité ont-ils des 'motivations ontologiques et protologiques'?" In U. Bianchi, editor, 83–98.

Guthrie, W. K. C. *A History of Greek Philosophy.* Vols. 1–6. Cambridge: Cambridge University Press, 1962–1981.

Gutzwiller, Kathryn J. *Poetic Garlands: Hellenistic Epigrams in Context.* Berkeley and Los Angeles: University of California Press, 1998.

Haas, Christopher. *Alexandria in Late Antiquity: Topography and Social Conflict.* Baltimore: The Johns Hopkins University Press, 1997.

Hadot, Ilsetraut. *Seneca und die griechisch-römische Tradition der Seelenleitung.* Berlin: Walter de Gruyter, 1969.

Hadot, Pierre. *Philosophy as a Way of Life: Spiritual Exercises from Socrates to Foucault.* Translated by Michael Chase and edited with introduction by Arnold I. Davidson. Oxford: Blackwell, 1995. Translated from *Exercices spirituels et philosophie antique*³, Paris: Institut d'études augustiniennes, 1993.

Hahm, David E. "The Ethical Doxography of Arius Didymus." *Aufstieg und Niedergang der römischen Welt* 2.36.4 (1990), 2935–3055.

———. *The Origins of Stoic Cosmology.* Columbus, Ohio: Ohio State University Press, 1977.

Hall, Peter. *Cities in Civilization.* New York: Fromm International, 1998.

Halperin, David M. "Plato and Erotic Reciprocity." *Classical Antiquity* 5 (1986), 60–80.

———. "Platonic *Erōs* and What Men Call Love." *Ancient Philosophy* 5 (1985), 161–204. Also available in N. Smith, editor, *Plato,* vol. 3, 66–120.

Hampton, Cynthia. "Pleasure, Truth, and Being in Plato's *Philebus:* A Reply to Professor Frede." *Phronesis* 32 (1987), 253–62. Also available in N. Smith, editor, *Plato,* vol. 4, 236–47.

Harder, Richard. *Ocellus Lucanus. Neue philologische Untersuchungen* I. Berlin: Weidmann, 1926. Reprint, Dublin: Weidmann, 1966.

Hatch, Edwin, and Henry A. Redpath. *A Concordance to the Septuagint and Other Greek Versions of the Old Testament.* Vols. 1–2. With a new introduction and index by Robert A. Kraft, Emanuel Tov, and Takamitsu Muraoka. Grand Rapids, Michigan: Baker Books, 1998. Originally published Oxford: Clarendon Press, 1897.

Hauck, Friedrich, and Siegfried Schulz. "πόρνη, πορνεία." *TDNT* vol. 6, 579–95, see G. Kittel et al., editors.

Hawthorne, Gerald F. "Tatian and His Discourse to the Greeks." *The Harvard Theological Review* 57 (1964), 161–88.

Hays, Richard B. *Echoes of Scripture in the Letters of Paul.* New Haven: Yale University Press 1989.

Heil, John Paul. "The Story of Jesus and the Adulteress (John 7,53–8,11) Reconsidered." *Biblica* 72 (1991), 182–91.

Heinemann, Isaak. *Philons griechische und jüdische Bildung: Kulturvergleichende Untersuchungen zu Philons Darstellung der jüdische Gesetze.* Breslau: M. & H. Marcus, 1932. Reprint, Hildesheim: Georg Olms, 1962.

Hengel, Martin. *Judaism and Hellenism: Studies in their Encounter in Palestine during the Early Hellenistic Period.* Translated by John Bowden. Philadelphia: Fortress Press, 1981. Originally published as *Judentum und Hellenismus,* Tübingen: Mohr, 1973.

———. *Property and Riches in the Early Church: Aspects of a Social History of Early Christianity.* Translated by John Bowden. Philadelphia: Fortress Press, 1974. Originally published as *Eigentum und Reichtum in der frühen Kirche: Aspekte einer frühchristlichen Sozialgeschichte,* Stuttgart: Calwer, 1973.

Héring, Jean. *The First Epistle of Saint Paul to the Corinthians,* translated by A. W. Heathcote and P. J. Allcock. London: Epworth Press, 1962. Originally published as *La première épitre de Saint Paul aux Corinthiens*[2], Neuchâtel: Delachaux & Niestle, 1959.

Hirschberg, Peter. *Das eschatologische Israel: Untersuchungen zum Gottesvolkverständnis der Johannesoffenbarung.* Düsseldorf: Neukirchener Verlag, 1999.

Horrell, David G. *The Social Ethos of the Corinthian Correspondence: Interests and Ideology from 1 Corinthians to 1 Clement.* Edinburgh: T & T Clark, 1996.

Horsley, Richard A. "The Law of Nature in Philo and Cicero." *The Harvard Theological Review* 71 (1978), 35–59.

Hoy, David Couzens, editor. *Foucault: A Critical Reader.* Oxford: Blackwell, 1986.

Humm, Michel. "Les origines du pythagorisme romain: Problèmes historiques et philosophiques, I–II." *Les Études classiques* 64 (1996), 339–53 and 65 (1997), 25–42.

Hunter, David G. "The Language of Desire: Clement of Alexandria's Transformation of Ascetic Discourse." *Semeia* 57 (1992), 95–111.

Inwood, Brad. *Ethics and Human Action in the Early Stoa.* Oxford: Clarendon Press, 1985.

———. "Rules and Reasoning in Stoic Ethics." In *Topics in Stoic Philosophy,* edited by Katerina Ierodiakonou, 95–127. Oxford: Clarendon Press, 1999.

———. "Why Do Fools Fall in Love?" In *Aristotle and After,* edited by R. Sorabji, 55–69. London: Institute of Classical Studies, 1997.

Irwin, Terence. *Plato's Ethics.* New York: Oxford University Press, 1995.

Jackson, Bernard S. "Liability for Mere Intention in Early Jewish Law." In his *Essays in Jewish and Comparative Legal History,* 202–34. Leiden: Brill, 1975.

Jacobson, Howard, editor, commentator, and translator. *A Commentary on Pseudo-Philo's* Liber antiquitatum biblicarum. Vols. 1–2. Leiden: Brill, 1996.

———. *The* Exagoge *of Ezekiel.* Cambridge: Cambridge University Press, 1983.

Jellicoe, Sidney. *The Septuagint and Modern Study.* Oxford: Clarendon Press, 1968.

Jones, A. H. M. *The Later Roman Empire 284–602: A Social, Economic, and Administrative Survey.* Vols. 1–2. Baltimore: The Johns Hopkins University Press, 1964.

Jouanna, Jacques. *Hippocrates.* Translated by M. B. DeBevoise. Baltimore: The Johns Hopkins University Press, 1999. Originally published as *Hippocrate,* Paris: Arthème Fayard, 1992.

Jouassard, G. "Requête d'un patrologue aux biblistes touchant les Septante." *Studia Patristica* 1 (1957), 307–27.

Judge, Edwin A. *The Social Pattern of the Christian Groups in the First Century: Some Prolegomena to the Study of New Testament Ideas of Social Obligation.* London: Tyndale Press, 1960.

Jungkurtz, Richard. "Fathers, Heretics, and Epicureans." *The Journal of Ecclesiastical History* 17 (1966), 3–10.

Just, Roger. *Women in Athenian Law and Life.* London: Routledge, 1989.

Kahn, Charles H. "Plato's Theory of Desire." *Review of Metaphysics* 41 (1987), 77–103.

Karavites, Peter. *Evil, Freedom, and the Road to Perfection in Clement of Alexandria.* Leiden: Brill, 1999.

Katz, Peter. *Philo's Bible: The Aberrant Text of Bible Quotations in Some Philonic Writings and Its Place in the Textual History of the Greek Bible.* Cambridge: Cambridge University Press, 1950.

———. "Septuagintal Studies in the Mid-Century: Their Links with the Past and Their Present Tendencies." In *The Background of the New Testament and its Eschatology,* edited by W. D. Davies and D. Daube, 176–208. Cambridge: Cambridge University Press, 1956.

Keesmaat, Sylvia C. *Paul and His Story: (Re-)Interpreting the Exodus Tradition.* Sheffield: Sheffield Academic Press, 1999.

King, Helen. *Hippocrates' Woman: Reading the Female Body in Ancient Greece.* New York: Routledge, 1998.

———. Review of *Eros: The Myth of Ancient Greek Sexuality,* by Bruce S. Thornton. *Bulletin of the History of Medicine* 72 (1998), 755–6.

Kingsley, Peter. *Ancient Philosophy, Mystery, and Magic: Empedocles and Pythagorean Tradition.* Oxford: Clarendon Press, 1995.

——. Review of *Philolaus of Croton: Pythagorean and Presocratic,* by Carl Huffman. *Classical Review,* n.s., 44 (1994), 294–6.

Kirchhoff, Renate. *Die Sünde gegen den eigenen Leib: Studien zu πόρνη und πορνεία in 1 Kor 6,12–20 und dem sozio-kulturellen Kontext der paulinischen Adressaten.* Göttingen: Vandenhoeck & Ruprecht, 1994.

Kittel, Gerhard et al., editors. *Theological Dictionary of the New Testament.* Edited and translated by Geoffrey W. Bromiley. Grand Rapids, Mich.: Eerdmans, 1964–1976. Originally published as *Theologisches Wörterbuch zum Neuen Testament,* Stuttgart: W. Kohlhammer, 1932–1979.

Klagge, James C., and Nicholas D. Smith, editors. *Methods of Interpreting Plato and His Dialogues.* Oxford Studies in Ancient Philosophy. Supplementary volume. New York: Oxford University Press, 1992.

Klassen, William. "Foundations for Pauline Sexual Ethics as Seen in 1 Thess 4:1–8." *Society of Biblical Literature 1978 Seminar Papers,* vol. 2, 159–81. Missoula, Mont.: Scholars Press, 1978.

Klaw, Spencer. *Without Sin: The Life and Death of the Oneida Community.* New York: Allen Lane, 1993.

Klein, George L. "Hos 3:1–3—Background to 1 Cor 6:19b–20?" *Criswell Theological Review* 3 (1989), 373–5.

Klosko, George. *The Development of Plato's Political Theory.* New York: Methuen, 1986.

Knight, George W. *The Pastoral Epistles: A Commentary on the Greek Text.* The New International Greek Testament Commentary. Grand Rapids, Mich.: Eerdmans, 1992.

Koch, Dietrich-Alex. *Die Schrift als Zeuge des Evangeliums: Untersuchungen zur Verwendung und zum Verständnis der Schrift bei Paulus.* Tübingen: J. C. B. Mohr, 1986.

Koester, Helmut. *Introduction to the New Testament* ², vols. 1–2: *History, Culture, and Religion of the Hellenistic Age* (vol. 1); *History and Literature of Early Christianity* (vol. 2). New York: Walter de Gruyter, 1995–2000. Originally published as *Einführung in das Neue Testament,* Berlin: Walter de Gruyter, 1980.

Kollwitz, Käthe. *Käthe Kollwitz: Die Meisterwerke aus dem Käthe-Kollwitz-Museum Berlin.* Weisloch, Germany: Kunstkreis Südliche Bergstrasse-Kraichgau, 1995.

Kramer, Samuel Noah. *The Sacred Marriage Rite: Aspects of Faith, Myth, and Ritual in Ancient Sumer.* Bloomington: University of Indiana Press, 1969.

Kruger, P. A. "Israel, the Harlot (Hos. 2:4–9)." *Journal of Northwest Semitic Languages* 11 (1983), 107–16.

Laks, André, and Malcolm Schofield, editors. *Justice and Generosity: Studies in Hellenistic Social and Political Philosophy.* New York: Cambridge University Press, 1995.

Lambrecht, Jan. *Second Corinthians.* Sacra pagina. Collegeville, Minn.: The Liturgical Press, 1999.

Lawler, Ronald, Joseph Boyle, Jr., and William E. May. *Catholic Sexual Ethics: A Summary, Explanation, and Defense* ². Huntington, Ind.: Our Sunday Visitor, 1998.

Le Boulluec, Alain. "L'allegorie chez les Stoïciens." *Poétique* 23 (1975), 301–21.

——. "La place des concepts philosophiques dans la réflexion de Philon sur le plaisir." In C. Lévy, editor, 129–52.

Lefkowitz, Mary. "Sex and Civilization." Review of *L'usage des plaisirs* and *Le souci de soi,* by M. Foucault. *Partisan Review* 52 (1985), 460–6.

Légasse, S. "Jésus et les prostituées." *Revue theologique de Louvain* 7 (1976), 137–54.

Lerner, Gerda. *The Creation of Patriarchy*. New York: Oxford University Press, 1986.

Levenson, Jon D. *The Universal Horizon of Biblical Particularism*. New York: American Jewish Committee, 1985.

Levine, Amy-Jill. "Tobit: Teaching Jews How to Live in the Diaspora." *Bible Review* 8.4 (1992), 42–51.

Levine, Michael P. *Pantheism: A Non-theistic Concept of Deity*. New York: Routledge, 1994.

Lévy, Carlos, editor. *Philon d'Alexandrie et la langage de la philosophie*. Turnhout, Belgium: Brepols, 1998.

Lévy, Isidore. *La légende de Pythagore de Grèce en Palestine*. Paris: E. Champion, 1927.

Liboron, Herbert. *Die karpokratianische Gnosis: Untersuchungen zur Geschichte und Anschauungswelt eines spätgnostischen Systems*. Leipzig: Komissionsverlag von Jordan & Gramberg, 1938.

Lietzmann, Hans. *Einführung in die Textgeschichte der Paulusbriefe an die Römer*[4]. Handbuch zum Neuen Testament 8. Tübingen: J. C. B. Mohr, 1933.

Lightman, Marjorie, and William Zeisel. "Univira: An Example of Continuity and Change in Roman Society." *Church History* 46 (1977), 19–32.

Lilla, Salvatore R. C. *Clement of Alexandria: A Study in Christian Platonism and Gnosticism*. New York: Oxford University Press, 1971.

Lindemann, Andreas. "Paul in the Writings of the Apostolic Fathers." In *Paul and the Legacies of Paul*, edited by William S. Babcock, 25–45. Dallas: Southern Methodist University Press, 1990.

Lloyd-Jones, David M. *Romans: An Exposition of Chapters 7.1–8.4. The Law: Its Functions and Limits*. Grand Rapids, Mich.: Zondervan, 1973.

Lloyd-Jones, Hugh. *The Justice of Zeus*[2]. Berkeley and Los Angeles: University of California Press, 1983.

Löhr, Winrich. "Karpokratianisches." *Vigiliae Christianae* 49 (1995), 23–48.

Lohse, Eduard. *Colossians and Philemon: A Commentary*. Translated by William R. Poehlmann and Robert J. Karris. Hermeneia. Philadelphia: Fortress Press, 1971. Originally published as *Die Briefe an die Kolosser und an Philemon*, Göttingen: Vandenhoeck & Ruprecht, 1968.

Long, A. A. "Language and Thought in Stoicism." In *Problems in Stoicism*, edited by A. A. Long, 75–113. London: Athlone Press, 1971. Reprint, with new introduction, London: Athlone Press, 1996.

———. "Soul and Body in Stoicism." *Phronesis* 27 (1982), 34–57. Also available in his *Stoic Studies*, 224–49. New York: Cambridge University Press, 1996; Berkeley and Los Angeles: University of California Press, 2001.

Louth, Andrew. "Apathetic Love in Clement of Alexandria." *Studia Patristica* 18.3 (1989), 413–19.

Macey, David. *The Lives of Michel Foucault*. New York: Pantheon Books, 1993.

Mack, Burton L. "Philo Judaeus and Exegetical Traditions in Alexandria." *Aufstieg und Niedergang der römischen Welt* 2.21.1 (1984), 227–71.

MacMullen, Ramsay. *Christianity and Paganism in the Fourth to Eighth Centuries*. New Haven: Yale University Press, 1997.

Magnien, Victor. "Le mariage chez les Grecs anciens. Conditions premières." *An-*

nuaire de l'Institut de Philologie et d'Histoire Orientales et Slaves de l'Université libre de Bruxelles 4 (1936), 305–20.

Malherbe, Abraham J. *The Cynic Epistles.* Sources for Biblical Study 12. Missoula, Montana: Scholars Press, 1977.

———. "Hellenistic Moralists and the New Testament." *Aufstieg und Niedergang der römischen Welt* 2.26.1 (1992), 267–333.

———. *Paul and the Popular Philosophers.* Minneapolis: Fortress Press, 1989.

Malina, Bruce. "Does Porneia Mean 'Fornication'?" *Novum Testamentum* 14 (1972), 10–17.

Manning, C. E. "Seneca and the Stoics on the Equality of the Sexes." *Mnemosyne,* 4th series, 26 (1973), 170–77.

Mantovani, Giancarlo. "La tradizione dell'enkrateia nei testi di Nag Hammadi e nell'ambiente monastico egiziano del IV secolo." In U. Bianchi, editor, *La tradizione dell' enkrateia,* 561–99.

Martin, Dale B. *The Corinthian Body.* New Haven: Yale University Press, 1995.

Martyn, J. Louis. *Galatians: A New Translation with Introduction and Commentary.* The Anchor Bible. New York: Doubleday, 1997.

Mattioli, Anselmo. *La realtà sessuali nella Bibbia: Storia e dottrina.* Casale Monferrato, Italy: Piemme, 1987.

Mayhew, Robert. *Aristotle's Criticism of Plato's* Republic. Lanham, Md.: Rowman and Littlefield, 1997.

Mazzaferri, Frederick D. *The Genre of Revelation from a Source-Critical Perspective.* New York: Walter de Gruyter, 1989.

Meeks, Wayne A. "'And Rose Up to Play': Midrash and Paraenesis in 1 Corinthians 10:1–22." *Journal for the Study of the New Testament* 16 (1982), 64–78.

———. *The First Urban Christians: The Social World of the Apostle Paul.* New Haven: Yale University Press, 1983.

Méhat, André. *Étude sur les 'Stromates' de Clément d'Alexandrie.* Paris: Éditions du Seuil, 1966.

Merlan, Philip. "Greek Philosophy from Plato to Plotinus." In *The Cambridge History of Later Greek and Early Medieval Philosophy,* edited by A. H. Armstrong, 14–32. Cambridge: Cambridge University Press, 1967.

Meyers, Carol L., and Eric M. Meyers. *Haggai, Zechariah 1–8.* Anchor Bible. Garden City, N.Y.: Doubleday, 1987.

Michel, Otto. *Paulus und seine Bibel.* Gutersloh, Germany: C. Bertelsmann, 1929. Reprint, Darmstadt: Wissenschaftliche Buchgesellschaft, 1972.

Millar, Fergus. "Porphyry: Ethnicity, Language, and Alien Wisdom." In *Philosophia Togata II,* edited by Jonathan Barnes and Miriam Griffin, 241–262. Oxford: Clarendon Press, 1997.

Minar, Edwin L. *Early Pythagorean Politics in Practice and Theory.* Baltimore: Waverly Press, 1942. Reprint, New York: Arno Press, 1979.

———. "Pythagorean Communism." *Transactions of the American Philological Association* 75 (1944), 34–47.

Mitsis, Phillip. "Natural Law and Natural Right in Post-Aristotelian Philosophy: The Stoics and Their Critics." *Aufstieg und Niedergang der römischen Welt* 2.36.7 (1994), 4812–4850.

Moore, George Foot. *Judaism in the First Centuries of the Christian Era: The Age of the Tannaim.* Vols. 1–3. Cambridge, Mass.: Harvard University Press, 1927–1930.

Morgan, Michael L. "Plato and Greek Religion." In *The Cambridge Companion to Plato,* edited by Richard Kraut, 227–47. New York: Cambridge University Press, 1992.

———. *Platonic Piety: Philosophy and Ritual in Fourth-Century Athens.* New Haven: Yale University Press, 1990.

Morris, Brian. *Anthropological Studies of Religion.* New York: Cambridge University Press, 1987.

Morrow, Glenn R. *Plato's Cretan City.* Princeton: Princeton University Press, 1960. Reprint, with a new foreword by Charles H. Kahn, 1993.

Mulhern, John J. "Population and Plato's *Republic.*" *Arethusa* 8 (1975), 265–81.

Müller, Mogens. *The First Bible of the Church: A Plea for the Septuagint.* Sheffield: Sheffield Academic Press, 1996.

Musti, Domenico. "Le rivolte antipitagoriche e la concezione pitagorica del tempo." *Quaderni urbinati di cultura classica* 65 (1990), 35–65.

Najman, Hindy. "The Law of Nature and the Authority of Mosaic Law." *The Studia Philonica Annual* 11 (1999), 55–73.

Neusner, Jacob. *The Idea of Purity in Ancient Judaism.* With a critique and commentary by Mary Douglas. Leiden: Brill, 1973.

———. "The Use of the Later Rabbinic Evidence for the Study of First-Century Pharisaism." In *Approaches to Ancient Judaism,* vol. 1, edited by William Scott Green, 215–28. Missoula, Mont.: Scholars Press, 1983.

Newman, Carey C., James R. Davila, and Gladys S. Lewis, editors. *The Jewish Roots of Christological Monotheism: Papers from the St. Andrews Conference on the Historical Origins of the Worship of Jesus.* Leiden: Brill, 1999.

Nikiprowetzky, V. *Le commentaire de l'Écriture chez Philon d'Alexandrie: Son caractère et sa portée.* Leiden: Brill, 1977.

Niven, W. D. Review of *St. Paul and Epicurus,* by N. De Witt. *The Expository Times* 67 (1955), 45.

Noonan, John T. *Contraception: A History of Its Treatment by the Catholic Theologians and Canonists*[2]. Cambridge, Mass.: Harvard University Press, 1986.

Nussbaum, Martha C. *The Fragility of Goodness.* Cambridge: Cambridge University Press, 1986. Reprint, with a new introduction, 2001.

———. *The Therapy of Desire.* Princeton: Princeton University Press, 1994.

O'Brien, Mary. *The Politics of Reproduction.* Boston: Routledge and Kegan Paul, 1981.

Oakley, John H. "The Anakalypteria." *Archäologischer Anzeiger* 97 (1982), 113–18.

Oakley, John H., and Rebecca H. Sinos. *The Wedding in Ancient Athens.* Madison: The University of Wisconsin Press, 1993.

Okin, Susan Moller. "Philosopher Queens and Private Wives: Plato on Women and the Family." *Philosophy and Public Affairs* 6 (1977), 345–69. Also available in N. Smith, editor, *Plato,* vol. 3, 174–93.

Olyan, Saul M. "'And with a Male You Shall Not Lie the Lying Down of a Woman': On the Meaning and Significance of Leviticus 18:22 and 20:13." *Journal of the History of Sexuality* 5 (1994), 179–206.

Orlinsky, Harry M. "The Septuagint as Holy Writ and the Philosophy of the Translators." *Hebrew Union College Annual* 46 (1975), 89–114.

Orr, William F., and James A. Walther. *1 Corinthians: A New Translation and Commentary*. The Anchor Bible. Garden City, N.Y.: Doubleday, 1976.

Osborn, Eric. "Philo and Clement." *Prudentia* 19 (1987), 34–49.

Osborne, Catherine. *Eros Unveiled: Plato and the God of Love*. Oxford: Clarendon Press, 1994.

Oulton, John E. L., and Henry Chadwick, editors and translators. *Alexandrian Christianity: Selected Translations of Clement and Origen*. London: SCM Press, 1954.

Parker, Robert. *Miasma: Pollution and Purification in Early Greek Religion*. Oxford: Clarendon Press, 1983.

Patterson, Cynthia B. *The Family in Greek History*. Cambridge, Mass.: Harvard University Press, 1998.

Patterson, Orlando. *Slavery and Social Death: A Comparative Study*. Cambridge, Mass.: Harvard University Press, 1982.

Peake's Commentary on the Bible. Edited by Matthew Black and H. H. Rowley. London: T. Nelson, 1962. Reprint, New York: Routledge, 1997.

Pender, E. E. "Spiritual Pregnancy in Plato's *Symposium*." *Classical Quarterly*, n.s., 42 (1992), 72–86.

Petersen, William L. *Tatian's* Diatessaron: *Its Creation, Dissemination, Significance, and History in Scholarship*. Leiden: Brill, 1994.

Petit, Alain. "Philon et le Pythagorisme: un usage problématique." In C. Lévy, editor, 471–82.

Pfister, Friedrich. "Die στοιχεῖα τοῦ κόσμου in den Briefen des Apostels Paulus." *Philologus*, n.s., 23 (1910), 411–27.

Piérart, Marcel. *Platon et la cité grecque: Theorie et realité dans la constitution des Lois*. Brussels: Palais des Académies, 1974.

Pierce, Christine. "Equality: *Republic* V." *Monist* 57 (1973), 1–11.

Pirenne-Delforge, Vinciane. *L'Aphrodite grecque: Contribution a l'étude de ses cultes et de sa personnalité dans le pantheon archaïque et classique*. Liège: Centre International d'Étude de la Religion Grecque Antique, 1994.

Pohlenz, Max. *Die Stoa: Geschichte eine geistiger Bewegung*[2]. Göttingen: Vandenhoeck & Ruprecht, 1959. Reprint, 1984.

Pomeroy, Sarah B. *Families in Classical and Hellenistic Greece*. Oxford: Clarendon Press, 1997.

Popper, Karl. *The Open Society and Its Enemies*[5]. Princeton: Princeton University Press, 1971.

Poster, Mark. "Foucault and the Tyranny of Greece." In D. Hoy, editor, *Foucault*, 205–20.

Pralon, Didier. "Les puissances du désir dans la religion grecque antique." In M. Bernos, editor, *Sexualité et religions*, 73–94.

Preisker, Herbert. *Christentum und Ehe in den ersten drei Jahrhunderten: Eine Studie zur Kulturgeschichte der alten Welt*. Berlin: Trowitzsch 1927. Reprint, Aalen, Germany: Scientia Verlag, 1979.

Press, Gerald A. *Who Speaks for Plato? Studies in Platonic Anonymity*. Lanham, Md.: Rowman and Littlefield, 2000.

Price, A. W. *Love and Friendship in Plato and Aristotle*. Oxford: Clarendon Press, 1989.

Prunet, Olivier. *La morale de Clément d'Alexandrie et le Nouveau Testament*. Paris: Presses universitaires de France, 1966.

Quispel, Gilles. *Makarius, Das Thomasevangelium und das Lied von der Perle.* Leiden: Brill, 1967.

Radice, Roberto. "Le Judaïsme alexandrin et la philosophie grecque." In C. Lévy, editor, 483–92.

Räisänen, Heikki. "Zum Gebrauch von ἐπιθυμία und ἐπιθυμεῖν bei Paulus." *Studia Theologica* 33 (1979), 85–99. Also available in H. Räisänen, *Jesus, Paul, and Torah: Collected Essays,* translated by David E. Orton, 95–111, Sheffield: Sheffield Academic Press, 1992.

Ranke-Heinemann, Uta. *Eunuchs for Heaven: The Catholic Church and Sexuality.* Translated by John Brownjohn. London: André Deutsch, 1990. Originally published as *Eunuchen für das Himmelreich,* Hamburg: Huffmann und Kampe, 1988.

Rathke, Heinrich. *Ignatius von Antiochien und die Paulusbriefe.* Texte und Untersuchungen 99. Berlin: Akademie Verlag, 1967.

Redfield, James. "Notes on the Greek Wedding." *Arethusa* 15 (1982), 181–201.

Reeve, C. D. C., translator. *Plato's Republic.* In *Plato: Complete Works,* edited by John M. Cooper. Indianapolis: Hackett Publishing, 1997.

Reverdin, Olivier. *La religion de la cité platonicienne.* Paris: E. DeBoccard, 1945.

Richardson, W. "The Basis of Ethics: Chrysippus and Clement of Alexandria." *Studia Patristica* 9 (1966), 87–97.

Richlin, Amy. "Foucault's History of Sexuality: A Useful Theory for Women?" In *Rethinking Sexuality: Foucault and Classical Antiquity,* edited by David H. J. Larmour, Paul Allen Miller, and Charles Platter, 138–70. Princeton: Princeton University Press, 1998.

———. *Pornography and Representation in Greece and Rome.* New York: Oxford University Press, 1992.

Riddle, John M. *Contraception and Abortion from the Ancient World to the Renaissance* Cambridge, Mass.: Harvard University Press, 1992.

Rist, John M. "Plotinus and Christian Philosophy." In *The Cambridge Companion to Plotinus,* edited by Lloyd P. Gerson, 386–413. Cambridge: Cambridge University Press, 1996.

———. "Seneca and Stoic Orthodoxy." *Aufstieg und Niedergang der römischen Welt* 2.36.3 (1989), 1993–2012.

———. *Stoic Philosophy.* London: Cambridge University Press, 1969.

Robertson, Archibald, and Alfred Plummer. *A Critical and Exegetical Commentary on the First Epistle of St. Paul to the Corinthians*[2]. Edinburgh: T & T Clark, 1914.

Robinson, Richard. "Plato's Separation of Reason from Desire." *Phronesis* 16 (1971), 38–48.

Rosner, Brian S. *Paul, Scripture, and Ethics: A Study of 1 Corinthians 5–7.* Leiden: Brill, 1994.

Roth, Norman. "The 'Theft of Philosophy' by the Greeks from the Jews." *Classical Folia* 32 (1978), 53–67.

Rousselle, Aline. *Porneia.* Translated by Felicia Pheasant. Oxford: Blackwell, 1988. Originally published as *Porneia,* Paris: Presses universitaires de France, 1983.

Rowley, H. H. "The Marriage of Hosea." *Bulletin of the John Rylands Library* 39 (1956–1957), 200–33.

Runia, David T. *Philo in Early Christian Literature: A Survey.* Minneapolis: Fortress Press, 1993.

————. *Philo of Alexandria and the* Timaeus *of Plato.* Leiden: Brill, 1986.

————. Review of *La philosophie de Moïse,* by Richard Goulet. *Journal of Theological Studies,* n.s., 40 (1989), 590–602.

————. "Was Philo a Middle Platonist? A Difficult Question Revisited." *The Studia Philonica Annual* 5 (1993), 112–40.

————. "Why Does Clement of Alexandria call Philo 'The Pythagorean'?" *Vigiliae Christianae* 49 (1995), 1–22.

Saffrey, H.-D. "Aphrodite à Corinthe: Réflexions sur une idée reçue." *Revue biblique* 92 (1985), 359–74.

Sandbach, F. *Aristotle and the Stoics.* Cambridge Philological Society 10. Cambridge: Cambridge University Press, 1985.

Sanders, E. P. *Paul and Palestinian Judaism: A Comparison of Patterns of Religion.* Philadelphia: Fortress Press, 1977.

————. *Paul, the Law, and the Jewish People.* Philadelphia: Fortress Press, 1983.

Sandmel, Samuel. *The Genius of Paul.* New York: Farrar, Straus, and Cudahy, 1958.

————. "Philo Judaeus: An Introduction to the Man, His Writings, and His Significance." *Aufstieg und Niedergang der römischen Welt* 2.21.1 (1984), 3–46.

Schmitt, John J. "The Gender of Ancient Israel." *Journal for the Study of the Old Testament* 26 (1983), 115–25.

————. "The Virgin of Israel: Referent and Use of the Phrase in Amos and Jeremiah." *The Catholic Biblical Quarterly,* 53 (1991), 365–87.

————. "The Wife of God in Hosea 2." *Biblical Research* 34 (1989), 5–18.

Schoedel, William R. *Ignatius of Antioch: A Commentary.* Philadelphia: Fortress Press, 1985.

Schofield, Malcolm. *Saving the City: Philosopher-Kings and Other Classical Paradigms.* New York: Routledge, 1999.

————. *The Stoic Idea of the City.* Cambridge: Cambridge University Press, 1991. Reprint, with a new foreword by M. Nussbaum and a new epilogue by M. Schofield, Chicago: University of Chicago Press, 1999.

Schrage, Wolfgang. *Der Erste Brief an die Korinther.* Vols. 1–4. Evangelisch-katholischer Kommentar zum Neuen Testament. Zurich: Benziger, 1991–2001.

————. *The Ethics of the New Testament.* Translated by David E. Green. Philadelphia: Fortress Press, 1988. Originally published as *Ethik des Neuen Testaments,* Göttingen: Vandenhoeck & Ruprecht, 1982.

Schürer, Emil, Geza Vermes, Fergus Millar, and Martin Goodman. *The History of the Jewish People in the Age of Jesus Christ.* Revised English version. Edinburgh: T. & T. Clark, 1973–1987.

Schweitzer, Albert. *The Mysticism of Paul the Apostle.* Translated by W. Montgomery. London: A & C Black, 1931. Originally published as *Die Mystik des Apostels Paulus,* Tübingen: J. C. B. Mohr, 1930.

Sedley, David. "The Origins of Stoic God." In *Traditions of Theology: Studies in Hellenistic Theology: Its Background and Aftermath,* edited by Dorothea Frede and André Laks, 41–83. Leiden: Brill, 2002.

Segal, Alan F. *Paul the Convert: The Apostolate and Apostasy of Saul the Pharisee.* New Haven: Yale University Press, 1990.

Seifert, Brigitte. *Metaphorisches Reden von Gott im Hoseabuch.* Göttingen: Vandenhoeck & Ruprecht, 1996.

Seland, Torrey. *Establishment Violence in Philo and Luke: A Study of Non-Conformity to the Torah and Jewish Vigilante Reactions.* Leiden: Brill, 1995.

Senft, Christophe. *La première épitre de saint Paul aux Corinthiens²*. Geneva: Labor et fides, 1990.

Sfameni Gasparro, Giulia. "Asceticism and Anthropology: Enkrateia and 'Double Creation' in Early Christianity." In V. Wimbush and R. Valantasis, editors, *Asceticism*, 127–46.

———. *Enkrateia e antropologia: Le motivazioni protologiche della continenza e della verginità nel cristianesimo dei primi secoli e nello gnosticismo.* Rome: Institutum Patristicum Augustinianum, 1984.

———. "Motivazioni protologiche dell'*enkrateia*." In U. Bianchi, editor, *La tradizione dell' enkrateia*, 239–52.

Sfameni Gasparro, Giulia, Cesare Magazzu, and Concetta Aloe Spada, editors. *The Human Couple in the Fathers.* Translated by Thomas Halton. New York: Pauline Books, 1998. Originally published as *La coppia nei padri*, Milan: Figlie di San Paolo, 1991.

Shapiro, H. Alan. "Dikē." *Lexicon iconographicum mythologiae classicae.* Vol. 3.1, 388–91. Zurich: Artemis, 1986.

Sherwood, Yvonne. *The Prostitute and the Prophet: Hosea's Marriage in Literary-Theoretical Perspective.* Sheffield: Sheffield Academic Press, 1996.

Shorey, Paul. "The Unity of Plato's Thought." *The Decennial Publications of the University of Chicago* (1903), 127–214. Reprint, as a monograph, New York: Garland Publishing, 1980.

Shorey, Paul, translator. *Plato's Republic.* In *Plato: The Collected Dialogues*, edited by Edith Hamilton and Huntington Cairns. Princeton: Princeton University Press, 1961.

Sim, David C. *The Gospel of Matthew and Christian Judaism: The History and Social Setting of the Matthean Community.* Edinburgh: T & T Clark, 1998.

Smith, D. Moody. "The Pauline Literature." In *It is Written: Scripture Citing Scripture*, edited by D. A. Carson and H. G. M. Williamson, 265–91. Cambridge: Cambridge University Press, 1988.

Smith, Janet E. Humanae Vitae *A Generation Later.* Washington, D.C.: The Catholic University of America Press, 1991.

Smith, Nicholas D, editor. *Plato: Critical Assessments.* Vols. 1–4. New York: Routledge, 1998.

Smith, William, and Henry Wace, editors. *The Dictionary of Christian Biography: Literature, Sects, and Doctrines.* London: J. Murray, 1880–1900. Reprint, New York: AMS Press, 1984.

Sorabji, Richard. *Animal Minds and Human Morals: The Origins of the Western Debate.* Ithaca, N.Y.: Cornell University Press, 1993.

Sourvinou-Inwood, Christiane. "A Series of Erotic Pursuits: Images and Meanings." *The Journal of Hellenic Studies* 107 (1987), 131–53.

Spada, Concetta Aloe. "Un' omelia greca anonima 'sulla verginità.'" In U. Bianchi, editor, *La tradizione dell' enkrateia*, 603–21.

Spelman, Elizabeth V. "Hairy Cobblers and Philosopher Queens." In her *Inessential Woman: Problems of Exclusion in Feminist Thought*, 19–36. Boston: Beacon, 1988. Also available in N. Tuana, editor, *Plato*, 87–107.

———. "Woman as Body: Ancient and Contemporary Views." *Feminist Studies* 8 (1982), 109–31.

Sperber, Alexander. "The New Testament and Septuagint." *Journal of Biblical Literature* 59 (1940), 193–293.

Staab, Karl, editor. *Pauluskommentare aus der griechischen Kirche: Aus Katenenschriften gesammelt und herausgegeben.* NT Abhandlungen 15. Münster: Aschendorff, 1933.

Stählin, Otto. *Clemens Alexandrinus und die Septuaginta.* Nuremberg: J. L. Stich, 1901.

Stalley, R. F. *An Introduction to Plato's* Laws. Indianapolis: Hackett Publishing, 1983.

Stead, Christopher. *Philosophy in Christian Antiquity.* Cambridge: Cambridge University Press, 1994.

Stephens, William O. "Epictetus on How the Stoic Sage Loves." *Oxford Studies in Ancient Philosophy* 14 (1996), 193–210.

Sterling, Gregory E. "Platonizing Moses: Philo and Middle Platonism." *The Studia Philonica Annual* 5 (1993), 96–111.

———. Review of *Establishment Violence in Philo and Luke,* by T. Seland. *Journal of Biblical Literature* 116 (1997), 368–70.

Still, Todd D. *Conflict at Thessalonica: A Pauline Church and Its Neighbours.* Sheffield: Sheffield Academic Press, 1999.

Stowers, Stanley K. *A Rereading of Romans: Justice, Jews, and Gentiles.* New Haven: Yale University Press, 1994.

———. "Romans 7.7–25 as a Speech-in-Character (προσωποποιία)." In *Paul in His Hellenistic Context,* edited by Troels Engberg-Pedersen, 180–202. Minneapolis: Fortress Press, 1995.

Striker, Gisela. *Essays on Hellenistic Epistemology and Ethics.* Cambridge: Cambridge University Press, 1996.

———. "Following Nature: A Study in Stoic Ethics." *Oxford Studies in Ancient Philosophy* 9 (1991), 1–73. Also available in her *Essays,* 221–80.

———. "Origins of the Concept of Natural Law." *Proceedings of the Boston Area Colloquium in Ancient Philosophy* 2 (1986), 79–94. Also available in her *Essays,* 209–20.

———. "The Role of Oikeiosis in Stoic Ethics." *Oxford Studies in Ancient Philosophy* 1 (1983), 144–67. Also available in her *Essays,* 281–97.

Stuhlmacher, Peter. *Paul's Letter to the Romans: A Commentary.* Translated by Scott J. Hafemann. Louisville, Ky.: Westminster John Knox Press, 1994. Originally published as *Der Brief an die Römer,* Göttingen: Vandenhoeck & Ruprecht, 1989.

Szesnat, Holger. "'Pretty Boys' in Philo's *De Vita Contemplativa,*" *The Studia Philonica Annual* 10 (1998), 87–107.

Szlezák, Thomas A. *Reading Plato.* Translated by Graham Zanker. New York: Routledge, 1999. Originally published as *Platon lesen,* Stuttgart: Frommann-Holzboog, 1993.

Tanner, R. G. "St. Paul and Stoic Physics." *Studia Evangelica* 7 (1982) in Texte und Untersuchungen 126, 481–90.

Tarrant, Harold. *Thrasyllan Platonism.* Ithaca, N.Y.: Cornell University Press, 1993.

Tate, J. "On the History of Allegorism." *Classical Quarterly* 28 (1934), 105–14.

Theissen, Gerd. *Social Reality and the Early Christians: Theology, Ethics, and the World of the New Testament,* 33–93, Translated by Margaret Kohl. Minneapolis: Fortress Press, 1992. Translated mainly from *Studien zur Soziologie des Urchristentums,* Tübingen: J. C. B. Mohr, 1979.

Thesleff, Holger. "On the Problem of the Doric Pseudo-Pythagorica: An Alternative Theory of Date and Purpose." In K. von Fritz, editor, 59–102.

Thistlethwaite, Susan Brooks. "'You May Enjoy the Spoils of Your Enemies': Rape as a Biblical Metaphor for War." *Semeia* (1993), 59–75.

Thom, Johan C. *The Pythagorean Golden Verses.* Leiden: Brill, 1995.

Thornton, Bruce S. *Eros: The Myth of Ancient Greek Sexuality.* Boulder, Colo.: Westview Press, 1997.

Throckmorton, B. H. "The ναός in Paul." *Studia Evangelica* 7 (1982) in Texte und Untersuchungen 126, 497–503.

Tieleman, Teun. *Galen and Chrysippus on the Soul: Argument and Refutation in the De placitis Books II–III.* Leiden: Brill, 1996.

Timothy, H. P. *The Early Christian Apologists and Greek Philosophy.* Assen: Van Gorcum, 1973.

Tomson, Peter J. *Paul and the Jewish Law: Halakha in the Letters of the Apostle to the Gentiles.* Minneapolis: Fortress Press, 1990.

Torhoudt A. "Épiphane." In *Dictionnaire d'histoire et de géographie ecclésiastiques,* vol. 15. Paris: Letouzey et Ané, 1963.

Toutain, J. "Le rite nuptial de l'anakalypterion." *Revue des études anciennes* 42 (1940), 345–53.

Tov, Emanuel. "Did the Septuagint Translators Always Understand Their Hebrew Text?" In *De Septuaginta,* edited by Albert Pietersma and Claude Cox, 53–70. Festschrift for John William Wevers. Mississauga, Ontario: Benben Publications, 1984.

Trapp, M. B. "Plato's *Phaedrus* in Second-Century Greek Literature." In *Antonine Literature,* edited by D. A. Russell, 141–73. Oxford: Clarendon Press, 1990.

Treggiari, Susan. *Roman Marriage: Iusti coniuges from the Time of Cicero to the Time of Ulpian.* New York: Oxford University Press, 1991.

Tsitrone, Abraham. "Sex et mariage dans la tradition juive." In M. Bernos, editor, *Sexualité et religions,* 95–133.

Tuana, Nancy. *Feminist Interpretations of Plato.* University Park, Pa.: The Pennsylvania State University Press, 1994.

Ussher, R. G., editor. *Aristophanes: Ecclesiazusae.* Oxford: Clarendon Press, 1973.

Valantasis, Richard. "A Theory of the Social Function of Asceticism." In V. Wimbush and R. Valantasis, editors, *Asceticism,* 544–52.

van den Hoek, Annewies. *Clement of Alexandria and His Use of Philo in the Stromateis: An Early Christian Reshaping of a Jewish Model.* Leiden: Brill, 1988.

———. "How Alexandrian was Clement of Alexandria?" *Heythrop Journal* 31 (1990), 179–94.

van der Kooij, Arie. *The Oracle of Tyre: The Septuagint of Isaiah XXIII as Version and Vision.* Leiden: Brill, 1998.

van der Waerden, B. L. *Die Pythagoreer. Religiöse Bruderschaft und Schule der Wissenschaft.* Zurich: Artemis, 1979.

Van Eijk, Ton H. C. "Marriage and Virginity, Death and Immortality." In *Epektasis,* edited by Jacques Fontaine and Charles Kannengiesser, 209–35. Festschrift for Jean Daniélou. Paris: Beauchesne, 1972.

Van Geytenbeek, Anton C. *Musonius Rufus and Greek Diatribe.* Rev. ed. Translated by

B. L. Hijmans. Assen: Van Gorcum 1963. Originally published as *Musonius Rufus en de griekse Diatribe,* Amsterdam: H. J. Paris, 1948.

Van Winden, J. M. "Quotations from Philo in Clement of Alexandria's *Protrepticus.*" *Vigiliae Christianae* 32 (1978), 208–13.

Vander Waerdt, Paul. "Philosophical Influence on Roman Jurisprudence? The Case of Stoicism and Natural Law." *Aufstieg und Niedergang der römischen Welt* 2.36.7 (1994), 4851–4900.

———. "Politics and Philosophy in Stoicism: A Discussion of A. Erskine, *The Hellenistic Stoa: Political Thought and Action.*" *Oxford Studies in Ancient Philosophy* 9 (1991), 185–211.

———. "Zeno's *Republic* and the Origins of Natural Law." In *The Socratic Movement,* edited by Paul Vander Waerdt, 272–308. Ithaca, N.Y.: Cornell University Press, 1994.

Viljoen, G. van N. "Plato and Aristotle on the Exposure of Infants at Athens." *Acta Classica* (1959), 58–69.

Vlastos, Gregory. *Platonic Studies*[2]. Princeton: Princeton University Press, 1981.

———. *Socrates, Ironist and Moral Philosopher.* Ithaca, N.Y.: Cornell University Press, 1991.

———. "The Theory of Social Justice in the Polis in Plato's *Republic.*" In *Interpretations of Plato,* edited by Helen F. North, 1–40. Leiden: Brill, 1977.

———. "Was Plato a Feminist?" *The Times Literary Supplement* 4485 (17–23 March 1989), 288–89. Also available in N. Tuana, editor, *Plato,* 11–23.

Vlastos, Gregory, editor. *Plato II: Ethics, Politics, and Philosophy of Art and Religion.* Garden City, N.Y.: Anchor Books, 1971.

Vögtle, Anton. *Die Tugend- und Lasterkataloge im neuen Testament, exegetisch, religions- und formgeschichtlich untersucht.* Münster: Aschendorff, 1936.

Völker, Walther. *Der wahre Gnostiker nach Clemens Alexandrinus.* Berlin: Akademie Verlag, 1952.

von Arnim, Hans. "Antipater." *RE* 1 (1894), 2515–16.

von Fritz, Kurt. *Pythagorean Politics in Southern Italy: An Analysis of the Sources.* New York: Columbia University Press, 1940. Reprint, New York: Octagon Books, 1977.

von Fritz, Kurt, editor. *Pseudepigrapha I: Pseudopythagorica, lettres de Platon, litterature pseudepigraphique juive.* Geneva: Fondation Hardt, 1972.

Vööbus, Arthur. *A History of Asceticism in the Syrian Orient I: The Origins of Asceticism.* Corpus Scriptorum Christianorum Orientalium, vol. 14. Louvain: E. Peeters, 1958.

Walker, William O. "The Burden of Proof in Identifying Interpolations in the Pauline Letters." *New Testament Studies* 33 (1987), 610–18.

Ward, Roy Bowen. "Musonius and Paul on Marriage." *New Testament Studies* 36 (1990), 281–9.

Washington, Harold C. "'Lest He Die in the Battle and Another Man Take Her': Violence and the Construction of Gender in the Laws of Deuteronomy 20–22." In *Gender and Law in the Hebrew Bible and the Ancient Near East,* edited by Victor H. Matthews, Bernard M. Levinson, and Tikva Frymer-Kensky, 185–213. Sheffield: Sheffield Academic Press, 1998.

Waterfield, Robin. *Plato's Republic.* Oxford: Oxford University Press, 1993.

Webb, W. J. "Unequally Yoked Together with Unbelievers. I. Who are the Unbelievers (ἄπιστοι) in 2 Corinthians 6.14?" *Bibliotheca Sacra* 149 (1992), 27–44.

———. "Unequally Yoked Together with Unbelievers. II. What is the Unequal Yoke
(ἑτεροζυγοῦντες) in 2 Corinthians 6.14?" *Bibliotheca Sacra* 149 (1992), 162–79.

Weems, Renita J. *Battered Love: Marriage, Sex, and Violence in the Hebrew Prophets.* Minneapolis: Fortress Press, 1995.

Weir, Terry, and Mark Carruth. *Holy Sex: God's Purpose and Plan for Our Sexuality.* New
Kensington, Pa.: Whitaker House, 1999.

Wendland, Paul. *Quaestiones Musonianae. De Musonio Stoico Clementis Alexandrini aliorumque auctore.* Berlin: Mayer & Mueller, 1886.

Wevers, John William. *Notes on the Greek Text of Deuteronomy.* Atlanta: Scholars Press,
1995.

———. *Notes on the Greek Text of Exodus.* Atlanta: Scholars Press, 1990.

Wey von Schwarzenbach, Heinrich. *Die funktionen der bösen Geister bei den griechischen
Apologeten des zweiten Jahrhunderts nach Christus.* Winterthur, Switzerland: Keller,
1957.

White, Nicholas P. "The Basis of Stoic Ethics." *Harvard Studies in Classical Philology* 83
(1979), 143–78.

White, Stephen A. Review of *The Hellenistic Stoa,* by A. Erskine. *Journal of the History of
Philosophy* 30 (1992), 294–6.

Wiesner-Hanks, Merry E. *Christianity and Sexuality in the Early Modern World: Regulating Desire, Reforming Practice.* New York: Routledge, 2000.

Wiles, Maurice F. *The Divine Apostle: The Interpretation of St. Paul's Epistles in the Early
Church.* London: Cambridge University Press, 1967.

Wilkes, K. V. "Aspects of Stoicism: From Revisionary to Reactionary Ethics." *Proceedings of the Sixteenth International Eirêne Conference* (1983), 183–88.

Williams, Bernard. *Ethics and the Limits of Philosophy.* Cambridge, Mass.: Harvard University Press, 1985.

Williams, Rowan. "Does It Make Sense to Speak of Pre-Nicene Orthodoxy?" In *The
Making of Orthodoxy: Essays in Honour of Henry Chadwick,* edited by Rowan Williams,
1–23. Cambridge: Cambridge University Press, 1989.

Wimbush, Vincent L. "The Ascetic Impulse in Early Christianity: Some Methodological Challenges," *Studia Patristica* 25 (1993), 462–78.

Wimbush, Vincent L., and Richard Valantasis, editors. *Asceticism.* New York: Oxford
University Press, 1995.

Winkler, John J. *The Constraints of Desire: The Anthropology of Sex and Gender in Ancient
Greece.* New York: Routledge, 1990.

Winston, David. "Philo's Ethical Theory," *Aufstieg und Niedergang der römischen Welt*
2.21.1 (1984), 372–416.

———. Review of *Establishment Violence in Philo and Luke,* by T. Seland. *Jewish Quarterly Review* 88 (1998), 372–4.

Wire, Antoinette C. *The Corinthian Women Prophets: A Reconstruction through Paul's
Rhetoric.* Minneapolis: Fortress Press, 1990.

Wolkstein, Diane, and Samuel Noah Kramer. *Inanna: Queen of Heaven and Earth: Her
Stories and Hymns from Sumer.* New York: Harper & Row, 1983.

Wyrwa, Dietmar. *Die christliche Platonaneigung in den Stromateis des Clemens von Alexandrien.* New York: Walter de Gruyter, 1983.

Yarbrough, O. Larry. *Not Like the Gentiles: Marriage Rules in the Letters of Paul.* Atlanta: Scholars Press, 1985.

Zhmud, Leonid. *Wissenschaft, Philosophie, und Religion im frühen Pythagoreismus.* Berlin: Akademie Verlag, 1997.

Ziesler, J. A. "The Role of the Tenth Commandment in Romans 7." *Journal for the Study of the New Testament* 33 (1988), 41–56.

INDEX

Ancient works are indexed, as appropriate, by author, author and title, or title. Modern works are indexed by author. Complete passage citations are provided in the notes designated.

REFERENCES TO ANCIENT WORKS

Acts, Book of, 18–19n49, 139n52, 275n3
Aeschylus: fr. 44, 65n25, 235n53; *Oresteia*, 142n62
Aëtius, 68n34, 69n40, 75n63, 233n44
Alexander of Aphrodisias: *De fato*, 73n56; *Mixt*, 68n34, 230n32, 232n39; *Top*, 75–6n66
Ambrose, 13n35
Ambrosiaster, 147n74
Anacreon: fr. 376, 66n27; fr. 413, 66n30; fr. 428, 65n26
ps.-Andronicus, 214n59
Antipater of Sidon, 237, 237n57
Antipater of Thessalonica, 237n57
Antipater the Stoic, 30n22, 83, 83n89, 85–6, 85n99, 87n105
Archilochus: fr. 191, fr. 193, 65n26
Aristocles, 70, 70n43
Aristophanes: *Lys*, 78n75
Aristotle: *Anim*, 102–3n19, 103–4n21; *Gen anim*, 108–9n30; *NE*, 79n80, 82n87; *Pol*, 47–8n77, 77n72
ps.-Aristotle: *Virt et vit*, 14n38
Aristoxenus: fr. 39, 100n15. *See also* Iamblichus, *vit Pyth*
Arius Didymus, 62n11, 63n13, 75n65, 75–6n66, 78n77, 79n79, 200n21, 280n12

Asclepiades: G-P 11, G-P 14, 74n57
Athanasius, 13n35
Athenaeus, 65n25, 75nn64, 65, 237n57
Augustine: *Civ dei*, 234n48

Barn, 18–19n49, 139n52, 178n43

Callimachus: G-P 4, 65n26; G-P 8, 66n27
Catullus, 237n57
Charondas, 107n29, 108, 206, 206n33
Chrysippus:
    SVF vol. 2: early Stoic cosmology, 68nn34, 36, 69nn38, 39, 40, 41, 72n50, 73n56, 75n63; Tatian's subversion, 230n32, 232n39, 233n44, 234n48
    SVF vol. 3: early Stoic ethics, 14n38, 29n19, 60n4, 62n9, 62n11, 71n46, 72n51, 73nn53, 54, 74nn58, 59, 61, 75n65, 75–6n66, 76n68, 78n77, 79n79, 80n83, 81n84, 81–2n85, 86n100, 97n6; Philonic and Christian Platonist reworking, 200n21, 214n59, 234n48, 266n54, 55, 280n12, 283n20, 284n24
    See also Alexander of Aphrodisias; Arius Didymus; Cicero; Dio Chrysostom; Diogenes Laertius, book 7; Galen, *PHP*; LS; Sextus Empiricus; Stobaeus

REFERENCES TO
MODERN WORKS

SUBJECT INDEX

6, 169–70, 169nn21, 22; difference
from prostitutes, 165–70, 165n11;
Jezebel, 163n8, 168–9; and Lord's
collective adulterous wives, 173, 173–
4, 173n29; prohibited as wives, 165–
70; rape victims and war captives,
167–8, 168n18; rebellious female insiders, 166; religiously alien women,
165–6, 166n12; role in spiritual fornication, 166–7, 166n12; as seductive stereotype, 167–8
   in Tatian: Helen of Sparta, 242; Sappho,
   237–8, 238n61, 294
will of God: as mutable criterion of sexual
   mores, 12, 158–9, 161–2, 186–9, 192,
   192nn5, 7, 9, 239–42, 270–1, 292–305;
   transformations in forbidden desire,
   152–7, 191–204, 255–66, 288–90
women's capabilities: diminished later Stoic
   engagement with, 84, 87, 87n102, 89;
   early Stoic affirmation of, 77–8, 80–1,

294; Plato's ambivalence toward, 29n20,
   42n64, 47–8n77
women's roles in: ancient warfare as sexual
   captives, 52n89, 167–8, 168n18, 252–3;
   Clement, 268–9; early Stoic city, 76–8;
   emergent church, 293–5; Paul, 146–52,
   170–3; Pentateuch and Prophets, 129–
   36, 165–70, 175–6, 176n37; Philo,
   211–12; Plato's Kallipolis, 44–7; Plato's
   Magnesia, 47–8; Tatian's encratite Christianity, 228–39

Zeno the Stoic: absence of sexual austerity,
   71n48, 91; ancient reactions to *Republic*,
   2, 2n4, 64–5, 89–90, 89–90n113; contents of *Republic,* 62n10; Sextus's testimony, 76–7, 80; and sexuality, 59–81
Zeus: in early Stoic cosmology, 68–70, 231–
   2; in Greek religion, 74; as the Lord's
   main rebellious demon, 229–30; as protector of marriage and family, 86

Compositor: G&S Typesetters, Inc.
Text: 10/12 Baskerville
Display: Baskerville
Printer and Binder: Maple-Vail Manufacturing Group